PRICE AND NONPRICE RIVALRY IN OLIGOPOLY

Also by Robert E. Kuenne

DYNAMICS AND CONFLICT IN REGIONAL STRUCTURAL CHANGE (*co-editor with Manas Chatterji*)

ECONOMIC JUSTICE IN AMERICAN SOCIETY

EUGEN VON BÖHM-BAWERK

GENERAL EQUILIBRIUM ECONOMICS: Space, Time and Money

MICROECONOMIC THEORY: Theoretical and Applied, Volumes I, II and III

MICROECONOMIC THEORY OF THE MARKET MECHANISM: A General Equilibrium Approach

MONOPOLISTIC COMPETITION THEORY: Studies in Impact (*editor*)

NEW FRONTIERS IN REGIONAL SCIENCE (*co-editor with Manas Chatterji*)

RIVALROUS CONSONANCE: A Theory of General Oligopolistic Equilibrium

THE ATTACK SUBMARINE: A Study in Strategy

THE ECONOMICS OF OLIGOPOLISTIC COMPETITION: Price and Nonprice Rivalry

THE POLARIS MISSILE STRIKE: A General Economic Systems Analysis

THE THEORY OF GENERAL ECONOMIC EQUILIBRIUM

WARRANTIES IN WEAPON SYSTEMS PROCUREMENT (*with P. H. Richanbach, F. Ridell and R. Kaganoff*)

Price and Nonprice Rivalry in Oligopoly

The Integrated Battleground

Robert E. Kuenne
Emeritus Professor of Economics
Princeton University

First published in Great Britain 1998 by
MACMILLAN PRESS LTD
Houndmills, Basingstoke, Hampshire RG21 6XS and London
Companies and representatives throughout the world

A catalogue record for this book is available from the British Library.

ISBN 0–333–73732–6

First published in the United States of America 1998 by
ST. MARTIN'S PRESS, INC.,
Scholarly and Reference Division,
175 Fifth Avenue, New York, N.Y. 10010

ISBN 0–312–21573–8

Library of Congress Cataloging-in-Publication Data
Kuenne, Robert E.
Price and nonprice rivalry in oligopoly : the integrated battleground / Robert E. Kuenne.
p. cm.
Includes bibliographical references and index.
ISBN 0–312–21573–8 (hardcover)
1. Oligopolies. 2. Pricing. 3. Competition. I. Title.
HD2757.3.K838 1998
338.8'2—dc21 98–15287
CIP

---

10 9 8 7 6 5 4 3 2 1
07 06 05 04 03 02 01 00 99 98

Printed and bound in Great Britain by
Antony Rowe Ltd, Chippenham, Wiltshire

To the memory of our lost princess

Olivia Michelle Kuenne
1991–97

Death lies on her like an untimely frost
Upon the sweetest flower of all the field

Contents

PART III THEORETICAL GUIDANCE TO AND USAGE OF MODELING METHODOLOGIES

List of Figures

List of Tables

Preface

Oligopolistic competition or rivalry is by its nature interdependent among industry firms, and its analysis therefore is one of general equilibrium or disequilibrium. Rather surprisingly, however, partial analysis is the rule when dealing with intrafirm competitive matters. Price determination, or advertising expenditures, or quality determination have been treated for the most part independently of each other, in part to feature the interfirm aspects of these decisions, but in greater measure to escape the complexity such analysis confronts.

This work is devoted to developing general equilibrium frameworks incorporating both levels of the competitive process: the interdependence of decisions among firms when those decisions include choices among prices and nonprice characteristics. I have used the term *integrated rivalry* to characterize this two-sided nature of oligopolistic incumbents' decision making, and have placed emphasis upon the intrafirm decisions concerning the prices and qualities of brands and the manner of their interactions with such aspects as the degree of tacit collusion within the industry.

The complexity of such analysis – especially when it is conducted with realistic numbers of firms rather than overemployed duopoly – rules out the exclusive use of closed, determinate theory. Recourse must be had to the construction of theory – and empirically-guided *models* whose parameters can be derived in numerical form from quantitative and nonquantitative data. Insights must be sought by simulative manipulation of the parameters in comparative statics exercises and their illumination accepted as limited to the specific industry for which the model is constructed or, when possible, as yielding conjectures about industries of similar structure. The search for generalizable theorems derived in theorem–proof sequences from closed theoretical structures must be reluctantly abandoned.

Further swallowing of theoretical pride as a prerequisite of making progress in this area is the need to develop methodologies for scaling qualities and attributes that are not measurable in the strict definition of that term, and of searching out methods of modeling the combinations of cooperation and competition that characterize oligopolistic industries. This book argues that game theory does not provide such a basis for determining the power structure of the industry that must be included firm by firm to analyze integrated rivalry. *Rivalrous consonance* is recommended and employed in the book to perform this function.

The contributions of the book, therefore, draw upon previous work but extend existing analysis in the development of a set of methodologies tailored to the study of specific industries' integrated rivalry as well as to the derivation of conjectures and hypotheses concerning behavior of sets of industries. This employment of "fuzzy" measurement techniques of scaling, the substantial abandonment of such widely accepted techniques as game theory, and the resort to simulation with parameter dependent structures will be judged harshly by those committed to the trappings of scientific formalism in microeconomic theory today. My appeal is to assert that the predominance of a limited general equilibrium approach in oligopoly analysis and the frequent dimensionality restriction to duopoly are tacit admissions of the limitations of such idealized methodologies, and urge investigations in less constraining – and hopefully useful – precincts. I am once more indebted to Macmillan for caring professionalism, and especially to T. M. Farmiloe and Sunder Katwala for their patience with prolixity. My thanks go out once more to Keith Povey for his careful editing of a difficult manuscript.

Princeton, New Jersey ROBERT E. KUENNE

Part I
Some Necessary Preliminaries

1 On Definitions and the Problems of Measurement

Since the late 1920s and the raising of microeconomic consciousness by Sraffa's (1926), Chamberlin's (1948) and Robinson's (1948) work,[1] it has been recognized that firms compete in many dimensions besides price, and that their decision making is complicated by the interdependence among price and nonprice strategies. Within the body of oligopoly analysis, differentiated oligopoly has come to be accepted as the dominant structure of interest. Yet progress in the formal integration of product properties into decision models and analysis of the social consequences of their presence lags behind that achieved in analyzing strategic pricing decisions by such techniques as game theory. This books attempts to make progress in the analysis of *integrated competition* through the use of both conventional and unconventional techniques, whose adoption and development are the products of some years of coping with the enigmas of oligopolistic decision making. Because the reader – and especially the younger reader – will find some of the nonconventional methods and the mindset that leads to their adoption unfamiliar and perhaps unworthy in this age of economic "scientism," some explanation of their genesis and rationalization is incumbent on the author.

1 A MANIFESTO

a Rivalrous Consonance

In the area of oligopoly we confront the inescapable – indeed, the defining – variational complexity: the interdependent decision making of identifiable, flesh-and-blood agents searching for an imprecisely acceptable point in a multidimensional price–quality space, under reactive scrutiny by a significant number of similarly motivated rivals. Each such agent (actually, a fictitious entity of contending and cooperating corporate bureaucracies) seeks uncertainly to balance a multiobjective goal set, where such goals differ among the agents or may be similar with different priorities.

A convenient, if oversimplified, manner of viewing the agents' motivations is in the framework of nonlinear programming: each seeks to maximize or minimize some primary objective (profits, revenues, growth, rate of return on capital or equity) subject to constraints which introduce the secondary goals as restraints. Each agent then seeks a constrained maximum or minimum that is acceptable to all other significant rivals in the search for an industry or product group stationary decision point. That process of a search for mutual acquiescence will involve the alteration of the sets of secondary goal constraints, or their restraints, or even the primary objectives of the agent – the *structures* of their decision making – as well as the price–quality variables acted upon in any given structure set.

The oligopoly becomes a *community*, like any other set of agents seeking stable relationships permitting mutual coexistence in the face of contending goals and opportunities for mutually beneficial cooperation. The members' actions, goals, and decision variable values are shaped by a mixture of rivalry and cooperation in varying degrees, the mixture varying with the industry, the personalities of the presently and historically active agents, the market strength of the contending firms, and the age or maturity of the industry. Over time a power structure emerges among the firms, unwritten rules of conduct come into force, mores and folkways shape behavior, and "rational conduct" becomes a more sophisticated concept than *homo oeconomicus* can convey. Rivalry may dominate the nature of the interdependence among the agents, but cooperation will temper that rivalry in nonignorable manners. There emerges, in short, a decision making environment in which a *rivalrous consonance of interests* is recognized by all participants.

b Game-theoretic Analysis

Economists in the last two decades have become increasingly concerned with this rivalrous consonance in oligopolies. Cooperative game theory has received increasing attention by the game-theoretic community, as the presentations in Kreps (1990), Myerson (1991), and Osborne and Rubinstein (1994) attest. I am critical of most of the game-theoretic approaches in this area, however, for reasons that are spelled out in more detail in Chapter 6. Briefly, I believe the approaches are excessively rational and therefore give too much emphasis on the competitive as opposed to the cooperative forces operative in realistic oligopolies; ignore the socio–political aspects of the relations and therewith the major formative elements in the industry's power structure; do not provide operational frameworks for empirical analysis of the industry; focus inordinate attention on he formation of the (excessively rational) strategic structure of the industry rather than the implications for its functioning.

Despite these criticisms, however, the book is in no sense an anti-game theory tract: it employs game theory frameworks and concepts in many of the analyses to follow. I do deplore the almost complete domination of modern oligopoly analysis by game theory, however, as I would any framework with claims of exclusive relevance. The approaches of this book are offered as alternatives or complements to game theory which have benefitted from its advances as well as critical reactions to it.

c Realistic Ambitions and Analytical Compromises

Variation in differentiated oligopolistic industries is featured by (1) high interdependence among prices and qualities within firms; (2) intense interdependence among firms; (3) the effects of idiosyncratic behavior by personalities in the industry; (4) a significant number of firms within the industry; (5) quality characteristics that are not measurable in a mathematically acceptable way; (6) multiobjective goals of rivals, some of which are difficult to define in function form; (7) constraints imposed in analytically nebulous fashion by the folkways and mores of the industry, qualifying the application of economic theory's beloved "rationality" assumptions; (8) a complicated and perhaps changing power structure defining the deference among firms in the product group; and (9) constraints resulting from potential or existent government regulation. Gone is the tractability of price and quantity determination only with negligible or nonexistent interdependence among faceless firms seeking singlemindedly to maximize profits.

Economic analysis enters, therefore, a qualitatively different arena and, reluctantly, compromises with its ambitions and scientific ideals in the hope of making inroads into the variational tangle. A first sacrifice is the hope of derivation of propositions that are generalizable as "laws of oligopolistic competition." Each oligopoly is *sui generis*, unique to itself in terms of the forces affecting its variables and attributes detailed above. At best we can gain insights into its structure and functioning, but extending those insights into some postulated "oligopolistic market structure" is to confuse structure with functioning. While structure may related closely to functioning in pure competition, monopolistic competition, and monopoly, even limited experience in oligopoly analysis reveals this to be false: like human beings, each oligopoly possesses the trait of individuality that registers as behavioral choice in a rich, multidimensional action field.

d Economic Theory and Simulative Theorizing

These circumstances have important implications for analytical research. They emphasize the usefulness of economic modeling methodology versus economic theory. In this book I will distinguish between the two in this manner. Economic theory seeks, in practice, to derive from a set of numerically undefined parameters and assumptions a set of their mutual implications in the form of numerically unspecified functions whose manipulation yields *qualitative* propositions concerning variable behavior. These propositions, of course, are relevant only under the regime of the postulated parameters and axioms, but to escape triviality these are generally designed to be applicable to a broad range of economic environments to make the theorems generalizable to a rather large class of economic variation. Indeed, some of the restrictive effects of the assumptions are frequently explicitly or implicitly omitted in the interpretation of the propositions to give the appearance of broader application than strictly permitted.

In this definition, economic theory deals with generalizable rules of variable behavior that are not "parameter dependent"; that is, propositions must be invariant to the numerical values of the parameters, or, to be less unbending, sensitive only to brackets defined by numerical values (e.g., "if parameter a is less than 50, then proposition *x* is true, otherwise proposition *y* is true").

As is well known, a problem with conventional theoretical techniques in comparative statics and dynamics is that dimensionality is severely restrictive in the derivation of qualitative theorems. Evaluation of numerically unspecified determinants as to sign becomes impossible, given acceptable restrictions in the assumptions, as the size of matrices rises above 2×2 or 3×3. But in oligopoly analysis dimensionality is rife. Realistic industries consist of at least 4 or 5 significant rivals, making decisions in price, multiple quality, and advertising dimensions within environments of intense rival interaction. Matrices become large and dense in nonzero elements, and insights in the form of qualitative propositions unobtainable.

The temptation of the theorist in these circumstances is to *partialize*: to reduce the dimensionality of the theory in order to salvage determinateness. In oligopoly analysis this frequently takes the form of reducing the industry to a duopoly, with firms having equal cost functions or demand functions or identical products. Such resorts are especially restrictive in oligopoly analysis whose very relevance consists in attaining insights into the implications of the interplay of decisions in a broad spectrum of agent circumstances (e.g., varying degrees of rivalry and cooperation) and opportunities. Such exercises leave one with disappointment at the sterile nature of the theorems and the inapplicability of the circumstances to reality, albeit, perhaps, admiration for the misguided ingenuity of the theoretical construction.

Economic modeling, or more exactly in this context in which we are not using empirically derived numerical data, what I have termed *simulative theorizing*, is distinguished from economic theory in the use of numerically specified parameters and assumed functions to derive quantitatively specific solutions and propositions. Two advantages derive from the method: first, it yields, with the proper function specifications, solutions giving quantitatively precise insights into the detailed anatomy and physiology of the analyst-designed oligopoly, and second the ability to design the industry means that the methodology can be tailored to the structure of real-world industry for operational empirical research or to confront more general industry structures of interest (e.g., product groups with wide differences in costs, or with clusters of firms close together in quality space, or with wide separations in such spaces). The major disadvantage, of course, is that the comparative statics propositions derived or the major outlines of the solutions are relevant only to the analyzed industry or closely structured industries. But the importance of this drawback should be judged against the limited ability of economic theory to derive generalizable theorems in an area of economics whose very nature defies generalization.

The technique of simulative theorizing is widely used in game-theoretic analysis, where strategic examples in both extensive and normal forms are used to depict rationalizable, Nash or Bayesian equilibria. In our terminology, therefore, such presentations are labeled simulative theorizing given their parameter dependence, numerical specification, and limited generalizability. As in the case of the approach in this book, such usage is a recognition of the complexity of oligopolistic (or, more generally, strategic) decision making that renders it for the most part beyond the remit of economic theory in our definition.

e On Scaling and Quasi-measurement

Another concomitant of analyzing differentiated oligopoly is the need to adopt quantitative units for such categories as product characteristics and power structures that are not susceptible of measurement in the rigorous mathematical definitions of the term. Because the remainder of the chapter deals at some length with this difficult problem, I will limit my discussion of it at this point to the reluctance of the economics profession, with the excessive devotion to the "scientific" procedures characteristic of fields that are troubled by the repressed realization they can never attain science stature, to resort to empirically justified scaling techniques employed by other fields confronted by similar problems.

Scaling techniques based on subjective judgment, visceral reactions, consumer preferences and the like, are used by a wide range of analysts on the frank basis of *faute de mieux* and empirical evidence of their usefulness. A notable example in education is the use of numerical grading procedures that must be frankly admitted to be scalings for which no rigorous justification exists for the arithmetic operations performed on them. Yet, in empirical usage, they are fairly reliable indicators of attainment. Our argument in this work will be that if progress is to be made in applying our mathematically-derived analytical techniques to the decision making in differentiated oligopoly, economists will have to be more accepting of such "quasi-measurement" procedures, and we will demonstrate such usage in the chapters to follow. Let us frankly accept the desirability of rigorous validation of scaling procedures in the sense to be defined in section 2, and never be satisfied with our makeshifts until we have done so, but absent that attainment let us be willing to compromise with the ideal to get on with the tasks of deriving insights into human behavior.

2 SOME CONCEPTUAL CHALLENGES

One reason, then, for the lag in progress in integrated competition analysis is this difficulty in quantification. Most product characteristics are not easily measurable in conventional manners, and in many instances finding a unit of measurement is difficult. The possession of an attribute may be binary in nature: it (for example, a brand name) is either present or not present, a 0–1 attribute.[2] Unlike price, quality characteristics are intended to affect consumer preferences or tastes as they are changed; hence, indifference maps will change rather than budget lines exterior to them. This makes analysis of characteristic alterations markedly more difficult. Indeed, a manner of distinguishing among price and nonprice variables or attributes is to term them preference-neutral and preference-altering.[3] Finally, even when characteristics are separable, their impact on consumer preferences will depend nonadditively on their bundling.

Indeed, alterations in characteristics may be so comprehensive as to constitute the creation of an new product – an "innovation." Although there were characteristics of the automobile that evolved from the horse-drawn carriage, it did constitute a new product. Formally, if one were to list the "core" or distinguishing characteristics of the auto and give each an axis in a "product space," one would have created a previously nonexistent space. By adding secondary or "non-core" characteristics – brand name, color, exterior design characteristics – one would find a *family* of existing products clustering in the space, but that family would not merely be distant from the carriage family, but it would be in a different space with some over-lapping characteristics no doubt. Alternatively, if one created a product space including all core and noncore characteristics of both families, the "distance" of the two families from each other would be so great as to reflect a qualitative distinction between them, militating against simple measurement distinctions.

I will include "time associated with consumption" in Becker's sense[4] as a quality and consequently as a competitive factor. When one purchases a method of language instruction the prospective time to completion of effective consumption and benefit is an important competitive feature among alternatives. Similarly, speed of checkout at supermarkets, time-to-delivery of mail order goods, speed of repair services, and so forth, are important qualities in a time-sensitive culture. This quality possesses a capacity for cardinal measurement, but should be depicted as a probability density function of possibly uncertain familial lineage, with expected value and variance, complicating inclusion in models.

Finally, attributes offer no self-evident or "natural" procedure for conventional measurement. How does one measure the ambience of restaurant *A* in a comparable fashion with that of restaurant *B*? What of the comparative "eye-pleasability" or "delectation" of their dishes, the "appeal" of their entertainment, the "compliance to standards" of their drinks? Each of these characteristics introduces a subjective complication in the form of individual preferences, so that even were some acceptable scaling devised for the individual, such scalings would not be interpersonally comparable. Clearly, attributes confront the theorist with the thorniest challenges to measurement manageability among characteristics, and given their ubiquity in oligopolistic nonprice competition some acceptable method of response must be developed before much progress can be made in modeling such competition formally. We treat such problems in sections 4 and 5 after addressing the nature of characteristics and the definition of brands or products in section 3.

3 TREATING THE PRODUCT

Another question is whether the product can be treated most fruitfully as (1) an alterable aggregate of individual characteristics or (2) an entity with immanent and fixed characteristics. In general this question will be answered by the purpose and scope of the analysis performed, or by the nature of the interdependence of the characteristics involved. When one is studying the effect of oligopolistic competition on the design of the product – its size or weight, the length of its mean time to failure, its sweetness, its convenience of packaging, and so forth – one will treat it as alterable in characteristics. Consumer preferences over characteristics must be specified or encapsulated in demand parameters, and profit maximization performed with their explicit or implicit incorporation. On the other hand, if the products can be treated as characteristics-unalterable, preferences among competing products or their reflections in demand functions, will suffice. One approach is a micro- and the other a macro-characteristics methodology.

One frequently employed technique of the macro variety is to use a spatial analogue as a simple characteristics space. In Hotelling's seminal analysis of location of firms in a linear market[5] and the large literature it inspired, space was used both literally as a product quality providing the sole quality variable among otherwise homogeneous products and as an analogue for a "characteristics space" measuring in some sense the similarity of products in the space. This spatial analogue approach has become one of the most popular methodologies in the field and will be discussed in Chapter 4 and employed in the analyses of Chapters 10–12. The method has the additional attraction of providing a "measurement" of consumer preferences for competing products on the same scale, nearness of consumers to products correlated cardinally with strength of preference for them.

A micro-characteristics approach at the other extreme of analytical methods is to view the product as a collection of characteristics as in Lancaster's approach or as a collection of core and noncore characteristics in my own work.[6] The micro disaggregation in Lancaster's work is carried into the preference specification, with consumers viewed as expressing preferences over a characteristics field whose members are then treated as substitutable to obtain indifference mappings of preferences for a unit of product consumption. In my own approach consumer preferences are expressed for products as a whole and change with alterations in the characteristics mix for movement between micro and macro treatments. These approaches are discussed in greater length in Chapters 2 and 5.

Is the good with the same separable physical and intangible characteristics identifiably linked to the individual good via brand name the same "product" when it is supported by advertising or other marking effort and when it is not? For purposes of analytic convenience, how can one distinguish among nonprice competitive practices that are "characteristics" of the product and those that are not? Both the warranty attached to a given automobile and the marketing effort expended on its sale are meant to change consumer preferences, and indeed consumer warranties are frequently more genuinely marketing ploys than contingent guarantees of repair services. Qualitatively distinctive impacts on consumer preferences, therefore, are not a promising classificatory criterion.

The means proposed in this book for defining the product by its characteristics is to include in the latter term only those tangible and intangible properties that can be identifiably and unambiguously linked to the proffered supply of the individual *unit* of commodity. The length of a warranty period is, therefore, under this definition a product quality, whereas selling costs expended for promotion of a specific type of good or of a group of such goods is not. In Chapter 12 they are treated as external supports for the sale of a product that affect the cognitive distances between products but are not internalized among its unit characteristics, as are also such expenditures as those for research and development or product innovation. Location of the product in time or space are treated as product qualities, identifiably associated with the unit of product.

4 THE MEASUREMENT AND SCALING PROBLEM

Central to the preparations for formal analysis of characteristics or product competition is measurement or scaling in the dimensions of characteristics or product space. I shall distinguish between "measurement" proper, which meets certain rigorous conditions to be discussed below and which can be distinguished by "degree of uniqueness," and "scaling," which is a heuristic procedure for association of a number scale and intensity of possession of a characteristic or product whose justification rests wholly on empirical usefulness.

a Some Theory of Measurement[7]

Formal measurement of the degree to which a product possesses a given characteristic rests on the proof of two types of theorem. The first – a representation theorem – establishes that the structure of the characteristic is similar (i.e., either *homeomorphic* or *isomorphic*) to the structure of the real number line. The representation is performed through a relational system which associates the property in a set of objects to be measured with positions on the number line. The second type of theorem establishes the "uniqueness" of the function that maps the relational system into or onto the real number system. That is, it characterizes the structure of alternative functions performing this mapping that could have been employed without sacrificing loss of information or the ability to perform mathematical operations on the resulting measurement.

For example, suppose we are interested in the degree to which a set of products possesses some characteristic. Assume, for example, that the set of products, A, with elements a_i, $i = 1, 2, \ldots n$, is a collection of brands of ice cream in cartons and that we choose the binary relation $\geq$, "at least to the same degree as" for the *relational* system, $\mathscr{E} = \{A, \geq\}$. We will leave the specific nature of the characteristics unspecified for the moment, but assume that it is possible to rank the brands from highest to lowest with respect to degree of presence of the given characteristic of interest. Assume, further, that without loss of generality the ranking is $a_1 \geq a_2 \geq \ldots a_n$.

To *measure* the ice cream brands with respect to this quality, however, it is necessary to determine some manner of deriving a function $f(a)$ which maps each brand's rank into real numbers in such manner that $f(a) \geq f(a')$ if and only if $a \geq a'$. But that mapping can be accomplished, if at all, with varying degrees of "similarity" to the real number system, a mapping which confronts some strict standards to which $f(a)$ may or may not conform.

To be technical, the mathematician views the real number system, $\mathbb{R}^n$, as a *complete ordered field*. A field, F, consists of a set with zero and unit elements and with two functions, $+$ and $\cdot$ defined on $F \times F$. The function $+$ maps all $x, y \in F$ into $x + y \in F$, where the function is commutative in addition ($x + y = y + x$). Analogously, function $\cdot$ maps all $x, y \in F$ into $xy \in F$. Define the set F' as the set of all nonzero elements in F: all elements of F' are commutative in multiplication ($xy = yx$) and, for elements $x, y, z \in F$, $x(y + z) = xy + xz$, i.e., the elements are distributive in multiplication.

An *ordered* field is one such that for every pair of elements $x, y \in F$, a relation over them exists such that (1) every such element is either positive, zero, or negative, (2) if $x > 0$ and $y > 0$, then $x + y > 0$ and $xy > 0$, and (3) $x > y$ if and only if $x - y > 0$. It will then follow that exactly one of the following relations will hold: $x > y$, $x < y$ or $x = y$; and if $x > y$ and $y > z$ then $x > z$ (i.e., the relation is asymmetric and transitive). A *complete ordered* field is simply one in which every nonempty subset of F which is bounded from above (below) has a least upper bound (greatest lower bound).

Suppose now that we have devised an $f(a)$ which is an ordered field, mapping the set of values, $s = f(a)$ onto some domain of R, preserving $+$, $\cdot$, and the relation $\geq$. Then $f(a + a') = f(a) + f(a')$, $f(a \cdot a') = f(a) \cdot f(a')$, and $a \geq a'$ implies that $f(a) \geq f(a')$. Intuitively, then, consider the real number line, R. It conforms to the specified behaviors under addition and multiplication: we can map into any point on it by summation or multiplication. Indeed, any function $f(a)$ that conforms to the requirements and retains the ranking of set elements *is* the real number line.

First, as an example, suppose that the characteristic in which we are interested is *weight* or the quality of "heaviness," and that to derive the ranking of ice cream package weights we have been clever enough to use a large spring which expands and contracts as packages of different weight are placed upon it. When the spring has no weight on it, the function $f(a)$ assigns a value of 0, but as ice cream packets are placed upon it and it is allowed to change its length freely we note the degree of expansion from its unextended position. To determine that degree of expansion, we pick up a stick of arbitrary length from the ground and record the number of "sticksfull," $s_i = f(a_i)$, that package a_i stretches the spring. We determine the greatest "stretch" as an upper bound and 0 as a lower bound, and note that $f(a)$ carries a into the real number line R over the whole domain of $f(a)$ and that the functions $+$ and $\cdot$ are preserved in the mapping. Finally the requirements for a completely ordered field are met. Then, indeed, the relation system $\mathscr{E}$ is *isomorphic* to the real number line R, which essentially means that its similarity to R is so close as to be identical.

This type of mapping is called a *ratio scale* because the ratios of $f(a)$ values are meaningful: that is, if one package has a value of 4 sticks and another a value of 2 sticks, it is meaningful to assert that the first package is twice the weight of the second. The term "meaningful" is defined to mean that any other scaling we obtained from this procedure would have differed from this scaling only because the size of the stick was different. If the stick we had chosen had been half as long as that we used, the scalings for the first and second packages would have been 8 and 4; had it been twice as long they would have been 2 and 1. In all such instances the relationship "twice as heavy" would have been maintained.

Suppose, however, that the characteristic of interest had been "degree of heat" or temperature of the ice cream packages, and that we had derived an empirical relation $\mathscr{E} = \{A, \geq\}$ on set A in the following manner. We insert a glass tube of colored alcohol into each packet and note the length of the alcohol in the tube when compared with the length displayed when the tube is at the point at which water just freezes. Let us set this as an "origin" of the scale on which *f(a)* is measured (say, 0) and as an arbitrary upper bound let us set the expansion of the alcohol when water boils at some value (say, 100). Then values of the ice cream's temperature *f(a)* are scaled as the percentage which their expansion is of the distance between these bounds.

Consider the representational function *f(a)* and the set *A*. That set is a partially ordered set, in that *f(a)* is transitive and asymmetric and $f(a) \geq f(a')$ if and only if $a \geq a'$. But *f(a)* is not a function that qualifies the pair $[A, f(a)]$ as a field. Two packs of ice cream, one of which registers 10 on the scale and one of which registers 20 do not have a combined temperature of 30, for example, nor is the product of their scalings meaningful. Moreover, although *f(a)* may *seem* to have a 0 value, that was assigned to it by us wholly arbitrarily: there is no "natural" origin of the scale. Hence this scaling is not "identical" to the real number line as was the case with weight, although is has some lesser degree of "similarity" to it.

Let $\mathbb{R}$ be the real number line. Then *f(a)* maps *A* on to $\mathbb{R}$, with a range that is potentially all of $\mathbb{R}$ including its negative values. Further, $f^{-1}(a)$ is the inverse of *f(a)*, and both of these functions are continuous. Under these conditions *f(a)* is termed a *homeomorphic mapping* or a *homeomorphism*. Its "degree of similarity" to the real number line is less than identity that we found in the isomorphism "measuring" weight.

Finally, suppose that we wish to measure the "sweetness" of the ice cream brands, and we succeed in ranking them from least to most sweet. It may prove convenient to attach numerals to the ranking, and suppose we choose any numbers from $\mathbb{R}$ that retain the ordering. Except for this restriction, any numbers on the real number line can be selected for the a_i. Let these numbers be denoted s_i.

Now, consider a function $f(s_i) = s_i/(1 + |s_i|)$. This function is clearly continuous with absolute values less than 1, so that the values *f(s)* lie in the open interval [–1,1]. Moreover, *f(s)* is negative, zero or positive as *s* is negative, zero or positive. If $f(s_i) = f(s_j)$, then $s_i = s_j$, so $f^{-1}(s)$ exists. Clearly, also, $f^{1}(s_j) = s_j/(1 - |s_j|)$. Hence, *f(s)* is a homeomorphic mapping of $\mathbb{R}$ on [–1, 1].

In our consideration of the isomorphic mapping of weight on $\mathbb{R}$ we asked the question whether ratios of *f(a)* were meaningful. Let us now approach the homeomorphic mappings with similar questions. First, with respect to temperature, note the absence of a *natural* zero value:[8] even though we assigned a zero value to an arbitrary degree of heat (the freezing point of water) we might just as well have assigned any other value (say, 32) to this benchmark point. Further, it was necessary to locate another anchoring bench mark which is discernible to the senses (say, the boiling point of water) and place some arbitrary value (greater than the value given the freezing point) on it (say, 212). This new scale, $f'(a)$, would now add proportions, r, of 180 to 32 to obtain its values.

Consider the functions $f(a)$ and $f'(a)$:

$$\begin{aligned} &1 \quad f(a) = 0 + r(100 - 0) = 100r \\ &2 \quad f'(a) = 32 + r(212 - 32) = 32 + 180r. \end{aligned} \tag{1.1}$$

First, let us test the meaningfulness of the ratios of these two measures of degrees of heat. The observations a_i and a_j will yield r_i and r_j in expansion proportions of the fixed intervals. These ratios are

$$\begin{aligned} &1 \quad \frac{f(a_j)}{f(a_i)} = \frac{100r_j}{100r_i} = \frac{r_j}{r_i} \\ &2 \quad \frac{f'(a_j)}{f'(a_i)} = \frac{32 + 180r_j}{32 + 180r_i} \end{aligned} \tag{1.2}$$

which are not the same, yet both functions are equally valid measures of temperature. Centigrade readings of 70 and 35 yield Fahrenheit values of 158 and 95 respectively, but

$$\frac{70}{35} \neq \frac{158}{95} \tag{1.3}$$

If, therefore, on either scale we derive two values, one of which is twice the value of the other, we cannot assert that the temperature of the first is twice that of the other. Any other equally valid choices of anchoring values for the scale would not have yielded the same ratio.

Note, from (1.2), that the problem is the choice of the "origin" of the scale: had we a "natural" zero we should have an isomorphism and a ratio scale. But this implies that any operation on these scales that eliminates the origin will be meaningful. For example, consider differences or "intervals" between values:

$$\begin{aligned} &1 \quad f(a_i) - f(a_j) = 100r_i - 100r_j = 100(r_i - r_j) \\ &2 \quad f'(a_i) - f'(a_j) = 32 + 180r_j - 32 - 180r_j = 180(r_i - r_j). \end{aligned} \tag{1.4}$$

The ratio of the intervals will always be in the ratio 1:1.8, the relative size of the "degrees" or units of the two scalings. Hence, a difference of 10° anywhere on the Centigrade scale will always convert to 18° on the Fahrenheit. Therefore, this type of homeomorphism is called an *interval scale* because intervals are meaningful in the sense that they are the "same" except for the arbitrary number of degrees into which a given length of expansion of the measuring liquid is converted.

Finally, let us study the scalings *f(a)* for the homeomorphism of the sweetness scale. Consider a_i and a_j, $a_i < a_j$. Then, we might have chosen $s_i = -2$, $s_j = -1$; alternatively, and equally capable of preserving the ranking, $s_i' = 10$ and $s_j' = 20$ might be designated. Then $f(s_i) = 0.67$, $f(s_j) = 0.50$, $f(s_i') = 0.91$ and $f(s_j') = 0.95$. It follows that

$$\frac{f(s_i)}{f(s_j)} = \frac{-0.67}{-0.50} = 1.34 \neq 0.97 = \frac{0.91}{0.95} = \frac{f(s_i')}{f(s_j')} \tag{1.5}$$

No ratio scale here, obviously. Consider, now, the intervals:

$$\begin{aligned} &1 \quad f(s_i) - f(s_j) \;=\; -0.67 + 0.50 = -0.17 \\ &2 \quad f(s_i') - f(s_j') \;=\; 0.91 - 0.95 \;=\; -0.04 \end{aligned} \tag{1.6}$$

Choose two more points with an interval equal to that between s_i and s_j, say $s_i'' = -10$ and $s_i'' = -9$. Then,

$$\begin{aligned} &1 \quad f(s_i'') - f(s_j'') = -0.909 + 0.90 = -0.009 \\ &2 \quad f(s_i') - f(s_j') \;=\; 0.91 - 0.95 \;=\; -0.04 \end{aligned} \tag{1.7}$$

Obviously,

$$\frac{f(s_i) - f(s_j)}{f(s_i') - f(s_j')} = \frac{-0.17}{-0.04} = 4.25 \neq .225 = \frac{f(s_i'') - f(s_i'')}{f(s_i') - f(s_j')}. \tag{1.8}$$

Intervals on the scale are not meaningful, so that the measures are not interval scalings. What is preserved is the sign of the intervals: by construction if $a_j > a_i$ then $s_j > s_i$, and if $a_j = a_i$ then $s_j = s_i$, it then follows that any scale we might have derived from our method would have preserved the ranking.

Isomorphic mappings on $\mathbb{R}$, therefore, are meaningful with respect to ratios of scale values, intervals between scale values, and, of course, the signs of intervals. Homeomorphic mappings on $\mathbb{R}$ never yield meaningful ratios, may yield meaningful differences between scale values, and always preserve meaningful signs of the differences.

These characteristics of the mappings of *A* on $\mathbb{R}$ can be translated into terms of the "uniqueness" of the measurement scales derived by these methods, and the proofs of these uniqueness theorems concerning meaningful ratios, intervals and signs of intervals yield the second set of validations of measurements. By *uniqueness* is meant a designation of the characteristics of the family of scalings that our methods are capable of yielding. That is, we have seen that the isomorphisms and homeomorphisms derived by the methods discussed above constrain the meaningfulness of the scalings possible from our methods to greater or lesser degrees. By defining the forms of the functions *f(a)* we can specify the uniqueness properties of the scalings exactly.

Consider, first, the isomorphism that yielded meaningful ratios:

$$f(a_i) = bs_i \tag{1.9}$$

Those ratios differed only by a positive scale factor, so that if any other function *f(a)* that preserves this highest degree of meaningfulness will have to differ from *f(a)* only through arbitrary choice of the size of the unit of measurement:

$$f'(a_j) = b's_i. \tag{1.10}$$

Hence, whether b is pounds or b' is ounces, the scalings s are the "same," in the sense that they yield identical ratios. Since *f(a)* can differ from *f′(a)* only by choice of b, the scalings are *unique up to a positive multiplicative constant*.

Second, let us designate the degree of uniqueness of homeomorphisms that are interval scale. If *f(a)* is a valid scale (say, the Centigrade scale), they any other scale that preserves the meaningfulness of intervals, *f′(a)* (say, the Fahrenheit scale), can differ from it only by addition of a constant and a different choice of unit of measurement. Let

$$f(a_i) = o + bs_i. \tag{1.11}$$

Then any other *f′(a)* derivable by the method of scaling must be

$$f'(a_i) = o' + b's_i. \tag{1.12}$$

This degree of uniqueness is designated *uniqueness up to a linear or affine transformation*.

Finally, consider homeomorphisms that merely preserve rankings, i.e., those in which only the signs of intervals are meaningful. If *f(a)* is such a function, then any other function that rises when *f(a)* rises, falls when it falls, and moves sideways when it retains the same value, will meet the constraint. That is, when *f′(a)* moves monotonically in the same direction as *f(a)*, then *f′(a)* preserves *f(a)*'s rankings. The degree of uniqueness, therefore, is *uniqueness up to a positive monotonic transformation*.

These three forms of measurement have been distinguished from each other by the terms *ordinal* and *cardinal* measurement. Ordinal measurement is unambiguously used to refer to uniqueness up to a positive monotone transformation. On the other hand, cardinality as used in the economics literature refers either to ratio scales only or includes both ratio and interval scales. Because the latter definition mixes isomorphisms with homeomorphisms, and because the same set of arithmetic operations cannot be performed on such scales, cardinal measurement will be reserved in this book for reference to uniqueness up to a positive multiplicative constant or ratio scales. Therefore, lineal or weight measurements will be referred to as cardinal, a von Neumann–Morgenstern index as unique up to a linear or affine transformation.

True measurement of objects' characteristics may be more or less "precise" in terms of uniqueness and the kinds of arithmetic operations that can be performed upon the derived scale. But it is "precise" mathematically in that a given type of measurement must be related as an isomorphism or homeomorphism to the real number line and the degree of uniqueness of the scale must be proven. Failure to establish these theorems means that arithmetic operations upon the scale are not only suspect: they must be rejected as valid measurements.

5 THE CASE FOR QUASI-MEASUREMENT OR SCALING

This conclusion, taken to heart by an economics profession striving desperately to attain the status of a natural science, closes the accessibility of much of characteristics analysis to the tool of economic analysis. Yet, in subscribing to such an exclusively deductive view, economists ignore another characteristic of modern scientific method: induction. Does a given method of scaling "work" in performing the tasks assigned it, even though representation and uniqueness theorems are unproved or unprovable? Does it consistently yield results that outperform alternative methods of making judgments? Less positively, does it mislead less frequently than alternative means, or does it provide support for those other means, and is its use properly qualified by its failure to conform to the rigors of the theory of measurement?

For example, psychologists seek insights into attitudes, ask subjects to scale handwriting in terms of "pleasingness," and require raters to score candidates in such qualities as "cooperativeness," "leadership," and "acting ability." None of these properties is truly susceptible to exact definition, not to mention capable of meeting the rigors of section 4. These scaling procedures, however, are those of *subjective estimate*, or blends of the scientific and the intuitive, and they are adapted for our purposes in this book.[9] Moreover, they are experimental in nature, and must establish their usefulness in practice.

I shall, then, frankly embrace the intuitive when the objective fails us: for example, I shall envision asking subjects whether the "flavor" of brand 1 is closer to that of brand 2 or brand 3 and by how much, where "flavor" is the primitive concept. It is fruitless to search for deeper concepts with which to define such qualities as "flavor" or "aroma"; and yet I hypothesize that the consumer will be able to answer such questions consistently with his or her fellow subjects within the confines of subjective probability theory and to the extent that the constructed scale may be treated as similar to an interval scale with useful results.

The use of "inexact" or quasi-measurement for practical scaling purposes has a long history in such fields as psychology and education. Indeed, in the academic community there is an inconsistency that verges on guiltless hypocrisy or, more generously, cognitive dissonance, in its condemnation of nonrigorous scaling methods and general professional practices. We may appeal to the practice of grading students in many course dimensions.

Consider the scoring of student achievement from 0 to 100 in a course of study. The characteristic to be "measured" is notable for its lack of precise definition: it is a connotative quality, drawing upon the experience, intuition and introspection of the grader for meaningfulness. Attempts to give it simple meaning lead one to balk: for example, conversion to the proportion of objective questions answered correctly (corrected or uncorrected for random guessing) leads to the objection that there is no readily plausible relation between percentage points on the correct-answers scale and percentage points of achievement.

If, therefore, the concept of a representational relation is at best fuzzy, what degree of uniqueness does such a student scoring system have? Is it at best unique up to a positive monotone transformation? Perhaps most of those who engage regularly in this judgment process would settle for the assurance that our scalings are that discerning. If so, however, the usual arithmetic operations performed on such grades are invalid: they cannot be added to other grades of the same grader or averaged and weighted. Are they equivalent to points on an interval scale, so that the 0 origin corresponds to no natural zero but intervals between individuals on the grade scale are meaningful? This would permit arithmetic operations of the weighted average variety, but would forbid such procedures as standardizing grades by use of standard deviations. Or, finally, would any of us maintain that the grading is isomorphic, with a 0 coincident with "absolutely no achievement" in a definable sense? Is the student who earns 80 assertively twice the achiever of the student who earns 40?

I would suspect that most experienced educators are quite humble in an admission confessing inability to prove a uniqueness theorem. Yet consider what the educational system does with such scalings. Not only does the individual teacher blithely add and weight and average such grades for course grades, but such course grades over a collection of grading instructors are added and averaged to obtain student career grade averages. A useless exercise at best, a distorting procedure at worst? Not at all: such grades and grade averages provide one of the best projectors of academic achievement that we have in higher education. Like the bumblebee whose structure dictates its theoretical inability to fly, the practical capability of the grading process belies its theoretical defects.

In this book I will suggest that an interpretation of the following type will validate the grading procedure and similar methodology in other characteristics areas. A teacher acquires through experience and training a good conception of the performance of an idealized student who has passed through the course or some segment of it with no practicably measurable accretion of knowledge. This idealized notion of null accomplishment he or she places at the 0 mark of his or her scale, and it can be interpreted as a "natural" zero for the individual teacher. At the other extreme, the idealized student who has mastered the material in a manner that could not be effectively surpassed in the time available is also present in the teacher's subconscious, and anchors the scale at the 100 mark. Hence the grading scale may be interpreted as *percentages of effective range (ER) of accomplishment*, and may be manipulated as a ratio scale.

If the "standards" of a teacher – the idealized definitions of 0 and 100 – are similar in some inevitably intuitive sense to the standards of other teachers, the grades may be averaged among courses over the academic lifetime of the student with meaningful results. Decisions of great importance to individuals, universities and society are made on the basis of such scalings and in the faith that their assimilated uniqueness is that of a ratio scale. The indefinable quality of academic excellence or achievement is scored in a "quasi-measurement" or scaling procedure reflecting intuitive–introspective knowledge, without formal proofs of isomorphic or homeomorphic relations to the number line or of uniqueness theorems, and with no scale validations by means of controlled stimuli.

The question to be faced frankly at this point is the following: can this experience with educational scaling, with its plausible if not provable foundations and its long record of accomplishment be projected with useful results into the untested area of characteristics scaling? It seems to me that any hope for progress in applying analytical techniques to qualities is dependent on an affirmative answer – an answer that can be rendered only by bold hypotheses and experimental attempts to validate usefulness. Some confidence is obtained by realization that the terrain is not wholly unexplored: psychologists, marketing researchers, and artificial intelligence workers intent on quantifying expertise have pioneered. With some hope of progress, then, I shall present the results of one extensive experiment and some proposed techniques in Chapter 2.

6 SUMMARY AND CONCLUSIONS

Nonprice properties of products, or *characteristics*, include *qualities*, or those that are continuously or discontinuously variable and can be scaled by measurement or quasi-measurement techniques, and *attributes*, those that cannot be scaled in other than a binary, 0, 1, present or not present manner. We distinguish between properties that are *extrinsic* to the product, such as warranties, location, or marketing services, and those that are *intrinsic*, such as flavor, packaging, color, and the like. And we also classify properties by *unit linkage*, or those that can be identifiably linked to the product unit, such as weight, color, location, consumption time duration, or packaging, and *unit nonlinkage*, which cannot be so linked, such as research and development services, marketing promotion, or patent protection services. And, finally, such properties are distinguished by their importance in defining one product from others: *core* characteristics are those judged vital in such a task, and *noncore* are those of a secondary nature in product definition.

Analysis of characteristics in decision making and competition is hindered by a variety of difficulties. One is the frequently difficult or impossible task of objectifying the property, which is its disentanglement from consumer preferences. Another is the decision to treat the characteristic as the unit of consumer concern or to center attention upon the product as a complex of characteristics. But by far the most troubling is the problem of measurement.

Bona fide measurement requires the proof of two theorems: the first, a *representation theorem*, is that a given relation system is related to the real number line as an *isomorphism* or a *homeomorphism*, and the second is to establish the *degree of uniqueness* of the homeomorphism. Formal measurement of characteristics is frequently – indeed, more often than not – impossible, and progress in analysis depends upon *scaling* or *quasi-measurement* techniques.

To these tasks the experiment detailed in Chapter 2 is dedicated. As will be seen, the results there are most encouraging. What seems to me to be a remarkable degree of consistency in sample characteristics and interbrand distance scalings emerged from the experiments, over a spectrum of poorly defined and abstract characteristics.

A call for the relaxation of scientific standards to make progress in a problem area cannot hope to be as ringing as an heroic summons to embrace their comforting if sterile rigor. But the results of these intuitive and heuristic methods are encouraging enough to permit hope that quasi-measurement techniques will permit us to make substantial progress in integrating nonprice competition with the body of microeconomic theory.

2 Core Characteristics Analysis

Most frequently economists have employed variants of five basic formal approaches to the analysis of product differentiation, and in the following chapters some important prototypes of these frameworks will be illustrated and adapted for use. The first and oldest of the techniques was referred to in Chapter 1 as drawing upon the notion of spatial extent both literally and analogically, with Hotelling's seminal article a point of departure in both usages.[1] One of the most important and most apparent differentiating characteristics of many products is the location of their producers, sellers or customers in geographic space. von Thünen (1929), Weber (1909, 1929), Predöhl (1928), Palander (1935), Lösch (1954), Isard (1956), and Beckmann and Puu (1985). produced landmark scholarship efforts on the path to modern spatial economic theory. There is now an extensive body of literature dealing with these literal spatial aspects of firms' strategies and there is no need to deal with it in the narrow confines of the present book. Therefore efforts in this area are limited to those analyses (1) that are importantly concerned with spatial competition within an oligopolistic context or (2) that use the spatial model as a metaphor for placement in a product space. This approach is discussed in Chapter 4. and used in Chapter 11 to model firms' decisions to relocate in a product space. Moreover, throughout our theory and modeling the notion of "cognitive distancing" of products in such a space is employed.

A second – and more recent – approach to the analysis of product characteristics is that of Lancaster (1966, 1971, 1972, 1975, 1979, 1991) which treats commodities as variable bundles of qualities within a linear characteristics space, with consumers' preferences defined over such variables rather than commodities *per se*. It is described in Chapter 5. Within this framework the analysis can draw upon the substantial body of techniques developed for the analysis of linear technologies, with attendant advantages and disadvantages.

Game theory has also contributed to the modeling of strategic interactive decision making with price and product characteristics rivalry, without, in my opinion, marked success in yielding insights. For reasons given in Chapter 1 and explained in more detail in Chapters 6 and 9, the framework for incorporating oligopolistic decision making in this work will be that of *rivalrous consonance*. It may be interpreted as a stand alone framework for oligopolistic analysis, as I believe it to be, or as a supplement to game-theoretic reasoning which translates the game theorist's equilibria into an operational model for comparative statics reasoning. In Chapter 3 I will illustrate its usage in both modes. Nonetheless, game theory is by all odds the mainstream framework for oligopoly, and no broad methodological survey of this terrain would be complete without attention paid to its accomplishments. Its contributions will be reviewed briefly in Chapter 6.

Fourth, important work in nonprice competition has been done using traditional types of neoclassical theory in which product differentiation is treated *implicitly*, meaning that the specific nature of quality differences among brands is ignored. Important work in this methodology deals primarily with monopolistic competition market structure in the strict sense of the term: that is, in the sense of E. H. Chamberlin's large group case and J. Robinson's tangency solution. This is a market structure in which I have little interest because I believe its attraction to analysts lies in its ability to yield determinate solutions rather than its relevancy to reality. Nonetheless, the analyses do have some bearing upon the tasks of this book. Seminal articles are those of Dixit and Stiglitz (1977) and Spence (1976). The monopolistic competition approach will also be discussed in Chapter 6.

In this chapter a fifth framework is presented that preserves the product as the unit of analysis but employs the notions of *core* and *noncore* characteristics to define product groups.[2] Differentiation among brands in a product group is then treated by using quasi-measurement techniques to obtain "distances" in the product group space and to measure consumer preferences with respect to such distances from preferred brands. It then draws upon spatial analogue techniques for its modeling. Acceptance or nonacceptance of the methodology depends upon the analyst's willingness or lack of willingness to accept quasi-measurement as a valid basis for metric measurement, as well as the meaningfulness of distances in multidimensional product space as an index of brand differences.

We will review the fundamental concepts, strengths and weaknesses of the first four approaches through examinations of some of their major representations in Chapters 3–6, without pretending to be exhaustive. The purpose of this chapter is to acquaint the reader with the core characteristics approach and to illustrate its application, because it forms the frame of the methodology of Part III of the book.

1 CORE CHARACTERISTICS ANALYSIS

It is appropriate to respond to the questions raised in Chapter 1 by presenting a methodology that was developed independently of and contemporaneously with Lancaster's characteristics approach.[3] That early interest in product differentiation was awakened when I attempted to build Chamberlin's large group case alongside pure competition in a general equilibrium model – a path that had been pioneered by Negishi (1961). In Kuenne (1967) I criticized Triffin (1949) for recommending that general equilibrium theory abandon the categories of the *industry* and the *product group* and analyze interfirm competition across products as indexed by such measures as cross-elasticities.[4] Such measurements have the advantage of incorporating consumer preferences into the definition of differentiation, but they extort too dear a price in the sacrifice of concepts which have existential validity in the decision making of economic agents for the uncertain utility of bloodless analytical categories derivative from those concepts.

So it seemed to me then and so it seems to me now. In that early work I defined characteristics (I used the term "qualities") in manners similar to those of Lancaster. They were taken to be physical attributes that were objective, measurable and definable independently of consumer preferences. A *product group* was distinguished by component goods that possessed a *core* of physical characteristics which differentiated its members *physically* from other goods in the consumer's preference field. Those core characteristics could differ in intensity among group members either continuously in cardinal measurement, in ordinal measurement, or attribute-wise in a 0–1 manner. The group goods could also possess *fringe* characteristics which could vary widely among products and whose intensity of presence played no role in defining the product group but might affect consumers' preferences among group goods. These distinctions were somewhat similar to relevant and irrelevant characteristics in Lancaster's analysis, although his treatment is much more extensive and satisfactory.

A topological approach was used to map points in characteristics space into feasible goods space, after characteristics measurable unique up to a linear transformation were normalized to yield quantities of intensity in the unit interval, whether or not a natural zero existed. Nonpresence was given a zero value and the content of the feasible good in which it had greatest intensity was indexed at 1. Attributes were assigned 0 or 1 values. Boldly, in accordance with the discussion of quasi-measurement of Chapter 1, homeomorphic measures that merely preserved rankings were normalized in the interval [0,1] and treated as cardinal. Although distances among the actual and hypothetical but feasible goods in goods space were not used in the formal modeling, it was suggested that a Euclidean metric could be employed to derive them in at least approximative manner for scaling in other uses.

The paper's methodology was constrained by its purpose, which was to incorporate nonrivalrous competitive behavior of the purely competitive and monopolistic competition proper forms into a Walrasian framework. Product competition was emphasized but largely implicit with "interaction functions" of firms set at zero values, ruling out oligopolistic interdependence. And although characteristics were treated primarily in physical terms, there was explicit reference to the extreme importance of attributes in product group definition and the need to bring in consumer perceptions to define them. The analysis was vague but indicates my discomfort at the time with defining characteristics independent of consumer preferences.[5]

With the completion of the paper, therefore, I was uncomfortable with two problems with which I felt I had not dealt adequately and which I perceived to be central problems in operational attacks upon realistic differentiated product analysis. The first was with the lack of empirical justification for the assumption that quasi-measurement techniques, as defined in Chapter 1, could be used with some confidence as at least workable if only approximative scalings in dimensions of product differentiation not susceptible of theoretically valid measurement. The second was the nagging belief that products could not truly be placed in a product space without integration of physical attributes with consumer perceptions and attitudes. I turned my attention to both problems as preliminaries to analyzing rivalrous competition among products in oligopolistic contexts in later work.

2 METHODOLOGIES FOR QUASI-MEASUREMENT OF CHARACTERISTICS: PREFERENCES EXCLUDED

One manner of proceeding in the investigation of quasi-measurement potential is to scale characteristics in a common homogeneous unit for comparability by employing the notion of distance in a characteristics space. Another approach, when appropriate, is to use the dollar as the alternative good to the group good when characteristics are defined through consumer preferences. Both methods scale characteristics on a [0,100] or [0,1] interval and treat such scalings as unique up to a positive multiplicative constant or a linear transformation, depending upon the arithmetic operations performed on them.

As a starting point I shall refine the distinctions among characteristics given in Chapter 1 as follows:

1 qualities capable of ratio or interval measurement
2 characteristics with intensities that vary in an absolute sense
3 characteristics with intensities that vary in a relative sense
4 attributes with 0,1 intensities.

In this section I will deal with the scaling of each of these categories in turn when consumer preferences are not involved. In section 3 preference-related characteristics will be treated.

a Qualities Capable of Ratio or Interval Measurement

For qualities whose measurement uniqueness is that up to a positive multiplicative constant or a linear transformation the task is that of converting true measures into a [0,100] scale. For such measures the procedure retains its true-measurement distinction. If the feasible brands of a product group can vary between 18 and 24 inches in length, for example, we place these values at 0 and 100 respectively and transform intermediate values to percentages of the effective range (ER) of 6 inches. If brand 1 is 21 inches long and brand 2 is 19 inches long their quality grades in this dimension are 50.00 and 16.67 respectively. The absolute difference between the brands of 2 inches is thus transformed to a distance of one-third of ER, which is also their relative distance in original units of inches.

Suppose, however, the quality is the recommended temperature at which different wines are served – a natural interval measure. We now enter the realm of quasi-measurement by specifying a maximum lower bound below which it is never served (say 42 F°) and a minimum upper bound above which it is normally never served (say 82 degrees F°). These values are converted to 0 and 100 respectively, and the interval thereby converted from 40 to 100, or by 2.5 times. The intermediate values are then given a scale value of $s = 2.5(T - 42)$, where T is the brand's recommended serving temperature in degrees Fahrenheit. If brand 1 has $T = 48$ it is scaled at 15 and if brand 2 has $T = 50$ a scale value of 20 is given. The distance between them is 5 percentage points of ER.

Note importantly that the scale values given the temperatures are invariant to the particular linear transformation of (say) Fahrenheit values used. Centigrade readings for the upper and lower bounds of the temperatures and for the brand temperatures would also have yielded 15 and 20 for the scalings of the brands, as would any other linear transformation. This is simply because differences between values of an interval scale eliminate the arbitrary origin and ratios of these differences are unique up to a positive multiplicative constant which cancels out of numerator and denominator. Hence, scalings of brands retain the uniqueness of a ratio scale, as will distances between pairs of them.

To demonstrate, let U be the upper and L the lower bounds of the interval, both in degrees Fahrenheit, and let T be an intermediate value in the bracket. Then, when normalized to a scale of 100, the scaling for the Fahrenheit values is

$$s = \frac{100}{(U - L)}(T - L),$$

For the Centigrade transformation of Fahrenheit values,

$$C = \frac{F-32}{1.8},$$

so the s' scaling using Centigrade degree values is

$$\begin{aligned} s' &= \frac{100}{\frac{(U-32)-(L-32)}{1.8}} \left(\frac{(T-32)-(L-32)}{1.8} \right) \\ &= \frac{180}{U-L} \left(\frac{T-L}{1.8} \right) \\ &= s. \end{aligned}$$

b Characteristics with Intensities that Vary in an Absolute Sense

A characteristic which is possessed by a given brand in greater or lesser intensity and which can be ranked only with respect to that intensity I shall view as differing *absolutely* among members of the product group. The inter-brand distance between goods on the scaling interval [0,100] represents a consensus among relevant agents of an economy at a particular time, reflecting their conceptual and perceptual differences and subjective uncertainties.

More explicitly, the state of mind of each participant is formalized as a subjective probability distribution over the ER scale, the probability value defining a degree of belief concerning positions of brands on the scale with respect to characteristic intensity. By asking each individual to locate three grades on the scale an attempt is made to estimate his or her probability distribution and its expected value. By taking some measure of central tendency for the values of the sample of individuals the final scale value is determined.

On a line segment with 0 and 100 as end points and with the quartiles marked as designated 25, 50 and 75, the subject is asked to place three points graphically:

1 L: a lower bound on degree of intensity below which he or she is in effect certain the given brand does not contain the characteristic
2 H: an upper bound above which he or she is effectively certain the characteristic intensity of the brand does not lie
3 M: the best point estimate of the location of the brand characteristic intensity on the interval the subject can make.

It is then assumed that the probability density over the interval can be approximated by a beta distribution, with parameters α and β and with mode M and range $H - L$:

$$\beta(s) = \left(\frac{\Gamma(\alpha + \beta + 2)}{\Gamma(\alpha + 1)\Gamma(\beta + 1)(H - L)^{\alpha+\beta+1}} \right) (s - L)^{\alpha} (H - s)^{\beta}. \qquad (2.1)$$

The expected value of the distribution is

$$E(s) = \frac{L + (\alpha + \beta)M + H}{\alpha + \beta + 2}, \qquad (2.2)$$

where the assumed mode is M:

$$M = \frac{\alpha H + \beta L}{\alpha + \beta}. \qquad (2.3)$$

Let $Z = \alpha + \beta$ and $K = (M - L)/(H - L)$. Then, from (2.2) and (2.3)

$$\alpha = ZK \qquad (2.4)$$

and (2.2) can be written

$$E(s) = \frac{L + ZM + H}{Z + 2}. \qquad (2.5)$$

To estimate Z another independent relation is necessary, and this is obtained from the formula for the variance of a beta distribution:

$$\sigma^2 = (H - L)^2 \left(\frac{Z^2K - Z^2K^2 + Z + 1}{(Z + 2)^2(Z + 3)} \right). \qquad (2.6)$$

$(H - L)$ is the range of the distribution and the further assumption is made that the beta distribution follows the normal distribution in including practically all of its range in an interval of 6σ.[6] Therefore, from (2.6):

$$\frac{(Z^2K - Z^2K^2 + Z + 1)}{(Z + 2)^2(Z + 3)} = \frac{1}{36}, \qquad (2.7)$$

from which Z may be treated as a function of K.

For the range of values for K and Z which are realistic for the unimodal beta distribution of this analysis (Table 2.1), I list the relations between σ and $H - L$, as well as v^*, the value of $H - L$ for which the 6σ relation holds exactly.

In my experience, K in the range of 0.30 to 0.50 and Z in the range of 3 to 4 have proved most relevant for subjects, and a distribution range $H - L$ of 30 to 40 is quite frequent. The estimate of range as 6σ, therefore, seems workably accurate.

Table 2.1 Values of beta distribution standard deviation for quartile values of K and realistic Z values, with range values for which the 6σ relation holds exactly

	K = 0.25 or 0.75			*K = 0.50*	
Z	σ	V^*	Z	σ	V^*
2	$0.22(H-L)$	27	2	$0.22(H-L)$	27
3	$0.14(H-L)$	43	3	$0.19(H-L)$	30
4	$0.17(H-L)$	35	4	$0.19(H-L)$	32
5	$0.37(H-L)$	16	5	$0.12(H-L)$	50

From (2.4) K is seen to be the ratio of distance from the mode to the lower bound divided by range. If the subject is reasonably symmetrical in his or her uncertainty this should approximate 0.50. If this is assumed, $K - K^2 \approx 2.85$. Further, when $K = 0.25$ or 0.75, $Z \approx 4.80$. By fitting a least squares regression equation to these three points the following estimating equation is obtained:

$$Z \approx 2.85 + 9.30G - 6.00G^2,\ G = \{K \text{ if } K \leq 0.50,\\ G = (1-K) \text{ otherwise}\}, \tag{2.8}$$

which can be substituted into (2.5) to obtain better estimates. This is the scale value sought.

Let us review briefly the weaknesses of the quasi-measurement. First, it will frequently be impossible to define the characteristic, so that the conceptualizations of the subjects must be relied on (e.g., feminine beauty). This immediately raises the question of common standards among the subjects and the uniqueness of the 0 origin of ER. Second, the subject is not responding to external stimuli under control of the experimenter. Methods of scaling based on fractionalization or equi-sectioning are denied us: the stimulus is wholly subjective, cannot be related functionally to a controlled stimulus, and the resulting scale, therefore, cannot be operationally validated to assure that equal distances along the scale line represent equal intervals of the stimulus.

Lastly, it is unclear the extent to which personal preferences intrude into the effective definition of the characteristic used by the subject, or perhaps worse, the extent to which it is desirable to try to include or exclude such preferences. As noted in section 1, much as we should like to be able to describe all members of product groups with vectors of such objective qualities or attributes as length, color, weight, temperature, and the like, there are characteristics whose scalings involve personal preferences intimately, and it is with a consensual judgment that we seek to locate the characteristic's scaling. The "tone" of a restaurant's customers, its quality of service, the diversity of its menu, and so forth, involve personal value judgments. Where it is desirable to minimize their impacts, the methods to be discussed in subsection 2c may be applicable; but frequently this will be undesirable as the degree of excellence is not the same as the degree of similarity.

c Characteristics with Intensities that Vary in a Relative Sense

In many cases characteristic measurement can be done only by comparing intensity attainment of the property by one brand relative to another. For example, the design of a container for brand 1 may be more or less similar to the design of brand 3's package than the design of brand 2's container. The characteristic "similarity of package design" must be graded on the basis of closeness to some chosen product's package as a standard. That standard is placed at 100 on the scale, and the individual is asked to choose the brand whose container is least similar to the standard in order to anchor the scale at 0. All intermediate brands are then located on the scale using the three-grade procedures of subsection 2b.

This type of measurement employing quaternary relations in the empirical relation system – "the difference between *A* and *B* is no greater than the difference between *C* and *D*: true or false?" – is frequently used in psychological scaling, usually with a controllable stimulus which varies continuously or in small discrete steps over the entire continuum of the scale. For example, this is true if the stimulus is the frequency of a tone in cycles per second and the scale is to depict a subject's awareness of pitch. Arbitrary maximum and minimum frequencies are selected to anchor the scale and subjects are asked to choose a frequency that bisects the scale. They are successively asked to locate the quartiles, the midpoints between quartiles and end-points, and so forth. The equal interval assumption permits a scale unique up to a linear transformation. Note that the procedure in psychometrics depends only upon the subjects' ability to *rank differences* between stimulus values, difference from one point being greater than, less than or equal to difference from an antipodal point. But it depends crucially on the ability to control the stimuli in continuous or near-continuous ways over the scale continuum. That frequently is not available in economic characteristics scaling.

Another difficulty is that "similarity to" is not an operationally defined concept, and my attitude to this objection is the pragmatic one of Luce and Galanter:

> The word "similar" used in the instructions is vague, and it is left that way because neither the experimenter nor the subject can verbalize very precisely what he means by it. Nonetheless, subjects respond non-randomly

when instructed in this way. That reproducible data can arise from a vague criterion should not surprise us when we think of how often we use equally vague criteria in everyday life, but in the long run a science is not likely to let reproducibility alone substitute for well analyzed and controlled experimental design.[7]

The support for quasi-measurement by these psychologists is similar to that presented in section 5 of Chapter 1 in terms of educational grading and, by extension, with respect to characteristics scaling. It is one, I believe, that economists must come to accept and respect to make progress in this field, preserving always, albeit somewhat skeptically, the hope for more scientific methods of defining and measuring product characteristics.

d Attributes with 0,1 Intensities

In the case of pure attributes interbrand distances are simply defined as 100. A Buick automobile and a Ford, *in the dimension of "brand"*, are the maximum distance apart. In practice, the number of pure attributes is not so large as one might think at first sight: many qualities that seem to fit the category can be interpreted as qualities varying along a scale (e.g., hue of color). Where an attribute shows this potential for variation it is graded as an attribute but relevant variations may be treated by the methods of subsections 2b and 2c. If three brands are dark red, light red, and blue in color, the first and second can be scaled on the attribute scale as a variable and the third placed at 100 from the first two.

3 METHODOLOGIES FOR QUASI-MEASUREMENT OF CHARACTERISTICS: PREFERENCES INCLUDED

In subsection 2a of Chapter 1 characteristics are presented as physical properties or as abstract properties in whose measurement the psychological attitudes of the subject entered only perceptually. Specifically, the tastes or *preferences* of the individual were assumed to be neutral. An alternative to seeking the distances of products among themselves in characteristics space is to bring the consumer's preferences as constrained by income explicitly into play, thereby adding one more psychological level of complexity to the perceptual.

The approach retains the viewpoint discussed in the introduction to this chapter: the product is adopted as an operationally indispensable concept and is distinguished by its possession of a core of distinctive and defining characteristics as well as a set of noncore fringe properties which do not enter into the delineation of the product group. I shall continue to deal only with core qualities and now further distinguish them by the notion of *appropriability*. An appropriable characteristic of a brand is one lying within the realm of competition, so that rival brands can copy it or approach it in a characteristics space. A *nonappropriable* property is one which is not capable of adoption by competitors by virtue, for example, of a patent or copyright.

Suppose that an industry consists of n firms with m appropriable characteristics, the first k of which are variables and the remainder of which are attributes. I then proceed following the comparative or relative techniques of subsection 2c.

a Preferences for Characteristics with Intensities that Vary in a Relative Sense

Arbitrarily, choose brand 1 as the anchoring brand for the analysis. To a large sample of potential customers for the product address the following question for brands 2, 3, … n:

> Suppose you were given a unit of brand 1 at no cost to you. If you were offered brand j instead, how many dollars would you have to receive or give up to make you feel as well off as you feel with brand 1?

Choose some measure of central tendency for the sample responses for brands j = 2, 3, … n, and term these the *indifference premia*, I_j, where $I_1 \equiv 0$ and $I_{j \neq 1}$ can take positive, negative or zero values. We proceed to decompose these I_j into additive components, I_{ij}, i = 1, 2, … m, by pursuing the following line of questioning of the subjects:

> Suppose once more you are given a unit of brand 1. Assume brand 1's quality i were changed from its present state to that of brand j's quality i state. How much would you have to receive or pay to feel equally well off as you feel with unchanged brand 1?

A representative measure of central tendency for the responses is chosen once more and the set of derived measures I_{ij} form the elements of the *quality indifference matrix* shown in Table 2.2. It is constructed by assuming that the indifference premia for the nonappropriable characteristics, I_{ej}, are residuals:

$$I_j \equiv \Sigma_i I_{ij} + I_{ej}. \tag{2.9}$$

I assume that the identity (2.9) will be approximated by the central tendency measures of the sample and neglect sample error: hence the aggregates are

Table 2.2 The quality indifference matrix, *I*, brand 1 base

	Brand (j)			
Quality (i)	*1*	*2*	.....	*n*
1	0	I_{12}	.....	I_{1n}
2	0	I_{22}	.....	I_{2n}
.	.	.	.	.
m	0	I_{m2}	.....	I_{mn}
Nonappropriable	0	$I_{\theta 2}$	.....	$I_{\theta n}$
Indifference premia	0	I_2	.....	I_n

treated as consistent and deterministic. Note that when characteristic i is an attribute this method is applicable because preferences are being measured rather than physical or perceptual attributes.

Next, let I_i be the range of indifference premia over all brands j for characteristic i:

$$I_i = \max_j I_{ij} - \min_j I_{ij}, \tag{2.10}$$

where I_{ij} values can be positive, zero or negative, and where $I_{i1} \equiv 0$. The I_{ij} values constitute absolute scale values, being signed distances from I_{i1} for the i characteristic dimension in dollars. Relative scale values can be obtained from

$$s_{ij} = \frac{I_{ij}}{I_i} \times 100, \tag{2.11}$$

when analysis requires such measures.

b Conceptual Content of the Method

The goal of the exercise in deriving the indifference matrix, *I*, is to obtain indices over characteristics which are ratio scales, measured in monetary or percentage units, and to derive them in an operational manner. The derivation of *I* is independent of prices, but it does mix the quality preferences of individuals as well as their marginal utilities of income or wealth. When the purpose of isolating the preferences is to gain insights into the firms' decision making, the intrusion of this factor is not unwelcome since it will influence consumers' decisions to buy. However, such preferences do not have the unsullied psychology of the indifference map: they are more akin to the preference mappings under conditions of risk, capturing a relevant attitude to the purpose for which they will be used.

Several other characteristics of the preference measurement framework also should be considered. It is possible, for example, to include as a brand in Table 2.2 a hypothetical product which does not exist but can be described as a characteristics complex to the subjects. Also, characteristics that may not be capable of independent consideration by consumers, being significantly associated physically or psychologically, may be combined into a single quality.

But deficiencies in the method provide some drawbacks. First, I have assumed a type of "additive transitivity." For quality i, if subjects indicate that moving from brand 1 to brand 2 in a given characteristic dimension requires a subsidy of I_{i2} and moving from brand 1 to brand 3 requires a subsidy of I_{i3}, then moving from brand 2 to brand 3 requires $I_{i2} - I_{i3}$. Even if this holds for an individual subject it is not necessarily true that it will hold for the aggregate central tendency measures. And it might not hold for the individual if characteristic i interacts with other characteristics in preferences. Combining characteristics may be useful in such cases but may not always be possible or desirable.

Second, I assume that the I_{ij} are independent of the quantity taken by consumers. This is a simplification which may or may not be an acceptable approximation, but it is a hypothesis that is at least initially desirable to retain an operational procedure. And, lastly, I treat the I_{ij} as aggregate deterministic values obtained by an averaging process. They are realistically seen as sample estimators of a population value, distributed as a sampling distribution with expected value and standard error.

4 THE COMPUTATION OF DISTANCES IN CHARACTERISTICS DIMENSIONS AND SPACES

As a last consideration of the treatment of products in characteristics and product spaces I shall discuss the calculation of distances among products in individual characteristics and in a global sense of location in a multidimensional characteristics space. Throughout this discussion I shall use the symbols s_{ij} for characteristic i, product j relative quasi-measure scalings in percentages for both preference-neutral and preference-impacted scales, and I_{ij} for the dollar scalings of preference-impacted quasi-measures of subsection 2a.

a Distances in a Characteristics Dimension

For the distance, d_{ij}, between two brands on a single characteristics dimension I shall use Euclidean distance:

$$\begin{aligned} &1\ \ d^{i}_{jk} = \sqrt{(s_{ij} - s_{ik})^2} \\ &2\ \ d^{i}_{jk} = \sqrt{(I_{ij} - I_{ik})^2}. \end{aligned} \tag{2.12}$$

For a one-dimensional space the Euclidean metric is the same as the "metropolitan or "linear" metric:

$$\begin{aligned} &1\ \ d^{i}_{jk} = \left| s_{ij} - s_{ik} \right| \\ &2\ \ d^{i}_{jk} = \left| I_{ij} - I_{jk} \right|. \end{aligned} \tag{2.13}$$

b Distances in a Characteristics Space

The problem of computing the distance between brands in a multidimensional characteristics space is much more complicated because of the question of the relative importance of the core characteristics that have been measured in defining the product. How does one obtain the relative weights that should be applied to the flavor of the ice cream and to its "texture" when defining the product? If brand 1 is very close to brand 2 in flavor but varies widely in texture, are the brands close or far apart in product space? Are not the priorities assigned by different subjects in such definition heavily influenced by individual preferences? Can one hope for a meaningful central tendency in subjects' weighting that at least would give hope that a consensus exists concerning the relative importance of core characteristics in distinguishing products? These questions can only be answered by empirical testing to see whether methods developed in this section yield results that are consistent and useful in analysis.

1 The Cross-factor Methodology

I use a cross-factor method that assures the comparison of every characteristic with every other in the determination of the weights. An $m \times m$ matrix of the characteristics is constructed as a tableau as illustrated in Table 2.3.

(a) Characteristic factors Methods *A* and *B*

To illustrate the methodology I present a four-characteristic cross-factor matrix in Table 2.4 with characteristic factors determined in the following manner by questioning subjects. The subject is asked to compare row characteristic i with column characteristic j and to grade as follows:

Table 2.3 The cross-factor tableau

Characteristic (i)	*Characteristic (j)*					
	1	*2*	*3*	*4*	.....	*m*
1	–					
2		–				
3			–			
4				–		
.					.	
.					.	
.					.	
m						–

4: Characteristic *i* is much more important than characteristic *j* in the definition of the product group
3: Characteristic *i* is more important than characteristic *j*
2: Characteristics *i* and *j* are of equal importance
1: Characteristic *j* is more important than characteristic *i*
0: Characteristic *j* is much more important than characteristic *i*.

Thus, the subject is asked to distribute 4 points between the two characteristics, so that in Table 2.4 the sum of cells *ij* and *ji* must equal 4. Assume that the subject's answers were those recorded in Table 2.4.

Table 2.4 The cross-factor matrix example: characteristics factor method *A*

Characteristic (i)	*Characteristic (j)*					
	1	*2*	*3*	*4*	*Sum*	*Weighting Method 1*
1	*****	3	0	1	4	0.17
2	1	*****	4	3	8	0.33
3	4	0	*****	2	6	0.25
4	3	1	2	*****	6	0.25
Totals					24	1.00

I have termed this method of deriving the matrix elements – the characteristics factors – Method *A*, and an alternative procedure Method *B*. The latter is simply to ask the subject to distribute 100 points between characteristics *i* and *j* in cells *ij* and *ji*. This permits a finer discrimination among characteristics when it is felt the subjects are capable of making such greater distinctions and the characteristics themselves support this capability. I will not use Method *B* in the examples to follow, nor have I used it in an extensive experiment to be detailed in section 5, but it should be included in the arsenal of the experimenter.

Of more importance is the procedure employed in deriving the characteristics weights from the factors, and in this regard I have employed three different procedures.

(1) Weighting Method 1 The simplest method of converting characteristics factors to weights indexing the relative importance of each characteristic in defining the product is illustrated in Table 2.4. Each row is summed and these row sums are normalized to sum to 1 by division by the total of the row sums. This total is $2m(m-1)$ for an $m \times m$ cross-factor matrix, or 24 for the example in Table 2.4. The normalized weights are displayed in the last column of the table.

While this may be an acceptable procedure in many cases, a difficulty with it is that no quality can exceed a weight of $2/m$, and this upper bound is independent of the amount distributed between conjugate cells. In smaller problems, such as that depicted in Table 2.4, this may be acceptable, because the limit is rather high. But as m rises it becomes increasingly restrictive, as is seen in row 1 of Table 2.5.

(2) Weighting Method 2 This limitation of Method 2 can be combatted by a procedure that adds more discrimination to the determination of weights, and therefore must be judged superior to that of Method 1. The method is illustrated in Table 2.6. Each row sum is divided by its maximum potential

Table 2.5 Maximum characteristics weights for methods 1, 2, and 3

	m				
Weighting Method	*3*	*4*	*5*	*7*	*10*
1	0.67	0.50	0.40	0.28	0.20
2	1.00	0.75	0.60	0.43	0.30
3	0.86	0.68	0.56	0.41	0.29

value of $4(m-1)$ so that the crude weighting factors are row scores as ratios to perfect scores. These values yield measures of the "importance" of each characteristic relative to a common standard, so that when characteristic i scores high against characteristic j it is now possible to determine the importance of that superiority in a common denominator. Therefore, for a given row, each element is multiplied by the relevant column weighting factor and a new sum is computed.[8] These sums are normalized by division by their grand total and the resulting ratios are the final characteristics weights recorded in the last column of the table.

In Table 2.6 note that characteristic 1's weight has been raised when compared with that of Method 1 because its strong characteristic factor with respect to characteristic 2 was weighted by the latter's heavy factor. On the other hand characteristic 3 declines in importance because its strong superiority was over characteristic 1, a relatively poor performer. The results differ from Method 1 which weights all characteristics equally.

The maximum weight attainable by a characteristic in Method 2 is given by

$$\frac{(m-1)(m-2)}{1\cdot 2+2\cdot 3+3\cdot 4+\ldots+(m-2)(m-1)}, \tag{2.14}$$

from which the values of the second row of Table 2.5 have been computed.

In addition to permitting some release from the tight restriction on maximum weights that Method 1 imposes, another advantage of Method 2 is that it enhances the independence of weights from irrelevant characteristics. Suppose, for example, we introduce a fifth characteristic into the example of Table 2.4 which is of no importance in defining the product group. This is illustrated in Table 2.7. Ideally, this should have no impacts on the weights derived for $n = 4$, but unfortunately some impact cannot be avoided. Method 2, by taking into account the relative performance of each characteristic with respect to a perfect score softens the impact of the irrelevant characteristic on the weights. This can be seen by comparing the weights obtained from the 5×5 matrix with those from the 4×4 matrix in parentheses for both methods.

(3) Weighting Method 3 One final method of determining weights deserves brief mention as it is recommended in studies where one or more row sums approach zero, as in Table 2.7. It differs from Method 2 only in that a unity value is placed in the diagonal cells *after* the row sums are computed. This permits the row quality's own relative weight to enter the weighted sums but permits a zero-scoring quality no weight at all. The maximum weight attainable by this method is

$$\frac{2m-3}{0.5m+2(m-1)^{-1}(1\cdot 2+2\cdot 3+3\cdot 4+\ldots+(m-2)(m-1))}, \tag{2.15}$$

Table 2.6 The cross-factor matrix example: characteristics weighting method 2

	Characteristic (j)							
Characteristic (i)	*1*	*2*	*3*	*4*	*Sum*	*Weight factor*	*Weight sum*	*Weights*
1	*****	3	0	1	4	0.33	2.50	0.22
2	1	*****	4	3	8	0.67	3.83	0.34
3	4	0	*****	2	6	0.50	2.32	0.20
4	3	1	2	*****	6	0.50	2.67	0.24
Totals					24		11.32	1.00

Table 2.7 The cross-factor matrix example: $n = 5$

	Characteristic (j)					*Weights in method:*		
Characteristic (i)	*1*	*2*	*3*	*4*	*5*	*1*	*2*	*3*
1	*****	3	0	1	4	0.20 (0.17)	0.20 (0.22)	0.20 (0.21)
2	1	*****	4	3	4	0.30 (0.33)	0.34 (0.34)	0.33 (0.32)
3	4	0	*****	2	4	0.25 (0.25)	0.22 (0.20)	0.23 (0.22)
4	3	1	2	*****	4	0.25 (0.25)	0.24 (0.24)	0.24 (0.25)
5	0	0	0	0	*****	0	0	0

which can be seen to be less than that of Method 2 but by an amount that approaches zero rapidly for $m > 10$, as illustrated in row 3 of Table 2.5. Method 3 weights are reproduced in Table 2.7 with its results for $m = 4$ in parentheses. The slightly greater stability of the results of the comparison of $m = 4$ and $m = 5$ for Method 3 versus Method 2 is apparent.

5 AN EXPERIMENT IN CHARACTERISTICS SCALING AND PRODUCT DISTANCE DETERMINATION

To illustrate these methods and to experiment with their workability, characteristics scalings and product distances were obtained for seven characteristics for five well-known brands of American candy bars from samples of subjects. The brands employed were:

1 Brand 1 – Plain Hershey bar
2 Brand 2 – Milky Way
3 Brand 3 – Life Savers, assorted fruit flavors
4 Brand 4 – Mounds
5 Brand 5 – Baby Ruth.

The sizes were the typical, over-the-counter package selling at the time of the experiments (1973) for about $0.10 and currently for about $0.25. The Hershey bar is a plain chocolate candy; Milky Way is a chocolate coated nougat bar with caramel; Life Savers are a hard fruit flavored candy in a distinctive small doughnut or Life Saver shape; Mounds are chocolate coated coconut cream bars; and the Baby Ruth bar is a chocolate coated, caramel with peanut centered bar. They were well-known brands to all of the subjects, and are staples in their product group.

The characteristics tested were the following:

1 Characteristic 1: net weight
2 Characteristic 2: package
3 Characteristic 3: external color
4 Characteristic 4: shape
5 Characteristic 5: sweetness
6 Characteristic 6: chewiness
7 Characteristic 7: flavor.

These characteristics were carefully chosen to include variables and attributes, objectively definable and determinable and subjectively definable and determinable, cardinally measurable and quasi-measurable, and absolute and relative scaling varieties. They range from the solidly defined and measured to the most ethereal and subjective properties.

Four samples of subjects were tested, and the same tests were performed on the combined samples (Sample *C*). Samples 1 and 2 consisted of U.S. Army lieutenant colonels and colonels, aged 40 to 45, with 22 and 24 subjects respectively. Samples 3 and 4 were Princeton graduate students in economics, between 20 and 25 years of age, with 17 and 16 subjects respectively. Sample C, then, had 69 subjects, ranging in age from 20 to 45. One interesting observation was that, after instruction, not one of the subjects balked at scaling any of the characteristics, so that it was concluded tentatively that the tasks were intuitively–introspectively meaningful for them.

a Characteristics Scaling

For characteristics 2, 4 and 7 (package, shape and flavor) the subjects were presented with a horizontal scale 10 cm long with the 0, 100 and quartile points marked and numbered. They were instructed to place brand 1 (Hershey Bar) at 100 in their mind's eye and in a relative scaling to mark *L–M–H* scalings in the manner of subsection 2c in terms of the similarity of the relevant brand characteristics to the Hershey Bar standard. They were also requested to anchor 0 on the scale as a hypothetical candy bar as far away from the standard in the characteristic as it could realistically be and still remain in the product group.

For qualities 3, 5 and 6 (color, sweetness and chewiness) the subjects were asked to imagine the highest and lowest possible attainment in candy bars of browness of color (only that color was scaled), sweetness and chewiness, and to mark *L–M–H* scores for each brand. For the color quality of browness Life Savers were ruled to be at a distance 100 or at the maximum distance possible from the other brands which were uniformly brown in color. Quality 1 (net weight) is a cardinally measurable characteristic and was given scores of 64, 88, 45, 82, and 80 for five brands respectively.

Table 2.8 lists, brand by brand, the mean scale values on each characteristic scale, derived as the means of expected values of beta distributions, for the four samples and the combined sample. Standard deviations are also recorded. The degree of correspondence among the four samples is surprisingly good.

An analysis of variance was performed on each of them, as well as on the combined sample *C*, with the results shown in Table 2.9. Pairs of the three factors in the experiment – brands, characteristics and subjects – were chosen by eliminating one of them to obtain the remaining two and provide variation within the resulting sets. For example, for the brand-characteristic pair analysis, the variation among subjects was ignored and the observations treated as replications by the same individual of the characteristic scalings for each brand. In the brand-subject analysis, characteristics are ignored and the observations treated as replications by subjects of the scaling of brands in

Table 2.8 Mean quality scalings for brands, with standard deviations, samples 1, 2, 3, 4, and *C*

		Mean					*Standard deviation*				
Brand	*Quality*	*1*	*2*	*3*	*4*	*C*	*1*	*2*	*3*	*4*	*C*
1	1	64.00	64.00	64.00	64.00	64.00	0.00	0.00	0.00	0.00	0.00
	2	100.00	100.00	100.00	100.00	100.00	0.00	0.00	0.00	0.00	0.00
	3	63.53	65.39	60.01	62.64	62.83	12.352	11.88	11.99	9.76	11.59
	4	100.00	100.00	100.00	100.00	100.00	0.00	0.00	0.00	0.00	0.00
	5	66.49	60.48	60.26	64.85	63.35	17.60	15.26	17.05	10.51	15.16
	6	33.37	35.63	37.65	33.57	34.93	10.98	14.28	15.39	18.40	15.68
	7	100.00	100.00	100.00	100.00	100.00	0.00	0.00	0.00	0.00	0.00
2	1	88.00	88.00	88.00	88.00	88.00	0.00	0.00	0.00	0.00	0.00
	2	57.65	52.53	58.00	62.85	57.90	15.42	15.06	16.06	12.94	15.13
	3	46.50	56.31	36.27	48.51	46.44	17.27	16.00	12.11	14.58	15.92
	4	58.15	47.30	53.96	55.14	54.22	18.09	15.23	18.69	15.62	16.25
	5	66.65	65.90	67.23	70.45	67.52	15.33	15.82	12.83	11.83	14.36
	6	58.83	63.93	69.92	63.12	63.52	14.28	14.92	12.09	11.60	14.01
	7	70.09	71.84	65.44	63.51	67.77	11.55	14.97	13.11	20.04	16.20
3	1	45.00	45.00	45.00	45.00	45.00	0.00	0.00	0.00	0.00	0.00
	2	28.13	40.50	18.94	22.09	26.98	28.25	25.48	13.16	8.54	20.94
	3	0.00	0.00	0.00	0.00	0.00	0.00	0.00	0.00	0.00	0.00
	4	15.43	15.19	10.98	26.84	16.93	13.77	10.27	6.67	20.97	14.17
	5	55.72	64.66	55.40	49.89	56.10	22.35	21.78	25.19	19.30	22.46
	6	25.29	17.13	10.95	27.68	20.65	19.33	22.91	5.16	28.17	22.37
	7	18.20	18.65	10.40	21.90	17.23	13.01	11.38	5.97	22.17	14.41

Table 2.8 continued

		Mean					*Standard deviation*				
Brand	*Quality*	*1*	*2*	*3*	*4*	*C*	*1*	*2*	*3*	*4*	*C*
4	1	82.00	82.00	82.00	82.00	82.00	0.00	0.00	0.00	0.00	0.00
	2	58.65	56.95	61.69	59.81	59.32	14.92	15.10	10.82	13.69	13.91
	3	79.14	85.79	78.77	80.23	80.65	9.11	12.19	7.11	11.46	11.05
	4	42.48	43.48	40.37	50.39	44.02	17.27	16.74	11.13	14.36	15.42
	5	56.25	52.19	56.03	58.61	55.92	16.61	16.15	20.99	16.46	17.61
	6	52.55	52.86	52.32	51.24	52.25	10.27	15.10	14.74	13.19	14.60
	7	50.66	53.98	47.48	51.10	50.65	21.55	19.26	16.32	18.61	18.52
5	1	80.00	80.00	80.00	80.00	80.00	0.00	0.00	0.00	0.00	0.00
	2	44.08	50.62	46.37	47.56	46.78	17.80	19.02	12.55	12.36	16.22
	3	53.02	59.83	55.12	59.21	56.35	13.92	13.72	10.96	9.14	12.26
	4	45.62	38.50	37.40	49.15	42.97	15.75	15.78	13.85	16.30	15.98
	5	50.19	62.85	52.88	48.54	53.04	13.95	14.90	18.80	10.55	15.35
	6	68.68	67.23	68.67	65.86	67.75	11.35	15.00	15.07	11.04	14.23
	7	45.48	47.59	51.64	55.50	51.78	14.94	16.43	13.45	14.12	15.37

Table 2.9 Analysis of variance, quality scalings, samples 1, 2, 3, 4, and *C*

	Sum of squares	*D.F.*	*Variance*	*F*	$F_{0.05}$
1 Sample 1					
Brand–Quality					
Between brands	93,286	4	23,321	118.98	2.37
Between qualities	175,438	6	29,240	149.18	2.10
Interaction ($B \times Q$)	140,076	24	5,875	29.97	1.52
Within sets	144,222	735	196		
Brand–Subjects					
Between brands	93,286	4	23,321	35.87	2.37
Between subjects	12,695	21	605	0.93	1.57
Interaction ($B \times S$)	18,886	84	225	0.34	1.27
Within sets	429,076	660	650		
Quality–Subjects					
Between qualities	175,438	6	29,240	43.51	2.10
Between subjects	12,695	21	605	0.90	1.57
Interaction ($Q \times S$)	18,946	126	150	0.22	1.22
Within Sets	346,864	516	672		
2 Sample 2					
Brand–Quality					
Between brands	55,866	4	13,967	66.82	2.37
Between qualities	98,141	6	16,357	78.26	2.10
Interaction ($B \times Q$)	109,473	24	4,561	21.82	1.52
Within Sets	95,239	455	209		
Brand–Subjects					
Between brands	55,866	4	13,967	202.42	2.37
Between subjects	7,276	13	560	0.69	1.73
Interaction ($B \times S$)	5,853	52	113	0.16	1.36
Within Sets	289,724	420	690		
Quality–Subjects					
Between qualities	98,141	6	16,357	27.03	2.10
Between subjects	7,276	13	560	0.92	1.73
Interaction ($Q \times S$)	16,108	78	207	0.34	1.28
Within Sets	237,194	392	605		
3 Sample 3					
Brand–Quality					
Between brands	83,579	4	20,895	130.59	2.37
Between qualities	158,888	6	26,481	165.50	2.10
Interaction ($B \times Q$)	123,948	24	5,165	32.28	1.52
Within Sets	89,568	560	160		
Brand–Subjects					
Between brands	83,579	4	20,895	30.01	2.37
Between subjects	7,407	16	463	0.66	1.65
Interaction ($B \times S$)	9,955	64	156	0.23	1.30
Within Sets	355,042	510	696		

Table 2.9 continued

	Sum of squares	*D.F.*	*Variance*	*F*	$F_{0.05}$
Quality–Subjects					
Between qualities	158,888	6	26,481	45.55	2.10
Between subjects	7,407	16	463	0.79	1.65
Interaction ($Q \times S$)	12,432	96	130	0.22	1.27
Within Sets	277,256	476	582		
4 Sample 4					
Brand–Quality					
Between brands	96,987	4	24,247	126.95	2.37
Between qualities	49,554	6	8,259	43.24	2.10
Interaction ($B \times Q$)	102,838	24	4,285	22.43	1.52
Within Sets	100,234	525	191		
Brand–Subjects					
Between brands	96,987	4	24,247	48.40	2.37
Between subjects	3,006	15	200	0.39	1.67
Interaction ($B \times S$)	9,185	60	153	0.31	1.32
Within Sets	240,435	480	501		
Quality–Subjects					
Between qualities	49,554	6	8,259	13.28	2.10
Between subjects	3,006	15	200	0.32	1.67
Interaction ($Q \times S$)	18,580	90	206	0.33	1.27
Within Sets	278,473	448	622		
5 Sample 5					
Brand–Quality					
Between brands	312,238	4	78,060	319.92	2.37
Between qualities	456,996	6	76,166	312.16	2.09
Interaction ($B \times Q$)	377,340	24	15,722	64.43	1.52
Within Sets	580,614	2,380	244		
Brand–Subjects					
Between brands	312,238	4	78,060	122.93	2.37
Between subjects	39,417	68	580	8.92	1.43
Interaction ($B \times S$)	61,357	272	226	0.36	1.13
Within Sets	1,314,176	2,070	635		
Quality–Subjects					
Between qualities	456,996	6	76,166	129.09	2.03
Between subjects	39,417	68	580	0.98	1.49
Interaction ($Q \times S$)	91,087	408	223	0.38	1.14
Within Sets	1,139,688	1,932	590		

a single quality. Finally, in the characteristic-subject analysis, brands were ignored and the observations treated as replications of subjects scaling a single brand in the set of qualities.

The statistical testimony is dramatically unambiguous. In all cases, the differences between subjects' scalings over brands, ignoring characteristics and characteristics, ignoring brands are statistically nonsignificant, as are the potential nonadditive interaction effects. On the other hand, the scaling differences between brands and characteristics as well as the interaction effects between them are significant in every instance.

We may conclude that (1) the subjects' scalings over brands and characteristics varied systematically in an other-than-random fashion, and (2) the scaling among subjects given brand and characteristic varied only randomly.

b Derivation of the Characteristics Weights

The characteristics weights were computed by cross-factor methods using factor method *A* and weighting methods 1, 2 and 3. The resulting means and standard deviations of the five samples are reproduced in Table 2.10.

The weights can be seen to be quite similar among samples and methods. Method 2, which does not include own-weights, tends to yield the largest weight for characteristic 7 (taste) and lower weights for the less important core qualities, but Method 3 for the combined sample provides exactly the same weights except with one exception. But the only significant difference among the methods is a slight tendency of Method 1 to lessen the standard deviations among individuals. Overall, however, in this experiment it seemed immaterial which characteristics weighting method was used. In view of this, only the weights from Method 2 were employed to compute interbrand distances in order to conserve space.

c Interbrand Distances

Finally, the interbrand distances of the individual scalings were weighted by Method 2 and the means and standard deviations of the distributions were computed. The results are given in Table 2.11, with the means listed in the upper row and the standard deviations in parentheses below them. The median distances were also computed but differed so little from the means that they are excluded from the table.

It was gratifying to note the close conformity of the distance measures among the five samples *in every interbrand distance* as well as the quite reasonable standard deviations. The subjects revealed an impressive consensus concerning distances of brands in an abstract characteristics space, given the abstruse nature of many of the characteristics considered and the differences in age and career backgrounds of the subjects. This initial

Table 2.10 Quality weights, computed by methods 1, 2, and 3 for samples 1, 2, 3, 4, and *C*

	Mean of samples:					*Standard deviation of samples:*				
Quality	1	2	3	4	*C*	1	2	3	4	*C*
1 Method 1										
1	0.14	0.10	0.10	0.11	0.11	0.05	0.05	0.06	0.06	0.06
2	0.08	0.10	0.12	0.10	0.10	0.05	0.06	0.06	0.04	0.05
3	0.10	0.11	0.12	0.10	0.11	0.03	0.06	0.04	0.03	0.04
4	0.18	0.10	0.11	0.10	0.10	0.02	0.04	0.04	0.04	0.04
5	0.18	0.19	0.16	0.19	0.18	0.04	0.03	0.06	0.04	0.04
6	0.18	0.17	0.17	0.17	0.17	0.04	0.05	0.05	0.05	0.05
7	0.24	0.24	0.22	0.23	0.23	0.05	0.06	0.06	0.03	0.05
2 Method 2										
1	0.13	0.09	0.10	0.10	0.11	0.06	0.04	0.06	0.06	0.06
2	0.08	0.10	0.11	0.09	0.09	0.05	0.07	0.07	0.04	0.06
3	0.09	0.10	0.12	0.09	0.10	0.04	0.08	0.05	0.04	0.05
4	0.08	0.09	0.11	0.09	0.09	0.03	0.04	0.05	0.04	0.04
5	0.18	0.19	0.16	0.20	0.18	0.05	0.05	0.07	0.05	0.06
6	0.18	0.17	0.17	0.18	0.18	0.07	0.06	0.07	0.07	0.06
7	0.27	0.27	0.23	0.25	0.25	0.07	0.09	0.08	0.03	0.07
3 Method 3										
1	0.13	0.09	0.10	0.10	0.11	0.06	0.04	0.06	0.06	0.06
2	0.08	0.10	0.11	0.09	0.09	0.05	0.07	0.07	0.04	0.06
3	0.09	0.10	0.12	0.09	0.10	0.04	0.07	0.05	0.04	0.05
4	0.08	0.09	0.11	0.09	0.09	0.03	0.05	0.05	0.04	0.04
5	0.18	0.19	0.16	0.20	0.18	0.05	0.05	0.07	0.05	0.05
6	0.18	0.17	0.17	0.18	0.18	0.04	0.06	0.07	0.07	0.06
7	0.26	0.26	0.23	0.25	0.25	0.07	0.09	0.08	0.03	0.07

experiment is encouraging, although it must be accepted that such revealed consistency even among a larger number of samples is not a sufficient condition to establish that we have in fact "measured" what we set out to measure.

6 SUMMARY AND CONCLUSIONS

In this chapter two types of scaling procedures for characteristics are presented, one for those that are relatively independent of consumer

Table 2.11 Interproduct distances in quality–space using method 1 weights, with standard deviations in parentheses

Distance of Brand i to Brand j	Sample 1	2	3	4	C
$D_{1,2}$	27.75 (5.47)	27.69 (8.45)	32.31 (8.04)	28.83 (5.24)	29.11 (7.06)
$D_{1,3}$	53.18 (6.61)	56.87 (10.57)	61.41 (10.43)	52.39 (7.48)	55.77 (9.45)
$D_{1,4}$	31.86 (10.13)	30.72 (7.20)	35.13 (5.52)	30.81 (5.32)	32.19 (7.77)
$D_{1,5}$	37.07 (8.12)	32.26 (8.80)	36.75 (5.87)	33.32 (6.34)	35.14 (7.67)
$D_{2,3}$	46.28 (8.08)	47.07 (8.69)	51.70 (7.46)	46.45 (10.21)	47.82 (8.89)
$D_{2,4}$	25.97 (8.17)	25.21 (9.36)	27.98 (5.35)	23.34 (7.41)	25.70 (7.84)
$D_{2,5}$	27.04 (7.81)	21.41 (8.50)	26.09 (7.54)	25.48 (5.38)	25.30 (7.68)
$D_{3,4}$	36.90 (8.65)	39.95 (8.20)	40.71 (6.38)	34.01 (9.90)	37.79 (8.77)
$D_{3,5}$	34.83 (9.44)	38.40 (9.67)	40.81 (7.34)	35.04 (9.75)	37.08 (9.44)
$D_{4,5}$	15.70 (5.73)	12.25 (5.71)	17.36 (5.09)	15.45 (2.98)	15.96 (5.12)

preferences and the other for those that are either inherently incapable of judgment without such tastes or conveniently analyzed when preferences are incorporated in the scales.

With the use of these quasi-measurements distances of *brands* of a given product, or those variants featuring different degrees of possession of core characteristics, from each other on a single characteristic dimension or in a multidimensional characteristics space are presented, using a *cross-factor* methodology. For multidimensional distances the additional complication of deriving weights for the characteristics that scale their importance in the definition of the product is confronted, and three methods of computing these weights are considered.

The ease with which all of these "unscientific" methods can be criticized and rejected, frequently by those who employ them most intensively in their professions out of necessity, has been noted in Chapter 1. Such critics bear the onus, however, of developing "scientific" methods of performing these tasks or of indicating informal alternatives that yield better analytical results. To this point those have not been forthcoming, and, hence, in the best traditions of scientific economics, nonmeasurability relegates characteristics analysis to the category of the ignorable. Given the importance of nonprice competition in differentiated oligopoly market structures this is not defensible. It is suggested that scaling techniques be pursued to test the randomness or consistency of their results in empirical analysis, and the potential usefulness of the methods compared with such alternatives as may exist.

To these tasks the experiment detailed in section 5 is dedicated. The results there are most encouraging. What seems a remarkable degree of consistency in sample characteristics and interbrand distance scalings emerged from the experiments, over a spectrum of poorly defined and abstract characteristics.

A call for the relaxation of scientific standards to make progress in a problem area cannot hope to be as ringing as a heroic summons to embrace their comforting but frequently sterile rigor. The results of these intuitive and heuristic methods are encouraging enough to permit hope that quasi-measurement techniques will permit us to make substantial progress in integrating nonprice competition with the body of microeconomic theory, and we will return to these themes in Chapter 10.

3 Rivalrous Consonance: An Approach to Mature Oligopolistic Competition

After the introductory considerations of Chapters 1 and 2, there remains the admittedly fearsome task of dealing with oligopolistic decision making in these areas of integrated competition, and the point has arrived at which the primary approach to be taken to this market structure must be presented in some detail. The framework discussed in this chapter has been presented in both theoretical and applied forms in an extensive literature.[1] As developed in this book it is designed to gain insights into the interdependent actions of firms that are in "mature" oligopolistic industry structures, a concept to be defined formally below, although it is capable of use in less settled, more aggressive environments, including active price and nonprice warfare. In the analysis of this work, however, with the exception of studies of entry in Chapter 11, the effort will be confined to mature industries, in which more peaceful patterns of competition and cooperation have emerged in the industry's patterns of decision making.

After several decades of modeling theoretical and empirical oligopolistic structures I have acquired a *vision* of realistic process in its potentially most complicated market form that shapes efforts in this work and that constrains my expectations from them. That vision comes closest to a rigorous fulfillment in a nonlinear dynamic model, with an internal structure that moves its behavior in the direction of chaotic patterns, revealing occasionally recurring but fleeting periods of stability. The state variables are also subject to frequent innovational, demand, and entrant exogenous shocks which serve to disturb and enhance the instability arising from the extreme interdependence of the decision making. That decision making has the game-theoretic properties associated with conflicting and interactive participant welfares in an environment of imperfect information, and is further complicated by the multiple objectives of the participants. Those objectives tend to be imperfectly defined, even in the consciousness of the players, and to be weighted differently in different states of the model.

But the salvaging observation is that realistic oligopolies do not tend toward chaos, and, indeed, reveal notably stable patterns of price and nonprice variables, despite these structural urgings. In chaos theory terms, as the system seeks to depart from a transitional period of stability, the structure itself generates forces to preserve that stable state or permit it to change within viable limits. In my view the only source for such compulsion toward homeostasis is that among the multiple objectives of the participants is the goal of achieving some degree of tacit cooperation to limit competition internal and (more rarely) external to the industry.[2] The industry acquires a form of "social capital" familiar to most forms of community that permits a more peaceable coexistence.

When these restraining forces are firmly embedded in the goal structure of the major incumbents of the industry, I term that industry a *mature* oligopoly. This concept is discussed in section 1 below. In my experience, the industry's complexity of structure and functioning is best encoded in a power structure matrix of binary relations among firms, as will be introduced formally in section 2.

Several implications affecting methodology flow from this shaping vision of the problem. The first is of the daunting complexity of the oligopolistic industry's physiology and the hopelessness of seeking to mock-up any useful theoretical portrayal of its dynamic functioning. I am, for example, extremely skeptical of employing "dynamic" game theory (extensive game forms) to formulate a model explaining the approach to this homeostatic equilibrium based largely or exclusively on egoistic motivation. In the first place, the process of attaining it is not of primary interest in analysis of industry functioning: rather it is the implications of that functioning for the state variables and the potential resistance to their values by power-disadvantaged firms. In the second place, in practical terms, the modeling cannot hope to incorporate the *development* or *evolution* of the homeostasis forces within the socio-historical context of the industry's development, absent deeper study of the industry in the sense discussed in Chapter 1. And, lastly, if the model does approach a steady state, there is little hope that it will depict adequately the results of firm-by-firm mixtures of competitive and cooperative behavior that shape the industry's state variables.

Hence the conviction that is rooted in this view of the extreme complexity of the problem is that any modeling of such industries must depend largely on deductive methods aided by historical research and informal polling of expertise within and without the industry. I have found large-scale econometric modeling attempts to disentangle the complicated interdependence futile.[3] Econometric methods can be helpful in pulling relatively simple relationships among oligopolists out of data, but in my view cannot be relied upon for major support when the more complicated relationships that form the core of the industry's structure are concerned.

Most importantly, in view of all of these modeling difficulties, my belief is that the most fruitful manner of obtaining insights into the structure and functioning of specific or generic cases of oligopoly is to concentrate skills and energies on the analysis of this homeostatic equilibrium of the mature industry. Because of the effective existence of industry cooperation to keep decision variables within viable limits, comparative static analysis has some limited hope of yielding valid qualitative responses to parameter changes. And if such states are those in which mature industries remain and to which immature industries are tending via inner propulsion, as I believe, they are also of greatest relevance in positive and normative studies of the implications of oligopoly.

1 MATURE OLIGOPOLY

Rivalrous consonance is a type of "reduced or normal game-theoretic form" view of the nature of the motivation of decisions by firms in oligopoly after some period of disequilibrium has subsided and a more permanent competitive structure has emerged in the industry. The keynote of that market structure, of course, is the realization by every major firm that its decisions will impact every other firm's welfare with an effect identifiable as to source of cause. An initiating firm must rationally anticipate such reactions before deciding on a course of action, and affected rivals must pursue modes of adaptation. From these characteristics of decision making arise the worrisome potentials of the oligopolistic environment: a pervasive uncertainty concerning competitor initiatives or responses, destabilization of the ruling price–quality profile, the possibility of aggressive new managements in a nonanonymous rivalry, and the amplitude of adverse competitive developments given the fewness of the firms over which they are distributed.

Over time firms strive to temper this incertitude in the manner of all human agents interacting in a communitarian context by enacting formal or informal "rules of the game" to define forms and limits of competing and cooperating. They realize that their relations with other incumbents in the industry are a blend of the competitive and the cooperative: that they are confronted with a *rivalrous consonance of interests*. They seek to institutionalize methods of restraining the rivalrous within viable bounds and to encourage the cooperative overtly or tacitly through active and passive signaling. A *power structure* or *pecking order* emerges among the firms to define binary patterns of deference or dominance between firms which are both enabling and constraining with respect to their decision making. Concern for "the good of the industry" masks the desire to achieve a stable status quo in which participants can function with greater joint control over the threats of chaos potential in their environment.

These patterns of behavior, formal and informal institutions, stable role expectations and bounds on actions give the industry a culture and a history that new managements absorb and perpetuate to constrain their innovatory strategies. All is not peace, of course, nor is all change absorbed smoothly in evolutionary fashion. Competition becomes fierce at times, exceeding the historical bounds over periods of some duration, whereas quiet and tacit cooperation wanes or waxes responsively. Occasionally aggressive newcomers may be disruptive and over the longer run must be absorbed and "tamed". Each oligopolistic industry experiences over time, therefore, a unique set of "events" that shapes and alters an ethos which importantly conditions its decision making.

As noted in Chapter 1, each such industry, therefore, is *sui generis*, but if it succeeds in reaching a period of "maturity" certain common characteristics emerge:

1 Every major firm is convinced of its "staying power" in the industry into the foreseeable future, so that survival over that horizon is not at issue.
2 The industry has achieved a period of coexistence within a context of active competition constrained by a discernible ethos that bounds firms' actions away from severe profit or market share destabilization. This does not preclude substantial disturbances caused by innovations or marketing initiatives, nor alterations in the power structure among major rivals; but it does rule out well mounted challenges to that ethos. That is, the *outcomes* of the process of mutual forbearance may vary with respect to firms' fortunes, but the *rules* defining that process must remain essentially unchanged.
3 The "industry" attains and retains a distinct *identity* over a period of maturity through continuity of its product's functions, dominant firms and its behavioral ethos that is recognized by its incumbents and which recognition tempers firms' narrowly egoistic decision making. Once more, much change and adaptation can be accommodated within the industry's continuity factors: products may change important characteristics; dominant firms may merge with or acquire lesser rivals and gain or lose market share; and the emphases on competition and cooperation within the ethos may alter somewhat. However, overriding these changes is a dominant hierarchy of producers, ever jockeying for market share leadership and profits, but acting within an informally accepted body of constraints, especially on price competition. These constraints constitute an implicit but active acceptance of the desirability of cooperation. That desirability is rooted deeply in the long-run profitability interests of the incumbents, perhaps after a history of painful disruptions from unconstrained rivalry, but may also have some basis in a genuine concern for the welfare of the industry as a communitarian concept due some allegiance from those incumbents.

Maturity, therefore, requires a stability over a long period of the identity and immutability of dominant firms; a continuity in the forms and functions of the relevant product group and their importance in the industry's customers' needs and preferences; the acceptance of an ethos that enforces important restraints on competition as a means of increasing long-run profitability through control of destabilizing rivalrous initiatives; and an external environment (featuring, for example, government regulatory or other relevant policy initiatives) which does not administer profoundly disturbing shocks to the industry's structure.

Mature oligopoly variable states are accepted as the longer-run industry "equilibrium" to which differentiated oligopolistic industries tend. One may view this as the hypothesized solution to a dynamic game which integrates into its axiomatic formulation the socio-historical factors in specific industries that are decision-relevant. The rivalrous consonance framework is designed to provide a flexible means of including in the analysis of an industry the decision-affecting peculiarities that make it *sui generis*. It does not seek to derive this end-state as a limiting state achieved by a dynamic process, as in dynamic game theory. Rather, it attempts through static analysis to discern this "equilibrium" by close study of the characteristics of the mature industry in order to incorporate them in the parameters, constraints and objective functions of the firms. In practice this permits (indeed, requires) the consideration and inclusion of much more information, especially of an informal character and perhaps with scaling of components, than the more rigorous strictures of game theory permit in actual applications.

In restricting attention to mature oligopoly, I do not mean to assert that rivalrous consonance theory cannot be used to analyze "immature" oligopolistic industries. Indeed, it is possible to employ it in studying models of such varied phenomena as price wars, price leadership, or altruistic protection of weak rivals, as will be illustrated in section 3. However, in this book we shall stay almost exclusively with the more prosaic cases of basic stability of industry form and function.

a A Formalization

To approach rivalrous consonance, define:

$\mathbf{P}$ = a vector of firms' prices, p_i, $i = 1, 2, \ldots I$
$\mathbf{X}$ = a vector of firms' outputs, x_i, $i = 1, 2, \ldots I$
$\mathbf{Z}$ = a vector of firms' quality levels, z_i, $i = 1, 2, \ldots I$
$\mathbf{Y}$ = a vector of relevant exogenous variables.

For simplicity we assume that the quality of each brand can be defined by a single characteristic.

Firms face demand functions that are given:

$$x_i = x_i(\boldsymbol{P},\boldsymbol{Z},\boldsymbol{Y}),\ i = 1,2,\ldots,I. \tag{3.1}$$

Assume also that inverse demand functions exist:

$$p_i = p_i(\boldsymbol{X},\boldsymbol{Z},\boldsymbol{Y}),\ i = 1,2,\ldots,I. \tag{3.2}$$

Total cost functions are defined as:

$$C_i = C_i(x_i, z_i),\ i = 1,2,\ldots,I. \tag{3.3}$$

Own-profit functions are simply:

$$\pi_i = p_i(\boldsymbol{X},\boldsymbol{Z},\boldsymbol{Y}) \cdot x_i - C_i(x_i, z_i),\ i = 1,2,\ldots,I. \tag{3.4}$$

The *power structure* of the industry is defined by a nonsymmetric matrix, Θ, whose elements are the *consonance coefficients*, θ_{ij}, where, in general, $\theta_{ij} \neq \theta_{ji}$, and $\theta_{ii} \equiv 1$. The coefficient θ_{ij} is the own-profit equivalent of \$1 of firm *j*'s profit in the reckoning of firm *i*. That is, if $\theta_{ij} = 0.25$, firm *i* values \$1 of firm *j*'s profit (loss) as equivalent to \$0.25 of its own profit (loss). This value is an index of the deference that firm *i* pays to firm *j* when firm *i* makes its price or output and quality decisions. The higher the value, the greater the weight firm *i* affords firm *j* in such decision making. The matrix Θ, therefore, depicts the power structure of the industry, or the set of binary relations of each firm to each of its rivals as depicted by the weight it affords those rivals' profits or losses in its decision making. Those coefficients reflect for the most part each firm's view of the capability of every other firm to punish it for initiatives that reduce that rival's profit or inflict losses on that rival. The decisions of each firm, therefore, are shaped by its *extended profit function*, not its *own-profit function*, where extended profits are defined as

$$\pi_i^e = \Sigma_{j=1}^{i} \theta_{ij}\pi_j,\ i = 1,2,\ldots,I. \tag{3.5}$$

The earning of profit by firms in the industry is treated as only one–albeit the major–objective of the firms. Each firm is treated in a multiobjective framework with such additional objectives differing in kind or in quantitative extent firm by firm. If we accept own-profits as a primary objective of firms, secondary objectives can be expressed in a firm-specific set of constraint functions of the form where r_{i1}, etc., are the restraints of the constraint functions, given as parameters and firm-specific. Such secondary goals are symbolized as constraint functions in (3.6):

$$\begin{aligned} g_{i1}(x_i, z_i) &\leq r_{i1} \\ g_{i2}(x_i, z_i) &\leq r_{i2} \\ g_{im}(x_i, z_i) &\leq r_{im} \\ g_{i(m+1)}(x_i, z_i) &\geq r_{i(m+1)} \\ g_{i(m+2)}(x_i, z_i) &\geq r_{i(m+2)} \\ g_{in}(x_i, z_i) &\geq r_{in} \\ x_i, z_i \geq 0,&\quad i = 1,2,\ldots,I. \end{aligned} \tag{3.6}$$

Secondary constraints might impose the conditions that quality z_i not fall below a given level, that price be above or below floors or ceilings, that market share be at least a specified value, that own-profit attain at least some minimum aspiration value, and so forth. The inclusion of constraint sets of this form, tailored to the objectives of each rival as revealed in the history of the industry or in discussions with its management yields two dividends to the user of the model: first, it incorporates the realistic observation that firms engage in multiobjective decision making, and second, it permits the model to attain greater flexibility in conforming to the peculiarities of specific firms and industries.

The model must then, after defining the firms' primary and secondary objectives, determine their price or output and quality decisions taking into account the power structure of the industry and, via an interdependence structure, search to attain a constrained Nash equilibrium industry-wide.

b The Short-run Model

In the short run it is assumed that firm i accepts its θ_{ij} as well as the ruling rivals' values of x_j and z_j, $j \neq i$, as parameters, and maximizes its extended profit function (3.5) with respect to p_i and z_i subject to its constraint set (3.6). As each firm determines its x and z variables in this fashion, the new variable values are taken as newly fixed parameters by firms remaining in the iterative round which have not yet acted to determine their extended profit maxima. A round is ended when all I firms have so acted. A new round then begins, followed by a sequence of rounds, terminated at a Nash equilibrium if and when the series of $\boldsymbol{P}$ and $\boldsymbol{Z}$ vectors converge to a stationary solution.

Each of the firms' models so parameterized is a nonlinear programming model, soluble for local or global maxima by any number of algorithms.[4] In terms of solution facility, two problems arise. The first is that some or all of the firms' models may not be convex, and hence fail to meet sufficiency conditions for global maxima. Indeed, in the real world it is highly unlikely that objective and constraint functions will meet Kuhn–Tucker conditions (or their equivalents), so that local maxima at best can be expected. Not only is a global maximum for each firm on each step in the sequences to local maxima not guaranteed, but convergence of the sequences is not guaranteed and the solutions obtained if any may be dependent on the order in which the firms' solutions are obtained.

Ultimately, if we accept the notion that in reality firms in mature oligopoly do arrive at stable solutions, the root cause of our failure to reproduce them must lie in a failure to attain a good specification of the industry's decision making. A failure to converge indicates that the conditions specified – objective functions, maximization-of-profit behavior, and constraint functions – cannot hold simultaneously. The firms, faced with such runaway solutions in reality, will essentially alter the structure of their goals and constraints with a flexibility that is difficult or impossible to simulate with rigid models simple enough to solve.

Failure to attain global maxima is somewhat less troublesome, from both a theoretical and practical viewpoint. It is an economist's fantasy that the world of decision making is a convex playground: in oligopolistic contexts solutions are in most instances samples from a substantial population of possibilities, with the sequencing of initiatives playing an important part in the sampling. This complication does foreclose the possibility of forecasting numerical results from the model, but hopefully will permit, with wise manipulation, qualitative movements of the variables yielding insights into the structure and performance of the industry.

c The Intermediate-run Model

Rather hesitantly I suggest that the model can be made more "intermediate-run" in nature if the θ_{ij} consonance coefficients are converted to endogenous variables and the firms' extended profit functions maximized with respect to them. This procedure meets an objection of economists I have frequently encountered that the rivalrous consonance coefficients should be endogenously derived under extended profit motivation rather than determined by an external analysis of power structure. The rationale is that firms will alter these coefficients in accordance with their egoistic interests in the longer run, insofar as enhancements of extended profits in general will increase own-profits within the bounds of mature oligopoly.

This viewpoint is based on two acceptable propositions concerning the nature of rivalrous consonance: the size of the coefficients is dictated in largest part by the firms' perceptions of their rivals' abilities to react in manners that reduce the firms' profits, and one must expect the power structure and hence the consonance coefficients to alter over time. However, whether in fact they will alter in accordance with own-profits is questionable.

My own belief is that over the longer period the coefficients should be altered to reflect changes in the same conditions which led to their initial determination. This requires a rather extensive study of such changes to which determination of the coefficients by maximizing extended profits with respect to them can only contribute. Determining them endogenously in general will be misleading, I believe, since in large part they reflect the willingness of incumbents to forego profits to purchase stability.

d The Consonance Coefficient Interval

In theory the firm's consonance coefficients are unbounded. If $\theta_{ij} < 0$, firm *i* values \$1 of firm *j*'s loss as the equivalent of \$$\theta_{ij}$ in its own profits. Firm *i* has taken a *predatory* stance toward firm *j*, therefore, and in its extended profit objective function will wage price and/or nonprice warfare against it. As noted above, in any specific industry application the rivalrous consonance framework would have no difficulty incorporating such behavior, but we will rule it out of a mature oligopolistic environment. Hence, the Θ-values are bounded away from negative values.

On the other hand, suppose the coefficient were greater than 1 in value. This means that firm *i* values $1 of firm *j*'s profits as the equivalent of more than $1 of its own. There may be instances of extreme dominance of an industry by one or more threatening firms in which such a θ_{ij} would be applicable; less dramatically, such a value might be useful in a price-leadership industrial pattern. Otherwise, however, such valuations would imply a completely unrealistic degree of industrial philanthropy on firm *i*'s part, and in a typical mature oligopoly it is not to be expected. Therefore, we place an upper bound of 1 on the Θ-values in that context.

In the analysis to follow, $\theta_{ij} \in [0,1]$, $i, j = 1, 2, \ldots, n$, $\theta_{ii} \equiv 1$. When $\theta_{ij} = 0$, firm *i* completely ignores the impacts of its decisions on firm *j*'s profits. If Θ is an $n \times n$ identity matrix, so that each firm acts to maximize its own profits (subject to constraints) and takes no heed of its impacts on any other firm, the resulting industry solution I have termed the *Cournot* solution, even when prices are the firms' target variables. The term denotes an extension of Cournot's myopia assumption that each firm assumes the actions of all others will be unchanged in the face of its own actions.

At the other extreme of the permissible interval, assume that all $\theta_{ij} = 1$. Every firm treats every other firm's profits and losses as equivalent to its own. The resulting solution I have termed the *Chamberlin* solution, in recognition of that economist's early treatment of the joint profit solution in oligopoly theory,[5] for that approaches the nature of the industry's actions under such conditions. In realistic applications it is to be expected that all firms will be operating in the interior of the [0,1] interval in determining their Θ-values for rivals. In the simulations to follow such expectations will constrain the parameterization of the consonance coefficients.

2 A SIMPLE DUOPOLY MODEL

To illustrate the rivalrous consonance methodology and demonstrate its welfare implications let us take the case of a duopoly with prices only as the decision variables and with no constraints other than nonnegativity restraints. Assume further that the demand functions for firms 1 and 2 are given below:

$$\begin{aligned} &1 \quad x_1 = 300 - 6p_1 + 2p_2 \\ &2 \quad x_2 = 100 - 2p_2 + p_1. \end{aligned} \tag{3.7}$$

The inverses can be written:

$$\begin{aligned} &1 \quad p_1 = 80 - 0.2x_1 - 0.2x_2 \\ &2 \quad p_2 = 90 - 0.1x_1 - 0.6x_2. \end{aligned} \tag{3.8}$$

The total cost functions are sums of fixed and variable costs:

$$\begin{aligned} &1 \quad C_1 = 600 + 30x_1 + 0.01x_1^2 \\ &2 \quad C_2 = 500 + 35x_2 + 0.02x_2^2. \end{aligned} \tag{3.9}$$

Extended profit functions may be written:

$$\begin{aligned} &1 \quad \pi_1^e = 50x_1 - 0.21x_1^2 - 600 + \theta_1(55x_2 - 0.62x_2^2 - 500) - \\ &\qquad (0.2 + 0.1\theta_1)x_1x_2 \\ &2 \quad \pi_2^e = 55x_2 - 0.62x_2^2 - 500 + \theta_2(50x_1 - 0.21x_1^2 - 600) - \\ &\qquad (0.1 + 0.2\theta_2)x_1x_2 \end{aligned} \tag{3.10}$$

If each firm zeroes its partial derivative with respect to own-price(since each firm has control over its own price only) and the resulting equations are solved, the following solutions are obtained:[6]

$$\begin{aligned} &1 \quad p_1^\circ = \frac{613.39630 + 2.584910\theta_1 - 39.396230\theta_2 - 16.981130\theta_1\theta_2}{12.03779 - 0.311340\theta_1 - 1.094300\theta_2 - 0.471740\theta_1\theta_2} \\ &2 \quad p_2^\circ = \frac{231.37930 - 4.034480\theta_1 + 8.877740\theta_2 - 6.112850\theta_1\theta_2}{4.00002 - 0.103460\theta_1 - 0.363620\theta_2 - 0.156750\theta_1\theta_2}. \end{aligned} \tag{3.11}$$

Numerical own-profit solution values for selected values of θ_1 and θ_2 are listed in Table 3.1, with firms listed in the rows and their rivals in the columns. Note that in the example firm 1's strategy of playing $\theta_1 = 0.6$ dominates $\theta_1 = 0$, 0.1, 0.2, and 0.3 and weakly dominates $\theta_1 = 0.4$ and 0.5, while firm 2's strategy $\theta_2 = 0.1$ strictly dominates all of its other strategies. The strategy pairs $\Theta = [0.5,0.1]$, $[0.6,0.1]$ and $[0.7,0.1]$ are indeed Nash equilibria. If a strategy pair did emerge, tacit or overt collusion has conducted the firms to a mutually beneficial solution, which in rivalrous consonance is depicted as the adoption of a pair of consonance coefficients. The game theorist would argue that by virtue of the Nash equilibrium we can confine our attention to the *core* of the solutions: firm 1 need not accept less than 1,551 and firm 2 no less than 295. That core contains the Pareto superior solutions.

But in rivalrous consonance the solution is indeterminate absent an analysis of the socio–politico–historical factors that determine the ethos of the industry. These factors, external to the payoff matrix values, might well lead firm 2 to a more deferential $\theta_2 > 0$, or might determine that firm 1 will follow a protection-of-the-underdog philosophy and determine θ_1 in the upper

Table 3.1 Profits for selected values of consonance coefficients, firms 1 and 2 (rounded to nearest thousand dollars)

	Firm 1/Firm 2										
θ_i	0.0	0.1	0.2	0.3	0.4	0.5	0.6	0.7	0.8	0.9	1.0
0.0	1511; 277	1545; 279	1580; 277	1615; 272	1652; 263	1689; 250	1727; 234	1766; 213	1806; 188	1848; 158	1890; 123
0.1	1513; 280	1547; 282	1582; 280	1618; 275	1655; 266	1693; 253	1732; 236	1772; 215	1812; 189	1855; 159	1898; 123
0.2	1514; 283	1548; 285	1584; 284	1620; 278	1657; 269	1696; 256	1736; 239	1777; 217	1819; 191	1862; 159	1906; 122
0.3	1514; 286	1549; 288	1585; 287	1622; 282	1660; 273	1700; 259	1740; 242	1781; 220	1824; 192	1868; 160	1913; 122
0.4	1515; 290	1550; 292	1587; 290	1624; 285	1633; 276	1702; 263	1743; 245	1785; 222	1828; 194	1873; 161	1919; 121
0.5	1515; 293	1551; 295	1587; 294	1625; 289	1664; 279	1704; 266	1746; 248	1788; 224	1832; 196	1878; 161	1925; 121
0.6	1515; 296	1551; 298	1588; 297	1626; 292	1665; 283	1706; 269	1748; 250	1791; 227	1836; 197	1882; 162	1930; 120
0.7	1514; 299	1551; 302	1587; 301	1626; 296	1666; 286	1707; 272	1749; 253	1793; 229	1838; 199	1885; 162	1934; 119
0.8	1514; 302	1550; 305	1588; 304	1626; 299	1666; 290	1708; 276	1751; 256	1795; 231	1841; 200	1888; 163	1937; 118
0.9	1513; 306	1549; 309	1587; 308	1626; 303	1666; 293	1708; 279	1751; 259	1796; 233	1842; 202	1890; 163	1940; 117
1.0	1511; 309	1548; 312	1586; 312	1625; 307	1665; 297	1707; 282	1751; 262	1796; 236	1842; 203	1891; 164	1941; 116

ranges of its bracket at $\theta_1 = 0.8$ or 1.0, since such a substantial benefit to firm 2 costs it very little. Or it might adopt a lower value for its coefficient to lower price and exploit what may be advantages reflected in its market share. The point is that only a deeper analysis of the power structure of the industry will permit us to make estimates of the coefficients, although such study of solution results guides us in isolating Schelling (1960) "focal points."

Let us briefly demonstrate the applicability of the rivalrous consonance framework to the "immature" case of a price war, or, more broadly, when rivals attach a positive value to their rivals' losses and are willing to sacrifice own-profits to inflict them. Table 3.2 reveals the solutions to the model when θ_1 and θ_2 are set to negative values.

In this case, where we assume that a tit-for-tat strategy is employed by both rivals, firm 2 fares much worse than firm 1. This is because firm 1, relatively speaking, is much less affected by firm 2's pricing actions than vice versa, by virtue of the relative size of own- and other-price coefficients in the respective demand functions. As the conflict intensifies, firm 1 suffers own-profit losses of about 18 percent, whereas firm 2 suffers a 82 percent fall in profit. The fall in firm 2's prices affects firm 1's output only minimally, and firm 1 must lower its prices only moderately to limit its loss in market share. On the other hand firm 2 increases its output by about 32 percent to prevent its profits from falling further. As firm 1 lowers prices, firm 2's demand curve shifts inward, increasing its elasticity, and inducing the listed price reductions. Such shifts in firm 1's demand function are much milder and decrease own-price elasticity less, accounting for the milder price declines. Both firms, however, suffer severely from such aggressive behavior, and in a state of mature rivalrous consonance should be expected to achieve a solution which blends rivalry with tacit cooperation.

Table 3.2 Solutions in cases of aggressive stances for firms 1 and 2

$\theta_1 = \theta_2$	p_1	p_2	x_1	x_2	π_1	π_2
–0.1	50.10	54.93	109.3	40.2	1477	270
–0.2	49.81	54.02	109.2	41.8	1444	260
–0.3	49.54	53.15	109.1	43.2	1412	247
–0.4	49.29	52.29	108.9	44.7	1391	233
–0.5	49.05	51.47	108.6	46.1	1351	217
–0.6	48.84	50.66	108.3	47.5	1323	199
–0.7	48.64	49.87	107.9	48.9	1295	179
–0.8	48.45	49.10	107.5	50.3	1268	158
–0.9	48.28	48.34	107.0	51.6	1241	135
–1.0	48.12	47.59	106.4	52.9	1216	48

3 SOCIAL WELFARE CONSIDERATIONS

On Figure 3.1 two different sets of price reaction functions are graphed – the set $R_{1,0}$ and $R_{2,0}$ reflecting $\Theta = [0,0]$ and the set $R_{1,1}$ and $R_{2,1}$ depicted for $\Theta = [1,1]$.[7] The purely competitive price outcome, where prices of each firm equal marginal production costs occurs at $p_1 = 33.48$ and $p_2 = 37.35$, is not graphed on the figure. As discussed in section 2, the intersection of $R_{1,0}$ and $R_{2,0}$ I have termed the Cournot point and the intersection of reaction functions $R_{1,1}$ and $R_{2,1}$ the Chamberlin point, *J*. The intersections [0,1] and [1,0] together with the Cournot and Chamberlin points form *a* "rivalrous consonance polygon" within which all other mature industry reaction function intersections will fall as the Θ-values take values in the interior of the unit square.

Table 3.3 lists outputs, prices, profits,consumers' surplus, and social welfare, consumers' surplus for selected symmetric values of θ_1 and θ_2. As the degree of cooperation rises the prices of both firms rise and quantities sold fall but profits of the firms for the most part move in opposite directions: the reductions in π_2 and consumers' surplus outweigh the rise in π_1 and so social welfare (the sum of profits and consumers' surplus) fall after $\theta_1 = \theta_2 = 0.2$.

Figure 3.2, based on the data of Table 3.1 and on solutions to $\Theta = [0,1]$ and [1,0] not recorded in the table, graphs the social welfare contours for p_1 and p_2 combinations that can be reached by θ_1 and θ_2 values in the unit interval permitted by mature rivalry. The figure and the data in the table

Table 3.3 Social welfare and consumer surplus values, quantities and prices for selected symmetric values of θ_1 and θ_2

$\theta_1 = \theta_2$	x_1	x_2	p_1	p_2	π_1	π_2	π	*CS*	*W*
0.0	109.3	38.7	50.41	55.87	1511	277	1788	1643	3431
0.1	109.3	37.0	50.74	56.85	1547	282	1829	1606	3435
0.2	109.2	35.4	51.09	57.87	1584	284	1868	1567	3435
0.3	109.0	33.6	51.48	58.94	1622	282	1904	1527	3431
0.4	108.8	31.8	51.89	60.05	1663	276	1939	1486	3425
0.5	108.5	29.9	52.33	61.22	1704	266	1970	1444	3414
0.6	108.1	27.9	52.81	62.45	1748	250	1998	1401	3399
0.7	107.6	25.8	53.32	63.75	1793	229	2022	1358	3380
0.8	107.0	23.6	53.87	65.13	1841	200	2041	1313	3354
0.9	106.4	21.3	54.47	66.60	1890	163	2053	1267	3320
1.0	105.6	18.8	55.12	68.16	1941	116	2057	1222	3279

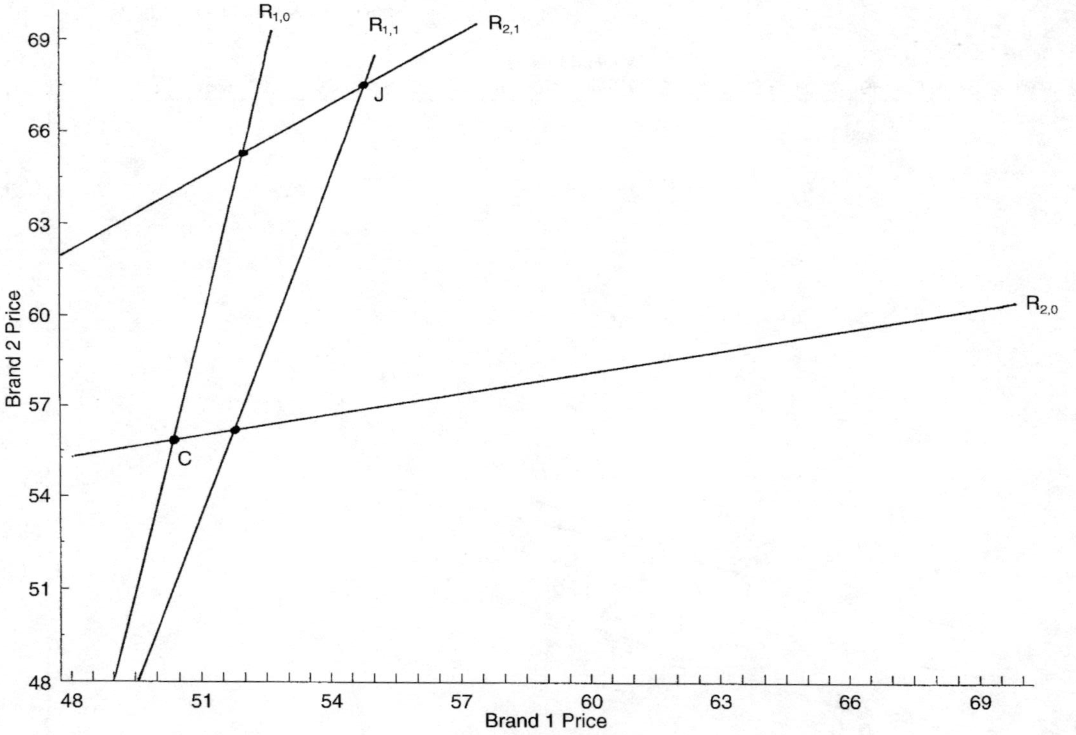

Figure 3.1 Price reaction functions

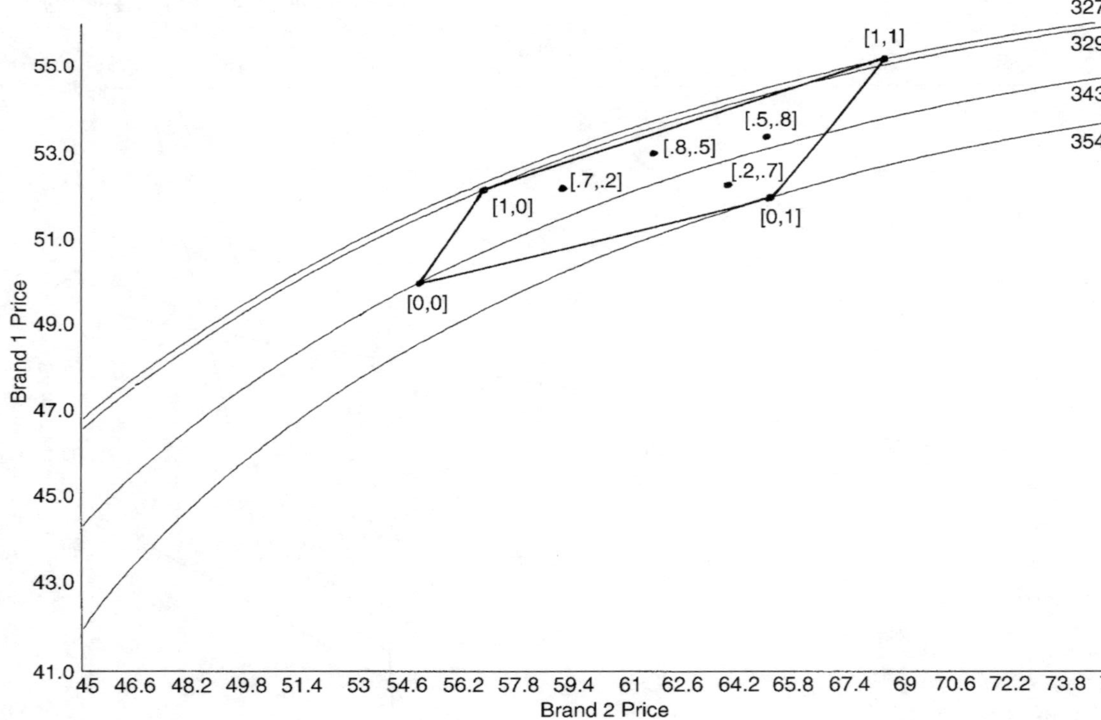

Figure 3.2 Welfare contours with prices

reveal that social welfare (W) and consumers' surplus (CS) fall uniformly as symmetric collusion increases. But social welfare reaches a maximum for these corner solutions at [0,1] because the unrequited cooperation of firm 2 increases firm 1's profits above the Θ = [0,0] level more than the fall in consumers' surplus below the Θ = [0,0] level. This is an instance of the faulty nature of social welfare as an index of societal benefit when oligopoly profits are involved, as will be discussed further below.

In Table 3.4 the forces behind the symmetric consonance results become discernible. In the table two symmetric consonance cases are analyzed: the movement of both coefficients from values of 0 to 0.1, and from 0.8 to 0.9. Firm 1's output is 3 to 5 times firm 2's and firm 1's other-price coefficient is twice that of firm 2's. When $\theta_1 = \theta_2 = 0.1$, the sum of marginal output and marginal consonance cost for firm 2 is \$38.67, versus firm 1's \$32.56; but when the consonance coefficients rise to 0.9 these costs are, respectively, \$55.00 and \$34.04. Firm 2 is hugely disadvantaged in its marginal consonance cost, which is, of course, the implied incremental monetary cost in forgone profits arising from tacit collusion.

For an interpretation of the results, therefore, it is useful to conjoin two marginal cost sources for the firms: marginal production cost and marginal consonance cost. Interestingly, consonance cost is an inversion of the economic concept of *externality*: it is an *internality* introduced by the firm itself

Table 3.4 Analysis of the motivation for consonance results for selected changes in consonance coefficients

Variable	$\theta_1 = \theta_2 = 0$	$\theta_1 = \theta_2 = 0.1$	$\theta_1 = \theta_2 = 0.8$	$\theta_1 = \theta_2 = 0.9$
p_1	50.41	50.74	53.87	54.47
p_2	55.87	56.85	65.13	66.60
x_1	109.3	109.3	107.0	106.4
x_2	38.77	37.0	23.6	21.3
$Revenue_1$	5510	5545	5766	5794
$Revenue_2$	2160	2105	1538	1417
MC_1	32.19	32.19	32.14	32.13
MC_2	36.55	36.48	35.94	35.85
AC_1	36.58	36.58	36.68	36.70
AC_2	48.71	49.24	56.65	58.93
Mar. Con. Cost$_1$	0	0.37	1.89	1.91
Mar. Con. Cost$_2$	0	2.19	17.13	19.15
π_1	1511	1547	1841	1890
π_2	277	282	200	163
ϵ_1	2.77	2.79	3.02	3.07
ϵ_2	2.89	3.07	5.52	6.26

into the cost structure which creates a phantom cost resulting only indirectly in a monetary cost, or, hopefully, by affecting the firm's demand function, its profit. Its size depends directly on (1) the size of its consonance coefficient, (2) its rival's output, and (3) the other-output coefficient in the rival's inverted demand function, and inversely on the value of the 2×2 principal minor of the system (i.e., $b_{11} b_{22} - b_{12} b_{21}$).[8] The latter, of course, is a measure of the interdependence of the demand functions, falling as the second product rises and the interdependence increases.

Panel a of Figure 3.3 illustrates the immediate impact of a firm's inclusion of marginal consonance cost in its decision making, before its rival responds by changing price or its Θ-value. The function MPC_1 is firm 1's marginal production cost and, if its $\theta_1 = 0$, its relevant cost function, whose intersection with the marginal revenue function (MR_1^0) dictates a profit-maximizing output of x_1 and price p_1. The resulting profit is p_1CFG *less* fixed costs. Suppose now that firm 1 adopts some $\theta_1 > 0$, so that marginal consonance cost (MCC_1^0) is positive and is added to MPC_1 to obtain the decision relevant marginal cost curve. Output falls to x_1^0 and price rises to p_1^0, and revenue falls by $BCx_1x_1^{0-}\ p_1p_1^0AB$. *But the firm's monetary costs are affected only by the move to the left on* MPC_1, for a fall of $EFx_1x_1^0$. Profits, therefore, are p_1^0 *AEG less* fixed costs, a decline of $BCFE\text{-}p_1^0ABp_1$ – the marginal consonance cost of the move from p_1 to p_1^0. The profit change is a loss because the firm had the option of operating at $[x_1^0, p_1^0]$ before it adopted a positive θ_1. The demand function, D_1^0, does not shift because by assumption firm 2 does not change p_2.

But, of course, the rise in firm 1's price to p_1^0 shifts firm 2's demand function to the right, decreasing its elasticity at the current price. With θ_2 constant, firm 2 should raise its price, which in turn shifts firm 1's demand function to the right, to D_1^1 on the graph in Figure 3.3b. Because firm 2's output can rise or fall, depending on the degree of shift it experiences in its demand function and that function's elasticity, and because firm 1's *MCC* rises or falls in response to that rival output movement, the graph shows no movement in *MCC*. However, firm 1's price rises to $p,^1$ and x_1^1 is shown as rising, although it may fall. The expectation is that firm 1's profit will rise to p_1^1BEG from p_1ACG, although it is possible that it will fall.[9] These interactions between the firms continue until a new equilibrium is reached at the given Θ-values.

In the longer run, if one accepts the notion of Θ responding to own-profit potentials, the expectation is that the rise in firm 2's profit will lead it to accept firm 1's signal to cooperate by raising θ_2 in its own self-interest. Figure 3.3c assumes that both firms adjust their Θ-values to the "equilibrium" levels appropriate to a steady state. Firm 1's consonance cost rises to MCC_1^2 by virtue of the increase in θ_2 and x_2 although it is to be expected that prices of both firms will have risen sufficiently high to reduce output below the

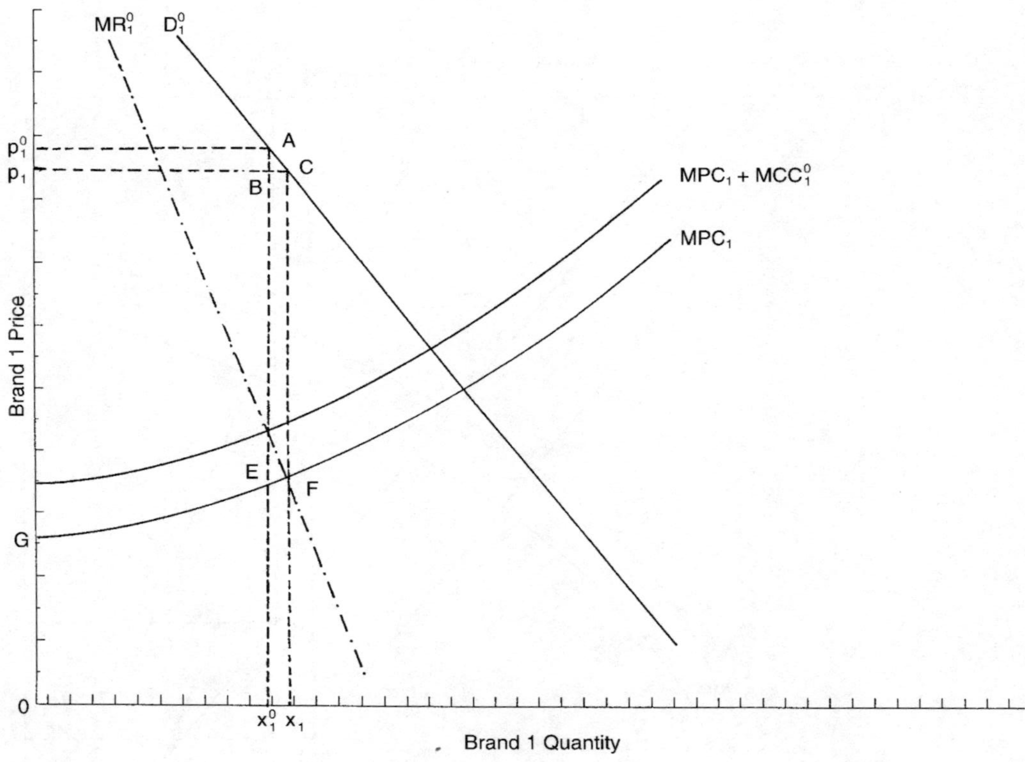

Figure 3.3a θ_2 and price constant

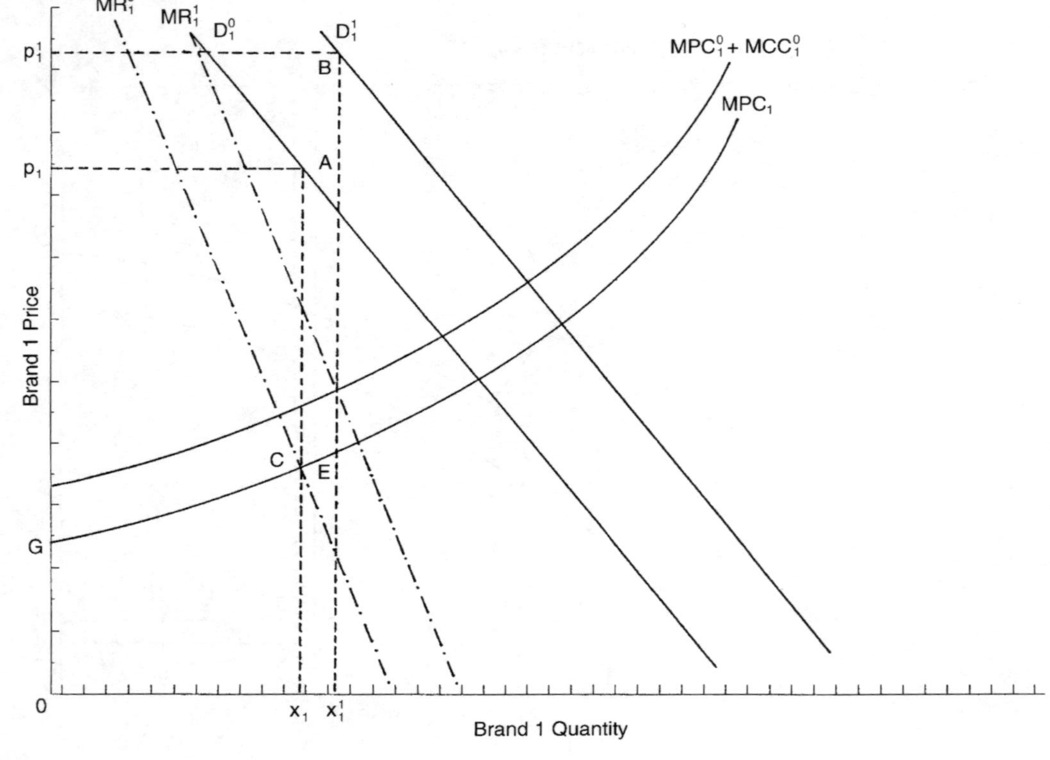

Figure 3.3b θ_2 constant, price rises

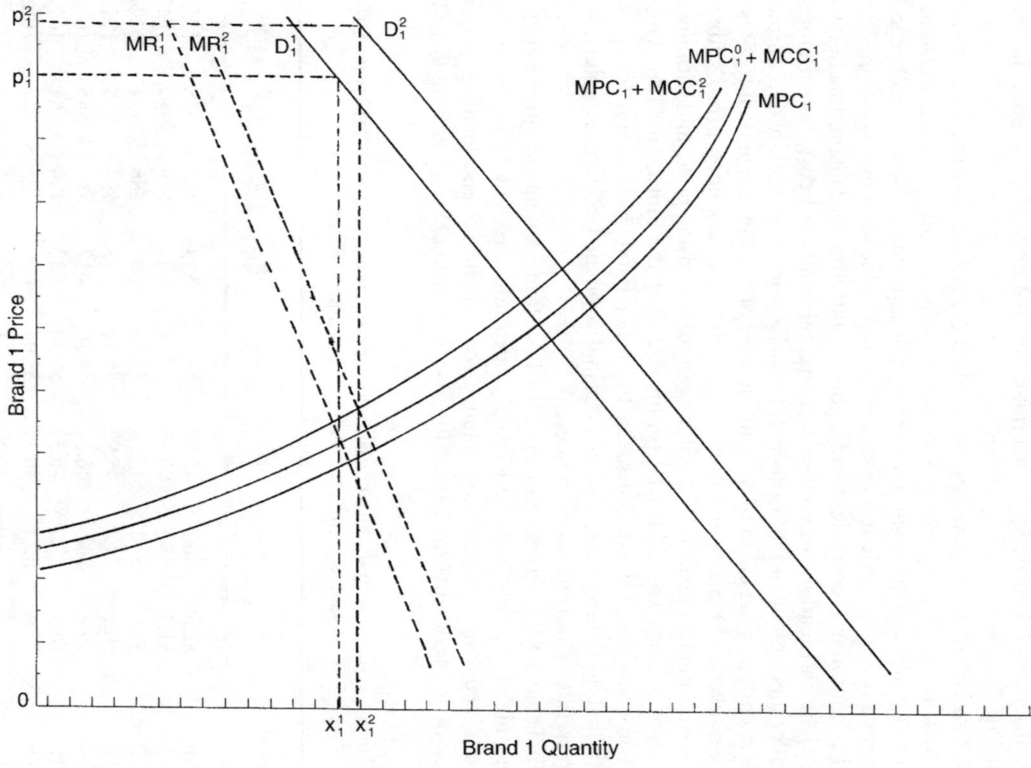

Figure 3.3c Both firms' θ's and prices vary

Figure 3.3b levels. The diagram depicts this assumed rivalrous consonance solution for firm 1, with price at p_1^1, an increase over p_1^2 , and output at x_1^2, somewhat higher than x_1^1 counter to expectations. Profit, of course, is shown as considerably increased over that of Figures 3.3a and 3.3b as the fruits of cooperation, although, as pointed out in section 2c this result is not certain in the absence of knowledge concerning the patterns of deference in the industry.

Let us return to our example in Table 3.3. Assume that the consonance coefficients rise symmetrically and, temporarily, x_1 and p_1 remain constant. Firm 2's combined marginal cost rises significantly, to intersect its unchanged marginal revenue curve at a higher price and reduced output solution. The higher consonance coefficient and higher p_2 shift firm 1's demand function to the right and lead also to a rise in marginal combined cost, but in much smaller amounts than that of firm 2. Firm 1's price rises slightly and output falls slightly as a net effect of the shift upward of combined marginal cost and shift outward of the demand function, which feeds back upon firm 2's functions with minor impacts. With falling output and rising price, and with near constant average costs, firm 1's profits rise over the unit interval for symmetric consonance coefficients. On the other hand, p_2 rises but less proportionately than x_2 falls, and its marginal combined costs rise rapidly, so that π_2 falls uniformly over the interval.

In Table 3.5 b_{12} is reduced from 2 to 1, so firm 1's demand curve benefit from higher p_2 falls by half. Firm 1's sales fall markedly from Table 3.3 values, reducing marginal consonance costs of firm 2 and leading to the rises in p_2. Indeed, firm 2's profits rise monotonically as θ_1 and θ_2 rise

Table 3.5 Social welfare and consumer surplus values, quantities and prices for selected symmetric values of θ_1 and θ_2 and $b_{12} = 1$

$\theta_1 = \theta_2$	x_1	x_2	p_1	p_2	π_1	π_2	CS	W
0.0	82.3	36.2	45.37	54.57	598	183	975	1756
0.1	81.7	35.7	45.55	54.95	603	186	954	1743
0.2	80.9	35.1	45.74	55.34	608	188	931	1727
0.3	80.2	34.4	45.93	55.75	613	191	909	1713
0.4	79.4	33.8	46.13	56.16	617	193	885	1695
0.5	78.5	33.2	46.35	56.60	622	194	861	1677
0.6	77.6	32.5	46.57	57.04	626	195	837	1658
0.7	76.7	31.8	46.80	57.51	630	195	812	1637
0.8	75.8	31.1	47.04	57.99	633	195	786	1614
0.9	74.7	30.3	47.29	58.48	636	194	759	1589
1.0	73.7	29.6	47.55	59.00	639	192	733	1564

symmetrically to Θ = [0.7,0.7], then fall gently for the rest of the interval. Firm 1's profits rise monotonically over the entire interval but only by about 4 percent. Of course, *CS* and *W* decline over the whole interval as the common values rise from 0 to 1.

In the example presented in this chapter, when collusion rises unambiguously (i.e., when both Θ-values rise together), consumers' surplus, *CS*, falls but social welfare, *W*, rises slightly before it declines. Is this a generalizable result of the model or is it dependent on the arbitrarily selected parameters of the example? When θ_i rises, θ_j constant, or when θ_i and θ_j rise together, can we expect *CS* and/or *W* to rise?

Consider *CS* first. The consumer surplus enjoyed from a brand is a function of its quantity, *x*, and the elasticity of its demand function. Define $p_i^* = p_{i,max} - p_i$, where $p_{i,max}$ is the price-axis intercept. Then, $CS_i = 0.5p_i^*x_i$ and for our example, from (3.8),

$$CS = 0.1x_1^2 + 0.3x_2^2. \tag{3.12}$$

But quantity is a negative function of own-price and a positive function of other-price. From Figure 3.1 if both Θ-values rise (fall) or if one rises (falls) while the other remains constant, both prices will rise (fall). When one Θ-value rises and the other falls, price of the firm which has increased Θ will rise and the price of the firm which has reduced the value will fall. If the rise is large enough and the fall small enough both prices may rise, but if the relative magnitudes are reversed both prices may fall.

Movements in *CS* do not depend upon the signs and values of price movements only, however. Differentiation of *CS* yields:

$$dCS = \frac{-b_{11}b_{22}x_1 + b_{11}b_{21}x_2}{b_{11}b_{22}}dp_1 + \frac{-b_{11}b_{22}x_2 + b_{12}b_{22}x_1}{b_{11}b_{22}}dp_2. \tag{3.13}$$

For each firm, a rise in own-price leads to a movement upward on the initial demand function and a fall in output, but the other-price coefficient shifts the demand function to the right and increases output. The sign of the net "shift and slope" result depends for firm *i* on the relative sizes of b_{ii} and b_{ij} in the demand function and the relative sizes of dp_i x_i and x_j. The own-price coefficient will in general be much larger in absolute value than the other-price coefficient, but initial quantities of the two goods are less predictable.

Consider the first term in (3.13), which is the contribution to total *CS* that (say) a rise in p_1 generates. This incremental *CS* can be rewritten

$$\left(x\frac{b_{21}}{b_{22}}x_2\right)dp_1.$$

The first term is the direct reduction in *CS* caused by dp_1 and the second term is the indirect *CS* offset resulting from the increase in p_2, or the amount of the shift in the demand function for good 1.[10] Normally it is expected that the sum of the two terms will be negative for all brands in the product group, but our example in (3.7) provides us with a perverse case, as will be shown below. It is possible, therefore, when the *CS* impact of one brand's price is perverse and the other prices' impacts are small enough, that a general rise in prices could increase *CS*, but this is highly unlikely with realistic demand functions and brand numbers in the product group.

Social surplus, *W*, includes firms' profits along with *CS*, and the rise in profits as the Θ-values rise with attendant tacit collusion may outweigh the fall in *CS* and lead to a rise in *W*. In Table 3.3 this happens as Θ rises from [0,0] to [1,1], the rise in π_1 with symmetric rises in Θ-values being outweighed by the fall in π_2 and *CS*. In general it is a close run balance between them, as the last column reveals, and, of course, one would generally expect *both* firms' profits to rise to make the outcome quite likely. In Figure 3.2, which graphs the welfare contours for prices for the extreme points of the unit square within which values of θ_1 and θ_2 for mature oligopoly must fall, note that *W* rises as we move from right to left on the diagram. The symmetric pairs [0,0] and [1,1] are "well behaved", with *W* larger for the first than the second. Moreover, as collusion rises from [0,0] to [1,0] and falls from [1,1] to [1,0] *W* is well behaved. But note that the contour containing the [0,1] collusion pattern has a higher welfare value than that for zero collusion, [0,0]. Indeed, the *W* value for the purely competitive solution (3,366, for $p_1 = 33.48$ and $p_2 = 37.35$, which is not graphed on Figure 3.2) lies below the contour containing the solution for Θ = [0,1] (because both firms' profits are negative)! Because firm 1 benefits so greatly from rises in firm 2's deference, it is the common occurrence that when θ_2 rises, θ_1 constant or rising, *W* rises. Note on the graph that any interior convex combination of [0,1] and [0,0] price solutions will yield *W* values above the noncollusion value.

Herein lies a flaw in the use of conventional welfare analysis in oligopoly analysis, but another difficulty also looms. Because interdependence leads to *shifts* in the demand functions changes in *W* and *CS* are not wholly reliable as indices of welfare changes. These shifts may involve nonnegligible external effects on other sectors of the economy that are not taken into account in the calculations. In all likelihood, this can be ignored. But more importantly, on nonefficiency grounds, taking some account of common notions of equity as public policy must it is difficult to accept the coordinate fairness of dollars of benefit flowing to consumers or to firms, when profit rises are due wholly to increases in tacit collusion among the firms. In both efficiency and equity aspects, consumers' surplus offers the prospect of a better tracker of the social harm of collusion that the sum of consumers' surplus and profits.[11]

With this hypothesis at hand, therefore, on Figure 3.4 the *CS* contours with respect to prices are graphed for the extreme points of the mature oligopoly polygon to provide the counterpart of Figure 3.2. The contours are

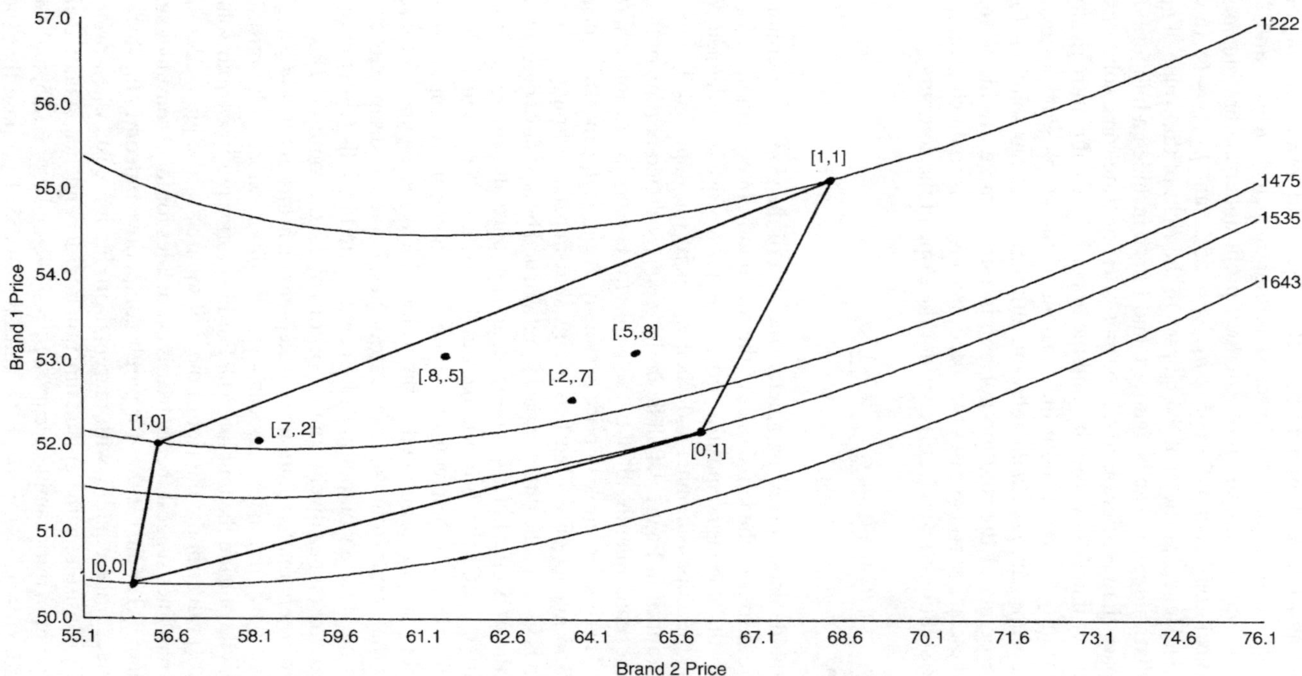

Figure 3.4 Consumers' surplus contours

ellipses[12] and I have presented both the upper and lower portions of the "lefthand" portions of the ellipses. The highest prices firms 1 and 2 will charge in their maximization of extended profit under mature oligopolistic conditions in our example occur at $p_{1,max1} = 55.12$ and $p_{2,max} = 68.16$ when $\Theta = [1,1]$. Hence, portions of the ellipses to the right of that value of p_1 and above that value of p_2 can be ignored, and I have included a bit more of the price space than is relevant to our purposes to illustrate some solutions that would occur if collusion went beyond the upper bounds of mature rivalry.

Importantly, however, both the portions of the graph with positive and negative slopes are *potentially* relevant, although all of our solutions for the extreme points of the solution polygon in our example are in the former area. These are perverse cases that occur because x_1 is so much greater than x_2 in the solutions. From (3.13) consider the slope of the contours:

$$\frac{dp_2}{dp_1} = \frac{b_{11}b_{22}x_1 - b_{11}b_{21}x_2}{b_{12}b_{22}x_1 - b_{11}b_{22}x_2} = \frac{3x_1 - 1.5x_2}{x_1 - 3x_2}. \tag{3.14}$$

Given the demand curves' parameters the sign of the slope is determined by the relative sizes of the initial sales of the two brands. In our example, for $0.5x_2 \leq x_1 < 3x_2$ the slope is nonpositive, otherwise it is positive or undefined. When $x_1 = 3x_2$, the slope is infinite, and when $x_1 = 0.5x_2$ the slope is 0. The extreme points graphed in Figure 3.4 all lie in the *positively* sloped portion of the contours, and, consequently, all of the solutions for Θ-pairs in the unit square will as well. This is an example of price perversity. A rise in p_1 generates a negative own-brand impact on *CS* but because its shift impact on brand 2's demand function is so great the direct impact is outweighed by a positive indirect effect. Hence the ΔCS effect of dp_1 is positive, and dp_2 must also rise to generate the compensating ΔCS that brings us back to the original *CS* contour.

Finally, since the behavior of outputs is so much more important when consumers' surplus is adopted as the welfare measure, Figure 3.5 charts the outputs that result from the pricing strategies. Perversity disappears as a rise (fall) in one brand's output must be compensated by falls (rises) in others'. Solutions are on negatively sloping portions of the *CS* contours. This graph is trimmed to eliminate solutions in which either firm's outputs are negative, but they have not been truncated to eliminate those solutions whose Θ-values lie outside the unit interval. For illustrative purposes, four solutions for $[\theta_1, \theta_2]$ values in the interior of the unit square are also graphed.

Two baselines suggest themselves as candidates for ideal consumer surplus attainments. The first is that for purely competitive outcomes in which both firms meet price equality with marginal production costs when prices are mutually consistent with demand function interdependence. As noted above, such a point in our example occurs at $p_1 = 33.48$ and $p_2 = 37.35$, and, we can now add, $x_1 = 173.84$, $x_2 = 58.77$, and $CS = 4{,}058$. I propose that such an

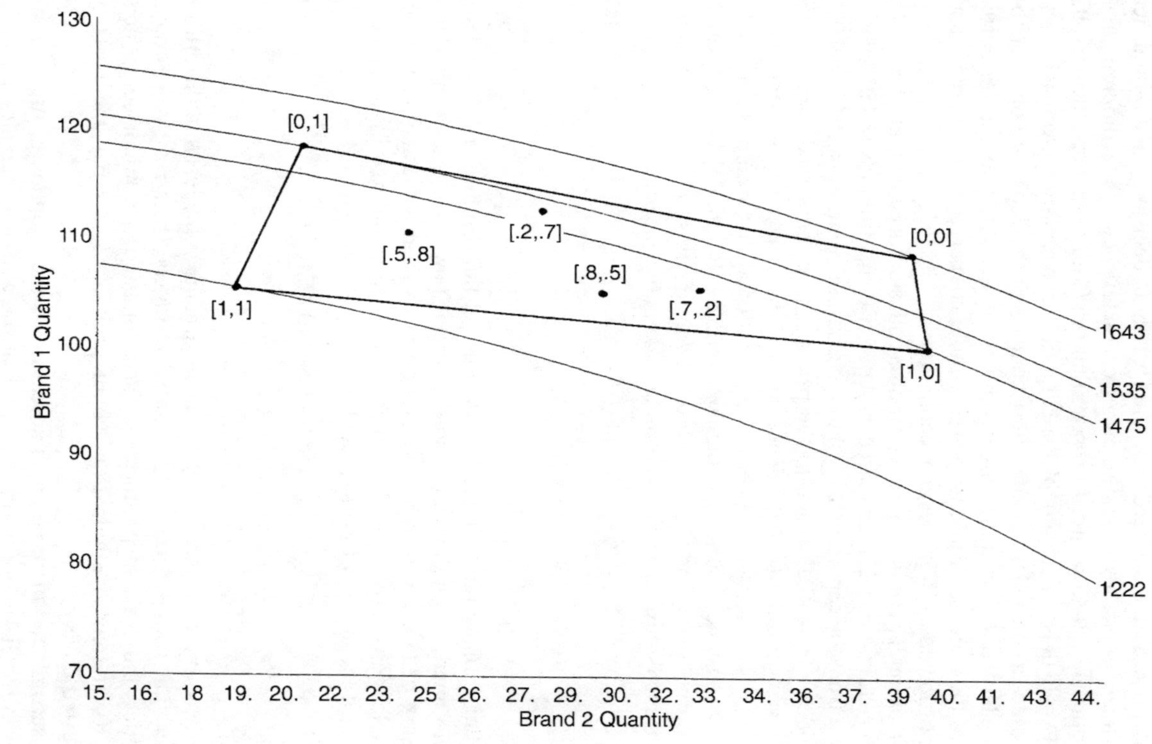

Figure 3.5 Consumers' surplus contours

ideal does not meet rational criteria in a realistic market economy, and therefore holds up a standard which is not truly a feasible policy goal. Oligopoly implies that rational agents are cognizant of the power of their brand price and the interdependence of their decisions, and would act irrationally were they to ignore either characteristic of their differentiated oligopoly market structure. I propose that the Cournot point, which results with $\Theta = [0,0]$ is a more suitable baseline from two realistic viewpoints. First, it provides a convenient manner of decomposing the departure of an oligopolistic level of *CS* from the purely competitive level into that portion ascribable to the exercise of pricing power without cooperation among rivals and that portion due to some level of cooperation.

For example, consider perfect mature collusion occurring at $\Theta = [1,1]$, which yields $CS = 1{,}222$ compared with purely competitive $CS = 4{,}058$. Then a move from the competitive level to the Cournot point, or from $CS = 4{,}058$ to 1,582 at $\Theta = [0,0]$ is due to the pricing power possessed by the rivals absent recognized interdependence, and the move from that Cournot point to $\Theta = [1,1]$ the social cost of rivals' cooperation at that level. Let CS_p be the level of consumers' surplus at the competitive solution, CS_c be the level at the Cournot point, and CS_r be the level of consumers' surplus at the rivalrous consonance solution. Then, in absolute and relative measure,

$$1 \quad (CS_p - CS_r) = (CS_p - CS_c) + (CS_c - CS_r) \tag{3.15}$$

$$2 \quad 1 = \frac{(CS_p - CS_c)}{(CS_p - CS_r)} = \frac{(CS_c - CS_r)}{(CS_p - CS_r)}$$

The first term on the right yields a measure of the absolute or relative level of consumers' surplus loss ascribable to pricing power and the second term a measure of loss due to tacit cooperation in rivalrous consonance. For our example, decomposing the loss in social welfare as indexed by consumers' surplus if the duopoly functions at $\Theta = [1,1]$:

$$\begin{aligned} &1 \quad 4058 - 1222 = (4058 - 1582) - (1582 - 1222) && (3.16)\\ &2 \quad 2836 = 2476 + 360 \\ &3 \quad 1 = 0.873 + 0.127. \end{aligned}$$

Clearly, in this case, most of the social disturbance is the result of the pricing power that springs from differentiated products, their relative customer loyalties and costs of production. Tacit collusion is a minor component and its attempted elimination would probably not repay the costs of dedicated policy.

A second, and more compelling reason for the adoption of the Cournot point as social welfare norm, is that a realistic welfare economics must take account of the permeation of markets by decision interdependence. On Figure 3.6 the rivalrous consonance polygon is superimposed on the same

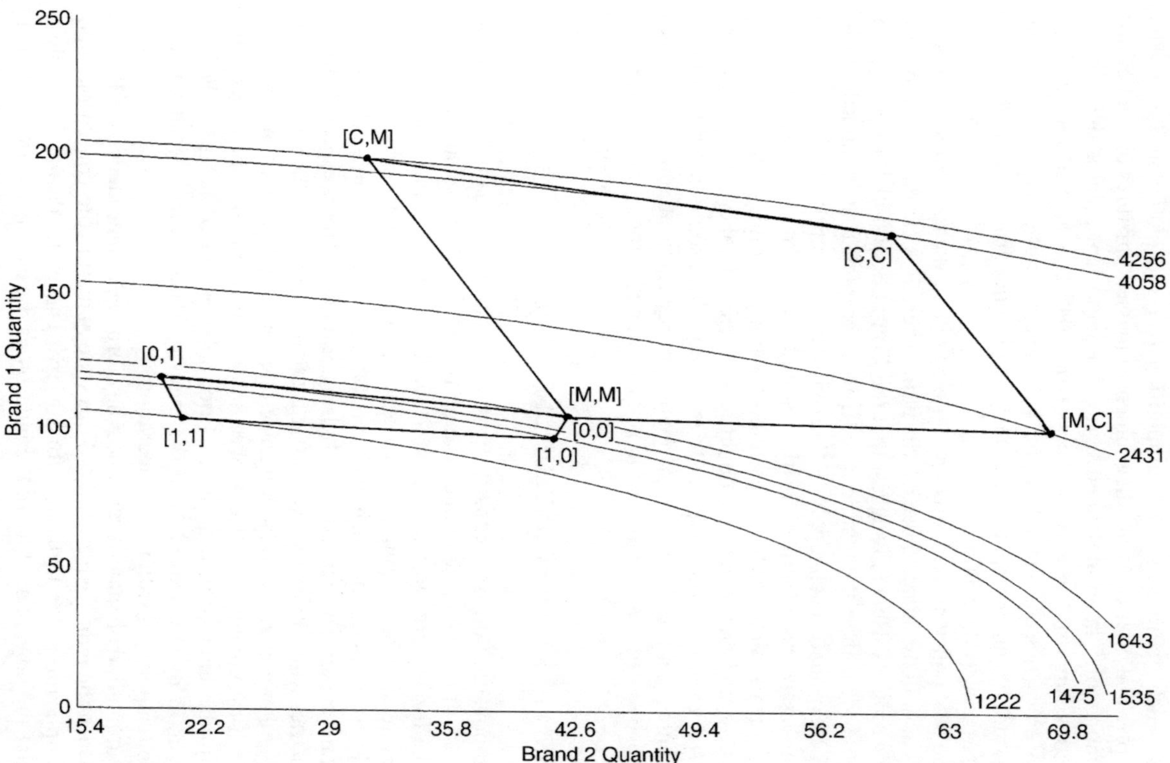

Figure 3.6 A comparison of welfare regions space

consumer surplus diagram as a polygon which encompasses much of traditional analysis of market structures' welfare implications in the absence of interdependence. The vertices represent the consumers' surpluses for two firms which operate in pure competition (C) and monopoly (M) in our example. The interior of the diagram encompasses "mixtures of competition and monopoly" in an ill defined sense. The important point is that the two polygons support one another only at the [0,0] consonance vector. Tacit collusion carries consumers' surplus values significantly below the "classic" polygon. The pure competition vertex [C,C] is quite distant – too far to serve as a realistic welfare guide.

The best policy makers can hope for is to reduce the tacit collusion among rivals and, in the ideal, approach the point where it is eliminated but pricing power remains. Hence, I suggest that the Cournot point [0,0] is a more reasonable ideal than the competitive, if it is accepted that it can seldom be reached in mature oligopoly but perhaps can be approached with policy incentives or disincentives. In the example in (3.16), the decomposition shows clearly that antitrust measures are not the solution in this industry structure, and that society can do little in a focussed policy sense to move the industry from the Cournot point to the competitive solution. Stimulation of new entry in a positive sense, or removal or lessening of entry barriers in a negative sense, are probably the most rational policy tools of relevance.

4 SUMMARY AND CONCLUSIONS

Oligopolistic industries consist of firms which are mutually aware of the impacts of their initiated policies upon rivals, and the expectation that they will be forced through self-interest to react to them. Actors in such communities, as in other communitarian contexts, will strive toward achieving a stable environment in which decisions can be made in manners that accommodate to pervasive fears of destabilizing initiatives. This is especially true of industries which have achieved a status of "maturity", in which wars of attrition and annihilation are no longer of relevance, and in which major players strive for mutually attractive or acceptable tacit cooperative behavior within the fundamental context of rivalry. Price policy is viewed as especially destabilizing in its implications, and the industry concentrates special attention upon tempering it with tacit cooperation.

Our method of analysis renounces any formal dynamic analysis of the path by which the industry has achieved this state of maturity to concentrate upon its implications for firms and for society. The methodology is simply to isolate the power structure of the industry as it exists in a period of time by determining a power matrix detailing the own-profit equivalent of rival firms' profits. Maximizing extended profit functions subject to secondary goals of the firms' decision making in the form of constraints is adopted as a flexible framework that can be tailored to the specifics of a specific industry. The power matrix contains consonance coefficients, Θ_{ij}, which specify the equivalent of other-profits in terms of own-profits, and maximization of extended profits that include own-profits plus the sum of rival profits discounted by relevant Θ-terms using price policies permits us to derive the industry price-output structure.

Because mature oligopolies are expected to adopt Θ-values that lie on the unit interval, we study the individual firm and social implications of pricing policies based on cooperation factors in this bracket. Because of the shortcomings of social surplus behavior in such decision making environments, we have chosen consumers' surplus as a more reliable index of social implications. In coming chapters, this framework, which has been presented wholly in price policy terms, will be used to analyze the joint implications of price and nonprice competitiveness among oligopolists.

Part II
Decision Making in Oligopoly: Approaches in the Literature

4 Hotelling Models and Other Spatial Analogs

1 SPATIAL ANALOGS

One of the unfortunate characteristics of the research that employs spatial analysis in dealing with product competition is that so much effort has been expended uselessly in analyzing the "large group" or "tangency solution" case of monopolistic competition.[1] As noted in the introduction to Chapter 2 the nature of these efforts will be discussed in Chapter 6. Its temptation is strong, for it permits the derivation of closed analytic price and brand numerical solutions and their examination for comparative static and social welfare considerations. In reality, monopolistic competition structure is not a frequent occurrence, with most firms in an industry acutely aware of rivals with whom they are in close competition. This is especially true of firms when spatial location is explicitly or implicitly present in actual or analogous usage. The assumption of equal and negligible competitive interdependence among differentiated products is not an acceptable assumption when neighboring firms must be expected to be in oligopolistic rivalry.

As will be developed more fully below, the concept of a zero-profit Nash price–brand number equilibrium with n firms equally spaced in a market or product space is simply not an interesting construct, especially when consumers are assumed to be uniformly distributed in that space with identical preferences and firms are assumed to have identical cost functions and to enjoy costless relocation. Hotelling (1929) was the first to implicitly impose this notional equilibrium (when short-run barriers prevent entry and zero-profit maxima) in duopoly, and d'Aspremont, Gabszcewicz and Thisse (1979) (hereafter, AGT) the first to criticize his failure to anticipate the Bertrand price competition that would render such equilibria unstable and nonsustainable.

In consequence, the interest of this study in examining this body of research is to benefit from its content that is independent of assumptions of monopolistically competitive market structure. Discussion of the body of methodologically ingenious but realistically irrelevant analysis of the equilibrium conditions that must hold in that market structure, the comparative statics theorems that are derivable for parameter displacements, and the social welfare characteristics of the equilibria is delayed until Chapter 6. Attention will focus on the valuable techniques these theorists have developed to define the broader problems of quality competition and to provide the tools necessary to cope with it in oligopolistic environments.

This chapter deals with three forms of spatial models, classified in terms of which variables are endogenous or exogenous: models in which prices are variable and locations are fixed, prices are fixed and locations are variable, and both variables are endogenous.

2 HOTELLING MODELS IN A LINEAR PRODUCT SPACE

In his classic paper Hotelling's point of departure was Sraffa's insight[2] that the nature of price competition in the real world did not conform to the Bertrand model in which firms' sales fell discontinuously to zero as rivals shaded prices slightly below ruling price. Rather, firms lost sales continuously as rivals reduced prices, revealing two important truths: (a) that consumers did not treat firms' products as homogeneous but preferred those of some producers to those of others, and (b) that firms possessed some pricing power over their products. Hotelling, therefore, is quite explicit about examining the implications of differentiated products, i.e., goods whose quality characteristics differ, for the pricing and product–space locations of competing firms, especially with respect to the existence or nonexistence of equilibria in these dimensions. Among the quality characteristics most prominently featured was seller location, but Hotelling explicitly employed distances in his linear spaces as a metric measuring differences in intensity of other characteristics, as we illustrated in section 5 of Chapter 2.

Hotelling discusses three models in his paper, which share the following common assumptions:

1 The "market" (product space) is linear and finite[3] with length λ
2 Buyers are distributed uniformly along the line
3 Firms produce at constant marginal and average total costs, hence no fixed costs exist, and for simplicity total costs are assumed to be zero
4 Demand is perfectly inelastic, with one unit of product consumed in each unit length of line each time period
5 Consumer preferences are driven wholly by delivered price and buyers choose the product at minimum delivered price
6 Prices are mill prices, with delivered prices f.o.b. firm locations and rising by c per unit of distance, where c is the constant "transport rate" which can be construed as the disutility cost to the consumer of departing from most preferred products in purchases; in this latter interpretation, the consumer's location is at the point of maximum quality satisfaction.

In Model 1:

7 Mill prices, p_i, are variable, are set by firms to maximize profits subject to conjectures about rival behavior, and are above constant marginal and average costs

8 Firm locations are fixed with no more than one firm at any location

9 Market structure is duopolistic with "Cournot expectations" (zero conjectural variation, or *ZCV*). That is, each rival expects the other to exhibit zero responses to policy initiatives.

In Model 2:

8′ Firm locations are variable and determined by maximum profit motivation, with zero cost of relocating.

9′ The dominant market structure is duopoly, with Cournot expectations, although Hotelling does discuss informally the solution for a three-firm industry.

In Model 3, which Hotelling discusses informally:

7′ Mill prices are fixed, at least tacitly, because Hotelling is ambiguous as to the behavior of prices, but since it is this model in which he discusses behavior for which prices are not relevant (e.g., political parties' choice of platforms) in situations in which they are relevant it seems clear that prices are held fixed

8′ Firm locations are variable and determined by maximum profit motivation, with zero cost of relocating

9′ The dominant structure involves two agents, with Cournot expectations, although Hotelling does discuss informally the solution for a multiagent locational problem.

In Model 1 firms 1 and 2 are located at 1 and 2 respectively on the line segment in Figure 4.1, so that the analysis is one where product brands are exogenous. With fixed locations, two cases can occur. Case 1 exists when $h_1 + h_2 = \lambda$, where h_i is a firm hinterland starting at the firm's location and terminating at an end point of the market; therefore, both firms are located at (nearly) the same point. As Hotelling indicated, in this case the commodities are no longer differentiated and Bertrand's criticism of Cournot is validated: each firm will find it advantageous to shade price until both prices equal marginal cost (0 in the present case) and a zero-profit Nash equilibrium occurs.

Case 2 is characterized by locations 1 and 2 having a potentially contested market area between them, so that $h_1 + h_2 < \lambda$. A necessary condition for an equilibrium is a price difference condition for $[p_1^\circ, p_2^\circ] : |p_1^\circ - p_2^\circ| < c(\lambda - h_1 - h_2)$, which is to require that neither firm in equilibrium be able to capture or share the other's hinterland. Were either of these latter conditions to occur, the aggrieved firm would find it advantageous to lower price, contradicting the assertion that the price vector was a Nash equilibrium.

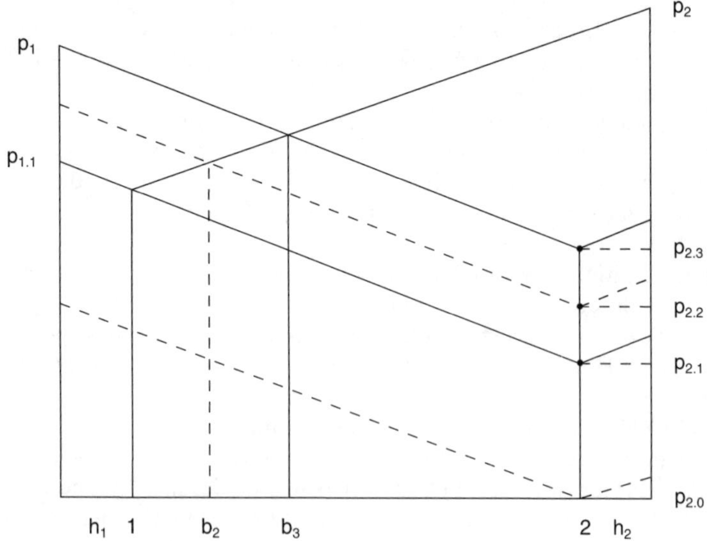

Figure 4.1 Small hinterlands condition

Two subcases arise under Case 2, one of which meets the price difference condition and one of which does not. For Case 2a, where neither firm's sales area penetrates the other's hinterland, AGT (1979) have proven that a necessary and sufficient condition for the existence of $[p_1^\circ, p_2^\circ]$ is:

$$
\begin{aligned}
&1 \quad \left(\lambda + \frac{h_1 - h_2}{3}\right)^2 \geq \frac{4}{3}\lambda(h_1 + 2h_2) \\
&2 \quad \left(\lambda + \frac{h_2 - h_1}{3}\right)^2 \geq \frac{4}{3}\lambda(h_2 + 2h_1)
\end{aligned}
\qquad (4.1)
$$

which implies the price difference condition. Case 2a's price solution meeting this necessary and sufficient condition is:

$$
\begin{aligned}
&1 \quad p_1^\circ = c\left(\lambda + \frac{h_1 - h_2}{3}\right) \\
&2 \quad p_2^\circ = c\left(\lambda - \frac{h_1 - h_2}{3}\right)
\end{aligned}
\qquad (4.2)
$$

In Case 2b the price difference condition is not met, one firm captures the other's entire inner market and intrudes into the hinterland; a price war begins, carrying both prices to zero. But then one of the firms may raise price, gaining nothing, but inducing the other to raise price to a level slightly below its rival's, setting off a new bout of price shading.

Hence a necessary and sufficient condition for an equilibrium in Case 2 is that (4.1) hold. It may be useful to illuminate these conditions with Figure 4.1. In the figure h_1 need not equal h_2 but $h_1 + h_2 < \lambda$. Assume p_1 is fixed at $p_{1,1}$, and initially $p_2 = 0$ so $\pi_2 = 0$. Obviously, π_2 will rise monotonically from 0 as p_2 is raised until p_2 reaches $p_{2,1} - \in$, $\in > 0$. A discontinuous break in the rise of Π_2 occurs at $p_{2,1}$ as firm 2 shares h_1 with firm 1, and two possibilities are presented here. First, firm 2 may find it unprofitable to raise price higher, say to $p_{2,2}$, where it has lost h_1 as well as the region between 1 and b_2 to firm 1 but has increased its revenue intake in its hinterland h_2 and its remaining contested region between 2 and b_2. In Case 2b the lost sales in h_1 are so large given the value of c that firm 2 pulls back price to $p_{2,1} - \in$. But of course firm 1 reacts with a reduction in p_1, from $p_{1,1}$ and a price war is on with no equilibrium occurring.

If h_1 is small, however, it may pay to raise price up to some level (say, $p_{2,3}$ before the balance of revenue lost and gained is equalized and profit is maximized. This is a temporary Case 2a occurrence. Once again, however, it is necessary to free p_1 to react to these intrusions if we are to find a Nash equilibrium, and if firm 1 faces similar circumstances to those experienced by firm 2 then a permanent $[p_1^\circ, p_2^\circ]$ occurs that permits a market boundary somewhere in the contested region between 1 and 2. These circumstances can be seen in conditions (4.1), which become harder to fulfill as the hinterlands come closer to equality and/or their sizes increase. This is to say that with locations fixed, an equilibrium with both firms in existence and positive prices can exist if and only if the firms are far enough apart so that the hinterlands are small. In terms of product characteristics, distances between the firms in product space must be sufficiently large. For $h_1 = h_2$ system (4.1) reveals this will occur for a common value less than 0.25λ.

In Chapters 9 and 10 the concept of "consumer benchmarking" of quality characteristics will be introduced. This assumes that in many cases of consumer purchasing, consumers acquire certain expectations of quality standards and react only to departures from these standards in either direction of improvement or depreciation. Under these circumstances, consumers would not be distributed uniformly over the linear quality scale but would be concentrated at the benchmark, perhaps in the manner of a frequency density function with narrow variance and mean or mode at the benchmark.

Because these benchmarks are presumed to be shaped by some sort of measure of central tendency of existing or recent levels of quality in the product group, one might expect that the "hinterlands" of firms are quite large and, in the limit, a Case 1 type of quality solution would emerge with firms clustering at the benchmarks. In Chapter 10, where a rivalrous consonance framework for duopolistic rivalry is employed, this does tend to happen for firms with identical cost and demand parameters as in the Hotelling cases. However, collusion prevents price from falling: indeed, prices rise steadily as the degree of tacit cooperation increases toward $\Theta = [1,1]$ in the example employed.

Hotelling has anticipated this possibility. To this point the Hotelling problem has been treated in terms of a noncooperative game (see Assumption 9 above). As Hotelling points out, however, in Case 2b interior solutions, it would be advantageous to both firms to cooperate and raise prices without limit to approach unlimited profit. This same potential exists for Case 1 and Case 2a: with price-invariant demand, tacit collusion with little signaling would result in a coordinated raising of prices above zero with a sharing of the market and profits. Indeed, it would be irrational for both firms not to recognize their interdependence and to exploit the capacity to profit. If they did, any location pair on the line would yield the same price solution and the degree of differentiation of product would be immaterial.

3 SALOP'S MODEL WITH PRICES VARIABLE, LOCATIONS FIXED

Salop (1979) has constructed a price–quality model that extends Hotelling's Model 1 in interesting directions. Most of his interest lies in examining what he calls a symmetric zero-profit Nash equilibrium (SZPE) in a circular market area, or a tangency solution in monopolistic competition for uniformly distributed consumers with identical preferences and firms with identical declining average cost functions.[4] In such equilibria firms are equally spaced with identical prices. Most of his results in this area will be ignored at this point to concentrate better on aspects most germane to oligopoly, but will be reviewed in the monopolistic competition discussion of Chapter 6.

Following a suggestion by Lerner and Singer (1937) Salop introduces a second industry (Industry 2) into his model to complement an industry with differentiated products (Industry 1). Industry 2 can be envisaged as producing a Hicksian composite commodity under fixed price conditions which absorbs consumers' residual incomes after their expenditures on the heterogeneous products of Industry 1. If a representative consumer spent all of his or her income Y on the composite good a utility s^*, measured in dollar units, would be obtained. Consumers are assumed to have unit potential demand functions for Industry 1's product, and therefore to buy either 0 or 1 unit of it as a function of prices, preferences and brand locations in product space. The value s^* provides a lower bound on consumer satisfaction, total utility rising above the minimum as good 1 is purchased as long as p_1 *plus* distances costs representing the disutility of having to buy a product which is not the most preferred good do not exhaust maximum satisfaction obtainable from it. Salop places great emphasis on the advantages of introducing Industry 2 into the model, although his enthusiasm is not clearly rationalized.[5]

For the differentiated products of Industry 1 the representative consumer has the utility function,

$$U = u - c\left|I_1 - I^\circ\right| \tag{4.3}$$

where U is calibrated in dollars, u is the maximum utility obtainable from consumption of a unit of product 1 when that product is located at I° in product space, the consumer's most-preferred brand location. The parameter c converts deviations from most-preferred brands into utility cost. For the circular model, $|I_i - I^\circ|$ is the minimum arc-length on the unit circle.[6]

Define

$$v = u - s^*, \tag{4.4}$$

or the maximum surplus above the utility afforded by an alternative purchase of Industry 2's product

Then, the consumer model is

$$\max_i Z = v - p_i - c\left|I_i - I^\circ\right|, \tag{4.5}$$

subject to:

$$Z \geq 0. \tag{4.6}$$

The firm's average cost function is defined as the sum of average variable cost, m_i and average fixed costs, F_i/x_i:

$$AC_i = m_i + \frac{F_i}{x_i} \tag{4.7}$$

where x_i is the firm's output. Average total cost is therefore declining, which is convenient for Salop's interest in the tangency solution case of monopolistic competition.

Given the long-run profitability of the firm ($p_i \geq AC_i$) the isolated firm's market configuration as a function of its price and the consumer model's functions may be illustrated in Figure 4.2. On the figure, v is the maximum attainable utility from good 1 were its price zero and firm i's location at I°. The value of Z shrinks toward zero as distance from the ideal increases, price fixed. When $Z = 0$ the last unit of good 1 is sold by firm i. At the boundary points, maximum utility attainable, u, is exhausted by the reservation utility from good 2, s^*, plus price, plus distance costs.

Consider, now, firm i's market configuration as it confronts a neighboring firm j with fixed price p_j. Three regime breakpoints are depicted in Figure 4.3. At any price $p_i \geq p_j^1$, firm i has a monopoly sales area with (neglecting the neighboring firm to the left of I_i) maximum half-size M.

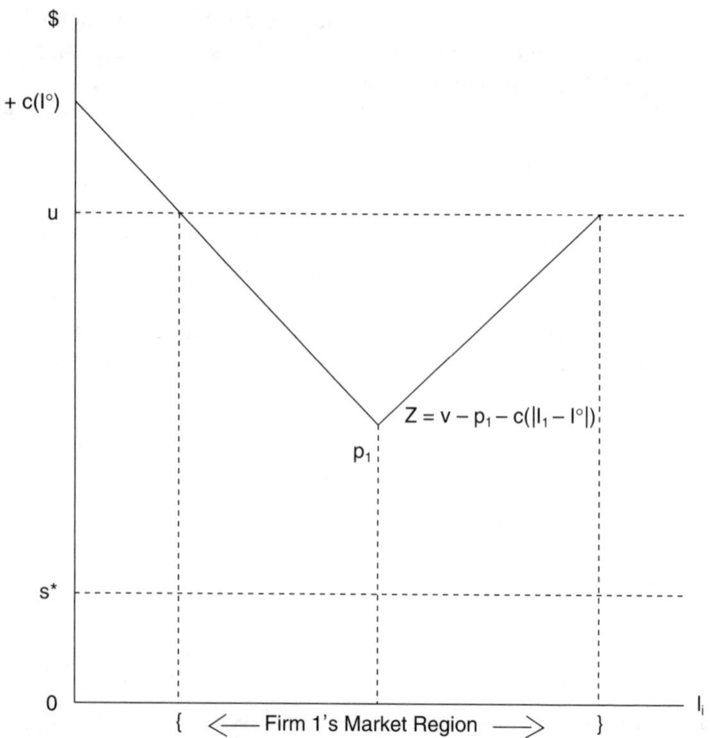

Figure 4.2 The isolated firm's spatial market

Given p_j, firm j will not invade this maximum potential sales area of firm i for $p_i \geq p_i^1$, although for $p > p_i^1$ some consumers in M will not purchase good 1 and will buy Industry 2's product instead.

At prices $p_i^3 \leq p_i \leq p_i^1 - \in$, firm i takes a portion of the market of firm j's sales area and gains sales (as p_i falls) at a slower rate than it does when it lowers prices in its own monopoly region. This region Salop terms the *competitive region*. Finally, at prices $p_i < p_i^3$, firm i takes the entire market of firm j and begins to invade the monopoly region of firm j's neighbor. This is the *super-competitive region*, in which firm j is eliminated and in which firm i accumulates sales at an ever slower rate that in the competitive region as it lowers prices. Firm i's demand function, therefore, has the piecewise linear shape depicted in Figure 4.4. Because of the interest of this book in examining oligopolistic behavior in mature oligopolies, in which rivals are not driven out of the industry, interest will focus on the monopoly and competitive regions.

Suppose locations of two firms on the unit linear product space are fixed, as is firm 2's price p_2, with $I_1 < I_2$. Both monopoly areas will include

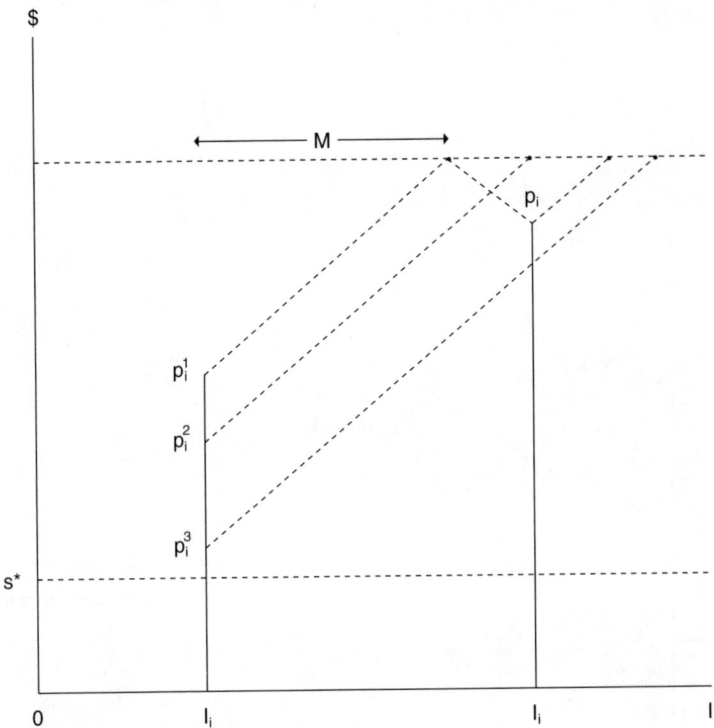

Figure 4.3 Neighboring firms' market areas

their *hinterlands*, $h_i = 0$ to I_1 for firm 1 and $h_2 = I_2$ for firm 2, in addition to potential sales areas in their *interior* regions on the sides facing rivals. Assuming that both firms' monopoly regions in the hinterlands end before the respective boundary points 0 and 1, we may define firm 1's sales region within its monopoly region as having lefthand and righthand boundaries

$$(B_{1,L})_m = \frac{p_1 + cI_1 - v}{c}, \qquad (B_{1,R})_m = \frac{v - p_1 + cI_1}{c}, \tag{4.8}$$

and a total sales area of $B_{1,R} - B_{1,L}$ or

$$s^m_{1,p_1} = \frac{2(v - p_1)}{c}. \tag{4.9}$$

Firm 1's sales at p_1 are then

$$x^m_{1,p_1} = \frac{2(v - p_1)L}{c}. \tag{4.10}$$

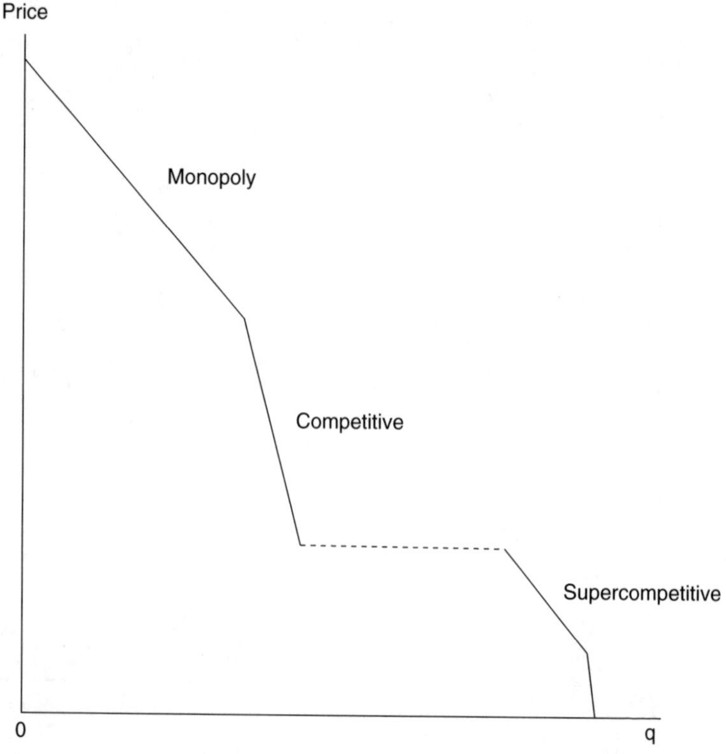

Figure 4.4 Firm *i*'s demand function

The slope of the demand curve in the monopoly region is

$$\left(\frac{dp_1}{dx_1^m, _{p_1}}\right) = -\frac{c}{2L}. \tag{4.11}$$

For firm 1's competitive sales region the boundary points are

$$\begin{aligned} &1 \quad (B_{1,L})_c = (B_{1,R})_m \\ &2 \quad (B_{1,R})_c = \frac{(p_2 - p_1) + c(I_1 + I_2)}{2c}, \end{aligned} \tag{4.12}$$

for a competitive sales area of

$$s_{1,p_1}^c = \frac{(p_2 - 3p_1) + c(I_2 - I_1) + 2v}{2c} \tag{4.13}$$

with sales of

$$x^c_{1,p_1} = \frac{[(p_2 - 3p_1) + c(I_2 - I_1) + 2v]L}{2c}. \tag{4.14}$$

The slope of the demand curve in the competitive region, therefore, is

$$\left(\frac{dp_1}{dx_1}\right)_c = \frac{2c}{3L}. \tag{4.15}$$

Hence, comparison of (4.11) and (4.15) reveals that the elasticity of the monopoly portion of the firm's demand function is greater than the competitive portion – an insight derived from Salop's analysis. Moreover, counterintuitively, the monopoly region is associated with higher, not lower, prices.

Figure 4.4's demand function for a given price, p_2, is generalized in Figure 4.5 to depict the family of firm 1's demand curves as p_2 is changed

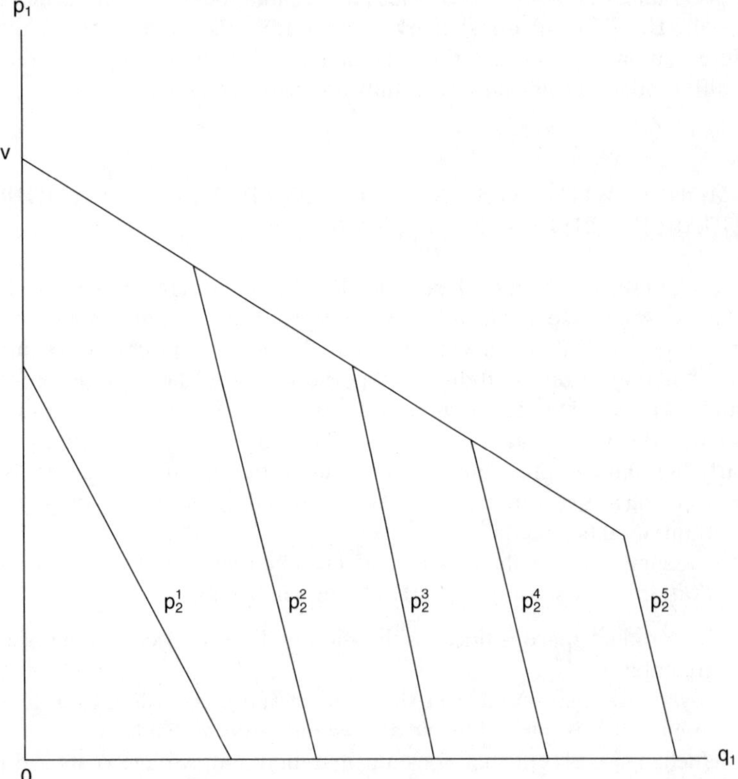

Figure 4.5 The family of firm 1's demand curve as p_2 changes

parametrically, shifting the competitive portions to the right as p_2 rises. Note the upper bound on p_1 at v and the elimination of Firm 1's monopoly region when p_2^1 obtains. The analysis can be extended for $n > 2$ to result, for non-peripheral firms in smaller monopoly regions with the same slope and more steeply sloped competitive regions. Salop's model escapes the potential indeterminacy of the solution when prices and location (product variety) are permitted to vary simultaneously by assuming equal spacing of firms at a zero-profit tangency (or, at the kink of the identical demand functions, a support equilibrium).[7] Introducing such joint variation in an oligopoly model, however, brings us face to face with the AGT problem of potential nonexistence of a Nash equilibrium, discussed in section 5 below and so we leave the Salop model at this point.

Salop's notable contribution to Model 1 Hotelling analysis is to provide a primitive general equilibrium dimension by incorporating a consumer model as an alternative manner of spending and obtaining utility to that given by the good under analysis that provides a minimum below which utility need not fall. By reducing firms' market areas this plays a role in reducing differentiation of products on the one hand, or, by eliminating firms, reducing differentiation even more forcefully on the other hand.

4 MODELS WITH F.O.B. PRICES FIXED, PRODUCT LOCATIONS VARIABLE: EATON AND LIPSEY'S MODEL

As noted in section 2 above, Hotelling (1929) did not treat a model in which mill prices were fixed and locations variable extensively, although his suggestion that oligopolistic firms with fixed and identical mill prices would cluster – the "minimum differentiation" hypothesis – was the most interesting feature of his article to researchers in diverse fields. Eaton and Lipsey (1975) treated and extended such a model to obtain definitive results that define clearly the limited applicability of minimum differentiation. Their analysis, like Hotelling's, is constrained by its failure to endogenize prices, but it yields important insights nonetheless.

The assumptions for their basic model can be presented best as additions or alterations to or substitutes for Hotelling's in Section 2:

- 1^{EL} The product space is linear with unit length ($\lambda = 1$) or a circle of unit circumference
- 2^{EL} Buyers are distributed over the product space according to a density function that is integrable and at least once differentiable
- 3^{EL} Unchanged, except that constant marginal and average costs are not assumed to be zero
- 4^{EL} Unchanged

5^{EL} Unchanged
6^{EL} "Transport" (or utility) costs rise with distance (not necessarily linearly)
7^{EL} Prices are fixed parametrically, identical for all firms, and are above average cost
8^{EL} Unchanged from 8′ for ZCV conjectures but location motivation for maximum loss conjectures (see 9^{EL} below) is maximin profit
9^{EL} Changed from 9′ to permit $n > 2$ with conjectures that are either (1) Cournot (ZCV) or (2) "maximum loss", implying that each firm i initiating a locational change expects one of its rivals to relocate in such manner as to maximize loss of firm i's market

Firms' market area boundaries, which delimit the two half-markets on either side of their sites, are of two kinds: *interior*, which are equidistant from the firm's location and one neighbor, and *exterior*, which are closer to the firm than to any other firm, or, effectively, the boundary of a half-market for firms closest to the ends of the linear market. A nonpaired *interior* firm has two half-markets extending one-half of the distance to its neighbors; a *peripheral* firm is one without an intervening neighbor between it and an end of the market line; and a paired *interior* firm is one with a zero-length half-market between it and a neighboring firm. Hence, paired firms have one half-market each which has (effectively) zero length.

a Model EL1

The Eaton–Lipsey Model 1 assumes the unit length linear market with rectangular customer distribution and ZCV. Importantly, two necessary and sufficient conditions are formulated for a (not necessarily unique) Nash equilibrium:[8]

Condition 1 No firm's whole market can be smaller than any other firm's half-market
Condition 2 Peripheral firms must be paired with an interior firm
The Nash equilibria for n firms which result when these conditions hold are the following:
1 $n = 1$, location is anywhere on the line
2 $n = 2$, peripheral firms are paired at the center (Hotelling's minimum differentiation result in duopoly)
3 $n = 3$, no equilibrium exists
4 $n = 4$, peripheral firms are paired at first and third quartiles
5 $n = 5$, peripheral firms are paired at $1/6$ and $5/6$ positions with an interior firm at the midpoint
6 $n > 5$, an infinite number of equilibria exists.

It is possible, when $n > 5$, to place lower and upper bounds on market areas, M:[9]

$$\text{1 Peripheral firm pairs: } \frac{1}{2n-4} \le M_p \le \frac{1}{n}$$
$$\text{2 Unpaired interior firm: } \frac{1}{2n-6} \le M_l \le \frac{2}{n+1}. \tag{4.16}$$

b Model EL2

The only change in the assumptions made in this model from Model EL1 is that the market is assumed to be the unit circumference circle. The major attendant innovation is the elimination of peripheral firms. Equilibria for n firms are:

1 $n = 1$, location is anywhere on the circle.
2 $n = 2$, an infinite number of equilibria exists, since no matter where firms locate each gets half of L.
3 $n = 3$, an infinite number of equilibria exists, but it is possible to delineate necessary conditions. On the circle, locate two firms arbitrarily at sites 1 and 2. Draw the diameters from these positions to terminate at C_1 and C_2 respectively. Then, any point in the arc C_1C_2 is an equilibrium, and any other point is disequilibrating.
4 $n > 3$, multiple equilibria exist, on which one can place lower and upper bounds:[10]

$$\frac{1}{2n-1} \le M_l \le \frac{2}{n+1}. \tag{4.17}$$

Two important conclusions emerge from Models EL1 and EL2. First, whether or not the market has end points is not of significant importance for $n > 5$, since a multiplicity of equilibria exists in both models. Only for $n = 3$ does one model yield no equilibrium and the other multiple equilibria. Second, minimum differentiation (as opposed to pairing) is not a typical characteristic of equilibria for $n > 2$. It must be expected to be an unusual occurrence, contrary to Hotelling's conjectures.

c Model EL3

This is Model EL1 with conjectures changed from ZTV to maximum loss. It will be recalled that this extremely conservative conjecture involves each firm believing that its locational moves will be countered by a rival's acting to maximize the market loss to the initiating firm. A rival inflicts this maximum loss by moving to pair with the firm on the side of its longer half-market.

Hence, a firm will locate in such manner as to minimize its larger half-market, which is to say, by equating the size of its half-markets.

The principle of location is therefore a simple one: each firm will locate at the midpoint of its market area with two equal half-markets of length $^1/_{2n}$ – with one exception. For $n = 1$, unlike Models EL1 and EL2, the firm's location is determinate at the market's midpoint. When $n = 2$ if either firm located at any points other than a pairing at the midpoint of the market line its rival would pair with it and capture a larger market: hence, both will pair at the center of the line. With the exception of this case maximum loss conjectures will lead to a socially optimal locational configuration that minimizes the sum of disutilities of consumers.

As a final consideration, assume now that incumbent firms now act to forestall entrants. When $n = 2$ each incumbent will fear that it will be "tombstoned" between its current and new rivals, and therefore will act to minimize the larger half-market the entrant would enjoy by moving to the quartiles, thereby bringing about the socially optimal solution in this case as well. Such action has already been taken by firms in all other cases and hence protection against potential entrants does not alter the solutions obtained when incumbents only were considered.

d Model EL4

Consider Model EL3 when the line is converted to the circle of unit circumference. Because peripheral firms followed the same location principles in that model as interior firms, one would suspect that this alteration would make no difference in the circular market model, and that is correct except for the cases of $n = 1$ and $n = 2$. In the former case, location is again indeterminate and in the latter case firms will cluster as a pair when deterrence of entry is not at issue and disperse to opposite points on the circumference when incumbents are protecting against potential entrants.

Both of our conclusions concerning Models EL1 and EL2 are relevant to Models EL3 and EL4: the shape of the one-dimensional market has little impact on the equilibria and minimum differentiation is not characteristic. However, in the latter two markets maximum loss conjectures in general lead to socially optimal locational patterns, except for duopoly, and even this case is included when incumbents include potential entrants into such conjectures.

e Model EL5

Assume the environment of Model EL1 with the exception of a nonlinear density function $c(x)$ meeting the requirements of Assumption 2^{EL}. Customers are no longer proportional to distance, so market and half-markets can be calibrated in either customers or distances, depending on context.

The necessary and sufficient conditions for Nash equilibria are:[11]

1 Condition 1: no firm's whole market can be smaller than any other firm's long-side half-market
2 Condition 2: peripheral firms must be paired
3 Condition 3: for interior firms marginal densities at the boundary points must be equal: $c(B_L) = c(B_R)$, where L and R denote left- and right-side half-markets
4 Condition 4: for peripheral firms marginal densities at the boundary points must meet the condition: $c(B_{SS}) \geq c(B_{LS})$, where SS and LS symbolize short-side and long-side half-markets.

For $n = 2$ an exception to Conditions 3 and 4 occurs, for an equilibrium will be established with a pairing at the median of $c(x)$ whatever the shape of the function. Suppose it to be rising monotonically over the market line. Then at the median Condition 4 will be violated for one of the firms, as $c(x)$ will be greater on its long-side half-market than on its short-side one. Nonetheless, by locating at the median each firm assures itself of half the customer market, and were one to move from that position the rival would relocate to pair with it and obtain a larger market.

For $n = 3$ Condition 2 is violated again because pairing of peripheral firms is not possible.

For $n > 3$ more interesting configurations arise. For example, when $n = 4$, no equilibrium exists for a unimodal symmetrical density function. It is necessary that such firms pair at the first and third quartiles of the density function to meet Conditions 1 and 2, but Condition 4 will not be met for the inner peripheral firms: they will gain marginal customers by moving inward toward the mode with disequilibrating results. More generally, Eaton and Lipsey propound the following theorem:

Theorem

With a variable customer density function that is not rectangular over any finite range of x, a necessary condition for equilibrium is that the number of firms does not exceed twice the number of modes of the density function.[12]

The implications of this theorem are quite interesting. When customers are not distributed over the linear spectrum of potential products uniformly, if such products are to be spaced with wide choice for the consumer there must be at least one concentration of consumers for each brand. More brands can exist in the long run if some or all of them are clustered in pairs. If, on the other hand, consumers are fairly uniformly distributed (i.e., an infinite number of modes exists), these limitations disappear and Conditions 1 and 2 dictate a wider choice of patterns.

Interestingly, however, whether uniform or nonuniform density functions exist, extreme brands must pair at either end of the spectrum. "Minimum differentiation" characterizes extreme brands. Extreme right-wing or left-wing political parties should exist in pairs, for example.

Indeed, in disequilibrium such systems should feature pairing, and this result may be more insightful than those emerging from equilibrium configurations. When the number of firms is within bounds, but an incumbent firm desires to move or an entrant intrudes, if its prospective market area does not include a mode it will desire to pair with an incumbent. If the number of firms exceeds the modal bounds sufficient modes do not exist to serve all firms and entrants will always seek to pair with another firm. Hence, in the words of Eaton and Lipsey: "This phenomenon of pairing in disequilibrium situations is so pervasive, especially in [two-dimensional] markets, that it seems reasonable to refer to a *principle of pairing* as a basic characteristic of disequilibrium models."[13]

One problem that arises when these results are taken into the analytical world of multicharacteristic products is that when weighted distances of such products from one another are computed on a line one seldom finds pairing. When such locations do occur it is difficult to interpret "likeness" in that two products might be quite diverse in all characteristics yet yield weighted distances that are identical. The problem may be somewhat less complicated for political parties, since even though two parties' positions on a variety of issues may differ somewhat, an overall cast of "right-wing" or "left-wing" might be an accurate macro description. For brands of economic goods, on the other hand, such unidimensional characterizations may not be possible.

f Model EL6

The proof of the bounding theorem (see n. 10) does not depend on Condition 2, which concerns peripheral firms. The results of Model EL5, therefore, hold without alteration when the linear market becomes finite but unbounded in the circle.

g Model EL7

Let us now change the conjectural assumption of Model EL 6 to the maximum loss mode, leading firms to minimize their large-side half-markets, if possible by equalizing the number of customers in both half-markets. It is now necessary to distinguish between *local* equilibria and *global* equilibria of firm locations.

1 Local Equilibria

Two types of these optima may occur, in one of which the firms' half-markets are equi-sized (Type I) and in the other in which they are not (Type II).

Type I

Two conditions must be attained for this equilibrium to hold for firm *i*:[14]

Condition 1: At x_i both half-markets are equi-sized:

$$\int_{B_L}^{x_i} c(x)dx = \int_{x_i}^{B_R} c(x)dx. \tag{4.18}$$

Condition 2: For interior and peripheral firms the following must hold:

$$\begin{aligned} &\text{Firm } i \text{ interior: } c(x_i) \geq 0.5c(B_L), 0.5c(B_R) \text{ or } \sim c(x_i) \leq 0.5c(B_L), 0.5c(B_R) \\ &\text{Firm } i \text{ lefthand peripheral: } c(x_i) \geq 0.5c(B_R) \\ &\text{Firm } i \text{ righthand peripheral: } c(x_i) \geq 0.5c(B_L). \end{aligned} \tag{4.19}$$

Type II

In Type I equilibrium the firm always locates at the center of its market area (when calibrated in customers, not distance). If , however, when Condition 1 holds but Condition 2 does not, the firm may be in equilibrium when market sides are unequal but the larger half-market is as small as possible. The conditions for Type II equilibrium are the following:

$$\begin{aligned} &1 \quad \text{If Firm } i \text{ is interior: Either } c(x_i) = 0.5c(B_R) \text{ and } c(x_i) \leq 0.5c(B_L) \\ &\quad\ \text{or } c(x_i) = 0.5c(B_L) \text{ and} c(x_i) \leq 0.5c(B_R) \\ &2 \quad \text{If Firm } i \text{ is righthand peripheral: } c(x_i) = 0.5c(B_L) \\ &3 \quad \text{If Firm } i \text{ is lefthand peripheral: } c(x_i) = 0.5c(B_R) \end{aligned} \tag{4.20}$$

When these conditions bind the short-side half-market is as small as possible.

Finally, because disutility costs are minimized when all firms are sited at the midpoints (customer-wise) of their markets, and because this only occurs when Type I equilibrium rules, the conditions of that type of equilibrium are necessary and sufficient for such a socially desirable outcome. As in the case of the uniform population distribution, maximum loss conjectural variation brings about a socially optimal spacing of product varieties.

h Model EL8

The conclusions of the linear model with nonlinear density functions and maximum loss conjectures are unaltered when the circular model is considered. Peripheral firms, of course, are not present, which simplifies the conditions.

We can now summarize the results for one-dimensional market models. These are drawn compactly by Eaton and Lipsey (1975, p. 39):

1 The results of this form of Hotelling model are most sensitive to changes in n and conjectural variations and to the distribution of customers. However they are surprisingly insensitive to the existence or non-existence of bounds on the one-dimensional market.
2 Minimum differentiation is a very special case of the linear market when $n = 2$.
3 With rectangular customer densities ZCV produces multiple equilibria which include socially optimal brand spacing on the circle but not on the line. On the other hand, maximum loss conjectures in both types of market produce a unique and socially optimal product spacing.
4 Nonrectangular customer density functions result in locational results that are quite different from rectangular, and cast much suspicion on the generalizability of much research based on the latter. With ZCV equilibrium cannot exist if the number of firms is greater than twice the number of modes, and under maximum-loss conjectures it may not exist and where it does it is not necessarily socially optimal.

i Model EL9

As a final exercise Eaton and Lipsey transform the market area into a disk (the circle and its interior) of unit radius (and area B) and limit their analysis to location under the assumptions of uniform customer distribution and conjectural conduct ZCV. The complexity of the problem when $n > 3$ grows so rapidly that most of their modeling was conducted by simulation. Their investigations were conducted with two types of models: a study of conjectured equilibrium patterns and a multistage or sequential location model to study the likelihood of convergence to such patterns.

For $n = 1$ or 2 the results are straightforward: a single firm may locate anywhere on the disk and in duopoly the Hotelling minimum differentiation pairing at the center occurs. For $n = 3$ Shaked (1975) confirms with proof the conjecture of nonexistence of an equilibrium. For $n = 3$ to $n = 17$, Eaton and Lipsey simulate to investigate the potential equilibrium nature of three conjectural patterns:

1 The n firms are in equilibrium at the corners of an n-sided regular polygon inscribed in a concentric circle with radius less than 1
2 All but one firm are located as in 1. but the nth is at the center of the disc
3 Regular hexagonal market areas occur with such areas along the boundaries of the disk incomplete.

For pattern 1 firms departed from the circle seeking to pair with rivals leading to an immediate breakup of the conjectured pattern. A similar result was obtained for pattern 2, with a strong tendency by firms seeking local optima to seek to pair with unwilling rivals. And for pattern 3 when $n > 1$ no hexagonal pattern was an equilibrium, nor were alternative patterns of regular polygons. The problem once more was that peripheral firms sought to pair with rivals and set off relocation efforts with no global equilibrium attained. This result is important because it establishes strong doubt that Lösch's[15] hexagonal market area result for unbounded spaces can be extended to bounded areas – a not infrequent assumption in the literature.

On the basis of these results Eaton and Lipsey advance the conjecture that no equilibrium exists for $n > 2$. To seek confirmation they proceed to simulations in which n firms are permitted to seek a maximum-profit location sequentially in an interactive process to determine whether such iterations converge to a steady-state locational pattern. Firm 1 is located at the center, firm 2 is paired with it, and then firms 3 through n are introduced singly to obtain their optima, all other firms remaining fixed. When all n firms have been introduced a new sequential cycle is begun, and so forth, until the model converges or it is clear no such pattern is emerging. The maximum value for n was 5, but the repetitive pattern of dispersing and pairing was so pervasive that their nonexistence conjecture was reinforced.

Location in two-dimensional space under these conditions, therefore, may be a succession of suboptimal disequilibria, with clustering of firms a strong tendency in such patterns. Equilibrium minimum differentiation is a special case of such tendencies that occurs in all 9 models only when $n = 2$. These results have their limitations for purposes of the present book. The lack of price competition is one of these, as is the assumption of perfectly inelastic demand functions. Potential effects of tacit collusion are also omitted. Circular markets in themselves have little application in treating product differentiation except as a substitute for unbounded linear markets. And multidimensional product spaces have a conceptual and analytical role in theoretical work, but for operational analysis different locations in such space must be reduced to Euclidean or other distances in a one-dimensional space.

But Eaton and Lipsey, in addition to giving many definitive answers for Hotelling models of this type, have clearly shown the complexity that faces the analyst and must surely intensify as price variation or other complications are introduced. Useful results will be forthcoming only if realistic constraints on relocation are introduced. We shall use a network approach to such problems in a linear quality space in Chapter 11. The rarity of minimum differentiation and the recurrence of disequilibrium clusters are valuable conjectures for such environments, as is the expectation of disequilibrium.

Not least in the list of their contributions is their willingness to resort to simulation in the absence of fruitful closed analysis, and the skill with which they executed such methodology.

5 MODELS WITH F.O.B. PRICES AND LOCATIONS VARIABLE

When lifted from its Hotelling Model 1 context of section 2 above, an important implication of the (AGT) analysis is to correct Hotelling's assertion that when price and location are variable, as they are allowed to be in Hotelling's Model 2, the duopolists would find a Cournot–Nash equilibrium at the midpoint of λ. We have seen that for Hotelling's Model 1 Eaton and Lipsey have established this result only for $n = 2$, although in two-dimensional space they detected strong evidence of disequilibrium clustering. However, this doctrine of *minimum differentiation*, which Hotelling asserted had broad implications for determination of product characteristics, is disproved by the analysis of Hotelling's Case 1 in section 2a above which reveals that both firms would price at 0 and make zero profits. It would, therefore, be preferable for them to disperse and enjoy positive profits. But, having dispersed, each would experience the motivation to increase hinterland by moving closer to the center at which point the cycle of dispersal and concentration would begin once again. In short: in the Hotelling problem, with prices and locations variable, there is no Cournot–Nash equilibrium. AGT show that if transport (disutility) costs are made quadratic in sales rather than linear a Cournot–Nash equilibrium will exist for all locations, but that firms will *maximize* distances between themselves and locate at the endpoints of the line.

6 LESSONS, CONJECTURES, AND POTENTIAL

We have merely sampled a huge literature that has been devoted to the "Hotelling model", a term which in itself is ambiguous. But the importance of the examined analyses is such that it permits us to draw certain conclusions that will help in shaping and constraining our own efforts in studying nonprice competition in oligopoly.

First, the conjectured tendency to minimum differentiated products equilibrium is a rare occurrence, both when prices are fixed and when they are variable. If equilibrium does occur it reveals in general a scattering of firms over a product space with a mixture of paired and unpaired brands. In one-dimensional markets, with which we shall be most concerned in our modeling, the exact configurations are sensitive to the number of firms, costs of production at different quality locations, the distribution of customers and conjectures held by rivals concerning their mutual reactions to locational initiatives. In Chapters 9 and 10 we will find that with price and qualities variable, benchmarking does lead to minimum differentiation. In Chapter 11, however, we will study purposive relocation and find greater cost-dictated product dispersion.

Second, there does seem to be a tendency for new and incumbent firms to seek to cluster near other incumbent firms, but such clustering is disequilibrating. Indeed, in multidimensional space, simulations suggest that the location of brands in a product space is a continuous disequilibrium process over time, casting some doubt on the utility of static equilibrium models. But we should suspect that rivalrous consonance forms of tacit collusion would arise to reestablish equilibrium.

Third, modeling product location is revealed to be an analytical problem of great complexity which frequently can be approached only by simulation techniques. In view of the seeming appropriateness of disequilibrium outcomes, that technique may offer advantages in deriving insights into multistage locational interdependence. In any event, we should be prepared to adopt simulation when necessary or germane.

Fourth, the spatial analog for brand location seems graceful and unforced. A product space with many quality dimensions and with brands scattered as points within it, is a natural extension of our familiar three-dimensional geographical space. Moreover, the ability to collapse this n-dimensional space into one-dimensional space through the use of a distance metric is so appealing that it fairly demands to be experimented with as a tool of analysis.

Certainly collapsing multidimensional spaces into unidimensional distance measurements, which is a form of weighted averaging, has its dangers, especially when quasi-measurement methods or cross-factor weight derivation must be employed. As indicated in Chapter 2, despite the seeming success of experiments with such methodology, only repeated efforts in analyses of real-world oligopolistic product location can validate the meaningfulness of the approach. Under such circumstances distance measures as averages must be treated as indices of complex differences in many dimensions of uncertain uniqueness. As such they afford considerable ambiguity of interpretation. Certainly their promise must be gauged in the light of alternative frames of investigation, and to initiate this comparison we turn to the "characteristics as consumption objects" approach in Chapter 5.

5 Characteristics as Objects of Consumer Preference

A most distinctive analytical approach to product differentiation has been developed and advocated by Kelvin Lancaster (1966, 1971, 1972, 1975, 1979, 1991) over a 25-year period beginning in the 1970s.[1] Other frameworks, examined in Chapter 2–4 and to be discussed in Chapter 6, view products as the objects of analysis, in the sense that consumer preference functions contain them as arguments, with product qualities employed largely as means of obtaining locational coordinates for brands within a product group characteristics space. Lancaster breaks new ground in arguing that consumers view the product as a mere carrier of different combinations of characteristics with which their active choice decisions are directly concerned. It is, therefore, characteristics which comprise the arguments in utility functions. A consumption technology structure depicts the characteristics content of product units, a preference structure captures the psychological attitudes toward characteristics, and this dichotomization permits product differentiation to be viewed as the conjunction of an objective and a subjective set of factors. Lancaster's contention is that such a structure can draw upon relatively simple frameworks – linear in large part and extensions of existing procedures otherwise – to derive new insights into product differentiation, including product design and consumer choice. Lancaster, in the series of works cited above, has developed and improved the structure over time for fruitful use in positive and normative analysis. In the process of doing so, he has derived a set of consistent definitions and instituted improvements and extensions of methodology, with results whose value is independent of one's judgment of the usefulness of his own frameworks. To study the contributions of his methodology as an alternative framing analysis for the field and its broader advances beyond that work it is incumbent that we devote a substantial amount of space to their detailed study.

1 THE CONSUMPTION TECHNOLOGY

a Some Preliminary Considerations

The most fundamental postulate of Lancaster's system is that consumers react psychologically to the *characteristics* derived from goods, the latter being merely convenient or technologically requisite packages of such qualities, preferences over which are simply derivative from the constituents. These characteristics are assumed to be *qualities* in the use of the term in Chapter 1: objectively measurable with ratio or interval uniqueness and clearly definable independent of consumer perceptions. Hence, attributes of a 0–1 nature are largely ignored in his formal analysis and such qualities as restaurant ambience would be excluded or broken down further into objective characteristics.[2]

Of necessity, characteristics are treated within the context of a *product group*, or a set of products whose characteristics components are sufficiently alike among themselves and sufficiently different from those of products outside that group that they may be viewed as essentially isolable. That is, the product group is significantly more similar in these characteristics respects among its members than with external products. Ideally, a completely separable product group is one in which all characteristics within the group are exclusive to the group: no product in the group contains a characteristic outside the group, and no characteristic in the group is possessed by a product outside the group. Realistically, product groups should possess a sufficiently close approximation to such *intrinsic group* ideals. Note that such criteria for definition of a product group exclude the Triffin cross-elasticity methodology because it involves consumer preferences which are subjective.

A further theoretical and practical problem of some importance to the employment of the framework is the choice of which characteristics of a product group are "integral" in some sense to its definition. Most products can be associated with a very large number of characteristics, most of which are not of significance in defining the functionality or distinctiveness of them. This distinction is essentially the same as that discussed in terms of core and noncore characteristics in Chapter 2. Because characteristics – and therefore product – definitions are definable and measurable objectively, independently of consumer preferences, the relevance filter is based upon functionality, both in Lancaster's theory and in his interpretation of realistic practice:

> In practice, of course, we use our common sense to tell us that a variation in an existing good which leaves the basic function of the goods more or less unchanged, but changes it in some minor way, will cause some change in demand conditions, but not very much. (Lancaster, 1971, p. 8)

In later work Lancaster recognizes two grounds for including characteristics in the relevant subset. The first springs from the relation of persons to characteristics via preferences: a characteristic may be ruled relevant on these grounds if ignoring it would lead to different predictions about choices or ordering goods by consumers (Lancaster, 1971, pp. 140–41). This inclusion does somewhat muddy the hitherto strict independence of characteristics from consumer preferences: although they are defined wholly on the basis of objective content, they may be ruled to be irrelevant if consumer preference-based reactions to them fail to meet certain demand criteria.[3] There remains the problem arising because characteristics are defined independent of the "persons–characteristics" relation yet may be highly relevant on its ground. Thus, the "beauty" of a good or the "congeniality" of a restaurant atmosphere is ruled out on the basis that it is not objective and is dependent on consumer preferences, yet that such a noncharacteristic may be quite relevant on the above definition.

It is natural, therefore, for Lancaster to emphasize the technological bases as a second ground for relevance, and it is here that he makes his most important contributions in respects relevance. His principles are the following:

1 If the content of a given characteristic in the product group is relatively small over a realistic range of quantities of the group goods, compared with the amounts of that characteristic derived from goods outside the group, it is ruled irrelevant for the group under analysis.
2 If the amount of a characteristic per dollar of expenditure contained by members of a product group as well as goods outside the group is relatively small, it may be ignored as irrelevant to defining the group.
3 If members of a product group possess a given characteristic to a like degree, so that choices among members cannot hinge upon its differential presence, it is irrelevant. For attributes, for example, if products in a group can be red (0) or blue (1), and if all are blue, or if a quality is possessed by all members of the group at some maximum level (e.g., the reliability of cigarette lighters in automobiles), such properties can be ignored.
4 A more technical consideration with respect to the number of relevant characteristics which is not wholly concerned with irrelevance is the number of characteristics included for consideration relative to the number of brands in the group. Consider a linear consumption technology, in which each brand, x_j, $j = 1, \ldots J$, is defined by a column vector of quantitative relevant characteristic requirements, z_i, $i = 1, \ldots I$, per unit of each brand.[4] Let $\mathbf{B} = [b_{ij}]$ be a matrix containing those vectors, $\mathbf{X}$ the vector $[x_j]$, and $\mathbf{Z}$ the vector $[z_i]$, so that the consumption technology can be written

$$\boldsymbol{Z} = \boldsymbol{B} \cdot \boldsymbol{X} \tag{5.1}$$

where $\mathbf{B}$ is a $I \times J$ matrix. When $I > J$, so that more characteristics exist than goods, the system is overdetermined and in general cannot be solved to yield a goods vector $\boldsymbol{X}$ that produces an arbitrarily given $\mathbf{Z}$ vector. Only if $I - J$

equations are eliminated and the remaining J form a linearly independent system can a goods vector be determined. The excluded z_i values are then determined from the b_{ij} and the solution values of the x_j levels of goods production obtained.

The problem in this case is that a given mix of characteristics Z can be derived from only one mix of goods X when feasible. It is the core of Lancaster's methodology that each combination of characteristics Z can be achieved by a variety of goods, the specific choice of which is to be made by a consumer maximizing preferences over characteristics subject to a budget constraint.

To illustrate the point, assume that $I = 1$ and $J = 2$, so that the system has one good and two characteristics. Figure 5.1 shows the mapping of the characteristics structure of a unit of the good in characteristics space.

Importantly, there is only one good vector, **Z**, in a two-dimensional characteristics space, so that no basis for spanning the space can be formed from unit goods images. Hence, the consumer desiring packages of the characteristics must move along the good vector: if he or she wants n units of z_1 the amount of z_2 obtained is not a matter of choice, and vice versa.

The approach offers little when the consumer is forced to choose among a discrete number of individual goods. Lancaster, therefore, assumes the

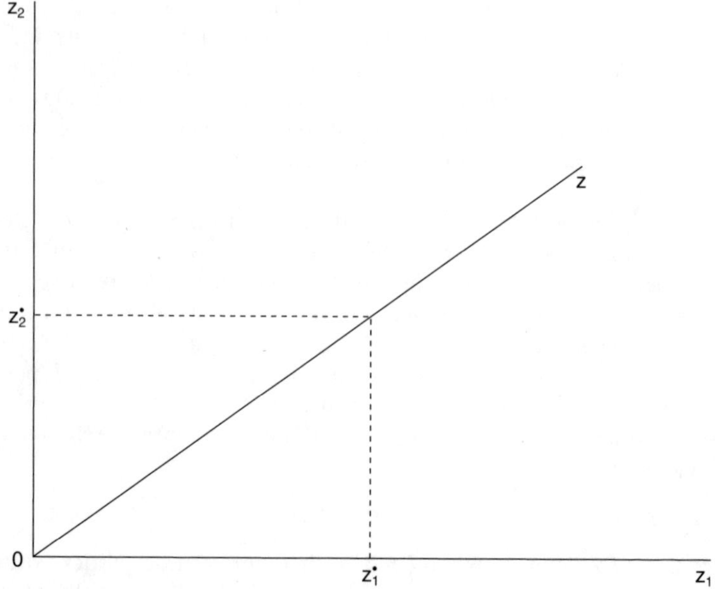

Figure 5.1 1 good in 2 characteristics space

problem away, asserting that in developed nations the number of goods will generally exceed the number of relevant characteristics (Lancaster, 1971, pp. 18–19).

b Defining the Feasible Region in Characteristics Space

In his earlier work, when he was dealing with consumer decision making in partial equilibrium frameworks, Lancaster imposed budget constraints on purchases of goods in a product group of the form

$$\boldsymbol{P} \cdot \boldsymbol{X} \leq y_g, \tag{5.2}$$

where $\boldsymbol{P}$ is an exogenously determined price vector and y_g is the income share to be devoted to purchases in the product group also given parametrically. The constraint is defined in goods space rather than characteristics space, and because $\boldsymbol{B}$ has dimensions $I \times J$ which in general are not equal, the inversion

$$\boldsymbol{X} = \boldsymbol{B}^{-1} \cdot \boldsymbol{Z}, \tag{5.3}$$

cannot be used to translate (5.2) into characteristics space. This is done indirectly, however, by creating a feasible region with the image of each good's vector with length y_g/p_j. Hence, each such vector represents the mix of characteristics that could be obtained by its purchase if all group income were spent wholly upon it. Linking the extreme points of these vectors with line segments creates the faces and edges of a polytope in I-space which constitutes the consumer's feasible characteristics region.

More recently Lancaster has turned to normative analyses with attendant need to adopt general equilibrium approaches.[5] Prices in such frameworks will be endogenous and hence do not form an invariant yardstick for product units. He adopts the expedient of assuming a fixed dedication of resources to the production of goods in the group, with each good's vector image in characteristics space having length proportionate to the amounts of characteristics producible if all such resources were expended exclusively on its production. It is not clear how such a procedure avoids the endogenous price problem, since if more than one type of resource is used the only manner such a complex can be treated as a single resource is to assume their relative prices are fixed. Further, in the analysis of the individual consumer this "resource" must be income, and the units of product producible by some arbitrary portion of that income which is determined by product price. Despite these questions, I will follow his choice of approach in detailing his derivation of a feasible region and its use in the derivation of preference measures for brands.

c Measuring Preferences of a Given Consumer among Brands in a Product Group

In defining the consumer technology two properties of goods within a product group are important. The first is that of *combinability* or *noncombinability*. Goods are combinable if their joint consumption yields combinations of their separate characteristics. For example, within the food product group, nutrients are characteristics which in general are combinable (and, in this case, additive). On the other hand automobiles and most consumer durables are not: two large cars do not yield double the size characteristic, nor do a large car and a small car combine to yield a medium size characteristic.[6] Hence convex combinations of such brands in characteristics space do not yield meaningful combinations of characteristics, so that analyses of consumer preferences is limited to comparisons of brand image vectors in such a space. In his analysis Lancaster limits his concerns almost wholly to noncombinable goods.

The second property is that of *divisibility* or *nondivisibility*. Divisible goods are those consumable in any quantity (coffee, cigarettes) and indivisible goods are used in a fixed package size (automobiles, refrigerators). For divisible goods in a group with I characteristics, the *specification* or definition of a brand can be obtained by choosing one characteristic as a numeraire and determining the I–1 ratios of other characteristics to it. This is because divisible goods can be treated yielding the characteristics in proportion to the number of units of product, so that λ units of product will have λ times the characteristics contained in the unit of the product. On the other hand, nondivisible goods must be specified by the absolute amounts of the I characteristics in a unit of the product because the fixed size of the units may differ among different brands. Consider, for example, two nondivisible goods that have identical characteristics ratios but differ in size, and therefore differ in the absolute amounts they contain. They cannot be considered to be identical brands, whereas if they were divisible they could be since one would simply be λ times the size of the other and therefore have λ times the characteristics content of the other. Lancaster focuses attention upon divisible goods, and from the discussion in the previous paragraph, divisible noncombinable brands.

The feasible region is then obtained by mapping the images of each actual or potential brand of given specification into characteristics space, the unit of the brand represented by the amount producible by the fixed level of resource which is taken to be the unit resource. Lancaster assumes that brands (potential or actual) can differ continuously in specification so that plotting the images for the available resources yields a continuous frontier or *product-differentiation curve* (PDC), as illustrated in Figure 5.2 for two characteristics for a fixed amount of resource and with two brand characteristics vectors, Z_1 and Z_2, illustrated. He assumes that diminishing returns in the production of characteristics will yield a concave PDC, but admits that no theoretical basis exists for this assumption.

Another important assumption: as the available resource expands by a factor of λ, every brand image expands by a common factor, but not necessarily by λ. That is, the shifts outward of the PDCs are parallel but not necessarily in proportion to the resource expansion. Such PDCs, therefore, are homothetic: economies of scale for all brands are equal but do not necessarily yield constant returns to the resource. To determine the consumer's most preferred product, his or her indifference map for characteristics is superimposed upon the relevant PDC depicting available "resource", and a tangency point determined. Figure 5.3 demonstrates that choice at $\mathbf{Z}^\circ = [z_1^\circ, z_2^\circ]$, the most preferred good to be that defined by $\mathbf{Z}^\circ$, and the amount of the most preferred good

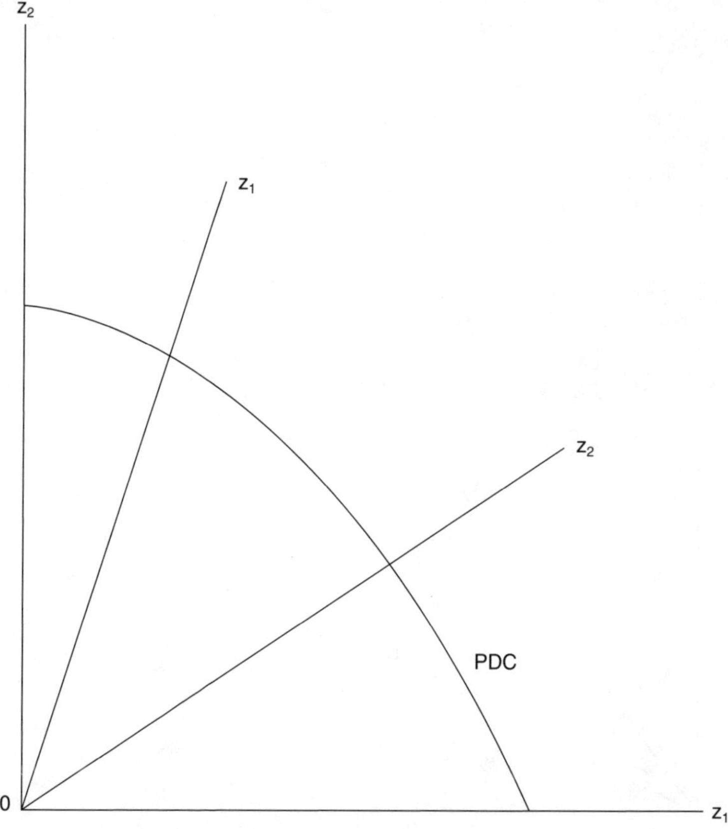

Figure 5.2 The product differentiation curve

necessary to achieve this indifference level to be $0A°$. Consider now any $\mathbf{Z}'$ that intersects the tangent indifference curve at a point such as the intersection at C, indicating that the amount of brand $\mathbf{Z}'$ that would yield equivalent satisfaction to that obtained from the most preferred brand $\mathbf{Z}°$ is $0C$. This lies on a higher product-differentiation curve, *PDC′*, and is currently infeasible for lack of dedicated resources. The *compensating ratio* of available brand $\mathbf{Z}'$ to most preferred brand $\mathbf{Z}°$, or the relative number of units of $\mathbf{Z}'$ to $\mathbf{Z}°$ necessary to just compensate for the nonavailability of $\mathbf{Z}°$ is $0C/0A$.[7] But consider the intersection of $\mathbf{Z}'$ with PDC at **B**: since $0B$ represents a unit of brand $\mathbf{Z}'$ and $0A$ a unit of brand $\mathbf{Z}°$ (see n. 9), this ratio may be written $0C/0B$. Finally, obtain the individual's *compensating function* by computing the compensating ratio for all available brands and taking its locus; obviously, it is computed with the most preferred good as a parameter.

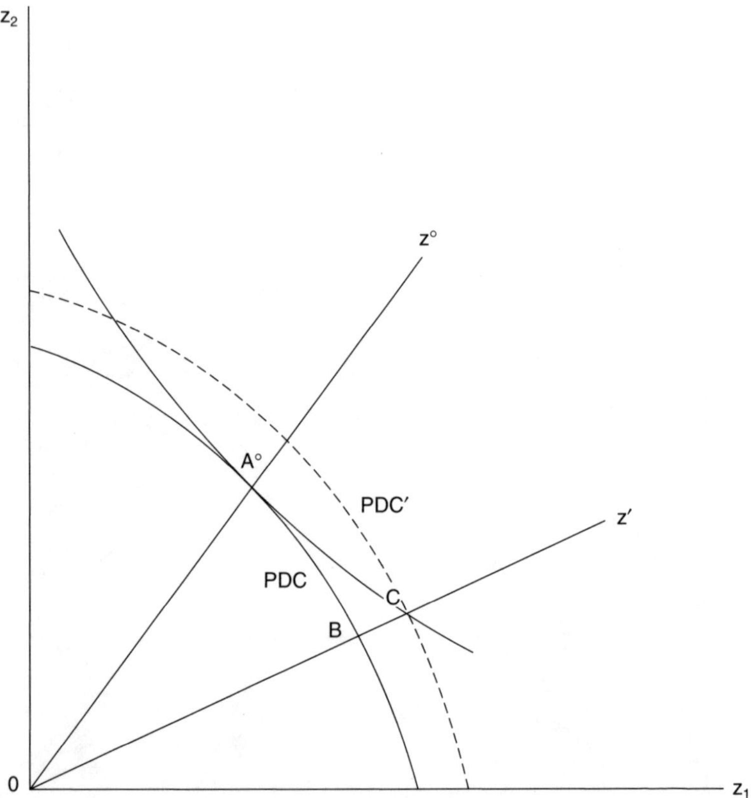

Figure 5.3 The derivation of compensating ratios

As a first heroic assumption in his analysis of consumer behavior Lancaster assumes that the consumer's preferences are homothetic over relevant ranges of variation of resources, so that as the resource is varied in quantity and new PDCs are attained the consumer's preferred good remains the same. The compensating ratios will remain the same along all PDCs and the compensating functions defined by the PDCs are homothetic in relevant domains of brand variations around the most preferred good. Then the PDCs are converted to a linear transformation by (1) measuring the total arc length of the PDC between the limiting feasible available goods, (2) measuring the arc distances between a limiting feasible available good and the intermediate available goods, and (3) replacing the available goods' specifications with the ratio of the value in (2) to the value in (1). By the homotheticity of the PDCs all of them will be converted to parallel straight lines of unit length with brands having the same specification ratios on all PDCs.

These transformations are illustrated in Figure 5.4. Note that the indifference curve yielding the most preferred good remains tangent to the relevant

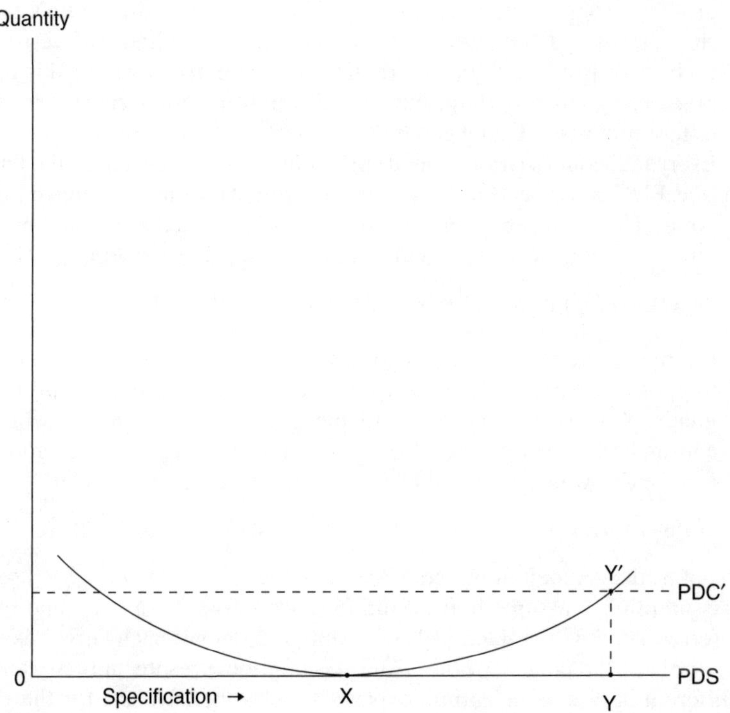

Figure 5.4 Normalization of product-differentiation curve

PDC at X but is typically made "more convex" as specifications are compacted from arc lengths to ratio measures. As each PDC for successively larger resource quantities is shrunk to unit size the distances between them represented by verticals represent the brand quantities and can be read from the vertical axis as such. Hence, $Y' - Y$ is the increment in quantity of the relevant available good necessary to compensate the consumer for failure to receive the most preferred good represented at X.

d Measuring Aggregate Preferences among Brands

To extend the measurement of brand preferences for the individual consumer to all consumers Lancaster retains the assumption that each consumer has homothetic PDCs and indifference curves and adopts a succession of equally implausible postulates. Given a distribution of consumers whose most preferred goods locate them on the specifications axis of Figure 5.4, the following properties are assumed to characterize their preferences:[8]

1 If two or more persons have the same most-preferred good within a product group their preferences are identical over the group's set of characteristics. Consumers' preferences, therefore, differ with respect to their most preferred goods, are alike for all persons within this most-preferred-good subgroup, but may differ from other consumers with different most-preferred goods.

2 Every individual's (transformed) indifference curve tangent at the linearized PDC is assumed to be symmetric around this most-preferred-good point. Therefore, the compensating ratio is a function of the absolute difference of an available good from the most preferred good.

$$h(x_1) = (h(x_2) \text{ if } \left|x_1 - x^0\right| = \left|x_2 - x^0\right|, \tag{5.4}$$

where $x°$ is the most preferred good and x_1 and x_2 are available goods.

3 Suppose consumer 1 and consumer 2 have different most-preferred goods. Let good x_1 be an available good for consumer 1 which is consumer 2's most preferred good x_2° and let x_2 be an available good for consumer 2 which is consumer 1's most preferred good x_1°. Then

$$h_1(x_2^0) = h_2(x_1^0). \tag{5.5}$$

That is, the compensating ratios are the same.

Assumption 1 assures that all indifference curves with the same most-preferred good will be identical. Assumption 2 defines such curves as symmetric about the tangency point. And Assumption 3 results in these tangent indifferent curves being carbon copies of each other. Hence, for the given PDC, tangent indifference curves will differ *only* with respect to location on the transformed linear PDC.[9] It follows, therefore, that the compensating functions of all persons can be represented by a single function, $h(|x - x°|)$, where x is an available good and $x°$ is a most preferred good. The set of most-preferred goods' specifications on the transformed PDC is the *preference spectrum* and is treated (in two-characteristics space) as a continuous function with a finite range.

This identity of compensating functions among individuals implies that, under the assumptions, it is possible to derive a single ordering of preferences from the compensating ratios recorded by groups of individuals. The assumptions, therefore, provide a method of deriving a social ordering of preferences from individual orderings, essentially by making all individuals identical.

Consider the example provided by Lancaster.[10] For 6 brands in a product group consumers A and B provide the information in Table 5.1 concerning their compensating ratios.

Then, with the ability to compare these ratios between individuals, it follows that:

1 3 and 19 must bound 11
2 23 and 47 must bound 11
3 3 and 19 must bound 23 and 47
4 11 and 12 must bound 19
5 11 and 12 must bound 23.

The ordering that preserves these conditions is 3, 47, 11, 23, 19, and 12.

However, by virtue of Assumptions 1, 2, and 3 the compensating ratios yield interval measurements of distance, because by making all individuals

Table 5.1 Listing of compensating ratios for brands in a product group by 2 individuals

	Compensating ratio for consumer:	
Good number:	*A*	*B*
3	1.12	n.a.
11	1.00	1.12
12	n.a.	1.12
19	1.12	1.00
23	1.04	1.04
47	1.04	n.a.

Note
n.a. = not available.

identical except as to location, equal intervals between locations anywhere on the transformed PDC have been rendered meaningful. From Table 5.1 and the ranking above the distance matrix in Table 5.2 records the distances between brands with relevance to consumer preferences.

2 A CRITIQUE OF THE CHARACTERISTICS APPROACH

Lancaster's creation is that of an integrated, explicit and carefully axiomatized synthetic structure to define product variation explicitly rather than implicitly; to treat it multidimensionally; to provide criteria for winnowing inessential properties from the whole body of properties; to split its objective and subjective variables into independent forces for fruitful analytical interface; and, most importantly, to derive operational theorems from positive and normative analyses. It is an ambitious architecture and constitutes the most impressive and influential contribution to the treatment of product differentiation since Hotelling's essential but limited definition of the problems it entails.

Nonetheless basic questions arise concerning the appropriateness and validity of its most fundamental concepts and postulates and the consequent usefulness of the methodology for treating nonprice competition in oligopoly. At the same time, its positive contributions to the process must be acknowledged, as well as the useful role it has played in stimulating debate and clearer concept definition and analysis.

a The Characteristic as Fundamental Unit of Consumer Concern

The most troubling element in Lancaster's approach is his isolation of the *characteristic* as an objectively definable and conventionally measurable property at the core of consumers' choice processes and from the plurality of which differentiated goods are synthesized as convenient by subordinate

Table 5.2 The interbrand distance matrix

Brands/Brands	*3*	*11*	*12*	*19*	*23*	*47*
3	–	12	36	24	16	8
11	12	–	24	12	4	4
12	36	24	–	12	20	28
19	24	12	12	–	8	16
23	16	4	20	8	–	8
47	8	4	28	16	8	–

packages in their consciousness. Characteristics are treated somewhat in the nature of Hegelian *categories* defining the *essence* or *being* of consumer preferences, objectified tentatively in the transitory *existence* of goods. Such properties as "sweetness," "durability," "size," and so forth, are the ultimate desiderata of the consumer but in general must be bundled in goods forms by virtue of convenience or technological constraints. In such form, the characteristics continue an independent existence with substitute goods differentiates that vary in quantitative content of such properties, to be disentangled in the consumption process and savored individually.

It is difficult to accept this atomistic view of product brands and their role in consumer choice, dictated by Lancaster's desire to separate rigorously the objective, observable, and measurable aspects of the characteristics from the subjective, nonobservable, nonmeasurable preference relation of the consumer to them. In turn, he desires this because of his goal of deriving a "new" theory of consumer demand employing maximization of budget-constrained consumer choice within a characteristics rather than a goods framework. But is it truly possible to separate the physical and the psychological? Is not the characteristic defined in part by the perception of the consumer? "Sweetness" is not desired in itself but only in association with other properties of a good or brand. The consumer may find it desirable in a soft drink but undesirable in a beer. Durability may be prized in an automobile but not in a style item of clothing.

In short, characteristics as qualities must be linked to specific product groups. Persons do not respond to categories but react preferentially to complexes of them interacting in complicated fashions to define a product or brand, where a nonisolable component of the product's distinguishing features is a subjective reaction of the consumer. Indeed, a consumer's preferences for a given brand may be shaped by its typical combination with nongroup goods: a taste for a given brand of breakfast cereal may be conditional upon its joint consumption with milk and sugar, for example.

b Placing Brands within a Product Group in a Product Space

Measuring distances between brands in a group as arc distance ratios along the PDC, therefore, is of questionable usefulness in placing brands in a product space for purposes of analyzing firm decisions in nonprice competition. In such a context, the important if not dominant factor in definition is consumer preferences among brands. Brand names gain their extreme importance in many product groups almost wholly by virtue of their consumer cachets. Attributes of this type, with their 0–1 measurability, fit badly into Lancaster's product space measurements, as he recognizes, but this is not wholly because of their nonquantitative nature. It is in large part because they are incapable of objective treatment in distancing brands absent consumer perceptions.

The PDC is a continuous product spectrum in terms of characteristics specifications with a finite number of such specifications embodied in available brands. Consumer preferences are continuous over the spectrum, however, in that each point on it is a most-preferred good for some group of consumers. As shown in Figure 5.4 the compensating ratio for the available good that is closest to a consumer's most preferred good represents the multiple of the available good unit that yields equivalent satisfaction to a unit of the most preferred good, where units of both brands are measured as the amount that could be "produced" by the "resource" available to the consumer for the product group. But that resource must be money income endogenously allocated between own-group goods and other-group goods – "all other goods" in the Hicksian fixed-prices definition – and measured by some arbitrary quantity of dollars' worth defined as the unit of each brand. The compensating ratio is the multiple of that unit expenditure that would have to be spent on the available good to equal the satisfaction to be gotten by spending the allocated amount on the most preferred good.[11]

One immediate problem arising when this analysis is used with money income as resource is that the price of the most-preferred brand is not known in general because that brand is usually not available and hence is hypothetical. Even when the "resource" is treated as some bundle of available factors the cost structure for hypothetical brands may not be known. When the resource is money income that ignorance is compounded in imperfect competition by inability to specify firms' pricing behavior.[12]

Ignoring this criticism for the present, the arc distance – in terms of proportionate amounts of the extreme available good on the spectrum – between the most-preferred good and the nearest available good is translated to a distance in the individual's preference space as a sum of money income necessary to compensate the consumer for second-best. By virtue of the three assumptions in section 1d, all consumers with the same most preferred good have identical indifference curves, those curves are symmetric, and they reflect equal compensating money amounts for equal distances anywhere along the characteristics scale. Hence, as noted above, aggregate consumer preferences are measurable by a ratio scale in "resource" – i.e., money – units.

It is interesting to compare these measurements in preference distancing of brands with those in the simplest Hotelling-type linear market space.[13] In the latter a limited number of brands in a product group is produced whose characteristics specifications are identical with the sole exception of location on the line segment. Hence, only location is a relevant characteristic, and it is indexed on the line segment as a ratio to the distance between feasible potential brands at 0 and 1. Thus, it is the counterpart of Lancaster's linearized PDC, although it is not conceptually identical as will be noted below.

A limited number of firms is located at fixed points on the continuous market space, giving rise to a limited number of differentiated available goods. On the other hand, as in Lancaster, we may assume that consumers are distributed continuously along the market line according to some density function and, unlike Lancaster, that they purchase one unit of a brand on the basis of minimum delivered price only. Distance "cost" (i.e., disutility cost of failing to obtain a most preferred good) is the only cost linked to characteristics that affects consumer preferences. Assuming *à la* Hotelling that transport (disutility) costs rise proportionately with distance at a rate of *c* per distance unit, we may then construct the compensating function in the following manner.

Following Salop in assuming a single good outside the product group under analysis (the *target-group*), and interpreting that outside good as a Hicksian fictitious aggregate good with components at fixed prices, we will treat it as "income." Figure 5.5 illustrates one manner of presenting the

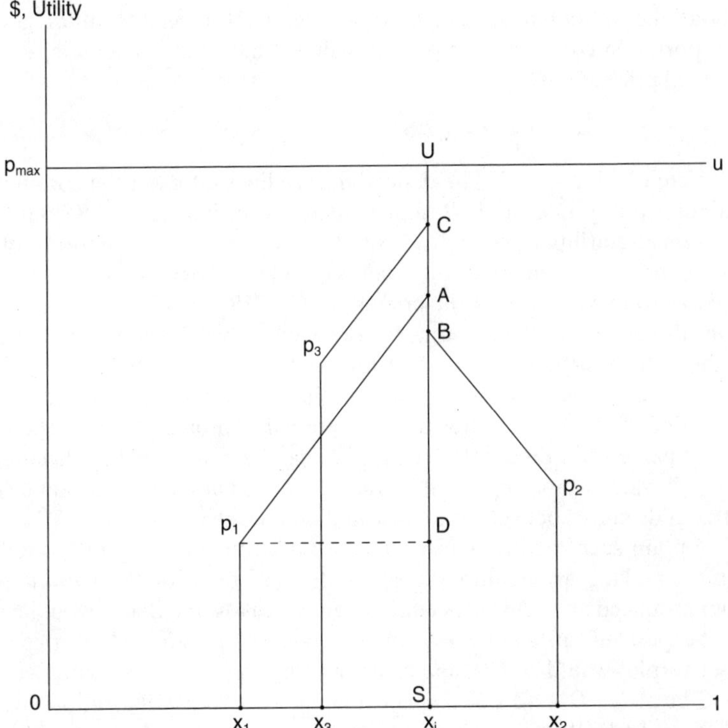

Figure 5.5 Compensating amounts and ratios for nonidentical brand prices

spacing of consumer preferences. Income, Y, is used as numeraire in which prices of own-group brands are measured. It is assumed that expenditure on the product group is relatively small, so that the utility of income for an individual can be approximated as linear in income over the relevant domain of actual and potential brand prices. The dollar, therefore, can function as a unit of measure with ratio scale uniqueness.

On the horizontal axis the characteristic line normalized to unit length with endpoints at extreme feasible brand locations is shown, with firms 1, 2, 3 producing at x_1, x_2, and x_3 brands that are identical in characteristics content with the exception of "spatial location." As in Lancaster the "PDC" is graphed on the horizontal axis, but unlike the Lancaster construct it has not been adjusted for differences in brand prices. Rather, prices are graphed at the indicated locations and read as dollars (utility units) against the vertical axis. Finally, consumer i's location is sited at x_i.

The consumer must choose between consuming a unit of own-group product whose costless consumption yields u_i in utility (i.e., the consumer would be willing to pay up to that delivered price, p_{max}, rather than do without the good but at p_{max} would spend all Y on the other good). Transportation costs rise at c per normalized unit of characteristic, so that delivered price at x_i is

$$p_{j,i} = p_j + c\left|x_j - x_i\right|, \quad j = 1,2,3, \tag{5.6}$$

as depicted on Figure 5.5. The delivered price lines intersect the consumer's maximum utility line at A, B, and C, and the ordinates AS, BS, and CS represent the utility opportunity costs paid in forgone consumption of all other goods were the relevant brands purchased. Respective consumer surpluses from purchases of the brands are UA, UB, and UC.

One direct measure in consumer i's preference space over brands 1, 2, and 3 is these three surplus values, which are simply differences between p_{max} and the $p_{j,i}$. The first is derivable by questioning the consumer and the $p_{j,i}$ are observable, so these measures are operational approximations to the consumer's perceived brand differences. They can be normalized by dividing by US (p_{max}) which would represent a brand produced at x_i and priced at 0. The matrix of distances between brands would then yield a ratio scale.

To obtain such measures using Lancaster's compensating ratio method requires making an assumption about the mill price of the hypothetical brand produced at x_i. One procedure might be to assume that p_i would equal the cheapest mill price of the available goods, or p_1. At such a price consumer surplus would be UD, and compensating amounts of goods 1, 2 and, 3 would be AD, BD, and CD respectively, and compensating ratios AS/DS, BS/DS, and CS/DS, all of which are expressed in or based on quantities of the outside good, money income.

Of course, the analysis of compensating amounts and ratios would be simpler if mill prices were identical for all brands. The compensating function for the individual would be linear in distance between the most-preferred and actual or hypothetical available goods over the continuous space. Also, it would be symmetric around the value of 1 at the consumer's location (although possibly truncated at an endpoint of the characteristic space). The function is illustrated in Figure 5.6.

Were we to adopt Lancaster's uniformity assumption these functions would be identical in shape and differ only (1) with respect to location of x_i and (2) in the level of u, the level of utility derived from the product by consumers at each location. With the assumption that all consumers have identical u the functions are displaced with location and equal distances along the characteristic spectrum yield the same characteristic ratio. The function differs from Lancaster's which follows a consumer indifference curve in strictly convex form.

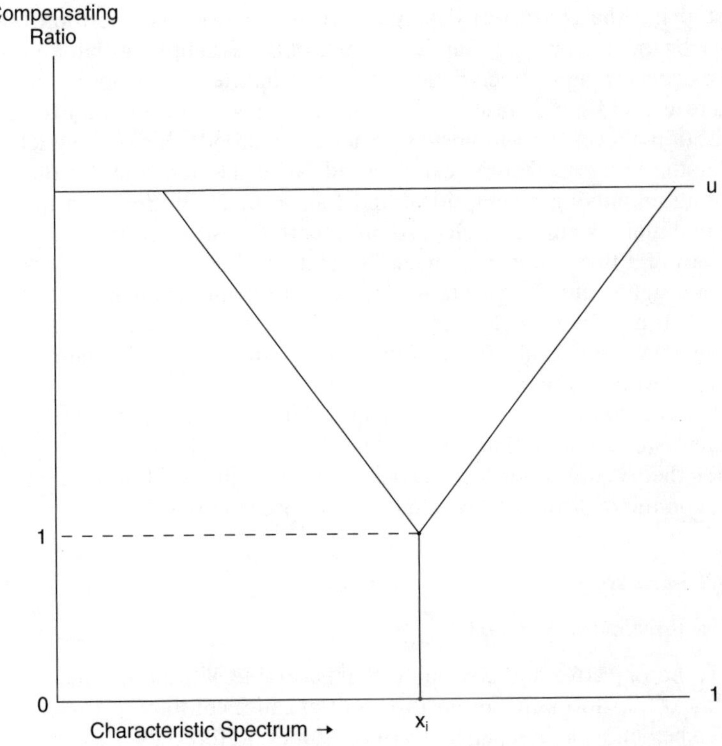

Figure 5.6 The compensating function with identical prices for all brands

The spatial model with outside good suggests an alternative method of locating brands within a product space that avoids most of Lancaster's heroic assumptions, averts the difficult task of isolating consumer indifference curves, and permits the treatment of brands rather than characteristics when deemed desirable. At the same time, it would permit analysis of the role of characteristics when fruitful. It is simply to ask consumers the maximum amount of money income they would pay for varying amounts of each brand or for each brand with an altered characteristic. Although it is not an acceptable basis to achieve Lancaster's more ambitious aims, among which is the goal of reconstructing neoclassical consumer theory using characteristics rather than goods as the primitives, it is suitable for the more limited goals of this work. This approach will be developed more fully in Part III.

c The Postulational Basis of Characteristics Theory

In studying the characteristics approach to nonprice competition one is struck by the number and simplistic nature of the assumptions that Lancaster makes concerning characteristics, consumer indifference maps, goods cost structures, and goods prices. Many of these have been mentioned in the exposition above, but will now be reviewed as a body. In so doing let it be understood that no theorist can proceed far in the derivation of theorems without simplifying assumptions, and Lancaster is entitled to a quota of instrumental assumptions. He also quite correctly stresses that the primary concern of a theory is not so much description of actual practices as it is in giving insights into the qualitative impacts of parameter changes. Although these two aspects of a theory of behavior are not independent, it may be possible to obtain valuable results in the latter sense with heroic compromises with reality in descriptive aspects.

That said, however, one must wonder whether the number and importance of Lancaster's assumption set, compared, for example, with standard consumer theory and other approaches to product differentiation, cast some doubt on the realistic validity of the derived propositions.

1 Characteristics

Characteristics are assumed:

1 To be objective and continuously measurable with uniqueness up to a linear transformation or positive multiplicative constant
2 To be definable independently of consumer preferences

3 To form product-differentiation curves that are continuous, concave and homothetic
4 To form product-differentiation curves that are specified using a unit measure which depicts the amount of each actual or potential brand capable of "production" with a unit of resource defined independently of prices
5 Not to exceed in their relevant form the number of goods feasible of production.

2 Goods

Goods are assumed:

1 To be produced with similar forms of economies-of-scale technologies
2 To have identical input functions (which are inverse production functions)
3 To possess, within a product group, identical characteristics in different proportions, none of which characteristics is shared with goods in another goods group
4 To be priced (in general, in his general equilibrium and welfare analysis) identically
5 To be noncombinable, that is, within a product group each consumer purchases only one brand at most.

3 Preferences

Preferences are assumed:

1 To be definable continuously in characteristics space
2 To yield indifference curves that are convex and homothetic
3 To yield indifference curves that are symmetric around most-preferred brands
4 To be identical for all consumers with the same most-preferred brand
5 To yield compensating functions with the same value for actual or potential goods that are equally distanced on the product-differentiation curves
6 To yield identical indifference curves at every most-preferred point on the product-differentiation curve, when such curves have already been assumed to be identical for all persons whose most-preferred brand is at those points (see 5.4)
7 To give rise to a unique compensating function over the preference spectrum.

4 Consumers

Consumers are assumed:

1 To be continuously distributed over the preference spectrum with uniform real or money incomes, except at end points of the spectrum to accommodate the peripheral–firm complication of finite preference spectra.

5 Group Competitive Structure

Brand firms ("the industry") are assumed:

1 To compete (in formal treatments) within the confines of monopolistic competition, either with perfect or imperfect information.

These are heroic assumptions indeed, and each of them can be challenged. Most tortuous is the preference set that is necessary to derive a single compensating function that can be used to obtain interval scalings for distancing brands in a preference space. One wonders if a more direct approach to such spacing – as, for example, the use of money income equivalences as suggested in section 2b – might not have been more transparent and less demanding in credibility.

d The Exclusion of Oligopolistic Analysis

Lancaster has the laudable goal of reconstructing general equilibrium theory with differentiated products in product group spaces with distances determined by consumer preferences over characteristics for purposes of gauging the impact of such products on social welfare. As in the cases of other theorists with similar social welfare ambitions in brand competition environments, he is led to such determinate solutions in monopolistic competition frameworks.

From the narrow standpoint of the interests of this work, a shortcoming of his analysis is that he all but totally excludes differentiated oligopoly from his body of research. His departures from the large group analysis consist of the impact of pure monopoly on product differentiation, the effects of "island monopoly" in which a subset of brands that are contiguous in preference space exists, and a discussion of strategies open to a monopolist seeking to deter entry of a rival into a product group.[14] Of course, these do not take us far, nor were they intended to go deeply into our area of interest. But we must add to our catalog of gifted and ingenious theorists who elected the path of determinate if irrelevant theory rather than intellectually less elegant but realistically relevant industrial structures. It should be clear from the discussion of this chapter, however, that this criticism does not detract from the many indirect insights and techniques Lancaster's frameworks have given to the differentiated oligopolist analyst. These will be summarized in the conclusion that follows.

3 CONCLUSIONS

Lancaster's carefully and skillfully constructed characteristics methodology and its architectural applications is the richest source of insights and techniques yet devised for the study of product differentiation. That they do not constitute the keys to the kingdom is at once a valid and foolish criticism. That they rest upon a body of simplifying assumptions is neither surprising nor in itself criticizable. That the kingdom to which they seek the keys is different from that we seek to enter and different searches imply different assumptions and techniques are also not grounds for criticism. But, at the same time, this last consideration does constitute an explanation of the necessity to filter Lancaster's approaches for their usefulness and relevance to a different goal.

I have questioned one basic premise of the characteristics approach that to my mind seriously jeopardizes its utility: that is the ability to *define* characteristics independently of consumer preferences. The whole notion of a product-differentiation curve based on "objectively" and continuously measurable and measured characteristics that is interfaced with an *independent* indifference mapping seems forced and conceptually questionable. Ultimately the truly relevant and useful implications of product variation are extracted from Lancaster's methodology: the measurement of distances between products on a preference spectrum that is based on consumer preferences over *goods*. These are the constructs that are basic to the further analysis of monopolistic competition theory in his work. One is led to wonder why they were not directly derived from preferences over goods.

Another aspect of Lancaster's structure that is subject to criticism is his failure to deal at length with problems of measuring characteristics without the aid of preferences. Attributes of a 0–1 nature are simply ignored and "characteristics" with subjective dimensions (ambience, comfort) are simply asserted to be capable of further decomposition into finer properties that are independent of consumer attitudes. More prosaically, even those characteristics acceptable of classification as "objective" confront the analyst with the problems of unit definition and uniqueness properties (color hues, design aspects, package convenience).

Lancaster's use of amounts of most-preferred products necessary to compensate consumers for the necessity of accepting available products also raises questions. If my preferred automobile is a Cadillac, how many Buicks would I have to be given to compensate me fully for forgoing a Cadillac? 1.75? But in most cases, were this number determinable, would it not be dictated by the amount of *income* (the alternate good) necessary to compensate me? Why not specify distances between goods in preference space directly by such dollar measures? This has the operational attraction of being more readily answerable by a consumer so queried.

Uniformity with symmetrical and identical preferences over goods differing only with respect to location of most-preferred brands – with all the supporting assumptions detailed above – seems a poor way of aggregating preferences on theoretical and operational grounds.[15] Alternative methodologies for so doing should be explored. Directly helpful, however, are Lancaster's techniques for screening characteristics for relevancy where characteristics retain an importance for defining brand choices. Some experimental methods for meeting these objectives have been discussed in Chapter 2.

6 Game-theoretic and Monopolistic Competition Analyses

1 INTRODUCTION

Because of the similarity of methodology, analytical goals and/or substantive content, two bodies of analysis must be compared with the rivalrous consonance approach of this book. Game theory is a well-developed body of techniques designed for a wide range of interdependence environments which has become the mainstream approach to oligopoly analysis in both microeconomic theory and industrial organization. It is distinguished by the devotion of many of the best theoretical analysts in economics, and outside the circle of this clerisy by that of a worshipful, if frequently uncomprehending, laity. Its devotees, in incautious moments, can be truly hegemonic in defining its relevance; Tirole (1993, p. 207), for example, asserts that "most problems of industrial organization can be solved with a handful of basic game-theoretic concepts." He is speaking at this point about conceptual problems in the scholarly field rather than empirical complexity, but even at the abstract level the assertion exudes excessive confidence.

Rivalrous consonance is a much simpler methodology when compared with game theory, which purports to yield insights into strategic decision making, and the necessity arises of explaining methodological points of difference between the two and agreements as well as their advantages and disadvantages. As will be shown in the chapters to follow, game theory contributes importantly to the *interpretation* of the results derived from rivalrous consonance frameworks, but it is in the *derivation* of those solutions that rivalrous consonance departs most significantly from game-theoretic approaches.

Another methodology of interest in these regards is that of monopolistic competition in the narrow sense. Theoretical interest in product differentiation and quality characteristics began in earnest with the publication of Chamberlin's and Robinson's monopolistic–imperfect competition analysis with their attention-capturing paradigm of the long-run tangency equilibrium. Recent interest in these frameworks revolves largely about the welfare implications of the degree of product differentiation achieved and the potentiality for market failure in providing too much or too little. With such concerns this body of analysis certainly has a kinship with the interaction of price and quality variables in firms' decision making discussed in the rivalrous consonance framework, but it departs importantly in its failure to confront oligopolistic interdependence. In my view, this disqualifies it from serious consideration as a realistically relevant body of analysis because in most instances of large numbers of firms producing differentiated products close analysis reveals clusters of firms which compete strategically with other members of the cluster. Nonetheless, a closer look at the modeling done in this area is warranted to discern potentially helpful insights in the oligopoly area.

2 GAME-THEORETIC METHODOLOGY

As described in Chapter 3, rivalrous consonance adopts as its core concept the notion that oligopolistic industries reveal mixtures of rivalry and co-operation that can run the gamut from self-punishing policies to inflict losses on rivals through a complete ignoring of rivals' experiences in face of any given firm's indicated actions to joint profit maximization. The game-theoretic frameworks that are most relevant to it, therefore, are those that study the manner in which firms' self-interest can lead them to various degrees of tacit collusion. Game theory is still – despite recent advances – directed primarily toward the solution and analysis of noncooperative games, which reduces its utility somewhat in the task for which rivalrous consonance is designed.[1] When cooperative game analysis is undertaken, it is assumed that players can negotiate effectively, frequently in manners that require overt rather than tacit contact or a "mediator" correlating strategies.[2]

One fundamental difference between the two approaches is that the game theorist is far more interested in the process that brings about the solution end-state than the exponent of rivalrous consonance. The latter assumes that the mature industry has settled into a steady-state solution reflected in the existing power structure which can be obtained by study of the current relationships in the industry or by modeling the industry and comparing the resulting solutions with real oligopoly behavior. It is the isolation of the power structure matrix and its implications for current decision making, whatever its genesis, that rivalrous consonance seeks to ascertain. Changes in the power structure in the intermediate run with the help of rationality considerations modified by more informal motivations, or changes in consumers' benchmarks in the long run with power structure constant, are studied largely through the use of comparative statics or less rigorous frameworks. In all such analysis it stresses the *environmental*[3] or *idiosyncratic* factors affecting the firm or industry that are for the most part external to the formal analyses of game theory. Such aspects of the problem are internalized in rivalrous consonance at the sacrifice of generality but in the interests of closer conformance to specific industry problems.

Of course, much of the interest of the game theorist in subgame perfection, sequential equilibrium or a variety of other refinements of Nash equilibrium in extensive form games inheres in the desire to deduce the nature of that solution end-state, or at least to restrict the potentially very large set of potential solutions to a more manageable subset. In this regard game theory is a more ambitious and more powerful technique than rivalrous consonance. Rivalrous consonance can be approached as a kind of "game with contracts," where the implicit contracts emerge from the socio–politico–economic matrix of the industry over a long time period, and are represented in the model via the consonance matrix, Θ. Consonance is not built into the game as a set of strategies, but as a concept that alters the concept of the equilibrium. In game theory the contracts are the result of negotiation and bargaining to obtain a correlated strategy or in the threats and rewards springing from coalition formation. In rivalrous consonance they are arrived at informally, tacitly, via signals: they frequently involve complex and intuitive reactions to rivals and may be "rational" only in rather forced interpretations of "utility." They evolve into a power structure that is perceived by rivals only in fuzzy, ill defined terms, whose formal approximation is the result of analysis by the rivalrous consonance practitioner.

The tendency of the game theorist – despite occasional disclaimers involving a confessed need to incorporate "external" considerations – is to interpret the formation of these contracts and their constraints on behavior in terms of narrow self-interest expressed in payoff matrices of "utilities." But in the real world such preference indices are at best sensed *ex post facto* from industry data rather than derived or more frequently assumed *ex ante facto*. The realistic nature of these correlated strategies is not that of probability density functions over a set of strategies or moves, but rather actions within the bounds of expected behavior best represented analytically by extended profits constrained by consonance coefficients and possible secondary goals of the firms.

For the most part game-theoretic constructions are abstract theoretical constructions in mathematical logic designed to generalize strategic decision making under certain stylized hypotheses defining environments. Except for the simplest forms of environment, they have little hope of giving rise to operational systems for coping with realistic oligopolistic decision making. Several constructions are central to equilibrium solutions. Most notable among these is that of the mixed strategy: despite the plain fact that firms in oligopolistic rivalry do not employ them. That in not doing so they are violating von Neumann–Morgenstern rationality axioms may disturb game-theoretic sensibilities, but this rates low on the scale of boards-of-directors' concerns.[4] Simple examples of the wisdom of mixing up the run and the pass plays in football or one's sequence of play styles in tennis cannot even purport to approach the environment of oligopolistic decision making.

Expected-value reasoning is far from a generally accepted valuation procedure. The Bayesian game form in games of incomplete information, where participants have private information known only to themselves, and in which each rival must have a probability density function over the "type" of every other rival, which function varies with that rival's own "type," where "type" can be identified with "private knowledge" or "personality structure" or other relevant characteristics, is an intellectually satisfying extension of expected value reasoning into situations of imperfect information, but is operationally uninteresting.[5]

In conditions of mature oligopoly, however, in which rivals have been engaged over relatively long periods, incomplete information may be a poor description of the environment. Firms will be well acquainted with opposing managements, their own initiation–reaction patterns, own- and other-costs and demand schedules, industry folkways, and so forth. Rivalrous consonance, therefore, approaches closer to the *supergame*, or a game with repeated plays in which this "state of nature" is singular, or subject to changes imposed parametrically by the analyst. A problem with such games is that a large number of strategies can lead to equilibria of widely varying natures, reflecting greatly varying allocations of industry profits. The explicit or implicit capacity to punish defectors from correlated strategies is central to deriving strategy solutions in supergames, and some of the potential equilibria in them may not be subgame perfect. That is, they will rest upon punitive actions on the parts of players that are not credible in the sense of sequential rationality.

In oligopolies, however, fundamental decisions are not altered realistically as such strategies require: prices and characteristics are not rapidly changed to conform to tit-for-tat, grim, getting-even, mutual punishment, or q-positional strategies. In addition, these punitive actions become complicated as the number of firms in the industry rises above two. Rather, in mature oligopolies, threats are largely low-key and accommodated in the socioeconomic norms reflected in the consonance coefficients. Nonconformist behavior is tolerated within wide tolerance brackets for profits without appeal to sequentially rational strategic reactions to achieve maximum advantages. This reluctance to disturb a longer-run stability to punish shorter-term misbehavior is reinforced by legal compunctions. A stabilizing inertia serves to preserve industrial peace and also avoids consumer and distribution network confusion caused by rapid price changes or brand reconfigurations.

Game theorists, of course, are aware of the need to step beyond the narrower confines of "rational" calculation to consider more informal but nonetheless important behavior constraints. For example, Osborne and Rubinstein (1994, p. 133), say that "The theory [of repeated games] gives us insights into the structure of behavior when individuals interact repeatedly, structures that may be interpreted in terms of a 'social norm'". See also the quotation from Myerson in n. 2 for an even more forceful statement of the importance of such external environments. In the view of the rivalrous consonance advocate these social norms that define the power structures which shape the behavior of firms in oligopolistic industries are of overriding significance in interpreting industry performance, even in industries which permit wide latitude to competition. Osborne and Rubinstein are correct in emphasizing that the goal of such game theoretical analysis should be to gain insights into individual behavior under constrained rational motivation rather than to focus upon profit allocation profiles as the desired output.[6]

a Isolating the Power Structure

But is game theory really helpful in isolating such patterns in industrial relations? To some extent yes, since self-interest must play a role in the intermediate- and long-run alterations in those social norms. But such contributions merely serve to bound expected behavior within broad brackets: much more institutional analysis is necessary to define the industry's consonance matrix and the secondary goals of firms. It is always possible to argue that such broader social relations and goals can be incorporated in repeated supergames by altering payoff utilities or by incorporating constraints as strategies: by definition, any strategic interaction can be viewed as a "game," and any framework that seeks to analyze it can be shoehorned conceptually into some normal, Bayesian normal, or extensive game framework. But such assertions do not move us far along the path to operational frameworks.[7]

The game theorist's dominating vision is shaped by the ultrarationality of an overriding competitiveness, the all-importance of striving for maximum utility defined by simple preference functions, the search for equilibria even when they can only be defined within the confines of rationality by use of probability mixtures of pure strategies with reliance on the employment or clear threat of employment of punitive measures against defectors from cooperative strategies. Such a vision has its useful place in analyzing oligopolistic interdependence, but it can mislead as well in ignoring the human if seemingly arational desire to temper the role of rational self-seeking with that of peaceful coexistence or improved equity.

One instance in which the sophisticated and frequently elegant techniques of cooperative game theory can be contrasted with the simpler analytical modes of rivalrous consonance is in the important area of isolating the power structure of the oligopolistic industry. As was made clear in Chapter 3 this is really the core problem of oligopoly analysis, and both game theorists and the advocate of rivalrous consonance recognize its centrality. The most familiar approaches in game theory are grounded in each rival's ability to deny payoffs to others by refusing participation in coalitions of subsets of the firms against their complements. The use of the concept of the "core" of the game, when at least one exists and they are not too plentiful, is common as an equilibrium concept with power implications, but the best known game-theoretic approach that seeks to obtain an explicit measure of such power for all firms in the industry is the calculation of the *Shapley value*.

1 The Shapley Value as a Measure of the Power Structure

Shapley (1953) sought a means of determining the payoffs that players in an n-person coalitional game could be expected to garner by their exercise of power in negotiations in coalition formation. These allocations of utility payoffs among the firms, $\mathbf{u(v)} = (u_1, u_2, \ldots, u_n)$, may be interpreted alternatively as the distribution of benefits an objective arbitrator would be led to assign on the basis of a contributory theory of equity.[8]

We begin the analysis of an n-person cooperative game with transferable utility and the possibility of coalition formation by placing the game in *characteristic form*. This is done by defining a characteristic function, v, defining the maximum utility payoff (*worth*) obtainable from each of the $(2^n - 1)$ coalition subsets, S, that can be formed from the coalition-of-the-whole to the singleton subsets containing each firm singly. For example, when $n = 3$, the whole set of coalitions consists of firms {1,2,3}, {1,2}, {1,3}, {2,3}, {1}, {2}, and {3}. The characteristic function would then be $v(\{1,2,3\}), v(\{1,2\}), \ldots, v(\{3\})$.

Shapley's approach to determining solution $\mathbf{u(v)}$ is to axiomatize the characterisitics of that solution that would have to be present for it to be acceptable. He specifies only three such axioms:

Axiom 1 (*Labelling Neutrality and Symmetry*): Labels given firms should play no role in determining the allocation, which should be the result wholly of the power relations within the coalitions. Thus, (1) whether a firm is designated player i or j should not influence the outcome, and (2) if firms i and j are in identical positions relative to the coalition structures they should emerge with the same allocation.

Axiom 2 (*Efficiency*): The sum of the allocations over individuals should exhaust the worth of the coalition-of-the-whole:

$$\Sigma_i u_i(v) = v(N) \tag{6.1}$$

That is, the allocation should be Pareto optimal: no firm or firms should be capable of receiving more utility without reducing allocations to one or more others. (6.1) accommodates the possibility that some firms may receive a 0 payoff if they are unable to contribute value to any coalition.

Axiom 3 (*Linearity*): Allocations are determined as linear functions of the worths of coalitions.[9]

Shapley proved that there was one and only one allocation vector **u(v)** in the $\{n,v\}$ game that conformed to the axioms and that it was based upon the weighted average of the marginal contributions of each firm to the worths of the coalitions. Let $S \subseteq n$ be a subset of firms with characteristic function value $v(S)$, where $i \notin S$. Then firm i's marginal contribution to the coalition $\{S \cup \{i\}\}$ is

$$v(S\ U\{i\}) - v(S). \tag{6.2}$$

The unique function that satisfies Shapley's axioms is

$$u_i(v) = \sum_{S \subseteq n-\{i\}} \left[\frac{|S|!(|n|-|S|-1)!}{|n|!} (v(S\ U\{i\}) - v(S)) \right]. \tag{6.3}$$

The term in parentheses outside of the fraction is simply the marginal contribution of firm i to the worth of the coalition consisting of subset S, as defined in (6.2). Let $|T|$ denote the number of firms in coalition T. Then we may turn to the interpretation of the fractional term: the denominator is simply the number of different permutations of n firms that could be obtained if such firms were arranged in an exhaustive manner in different orderings. The numerator is explained in the following manner. Suppose we select a specific coalition S (i.e., specifying the $|S|$ firms by their names) and a specific firm i whose marginal contribution to coalition S we wish to determine. Now, let us place the names of all n firms in a box, and exhaustively order them in all possible sequences. There would be $n!$ such sequences.

For example, suppose first $|n| = 3$. Then we can list the 6 sequences as (1, 2, 3), (1 ,3, 2), (2, 1,3), (2, 3, 1), (3, 1, 2), and (3, 2, 1). Suppose, now, we choose firm $i = 2$ as the firm whose marginal contributions to coalitions S which do not contain it we wish to isolate. There is only one coalition of two firms (firms 1 and 3) which can be formed, but it can occur in the sequences {1,3} or {3,1}. That is, the number of permutations of the 3 firms in which firms 1 and 3 can precede 2 in the ordering is $|S|! = 2$. But these each can occur with $(|n| - |S| - 1)! = 1$ of the remaining relevant firms (i.e., other than firm $i = 2$). Hence, the number of joint permutations for coalition S and its complement in $n - S - 1$ is $|S|!(n - S - 1)!$. In our illustration, when $|S| = 2$ this joint product is $2!0! = 2$. If this is divided by $|n|! = 6$, the probability of firm $i = 2$ joining the coalition $S = \{1,3\}$ is 1/3, and this is the weight applied to the marginal contribution of firm 2 to that coalition.

If we set $|S| = 1$, then two coalitions become potential partners for firm i, {1} and {3}. For each taken singly the joint probability is $1!1!/3! = 1/6$, and the weight for the marginal contributions of $i = 2$ to each coalition {1,2} and {2,3} is 1/6. Finally, when $|S| = 0$, so that firm $i = 2$ is the first name drawn in the sequence, and the resulting coalition is the singleton $\{i\}$, the probability is $0!2!/3! = 1/3$. We define $v(\phi) = 0$, where ϕ is the null set, so that this probability is applied to $v(S + 2)$ to obtain the expected marginal contribution of firm $i = 2$ to the Shapley value. Hence, the Shapley value is the weighted average of the marginal contributions of the given firm i to all of the possible coalitions that exclude it, where the weights are the probabilities of those coalitions forming on a random basis.

Several difficulties arise in consideration of the Shapley value as a measure of the power structure within the context of functioning oligopoly. First, the Shapley value for a firm depends upon its marginal contribution to every potential coalition capable of formation in the industry. In realistic situations where a coalitional game with transferable utility is applicable, it is likely that marginal contributions to a limited number of coalitions dictated by external considerations will be determining. Such environmental factors as geographical proximity or similarity of management attitudes may play important roles in weighting the likelihood of contributory payoffs.

But more fundamentally, the whole concept of coalition formation within the body of oligopolistic competition analysis is suspect. Even in those relatively rare instances in which coalition cartels are existent, as in the OPEC petroleum cartel, participants demand much more freedom of decision making than rigid divisions of coalition profits permit. In most market economies such formal arrangements to distribute profits among cartel participants are illegal, as are attempts by mediators like trade associations to enforce or monitor them. Effective means to bring about cooperation among industry members must be tacit rather than overt, implicitly rather than explicitly accepted, subtle constraints on competition rather than contractual agreements to distribute joint earnings. Such relationships are more faithfully reproduced in rivalrous consonance, and therefore, the power structure derived with a greater realism and with more operational relevance, than possible in coalitional game theory.

2 The Consonance Coefficient Matrix, Θ, as a Measure of the Power Structure

In Chapter 3 a discussion of the rivalrous consonance framework introduced the notion of the consonance coefficient matrix as a detailed presentation of the power structure of the industry. The matrix, whose elements are the consonance coefficients, θ_{ij}, presents that structure as a set of binary relationships between firms, where $\theta_{ij} \neq \theta_{ji}$ and $\theta_{ii} \equiv 1$, and which depict the degrees of consideration firms accord each rival in incorporating the welfares of those rivals in their decision making. In determining realistic values for these coefficients various formal measurement and quasi-measurement techniques should be employed, because in realistic industry contexts they are determined by mixtures of "rational" (i.e., profit-maxization) motivations and "environmental" or "idiosyncratic" factors which add enhanced dimensions of more informal types serving to temper the former motivations. In Chapter 3 an example of the use of cross-factor analysis to estimate the consonance coefficients for the OPEC cartel in the 1970s was quoted and may be considered a means of illustrating methods of calibrating the idiosyncratic factors.[10]

At this point one means of deriving the rational determinants of the power structure as an alternative to the coalitional analysis of Shapley and like efforts[11] employing the rivalrous consonance methodology will be presented. Analogously to game-theoretic usage, it assumes that the payoffs to firms under zero cooperation conditions can be determined. These are assumed to be derived from demand and cost functions using own-profit maximization techniques. Utility is assumed to be linear in the relevant regions of potential cooperation determined by consonance coefficients $\theta_{ij} \in [0,1]$, as explained in Chapter 3. In empirical derivation of such functions econometric problems will arise if industry data reflect active patterns of cooperation, and we will share with game theory the difficulties of filtering out such impediments. At the theoretical level we shall revel in the economist's carefree world of assumption.

Assume the case of duopoly for ease of presentation. Reduce the infinity of consonance coefficients that will define the firms' action sets on the unit interval to a finite number by defining a mesh sufficiently fine to permit acceptable estimation of profits for gaps in the mesh. Then, by selecting each pair of consonance coefficients $[\theta_{1,2}, \theta_{2,1}]$ in turn use extended profit maximization to derive the profits that would accrue were the firms to engage in those degrees of cooperation. The results will define a payoff matrix in dollar profit terms over the mesh of consonance coefficients.

In Table 6.1 an example of the results of this technique. It is abstracted from a model developed and presented in full detail in Chapter 9, whose results are detailed in Table 9.9. The model reflects both price and quality competition, and its derivation and interpretation with several different variants will be developed at that point. Table 6.1 presents only the profit results on the mesh defined for 0.2 increments of the coefficients. We may interpret the payoffs as calibrated in millions of dollars, with firm 1's profits in front of the semicolon and firm 2's behind.

Note that firm 1's strategies 0, 0.2, 0.4 and 1.0 are dominated, as are firm 2's strategies 0, 0.4, 0.8 and 1.0. In this example a Nash equilibrium exists with strategies $\Theta = [0.6,0.2]$ which is proposed as a focal point in the isolation of the power structure. Firm 2 is the stronger firm and receives a good deal of deference from firm 1 in its decision making. But we note that $\Theta = [0.8,0.4]$ is Pareto superior, and remaining with arguments based on sheer rationality we should also tag it as a potential focal point even though it is in a dominated strategy. However, as we stressed in Chapter 3 and will emphasize once more in Chapter 9, more informal factors must be considered that could well move

Table 6.1 An example of the derivation of rational components of the power structure in a duopoly

		θ_{21}					
		0	0.2	0.4	0.6	0.8	1.0
	0	5.146;11.366	5.297;11.442	5.473;11.300	5.675;10.890	5.909;10.115	6.185;8.801
θ_{12}	0.2	5.160;11.504	5.312;11.582	5.489;11.440	5.693;11.030	5.928;10.250	6.197;8.923
	0.4	5.146;11.366	5.322;11.702	5.498;11.588	5.701;11.731	5.939;10.389	6.218;9.056
	0.6	5.169;11.796	5.323;11.881	5.500;11.740	5.691;11.271	5.944;10.434	6.215;9.187
	0.8	5.163;11.952	5.315;12.038	5.495;11.899	5.701;11.482	5.940;10.685	6.221;9.331
	1.0	5.147;12.114	5.302;12.203	5.480;12.065	5.686;11.642	5.928;10.844	6.208;9.478

the equilibrium to other solutions. For example, if firm 2 is somewhat more aggressive it might insist that $\Theta = [0.8,0.2]$, where it would it would gain substantially at little cost to firm 1.[12]

Rationality in realistic contexts is tempered by caution, considerations of equity, and uncertainty about rivals' responses. There may also be a certain concern for the welfare of the industry as a whole, and worry about the effects on it of instability or competitive turmoil.

The important point at this juncture is that such strategy pairs have a more realistic claim to depict the power structure in the industry than the family of Shapley values, based as they are on coalition behavior, on expected value reasoning, and with difficult-to-decipher motivations. Profit profiles in such matrices can be readily checked against realized profiles in the actual functioning of the industry so that the power structure selected has empirical validity.

b The Strengths and Limitations of Game Theory in Oligopoly Analysis

Game theory in its purest mathematical statements is an ultrarationalist approach to a wide spectrum of decision making contexts, involving welfare interdependence of agents. As such its remit is much broader than our narrower concerns about the functioning of oligopolists within liberal societies. The behavior of such industries of necessity are conducted within the liberties and constraints of social institutions – notably the legal – and, more broadly, an ethos incorporating the core values and beliefs of that society. These are externalities to game theory and microeconomic theory in general.

It is not to argue in an Institutionalist or Neo-Idealist vein that the evolution of such institutions and folkways is the primary concern of the social scientist to insist that they should be endogenized to relevant degrees in such theories. This is particularly true where market power is identifiable, seriously interferes with other agents' welfares when exercised, and is potentially destabilizing to a community of decision makers in continuous rivalry. In mature communities of rivals, therefore, where cooperation may benefit all and unrestrained rivalry be destructive of individual wellbeing, tacitly accepted and informally enforced sanctions and rewards support an industry ethos of importance in projecting potential industry decision profiles.

As indicated in the introduction of this chapter, many – perhaps most – game theorists recognize the necessity and, indeed, importance of approaching game-theoretic equilibria as plausible focal points that may be substantially compromised by externalities. The basic problem, however, is that the game theoretic framework is so ultrarationalist in structure that these concerns are not capable of true endogenization and remain vague *obiter dicta*. The contribution of game theory to the study of oligopoly is undeniable, which is to say that rivalry is the dominant force in such industries, and therefore that rationality especially in the intermediate and long runs is a necessary ingredient in the search for motivations. The question is whether it is the best framework to incorporate the dualistic force of cooperation.

The concept of the consonance coefficient permits both forces to be introduced in a continuous fashion, as well as to accommodate the multi-objective goals of firms. Initial estimates of this power structure based upon study of the specific industry and usage of such techniques as cross-factor analysis can be used to modify rationality-based estimates, and iterative procedures used to approximate the price and nonprice data of the functioning industry. It permits, therefore, the interplay of deductive and inductive procedures to simulate the complex motivations and goals, frequently ill defined in the cognition of the agents themselves, that underlie the actions of firms in oligopolistic communities. Rivalrous consonance techniques recognize that human motivation in such environments may not really be capable of codification by deductive techniques, and offers a set of parameters in the form of consonance coefficients that summarize approximatively the resultants of those unobservables. An apt analogy, perhaps, is the case where consumer preferences may be practically incapable of isolation so that the modeler must begin with observable demand functions to make progress in the analysis of market decisions.

3 MONOPOLISTIC COMPETITION METHODOLOGY

Monopolistic competition theory – by which we distinguish the market structure of Chamberlin's "large-group case" as opposed to the broader usage that the term has acquired in recent years – has the virtue from the vantage point of the present study of concentrating its analysis on the implications of product differentiation. Fortunately, the major contributions of potential relevance to oligopoly theory are also concentrated in the seminal work of Spence (1975, 1976, 1984), Dixit and Stiglitz (1977), and Hart (1974, 1980); we shall, therefore, limit the discussion of the newer developments in this market structure to their pathbreaking works.

Several unifying themes in these works are of interest in defining its strengths and weaknesses. First, as noted in previous chapters, the market structure as one of slightly differentiated and highly substitutable products within their product group offered by many small firms each of which has negligible impacts on the sales of any other competitor, limits its realistic relevance.[13] It may be useful in gaining some insights in the analysis of the "competitive fringe" of oligopolistic industries, but even in these cases the neglect of the interdependence among "dominant firms" and these junior rivals can be punishing to the analysis, and, frequently, the fringe itself contains clusters of tightly competing subsets.

The attractions to the theorist of the market structure are several. First, it permits closed analysis of the implications of fixed costs and falling average costs on industrial equilibria; and, in many cases, those equilibria are determinate and capable of yielding such interesting variable values as the number of firms or brands extant. Second, of course, it permits abstraction in its pursuit of these objectives from the complications of oligopolistic interdependence. Third, the use of symmetric or representative firms with consequent exploitation of simple graphical presentations does not strain the structural environment. And, lastly, it provides an ideal environment to study the social welfare implications of industry decisions because zero-profit equilibrium reduces such comparisons to those of consumers' surplus.

a The Dixit–Stiglitz Study

One of the papers that emerged in a group in the middle 1970s to revive an interest in this market structure was that of Dixit and Stiglitz, (1977). It typified the "new" studies of the large group case in that it applied modern analytical techniques to seek clearer answers to the "excess-capacity" debate of the 1930s. Does the failure of long-run equilibrium tangencies of demand and average cost curves to occur at the minimum of such cost functions indicate that heterogeneous products in a product group bring about a misallocation of resources? Are there too many brands of corn flakes being produced by too many firms on the descending portion of average cost curves when compared with the hypothetical production of a homogeneous product at the minimum of such cost curves? Do the welfare contributions of variety outweigh the higher costs? Indeed, could there be too few brands rather than too many, and, if so, are there consistent biases against the production of certain types of goods?

These studies feature product groups with fixed costs and monotonically declining average total costs in relevant output domains, and start with the definition of social surplus as the sum of consumers' surplus and producer surplus. A dilemma arises in a market system: social welfare dictates that a product should be produced if social surplus is positive, while production occurs in the market economy only if profits alone are nonnegative. Thus, it may well happen that certain socially desirable goods will not be produced when in fact their negative potential profits are outweighed by the consumers' surplus associated with them. In such circumstances too few brands will be forthcoming rather than too many.

1 Constant Elasticity of Substitution among Brands: Symmetric Firms

Dixit and Stiglitz (hereafter, D–S) begin with firms whose cost functions are identical, with equal fixed costs and constant marginal cost c. Moreover, the social utility is a function of a numeraire "other" good, x_0, and a CES function that treats all firms in the product group symmetrically:

$$u = U\left(x_0, \left[\sum_i x_i^\rho\right]^{\frac{1}{\rho}}\right), \qquad (6.4)$$

where $0 < \rho < 1$. The function argument with unity in the numerator of its outside exponent indicates that the function is linear homogeneous and therefore homothetic, and this latter quality is extended by assumption to the function U. The restraint in the budget constraint, I, consists of the fixed amount of x_0 *plus* positive or negative profits of the firms. The elasticity of substitution between any pair of commodities is $(1/(1 - \rho))$.

One of the simplifications possible with a CES function which is linear homogeneous in its arguments is that it is characterized by *homogeneous separability* and, therefore, demand functions can be derived in two stages.[14] In the first stage, the brands in the product group can be aggregated into a quantity index and their prices into a price index, and the amount demanded, the price index for the group, and the share of I spent of the group derived by straightforward constrained maximization of U. Detailed demands for each of the goods taken separately can then be derived in the second stage by maximizing the CES function with respect to each of the goods constrained by the sum of their values equalling the share of I previously determined to be spent on them.

D–S compare the familiar profit-maximizing market equilibrium with two social welfare alternatives: a maximization of social utility subject to each firm having nonnegative profits (if negative they must be subsidized by means other than a lump sum grant), and a maximization of social utility unconstrained by such a profit restriction. The market equilibrium and the constrained maximum solution are identical, with the same number of firms, n, all firms producing equal output amounts and the same amounts in both solutions, and all firms pricing identically and with equal values in both solutions. Maximization of social utility constrained only by a nonnegative profit condition yields a second-best solution identical to that of the large group solution of the market. Neither overproduction nor underproduction of variety characterizes the decentralized market solution.

Comparison of the market equilibrium with the unconstrained maximum utility solution reveals that the latter will attain a greater social utility with a larger number of firms, but each of the firms will produce the same amount of output as in the market equilibrium – that determined by the equality of price and marginal cost c. Each firm covers its variable costs in the unconstrained maximum solution, but total lump sum subsidies must cover the losses undergone by producing at prices that cover only average variable costs. Hence, for this case, D–S establish that the market equilibrium delivers *less – not more* – variety than a first-best social optimum requires, but that each active firm does not increase its output beyond the point that the market equilibrium does.

2 *Variable Elasticity of Substitution among Brands: Symmetric Firms*

D–S next consider a utility function with a power function form:

$$u = x_0^{(1-\gamma)}\left(\sum_i v(x_i)\right)^{\gamma}, \tag{6.5}$$

where $0 < \gamma < 1$ and the $v(\cdot)$ are increasing and concave. Because the product group function enclosed in parentheses is no longer homothetic, the two-stage solution process is not possible, and derivation of results is more complicated.

A comparison between the common p and x values, as well as the number of firms n, in the Chamberlin market equilibrium and the constrained optimum solution is not so straightforward in the variable elasticity case as in the constant elasticity case. The relation of the prices and the number of firms in the two cases is derivative from the relation of the outputs x in them. Since both x-solutions lie on the same average cost curve, if the market equilibrium x is greater, then p in that state must be smaller. Those $[x,p]$ solutions lie at tangencies of the Chamberlin *dd* demand functions (which are the firm's perceptions of its sales at each price if all other firms hold their prices constant) with the average cost function, at which points the Chamberlin *DD* demand functions (which depict the behavior of industry sales if all firms move prices together) intersect the tangencies. The *DD* functions are steeper than the *dd* functions, and if we assume that when a new firm enters the industry it shifts the incumbents' *DD* function leftward, then the solution with the larger x value will have the smaller n. Therefore, with subscripts e and c denoting the market and constrained optimum solutions, we conclude:

$$\begin{aligned} &x_e > x_c \rightarrow p_e < p_c \text{ and } n_e < n_c \\ &x_e < x_c \rightarrow p_e > p_c \text{ and } n_e > n_c. \end{aligned} \tag{6.6}$$

Which of these two cases occurs hinges upon the slope of the elasticity of utility of the *DD* curve, on which all firms will have the same x and p:

$$\varrho_x = \frac{xv'(x)}{v(x)}. \tag{6.7}$$

D–S assert that it can be shown that

$$\begin{aligned} &1 \quad \varrho'(x) > 0 \rightarrow x_e < x_c \\ &2 \quad \varrho'(x) < 0 \rightarrow x_e > x_c. \end{aligned} \tag{6.8}$$

They hypothesize that if n decreases so that x increases, the utility of x will rise, so that $\varrho'(x) > 0$ in the market equilibrium (6.8.1) will hold. In that case, the market will establish fewer firms (and brands) than would be optimal in the constrained optimum – once again challenging the notion that product differentiation would be excessive in the tangency solution.

Finally, in the unconstrained optimum, price is set at marginal cost, which is below the levels of the market equilibrium and constrained optimum that lie on the average cost curve (in general, at different points). Output comparisons with the constrained optimum will be related to marginal elasticity of utility as in (6.8):

$$\begin{aligned} &1 \quad \varrho'(x) > 0 \rightarrow x_u < x_c \\ &2 \quad \varrho'(x) < 0 \rightarrow x_u > x_c, \end{aligned} \tag{6.9}$$

with the relations to x_e implied by (6.8). Finally,

$$\begin{aligned} &1 \quad x_u < x_c \rightarrow n_u > n_c \\ &2 \quad x_u < x_e \rightarrow n_u > n_e. \end{aligned} \tag{6.10}$$

But this does not rule out the possibility that both x_u and n_u could be larger than their equilibrium and constrained optimum counterparts.

3 *Variable Elasticity of Substitution among Brands: Asymmetric Firms*

As a last case, D–S investigate an area in which A. M. Spence (1975, 1976, 1984) pioneered: the existence of a bias in the market equilibrium against production of brands which have an inelastic demand curve. As noted in the introduction to this section, the problem is inherent in the market system because decisions to produce a brand are based upon attaining nonnegative profits with it, whereas the social optimum requires that it be produced even with a negative profit if the consumer surplus outweighs that loss. Because that potentiality occurs most frequently with goods with inelastic demands, whose consumer surplus tends to be large, the market failure is expected to occur most frequently with them.

D–S specify a utility function with two subgroups of brands in the product group, all of which are perfect substitutes for one another, along with the numeraire good. Elasticities of substitution and cost functions are uniform for firms within each subgroup but different between the two. Each, therefore, is included in a separate CES function, and the two are related in a Cobb–Douglas manner to the numeraire good in the utility function:

$$u = U(x_0^{(1-s)} \left(\left[\sum_{i_1=1}^{n_1} x_{i_1}^{\rho_1} \right]^{\frac{1}{\rho_1}} + \left[\sum_{i_2=1}^{n_2} x_{i_2}^{\rho_2} \right]^{\frac{1}{\rho_2}} \right)^s \tag{6.11}$$

Each firm in a subgroup has a cost function $a_i + c_i x_i$.

Because the members' subgroups are related in *CES* functions, which are homogeneously separable, it is possible to obtain indices of quantities and prices which can be used as aggregates in profit or utility maximization. Letting p_i^* denote the price index for subgroup i, brands from that subgroup will be produced with zero product of subgroup j brands if and only if

$$p_i^* < \frac{sc_j}{s - a_j}. \tag{6.12}$$

In the constrained utility optimum which subgroup is favored depends upon which yields the higher aggregate utility value, and those values are determined by

$$u_i^* = s^s (1-s)^{(1-s)} p_i^{*-5}. \tag{6.13}$$

Hence utility is inversely related to the aggregate price index of the subgroup. But that price index is closely related to the elasticity of demand curves for firms in the subgroup:

$$\begin{aligned} &1 \quad p_i^* = p_i n_i^{-\beta_i} = c_i (1+\beta_i)^{1+\beta_i} \left(\frac{a_i}{s} \right)^{\beta_i} \\ &2 \quad \varepsilon_i = \frac{(1+\beta_i)}{\beta_i}, \end{aligned} \tag{6.14}$$

where ε_i is the (absolute value of the) common own-price elasticity of the demand functions of subgroup i, p_i is the common price of firms in subgroup i if it is chosen, and n_i is the number of active firms in the equilibrium. β_i is inversely related to ε_i, p_i^* is negatively related to β_i, and u_i (from (6.13)) is inversely related to p_i^*. Thus, a rise in ε_i lowers the utility of the subgroup. Also, be it noted, that p_i^* is positively related to changes in a_i and c_i.

It follows from (6.12)–(6.14) that the choices of the subgroup in both market equilibrium and the constrained utility solution can be depicted in terms of the values of p_i^*, or graphically in $p_i^* \times p_j^*$ space. Figure 6.1 is reproduced from D–S to illustrate the potential conflicts between the subgroups chosen in the two solutions. Consider, first, regions A and B of the diagram: in them both subgroups meet the conditions for market equilibrium stated in (6.12). On the 45° line that separates the two regions $p_1^* = p_2^*$ so that either meets the utility optimality condition of (6.13). Therefore, either good would satisfy both solutions.

But starting from a point on the 45° line suppose the elasticity of subgroup 2 increases, or a_1 or c_1 increases, so that the point moves from the line into region A. The rise in p_2^* makes the more inelastic subgroup 1 optimal but as long as the point remains within A it is possible that subgroup 2 could be chosen in the market equilibrium. A bias could occur against brands with more inelastic demands. As the named parameters continue to change in the indicated directions p_2^* continues to grow and with large enough changes

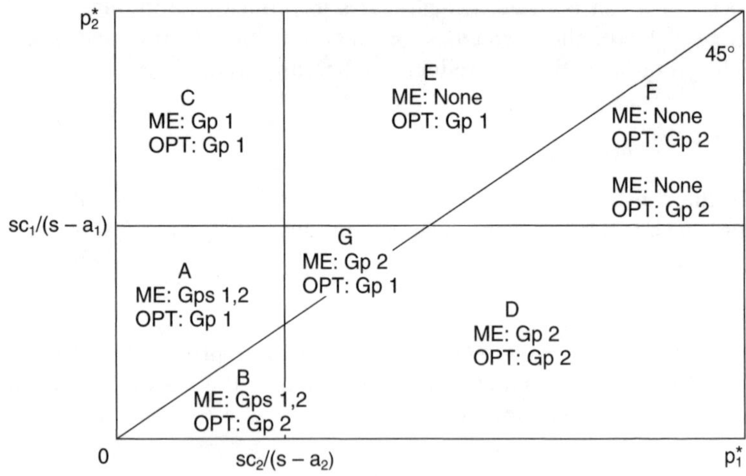

Figure 6.1 Comparison of solution groups

crosses into region *C* where the potential conflict is eliminated. A symmetric analysis would hold if any of the parameters for subgroup 1 were changed and p_1^* moved from the 45° line into a zone of potential conflict, *B*, and through it to resolution in region *D*.

In region *G* one encounters a zone of unambiguous conflict between solution conditions and ensuing bias against the inelastic subgroup. It arises because of the higher costs of subgroup 1 and the consequent larger latitude subgroup 2's price index has to meet the market equilibrium conditions. This zone would disappear if the righthand sides of (6.12) were equal.

In zones *E* and *F* neither good can meet the conditions for a market equilibrium but conditions for a constrained optimum require that goods from subgroup 1 or 2 respectively be produced. Market intervention by government may be required to dictate the more desirable subgroup be chosen.

4 *Insights from the Dixit–Stiglitz Models*

In this elegant analysis D–S offer four interesting and potentially powerful demonstrations concerning the market's choices of numbers and types of differentiated products under conditions of nonstrategic decision making:

1 In conditions where firms have symmetric cost functions and demands characterized by finite but identical elasticities of substitution, the market equilibrium and utility maximization constrained only by a nonzero profit constraint will feature solutions with identical prices, outputs and numbers

of brands. The excess capacity charge levied against Chamberlin's large-group tangency solution is contradicted: firms will operate at the same point on the average total cost function and socially excessive differentiation will not occur.

2 In the cost and demand conditions of 1, the unconstrained utility-maximization solution (which permits negative profits with marginal cost pricing) will feature a larger number of brands produced but, surprisingly, each producing firm will produce at the same output level as the market equilibrium and constrained utility-maximization solution. Economies of scale are not pushed beyond those of the previous two solutions and differentiation will be greater than in the latter two cases. Once more, therefore, the market equilibrium escapes the charge of excessive differentiation.

3 For firms with variable elasticities of substitution outputs in the market equilibrium and constrained optimization cases may vary in either direction depending upon the marginal elasticity of substitution of the brands, and prices and numbers of brands relations will vary inversely with outputs. D–S speculate that the market equilibrium will feature fewer firms with larger outputs than the constrained equilibrium, to cast more doubt on excessive differentiation arising under the former. The unconstrained optimum will feature price at marginal cost and hence lower than the other two solutions but other results are ambiguous.

4 Most importantly, for an asymmetric case, they demonstrate the possibility of biases against brands with inelastic demands arising in the market's equilibrium, an affirmation of Spence's prior analysis.

It is difficult to establish the degree to which these relationships depend upon the specific forms of the functions employed. Moreover, even in the asymmetric cases, the differentiation manifests itself only in elasticity of demand among firms, with characteristics remaining merely implicit rather than fully dimensioned. Nonetheless, the work must be ranked as among the most important in the area of price and nonprice competition under the determinate conditions of nonrivalrous competition.

b Spence's Analysis of Monopolistic Competition Goods Numbers and Biases

Spence, in a series of seminal articles (1975, 1976, 1984) investigating the role of fixed costs in defining industry structure, equilibria, and firm makeup, initiated a new concern with the excess capacity hypothesis about Chamberlin's large-group case as well as a deeper probing into the nature of its equilibria. Spence's key insight was to see that in monopolistic competition two forces operated to warp the tangency solution from the social optimum: (1) socially desirable goods might fail to be produced even though incremental social surplus was positive because profits were negative, and (2) entering firms impacted incumbent firms' demand functions and profits, but such impacts were ignored as pecuniary externalities to the new firms and opened the possibility that too many (if goods were substitutes) or too few (if goods were complements) brands would be produced from the viewpoint of social desirability.

In the most pathbreaking of his articles (1984) Spence's methodology shows that under certain conditions the firms' profit maximization results in the maximization of a fictitious or virtual objective function, and compares that virtual function with the social surplus function in order to denote qualitative and quantitative differences.

Most simply, Spence discusses the fact that were the firms capable of first-degree price discrimination in their individual, product-differentiated markets, limiting output by equating the price of the marginal unit to marginal cost which profit maximization would lead them to do would coincide with the conditions necessary for a maximization of social surplus. Each firm's equilibrium contribution to the total surplus will equal its profits (which, of course, incorporates all of what would constitute consumer surplus were it to price at marginal cost for all consumers), and the industry result could constitute a Nash equilibrium in that no firm could change output in such manner as to increase total surplus. The interesting insight is that *each* firm acts in its profit maximization as if it were maximizing *total* surplus over the total market for these highly substitutable products. Consumers in each market are giving up in income the maximum amount they would be willing to spend on the product, and therefore are on the margin of indifference about purchasing it. However, if the product brands are all pairwise substitutes, the value to the consumers as a whole of having access to products of the industry is greater than the sum of the firms' marginal contributions to the surplus. Intuitively, as firms leave the industry and total surplus falls in gross fashion by the amounts of their contributions, the demand functions of remaining firms shift outward to increase their contributions to surplus and raise the attractiveness of remaining products to consumers.

Spence's analysis of complementarity is best interpreted as complementary relationships between two product groups in monopolistically competitive market structures producing brands of distinctively different goods (e.g., peanut butter and jelly).[15] When such cross-industry relations are such that an increase in the output of a brand in one industry increases the marginal revenue of firms in the other, the market equilibrium will feature too few firms each of which produces too small an output to be socially optimal. If a firm in product group 1 experiences negative profits it will leave the industry, which shifts the marginal revenue of firms in the other industry down, inducing (1) brands in product group 2 which move into negative profit positions to leave the industry and (2) surviving firms to reduce output. This in turn feeds back into product group 1 to induce the same movements and to set up a cumulative cycle converging to a market equilibrium in both industries characterized by too few firms each of which produces too few units of output (and setting up the prospect of joint production in oligopolistic environments).[16]

But the major contribution of Spence's work concerns the single monopolistically competitive industry with strong intraindustry substitutability. As noted above, its methodology employs the search for a virtual objective function which the equilibrating processes of the industry featuring profit maximization implicitly maximize. This function – which Spence terms the *wrong surplus function* – is then compared with the true surplus function to denote differences in their configurations and potential biases against types of products which would be chosen in the latter solution but which are not selected in the former. This is a different approach from that of D–S in that it is a partial equilibrium analysis and isolates a more general form of function to depict firms' substitutability relations than D–S.

Define the vector $x = [x_1, x_2, \ldots, x_n]$ as output of the n firms (brands) in the industry and the *benefit function* $u(x)$ which is the aggregate dollars of consumer surplus plus revenue accruing from the output vector x. The partial derivatives $u_i(x)$ are the inverse demand functions of firms i. Spence discerns a form of the benefit function (1975, (20), p. 222) whose existence guarantees the existence of a wrong surplus function implicitly maximized by the industry in its equilibrium. We will continue to state the nature of the functions in qualitative terms and to repeat the more important of the theorems derived from them. For the more detailed presentation see Spence (1975).

Two specific forms of the more generally acceptable benefit function are the quadratic form

$$u(x) = ax - xAx \tag{6.15}$$

and the generalized quadratic,

$$u(x) = \Sigma_i \phi(x_i) - \Sigma_{ij} G_{ij}(x_i x_j), \tag{6.16}$$

where the ϕ_i are assumed to be concave, the G_{ij} are assumed to be convex, and the $G_{ii}(x_{ii}^2) = 0$. Spence uses (6.16) to show that the gross contribution of x_i to the surplus is above the revenue of the firm, which opens the *possibility* that the product may not be produced, and that the x_i of the market equilibrium will be below the socially optimal levels, given nonmarginal cost pricing.

To demonstrate the product biases that exist in this family of functions, Spence specifies (6.16) with $\varphi_i = a_i x_i^{\beta_i}$ and $G_{ij} = A_{ij} x_i x_j$. Further, marginal cost for each good is assumed constant at c_i. β_I is the ratio of the firm's profits to the contribution of the firm to social surplus, when both quantities are maximized. It is the crucial measure determining the susceptibility of brand i to bias in market selection – not the price elasticity of demand or the slope of the demand curve. Low values of β_I bias the product against selection, and since β_I does tend to vary directly with demand elasticity, inelastic demand functions do tend to inject product bias. Moreover, if we eliminate the influence of β_I in product selection by choosing two brands with equal βs, fixed costs are seen to exert an independent bias in product selection. Then, if product quality tends to increase fixed costs, the bias against selection extends to high quality products.

Spence discusses two possible sources of inelastic demand curves. The first is that products so characterized appeal to a narrow segment of purchasers who have widely varying valuations of the brand. The other is that a brand has a group of close competitors which bid away demand for the brand at higher prices. Both cases are characterized by widely varying valuations of the product, and it is this characteristic of consumer demand rather than appeal to a narrow audience that leads to a low β_I, low price elasticity and selection bias.

Finally, like D–S, Spence is drawn to generalized *CES* functions for product group brands, remaining at a partial equilibrium level rather than introducing a numeraire good into the utility function. The attraction of such functions, as seen in section 3a, is in the calculability of the market equilibrium and comparisons with the social surplus optimum. In its most general form, Spence's function is

$$u(x) = G\left[\int_i \phi_i(x_i)di\right] \tag{6.17}$$

with G and ϕ_i concave. In more specific usage this can be converted to a *CES* function of conventional form

$$u(x) = \left[\int_i a_i x_i^{\beta_i}\right]^{\theta} \tag{6.18}$$

where $0 < \beta_i < 1$. The benefit function $u(x)$ can be viewed as a utility function whose partial derivatives are inverse demand functions, or for the generalized form $\rho_i = u_i = G'(m)\varphi_i'(x_i)$, where $m = \int_j \varphi_j(x_j)d_j$. Because G is concave, G' decreases as m rises, so that the inverse demand functions of firms shift downward as the number of firms in the product group rises. Spence terms it an index of the congestion in the product group

$$G'(m) \geq \left[\frac{c_i(x_i) + F_i}{x_i\varphi_i'(x_i)}\right]. \tag{6.19}$$

Profits are simply $G'\varphi_i'x_i - (c_i(x_i) + F_i)$. For a given value of m the ability of firm i to survive (obtain nonnegative profits) depends upon how low the right side of (6.19) can be made. Therefore, define the *survival coefficient* of firm i as

$$s_i = \min_{x_i}\left[\frac{c_i(x_j)+F_i}{x_i\phi_i'(x_i)}\right]. \tag{6.20}$$

At the firm level, with given m, profit is maximized with the firm active when

$$G'[\varphi_i' + x_i\varphi_i''] = c_i(x). \tag{6.21}$$

At the product group level m is determined as $\int_j \varphi_j(x_j)d_j$ for active firms and (6.21) simultaneously determines x_i's. To determine the industry equilibrium, rank the s_i in ascending order and introduce them as active in that order. As this procedure continues, m rises, G' falls, and s_i falls until firm n, the marginal firm, just breaks even, at which value $G'(m) = s_n$. The equilibrium is graphed in Figure 6.2.

Total surplus is simply the benefit function *less* the sum of costs of firms which are active when surplus is maximized, or from (6.17) and the definition of m

$$T = G(m) - \int_{i\in\Gamma} c_i(x_i) + F_i, \tag{6.22}$$

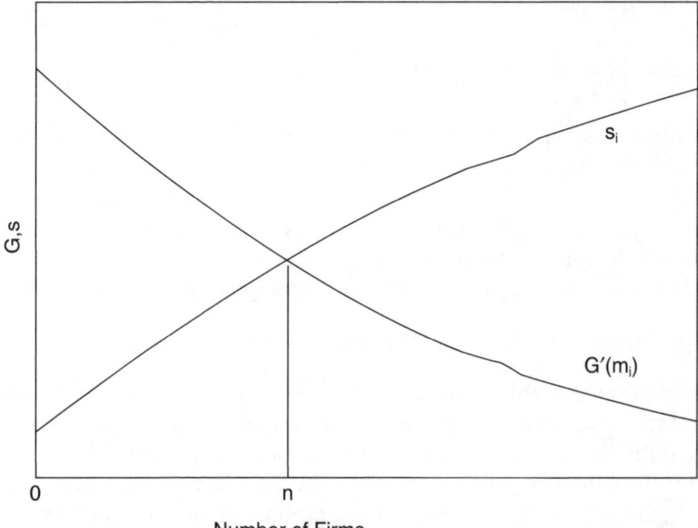

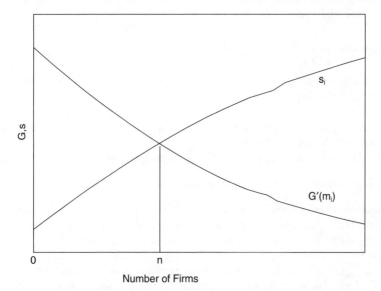

Figure 6.2 Determination of number of firms

where Γ is the set of active firms in the optimum. Spence solves the problem indirectly by setting m parametrically and minimizing costs, to obtain the objective function

$$c - \int_{i \in \Gamma} \left(\frac{c_i + F_i}{\phi_i} \right) \phi_i = 0 \tag{6.23}$$

which is minimized subject to

$$m - \int_{i \in \Gamma} \phi_i(x_i) \geq m*. \tag{6.24}$$

Let the set of coefficients defined by this minimization problem be

$$\rho_i = \min_i \left[\frac{c_i(x_i) + F_i}{\phi_i(x_i)} \right], \tag{6.25}$$

which can be ranked in ascending order as we treated s_i above. If it be substituted for the s_i curve in Figure 6.2, and its intersection be determined with a new G' function, then $n°$, the number of firms (brands) selected in the optimal surplus solution, is determined. The maximum surplus, $G_m - c(m)$, is obtained when $\rho_n = c'(m)$, which is to say marginal cost pricing holds for the marginal firm. But $G'\phi_i' = \rho_i = c_i' = c'(m°)$, so that marginal pricing holds for each of the active firms in the optimum.

In the comparison of the market equilibrium's choice of products with that of the optimum surplus, Spence reverts to the specific case of the generalized quadratic where $\varphi_i = a_i x_i^{\beta_i}$. Then

$$s_i \min_{x_i} \left[\frac{c_i + F_i}{x_i \varphi_i'} \right] = \min_{x_i} \frac{1}{\beta_i} \left[\frac{c_i + F_i}{\varphi_i} \right] = \frac{\rho_i}{\beta_i} \tag{6.26}$$

Because $\beta_i < 1$, $s_i > \rho_i$, so for goods with small β_i the rank of s_i by the market will be significantly higher than its optimum surplus ranking, and have a relatively smaller chance of selection. Since β_i is inversely related to the steepness of the inverse demand function, therefore, it is the brand with low elasticity of demand that is disadvantaged.

When the more general form of $\varphi_i(x_i)$ is adopted, ρ_i/s_i tends to smallness for goods whose $\frac{x_i \varphi_i'}{\varphi_i}$ is small. This means the ratio of revenues to product i's contribution to surplus is small, and the potentiality for negative profits is higher. Once more, then, bias is demonstrated for such goods whose markets may be quite restrained or featured by wide variance of demand.

As for the extent of product differentiation, Spence distinguishes two sets of conflicting sources in the market's operation. On the one hand, fixed costs make it more difficult for revenues to render positive profits, and so serve to limit the number of brands produced. On the other hands, two forces operate to expand the number. Pricing power keeping price above marginal cost gives greater scope for entry, and firms enter without considering the impacts of their entry on the consumers' and producer surplus of incumbent firms. Higher cross-elasticities of demand, which are expected in this market structure, would lead to the expectation that the second group of forces would dominate, and excess differentiation would be more common.

Consider the symmetric case where $\varphi_i(x_i)$ and cost functions are the same for all firms and, additionally, $\varphi_i(x) \equiv \varphi(x) = ax^{\beta}$. Then, the optimum has *more* products than the market equilibrium, outputs of each product are equal for both solutions (so firms operate at the same points on their common cost functions), and profits are negative in the optimum.

If the symmetry assumption is retained with an arbitrary concave function, ambiguities arise. If $\frac{x\varphi'}{\varphi}$ is a decreasing function, too few products will be produced in the market equilibrium but active firms produce larger output levels, thereby pushing production past the point on the average total cost curve that yields the optimum. If $\frac{x_i\varphi_i'}{\varphi_i}$ is increasing optimal firm quantities are above those of the market equilibrium but the value of m – and therefore the optimal number of brands – is ambiguous. When $\frac{x\varphi'}{\varphi}$ is decreasing revenues as a function of benefits decline as price falls and quantity increases. If this be accepted as the more likely prospect then monopolistic competition would be characterized normally by larger than optimal firm outputs of a smaller than optimal number of brands.

1 Insights from Spence's Analysis

Spence's investigations into the social welfare aspects of noncompetitive pricing must be ranked among the virtuoso performances in modern applied microeconomics. In his early work on monopoly and regulation (1975) he identified the lack of correspondence of market equilibria and social welfare as a form of market failure in that the *marginal* benefit of product quality is equated with its marginal cost rather than the *average* benefit. That is, when the average valuation of quality is greater that its marginal valuation firms set quality too low. This will occur when the marginal benefit of quality enhancements declines with rises in output, i.e., when $p_{qx} < 0$, where q is quality and x output.

From this fundamental insight Spence demonstrates in his later work the bias against selection of goods with inelastic demands and those whose introduction is characterized by pecuniary externalities on other firms' profits, as well as the existence of contending forces discussed above whose net resultant is product variety greater or less than socially optimal.

c Contributions of Monopolistic Competition Theory to Integrated Competition in Oligopoly

To a greater degree than game-theoretic analysis, and somewhat paradoxically, the new monopolistic competition analysis yields some potentially applicable insights into oligopolistic price–nonprice competition. These are, of course, more in the nature of an interrogation methodology than directly transferable propositions. The more esoteric concerns, such as the potential for nonproduction of complementary products by virtue of pecuniary externalities, seem even less likely of occurrence in oligopoly than in monopolistic competition, given the expectation of larger firms with greater resources for joint production and product development. Rather more interesting for our purposes is the study of quality variation as demand functions vary in price elasticity and as tacit collusion changes with consonance coefficients.

To what extent may improvements in product quality offset declines in consumers' surplus as prices rise? In many of our simulations to be discussed in Chapters 8 and 9, price and quality characteristics tend to rise together, and attention will focus on net consumers' surplus changes as they vary. The monopolistic competition analysis sensitizes us to study patterns of change in these variables resulting from the pecuniary firm externalities internalized by the industry via tacit collusion.

For reasons stated in the introduction to section 3, monopolistic competition equilibria and the propositions based on convenient functional forms concerning excesses or shortfalls in product differentiation are not of major realistic interest, in our judgment. Comparisons of rivalrous consonance or other types of oligopolistic equilibria with marginal cost pricing we have treated as especially unhelpful and, indeed, misleading in terms of policy formation. But the monopolistic competition analyses will lead us to compare industry equilibria under varying assumptions about tacit collusion with zero-collusion equilibria with respect to product quality and social welfare.

7 Pure Competition and Monopoly: A Beginning

To gain a foothold in the analytics of the firm's decisions we will begin with firms that are either price takers in their markets or, at the other extreme, monopolists. Such firms make decisions concerning price, quantity and quality policy variables for their brands, which are treated in 1 to 1 correspondence with firms. In this chapter quality is viewed as a one-dimensional variable which is measurable with uniqueness up to a positive multiplicative scalar, where z denotes units of its intensity. The implications of the firms' decisions for their own profit, for consumers' surplus, and for social surplus are considered under varying structural conditions.

1 SEPARABLE PRICING OF CHARACTERISTICS

One of the complicating factors in analyzing quality characteristics is that they are not in general priced explicitly in markets, with choices of amounts taken made by consumers in accordance with preferences for them and their prices. Rather, as noted in Chapter 5, they are usually bundled in packages whose prices are stated in dollars per package unit, with differences in quality intensities among such packages treated as different brands or distinguishable brand variants within an overarching trademark.[1] The rare product in the world of standardized products is capable of explicit quality component pricing; however, the purchase of a "basic" automobile model with listed options, or a tailored suit with choice of fabric, hand- or machine-stitching, number of fittings, and so forth, are instances of such exceptions. In this section we study the positive and normative implications of firms' decisions in such market conditions, and for simpler presentation purposes we assume that different firms produce the basic product and the quality add-ons. As an example, we may concretize the situation as that in which one firm produces and sells an automobile with a minimum warranty period and another firm sells extended warranties at an independent price per unit.

Consider firms with separable inverse demand functions for quantities, x, with some minimum quality intensity but capable of quality supplements above that minimum, z. The unit of z will be taken to be a month of warranty with price p_z.[2] Demand functions for x and z can be written

$$\begin{aligned} &1\quad x = x(p_x) \\ &2\quad z = z(p_z) \text{ if } x > 0,\ 0 \text{ otherwise,} \end{aligned} \tag{7.1}$$

with inverses $p_x = p_x(x)$ and $p_z = p_z(z)$ when $x > 0$.

Total cost functions are defined as

$$\begin{aligned} &1\quad C_x = C_x(x),\ C_x' > 0,\ C_x'' \geq 0 \\ &2\quad C_z = C_z(z),\ C_z' > 0,\ C_z'' \geq 0, \end{aligned} \tag{7.2}$$

where $C_x' = dC_x/dx$ and $C_z' = dC_z/dz$, etc.

Profits for the combined firms are

$$\pi = p_x(x) \cdot x + p_z(z) \cdot z - C_x(x) - C_z(z), \text{ when } x > 0,\ 0 \text{ otherwise,} \tag{7.3}$$

and consumers' surplus, S, is defined over both firms when $x > 0$ as

$$S = \int_0^x p_x(v)dv + \int_0^z p_z(y)dy - p_x \cdot x - p_z \cdot z. \tag{7.4}$$

Given $x > 0$, social welfare, W, is

$$W = S + \pi = \int_0^x p_x(v)dv + \int_0^z p_z(y)dy - C_x(x) - C_z(z). \tag{7.5}$$

When S and π are strictly concave, necessary and sufficient first-order conditions for a global maximum of W are:

$$\begin{aligned} &1\quad \frac{\delta W}{\delta x} = \frac{\delta S}{\delta v} + \frac{\delta \pi}{\delta x} = p_x - C_x' = 0 \\ &2\quad \frac{\delta W}{\delta z} = \frac{\delta S}{\delta z} + \frac{\delta \pi}{\delta z} = p_z - C_z' = 0, \end{aligned} \tag{7.6}$$

Independently determined profits, however, reach a maximum when marginal revenues and marginal costs are equated, firm by firm:

$$\begin{aligned} &1\quad \frac{\delta \pi}{\delta x} = p_x' \cdot x + p_x - C_x' = 0 \\ &2\quad \frac{\delta \pi}{\delta z} = p_z' \cdot z + p_z - C_z' = 0, \end{aligned} \tag{7.7}$$

a The Firms as Price Takers

Figure 7.1 illustrates the elliptical contours of the welfare function W when demand functions are linear, cost functions are quadratic in quantities, and both function sets are separable.[3] Social surplus increases as we move

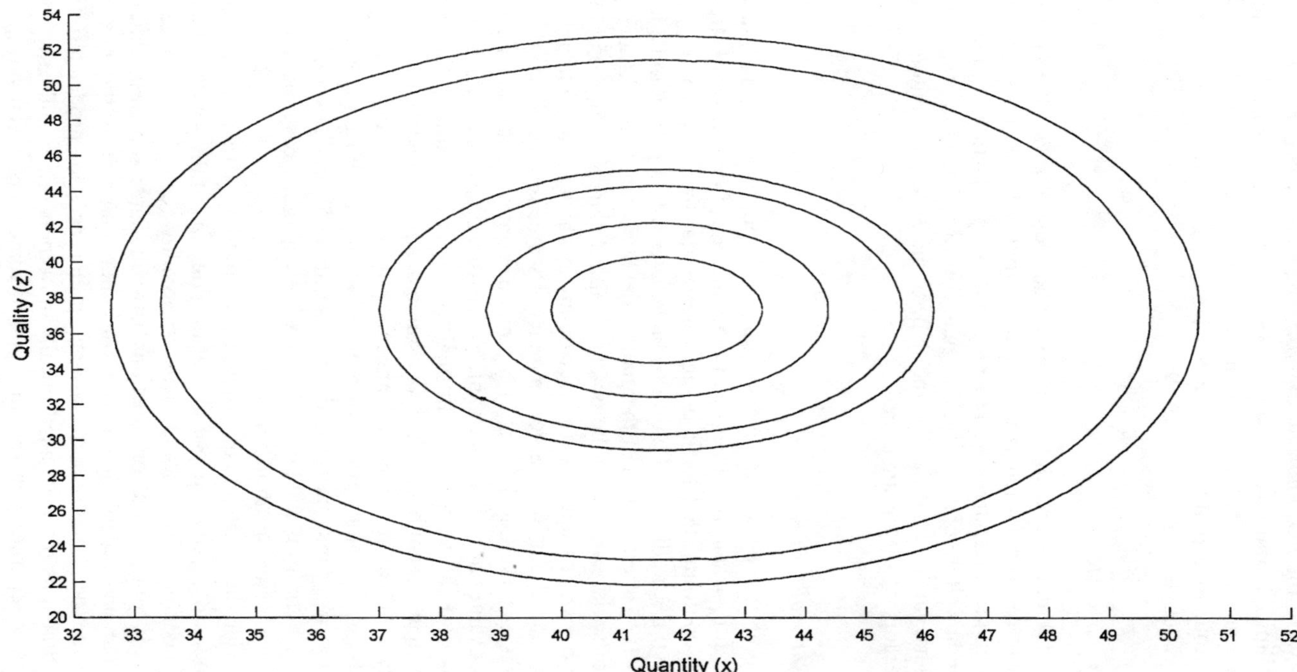

Figure 7.1 *W*-function contour ellipses

inward toward the *maximum maximorum* (W_{max}) at the center of the concentric ellipsoid contours, at which punctiform contour social surplus is maximized meeting conditions in (7.6). From (7.5) the slope of an "isosurplus" contour at a point $[x,z]$ (the marginal rate of welfare substitution between goods) is

$$\frac{dz}{dx} = -\frac{p_x - MC_x}{p_z - MC_z}. \tag{7.8}$$

The loss of a unit of x results in a gross welfare loss of p_x *less* the savings in the value of resources when dx is no longer produced: net loss is the difference. When these resources are redeployed to the production of z they yield a net gain in welfare of p_z *less* the marginal cost of z. Therefore, the ratio of net marginal gain and loss dictates the slope of the isosurplus contours. From (7.6), the slope at W_{max} is undefined.

1 The Rationality Region

If we assume that $p_z = 0$ and z costs nothing to produce, the maximum W attainable for parametric values of x lies on a locus of tangencies of straight lines with contours, that locus being a horizontal line through W_{max} (the major axis). Each ellipse will have two tangencies with a higher and a lower value of x (i.e., at either end of the major axis) hence on Figure 7.1 an equal amount of social surplus can be obtained with a common value of z but a higher and a lower value of x. In an economy in which greater amounts of x can be produced only with larger amounts of scarce resources, whether the economy is a market mechanism or command economy, only the tangencies with lower values of x will be relevant. Hence, those portions of the contours to the right of the vertical line through W_{max} can be ignored. An exactly symmetrical argument holds when we assume that $p_x = 0$ and we treat z parametrically to trace out a locus of tangency points as a vertical straight line through W_{max} (the minor axis). Portions of the ellipses above the horizontal line through W_{max} may be ignored. In these discarded regions, (7.6) shows that one or both firms will be producing where marginal costs exceed price, violating profit maximization behavior.

If we divide the figure into quadrants by use of these perpendicular boundaries through W_{max}, only the portions of the contours in the southwest quadrant are economically rational. This "rationality region", is depicted in Figure 7.2. It contains tradeoff functions between x and y somewhat different from the familiar tradeoff functions of consumer and producer theory in that they combine the effects of both consumer preferences and production costs. For cost functions that rise quadratically in outputs one would expect that the distances separating curves for equal increments of social surplus will

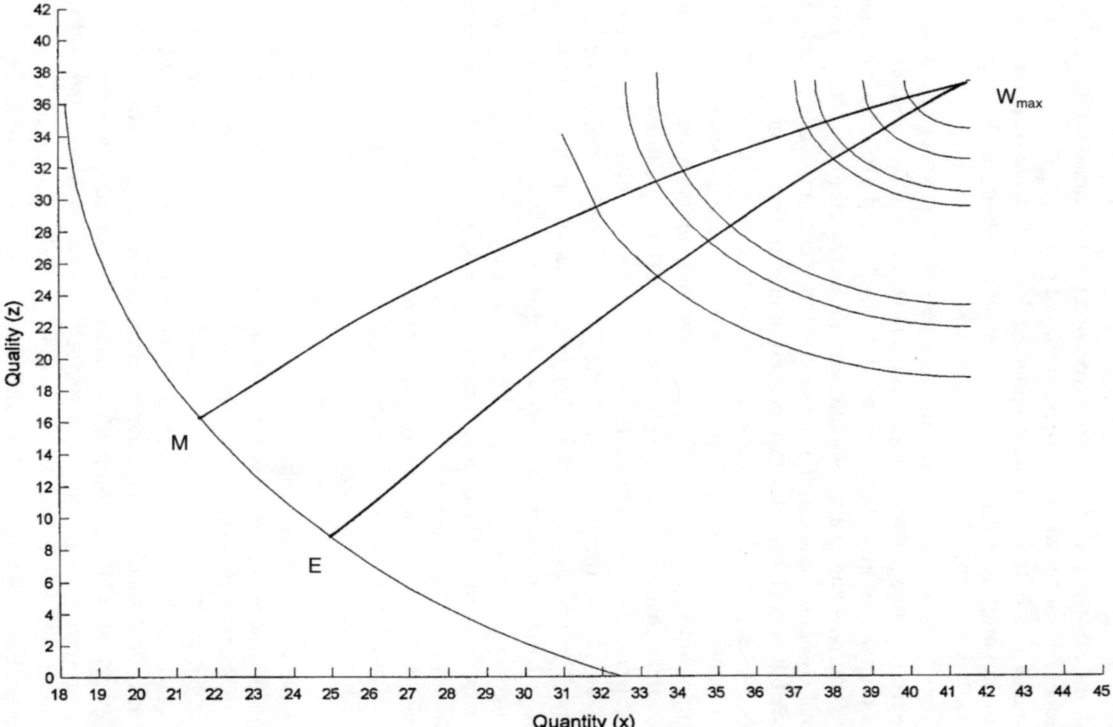

Figure 7.2 Isosurplus contours

tend to become smaller as costs increase more than linearly with x and z. Some interpretations of the economic meaning of the curves are familiar: for example, as noted above, the slopes represent marginal rates of welfare substitution between quality and quantity. However, significant differences do exist.

First, the isosurplus curves fall to zero when $x = 0$ because positive values of z cannot be associated with zero quantities of product.

Second, when outputs are determined under motivation of profit maximization in purely competitive markets, the only contour that has relevance is the satiation or "bliss" point at the *maximum maximorum*, W_{max}, where conditions (7.6) are met: at the optimal outputs of product and quality, marginal costs are equated to prices. The analytical usefulness and relevance of suboptimal contours, therefore, must be established explicitly. On such contours outputs and quality amounts are not increased to the levels where marginal costs are equated to given prices. One such purpose is to analyze the shortfall in social surplus experienced in environments where firms are not price takers. Another might occur in planned or regulated economies where planning or regulatory boards decide to produce amounts of outputs that compromise between purely competitive and monopoly quantities, and set price–marginal cost differences to bring about those quantities efficiently. A more practical goal might be to increase profits at the expense of consumers' surplus in the short run to encourage growth in noncompetitive markets. The important point is that interest in suboptimal contours is derivative from constraints defining goals that foreclose the possibility of attaining maximum surplus, and this is not easily motivated in purely competitive markets. These concerns will occupy us in the monopolistic conditions of section b. below.

When both firms achieve long-run purely competitive equilibrium with U-shaped average cost functions, social welfare will be optimized at W_{max} with prices equal to marginal and average costs. The *average* quality will be $q = z/x$, but behind that average each consumer purchasing an automobile will be able to obtain the size of warranty period that is optimal for him or her at p_z, the social cost of a month of warranty. Firms will receive no rents but consumers' surplus will represent the rents that result because each consumer pays for a car and unit of warranty the marginal benefit received by the least eager purchaser. Average consumer benefit is above marginal social benefit, and consumers' surplus is maximized as a social magnitude at W_{max}. Competition permits the consumer to extract every unit of product from producers at the very lowest price the firms will be able to sell and survive. In the short run W_{max} will contain profits of the firm as well as consumer surplus, with prices equal to marginal but above average cost.

b The Firms as Monopolists

Consider, now, the case of monopoly with the firms producing x and z as sellers. Unconstrained, the firms will maximize separate and joint profits (since their demand and cost functions are independent) where marginal revenue equals marginal cost:

$$1\ \frac{\delta\pi_x}{\delta x} = p_x + p'_x \cdot x - C'_x = 0$$

$$2\ \frac{\delta\pi_z}{\delta z} = p_z + p'_z \cdot z - C'_z = 0. \tag{7.9}$$

This solution is graphed as point M on Figure 7.2, which is the punctiform contour for *maximum joint profit* serving as the center of concentric ellliptical contours of the joint profit function $\pi = \pi_x + \pi_z$. These are not drawn to reduce clutter.

Let us return now to our consideration of social policy. Suppose a goal entailed attainment of a given level of welfare, W which could be met by any of the alternative mixtures on the relevant contour. Which is the socially most desirable mix of x and z? One goal that suggests itself on grounds of social efficiency is to produce on W where costs are minimized:

$$\min C = C(x) + C(z)$$

Subject to: (7.10)

$$\int_0^{p_x} p_x(v)dv + \int_0^{p_z} p_z(y)dy - C(x) - C(z) - W = 0.$$

Then, assuming the C-functions and CS are concave, necessary and sufficient conditions for such an optimum are:

$$\frac{p_x - C'_x}{p_z - C'_z} = \frac{C'_x}{C'_z}. \tag{7.11}$$

That is, prices must be proportionate to marginal costs of the goods, or, price per unit of marginal cost must be equal for both goods. These conditions may also be written:

$$\frac{p_x}{p_z} = \frac{C'_x}{C'_z}. \tag{7.12}$$

At the solution mix on W the ratio of prices must equal the ratio of marginal costs.

If we choose W to be the isosurplus contour on which M is resident, that efficiency mix might be at E on Figure 7.2. As we permit W to rise parametrically we envisage the optimal efficiency points to lie on the locus EW_{max}.

Note that at M the ratio of marginal costs is smaller (absolutely) than at E because x is reduced and z increased, lowering C'_x and raising C'_z. At M the *ratio of marginal revenues* is equal to the ratio of marginal costs, but the slope of W at M is steeper than at E, so the *ratio of prices* is greater than the marginal cost ratio $(p_x)/(p_z) > C'_x/C'_z$. As movement occurs on W towards E, p_x falls and C'_x rises as x rises, p_z rises and C'_z falls as z falls, and (7.12) is established at E. Finally, if we allow W to vary parametrically the line of tangencies established by (7.12) with the constraint that W be attained will be similar to EW_{max} on Figure 7.2. This locus can also be obtained by maximizing W in (7.5) subject to a joint cost constraint.

Point M on Figure 7.2 is the point of maximum *joint* profit. The isosurplus contour lines, identified with the value of W, which is maximized at W_{max} and declines with distance from that maximum, can be indexed with values of deadweight loss, DWL. For a contour line W^n

$$\begin{aligned} DWL^n &= W^n - W^{max} \\ &= (S_x^n + S_z^n + \pi_x^n + \pi_z^n - S_x^{max} + S_z^{max} + \pi_x^{max} + \pi_z^{max}). \end{aligned} \tag{7.13}$$

Another welfare policy goal might be to accept monopoly rents as unavoidable, or even desirable, but to control their deadweight loss. For example, policy might be to maximize W subject to permitting a specified amount of joint profits, which is identical to maximizing consumers' surplus CS for that specified profit constraint. The same outcome could be obtained by maximizing profits subject to being on a specified W contour.

Consider now the W contours that lie between W_{max} and the M-resident contour. As in the case of pure competition these can never contain a pure, two-firm joint monopoly solution, since it will always lie at M. The locus of such constrained monopoly solutions is the line MW_{max} on Figure 7.2. The joint profit function is an ellipsoid (not drawn on Figure 7.2) with maximum at M and elliptical contours whose portions to the left of a vertical line through M perpendicular to the horizontal axis may be ignored. This is because to the left of M profits and welfare decline so no $[x,z]$ solution can lie on these portions of the contours. The constrained maximum for a given π will lie at the tangency of its isoprofit contour and an isosurplus contour.

The slopes of the isosurplus contours are independent of market structure and remain the (negative of) the ratio of prices *less* marginal costs, as depicted in (7.8). But the slope of the isoprofit contours will be the ratio of marginal revenues *less* marginal cost. Therefore, at the tangencies of the isoprofit and isosurplus contours, the marginal rate of substitution of x and z for joint profits equals their marginal rate of substitution for welfare:

$$\frac{p_x + p'_x \cdot x - C'_x}{p_z + p'_z \cdot z - C'_z} = \frac{p_x - C'_x}{p_z - C'_z}, \tag{7.14}$$

or

$$\frac{p_x - C'_x}{p'_x \cdot x} = \frac{p_z - C'_z}{p'_z \cdot z}. \tag{7.15}$$

The interpretation of (7.15) permits us to introduce a concept that will be employed throughout the remainder of this work. This is the notion of *marginal policy cost*, as represented in the denominators of (7.15). Both of these firms are assumed to be determining price policies of joint profit maximization under conditions of constrained monopoly. The *marginal production costs* of their pricing actions are C'_x and C'_z but there is an additional cost to (say) lowering price to sell more output. That is the reduction in the revenue collected on intramarginal sales, or $p'_x \cdot x$ and $p'_z \cdot z$. These terms are negative and could be added to marginal production costs to obtain marginal total costs, i.e., marginal production cost plus marginal policy cost. Marginal profit is then simply price *less* marginal total costs.[4]

Condition (7.15) then is interpreted as requiring, for a maximization of W or CS subject to a fixed profit constraint, that the marginal gross profit of each good per dollar of marginal policy cost be equal. At M, both sides of (7.15) equal 1. The last dollar of revenue lost by price reduction of each good must yield the same incremental gross profit. The locus of these points of tangency lie on the line MW_{max} on Figure 7.2.

Under conditions of complete separability that characterizes the two monopolists in our example, were the regulatory goal for W separated into two additive portions, W_x and W_z, that coincide with the contributions they make under condition (7.15), and the distribution of the fixed level of profits between the firms indifferent to the regulators, such policies would lead to the locus of tangencies MW_{max}. However, in general, the distribution of the fixed level of profits will be an additional constraint on the solution. For arbitrary distributions of the desired level of B between the firms, therefore, the solution will lie on the relevant isoprofit contour at an intersection with an isosurplus contour rather than a tangency. Smaller welfare will result than would occur were profit distributed according to condition (7.15).

Suppose firms maximize profits in an unconstrained manner, so $\delta\pi/\delta x = \delta\pi/\delta z = 0$. Then, from (7.6)

$$\begin{aligned} &1 \quad \frac{\delta W}{\delta x} = \frac{\delta S}{\delta x} = \frac{d\int_0^x p_x(v)dv}{dx} - p_x - p'_x \cdot x = -p'_x \cdot x \\ &2 \quad \frac{\delta W}{\delta z} = \frac{\delta S}{\delta z} = \frac{d\int_0^z p_z(y)dy}{dz} - p_z - p'_z \cdot z = p'_z \cdot z \end{aligned} \tag{7.16}$$

where $p_x' = dp_x/dx$, etc., so

$$\begin{aligned} &1 \quad \delta W = -p_x' \cdot x \cdot \delta x \\ &2 \quad \delta W = -p_z' \cdot z \cdot \delta z, \end{aligned} \tag{7.17}$$

Because $p_x(x)$ and $p_z(z)$ are negatively sloped, $\delta W/\delta x$ and $\delta W/\delta z > 0$. Hence (7.17) is readily interpreted: the differentials are simply the amounts by which consumers' surplus is increased with small increments in the decision variables in the neighborhood of the monopolistic solution. A portion of this is at the expense of the monopolist's profits and another portion recaptures deadweight loss.

On Figure 7.3 the quality rays q_{max} and q_M for the competitive and monopoly equilibria respectively are drawn. Note that as drawn the average quality of product (equals the average length of warranty per automobile) is greater in the monopoly equilibrium than the purely competitive. The demand and cost conditions for producing automobiles permit a higher margin of price above marginal cost for x than is available for z. Hence, the monopoly equilibrium occurs higher on the monopoly W-contour than would be true if the opposite held true. The consumers as a whole receive less of both goods than in the competitive equilibrium and are less well off with fewer automobiles of higher quality on average. However, individual consumers will choose autos of higher or lower quality than average in both competitive and monopoly equilibria, but will always be on a lower indifference curve on

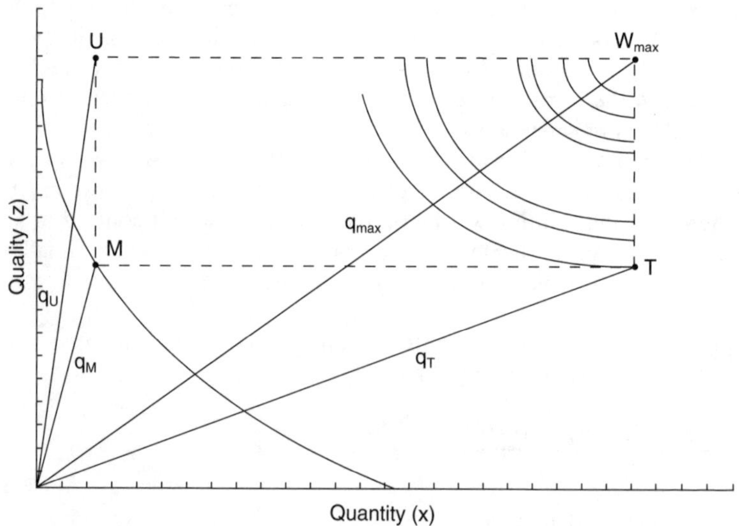

Figure 7.3 Equilibria and average quality

their own indifference maps at the monopoly equilibrium prices than at competitive prices.

Suppose, now, that at the monopoly solution at M on Figure 7.2 government regulators place a price ceiling on (say) x, so that $p_x < p_{max}$, where p_{max} is the price of x at M. The new solution occurs at an intersection of a higher W contour and a lower profit contour with higher x but the same z. This is because for independent firms x and z have no interaction in demand or cost functions. Hence, on Figure 7.3, the new optimum will move to the right on MT to a higher W-contour. Profits are reduced, of course, but consumer surplus rises by more than this decline to result in a higher social surplus. However, q declines, as the same z is spread over a larger x, so that a larger amount of a lesser quality product is produced.

c One Monopolist, One Competitor

Next, assume the constraint on p_x is lowered parametrically, increasing x and raising C'_x so that the solution approaches $p_x - C'_x = 0$, as the producer of z (the warranty firm) remains an uncontrolled monopolist. The solutions move along the line MT on Figure 7.3 approaching T, at which:

$$1 \quad \frac{\delta \pi_x}{\delta x} = p_x - C'_x = 0$$

$$2 \quad \frac{\delta \pi_z}{\delta z} = p_z - p'_z \cdot z - C'_z = 0. \tag{7.18}$$

At T, x is the competitive output and z the monopoly output, yielding q_T lower than q_M or q_{max} because x has expanded to its competitive level and z is restricted to its monopoly level.

If we reverse the roles of price taker and price maker, the equilibrium basket is graphed as point U on Figure 7.3 with x at its monopoly level but z at its competitive value. Quality q_U is even steeper than q_M.

Lastly, if regulatory authorities place a maximum price constraint on the monopolist producing z while the production of x remains purely competitive, parametric changes of the price constraint will move equilibria along TW_{max} to W_{max} as a limit, raising W and consumers' surplus and lowering producer surplus from their values at M. But, as remarked earlier, q may rise or fall.

It follows that in the optimal social welfare product configuration at W_{max} it is not generally true that the product is of the highest quality attainable in the framing region, where degree of quality is defined as the content of the characteristic per unit of product. That distinction will usually occur when either or both variables are restricted to a greater or lesser degree. On Figure 7.3 that occurs when output x is at monopoly level while z is produced competitively. Even when both variables are monopolized a higher quality product is manufactured that at W_{max}. Maximum social welfare does not imply the highest feasible degree of product quality.

d A Summary of Welfare Implications of Independent Firms

Besides permitting us to develop a framework for dealing with the welfare aspects of price and nonprice decision making in the simplest possible way, the analysis of independent firms has several advantages. More germane to present goals, it has permitted us to develop bounds of relevance for the analysis of oligopolistic market structure and characteristics decisions to follow in future chapters. On Figure 7.3, the rectangle $UMTW_{max}$ must be expected to frame the $[x,z]$ and implied $[p_x,p_z]$ solutions for mature oligopolies under conditions of complete separability. As developed in Chapter 3, we will view such solutions as results of mixtures of competition and co-operation, or solutions bounded by joint profit maximization at M, both firms as pure competitors at W_{max}, and one firm as monopolist and the other as price taker at U and T.

Quite apart from the purposes at hand, this framework provides a means of analyzing the price decisions of firms which produce in wholly different product groups and in widely different market structures. That is, it affords an avenue of approach to the daunting task of constructing a far-reaching welfare economics of imperfect competition.

The isosurplus contours can be labeled to reveal total welfare in cardinal dollar measures or deadweight loss as prices depart from marginal cost on contours that approach the M-resident limiting contour. Also, the locus of solutions under planning strategies translated into margins of price above marginal cost can be traced out on the figure, as for example, on Figure 7.2.

Also, on Figure 7.3, suppose government regulators permit the automobile monopolist to function as such, but desire to protect consumers by restraints on average safety quality. As they raise those minimum average warranty periods per automobile from q_M toward a maximum feasible level q_U, the intercepts of isocontour lines that intersect UM (not drawn) will trace out the rise in welfare attendant on those constraints as well as the margin of price over marginal cost enforced to achieve them. Interestingly, were z some important safety characteristic, government regulators might find point U and implied q_U superior to W_{max}, being willing to accept safer cars instead of a larger number of cars with lower average quality. The monopoly decisions of the automobile industry would be socially desirable in their view despite consumer preferences. When one or both firms are monopolists, government regulation may impose ceiling prices below monopoly prices to increase output of the monopolized variables and increase W. Similar results may be obtained by placing ceiling quantity restrictions on monopolized variables.

One welfare interpretation that we challenged on realistic grounds in section 4 of Chapter 3 and illustrated in Figure 3.6 bears repeating in its depiction in Figure 7.3. The punctiform contour W_{max} at the apex of the diagram naturally emerges as an ideal norm against which to measure the welfare costs of lapses from purely competitive decisions. But in realistic terms where strategic interdependence among firms is the rule rather than an idiosyncratic and deplorable lapse from the ideal, this may be a misleading policy guide. The ideal should be redefined to be some point on a lower W-contour that is realistically achievable by policy measures in a market economy rather than ignore the rationality of interdependent price–quality decision making. Perhaps, for example, in the case at hand, where both firms are in oligopolistic markets, a Cournot solution as defined in section 2c of Chapter 3 for each industry may be a realistic ideal against which degrees of departure in social welfare can be judged. Rivalrous consonance will permit us to move systematically into the interior of the rivalrous consonance polygon toward the development of a more relevant social welfare analysis.

2 NONSEPARABLE PRICING OF CHARACTERISTICS

a Extrinsic Characteristics

We approach closer to reality by assuming that the producing firm of a commodity simultaneously determines its qualities. As a first case assume that the characteristic under consideration is one like warranties, which consumers pay for independently, or advertising, which affects the firm's demand curve without becoming an object of consumer choice. In the case of market costs like advertising, of course, z becomes an amount demanded rather than supplied by the firm and in the surplus function it affects the W contours by impacting demand functions for the commodity as well as cost functions.

We will ignore competition from other automobile producers and assume that the firm is a monopolist of an isolated product in product space. Market demand for the product is

$$\begin{aligned} &1 \quad x = x(p_x, p_z) \\ &2 \quad z = z(p_x, p_z), \end{aligned} \tag{7.19}$$

with inverses assumed derivable:

$$\begin{aligned} &1 \quad p_x = p_x(x, z) \\ &2 \quad p_z = p_z(x, z). \end{aligned} \tag{7.20}$$

For simplicity of graphical presentation the forms of (7.19) and (7.20) are assumed to be linear:

$$\begin{aligned} &1 \quad x = a_1 - b_1 p_x + c_1 p_z \\ &2 \quad z = a_2 - b_2 p_z + c_2 p_x, \end{aligned} \qquad (7.21)$$

with inverses

$$\begin{aligned} &1 \quad p_x = \frac{[b_2 x + c_1 z - (a_1 b_2 + a_2 c_1)]}{c_1 c_2 - b_1 b_2} \\ &2 \quad p_z = \frac{[c_2 x + b_1 z - (a_1 c_2 + a_2 b_1)]}{c_1 c_2 - b_1 b_2} \end{aligned} \qquad (7.22)$$

Cost functions remain those of (7.2).

The isosurplus contours of the social surplus function can then be derived in the manner of section 1, the sole difference being that the demand and/or the cost function now contain interdependence terms through inclusion of other-prices in the demand functions and, perhaps, interdependence relations in the cost functions whose effect is to give rise to nonzero xz terms in the quadratic. This makes the axes of the concentric ellipses oblique to the axes of the graph, as shown in Figure 7.4.[5] The decision making of the firm now incorporates both price and quality variables under competitive or monopolistic market structures for either variable. In the general case, extrinsic characteristics are continuous in nature, so that such qualities can be provided in any quantity the consumer or firm decides explicitly or implicitly is desirable. Analysis proceeds along the lines discussed in section 1, with the exclusion of consideration of the non-rationality region, the derivation of the EW_{max} and MW_{max} loci, as shown on Figure 7.2, and the bounding of relevant regions by the joint pure competition and monopoly solutions and the two pure competition–monopoly hybrid solutions (Figure 7.3).

These boundaries will now "tilt" to reflect the interdependence of the firm's decisions in x and z. On Figure 7.5 the rationality region is magnified and the $UMTW_{max}$ vertices are displayed for this case.

Also displayed are the implied quality intensities of the product under different regulatory or industry structure regimes, assuming that the firm produces only one "brand" in each environment.

Several differences in the "framing region" $UMTW_{max}$ in Figure 7.5 from that of Figure 7.3 are evident. The "tilt" in the region on Figure 7.5 is negative, revealed most clearly in the slopes of the boundaries of the framing region. The marginal revenue terms now incorporate the impact of a change in one variable on the price of the other. For example,

$$\frac{\delta\pi}{\delta x} = \frac{\delta(p_x \cdot x + p_z \cdot z - C)}{\delta x} = \frac{\delta(p_x \cdot x)}{\delta x} + \frac{\delta p_z \cdot z}{\delta x} - C_x. \qquad (7.23)$$

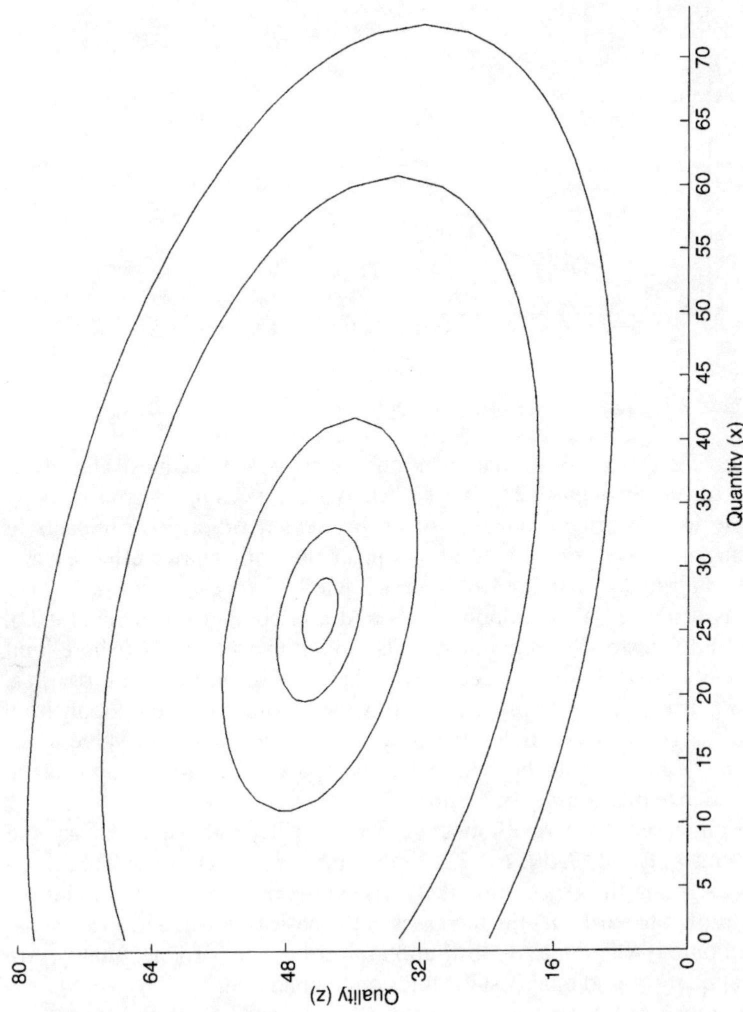

Figure 7.4 Single-firm welfare analysis

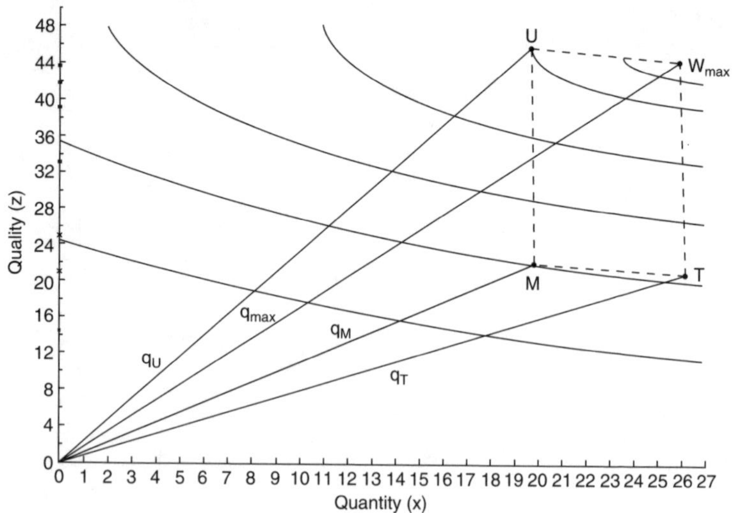

Figure 7.5 Single-firm isosurplus contours

In Figure 7.5 $dz/dx < 0$, so that as output x increases, z declines. This effect can be traced through (7.21) and (7.22). When x rises p_z rises, as does p_x. The rise in own-price reduces z, offset by weaker other-price impacts of p_x raising z. If own-price effects are stronger than other-price effects, x and z will be negatively correlated as Figures 7.4 and 7.5 reveal.

If x is produced at monopoly levels and z at competitive levels (at *U*), z rises and x, instead of remaining at its monopoly value at *M* (where joint monopoly rules) will be reduced to its value at *U* by virtue of the rise in z. Similarly, if x is produced at its competitive level and z at its monopoly level (at *T*), the rise in x will pull z down below its joint monopoly value at *M*. Thus, $UMTW_{max}$ is "on the bias" when compared with this region in the independence relationship of Figure 7.3.

The direction of the relation between x and z depends upon the signs of $\delta x/\delta p_z$ and $\delta z/\delta p_x$ in (7.19). In (7.20) other-price modifiers have been given positive signs, in the expectation that a rise in the price of quality will induce a substitution toward quantity increases in the basic product, and a rise in the price of output will induce a substitution toward greater product quality. Are product quantity and quality substitutes or complements?

The answer will depend upon the nature of the product. With a rise in the price of a given level of durability in an automobile, do consumers shift to buying larger numbers of the basic minimal-durability automobiles with shorter lives and higher maintenance cost? Or do they reduce their expenditures on all aspects of automobile ownership and buy fewer basic automobiles?

In important part, the answer depends on the significance of quality differentials in the consumer's preferences. For necessities like automobiles in a developed economy, with the effective lack of close substitutes outside the product group, one would give higher credence to the substitutability hypothesis. On the other hand, were the price of diamonds of a given carat size and color quality to rise, the opposite may be true: the functionality of ostentation outweighs that of basic decoration, and greater cost of higher quality forms may reduce the demand for diamonds in general. Consumers might shift, perhaps, to high-quality pearls or emeralds, where the cost of differentials in quality may be less.

A second consequence of the "interdependence tilt" in our framing region is that a higher quality product is produced in the purely competitive W_{max} solution than in the joint monopoly solution, unlike the result in Figure 7.3 with independent x and z. Either result is possible depending upon the relative rise or fall in x when z falls or rises when they are substitutes. It would not occur when the two variables are complements, rising and falling together.

3 THE WELFARE IMPLICATIONS OF SIMPLE OLIGOPOLY UNDER RIVALROUS CONSONANCE: A COMPARISON

It is time now to move into analyses of differentiated oligopoly under rivalrous consonance regimes and with explicit consideration of characteristics. A useful manner of doing so is to compare the welfare characteristics of various social policies under the conditions of monopoly, pure competition and mixtures of them on the one hand, as developed in this chapter, and simple oligopoly as discussed in Chapter 3.

One of the themes in Chapter 3, which is meant to be a primary conclusion of our analyses, is that with the recognition of differentiated oligopoly as the dominant market structure in developed economies, welfare economics and the norms it presents to policy makers should be revised in the interest of relevance. Social policy must also incorporate "rationalizable" expectations of firms' strategies, and the ignoring of impacts of rivals' actions does not meet such standards.

As an illustration of the quite dramatic differences the incorporation of oligopolistic implications into welfare economics can make, we will use the example of section 3 of Chapter 3, with parameters and functions defined in (3.7)–(3.9). In section 4 of that chapter we argue for consumers' surplus as a better guide to social welfare than social surplus, and in this chapter we have extended its maximization as a policy goal to permit its constraint by profit ceilings. In this analysis we will present a comparison of regions of the consumers' surplus functions of the example traced out by the bounds we have placed on consonance coefficients in duopoly, as shown in Figure 3.5, with the region defined by the combinations of monopoly and pure competition used in this chapter. Figure 3.6 reproduces the region of Figure 3.5 bounded by dotted lines and superimposes the $UMTW_{max}$ region of Figure 7.5 translated into consumer surplus space. Figure 7.6 reveals more dramatically the practical imbalance of W_{max} by comparing its contour with the contours of the consonance polygon. The values of the contours and the coordinates of the extreme points of both polygons are reproduced in Table 7.1.

The W_{max} value of *CS* is far beyond the capability of attainment under rivalrous consonance in duopoly. The Cournot point [0,0] yields the highest attainable *CS* value and it may be the ideal goal for social policy. However, in our example, it would yield a *CS* value only about 11 percent above a market structure with twin monopolies.[6]

Duopoly is much more punishing to consumers in the example even at the Cournot point when firms ignore the impacts of their policies on rivals' profits, when compared with joint pure competition, because firms do vary prices to maximize profits. The intrusion of monopolies into the two-firm

Table 7.1 Coordinates and consumer surplus values for extreme points of relevant regions

1 Monopoly and pure competition						
Symbol	*Market structure*	x_1	x_2	p_1	p_2	*Consumers' surplus*
M	Monopoly, Monopoly	109	39	\$50.41	\$55.87	\$1,643
U	Monopoly, Pure Comp.	96	71	46.62	37.84	2,431
T	Pure Comp., Monopoly	199	31	33.99	51.61	4,256
W_{max}	Pure Comp., Pure Comp.	174	59	33.48	37.35	4,058
2 Oligopoly						
Symbol	*Market structure*	x_1	x_2	p_1	p_2	*Consumers' surplus*
[1,1]	[1,1]	106	19	55.12	68.16	\$1,222
[1,0]	[1,0]	100	39	52.03	56.30	1,475
[0,1]	[0,1]	119	20	52.16	65.84	1,535
[0,0]	[0,0]	109	39	50.41	55.87	975

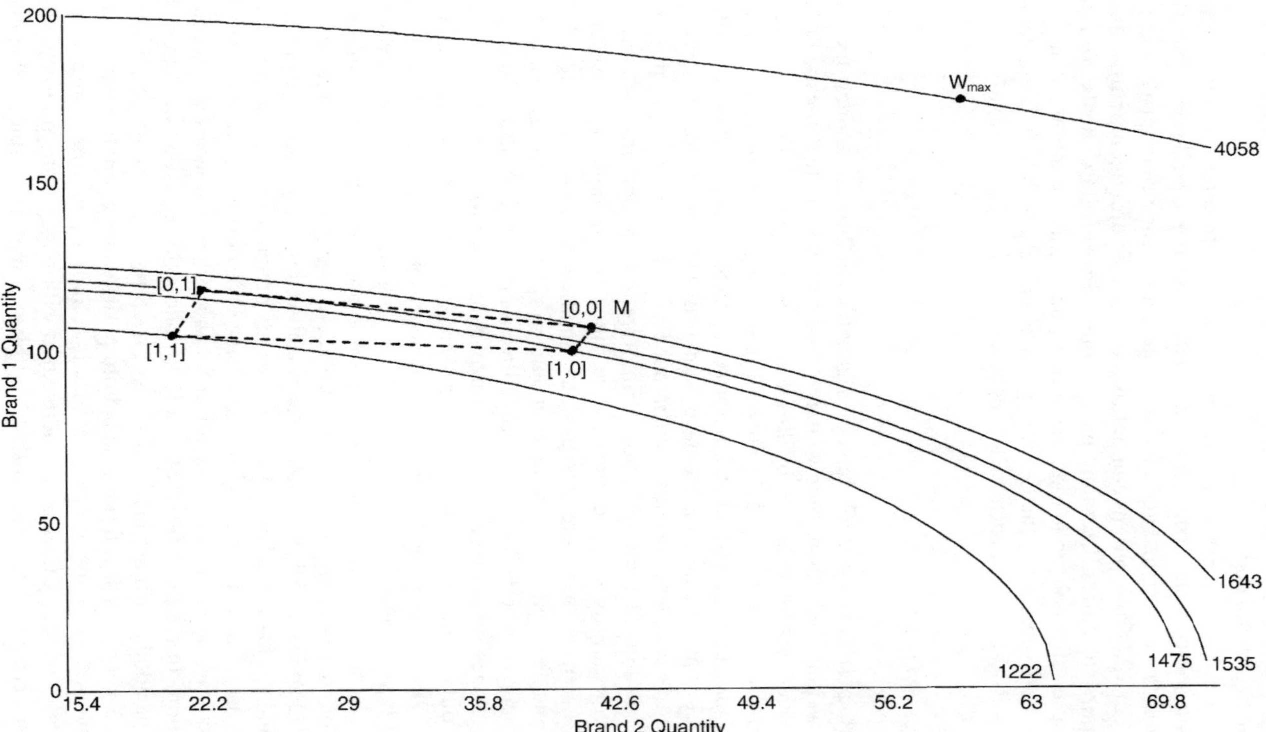

Figure 7.6 Welfare in competition and oligopoly

structure damages consumers' welfare, but does not offer the obstacle to it that tacit collusion does.

The example may exaggerate the differential welfare results from oligopoly and non-collusive structures, but it does make the central point: mature oligopolistic decision making can lead to quite different welfare profiles from those derived from purely competitive or mixed purely competitive and monopoly structures. Certainly purely competitive welfare ideals are not realistic in oligopolistic market economies, and more attention should be paid by policy makers to the Cournot point as a ideal which is itself unattainable realistically but a benchmark to approach as closely as possible.

4 A SUMMARY

This chapter develops and deploys a general equilibrium framework for social welfare analysis in purely competitive and monopoly contexts. Price and product quality decisions by different firms or the same firm have been studied with respect to welfare implications through manipulation of parameters that move output (x) and nonprice characteristics (z) between isosurplus and isoprofit contours. We have remained within monopoly and purely competitive contexts, permitting combinations of these market structures to occur, but omitting consideration of intermediate competitive structures. These comparative statics exercises were conducted by imposing constraints upon the firms that were designed to simulate regulatory policies that governments might impose in an economic world that was recognized to be and accepted as imperfect in its competitive aspects. The solutions occurred at tangencies or intersections of isosurplus and isoprofit contours which traced out certain loci of interest as constraints were altered parametrically.

These exercises provided some welcome insights into the efficiency of second-best solutions, most particularly in the relation of profit maximization and social welfare when pure competition is not achievable (or desirable, given other regulatory ends). One extremely valuable result for work in future chapters is the importance for social welfare efficiency of equating marginal profits or social welfare of various policies per unit of *marginal policy* cost of those policies. This type of cost is distinguished from marginal production cost which will be identical for the different policies under consideration. In the analysis of oligopoly to follow this equation of marginal profit per dollar of marginal policy cost for all price and nonprice policies adopted will play a significant role in both positive and normative modes. In the attempt to shape a realistic social welfare framework for market economies whose structures are permeated with oligopolistic interdependence this construct of policy cost should play an important role in shaping policies whose goals are the increase in social welfare efficiency.

In section 3 a comparison of the industry structures considered is made with a duopoly structure in rivalrous consonance, when nonprice characteristics were absent. The purpose is to demonstrate the potential differences in welfare measures that arise in oligopolistic and monopolistic structures, and the consequent need to accommodate welfare analysis to the results inherent in oligopolistic decision making.

Beyond the narrower aims of this work, the approach developed in this chapter should be fruitful in the study of firms' price and output decisions when such firms operate in wholly different product groups, apart from or in conjunction with normative implications. The framework is generalizable from 2 to n firms and affords a convenient means of simulating and studying the implications of realistic regulatory policy intervention. In the present work, however, we must now adapt the framework to the study of oligopolistic decision making in the price and nonprice area.

Part III
Theoretical Guidance to and Usage of Modeling Methodologies

8 The Isolated Firm and Consumer Benchmarking of Measurable Characteristics[1]

In this chapter we develop a framework within which characteristics choices can be incorporated with price/output decisions and solved through the use of closed and simulation analysis when cardinal measurement of characteristics is appropriate. The characteristics discussed are "core qualities" in the sense discussed in Chapters 1 and 2. In this chapter the firm is considered in isolation from rivals under the assumption that it produces a differentiated product but treats other firms' prices as parameters and anticipates no feedback from them as it makes its decisions. Such analysis would be most appropriate in dominant firm oligopoly. Interactive competition within an oligopolistic context will be dealt with in Chapter 9, but the current chapter will establish a base for that more difficult modeling.

The methodology developed in this chapter is recommended as a demonstration of means of analyzing specific firms in specific circumstances, as opposed to deriving universal theorems of price–nonprice variable behavior. We analyze two quite different parameter sets for isolated firms in this chapter whose solutions reveal significantly different relationships among the decision variables, especially as related to the strengths of direct and indirect paths of impact. As in the case of game theory, the analysis uses simulation with differing parameters to demonstrate the variety of solutions one can expect in conditions of complicated interdependencies among decision variables.

One dimension of product quality is product durability, measured by "mean time to failure" (*MTTF*). It is modeled in this chapter for two types of products: those whose breakdowns occur within an electronic regime with a negative exponential time-to-failure density function and those which wear out continuously with age and whose density function is a Weibull distribution.[2] *MTTF* reflects internal forces of destructiveness only, not environmental factors, based on a "normal" set of operating conditions.

It is assumed that the consumer's preference for durability in the sense of time-to-failure is a function of the difference between a product's *MTTF* (symbolized μ_i) and some industry standard *MTTF*, (μ), interpreted in this book as the sales-weighted average of those of firms in the industry. Further, consumers' preferences for a second dimension of quality are related to the difference between the standard deviation of a product's time-to-failure distribution and the sales-weighted average of that variable for industry products. If all consumers are risk-averse, of two products with the same *MTTF* they will individually and collectively prefer to have one with less variance (i.e., "more consistency") to one with more, and may be willing to trade off a reduction in *MTTF* for a reduction in variance in some domains. Lastly, the same methodology is employed with respect to a final quality variable in the consumer preference field, the length of warranty period. Notably, all three qualities are cardinally measurable and require no quasi-measurement scaling. Other qualities and attributes are treated implicitly as noncore characteristics and are ignored.

This approach incorporates "consumer benchmarking" as an important assumption about economic reality. In a state of imperfect information the consumer will have somewhat fuzzy notions of the average time the typical industry product experiences before breakdown as well as the average "consistency" of the industry's product as measured by average standard deviation. Warranty period lengths may be known with greater accuracy. With the passage of a relatively short period of time the consumer is assumed to gain a fairly accurate picture of these three dimensions for a specific product, and therefore for its differential advantages or disadvantages compared with the "standard" product of this type.

Section 1 analyzes the firm's decision making when the product has a "Markov memory," i.e., when the likelihood of failure at any instant of time does not change with age or usage. As noted above, this is characteristic of many types of electronic equipment or components. Further, it is assumed in this section that no warranty period is offered on the product. Section 2 complicates the model by introducing the length of the warranty period as a decision variable for the firm. Sections 3 and 4 construct analogous models for products which age and wear out, the first excluding and the second including warranties. Section 5 contains conclusions concerning the firm's decisions in the four models constructed and discusses some implications and conjectures for richer models featuring oligopolistic competition in theoretical frameworks that include rivalrous consonance which will be presented in the next chapter.[3]

Obviously, real products combine components which are subject to aging and nonaging as well as aging at different rates, so the models presented here are simplifications. Nonetheless, a good deal of realism is attainable through use of the Weibull distribution as a means of designing average quality factors over multiple components into the product.

1 UNWARRANTIED PRODUCTS WITH NONAGING CHARACTERISTICS

Assume firm i's demand function may be written in the general case as[4]

$$x = a - b_{ii}p + \Sigma_j b_{ij}p_j + m(\mu_i - \mu) - n(\mu_i - \mu)^2 - r(\sigma_i - \sigma) - s(\sigma_i - \sigma)^2 + \tau(w_i - w) - \kappa(w_i - w)^2, \tag{8.1}$$

where the subscript i has been suppressed to reduce notational clutter, except where necessary to prevent confusion, and where

μ_i = product i's *MTTF*
μ = the industry sales-weighted average *MTTF*, a parameter
σ_i = standard deviation of product i's time-to-failure probability density over time to failure
σ = the industry sales-weighted average standard deviation of time to failure density, a parameter
w_i = the length of warranty period adopted by firm i
w = the industry sales-weighted average warranty period, a parameter.

Other terms are parameters.

(8.1) formalizes benchmark concerns. The quadratic terms in the quality factors of demand reinforce the firm's motivation to move its quality characteristics closer to the benchmarks. In (8.1) the consumer is concerned wholly with the difference a given firm's quality variable is from those norms. The larger the parameters n, s and κ the more is the firm punished or the less is it rewarded for moving away from the benchmarks in *either* direction. As μ_i is reduced below μ, the amount demanded falls by increasing amounts; but, also, as μ_i rises above μ the perceived benefit is subjected to severer diminishing returns as consumers confront a product that departs from their collective experience. The symmetrical treatment of departures from benchmarks operates similarly for warranty periods and in the opposite direction for decreasing and increasing values of $(\sigma_i - \sigma)$. This "benchmark effect" will be seen to be an important factor in forcing the firm's conformance to industry standards, especially in the long run.

Finally, amounts demanded are assumed to be linearly related to own-price and other-price magnitudes. The firm's four policy decisions, therefore, are its choices of price (p), *MTTF* (μ_i), standard deviation (σ_i) and warranty period (w_i), which emerge simultaneously in a profit maximization calculation.

In the general case firm i's total cost function may be written

$$C = F + J\mu_i + K\mu_i^2 - U\sigma_i - V\sigma_i^2 + (o + j\mu_i + k\mu_i^2 - u\sigma_i - v\sigma_i^2)(x + hx^2) + q[(1 - e^{-(w/b)^c})x](gw_i + zw_i^2), \tag{8.2}$$

where

F = fixed costs
J, K, U, V = coefficients in cost factors that vary with their respective quality variables but not with output levels
j, k, u, v = coefficients in variable cost factors that are sensitive to levels of their quality variables and interact with output volume as well
o = a coefficient in a variable cost factor that varies with output but is not sensitive to levels of quality variables
q = fraction of eligible output (units failing during warranty period) actually returned for repair or replacement
g, z = parameters determining the cost of warranty repair or replacement as a function of warranty period, w_i.

By assumption, in section 1 the product is nonaging, so time to failure follows the exponential density function:

$$\Pr(t) = \left(\frac{1}{\mu_i}\right) e^{-\left(\frac{1}{\mu_i}\right)t}, \tag{8.3}$$

where t is time of product failure. Since no warranty decision occurs in this section and because $\mu_i = \sigma_i$ in an exponential function, (8.1) may be rewritten as

$$x = a - b_{ii}p + \Sigma_j b_{ij}p_j + (m-r)(\mu_i - \mu) - (n+s)(\mu_i - \mu)^2, \tag{8.4}$$

where the quality terms contain two contending forces because a rise in μ_i results in a equivalent rise in the dispersion of the density function as well. Also, for the present case (8.2) may be written

$$C = F + (J-U)\mu_i + (K-V)\mu_i^2 + (o + (j-u)\mu_i + (k-v)\mu_i^2)(x + hx^2) \tag{8.5}$$

Profits are

$$\pi = px - C. \tag{8.6}$$

Define:

1 $\alpha = \{(m-r) + 2(n+s)\mu\}$
2 $\beta = x + b_{ii}p$
3 $\omega = \{o + (j-u)\mu_i + (k-v)\mu_i^2\}$
4 $\delta = (m-r) - 2(n+s)(\mu_i - \mu)$
5 $\eta = (j-u) + 2(k-v)\mu_i$
6 $\Omega = p - \omega(1 + 2hx)$.

First-order necessary conditions for a profit maximum may be written:

$$1 \quad p = \frac{\beta + b_{ii}\omega(1+2h)\beta}{2b_{ii}(1+b_{ii}h\omega)}$$

$$2 \quad \mu_i = \frac{p\alpha - (J-U) - x(1+hx)(j-u) - \delta\omega(1+2hx)}{2[(n+s)p + x(1+hx)(k-v) + (K-V)]} \qquad (8.7)$$

In the simulations, using a set of base case parameters reproduced in Table 8.1, (8.7.1) was solved for p with an initial estimate of μ_i, these two values were substituted in (8.4) to obtain an estimate of x, and the three values were substituted into the righthand side of (8.7.2) to get a new value of μ_i. This diagonalization procedure was iterated until convergence of both p and μ_i occurred.[5]

The elements in the Hessian matrix may be written:[6]

$$1 \quad A_{11} = -2b_{ii}(1+b_{ii}h\omega)$$

$$2 \quad A_{12} = \delta(1+2b_{ii}h\omega) + b_{ii}(1+2hx)\eta \qquad (8.8)$$

$$3 \quad A_{22} = 2[h\delta^2\omega + \Omega(n+s) + (K-V) + x(1+hx)(k-v)] - \eta\delta(1+2hx).$$

Table 8.1 Base case parameters – isolated firm, exponential density function, without warranty period

	1 Demand function parameters	
$a = 5{,}000$		$b_{1,1} = 30$
$p_2 = 450$		$b_{1,2} = 5$
$p_3 = 500$		$b_{1,3} = 6$
$p_4 = 550$		$b_{1,4} = 7$
$p_5 = 600$		$b_{1,5} = 8$
$m = 250$		$n = 10$
$r = 50$		$s = 5$
	$\mu = 3.5$	
	2 Cost function parameters	
$F = 600{,}000$		$J = 1{,}750$
$U = 500$		$K = 80$
$V = 10$		$o = 60$
$j = 10$		$u = 7$
$k = 0.06$		$v = 0.03$
	$h = 0.00015$	

For illustrative purposes, I have reproduced the exponential density function for the base case in Figure 8.1 and the cumulative density function in Figure 8.2.

The optimal *MTTF* determined by (8.7) was 3.608 years, optimal p was \$418.85, and $x = 6{,}356$. In (8.7) the marginal revenue of each policy equals its marginal cost. In Figure 8.3 the base case "policy reaction functions" are illustrated, graphing the optimal values for each given the values of the other. The function $p = g(\mu_i)$ intersects $\mu_i = f(p)$ from above to yield a stable optimal pair $[p°, \mu_i°]$.

From (8.7) we may write

$$\begin{aligned} &1 \quad p = \omega(1+2hx) + \frac{x}{b_{ii}} \\ &2 \quad p = \omega(1+2hx) + \frac{[(J-U)+2(K-V)\mu_i + x(1+hx)\eta]}{\delta}, \end{aligned} \tag{8.9}$$

which have interesting implications, imposing the conditions that optimal price (marginal gross revenue of the policy) be equated to the sum of (1) the *marginal production costs* of the policy-linked output and (2) the *marginal cost per marginal unit* of the output of the policy. We may distinguish these as the *indirect* and *direct* policy costs respectively. In the case of price policy the marginal policy cost is the loss a reduction in price imposes on prior sales and for quality policy it is the marginal policy costs of a change in *MTTF*. (8.9) impose the condition that at the profit optimum the direct marginal policy costs must be equated. Note that Ω is gross revenue minus the indirect marginal production costs of the policies, which is common to all policies at the margin, and rewrite system (8.9) as

$$\begin{aligned} &1 \quad \Omega = \frac{x}{b_{ii}} \\ &2 \quad \Omega = \frac{(J-U)+2(K-V)\mu_j + x(1+hx)\eta}{\delta}. \end{aligned} \tag{8.10}$$

Consider the definition of price elasticity of demand: the numerator (pdx) is the "gross" marginal revenue from a decrease in price and the denominator (xdp) is the "marginal policy cost" of such action by virtue of the "loss" of revenue on prior sales.

$$\varepsilon = \frac{pdx}{xdp},$$

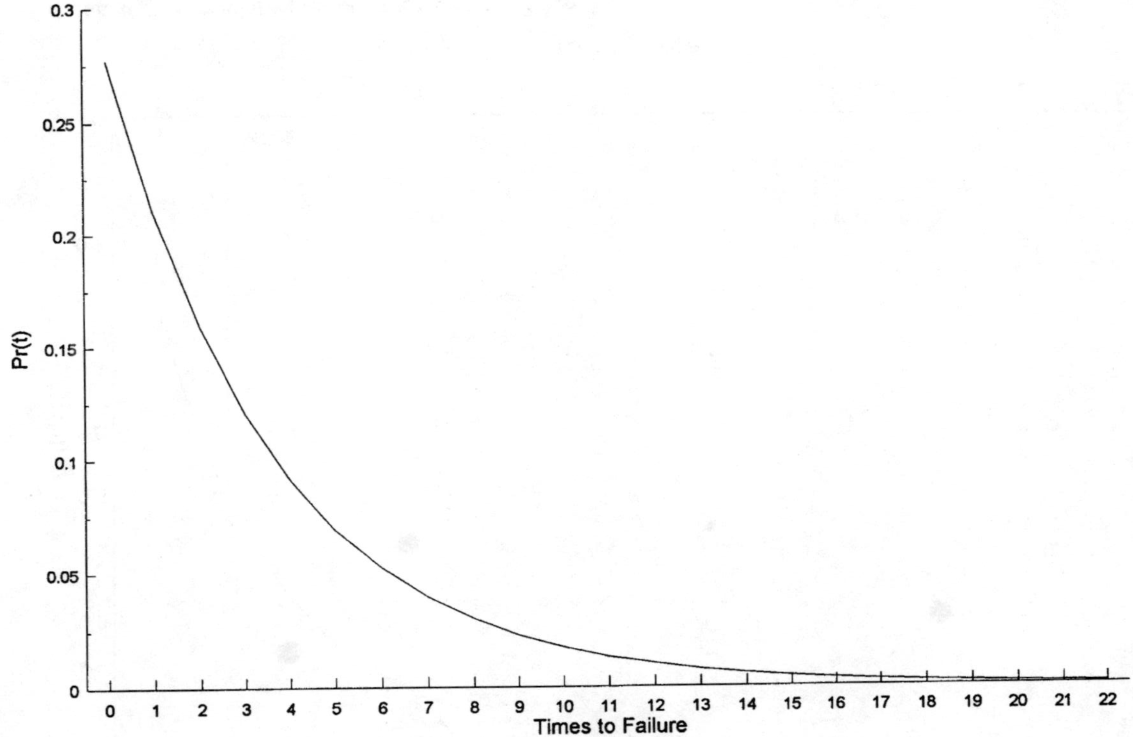

Figure 8.1 Exponential distribution, mean = 3.608

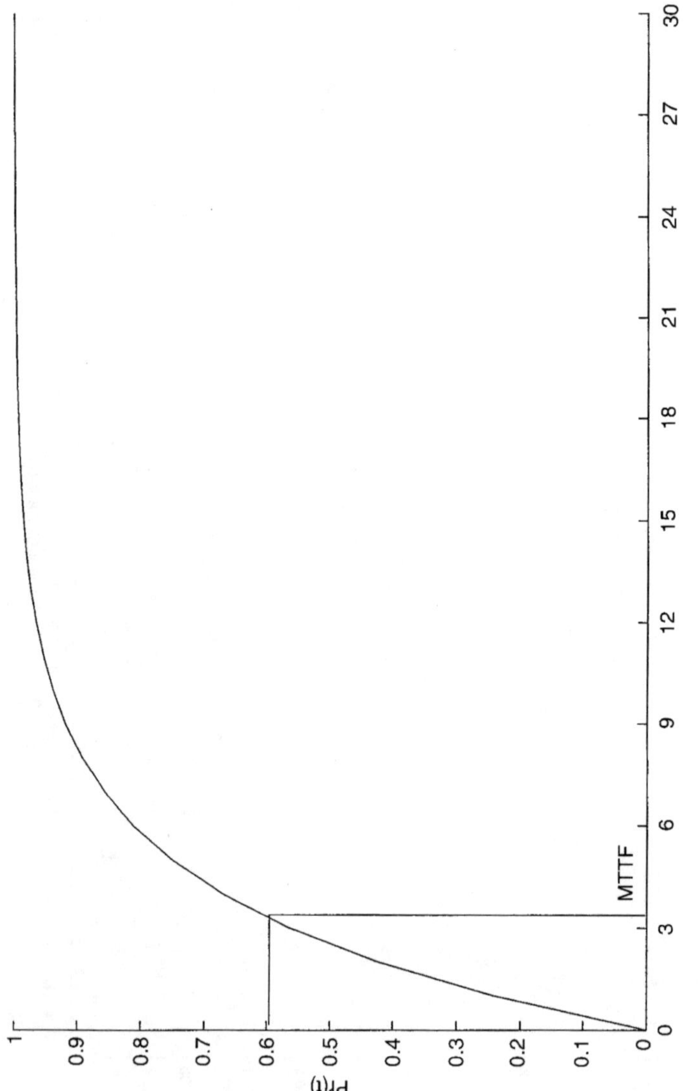

Figure 8.2 Cumulative exponential, mean = 3.608

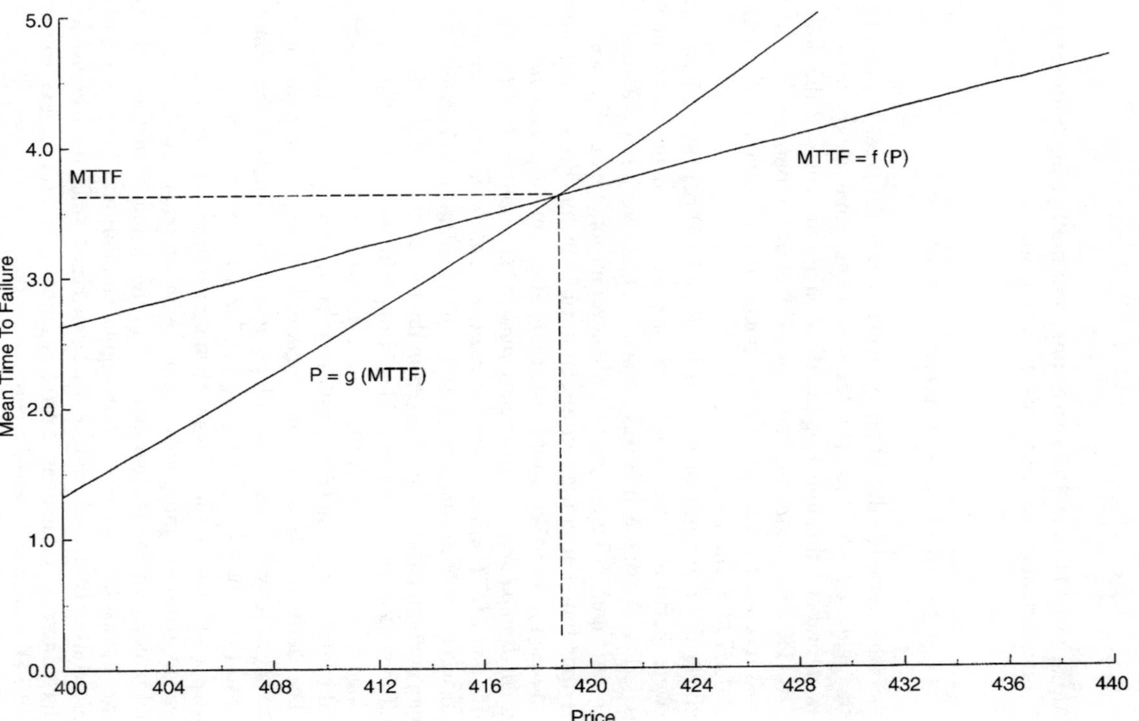

Figure 8.3 Policy reaction functions, base case

or, for a linear demand function,

$$\varepsilon = p \cdot \frac{b_{11}}{x}.$$

Substituting (8.10.1) in (8.10.2), inverting, and multiplying both sides by p we obtain a variant of the Dorfman–Steiner theorem:[7]

$$-\varepsilon = \frac{\delta p}{(J-U)+2(K-V)\mu_i + x(1+hx)\eta}, \tag{8.11}$$

where $-\varepsilon$ is the absolute value of the price elasticity of demand. The numerator on the righthand side of (8.11) is the value of marginal sales generated by a rise in μ_i and the denominator the direct marginal costs of the policy. Hence, (8.11) simply states the requirement that at the optimum the marginal gross revenue per unit of marginal policy cost be equal for all policies (price and *MTTF* in this instance).

Parameter displacements of +100 percent and –50 percent of base case values were performed and for the most part yielded unexceptionable responses. The Hessian matrix was negative definite for all of the displacements. From Figure 8.3 it is clear that whenever any parameter displacement moves either function in a given direction or both functions in the same direction p and μ_i will also move in the same direction. *In general, therefore, to the extent demand and cost parameters impel the functions in the same direction, price and MTTF will be complementary, not substitutional, although, of course, σ_i will move identically with μ_i with opposite quality implications.*

Among demand parameters, changes in the intercept a and the rival-sales sum will move the two policy variables in opposite directions. This can be enlightened by considering only the *direct* impacts of changes in a on p and μ_i obtained by differentiating (8.9.1) with respect to p and (8.9.2) with respect to μ_i. The derivative $\delta p/\delta a_i$ is unambiguously positive and $\delta u_i/\delta a_i$ is unambiguously negative.[8] A rise in a, holding μ_i constant, will shift the demand function to the right making it more price inelastic. At the former equilibrium price, x will have to rise along with marginal production cost, requiring p to rise to reequate marginal revenue with marginal production *plus* marginal policy cost. With a parallel shift in the demand function, x at the higher price must have risen over the original equilibrium x. As noted, had p remained constant, μ_i would have moved downward, since the increase in a would have increased x, increased production costs, and reduced Ω, so that, from (8.10.2), μ_i would have to decrease.

Now let us consider the interdependence among the variables. When p rises with the parallel shift in the demand curve, it will do so in greater degree than the rise in costs incumbent to the rise in x. Therefore, Ω will rise, and μ_i will have to increase its marginal policy cost to reequate it with Ω. This will cause μ_i to rise somewhat from its initial fall, which in turn will lead to the demand function shifting outward in parallel fashion, leading to a further rise in p from its initial move. These waves of interdependence will continue until the final solution $[p,\mu_i]$ is reached, with the possibility that the secondary waves will be sufficiently strong to reverse the immediate direct effects of the parameter change. They did not do so in the displacements of the present example.

On the cost side consider increases in $(j-u)$ or $(k-v)$. Following the same procedure as that outlined above, we conclude that $p = g(\mu_i)$ shifts rightward and $\mu_i = f(p)$ downward, to lower the optimum μ_i and raise optimum p. If $(J-U)$ or $(K-V)$ rise, on the other hand, $p = g(\mu_i)$ is initially unaffected but $\mu_i = f(p)$ shifts down, shifting $p = g(\mu_i)$ down and setting off reinforcing waves of diminishing strength so that both μ_i and p fall in the new equilibrium.

Interestingly, therefore, policies initiated by the firm to shift its demand function to the right and to decrease its elasticity, such as advertising or other marketing effort, can reduce quality when there exist costs that vary with both quality levels and output quantities. The phenomenon does not arise because of marginal costs of production that rise with output levels, nor because of rising marginal costs in function of quality levels only. Its source is in the joint interaction of quality and output levels. The complicated patterns of interdependence among the policy variables discussed above recurs in all of the models and base cases in the chapter.

a Some Welfare Considerations

Consumers' surplus (CS) for the model of the single firm with no rival interaction is

$$CS = \frac{0.5x^2}{b_{ii}}, \tag{8.12}$$

and profits, $\pi = px - C$, so social welfare becomes

$$W = \frac{0.5x^2}{b_{ii}} + p \cdot x - C. \tag{8.13}$$

Contours of W are graphed in $\mu_i \times p$ decision space on Figure 8.4, consisting of those portions of the ellipses that yield nonnegative profits and are therefore feasible solutions in a market economy. The line labeled $\pi = 0$ is the locus of zero profit solutions for parameterized values of W, and is also, of course, the locus of maximum CS for such constrained W-contours.

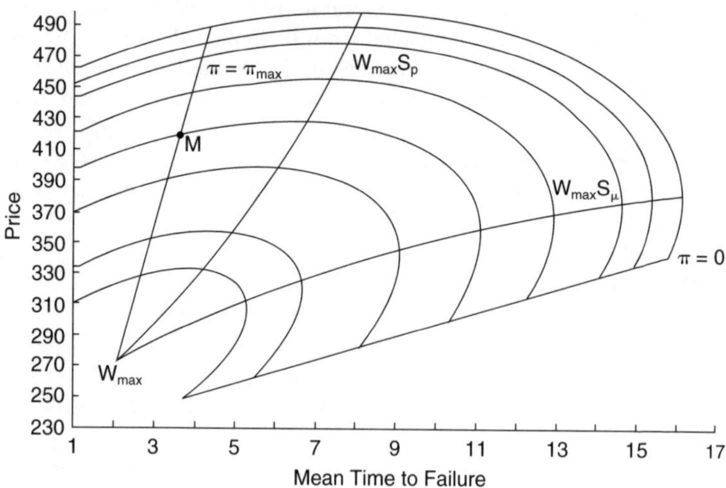

Figure 8.4 Welfare contours, exponential case

The point contour W_{max} is the maximum social welfare solution $[\mu_i, p]$ where price is equated to the marginal *social* costs of output and *MTTF*. By this term is designated those costs that absorb social resources to produce goods and characteristics. From (8.9) and (8.10) note that the marginal policy cost for μ_i involves solely those costs that arise from the use of resources to produce improvements in *MTTF*. On the other hand, the marginal policy cost for price, x/b_{ii}, arises from the "antisocial" exercise of market power only. In maximizing *profits* the firm includes it as a cost for self-serving reasons, reducing output below socially desirable levels. Thus, in *welfare* maximization, marginal policy cost for p is excluded from cost as a monopoly rent. The locus of solutions that maximize profits for given W-contours, with the *maximum maximorum* occurring at M, is labeled $\pi = \pi_{max}$.

The slope of a W-contour at any point is

$$\frac{dp}{d\mu_i} = \frac{\frac{x\delta}{b_{ii}} + \delta[(p - \omega(1+2hx)) - ((J-U) + 2(K-V)\mu_i + x\eta(1+2hx))]}{-b_{ii}(p - \omega(1+2hx))},$$

$$= \frac{\frac{x\delta}{b_{ii}} + \delta\left[\Omega - \frac{MC_{\mu_i}}{\delta}\right]}{-b_{ii}\Omega} \tag{8.14}$$

which, from (8.9), (8.10) and (8.13) is simply the ratio of the marginal contribution to consumers' surplus and profits of small changes in price and μ_i.

Policy makers may aim to achieve a given p/μ_i, which achieves maximum social welfare at an intersection of a ray from the origin with the contour closest to W_{max} that has a segment between the π_{max} and $\pi = 0$ loci, or some other defined region. If policy is to set a maximum price, the policy maker will desire to attain a tangency of a horizontal line at the specified price with a contour, indicating that μ_i has reached a welfare maximizing value for *MTTF* at that price. At this price, of course, the firm will desire to reach the intersection of the horizontal line at the selected p with its maximum profit line $\pi = \pi_{max}$ so that some disincentive to attaining it must be imposed. The locus of welfare maximizing μ_i for parameterized p is drawn on Figure 8.4 as the line $W_{max}S_{\mu}$. On the other hand, if the policy is to set quality levels μ_i, the welfare maximizing price will be achieved at tangencies of vertical lines at the designated μ_i levels with welfare contours. The locus of such points is depicted by the line $W_{max}S_p$. The firm would at this fixed level of *MTTF* attempt to move to the intersection of the relevant vertical line with $\pi = \pi_{max}$ or closer to that line and again must be constrained.

2 WARRANTIED PRODUCTS WITH NONAGING CHARACTERISTICS

Warranties are introduced into the quality decision space by altering the demand and cost functions appropriately. From (8.1) for non-aging products

$$x = a - b_{ii}p + \Sigma_j b_{ij}p_j + (m-r)(\mu_i - \mu) - (n+s)(\mu_i - \mu)^2 + T(W_i - w) \\ -\kappa(w_i - w)^2 \qquad (8.15)$$

In like fashion the cost function is altered from (8.2) to

$$C = F + (J-U)\mu_i + (K-V)\mu_i^2 + (o + (j-u)\mu_i + (k-v)\mu_i^2)(x + hx^2) \\ +q\left[\left(1 - e^{\frac{-w_i}{\mu_i}}\right)x\right](gw_i + zw_i^2). \qquad (8.16)$$

From (8.6) the first-order maximum conditions may be written

$$1 \quad p = \frac{\beta + b_{ii}(\omega(1+2h\beta) + \lambda)}{2b_{ii}(1 + b_{ii}h\omega)}$$

$$2 \quad \mu_i = \frac{(p - (\lambda + \omega(1+2hx)))\alpha - (J-U) - \eta(x + hx^2) + q(gw_i + zw_i^2)x\left(\frac{w_i}{\mu_i^2}\right)e^{\frac{-w_i}{\mu_i}}}{2((n+s)(p - \lambda - \omega(1+2hx)) + (K-V))} \qquad (8.17)$$

$$3\quad w_i = \frac{(T+2\kappa w)(p-\omega(1+2hx)-\lambda) - qx\left(\left(1-e^{\frac{-w_i}{\mu_i}}\right)g + \left(\frac{zw_i^2}{\mu_i}\right)e^{\frac{-w_i}{\mu_i}}\right)}{2\kappa(p-\omega(1+2hx)-\lambda)+qx\left(2z\left(1-e^{\frac{-w_i}{\mu_i}}\right)+\frac{g}{\mu_i}e^{\frac{-w_i}{\mu_i}}\right)}$$

where

$$\lambda = q\left(1-e^{\frac{-w_i}{\mu_i}}\right)(gw_i + zw_i^2).$$

Unfortunately the warranty cost term has the capability of destroying the concavity of the profit function for realistic parameters, so system (8.17) is best solved by parameterizing w_i and allowing it to rise from zero until π attains a maximum. By using finer and finer grids for incremental values of w_i a close approximation to the profit maximum is achieved.

(8.17) can be rewritten as in (8.9) to equal the sum of a common direct marginal production cost of induced output and a marginal policy cost per unit of output. By substituting to eliminate this Ω-term we derive the *mutatis mutandis* policy reaction functions for μ_i and w_i, where price is adjusting to optimum levels as μ_i and w_i change:

$$1\quad \mu_i = \frac{\alpha - \frac{b_{ii}}{x}(J-U) - b_{ii}\varepsilon(1+hx) + b_{ii}q(gw_i + zw_i^2)\left(\frac{w_i}{\mu_i^2}\right)e^{\frac{-w_i}{\mu_i}}}{2\left((n+s)+\frac{b_{ii}}{x}(K-V)\right)} \tag{8.18}$$

$$2\quad w_i = \frac{T+2\kappa w - qb_{ii}\left(g\left((1-e^{\frac{-w_i}{\mu_i}}\right)+\frac{zw_i^2}{\mu_i}e^{\frac{-w_i}{\mu_i}}\right)}{2\kappa + qb_{ii}\left(2z\left(1-e^{\frac{-w_i}{\mu_i}}\right)+\left(\frac{g}{\mu_i}\right)e^{\frac{-w_i}{\mu_i}}\right)}.$$

These reactions functions were derived for a base case to whose parameters in Table 8.1 are added the warranty-relevant parameters in Table 8.2.

They are graphed in Figure 8.5, and optimal price is graphed as the intersection of (8.18.1) and a 45° line in Figure 8.6. The seeming multiple intersections of the functions in Figure 8.5 are a distortion because of the discrete nature of the solution values. The base case solution values are found in row 1 of Table 8.4.

Table 8.2 Base case parameters – isolated firm, exponential density function, with warranty period, additional parameters to those in Table 8.1

	1 Demand function parameters	
$T = 400$	$w = 0.2$ $\kappa = 10$	$\eta = 10$
	2 Cost function parameters	
$g = 200$	$z = 5$	$q = 0.95$

Table 8.3 Signs of partial derivatives of the first-order conditions

	With respect to:		
Sign of the derivative of:	p	μ_i	w_i
p	*****	+	+
μ_i	+	*****	–
w_i	+	–	*****

The reaction functions of (8.18) and Figure 8.5 are *mutatis mutandis* functions because p adjusts to the values of μ_i and w_i as they vary. This is important because the partial derivatives of (8.17), which permit only one policy variable to vary as others are treated as parameters, have the signs shown in Table 8.3.

While these results are dependent upon the specific parameters of the base case, I believe they are consistent with feasible values of the parameters. Table 8.3 reveals that while the *mutatis mutandis* reaction functions of Figure 8.5 are positively sloped, the *ceteris paribus* reactions of μ_i and w_i are negatively sloped. Hence it is the general equilibrium impact of p upon μ_i and w_i that dictates the positive slopes of the functions in Figure 8.5, overcoming the direct negative relations of μ_i and w_i.

Strategic parameters were increased and decreased by 100 and 50 percent respectively, with the results listed in Table 8.4. Several aspects of the simulation results are of interest. For warranty costs that are felt to be realistic for a

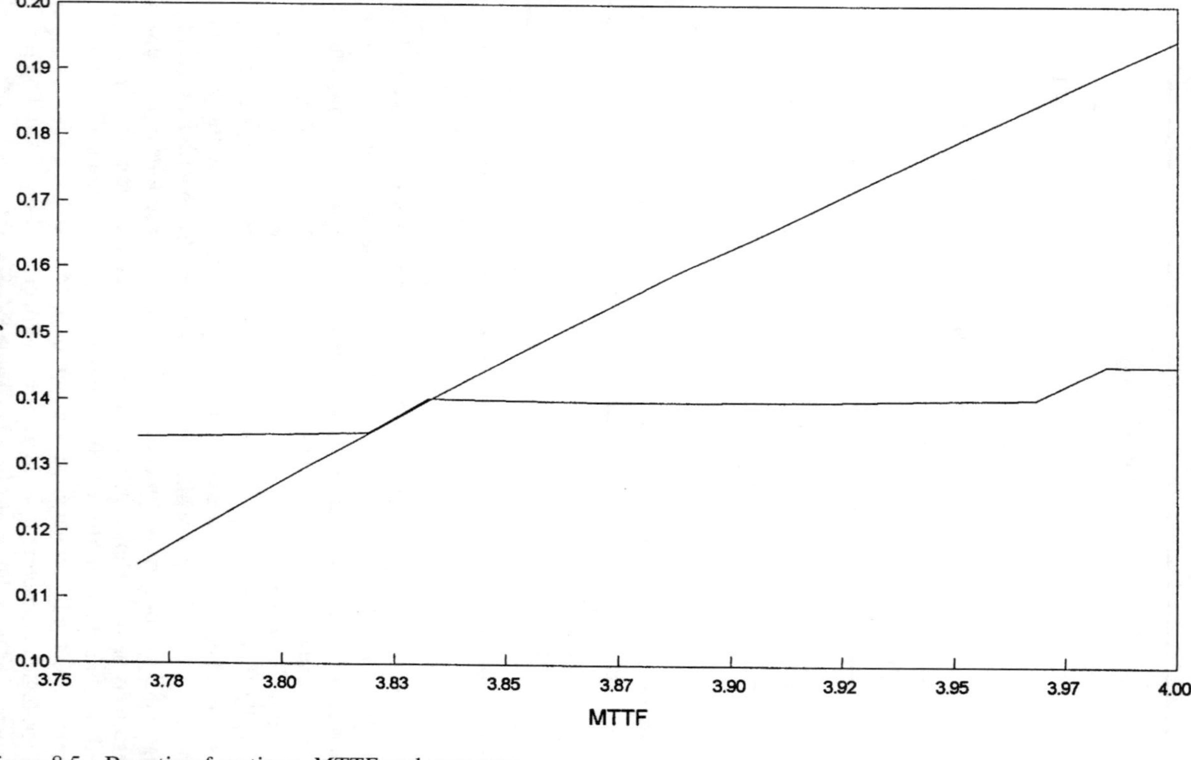

Figure 8.5 Reaction functions, *MTTF* and warranty

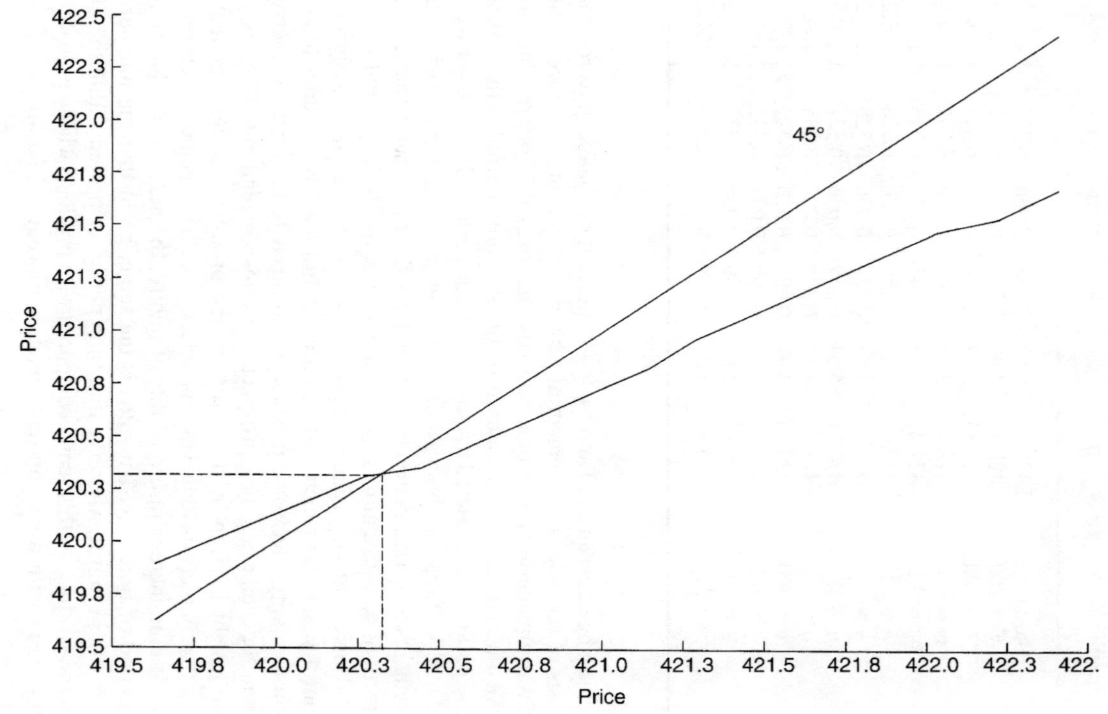

Figure 8.6 Profit-maximizing price

Table 8.4 Parameteric displacements of base case for the isolated firm, exponential function, warranties case

Run	*Parameter changed*	p	μ_i	w_i	w_i/μ_i	x	π
0	Base Case	\$420.36	3.83	0.138	0.036	6,328	\$1,161,261
1	$T = 800$	428.93	4.46	0.326	0.073	6,312	1,163,387
2	$T = 200$	418.85	3.67	0.060	0.016	6,341	1,165,444
3	$w = 0.4$	418.86	3.85	0.140	0.036	6,297	1,144,290
4	$w = 0.1$	421.21	3.83	0.141	0.037	6,343	1,169,712
5	$\kappa = 20$	420.42	3.83	0.139	0.036	6,328	1,161,252
6	$\kappa = 5$	420.39	3.83	0.138	0.036	6,328	1,161,265
7	$q = 1$	420.61	3.84	0.139	0.036	6,327	1,160,941
8	$q = 0.4$	424.84	4.11	0.378	0.092	6,335	1,169,709
9	$g = 400$	420.16	3.84	0.099	0.026	6,322	1,157,731
10	$g = 100$	423.76	4.05	0.299	0.074	6,332	1,167,230
11	$z = 10$	420.43	3.83	0.139	0.036	6,328	1,161,238
12	$z = 2.5$	420.42	3.83	0.139	0.036	6,328	1,161,270

product selling between \$420 and \$430 – 95 percent of eligible units returned with costs of repair or replacement at \$200 per output unit per incremental unit of warranty period plus a quadratic cost that rises at \$5 per returned unit and which accelerates as the square of the warranty period – the optimal warranty period was restricted to quite short time periods. In the base case for example, $w_i = 0.138$, or about 50 days when w_i is measured in years. In the displacements w_i varied between 0.060 and 0.378, or between about 1.6 and 9.2 percent of μ_i, with a more representative range of 3.6–3.7 percent.

This is somewhat surprising for a product whose average life is designed to be about 4 years and which suffers no wear and tear. But it does tend to conform to reality: electronic products seem rarely to be warranted beyond 3–12 months, even when their prospective lifetimes extend to 8–10 years.

Some insight is given by the nature of the product and the exponential function that depicts its longevity characteristics. Since such products reveal a constant time increment probability of failure, the number of failures in a given period of time (say, 1 month) is the same, given that the number of survivors will permit it, wherever that time period is located within the lifetime of the product. In this sense, compared with products whose probability of failure rises with wear and tear, electronic products' failures are front-loaded.

This fact is brought out dramatically in Table 8.5 where 20 representative combinations of w_i and μ_i from Table 8.4 are analyzed for expected proportions of eligible returns with exponential functions on the one hand

and Weibull functions on the other. Hypothetical values for w_i are also compared for both types of longevity conditions. Weibull functions become increasingly peaked as c, a shape parameter, rises, and I have selected values of 1 (which yields the exponential function), 3 and 6 to illustrate its impact upon expected eligible warranty returns. It is a useful guide to the shapes obtained by the Weibull to remember that it approximates the normal density function when $c \approx 3.34$.

Note that for relatively small warranty periods expected failures for the exponential distribution are quite large relative to those for Weibull distributions depicting longevity for aging products. Only when c grows substantially and the warranty period is expanded, frequently to exceed μ_i, do the Weibull distributions' expected eligibles surpass those of the exponential.

Table 8.5 Comparison of eligible warranty returns for exponential and Weibull functions at selected lengths of warranty periods

		Expected proportion of eligible output for c=:		
μ_i	w_i	*1*	*3*	*6*
3.67	0.060	0.018	0	0
	2.0	0.420	0.109	0.603
	4.0	0.664	0.603	0.661
	5.0	0.743	0.835	0.984
3.83	0.138	0.035	0	0
	2.0	0.407	0.097	0.013
	4.0	0.648	0.556	0.568
	5.0	0.729	0.795	1.000
3.84	0.099	0.025	0	0
	2.0	0.406	0.096	0.013
	4.0	0.647	0.553	0.562
	5.0	0.728	0.793	0.957
4.11	0.378	0.088	0.001	0
	2.0	0.385	0.079	0.009
	4.0	0.622	0.482	0.423
	5.0	0.704	0.723	0.877
4.46	0.326	0.070	0	0
	2.0	0.361	0.062	0.005
	4.0	0.592	0.402	0.286
	5.0	0.674	0.634	0.723

A second characteristic of the sensitivity results in Table 8.4 is the positive relation between optimal μ_i and w_i. When μ_i rises, it pays the firm to raise w_i and vice versa. This holds for all but one run in Table 8.4 in the weaker sense that μ_i rises with w_i or remains unchanged, or vice versa. The exception occurs when direct warranty costs rise dramatically. I have already indicated that this result is generated in almost all cases by the indirect effects of p. This is behind the flat reaction of w_i to changes in μ_i compared with its companion reaction function. Both functions appear near-linear in Figure 8.5 for this base case, although neither is in general and both can be badly behaved in regions.[9] Hence, in a nonstrict sense, it is w_i that does "most" of the determining of the optimum, in that Table 8.4 demonstrates that its unresponsiveness keeps movements of w_i from the base case within narrow bounds of the base case optimum. A great deal of this "stickiness" is generated by the contradictory influences of changes in p and μ_i upon w_i.

3 UNWARRANTIED PRODUCTS WITH AGING CHARACTERISTICS

a The Weibull Density Function

Suppose now the product is mechanical in nature and therefore suffers wear and tear in usage and in aging. The *MTTF* of such goods follows the Weibull density function:

$$\Pr(t) = \left[\frac{ct^{c-1}}{b^c}\right] e^{-\left(\frac{t}{b}\right)^c}, \qquad t\varepsilon[0,\infty] \tag{8.19}$$

where b is a parameter specifying the scale of measurement on the fractile axis, and c is a parameter controlling the shape of the distribution, notably the "peakedness" of the function. The exponential term is the probability that the unit will survive to time t (the *survival* function). The bracketed term is the probability density that, having survived, the product will fail in the interval $t + dt$ (the *hazard* function) . The former term declines monotonically and the latter rises monotonically for $c > 1$. The function rises to the mode, where the rates of change of the counteracting probabilities cancel to zero, after which the negative survival term dominates and Pr(t) falls. For a base case to be introduced in Table 8.6 the hazard and survival functions are graphed in Figure 8.7.

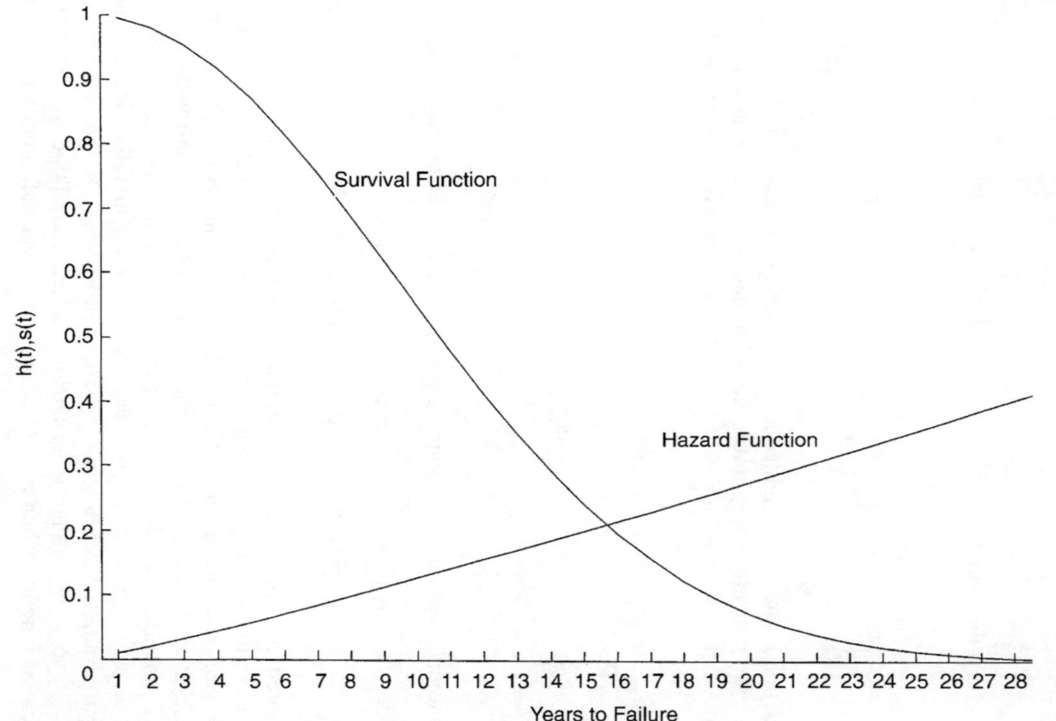

Figure 8.7 Base Case hazard and survival function

The expected value or mean of the density function is

$$\mu_i = b\Gamma\left(\frac{c+1}{c}\right), \tag{8.20}$$

where $\Gamma(\cdot)$ is the gamma function. The standard deviation is

$$\sigma_i = b\sqrt{\left[\Gamma\left\{\frac{(c+2)}{c}\right\} - \left(\Gamma\left\{\frac{(c+1)}{c}\right\}\right)^2\right]}. \tag{8.21}$$

I will define μ and σ as weighted industry averages as was done in section 1 above, but indicate once more the legitimacy of use of any industry standard. Let $z_1 = (c + 1)/c$ and $z_2 = (c + 2)/c$, and rewrite terms in (8.20) and (8.21):

$$1 \; = \Gamma\left[\frac{(c+1)}{c}\right] = \Gamma(z_1) \tag{8.22}$$

$$2 \; = \Gamma\left[\frac{(c+2)}{c}\right] = \Gamma(z_2).$$

A polynomial approximation to these gamma functions is the following:[10]

$$\Gamma(z) = \{z + 0.5772157z^2 - 0.6558781z^3 - 0.0420026z^4 + 0.1665386z^5 - 0.0421977z^6 - 0.0096219z^7\}^{-1}. \tag{8.23}$$

As noted in section 1, the exponential function is the Weibull function for $c = 1$. For products subject to aging, $c > 1$. Thus, from (8.20) the argument for the gamma function in (8.22.1) will lie in the interval]1,2[, and that for (8.22.2) in the interval]1,3[. Since $\Gamma(1) = \Gamma(2) = 1$, and because the gamma function over the interval reaches a minimum of about 0.886 at 1.46, the mean, μ_i, will fall between $0.886b$ and b in value. Hence that position parameter can be closely associated with μ_i. On the other hand, $\Gamma(3) = 2$, so σ_i will range from $0b$ for c indefinitely large to b (for the exponential function when $c = 1$). Moreover, σ_i will fall monotonically as c rises.[11]

The cost function (8.2) is now interpreted to define F, the fixed cost, and o, a variable cost term, as including the cost of producing products with a very small time-to-failure density function variance. One change made in the cost function is to change the quadratic terms involving V and v to positive rather than negative terms. That is, the policy costs of σ_i fall as σ_i rises but by *decreasing* rather than increasing amounts. It was felt that when σ_i was freed to attain larger values that this would be a more accurate characterization of the cost function within the relevant bracket of values that were likely. This may or may not be empirically correct, but for the parameters of the base case solutions are little affected by the change.

Note that the only innovation arising from the Weibull density is the introduction of a σ_i which is not identical to μ_i when $c > 1$. Define:

$$1 \quad \omega^* = o + j\mu_i + k\mu_i^2 - u\sigma_i + v\sigma_i^2 \qquad (8.24)$$

$$2 \quad \Omega^* = p - \omega^*(1 + 2hx).$$

Then, first-order maximization-of-profit conditions are

$$1 \quad p = \frac{\beta + b_{ii}\omega^*(1 + 2h\beta)}{2b_{ii}(1 + hb_{ii}\omega^*)} \qquad (8.25)$$

$$2 \quad \mu_i = \frac{\Omega^*(m + 2n\mu) - J - jx(1 + hx)}{2(n\Omega^* + K + kx(1 + hx))}$$

$$3 \quad \sigma_i = \frac{-\Omega^*(r - 2s\sigma) + U + ux(1 + hx)}{2(s\Omega^* + V + vx(1 + hx))},$$

whose similarity of structure with those in (8.7) is apparent. The *ceteris paribus* reaction functions for μ_i and σ_i, which assume that p is fixed at its optimal value, are graphed in Figure 8.8. Conditions (8.25) may be rewritten:

$$1 \quad \Omega^* = \frac{x}{b_{ii}} \qquad (8.26)$$

$$2 \quad \Omega^* = \frac{2(K + kx(1 + hx))\mu_i + (J + jx(1 + hx))}{m - 2n(\mu_i - \mu)}$$

$$3 \quad \Omega^* = \frac{-2(V + vx(1 + hx))\sigma_i + (U + ux(1 + hx))}{r + 2s(\sigma_i - \sigma))},$$

whose structure repeats that discerned in system (8.10) for the analysis of section 1 in terms of indirect product and direct policy specific marginal costs. And, as in that prior analysis, note that from (8.26) a necessary condition for optimal decisions is that the marginal *direct* costs of each strategy be equalized.

The *mutatis mutandis* policy reaction functions for μ_i and σ_i are derivable by substituting from (8.26.1) into (8.26.2) and (8.26.3):

$$1\quad \mu_i = \frac{m + 2n\mu - \frac{b_{ii}}{x}(J + jx(1 + hx))}{2\left(n + \frac{b_{ii}}{x}(K + kx(1 + hx))\right)} \qquad (8.27)$$

$$2\quad \sigma_i = \frac{r - 2s\sigma - \frac{b_{ii}}{x}(U + ux(1 + hx))}{2\left(s + \frac{b_{ii}}{x}(V + vx(1 + hx))\right)}.$$

Figure 8.9 depicts the base case optimal μ_i and σ_i as the intersection of the *mutatis mutandis* functions of (8.27). They should be compared with the *ceteris paribus* functions of Figure 8.8, which are determined at a price fixed at its Table 8.6 base case optimal value.

The solution values for the base case are listed in Table 8.7.

Table 8.6 Base case parameters – isolated firm, Weibull density function, without warranty period

	1 Demand function parameters	
$a = 90{,}000$		$b_{1,1} = 20$
$p_2 = 20$		$b_{1,2} = 5$
$p_3 = 25$		$b_{1,3} = 6$
$p_4 = 30$		$b_{1,4} = 7$
$p_5 = 35$		$b_{1,5} = 8$
$m = 500$		$n = 30$
$r = 700$		$s = 200$
$\mu = 9$		$\sigma = 3.5$
	2 Cost function parameters	
$F = 35{,}000$		$J = 1{,}750$
$U = 500$		$K = 80$
$V = 10$		$o = 110$
$j = 1$		$u = 20$
$k = 0.06$		$v = 0.9$
	$h = 0.00015$	

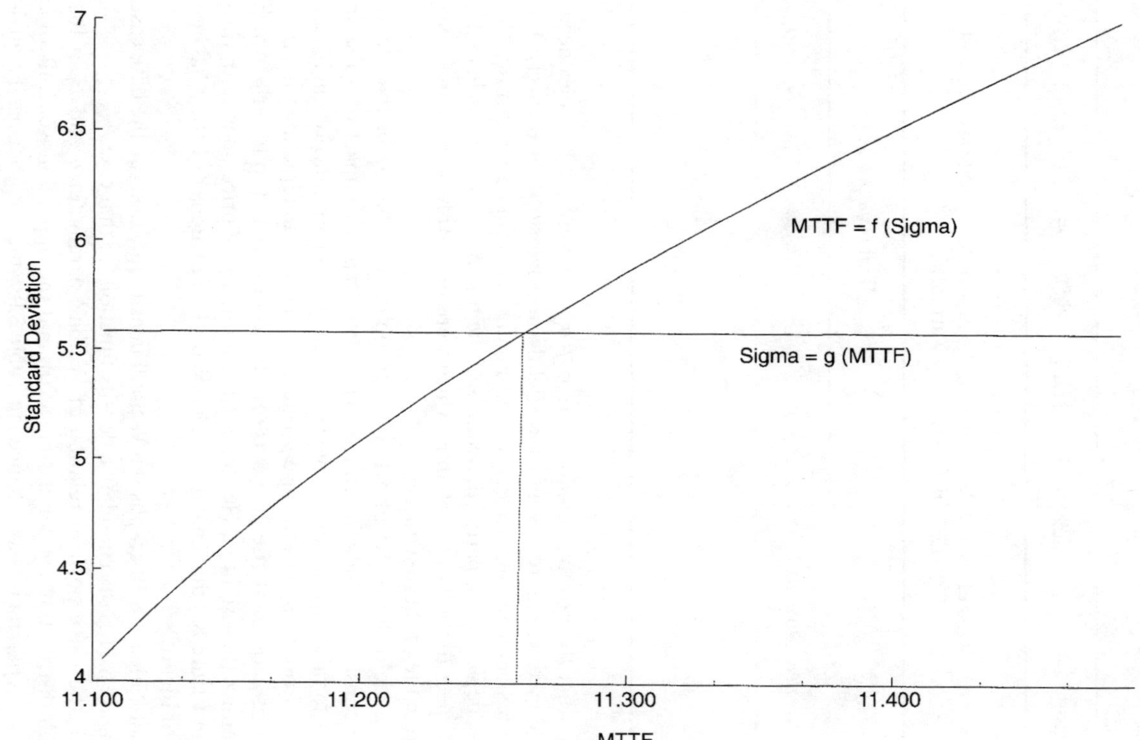

Figure 8.8 *Ceteris paribus* reaction functions

Table 8.7 Base case solution values for Table 8.6 parameter set

	p	μ_i	σ_i	x	b	c
Base case	\$2,889.86	11.26	5.59	44,751	12.72	2.12

Table 8.8 Signs of partial derivatives of the first-order conditions, Weibull density function, no warranties

	With respect to:		
Sign of the derivative of:	p	μ_i	σ_i
p	*****	+	−
μ_i	+	*****	+
σ_i	−	+	*****

Note that the positive relation of $\mu_i = f(\sigma_i)$ in Figure 8.8 becomes negatively sloped in Figure 8.9 and the slightly positive slope of $\sigma_i = g(\mu_i)$ in Figure 8.8 becomes slightly negative in Figure 8.9. Table 8.8 motivates this change, depicting the partial derivatives of the first-order conditions in (8.25) with respect to the policy variables which were not involved in their derivation from the profit function.

These yield the direct effects of each policy variable upon the others before considering indirect effects. The *ceteris paribus* impact of a rise in $\mu_i(\sigma_i)$ is to raise $\sigma_i(\mu_i)$, yielding the positive slopes of both functions in Figure 8.8. But a rise in μ_i acts to raise p which lowers σ_i, counteracting the direct impact of μ_i on σ_i. A rise in σ_i acts directly to raise μ_i but to lower p, which counteracts the rise in μ_i. Hence, it is the influence of price upon both variables in Figure 8.8 that changes the slope of the functions of Figure 8.8 into those of Figure 8.9.

Finally, Figure 8.10 graphs the Weibull density function for the base case and Figure 8.11 is the cumulative density function for that case.

Note the close positive relation of Weibull parameter b and μ_i in the Weibull distribution, as defined in (8.20), and the implied movements of b and c when parameters are changed in Table 8.9, which reproduces the qualitative results of the indicated parametric displacements for nonwarrantied products. When possible, parameters were raised by 100 percent and lowered 50 percent to generate the new solutions. For the base case the price

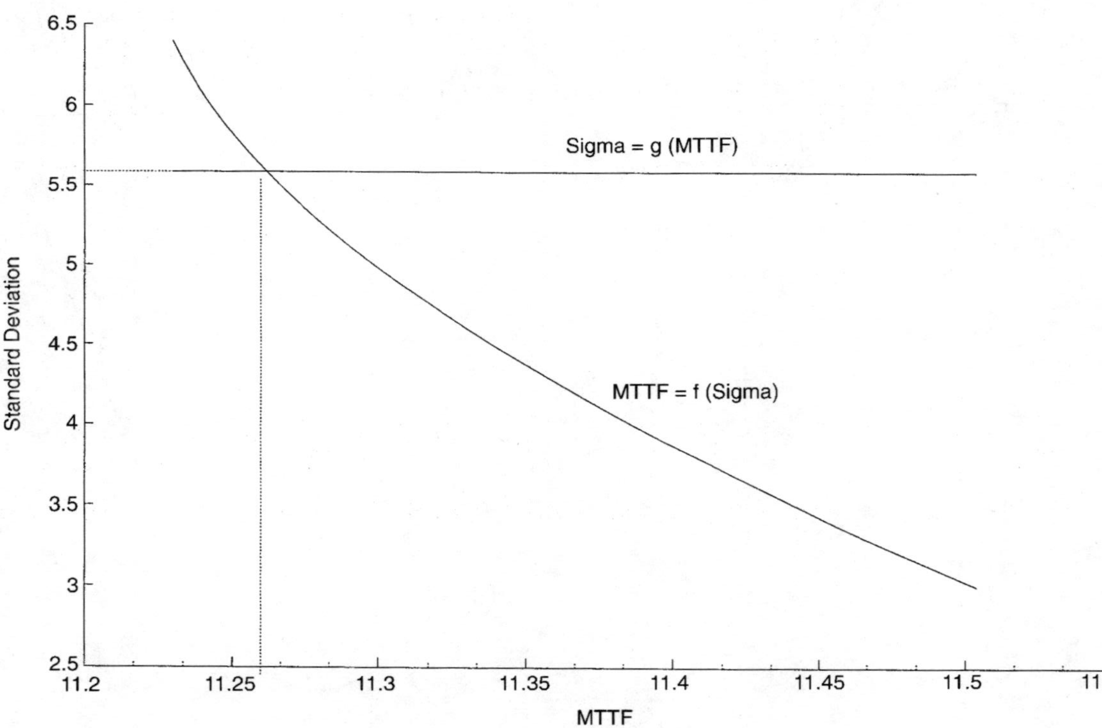

Figure 8.9 *Mutatis mutandis* reaction functions

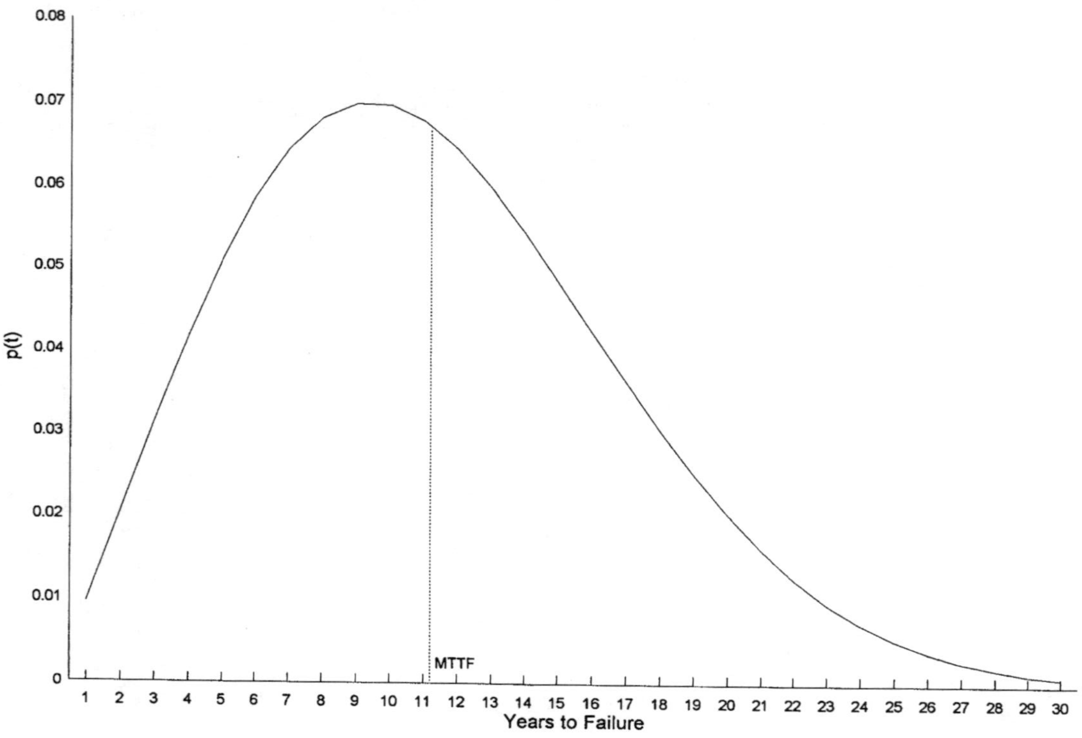

Figure 8.10 The Base Case Weibull density function

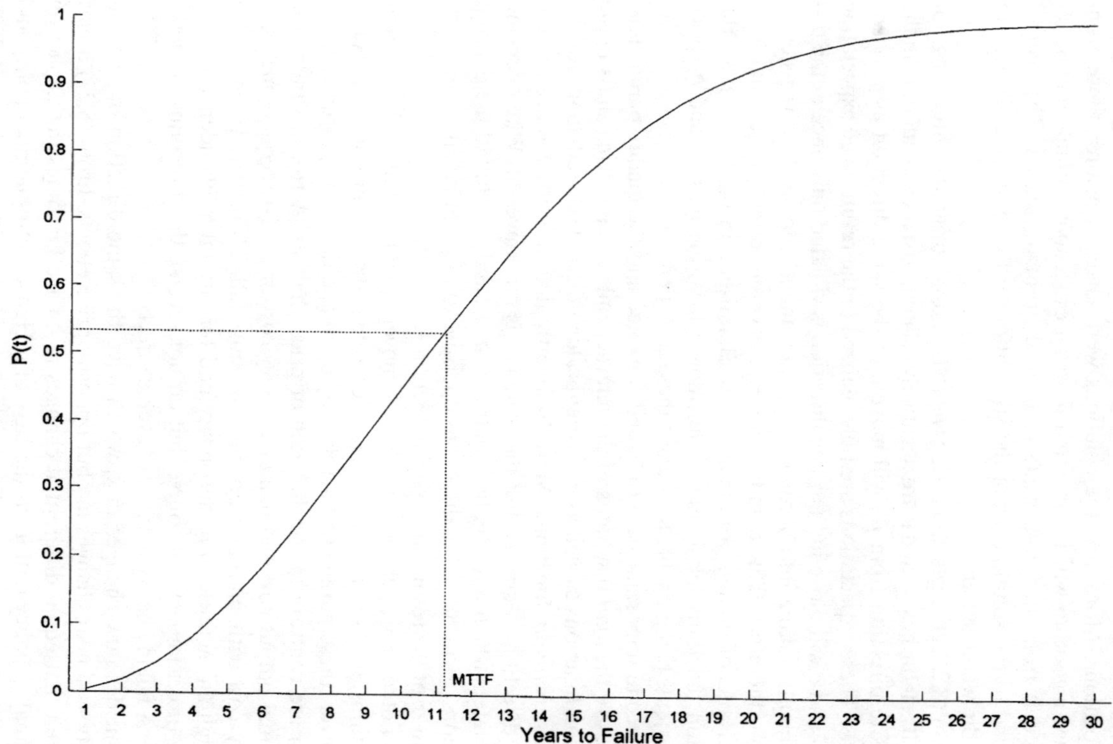

Figure 8.11 Base Case cumulative density function

policy-*MTTF* policy subsystem yielded a negative definite Hessian matrix, but a positive (rather than nonpositive) determinant (third nested principal minor). However, for all parameter displacements to be discussed below, the solutions for all three policies converged quickly from widely dispersed starting positions. Moreover, the solutions were checked against those from another algorithm which converted σ_i to an exogenous variable and incremented it from an initial value of 0 until profit decreased. They corresponded to the solutions from the straightforward diagonal matrix used to solve the whole system.

From (8.21) changes in μ_i, *ceteris paribus*, move b in similar directions, but as n.10 establishes, σ_i and c are negatively related, so a movement of σ_i in the opposite direction from μ_i, will move c in the same direction as b, *ceteris paribus*. These expectations are fully realized in the results. The expectation that b and c will move in the same direction is violated only once in the displacements, taking into account some movements too small to register. It follows, therefore that μ_i and σ_i move in opposite directions, so that both dimensions of quality are enhanced or diminished in tandem. x falls, the reaction functions for μ_i and σ_i shift down, lowering both μ_i and σ_i, price movements being unable to counter these direct effects.

A second important pattern is that for price and the quality parameters. These are the *total* resultants of the interdependence, involving shifts in the reaction functions as well as movements along them discussed above for the *mutatis mutandis* functions. More frequently than not, price moved in the same direction as quality, but the tendency is not universal. When demand parameters which were "policy neutral" – a, b_{ij}, and p_j – shifted the demand function, prices moved in directions opposite to those of quality – an extension to σ_i of the results discussed in section 1.

As noted above, changes in j and k moved quality variables in different directions, worsening *MTTF* but lessening dispersion, or vice versa. However, these parameters act directly upon and dominate μ_i's movements which are contrary to the direction of price changes. A rise in j raises the marginal output cost and marginal policy cost of μ_i. To reequate marginal policy cost with marginal revenue, μ_i must fall. Moreover, Ω_i^* must rise through an increase in p. Secondary and tertiary interdependence temper these direct impacts, of course, but do not reverse the directions of movement. A fall in j has symmetrical inverse effects.

Consider now changes in k, which have the same direction impacts on quality as similar changes in j but opposite price effects. From (8.27) it may be seen that equal differential changes in k have $2\mu_i$ times the impact on marginal μ_i policy cost as in the case of j. Hence both marginal policy and marginal output costs rise by more than j changes would cause. From (8.23.2) these cost rises put immediate pressure on p to rise to conform to the higher policy cost, reducing x. But with the shift leftward of the demand function in

Table 8.9 Directions of movement of variables for demand and cost parameter increases, Weibull model, no warranties

Parameter	p	μ_1	σ_1	x	b	c
			1 Demand Parameters			
a = 180,000	+	−	+	+	−	−
a = 45,000	−	+	−	−	+	+
$b_{1,1}$ = 40	−	−	+	−	−	−
$b_{1,1}$ = 10	+	+	−	+	+	+
$b_{1,j}$ = 2x	+	−	+	+	−	−
$b_{1,j}$ = 0.5x	−	+	−	−	+	+
p_j = 2x	+	−	+	+	−	−
p_j = 0.5x	−	+	−	−	+	+
m = 1,000	+	+	0	+	+	+
m = 250	−	−	+	−	−	−
n = 60	−	−	0	+	0	0
n = 15	+	+	−	−	+	+
r = 1,400	+	+	−	−	+	+
r = 350	−	−	+	+	−	−
s = 400	+	+	−	−	+	+
s = 100	−	−	+	+	−	−
μ = 18	+	+	−	−	+	+
μ = 4.5	−	−	+	+	−	−
σ = 7	−	−	+	+	−	−
σ = 1.75	+	+	−	−	+	+
			2 Cost Parameters			
h = 0.003	−	−	+	−	−	−
h = 0.000075	−	+	−	+	+	+
j = 2	+	−	−	−	−	−
j = 0.5	−	+	+	+	+	+
k = 0.12	−	−	−	−	−	−
k = 0.03	+	+	+	+	+	+
u = 40			*Meaningless solution*			
u = 10	+	+	−	−	+	+
v = 1.8	+	+	−	−	+	+
v = 0.45	−	−	+	+	−	−
o = 220	+	+	−	−	+	+
o = 55	−	−	+	+	−	−
F = 132m	0	0	0	0	0	0
F = 32.5m	0	0	0	0	0	0
J = 3,500	−	−	0	+	−	0
J = 825	−	+	0	+	0	0

Table 8.9 continued

Parameter	p	μ_1	σ_1	x	b	c
$K = 40$	–	+	0	+	0	0
$K = 10$	+	+	0	–	+	0
$U = 1{,}000$	–	0	0	+	0	0
$U = 250$	+	0	0	–	0	0
$V = 1.8$	+	+	–	–	+	+
$V = 0.45$	–	–	+	+	–	–

$[p,x]$ space induced by the fall in μ_i elasticity rises, and the extent of the rise in p is excessive, so that p falls and sufficiently, after secondary and tertiary reactions, to result in a net fall in price. A fall in k has symmetrical impacts in the opposite directions.

Doubling and halving parameters J, K, U, and V have very small impacts on the policy variables: maximum price change was \$0.72, maximum *MTTF* change was 0.01, and no change was registered in σ_i. The decline in J and rise in K resulted in contrary movements in p, μ_i and σ_i, but by negligible amounts.

Finally, in almost all cases, quality and profits moved inversely, somewhat surprisingly. On the other hand, as expected, price and profits moved in the same direction as changes in demand parameters and in opposite directions for cost parameter changes.

4 WARRANTIED PRODUCTS WITH AGING CHARACTERISTICS

With the introduction of warranties, the firm's demand and cost functions are defined in the general forms of (8.1) and (8.2). Let

$$\Omega^{**} = \rho - \omega^{*}(1 + 2hx) - \lambda$$

The first-order necessary conditions are straightforward:

$$1\quad p = \frac{\beta(1 + 2b_{ii}h\omega^{*}) + b_{ii}(\omega^{*} + \lambda)}{2b_{ii}(1 + b_{ii}h\omega^{*})} \qquad (8.28)$$

$$2\quad \mu_i = \frac{\Omega^{**}(m + 2n\mu) - J - jx(1 + hx)}{2[n\Omega^{**} + K + kx(1 + hx)]}$$

$$3\quad \sigma_i = \frac{-\Omega^{**}(r - 2s\sigma) + U + ux(1 + hx)}{2[s\Omega^{**} + V + vx(1 + hx)}$$

$$4\quad w_i = \frac{\Omega^{**}(T+2kw) - qx\left[g\left(1-e^{-\left(\frac{w_i}{b}\right)^c}\right) + zw_i^2\left(\frac{c}{b}\right)\left(\frac{w_i}{b}\right)^{c-1} e^{-\left(\frac{w_i}{b}\right)^c}\right]}{2\Omega^{**}K + qx\left[2z\left(1-e^{-\left(\frac{w_i}{b}\right)^c}\right) + g\left(\left(\frac{c}{b}\right)\left(\frac{w_i}{b}\right)\right)^{c-1} e^{-\left(\frac{w_i}{b}\right)^c}\right]}$$

To obtain the *mutatis mutandis* reaction functions we rewrite (8.28):

$$1\quad \Omega^{**} = \frac{x}{b_{ii}} \tag{8.29}$$

$$2\quad \mu_i = \frac{(m+2n\mu) - \frac{b_{ii}J}{x} - b_{ii}j(1+hx)}{2\left[n + \frac{b_{ii}K}{x} + b_{ii}k(1+hx)\right]}$$

$$3\quad \sigma_i = \frac{-(r-2s\sigma) + \frac{b_{ii}U}{x} + b_{ii}u(1+hx)}{2\left[s + \frac{b_{ii}V}{x} + vb_{ii}(1+hx)\right]}$$

$$4\quad w_i = \frac{(T+2\kappa w) + b_{ii}q\left[g\left(1-e^{-\left(\frac{w_i}{b}\right)^c}\right) + zw_i^2\left(\frac{c}{b}\right)\left(\frac{w_i}{b}\right)^{c-1} e^{-\left(\frac{w_i}{b}\right)^c}\right]}{2K - b_{ii}q\left[2z\left(1-e^{-\left(\frac{w_i}{b}\right)^c}\right) + \left(\frac{c}{b}\right)\left(\frac{w_i}{b}\right)^{c-1} e^{-\left(\frac{w_i}{b}\right)^c}\right]}$$

(8.27–2,3,4) are the policy reaction functions for μ_i, σ_i, and w_i respectively.

The profit function is not globally concave; indeed, the introduction of warranties results in a badly behaved objective function. Recourse to simulation was necessary after several algorithms proved unreliable or excessively time-consuming. This is an excellent example of the position taken in Chapter 2 on simulative theorizing. In many instances of oligopoly, the complexity of the functions becomes so great and their structures so dependent on parameter values that analytical solutions are unattainable or, even if attainable, theorems are extremely parameter-dependent. Ambitions for "general" theorems in oligopolistic decision making, especially in integrated rivalry, must yield to the search for frameworks that can be employed to attack parameter-specific problems.

A base case was constructed with parameter values listed in Table 8.10 and solution values given in Table 8.11. Parameter displacements were once more performed, consisting of 20 percent increases and decreases around base case values (except for q which cannot exceed 1) and the results were converted to ratios to relevant base case values.

The algorithm used yielded global maxima through application of exhaustive search techniques. For each displacement, w_i was parameterized and used to solve (8.28.1, 2, and 3) for $[p,\mu_i,\sigma_i]$. These relations converged quickly, and from μ_i and σ_i, the Weibull parameters b and c were obtained to complete the data necessary to compute the cost function values for use in the iteration. By choosing w_i to maximize profits in successive iterations to determine $[p,\mu_i,\sigma_i]$, global maxima for each of the 50 displacements were obtained. Their normalized values provided the data for the analyses to follow.

As in section 3, major interest lies primarily in the qualitative covariation of prices and the values of the three quality characteristics. To what extent do they move in similar or opposite directions as parameters vary? Does the firm tend to increase or decrease some or all of the qualities as it raises or lowers prices, so that they are "competitive complements", or does it move

Table 8.10 Base case parameters – isolated firm, Weibull density function, with warranty period

	1 Demand function parameters	
$a = 90{,}000$		$b_{1,1} = 20$
$p_2 = 4{,}000$		$b_{1,2} = 3.475$
$m = 350$		$n = 90$
$r = 700$		$s = 250$
$T = 450$		$\kappa = 3$
$\mu = 9$		$\sigma = 3.5$
	$w = 1$	
	2 Cost function parameters	
$F = 65{,}000{,}000$		$J = 1{,}750$
$U = 1{,}000$		$K = 80$
$V = 10$		$o = 50$
$j = 1$		$u = 10$
$k = 0.06$		$v = 0.9$
$g = 800$		$q = 0.95$
$z = 10$		$h = 0.00015$

some or all quality characteristics in opposite directions from prices? Under which parameter changes does it tend to do one or the other?

Table 8.12 reproduces the gross correlation matrix for values of price, the quality variables, quantity and profits. The policy variables p_i, μ_i, σ_i, and w_i reveal qualitative relationships that will be shown to be consistent with expectations derived from the first-order optimization conditions and from detailed analysis of the 50 displacements, despite the coarseness of gross correlation analysis. Price is positively associated with quality improvements in all quality variables (which implies *reductions* in σ_i), and each of the quality variables reveals the same pattern with price and its two companion qualities. Most highly intercorrelated with other policy variables is w_i, while μ_i and σ_i reveal weak relations with the other two. A portion of the causes of this rests with the parameter values, of course, but this is also true because the impacts on cost of μ_i and σ_i are scattered in the cost equation among several parameters, whereas w_i's impact is highly concentrated. Any one of the parameter changes that affects the former two in the cost equation, therefore, will not deliver the degree of shock that a change in a coefficient in the warranty cost term will do. Their influence will be much more vulnerable to indirect feedbacks of the opposite sign. Were all of the parameters in the cost equation having a direct impact on μ_i or on σ_i changed simultaneously the outcomes would have been much stronger.

Table 8.11 Base case solution values for Table 8.10 parameter set

	p	μ_1	σ_1	x	w_1	π_1	b	c
Base case	\$3,040.61	10.942	2.10	45,544	4.704	5.4578E07	11.788	6.063

Table 8.12 Correlation matrix for variables in the displacement solutions, 50 observations

	p_1	μ_1	σ_1	w_1	x_1	π_1
p_1	1	+0.0570	–0.0666	+0.2170	+0.7196	+0.9370
μ_1	+0.0570	1	–0.0001	+0.6815	–0.0349	–0.0047
σ_1	–0.0666	–0.0001	1	–0.7022	+0.0396	+0.0027
w_1	+0.2170	+0.6815	–0.7022	1	+0.0626	+0.1276
x_1	+0.7196	–0.0349	+0.0396	+0.0626	1	+0.8818
π_1	+0.9370	–0.0047	+0.0027	+0.1276	+0.8818	1

To permit study of the parametric ranging in more detail, Table 8.13 summarizes the correspondence between qualitative movements of price and the quality variables taken pairwise for the 50 experiments. A (+) indicates that row and column variables moved in the same direction, a (–) denotes contrary movement, and a 0 signifies reactions of one or both variables that were too weak to register in three decimal places. These entries present the net movements in variables taking into account direct and indirect impacts captured in the general economic interdependence of the system. Table 8.14 on the other hand reproduces the signs of the partial derivatives of (8.28.1, 8.28.2, 8.28.3 and 8.28.4) which represent only the *direct* impacts of one variable on the other as parameter shocks occur. In Table 8.13 the directions of movement in each cell that correspond to that associated with the direct

Table 8.13 Directional movement of the policy variables in the displacements, 50 observations

	Directions of movement with changes in:											
	p			μ_1			σ_1			w_1		
	+	–	*0*	+	–	*0*	+	–	*0*	+	–	*0*
p	***	***	***	**19**	4	27	1	**25**	24	**37**	11	2
μ_1	**19**	4	27	***	***	***	4	**16**	30	**16**	6	28
σ_1	1	**25**	24	4	**16**	30	***	***	***	3	**23**	24
w_1	**37**	11	2	**16**	6	28	3	**23**	24	***	***	***

Table 8.14 Signs of partial derivatives of policy variables, Weibull density function, with warranties

Sign of derivative of:	*With respect to:*			
	p_1	μ_1	σ_1	w_1
p_1	***	+	–	+
μ_1	+	***	–	+
σ_1	–	–	***	–
w_1	+	+	–	***

impelling of the relevant variables as shown in Table 8.14 have been printed in bold face.

Comparison of the two tables discloses that direct effects are dominant in all cases, considering only nonzero entries – a result differing significantly from the base case in section 3. With the parameter set of Table 8.10, sign reversals due to interdependence tended to occur with changes in cost parameters for reasons discussed above: when they were changed singly small changes in marginal costs occurred although they set afoot forces that ramified through the model and from time to time upset the sign expectation derived from the direct impacts. By and large, however, the model as presently parameterized is demand-driven.

The evidence from Tables 8.12, 8.13, and 8.14 is in agreement: as in section 3, prices and the quality variables tend to move in positive directions, taking this to mean that p_i, μ_i, and w_i move in the same direction and σ_i in the opposite direction when responding optimally to parameter changes. Costs are not the dominant driving forces leading to this result. The firm finds it advantageous to offset price rises with hikes in quality and, generally, in all dimensions of quality: it does not raise price and reduce one or more quality characteristics.

Figures 8.12–8.14 provide a graphical view of the outcomes of the 50 displacements and the base case. They provide idealized continuous surfaces that bring out more clearly the consistencies among variable relationships, but illustrate as well the difficulty of specifying precise propositions that describe the nature of the relations in all domains. Figure 8.12 relates profit to price and output which are shown to be, in Table 8.12, and not surprisingly, highly intercorrelated. Although the table shows a positive correlation coefficient of +0.937, the figure reveals some tendency for profits to rise as price rises to the neighborhood of the base case price but then to decline as price continues to rise. Indeed, for prices that are at the low end of the range, profits take a sharp dip and then rise for lower output levels. These very low prices arise from changes in two parameters that directly and importantly affect the demand function: a reduction in its intercept (a) and an increase in its own-price slope ($b_{i,i}$). These inflicted severe reductions in price and output and therefore profits. Symmetrically, the sharp spike upward in profits occurred when $b_{i,i}$ was reduced and the maximum profit level on the surface at $x = 53{,}340$ resulted from a 20 percent rise in a.

A total of 14 of the 20 demand function parameters registered price and profit movements in the same direction, and their relative strengths of impact account in largest measure for the high positive correlation between p_i and π_i. Fully 20 of the 30 cost parameter shocks determined negative movements in these two variables, but of smaller absolute magnitude in general than their demand counterparts. Surprisingly, none of the cost

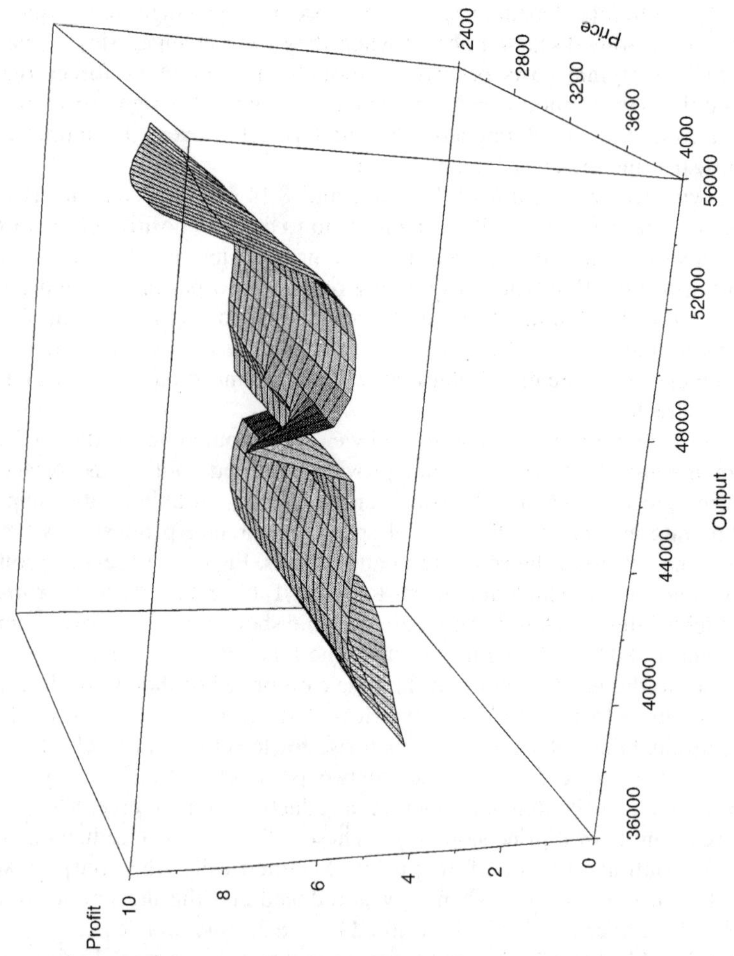

Figure 8.12 Profit, price, and output

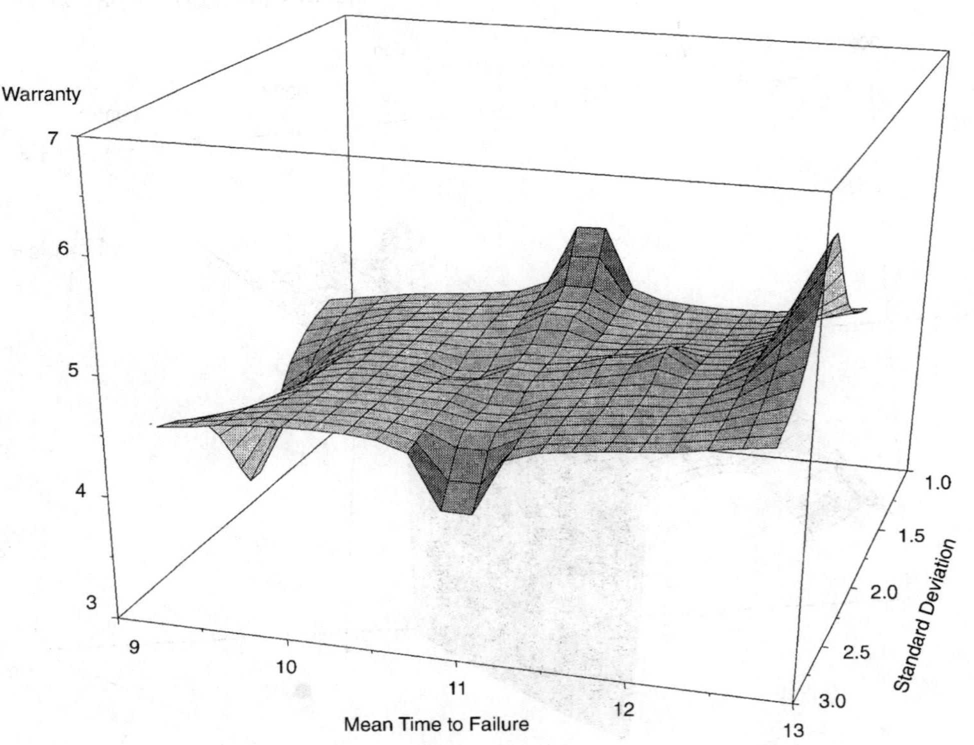

Figure 8.13 Quality variables surface

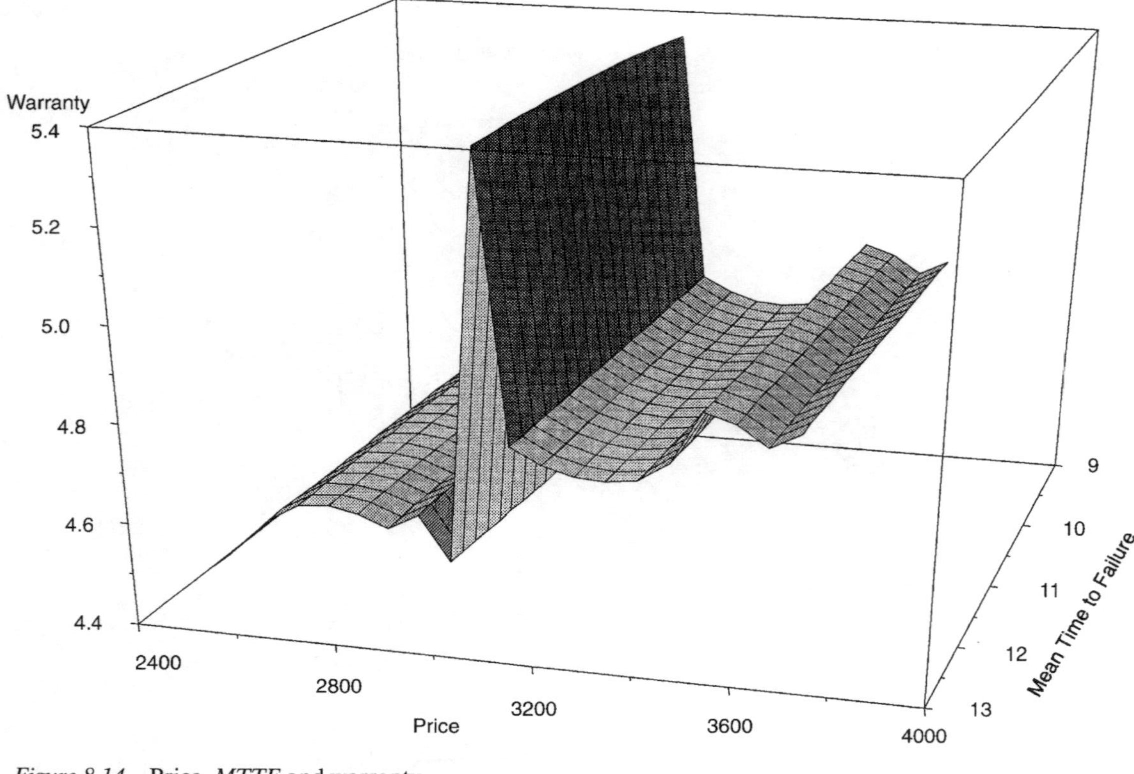

Figure 8.14 Price, *MTTF* and warranty

parameters associated with warranties exercises much price or output effect, although all but one moved p_i and π_i in the same direction.

From Figure 8.12, therefore, an initial lesson is that aggregate measures of association among variables are untrustworthy, and that results are highly parameter-specific. In demand-driven systems like the one presented in this section, in general p_i and π_i will be positively associated when demand parameters are changed and negatively associated for cost parameter changes. Demand parameters raise or lower p_i and π_i by more than increased x_i raises or lowers cost. On the other hand cost reductions or increases incumbent on cost parameter changes tend to be smaller than demand-inspired revenue changes.

Of more interest is the quality variables surface in Figure 8.13. Tables 8.12–8.14 support the notion that the movements of μ_i, σ_i and w_i are positively correlated in their product improvement implications (implying negative correlation with σ_i). This is borne out by the surface with four rather dramatic intensifications at the extremities. In the neighborhood of base case values, μ_i, w_i and σ_i are sharply and symmetrically impacted by a 20 percent rise in σ (the standard consistency benchmark) from its base case value and a 20 percent fall from that level. And at highest and lowest levels of μ_i, symmetrical moves in w_i in the neighborhood of σ_i base case values show intensified positive associations of μ_i and w_i. These are caused by changes in *MTTF* standard benchmark μ in 20 percent negative (on the left side of the document) and positive directions.

The dramatic changes in an otherwise tranquil and consistent 3-way relationship are caused by these benchmarks. Changes in the remaining benchmark, w, have slight impacts on the surface – again, somewhat surprising in that w_i is the most volatile of the quality variables, unlike the experience noted in section 2. This leads to the belief that w_i is largely a *reactive* variable, highly affected by μ_i and σ_i as they alter x_i, but whose autonomous changes have minor impacts on the other quality variables. Finally, the symmetrical minor dips and peaks in the middle of the surface result from an increase and decrease in n_i respectively, which is the quadratic coefficient for μ_i in the demand function. This enhances the view of w_i as reactive and explains the large correlation coefficient for μ_i and w_i in Table 8.12.

Finally, the rather anomalous relation of μ_i and p_i revealed in their low correlation coefficient in Table 8.12 and the small correlation of w_i and p_i compared with the dominant number of positive movements between them in Table 8.13 led to a graphing of the $[\mu_i, p_i, w_i]$ surface in Figure 8.14. Like Figure 8.12 and unlike Figure 8.13 it reveals the potential ambivalence in such relations lurking behind macro measures of association or a mere counting of joint qualitative movements.

For given values of μ_i, variables p_i and w_i exhibit rather sudden reversals in their direction of covariation – a pattern that is uniform as μ_i changes parametrically. From its base case values for p_i and w_i, w_i jumps sharply to a maximum as p_i rises slightly and falls just as sharply to its minimum as price falls slightly. As might be expected from the discussion of Figure 8.13, these movements are those associated with 20 percent increases and decreases in μ, once more underscoring the extreme one-way causal forces *MTTF* exercises on warranties. At the same time μ's changes affect p_i and π_i by less than 1 percent. It is through changes in x_i for the most part that, w_i is moved so sharply, although that is not clearly revealed in Table 8.12.

The erratic path of w_i and p_i beyond this pinnacle area shows at least six reversals of direction of movement in w_i as p_i increases. These reversals are dictated by the behavior of x_i as p_i changes, rising or falling with price as the nature of the parameter causing movement dictates. The size of w_i varies directly with μ_i, for greater *MTTF* makes the warranty period less costly to the firm; on the other hand, larger output by itself makes warranties more costly as their marginal cost rises. As Figure 8.13 shows, μ_i changes within narrow limits over most of the surface and warranties respond equally sluggishly except at the extremities. Thus, the erratic responses of w_i to p_i in Figure 8.14 reflect the changes in x_i associated with p_i, which are positive in 17 cases but negative in 25, and it is these variations in output that account for the changes in directional movements of p_i and w_i that account for the changes in direction in the $p_i - w_i$ dimension of Figure 8.14.

5 SOME CONCLUSIONS AND CONJECTURES

The conclusions just derived concerning the complicated interdependence among the four policy variables and the parameter-specific outcomes are among the most important of the study. But it will be useful to summarize several other results and to suggest plausible hypotheses or to conjecture concerning more general implications.

First, for nonaging products, *ceteris paribus* and *mutatis mutandis* movements in μ_i and σ_i are identically and trivially positive since they are equal. Improvements in *MTTF* necessarily result in reduced consistency. In the case of aging products without warranties, the direct impact of μ_i on σ_i and vice versa are also positive, but the relations are reversed by price relationships. In the base case for aging products when warranties are introduced, however, the direct relationships between μ_i and σ_i which are positive in the nonaging case, are negative in the aging cases. Moreover, p and μ_i are positively correlated in relevant regions. Hence, changes in demand or cost parameters that raise price will tend to raise *MTTF* (and increase consistency).

One caveat is necessary concerning this conclusion, however. If the marginal production costs rise as a function of output level and the marginal policy cost of μ_i rises as it increases, the joint interaction of these rising costs may result in a rise in p and a fall in μ_i. In such cases, rises in demand can result in a rising price and lower quality.

A striking result of the analysis of optimal warranty periods in conditions of nonaging is the relatively small size of such periods relative to *MTTF*, compared with what would be expected were such products subject to aging. An explanation for this is found in the constancy of the probability of failure during a small interval of time over the life of the product, and the consequent front-loading of failures for such products. On the other hand, in the Weibull case when warranties are included, the size of the warranty period was the most volatile of the quality characteristics. Although parameter differences were a portion of the explanation for the difference, the nature of the aging process and the greater sensitivity of eligible units to warranty period length was a more important factor. Nevertheless, despite this greater volatility, warranty periods continued to move within surprisingly narrow limits, reflecting their importance in cost relationships.

Another complexity introduced with the analysis of warranties is the introduction of a nonconvexity into the profit function, so that it is no longer concave. This necessitates the design of algorithms to circumvent the problem and to obtain convergence to global solutions for models whose parameters are realistic.

With the phenomenon of aging occurs a good deal of independence between μ_i and σ_i and with it increasing complexity in the qualitative relationships among the policy variables discussed at length in section 4. The positive *ceteris paribus* relation between μ_i and σ_i persists when warranties are not present but in the simulations of this study is overridden by the negative relation between p and the two variables.

The analysis of the isolated firm's nonprice decisions and their relations to the price decision is a prelude to the construction of a rivalrous consonance model for oligopolistic rivalry. Adding another layer of interdependence to the several layers revealed in this chapter promises yet more challenges but rich analytical payoffs as well. Especially intriguing is the question of the role of benchmarking as industry standards vary with competitors' decisions concerning quality variables.

Lastly, one can merely conjecture concerning the insights our analysis yields into the firm's decisions with respect to qualities that do not lend themselves to such neat quantitative depiction as those used in this paper. One is led to suspect that the important mutual interdependence uncovered would also characterize such decisions as taste or color or research effort. Our initial efforts to analyze such quality dimensions certainly supports that suspicion, as will be demonstrated in Chapter 10.

9 Oligopolistic Competition and Consumer Benchmarking in a Rivalrous Consonance Market Structure: Measurable Characteristics[1]

1 PURPOSE AND STRUCTURE OF THE MODEL

Chapter 8 dealt with optimization models for price and core quality characteristics of an isolated firm when those core characteristics were the extent and consistency of product durability and the length of warranty period, and were for products which do not age or wear out with time and those that do. This chapter extends this decision making into a duopolistic model of strategic interdependence under the regime of rivalrous consonance described and illustrated in Chapter 3. As in Chapter 8, firms' decisions involve p_i, μ_i, σ_i and w_i, or price, mean time to failure (*MTTF*), the standard deviation of the *MTTF* density function, and length of warranty period. In the interest of focussing on the implications of duopolistic rivalry, the models in this chapter will deal only with the case of products that suffer wear and tear with age, so that the probability of failure rises with the age of the product.

The purposes of the modeling are to derive insights by closed analysis and by simulation into the implications of four behavioral aspects of duopolistic firms in this form of market structure:

1 Patterns of interdependence among the four target variables for a given degree of competition/cooperation (i.e., rivalrous consonance) and fixed benchmarks.
2 Patterns of change in the variables as the level of rivalrous consonance is varied parametrically, benchmarks remaining fixed.
3 Patterns of change in industry profitability as the level of rivalrous consonance varies, benchmarks fixed.

4 Patterns of change in price and quality variables and in profitability as consumer benchmarks adapt to firms' quality decisions and the level of rivalrous consonance is varied parametrically.

It will come as no surprise given the experience in Chapter 8 that the interdependent variation in the oligopoly models become so complex even in duopoly with results so dependent on parameter values that closed analysis cannot be relied on exclusively. While the theoretical analysis gives us the clues with which to interpret solutions, specific results depend on the numerical specification of the model. When this occurs parameters have been chosen for the simulations with the purpose of realistic depiction of relative demand and cost conditions in real world firms.

2 THE MODEL

Assume that the demand for firm *i*'s product is written:

$$x_i = a - b_{ii}p_i + b_{ij}p_j + m_i(\mu_i - \mu) - n_i(\mu_i - \mu)^2 - r_i(\sigma_i - \sigma)$$
$$-s_i(\sigma_i - \sigma)^2 + T_i(w_i - w) - \kappa_i(w_i - w)^2, \ i = 1,2, \tag{9.1}$$

where terms have been defined in section 1 of Chapter 8. An important characteristic of this demand function is that although p_j enters directly in firm *i*'s demand function, μ_j, σ_j, and w_j are present only implicitly and partially in μ, σ, and w, the quality benchmarks. These industry standards are treated in two manners in the chapter. In a long-term model, in which sufficient time is assumed to pass to permit consumers to absorb changed standards, they are determined within the model as the sales-weighted averages of the quality variables' values for the two firms and vary as those endogenously determined decision variables change. In short- and medium-run models in which insufficient time has passed to permit such consumer cognition, the standards are set at initial values exogenously or may be interpreted as being imposed by external (e.g., foreign) competitors.

The firm's cost function is given as follows:

$$C_i = F_i + J_i\mu_i + K_i\mu_i^2 - U_i\sigma_i - V_i\sigma_i^2 + (o_i + j_i\mu_i + k_i\mu_i^2 - u_i\sigma_i + v_i\sigma_i^2)$$
$$(x_i + h_i x_i^2) + q_i[(1 - e^{-(w_i/b_i)^{c_i}})x_i](g_i w_i + z_i w_i^2), \ i = 1,2, \tag{9.2}$$

whose terms are interpreted in section 1 of Chapter 8.

Two unusual complexities in the cost function should be highlighted again. The quality variable cost factors for μ_i and σ_i as well as the variable cost factor o_i interact multiplicatively with the scale of output x_i. Quality variable cost components, therefore, are assumed to rise with improvements in quality, output constant, or with constant quality factors and rising output, or both, and to do so quadratically on both counts.

The second characteristic of note concerns the warranty cost term. The brackets in (9.2) enclose the cumulative Weibull density function. As developed in Chapter 8, the time-to-failure density function for a product whose probability of failure in an increment of time dt rises with age t is a Weibull distribution:

$$\Pr(t_i) = \left[\frac{c_i (t_i)^{c_i - 1}}{b_i^{c_i}}\right] e^{-\left\{\frac{t_i}{b_i}\right\}^{c_i}}, \; t_i \in [0, \infty], \; i = 1,2, \tag{9.3}$$

where t_i is age at failure. The warranty period cost component consists, therefore, of the proportion of warranty-eligible output units expected to be delivered for repair or replacement (q_i) times the eligible number of units with a given warranty time w_i times the unit cost of repair-replacement which rises quadratically with length of warranty period (and, hence, average age at failure).

Firm i's profit function is then:

$$\pi_i = p_i x_i - C_i, \; i = 1,2 \tag{9.4}$$

but in a rivalrous consonance duopolistic market structure this function becomes an *extended profit function* consisting of own-profit plus discounted firm j profits:

$$\pi_i^e = \pi_i + \theta_{ij} \pi_j, \; i = 1,2, \; j \neq i, \tag{9.5}$$

where, as developed in detail in Chapter 3, θ_{ij} is a *consonance coefficient* in the interval [0,1] which designates firm i's readiness to take into account in its decision making the impact of those decisions on firm j's profits. This framework within which to confront oligopolistic decision making assumes that in a mature oligopoly there develops largely out of self-protective motives a communitarian mixture of competition and tacit collusion. The matrix Θ, with $\theta_{ii} \equiv 1$, details the power structure that emerges in the industry to encapsulate each firm's deference to every other firm, motivated largely by the perceived capability of rivals to retaliate against the initiating firm.[2] In a duopoly we may simplify notation by dropping the second subscript in the consonance coefficients.

Finally, each firm is viewed as maximizing its extended profit function subject to a set of constraints that may be unique to the individual firm. In this manner as well as in the determination and inclusion of the power structure it is possible to tailor the model to the specifics of individual industries.

3 FIRST-ORDER CONDITIONS

For firm i the model consists of

$$\text{Max}_{p_i,\,\mu_i,\,\sigma_i,\,w_i}\ \pi_i^e \tag{9.6}$$

Subject to:

$$\mu^* - \mu_i \le 0, \qquad \mu_i - \mu^\circ \le 0$$

$$\sigma_i - \sigma^* \le 0, \qquad \sigma^\circ - \sigma_i \le 0$$

$$w^* - w_i \le 0, \qquad w_i - w^\circ \le 0$$

$$p_i, \mu_i, \sigma_i, w_i \ge 0, \quad i = 1, 2,$$

where the starred restraints in the constraints are self-imposed minimum quality standards meant to protect the brand's reputation, and the degree-marked restraints are technologically-imposed bounds on the ability of quality characteristics to be improved.

To solve the model the Lagrangean form is set up:

$$\text{Max}_{p_i,\,\mu_i,\,\sigma_i,\,w_i}\ \mathcal{L} = \pi_i^e - \lambda_1(\mu_i - \mu^*) + \lambda_2(\sigma_i - \sigma^*) - \lambda_3(w_i - w^*) - \lambda_4 (\mu_i - \mu^\circ) + \lambda_5(\sigma_i - \sigma^\circ) - \lambda_6(w_i - w^\circ), \ i = 1, 2 \tag{9.7}$$

The Kuhn–Tucker first-order maximization conditions are:

1 $\dfrac{\delta \mathcal{L}}{\delta p_i} = \dfrac{\delta \pi_i^e}{\delta p_i} \le 0,$ 2 $p_i\left(\dfrac{\delta \pi_i^e}{\delta p_i}\right) = 0$

3 $\dfrac{\delta \mathcal{L}}{\delta \mu_i} = \dfrac{\delta \pi_i^e}{\delta \mu_i} + \lambda_1 \le 0,$ 4 $\mu_i\left(\dfrac{\delta \pi_i^e}{\delta \mu_i} + \lambda_1\right) = 0$

5 $\dfrac{\delta \mathcal{L}}{\delta \sigma_i} = \dfrac{\delta \pi_i^e}{\delta \sigma_i} - \lambda_2 \le 0,$ 6 $\sigma_i\left(\dfrac{\delta \pi_i^e}{\delta \sigma_i} - \lambda_2\right) = 0$

7 $\dfrac{\delta \mathcal{L}}{\delta w_i} = \dfrac{\delta \pi_i^e}{\delta w_i} + \lambda_3 \le 0,$ 8 $w_i\left(\dfrac{\delta \pi_i^e}{\delta w_i} + \lambda_3\right) = 0$

9 $\dfrac{\delta \mathcal{L}}{\delta \lambda_1} = (\mu_i - \mu^*) \ge 0,$ 10 $\lambda_1(\mu_i - \mu^*) = 0$

$$11\quad \frac{\delta\mathcal{L}}{\delta\lambda_2} = (\sigma^* - \sigma_i) \geq 0, \qquad 12\quad \lambda_1(\sigma^* - \sigma_i) = 0$$

$$13\quad \frac{\delta\mathcal{L}}{\delta\lambda_3} = (w_i - w^*) \geq 0, \qquad 14\quad \lambda_3(w_i - w^*) = 0$$

$$15\quad \frac{\delta\mathcal{L}}{\delta\lambda_4} = (\mu_i - \mu^\circ) \geq 0, \qquad 16\quad \lambda_4(\mu_i - \mu^\circ) = 0$$

$$17\quad \frac{\delta\mathcal{L}}{\delta\lambda_5} = (\sigma_i - \sigma^\circ) \geq 0, \qquad 18\quad \lambda_5(\sigma_i - \sigma^\circ) = 0$$

$$19\quad \frac{\delta\mathcal{L}}{\delta\lambda_6} = (w_i - w^\circ) \geq 0, \qquad 20\quad \lambda_6(w_i - w^\circ) = 0$$

$$21\quad p_i,\ \mu_i,\ \sigma_i,\ w_i,\ \lambda_k \geq 0, \quad k = 1,2,\ldots,6,\ i = 1,2. \tag{9.8}$$

If we assume that none of the constraints is binding at the optimum, for purposes of iterative algorithmic solution these first-order conditions may be written

$$1\quad p_i = \frac{\beta_i(1 + 2h_i b_{ii}\omega_i) + b_{ii}(\omega_i + \psi_i) + \theta_i\Omega_j b_{ji}}{2b_{ii}(1 + h_i\omega_i b_{ii})}$$

$$2\quad \frac{\Omega_i\left(1 - \frac{\delta\mu}{\delta\mu_i}\right)(m_i + 2n_i\mu) - J_i - (x_i h_i x_i^2)j_i - \theta_i\Omega_j(m_j - 2n_j(\mu_j - \mu))\frac{\delta\mu}{\delta\mu_i}}{2\left[n_i\Omega_i\left(1 - \frac{\delta\mu}{\delta\mu_i}\right) + K_i + k_i\left(x_i + h_i x_i^2\right)\right]}$$

$$3\quad \sigma_i = \frac{\left(1 - \frac{\delta\sigma}{\delta\sigma_i}\right)\left(-r_i + 2s_i\sigma\right)\Omega_i + U_i + u_i\left(x_i + h_i x_i^2\right) + \theta_j\Omega_j\left(r_j + 2s_j(\sigma_j - \sigma)\right)\frac{\delta\sigma}{\delta\sigma_i}}{2\left[s_i\Omega_i\left(1 - \frac{\delta\sigma}{\delta\sigma_i}\right) - V_i + v_i\left(x_i + h_i x_i^2\right)\right]}$$

$$4\quad w_i = \frac{\Omega_i\left[T_i + 2\kappa_i w\left(1 - \frac{\delta w}{\delta w_i}\right)\right] - q_i x_i\left[E_{i1}g_i + E_{i2}z_i w_i^2\right] - \theta_i\Omega_j\left(T_j - 2\kappa_j(w_j - w)\right)\frac{\delta w}{\delta w_i}}{\left[2\kappa_j\left(1 - \frac{\delta w}{\delta w_i}\right)\Omega_i + q_i x_i\left(2z_i E_{i1} + g_i E_{i2}\right)\right]},$$

$$i = 1,2,\ \ j \neq i \tag{9.9}$$

where

$$\beta_i = x_i + b_{ii}p_i \qquad \omega_i = o_i + j_i\mu_i + k_iu_i^2 + u\sigma_i + v_i\sigma_i^2$$

$$E_{ii} = 1 - e^{-\left(\frac{w_i}{b_i}\right)^{c_j}} \qquad E_{ij} = \left(\frac{c_i}{b_i}\right)\left(\frac{w_i}{b_i}\right)^{c_i - 1}(1 - E_{ii})$$

$$\Psi_i = q_iE_{ii}(g_iw_i + z_iw_i^2) \qquad \Omega_i = p_i[\omega_i(1 + 2h_ix_i)\Psi_i] \quad i = 1,2, i \neq j.$$

System (9.9) can be rewritten in the following helpful way:

$$1 \quad \Omega_i = \frac{x_i}{b_{ii}} + \frac{\theta_i b_{ii}\Omega_j}{b_{ii}}$$

$$2 \quad \Omega_i = \frac{J_i + 2K_i\mu_i + (j_i + 2k_i\mu_i)x_i(1 + h_ix_i)}{[m_i - 2n_i(\mu_i - \mu)]\left(1 - \frac{\delta\mu}{\delta\mu_i}\right)} + \frac{\theta_i\Omega_j[m_j - 2n_j(\mu_j - \mu)]\left(\frac{\delta\mu}{\delta\mu_i}\right)}{[m_i - 2n_i(\mu_i - \mu)]\left(1 - \frac{\delta\mu}{\delta\mu_i}\right)}$$

$$3 \quad \Omega_i = \frac{U_i + 2V_i\sigma_i + (u_i - 2v_i\sigma_i)x_i(1 + h_ix_i)}{[r_i + 2s_i(\sigma_i - \sigma)]\left(1 - \frac{\delta\sigma}{\delta\sigma_i}\right)} + \frac{\theta_i\Omega_j[r_j + 2s_j(\sigma_j - \sigma)]\left(\frac{\delta\sigma}{\delta\sigma_i}\right)}{[r_i + 2s_i(\sigma_i - \sigma)]\left(1 - \frac{\delta\sigma}{\delta\sigma_i}\right)} \qquad (9.10)$$

$$4 \quad \Omega_i = \frac{q_ix_i[E_{i1}(g_i + 2z_iw_i) + E_{i2}(g_iw_i + z_iw_i^2)]}{\left[(T_i - 2\kappa_i(w_i - w)\left(1 - \frac{\delta w}{\delta w_i}\right)\right]} + \frac{\theta_i\Omega_j[T_j - 2k_j(w_j - w)]\left(\frac{\delta w}{\delta w_i}\right)}{[T_i - 2\kappa_i(w_i - w)]\left(1 - \frac{\delta w}{\delta w_i}\right)},$$

$i = 1,2, j \neq i.$

The pattern in the four equations of (9.10) is consistent with the analogous relations in Chapter 8, with an extension. Three additive components of cost are identifiable for each of the four policy options:

1 *Marginal output costs*, or the marginal production cost of the output of a unit of policy change, where the policy units are dollars of price reduction and units of change in μ_i, σ_i, and t_i respectively. This component is common to all four policies and has been transposed to the lefthand side of the equations, to be found in the negative term of Ω_i.
2 *Marginal policy costs*, or the costs of effecting a unit policy change per unit of output resulting from that policy change. These are distinguished

from marginal output costs by the limitation to those costs that are variable with respect to the relevant policy only. As introduced in Chapter 8, for price policy this marginal policy cost is the dollars lost through a price reduction on pre-reduction sales per unit of increased sales ($x_i dp_i / dx_i$). The interpretation for the other policies is straightforward. These terms are the first on the righthand side of the equations in (9.10).

3 *Marginal consonance costs*, or the internalized costs of tacit collusion per unit of policy induced sales. Firm i has tacitly agreed to impute proportion θ_i of firm j's losses from its (firm i's) initiated strategies. Those losses are inflicted via the rise in firm j's policy costs caused by the impact of the policy change on the policy benchmark (in the cases of the 3 quality variables) or the reduction in p_i for price policy. For example, in the second term or consonance term on the righthand sides of the relations for μ_i, σ_i, and w_i, Ω_j is the gross marginal revenue net of marginal output cost, the bracketed term in the numerator is the reduction of x_j due to the rise in the benchmarks caused by firm i's policies, the denominator puts this loss of revenue on a per unit of firm i's marginal output gain, and θ_i converts this to the percentage of loss per unit of gain x_i imputed if firm i raises μ_i or w_i or lowers σ_i. Thus, θ_i is the proportion of the change in firm j's marginal profits (losses) per unit of firm i's changed marginal sales accepted by firm i as a cost of cooperation, impacting the extent of the policy change to protect firm j. The denominator on these terms is the change in firm i's marginal sales induced by its policy.

In (9.10.1), a reduction in p_i induces a fall in x_j of $b_{ji} dp_i$ and a fall in profit of this amount multiplied by Ω_j. Division by b_{ii} places the loss on a per marginal unit of firm i's sales rise, and θ_i is the proportion of this fall in profits imputed by firm i as a cost to itself and a deterrent to the fall in p_i.

System (9.10), therefore, expresses the necessary conditions for the firm's optimum when reputation or technology constraints do not bind as the equality of the sum of marginal policy and consonance costs to marginal gross revenue *less* marginal output costs. By extension, the sum of the marginal policy and consonance costs must be equal in the optimum for all policies.

As discussed in Chapter 8, the necessity of marginal policy costs of each quality characteristic, inclusive now of induced marginal consonance costs, to equal the identical value Ω_i is a most useful insight into the relations among prices and quality variables under parametric ranging. We will rely on its guidance in interpreting the simulation results of the five cases to be studied in the remainder of the chapter.

4 ALGORITHM TO SOLVE THE MODEL

The 4×4 Hessian matrix of second-order partial derivatives of profit with respect to p_i, μ_i, σ_i, and w_i has a diagonal with negative elements, meeting necessary conditions for a negative definite matrix and a global profit maximum.[3] Unfortunately, however, the off-diagonal elements, controlling indirect interdependence, are subject in their joint impacts on the signs of nested principal minors to the values of the parameters. In the simulations done to date, the 3×3 matrices of the first three variables were negative definite for all solutions. The method of solution adopted, therefore, as in Chapter 8, is to parameterize w_i and solve the reduced system by a diagonalization algorithm for p_i, μ_i, and σ_i, increasing or decreasing w_i after each iteration until profits reach a maximum. The algorithm adopted proved to be quite efficient.

a Analytical Periods

The structure of the conditions in (9.9) and (9.10) permits some important insights into the behavior of firms. I will distinguish three periods defined by consumers' lengths of adjustment to changing benchmarks and those of firms to changing consonance coefficients:

1 *The short run*: Quality standards are fixed as parameters because too little time elapses to allow ruling quality values in the industry to affect consumer consciousness. Further, θ values for the firms – collectively a depiction of the industry power structure – are fixed.
2 *The intermediate run*: A sufficient period of time elapses to permit firms to adjust θ values (if desired by the analyst) to achieve maximum profit, but quality standards remain fixed.
3 *The long run*: A long time elapse permits quality standards to adjust to changing sales-weighted averages of firm values and to accommodate to game-theoretic determination of θ-values if deemed appropriate.

1 The Short Run

The short- and medium-run models are distinctive in that consonance factors directly affect only price because quality standards – the benchmarks – are fixed. Marginal consonance costs, therefore, are zero for the determination of μ_i, σ_i, and w_i, and their magnitudes are affected indirectly only by displacements of p_i (and hence, Ω_i). This is an important feature of these two models: tacit cooperation among firms has *direct* impacts on quality competition only through its effect on the benchmarks. Interfirm rivalry in quality variables is activated to an intense and direct degree only when rivals' choices in these characteristics are perceived by consumers and incorporated in the demand function. In turn, firms factor their quality decision impacts on standards into their maximizing behavior. This simplifies the analysis of reactions of policy variables to endogenous or exogenous changes in θ_i.

Consider, now, (9.10.1) for the short-term model. The term Ω_i is price *less* marginal output cost, or the gross marginal profit that must be equated with the sum of marginal policy and consonance costs, as shown in Figure 9.1, where MC_o is marginal output cost and MC_c is marginal consonance cost. In the case of price policy, marginal policy cost is simply the difference between average and marginal revenue, and is drawn as MC_p. For our purposes we transpose it to the lefthand side and obtain the condition that p_i minus the sum of marginal output, policy and consonance cost must equal zero at the profit optimum. On Figure 9.1 this is indicated where the marginal cost curve $MC_i = MC_o + MC_p + MC_c$ equals p_i.

Assume now that θ_i is changed as a parameter, θ_j constant. Then MC_c shifts upward and MC_i does as well by an equivalent amount. Since the demand curve has some own-price elasticity p_i rises by a smaller amount, so p_i-MC_i falls but Ω_i rises because p_i rises and x_i is reduced. As far as μ_i is concerned, because from (9.10.2) Ω_i has increased and marginal consonance cost is zero, the marginal policy cost per unit of marginal policy induced sales

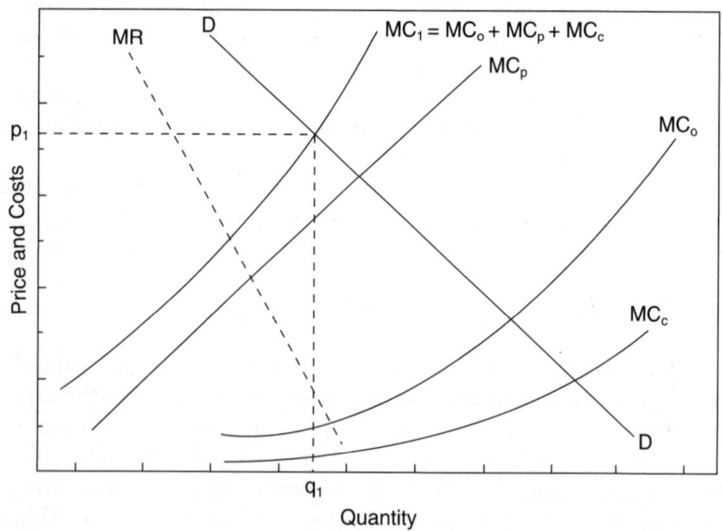

Figure 9.1 The firm's consonance optimum

must rise, as (9.10.2) shows. But if μ_i rises (falls), both numerator and denominator of (9.10.2)'s righthand side must rise (fall) since the consonance term is inoperative. Therefore, whether the righthand side rises or falls with an increase in μ_i depends upon the relative sizes of the numerator (cost effect) and the denominator (sales effect). That is, it depends on whether the marginal cost of μ_i *per unit of marginally induced sales* rises or falls. In general we expect such marginal policy cost to rise, so a rise in Ω_i will require an increase in μ_i to reequate the lefthand side and righthand side. Similar statements follow from (9.10.3) and (9.10.4) for changes in σ_i and w_i, although σ_i's moves will be in opposite directions from μ_i and w_i. I neglect the rise in the marginal output cost caused by the induced rise in x_i and remain with direct and first-order indirect effects.

This yields a counter-intuitive proposition: *as tacit collusion rises in industries whose policy costs rise with μ_i, σ_i, and w_i, benchmarks constant, improvements in quality will tend to increase as Ω_i rises.*

Consider the case where μ_i and w_i must rise and σ_i must fall. If secondary and tertiary indirect induced impacts of these quality improvements caused by a rise in MC_o and a fall in Ω_i do not outweigh the primary indirect effects, the rise in price and marginal output cost will lead to an improvement in all quality variables. This also is a most interesting proposition: *consumer welfare is negatively impacted by tacit collusion because of implied price rises and output reduction but may be positively affected because the quality of products is improved when benchmarks are given exogenously*. If consumer welfare is measured by consumers' surplus (an alternative discussed in Chapters 3 and 8) the positive impacts of quality changes (under conditions specified above) are effected by outward shifts of the demand function as μ_i, σ_i and w_i improve and the negative changes by price rises induced by cost increases and decreased elasticity of the shifted demand curves. Hence, *if demand is sufficiently sensitive to improved quality variables, it is possible that rivalrous consonance with exogenous benchmarks could yield higher consumers' surplus.* Because, as will be shown, profits of both firms rise monotonically as θ_i and θ_i rise by identical amounts, it would follow that social surplus, or the sum of consumer and producer surplus, would rise in the same circumstances. However, for these effects to occur, demand must be quite sensitive to quality improvements, which will militate against the need for marginal policy cost to rise more proportionately than marginal sales – a requirement for the initial hypothesis.

(a) The short run: symmetrical firms with identical u-values

Consider, for example, a simulation with both rivals' demand, cost, reputation and technology parameters identical and those listed in Table 9.1 for three short-run cases to be treated.

Table 9.1 Base case parameters for Cases 1, 2 and 3, symmetric cases

Demand parameters				*Cost parameters*				*Reputation parameters*			
Parameter	*Case 1*	*Case 2*	*Case 3*	*Parameter*	*Case 1*	*Case 2*	*Case 3*	*Parameter*	*Case 1*	*Case 2*	*Case 3*
a_i	90,000	90,000	90,000	o_i	50	50	50	μ_i^*	8	8	8
$b_{i,i}$	20	20	20	j_i	1	1	1	σ_i^*	3.5	3.5	3.5
$b_{i,j}$	3.475	10	12	k_i	0.06	0.06	0.06	w_i^*	1	1	1
$b_{i,k}$	–	–	–	u_i	10	10	10	μ^c	20	20	20
p_j	Variable	Variable	Variable	v_i	0.9	0.9	0.9	σ^c	2	2	2
p_k	–	–	–	F_i	\$65 m	\$65 m	\$65 m	w^c	10	10	10
m_i	350	350	700	J_i	1,750	1,750	1,750				
n_i	90	90	45	K_i	80	80	80				
r_i	700	700	900	U_i	1,000	1,000	1,000				
τ_i	450	450	900	V_i	10	10	10				
κ_i	3	3	1.5	q_i	0.95	0.95	0.95				
μ	9	9	9	g_i	800	800	800				
σ	3.5	3.5	3.5	z_i	10	10	10				
π	1	1	1	h_i	0.00015	0.00015	0.00015				

(1) Case 1: symmetric firms, low firm interaction Case 1 is a duopoly model where both firms' parameters are those of the base case in section 4, Chapter 8. Each firm now has only one rival rather than four, and the other-price coefficient $b_{ij} = b_{ji}$ has been set in this case at the value that in the prior model of Chapter 8 would yield the same contribution to sales. Of course, in the present model rival firms' prices adjust continuously to each other's variable changes. Solution values for Case 1 are given in Table 9.2 for chosen values of θ. Values for μ_i, σ_i and w_i are stated per firm, while consumers' and social surplus are summed over both firms.

Case 1 reveals an unexceptional case of duopoly behavior under rivalrous consonance. As tacit collusion rises (with increases in $\theta_i = \theta_j$) p_i and π_i rise and x_i falls. Despite the fact that the model is demand-driven (as developed in Chapter 8) all of the quality characteristics improve as collusion intensifies. Collusion does not lead the firms to reduce product quality, but rather to increase it, as Ω_i rises with the common θ. Output falls monotonically as profits rise, and with it consumers' surplus, which falls more than profits rise, so that social surplus declines as θ increases.

Note that the interaction between the firms is rather weak, with $b_{ij}/b_{ii} = 0.174$. Rises in one rival's price, therefore, shift the other firm's demand function by relatively small amounts, so price and nonprice variables do not change dramatically as collusion increases. In the limit, were $b_{ij} = b_{ji} = 0$ and yet a firm extended protection via θ_i to another firm (perhaps a customer or supplier), the magnanimous gesture would result in a reduction of profits due to a rise in price above its maximum-profit level and the induced improvements in quality characteristics. Interaction in Case 1 is strong enough to benefit each firm profitwise but relatively weakly: with a rise from the Cournot point to the Chamberlin point firms' profits increase by less than 3 percent, so that this is a case of rather benign tacit collusion.

Consumers' surplus – as a function of x_i only, given demand function own-price parameters[4] – declines monotonically as the θ values rise, and by amounts that the rise in joint profits does not dominate, so that social surplus declines as well. These declines are relatively gentle in both cases, or about 15 and 6.5 percent respectively over the range of θ values. The importance of the quality variables in the determination of consumers' surplus is listed in Table 9.3, which compares consumers' surplus with its value after the impact of quality variation has been eliminated in both absolute and percentage terms.[5] The quality variables add to consumers' surplus by expanding sales even as consumers' surplus declines with the reduction in output, so that the quality characteristics become increasingly more important as tacit collusion increases. Still, their contribution remains quite small in this example. But, as noted in Chapter 8, it is conceivable that if the quality variables contributed greatly to sales, the rise in consumers' surplus on their account could

Table 9.2 Case 1 solutions for the symmetric duopoly, for selected θ-values

θ	p_i	μ_i	σ_i	w_i	π_i	Ω_i	x_i	*Consumers' surplus*	*Social surplus*
0.0	$2,802.28	9.156	3.326	1.816	$44,762,690	$2,211.21	44,224	$97,788,110	$187,313,500
0.1	2,830.59	9.194	3.308	2.134	45,011,150	2,234.86	43,921	96,452,410	186,475,000
0.2	2,852.57	9.232	3.289	2.176	45,192,860	2,258.45	43,599	95,043,640	185,429,400
0.3	2,874.62	9.270	3.270	2.198	45,344,610	2,282.35	43,268	93,605,990	184,295,200
0.4	2,897.58	9.308	3.250	2.250	45,507,750	2,307.03	42,934	92,166,420	183,181,900
0.5	2,920.69	9.346	3.230	2.287	45,646,980	2,332.14	42,591	90,699,660	181,993,600
0.6	2,944.29	9.384	3.210	2.326	45,770,630	2,357.79	42,240	89,210,880	180,752,200
0.7	2,968.35	9.423	3.190	2.361	45,868,560	2,383.92	41,880	87,696,720	179,433,800
0.8	2,993.04	9.461	3.170	2.413	45,973,550	2,410.90	41,516	86,178,910	178,126,000
0.9	3,018.13	9.499	3.149	2.454	46,042,630	2,438.30	41,140	84,624,980	176,710,200
1.0	3,043.95	9.537	2.128	2.506	46,096,810	2,466.39	40,757	83,056,660	175,250,300

Table 9.3 A comparison of consumers' surplus and contribution of quality variables to its value for Case 1

		Quality contribution	
θ	*Consumers' surplus*	*Value*	*Percentage of total*
0.0	97,788,110	2,337,890	2.39%
0.1	96,452,710	3,033,290	3.14
0.2	95,043,640	3,190,280	3.36
0.3	93,605,990	3,304,150	3.53
0.4	92,166,420	3,472,010	3.77
0.5	90,699,660	3,606,150	3.98
0.6	89,210,880	3,703,123	4.33
0.7	87,696,720	3,859,010	4.40
0.8	86,178,910	4,003,760	4.65
0.9	84,624,980	4,071,480	4.81
1.0	83,056,660	4,258,880	5.13

outweigh the fall on price account and lead to an increase in consumers' surplus (and social surplus) as consonance increases.

(2) Case 2: symmetric firms, high firm interaction Case 2 depicts a duopolistic product group with stronger interfirm rivalry. All demand and cost parameters are identical with those of Case 1 except that $b_{i,j}$ has been raised from 3.475 to 10, so that rivals' prices have much greater impacts on firms' sales than in the earlier case. Profits of both firms begin at higher levels in the $\theta = 0$ situation and rise rapidly as tacit collusion increases. Solutions for the selected values of θ-values are given in Table 9.4.

The returns to cooperation are much more rewarding to the firms when compared with those of Case 1. Price rises are substantially higher despite the fact that costs are unchanged from the earlier case, but note that the quality variables in the $\theta = 0$ solution are less satisfactory from the viewpoint of the consumer despite the existence of higher Ω_i values. The larger x_i values in this case reduce the degrees of improvements in the quality characteristics necessary to reequate the righthand side and lefthand side of (9.10), since x_i affects only the numerators of the marginal policy cost terms. Only when the θ values attain 0.5 (for μ_i and σ_i) or 0.4 (for w_i) does x_i decline sufficiently to permit these variables to improve over their respective Case 1 values. This is an interesting insight: the greater the interaction and interdependence of rivals, the larger the sales of each rival and the less improvement therefore that the quality characteristics must undergo, although they do improve as consonance increases.

Table 9.4 Case 2 solutions for the symmetric duopoly, for selected θ-values

θ	p_i	M_i	Σ_i	w_i	π_i	Ω_i	x_i	*Consumers' surplus*	*Social surplus*
0.0	$3,467.94	8.811	3.487	1.237	$106,435,500	$2,768.27	55,367	$153,275,200	$366,146,300
0.1	3,564.39	8.932	3.433	1.248	109,061,500	2,867.85	54,489	148,452,600	366,575,600
0.2	3,686.44	9.051	3.300	1.973	112,484,200	2,981.63	53,670	144,023,500	368,991,900
0.3	3,797.38	9.173	3.319	2.027	115,145,400	3,097.73	52,662	138,664,300	368,955,100
0.4	3,936.32	9.295	3.258	2.620	118,004,300	3,225.51	51,608	133,169,300	369,177,900
0.5	4,067.39	9.419	3.193	2.760	120,546,700	3,362.04	50,431	127,164,300	368,257,700
0.6	4,208.27	9.543	3.126	2.877	122,882,300	3,510.11	49,142	120,746,800	366,511,400
0.7	4,362.94	9.666	3.055	3.066	125,054,600	3,672.48	47,742	113,964,900	364,074,100
0.8	4,530.45	9.790	2.982	3.234	126,858,900	3,850.11	46,202	106,731,200	360,449,100
0.9	4,712.48	9.913	2.906	3.386	128,207,600	4,045.80	44,504	99,030,290	355,445,500
1.0	4,913.22	10.035	2.827	3.557	128,907,900	4,262.25	42,623	90,836,010	348,651,800

Table 9.5 A comparison of consumers' surplus and contribution of quality variables to its value for Case 2

		Quality contribution	
θ	*Consumers' surplus*	*Value*	*Percentage of total*
0.0	153,275,200	255,552	0.17%
0.1	148,452,600	723,700	0.49
0.2	144,023,500	3,109,984	1.98
0.3	138,664,300	3,325,700	2.40
0.4	133,169,300	4,965,500	3.73
0.5	127,164,300	5,511,100	4.33
0.6	120,746,800	5,942,100	4.92
0.7	113,964,900	6,456,400	5.67
0.8	106,731,200	6,845,380	6.41
0.9	99,030,290	7,115,910	7.19
1.0	90,836,010	7,325,280	8.06

Profits to cooperation among intensely interactive firms rise rapidly not only because prices are raised higher than in less interactive environments but because rivals are not led to high degrees of product quality enhancement. This advantage does diminish or disappear as θ rises and outputs shrink sufficiently as Table 9.5 illustrates in the rapidly rising portion of consumers' surplus contributed by quality improvements.

Most interestingly, when $\theta \in [0,0.3]$ social surplus *rises* as output shrinks despite the monotonic fall in consumers' surplus. Thus, it does not occur because of a rise in consumers' surplus due to improvements in brand qualities, but simply because oligopoly rent increases outweigh slightly those falls in consumers' surplus. However, a weak incidence of this potential is exhibited in Table 9.5 for $\theta = 0.1$ and 0.3: if the fall in consumers' surplus corrected for quality variation is compared with the rise in profits in these two instances, it is seen that the fall in such corrected consumers' surplus outweighs the rise in profits and this form of social surplus would fall. That is, in these two instances, if quality variables had not improved social surplus it would have revealed its expected decline as collusion increased.

(3) Case 3: symmetric firms, enhanced demand parameters As a last symmetric model Case 3 was set up to explore the implications of increasing the demand effects of quality characteristics improvements. Parameters of Case 2 are adopted except for increases in the linear term coefficients for quality variables and decreases in their quadratic terms, so that favorable increases

Table 9.6 Case 3 solutions for the symmetric duopoly, for selected θ-values

θ	p_i	M_i	Σ_i	w_i	π_i	Ω_i	x_i	*Consumers' surplus*	*Social surplus*
0.0	$3,810.39	11.648	3.182	5.059	$122,558,100	2,866.80	57,336	$164,370,900	$409,487,100
0.1	3,929.70	11.901	3.095	5.346	126,556,800	2,978.00	56,582	160,076,100	413,189,700
0.2	4,058.78	12.159	3.001	5.670	130,629,100	3,097.91	55,762	155,470,000	416,728,300
0.3	4,195.09	12.422	2.901	6.001	134,799,200	3,227.96	54,875	150,563,300	420,161,700
0.4	4,340.70	12.691	2.793	6.334	138,929,100	3,368.47	53,896	145,239,000	423,097,200
0.5	4,498.98	12.964	2.676	6.714	143,096,000	3,521.88	52,828	139,539,900	425,731,900
0.6	4,657.99	13.243	2.551	6.979	147,177,500	3,689.45	51,649	133,381,000	427,736,000
0.7	4,783.00	13.534	2.411	6.543	149,777,300	3,860.81	50,193	125,966,900	425,521,500
0.8	4,952.80	13.829	2.260	6.431	151,822,300	4,047.41	48,571	117,957,100	421,601,700
0.9	5,183.86	14.115	2.103	7.144	155,909,200	4,279.39	47,051	110,689,800	422,508,200
1.0	5,389.91	14.417	1.926	6.980	156,050,200	4,500.74	45,007	101,281,500	413,381,900

over benchmark values yield more sales to the firm and the sales "decay" more slowly as this gap between the relevant quality and its benchmark increases.

Results of the runs are for the most part unexceptionable. Profits are larger than in Case 2 for each θ, although, as in that case, they rise by decreasing amounts as costs rise and the quadratic terms in the demand terms for quality characteristics take their toll on sales. Product characteristics are substantially improved over Case 2 values, but the most interesting aspect of the solutions is the reduction in w_i for θs of 0.7, 0.8 and 1.0. In these higher reaches of collusion, x_i has declined to so low a value that marginal policy costs per unit of marginal sales fall, so w_i must fall to reequate the lefthand side and righthand side of (9.10.4). With the larger outputs of Case 3, consumers' surplus is larger than that of Case 2 and declines monotonically with θ, and the decline in social surplus occurs at $\theta = 0.7$ in Case 3 rather than 0.4 by virtue of the higher profits in the former case; however, in that case the rise in w_i between $\theta = 0.8$ and 0.9 interrupts the decline.

Table 9.7 presents the contribution of the enhanced quality variables to consumers' surplus, and the results are best compared with those of Case 1 in Table 9.3. The more meaningful comparability with that case rather than Case 2 arises because Case 2 increases the importance of interfirm price interaction, obscuring the impact of improved quality with price factors unchanged. Cases 1 and 3 differ only in the importance given the quality

Table 9.7 A comparison of consumers' surplus and contribution of quality variables to its value for Case 3

		Quality contribution	
θ	*Consumers' surplus*	*Value*	*Percentage of total*
0.0	$164,370,900	$12,758,580	7.76%
0.1	160,076,100	13,288,740	8.30
0.2	155,470,000	13,791,140	8.87
0.3	150,563,300	14,184,560	9.42
0.4	145,239,000	14,446,600	9.95
0.5	139,539,900	14,667,890	10.10
0.6	133,381,000	14,495,460	10.87
0.7	125,966,900	12,734,780	10.11
0.8	117,957,100	11,509,720	9.76
0.9	110,689,800	11,793,490	10.65
1.0	101,281,500	10,177,410	10.05

variables in the parameters of the demand function. As quality variables rise with tacit collusion, demand functions shift to the right and become more inelastic in step with the size of the demand function parameters for the quality variables. This permits firms to raise prices without suffering the larger relative sales losses that would occur in the absence of these parameter changes. Case 3, therefore, reveals higher consumers' surplus as a consequence. Relative contributions of the quality variables to that welfare index are uniformly higher in Case 3 than in Case 1, as would be expected. However, the contribution declines in the higher consonance coefficient ranges in Case 3 whereas it rises monotonically in Case 1. This results from the reduction in w_i when $\theta = 0.6$ and the failure of that variable to rise much or its tendency to actually fall over most of the $\theta = 0.7$ to 1.0 range.

(b) The short run: Case 1 revisited with nonidentical θ-values

Table 9.8 presents the solutions in cases where the firms share Case 1 parameter values but may have different fixed θ-values. To keep the presentation manageable pairs of θ-values are incremented by 0.2 instead of 0.1.

In the short-run we approach Table 9.8 with the question: "What price and quality variable profiles would combinations of consonance coefficients imply if those combinations were fixed by forces inherent in the folkways, mores and history of the industry?" It turns out that an introduction to answering this question is offered by approaching the matrix of Table 9.8 as a normal game form with profits as payoff utilities.

A rival's increase in its θ value is no guarantee that a firm's profit will benefit. Monotonic rises in firm 1's profits as firm θ raises θ_2 occur only for $\theta_1 = 0$ and 0.6. Firm 1's best payoff occurs at $\theta = [0.4,1]$ (and, of course, given the identical demand and cost functions of the firms, firm θ's at $\theta = [1,0.4]$), and those choices might be likely as *dominant firm* strategies under rivalrous consonance. The rather unpredictable behavior of profits and with them the price and quality variables is highlighted by Figure 9.2. The global maximum for π_1 occurs at [0.4,1] substantially higher than at [1,1], and this occurs because the quality variables at the former point are considerably lower in the quality scale than at the latter point; this would not have happened in Chapter 3 where price competition only was operative. Consider also the local minimum in the neighborhood of [0.2,8]: this θ-conjuncture features a large jump in price and strong improvements in the quality of Firm 1's output conjoined with a sharp falls in Firm 2's prices and product quality to reduce Firm 1's profits below those of its immediate neighbors and to raise Firm 2's profits. The reasons for such sharp breaks are extremely difficult to isolate. In general, the billowing nature of the profit surface gives visual evidence that profits and the underlying price–nonprice optima are not simple monotonic relations with the size of own- or other-θ values.

Table 9.8 Solution values for selected nonidentical θ-values, Case 1

			θ_2			
θ_1	*0*	*0.2*	*0.4*	*0.6*	*0.8*	*1.0*
0	μ:9.156;9.156 σ:3.326;3.326 w:1.816;1.816 p:2802.28;2802.28 π:4.47627;4.47627 x:44,224;44,224 Ω:2,211;2,211	μ:9.154;9.234 σ:3.327;3.288 w:1.979;2.064 p:2809.87;2845.92 π:4.51125;4.48751 x:44,295;43,536 Ω:2,215;2,255	μ:9.152;9.312 σ:3.328;3.248 w:1.967;2.126 p:2813.42;2886.52 π:4.54261;4.48754 x:44,359;42,810 Ω:2,218;2,300	μ:9.150;9.390 σ:3.329;3.208 w:1.965;2.206 p:2817.40;2928.97 π:4.57508;4.48110 x:44,424;42,055 Ω:2,221;2,348	μ:9.148;9.467 σ:3.330;3.166 w:1.967;2.290 p:2821.56;2973.03 π:4.60943;4.46702 x:44,494;41,270 Ω:2,225;2,397	μ:9.146;9.545 σ:3.331;3.123 w:1.957;2.375 p:2825.71;3018.68 π:4.64407;4.44428 x:44,563;40,451 Ω:2,228;2,448
0.2	μ:9.234;9.154 σ:3.288;3.327 w:2.064;1.979 p:2845.92;2809.87 π:4.48751;4.51125 x:43,536;44,295 Ω:2,255;2,215	μ:9.232;9.232 σ:3.289;3.289 w:2.176;2.176 p:2258.45;2258.45 π:4.51929;4.51929 x:43,599;43,599 Ω:2,258;2,258	μ:9.230;9.310 σ:3.290;3.249 w:2.041;2.127 p:2853.18;2890.47 π:4.54869;4.51744 x:43,658;42,869 Ω:2,261;2,304	μ:9.228;9.388 σ:3.291;3.209 w:2.037;2.207 p:2857.12;2932.90 π:4.58174;4.51169 x:43,724;42,114 Ω:2,265;2,351	μ:9.466;9.226 σ:3.167;3.292 w:2.198;2.040 p:2975.06;2861.24 π:4.49635;4.61405 x:43,787;41,325 Ω:2,268;2,400	μ:9.224;9.543 σ:3.293;3.124 w:2.035;2.375 p:2865.68;3022.77 π:4.65104;4.47459 x:43,861;40,507 Ω:2,272;2,451
0.4	μ:9.312;9.152 σ:3.248;3.328 w:2.126;1.967 p:2886.52;2813.42 π:4.48754;4.54261 x:42,810;44,359 Ω:2,300;2,218	μ:9.310;9.230 σ:3.249;3.290 w:2.127;2.041 p:2890.47;2853.18 π:4.51744;4.54869 x:42,869;43,658 Ω:2,304;2,261	μ:9.308;9.308 σ:3.250;3.250 w:2.250;2.250 p:2897.58;2897.58 π:4.55078;4.55078 x:42,934;42,934 Ω:2,307;2,307	μ:9.306;9.386 σ:3.251;3.209 w:2.115;2.195 p:2898.31;2936.79 π:4.58191;4.54241 x:42,995;42,173 Ω:2,310;2,354	μ:9.464;9.304 σ:3.168;3.252 w:2.286;2.122 p:2981.11;2902.76 π:4.52891;4.61623 x:43,062;41,387 Ω:2,314;2,403	μ:9.302;9.542 σ:3.253;3.125 w:2.111;2.394 p:2907.05;3027.24 π:4.65140;4.50795 x:43,130;40,569 Ω:2,318;2,456

Table 9.8 continued

θ_1	θ_2: *0*	*0.2*	*0.4*	*0.6*	*0.8*	*1.0*
0.6	μ:9.390;9.150 σ:3.208;3.329 w:2.206;1.965 p:2828.97;2817.40 π:4.48110;4.57508 x:42,055;44,424 Ω:2,348;2,221	μ:9.388;9.228 σ:3.209;3.291 w:2.207;2.037 p:2932.90;2857.12 π:4.51169;4.58174 x:42,114;43,724 Ω:2,351;2,265	μ:9.386;9.306 σ:3.209;3.251 w:2.195;2.115 p:2936.79;2898.31 π:4.54241;4.58191 x:42,173;42,995 Ω:2,354;2,310	μ:9.384;9.384 σ:3.210;3.210 w:2.326;3.326 p:2944.29;2944.29 π:4.57706;4.57706 x:42,240;42,240 Ω:2,358;2,358	μ:9.383;9.462 σ:3.211;3.169 w:2.199;2.282 p:2945.45;2985.32 π:4.60954;4.56147 x:42,308;41,448 Ω:2,361;2,407	μ:9.381;9.540 σ:3.212;3.126 w:2.201;2.354 p:2949.99;3031.07 π:4.64497;4.53718 x:42,370;40,623 Ω:2,365;2,412
0.8	μ:9.467;9.148 σ:3.166;3.330 w:2.290;1.967 p:2973.03;2821.56 π:4.46702;4.60934 x:41,270;44,494 Ω:2,397;2,225	μ:9.226;9.466 σ:3.292;3.167 w:2.040;2.198 p:2861.24;2975.06 π:4.61405;4.49635 x:41,325;43,787 Ω:2,400;2,268	μ:9.304;9.464 σ:3.252;3.168 w:2.122;2.286 p:2902.76;2981.11 π:4.61623;4.52891 x:41,387;43,062 Ω:2,403;2,314	μ:9.462;9.383 σ:3.169;3.211 w:2.282;2.199 p:2985.32;2945.45 π:4.56147;4.60954 x:41,448;42,308 Ω:2,407;2,361	μ:9.461;9.461 σ:3.170;3.170 w:2.413;2.413 p:2993.04;2993.04 π:4.59736;4.59736 x:41,516;41,516 Ω:2,411;2,411	μ:9.573;9.459 σ:3.127;3.171 w:2.370;2.281 p:3035.80;2994.40 π:4.57251;4.63046 x:41,578;40,689 Ω:2,415;2,462
1.0	μ:9.545;9.146 σ:3.123;3.331 w:2.375;1.957 p:3018.68;2825.71 π:4.44428;4.64407 x:40,451;44,563 Ω:2,448;2,228	μ:9.543;9.224 σ:3.124;3.293 w:2.375;2.035 p:3022.77;2865.68 π:4.47459;4.65104 x:40,507;43,861 Ω:2,451;2,272	μ:9.542;9.302 σ:3.125;3.253 w:2.394;2.111 p:3027.24;2907.05 π:4.50795;4.65140 x:40,569;43,130 Ω:2,456;2,318	μ:9.540;9.381 σ:3.126;3.212 w:2.354;2.201 p:3031.07;2949.99 π:4.53718;4.64497 x:42,370;40,623 Ω:2,365;2,412	μ:9.459;9.573 σ:3.171;3.127 w:2.281;2.370 p:2994.40;3035.80 π:4.63046;4.57251 x:40,689;41,578 Ω:2,462;2,415	μ:9.537;9.537 σ:2.128;2.128 w:2.506;2.506 p:3043.95;3043.95 π:4.60968;4.60968 x:40,757;40,757 Ω:2,466;2,766

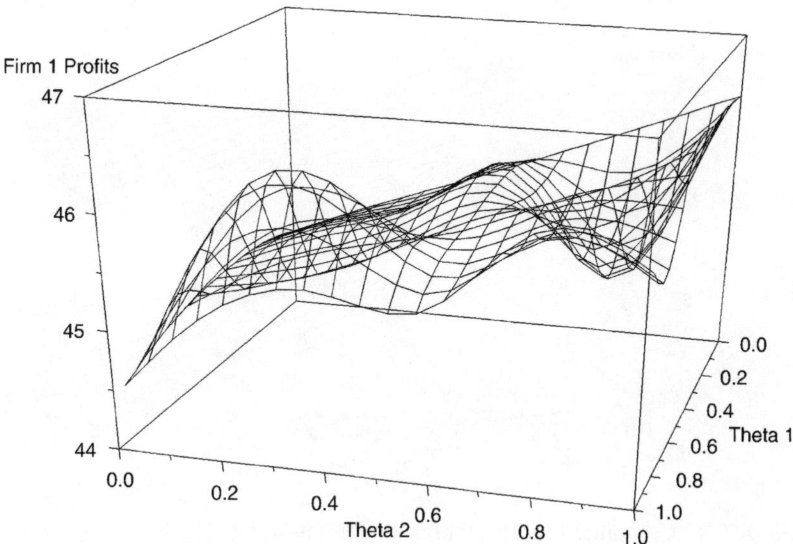

Figure 9.2 Firm 1 profits, case 1

In general, the established relations between prices and the quality variables discerned in Chapter 8 and in Cases 1, 2 and, 3 of this chapter in which quality characteristics move in the directions of improvement as prices rise and deterioration as prices fall become more complex with differing θ-values. Consider the table from the viewpoint of firm 1 as firm 2 increases θ_2, so that we travel across the rows in Table 9.8 or from left to right along a θ_1 contour in Figure 9.2. In general, both firms' prices rise as firm 2 increases its consonance coefficients for a fixed firm 1 coefficient. But firm 1's output in most cases rises while that of firm 2 falls as θ_2 falls, which increases the marginal policy costs of quality variables, especially for μ_1 and σ_1 which are especially sensitive to quantity changes. Therefore, firm 1's quality variables fall in order to equate righthand sides to Ω_1, which rises but by small amounts. Firm 1 is permitted to enjoy rising profits from firm 2's increasing deference while reducing the quality of its product. In Cases 1, 2, and 3 when firms raised their consonance coefficients in lockstep, prices and quality rose together, but in the present case of nonidentical θ-values a firm benefitting from a rival's enhanced deference is able to depreciate its product quality in order to maximize its profits.

(1) Some social welfare consequences On the other hand, consumers' and social surplus are related to the consonance coefficients in near-linear manners. Figure 9.3 depicts consumers' surplus as a function of θ_1 and θ_2, with

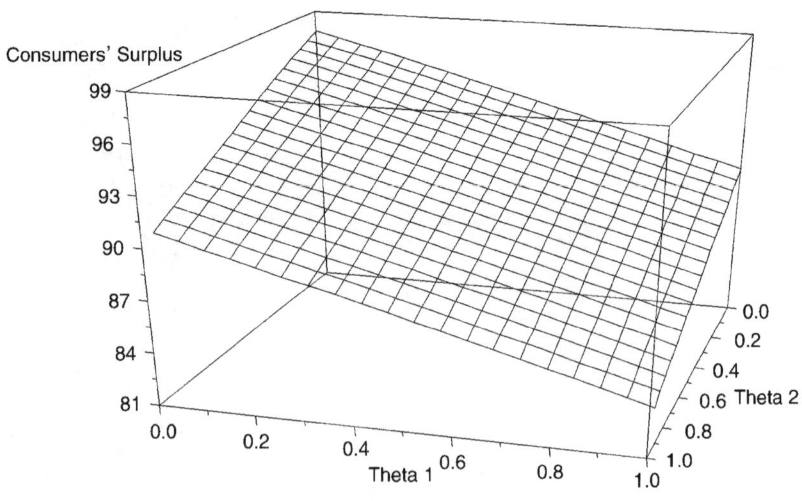

Figure 9.3 Consumers' surplus for selected θ-values

a global maximum at [0,0] and minimum at [1,1], with intermediate and equal values at the dominant firm strategies of [1,0] and [0,1]. With the addition of profits to obtain social surplus, a slightly less planar aspect is given to social surplus, and indeed some small rises and dips do occur in the contours. Nonetheless the socially harmful effects of rivalrous consonance as measured by social surplus are effectively demonstrated. Figure 9.4 displays the social surplus surface.

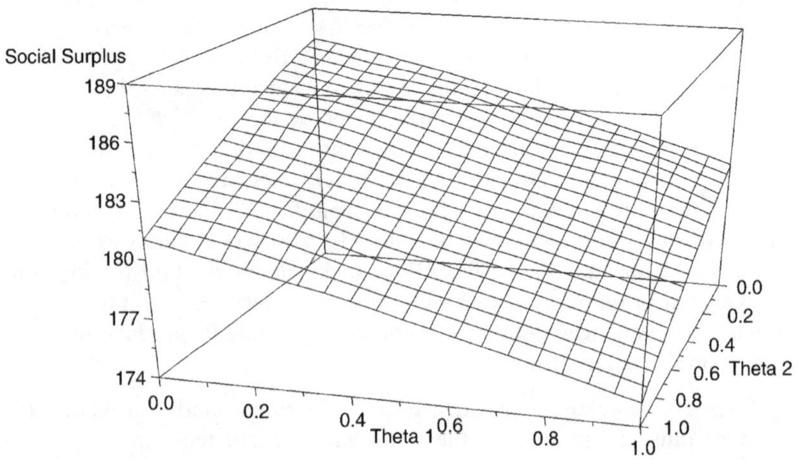

Figure 9.4 Social surplus for selected θ-values

2 *The Intermediate Run*

(a) The short run revisited

We may begin our discussion of the intermediate run adjustments of duopolistic firms by treating Table 9.8 in an intermediate- rather than short-run context. Readers with a strong game-theoretic bent may view the table as a two-person, nonzero sum payoff matrix in a normal game form and interpret the implications of the model in reactive strategic terms. Of course, the arguments in Chapter 3 in support of the rivalrous consonance approach oppose this view in short-term and medium-term analysis with the assertion that the cell of the matrix that will rule must be determined largely by the power structure of the specific oligopoly under analysis and by other associated politico–sociological factors in the industry's environment. These determinants may well lead to violations of the axioms of "rational" choice that underlie decision theory. The ultrarationalistic game-theoretic outlook in the intermediate run analysis is adopted only hesitantly because I believe these factors will continue to exercise their important conflict-tempering influences, which are "arational" in the narrow sense of the term. Nevertheless, the game theorist's approach has something to contribute in the intermediate run since the self-interest aspect of firms' actions will play one of many roles in determining the power structure of the industry and should not be ignored. However, the destabilizing potential of such power struggles will be constrained by the tempering forces of cooperation in mature industries – a possibility that cooperative game theory is increasingly recognizing.

In the intermediate run firms are assumed to be able to alter their θ values to institute structural changes in the power structure of the industry. As indicated in Chapter 3, any of a number of motivations can account for fundamental shifts in the patterns of deference rivals develop among one another, but unquestionably one of the important factors impelling such moves will be the profit motive. In this I am in accord with the game theorist who focusses primarily upon rather straightforward profit (or utility) payoffs; however, it is the inherent nature of game theory in its search for generalizable patterns of action and reaction (rather than the broader notion of *interaction*) to focus on such simplisitic measures and to neglect the subtler determinants of cooperation and competition that operate in realistic oligopolistic contexts. In this section, however, I will follow the game theorist's lead and assume that in the intermediate run powerful drives toward greater profitability will be dominant in dictating consonance coefficients.

Somewhat surprisingly, perhaps, neither firm in the case whose solutions are summarized in Table 9.8 exhibits a dominant strategy nor does a Nash equilibrium exist. One might expect that strategy set [1,1] would exhibit both qualities, but such is not the case, and it is the quality variables that afford the greatest barrier to their emergence. Also, the parameter symmetry of the firms militates against their attainment. As noted in the discussion of the table in short-run contexts, in general, for a given firm i θ-strategy, increases in firm j's θ do not necessarily benefit firm i's profit. Monotonic rises in firm 1's profits as firm 2 raises θ_2 occur only for $\theta_1 = 0$ and 0.6. Firm 1's best payoff occurs at $\theta = [0.4,1]$ (and, of course, firm θ's at $\theta = [1,0.4]$), and those choices might emerge as *dominant-firm* strategies under rivalrous consonance.

Where the game theorist might have recourse to mixed strategies in non-cooperative games, rivalrous consonance would have an initial expectation that the duopoly over successive plays would adopt some intermediate compromise power structure despite its potential instability in a type of cooperative game. Strategy set [1,1] – the Chamberlin point – seems a likely compromise, with both firms sacrificing about 1 percent of their maximum profits to attain a steady state in which they earn returns exceeded in only 7 of the cells of the payoff matrix, all of which inflict substantial sacrifices on the rival which makes their attainment a nonrational expectation. In general, we should expect that in symmetric firm rivalry, a "focal point" will occur at the Chamberlin solution.

(b) Case 4: Nonsymmetric firms with variable θ-values

In the study of behavior in the intermediate run, the case just considered is a construction in which the firms are symmetric in demand and cost conditions but nonsymmetric in consonance coefficients. In Case 4, to which we now turn, the model assumes asymmetry in both respects: firms 1 and 2 have Case 1 and Case 2 demand–cost parameters (as listed in Table 9.1) respectively and in general have different consonance coefficients as well.

Firm 1 differs from firm 2 wholly in its demand factors. It is much less favored by consumers than firm 2, and therefore is the weaker rival. It is believed that this is the more usual case among mature rivals, in that all have access to quite similar technologies and equally efficient factor services, so that costs for similar quality mixes are about the same. Mature firms are more likely to be differentiated by the strength of demand among their consumer bases with sources in such factors as reputation, marketing skills and design, none of which is explicitly included in the mix of qualities we are analyzing. Because we are interested in illustrating the frame-work and deriving broader interpretations of variable behavior using a single simulation, it was deemed more useful to distinguish the firms on this basis.

Once more a mesh of 0.2 for consonance coefficients has been employed in 36 runs to obtain the solutions for strategy sets $\Theta = [\theta_1, \theta_2]$, and they are presented in normal game theoretic form in Table 9.9. Our interest, however, will not be exclusively in "solutions" and their plausibility, but will be directed extensively to that which has interested us from the beginning: the behavior of prices and quality characteristics as they interact to maximize profit through changes in the θ's with fixed industry standards μ, σ and w. The methodology for solution of Case 4 is an extension of that used for the symmetric Cases 1, 2, and 3 analyzed in normal form in Tables 9.2, 9.4, and 9.6, as well as for a case in Table 9.8 in which two firms having the same Case 1 demand–cost parameters have different θ values.

Not surprisingly, it is firm 1 – the "weaker" rival – that gains most from increases in tacit collusion. For example, a comparison of profits between $\Theta = [0,0]$ and $\Theta = [1,1]$ in Table 9.9 reveals that firm 1's profits rise by 20.6 percent whereas firm 2's profits *fall* by 16.6 percent. Figure 9.5 reveals rather dramatically how firm 1 benefits from higher θ coefficients. On it the θ_1 axis forms the north–south dimension of the base plane and the θ_2 axis the east–west dimension, with firm 1 profits on the vertical axis. For any value of θ_1 the contour formed by varying θ_2 between 0 and 1 rises monotonically with a slightly convex configuration. The contours formed by constant θ_2 values are gently strictly concave, with profits rising to $\theta_1 = 0.4$ or 0.6 and falling barely perceptibly on the graph to $\theta_1 = 1$ with an occasional small reversal of direction. Firm 1 profits are maximized at $\Theta = [0.8,1]$, or at near-complete rivalrous consonance.

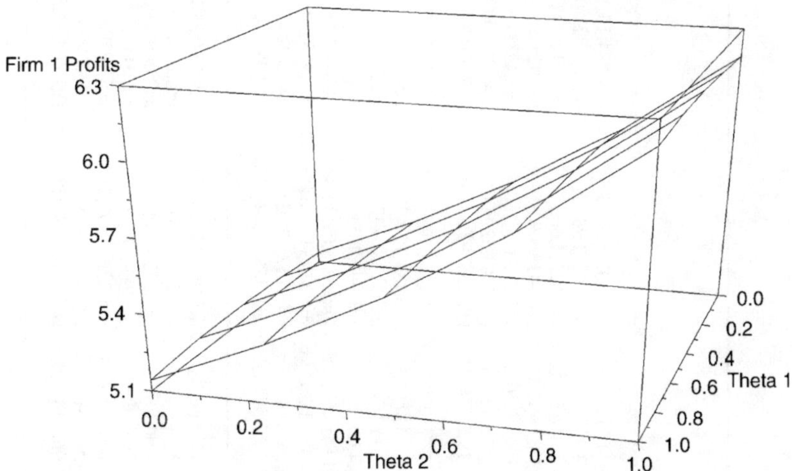

Figure 9.5 Firm 1 profits as a function of θ-coefficients

Table 9.9 Solution values for selected nonidentical θ-values, nonsymmetric case

θ_1	θ_2: *0*	*0.2*	*0.4*	*0.6*	*0.8*	*1.0*
0	μ:9.114;11.738 σ:3.347;3.152 w:1.934;4.000 p:2,886.18;3,663.16 π:5.146109;11.36634 x:45,564;55,935 Ω:2,278.19;2,796.74	μ:9.105;12.419 σ:3.351;2.902 w:1.925;4.000 p:2,903.98;3,854.48 π:5.297315;11.441830 x:45,863;52,806 Ω:2,292.93;3,000.35	μ:9.094;13.126 σ:3.357;2.604 w:1.911;4.000 p:2,924.60;4,075.00 π:5.472907;11.300020 x:46,203;49,110 Ω:2,310.17;3,230.92	μ:9.082;13.844 σ:3.362;3.251 w:1.899;4.000 p:2,948.21;4,327.32 π:5.675021;10.890480 x:46,595;44,782 Ω:2,329.74;3,498.63	μ:9.068;14.558 σ:3.369;1.837 w:1.877;4.000 p:2,975.11;4,616.95 π:5.909407;10.115020 x:47,045;39,700 Ω:2,352.23;3,817.30	μ:9.051;15.245 σ:3.377;1.362 w:1.871;4.000 p:3,006.79;4,953.82 π:6.185178;8.801451 x:47,568;33,661 Ω:2,378.42;4,207.59
0.2	μ:9.193;11.724 σ:3.308;3.157 w:2.005;4.000 p:2,927.81;3,676.68 π:5.160448;11.50388 x:44,859;56,154 Ω:2,323.70;2,807.68	μ:9.184;12.407 σ:3.313;2.907 w:1.997;4.000 p:2,946.09;3,868.87 π:5.312347;11.581560 x:45,152;53,015 Ω:2,338.90;3,012.20	μ:9.174;13.115 σ:3.318;2.609 w:1.987;4.000 p:2,967.11;4,090.41 π:5.488721;11.439740 x:45,491;49,305 Ω:2,356.41;3,243.75	μ:9.162;13.835 σ:3.324;2.256 w:1.984;4.000 p:2,991.28;4,343.84 π:5.693012;11.029910 x:45,879;44,964 Ω:2,376;3,512.78	μ:9.149;14.551 σ:3.330;1.842 w:1.964;4.000 p:3,018.80;4,634.89 π:5.928219;10.249650 x:46,323;39,862 Ω:2,399.53;3,832.88	μ:9.133;15.241 σ:3.338;1.366 w:1.915;4.000 p:3,049.76;4,972.82 π:6.197276;8.922771 x:46,825;33,795 Ω:2,425.56;4,224.33
0.4	μ:9.273;11.709 σ:3.268;3.162 w:2.082;4.000 p:2,971.03;3,690.71 π:5.168451;11.64730 x:44,125;56,381 Ω:2,371.06;2,819.05	μ:9.264;12.396 σ:3.273;2.911 w:2.072;4.000 p:2,989.84;3,885.82 π:5.322405;11.701650 x:44,418;53,193 Ω:2,386.76;3,022.35	μ:9.254;13.104 σ:3.278;2.614 w:2.060;4.000 p:3,011.02;4,106.12 π:5.497935;11.587530 x:44,748;49,510 Ω:2,404.53;3,257.27	μ:9.243;13.826 σ:3.283;2.261 w:2.030;4.000 p:3,035.31;4,360.73 π:5.700527;11.730700 x:45,127;45,149 Ω:2,424.89;3,527.26	μ:9.230;14.544 σ:3.290;1.846 w:2.030;4.000 p:3,063.66;4,653.32 π:5.938961;10.388510 x:45,569;40,028 Ω:2,448.63;3,848.87	μ:9.215;15.236 σ:3.298;1.370 w:2.025;4.000 p:3,096.62;4,993.52 π:6.217885;9.055638 x:46,081;33,941 Ω:2,476.12;4,424.58

Table 9.9 continued

θ_1	θ_2: *0*	*0.2*	*0.4*	*0.6*	*0.8*	*1.0*
0.6	μ:9.352;11.694 σ:3.228;3.167 w:2.162;4.000 p:3,015.86;3,705.34 π:5.169467;11.79578 x:43,362;56,615 Ω:2,420.42;2,830.77	μ:9.344;12.380 σ:3.232;2.917 w:2.160;4.000 p:3,034.95;3,899.08 π:5.322791;11.880770 x:43,648;53,459 Ω:2,436.37;3,037.43	μ:9.334;13.092 σ:3.237;2.619 w:2.142;4.000 p:3,056.66;4,122.56 π:5.500458;11.740011 x:43,977;49,722 Ω:2,454.73;3,271.17	μ:9.324;13.280 σ:3.242;2.265 w:2.137;4.000 p:3,079.87;4,372.02 π:5.691117;11.271370 x:44,327;45,276 Ω:2,474.28;3,537.17	μ:9.311;14.537 σ:3.249;1.851 w:2.125;4.000 p:3,110.61;4,672.60 π:5.944248;10.434440 x:44,788;40,202 Ω:2,500.00;3,865.60	μ:9.297;15.230 σ:3.256;1.373 w:2.021;4.000 p:3,142.81;5,013.93 π:6.215007;9.187163 x:45,275;34,085 Ω:2,527.23;4,260.58
0.8	μ:9.431;11.678 σ:3.186;3.172 w:2.249;4.000 p:3,062.42;3,720.44 π:5.163031;11.95162 x:42,567;56,860 Ω:2,471.95;2,843.02	μ:9.423;12.366 σ:3.190;2.922 w:2.226;4.000 p:3,081.54;3,914.95 π:5.315415;12.038180 x:42,846;53,691 Ω:2,488.15;3,050.62	μ:9.414;13.080 σ:3.195;2.625 w:2.226;4.000 p:3,104.02;4,139.60 π:5.494748;11.899350 x:43,172;49,941 Ω:2,507.07;3,285.61	μ:9.404;13.806 σ:3.200;2.720 w:2.213;4.000 p:3,129.55;4,396.88 π:5.700914;11.481520 x:43,543;45,546 Ω:2,528.65;3,558.25	μ:9.392;14.529 σ:3.207;1.856 w:2.199;4.000 p:3,158.93;4,692.44 π:5.939689;10.685320 x:43,970;40,381 Ω:2,553.43;3,882.82	μ:9.378;15.225 σ:3.214;1.378 w:2.189;4.000 p:3,193.18;5,036.22 π:6.220793;9.331405 x:44,467;34,242 Ω:2,582.30;4,280.23
1.0	μ:9.510;11.662 σ:3.143;3.178 w:2.330;4.000 p:3,110.60;3,736.03 π:5.147244;12.11408 x:41,737;57,115 Ω:2,525.69;2,855.74	μ:9.502;12.352 σ:3.147;2.928 w:2.326;4.000 p:3,130.45;3,931.72 π:5.301559;12.202580 x:42,014;53,932 Ω:2,542.46;3,064.34	μ:9.494;13.067 σ:3.152;2.630 w:2.315;4.000 p:3,153.23;4,157.34 π:5.480313;12.065360 x:42,333;50,169 Ω:2,561.75;3,300.61	μ:9.484;13.796 σ:3.157;2.277 w:2.252;4.000 p:3,178.16;4,415.51 π:5.686404;11.641530 x:42,698;45,750 Ω:2,583.77;3,514.23	μ:9.473;14.521 σ:3.164;1.861 w:2.296;4.000 p:3,209.41;4,713.16 π:5.927690;10.843610 x:43,121;40,568 Ω:2,609.42;3,900.81	μ:9.459;15.219 σ:3.171;1.382 w:2.272;4.000 p:3,244.24;5,058.75 π:6.208111;9.477958 x:43,607;34,401 Ω:2,638.86;4,300.10

On the other hand, Figure 9.6 shows a quite different profits pattern for firm 2. With θ_2 graphed on the north–south base plane axis and θ_1 the east–west, the graph shows θ_2 contours that rise monotonically and reach a local maximum on the $\theta_2 = 0.6$ contour at $\theta_1 = 0.4$. The θ_1 contours rise to maxima at $\theta_2 = 0.2$ and fall thereafter, indicating firm 2's inability to benefit much from other than mild tacit collusion. Indeed, firm 2 attains its global maximum at $\Theta = [1,0.2]$, at which configuration the firm's further cooperation is costly in profit terms.

A Nash equilibrium exists at $\Theta = [0.6,0.2]$. This may be seen by noting that only strategies $\theta_1 = 0.4$, 0.6, and 0.8 are undominated for firm 1 and $\theta_2 = 0.2$ and 0.6 for firm 2. The reduced matrix is presented in Table 9.10. Firm 1 is led, as the weaker firm, to defer to firm 2, but both firms benefit when compared with the noncollusive strategy set $\Theta = [0,0]$, firm 1 by 3.4 percent and firm 2 by 4.5 percent. Were firms in the intermediate run to be motivated wholly by the search for profit floors below which rivals could not reduce them, they would search out these joint strategies.

But, without belaboring the point, we urge again that the burden of rivalrous consonance is that the motivations of firms seeking a mature stability may be quite different from the Nash equilibrium, as game theorists themselves admit.[6] Consider, for example, $\Theta = [0.8,0.4]$ or $[1,0.4]$. Both of these are Pareto superior to the Nash equilibrium in that both firms improve their

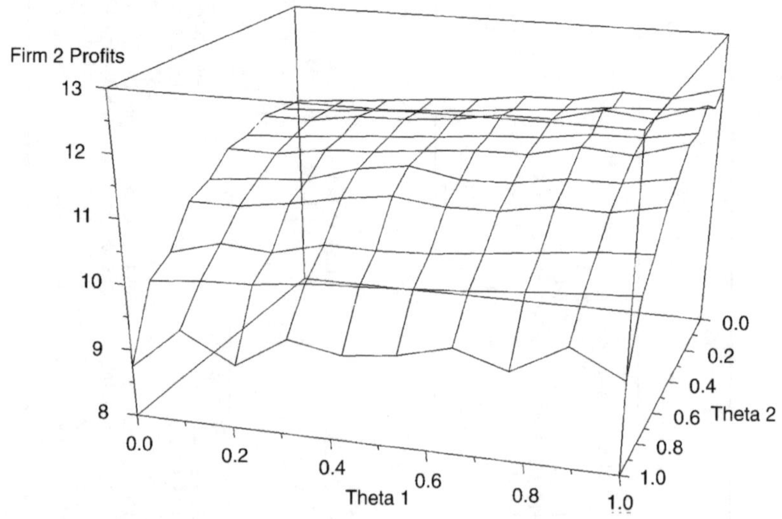

Figure 9.6 Firm 2 profits as a function of θ-coefficients

Table 9.10 Reduced payoff matrix, nonsymmetric case

		θ_2	
		0.2	0.6
	0.4	μ:9.264;12.396 σ:3.273;2.911 w:2.072;4.000 p:2,989.84;3,885.82 π:5.322405;11.701650 x:44,418;53,193 Ω:2,386.76;3,022.35	μ:9.243;13.826 σ:3.283;2.261 w:2.030;4.000 p:3,035.31;4,360.73 π:5.700527;11.730700 x:45,127;45,149 Ω:2,424.89;3,527.26
θ_1	0.6	μ:9.344;12.380 σ:3.232;2.917 w:2.160;4.000 p:3,034.95;3,899.08 π:5.322791;11.880770 x:43,648;53,459 Ω:2,436.37;3,037.43	μ:9.324;13.280 σ:3.242;2.265 w:2.137;4.000 p:3,079.87;4,372.02 π:5.691117;11.271370 x:44,327;45,276 Ω:2,474.28;3,537.17
	0.8	μ:9.423;12.366 σ:3.190;2.922 w:2.226;4.000 p:3,081.54;3,914.95 π:5.315415;12.038180 x:42,846;53,691 Ω:2,488.15;3,050.62	μ:9.404;13.806 σ:3.200;2.720 w:2.213;4.000 p:3,129.55;4,396.88 π:5.700914;11.481520 x:43,543;45,546 Ω:2,528.65;3,558.25

earnings. Given the greater market power of firm 2 the second might be considered a more likely prospect, but firm 2 might elect the first to help firm 1 in resisting the temptation to defect from the tacit agreement, although both firms have those temptations when profits alone are considered. In repeated play, this neighborhood might well be settled into by the industry. Also, at the Nash equilibrium firm 1 has the ability to punish firm 2 severely at small cost to itself by moving to Θ = [0.4,0.2] if firm 2 refuses to move to [0.8,0.4]. More importantly, as stressed in Chapter 3, a wide variety of other historical and socio–political–economic determinants of long-run market structure might well temper the drive to maximize straightforward profits and stabilize the industry in bounded rationality contexts.

Of more interest than these attempts to predict intermediate-run market structure are the patterns of price and nonprice movements under various strategy conjunctures. At the highest level of generalization, the general rules are that when a firm's θ is fixed and the rival's θ rises:

1 own- and rival-prices rise
2 own-qualities are degraded and rival-qualities improve or remain unchanged
3 own-profits rise and rival-profits rise in the lower values of own θ but fall for most values
4 own-outputs rise and rival-outputs fall.

Interestingly, as a firm extends deference to a nonreciprocating rival it does not reduce prices to enhance its competitiveness with its rival as that rival raises price. Rather, the deferring firm competes by increasing product quality , as its rival depreciates the quality of its product. This permits the firm with rising θ to limit its losses, but nonetheless in general its profits decline: costs rise to squeeze its profit margin. However, the rival's profits may rise over a portion of its θ = [0,1.0] domain (or else, of course, there could be no Nash equilibrium other than at Θ = [0,0]).

A most interesting outcome in Table 9.9 is that as such unreciprocated deference increases the benefiting firm *increases* output, certainly not a result anticipated in collusive market structures. Part of the reason for this unexpected outcome can be found in the simplicity of the model, which assumes that with every dollar of rise in a rival's price a firm's demand function shifts by undiminished amounts. The firms are essentially assumed to have unlimited opportunities to lift each other up by the bootstraps in terms of sales. But even if we placed nonlinear "drag" terms in the other-price portion of the demand functions, within the relatively small range within which prices change in the solutions of Table 9.9 one would expect such outcomes to occur. In welfare terms, combined outputs of the firms decline as rival's θ rises, so that consumers' surplus falls on the score of decreased quantities, although these will also reflect the shifts in the demand functions caused by changes in quality variables. But it would be quite possible if rival j's demand function were very qualities-elastic and firm i's very inelastic that both firms' outputs could rise and increasing collusion could lead to larger consumers' surplus. This possibility has been alluded to already in Chapter 8 and in this chapter.

3 The Long Run

If we disaggregate the quality variables we find that when θ_1 is fixed, θ_2 variable, μ_1 falls and σ_i rises in all solutions as θ_2 rises in all solutions, while μ_2 rises and σ_2 falls without exception.

General rule 2 holds without exception with respect to these two quality variables. For warranty periods w_i the record is a bit more complicated. When θ_1 is fixed, w_1 does fall as θ_2 rises except for 3 instances. When $\theta_1 = 0.4$ and θ_2 rises from 0.6 to 0.8, and when $\theta_1 = 0.8$ and θ_2 rises from 0.2 to 0.4, w_1 remains the same, and $\theta_1 = 0.1$ and θ_2 changes from 0.6 to 0.8, it increases. The rule holds, therefore, in 35 of 36 solutions. When θ_2 is fixed w_2 is constant at 4.0 for all solutions: the equilibrating movements in that variable necessary to equate marginal policy cost per unit of output to Ω_2 are too small to register at the 3-decimal-place level because of the extreme sensitivity of demand to w_2. Therefore, in this case too general rule 2 holds in its weak form. With few exceptions, therefore, each of the policy variables taken separately conforms to general rule 2. When θ_1 is variable and θ_2 fixed, the same qualities distinguish movements of μ_1, μ_2, σ_1, and σ_2 as in the prior pattern, so that general rule 2 again holds. For w_1 only two exceptions to the rule occur.

The relations among p_1, μ_1, and σ_1 are displayed graphically in the convoluted configuration of Figure 9.7. The figure ignores the relationships of θ_1 and θ_2 to these variables. We have seen above that this does not matter in the relations of μ_1, and σ_1 because the negative correlation holds universally rowwise and columnwise in Table 9.9. This relation is reflected in the negative slope of the edges from front to rear in the figure. But for p_1 and σ_1 a positive relation characterizes the data rowwise and a negative one columnwise. Half of these observations, therefore, reveal a positive and half a negative correlation, and the result is the sawtooth surface of Figure 9.7. A rise in price may raise or lower σ_1 depending on a movement along a row or

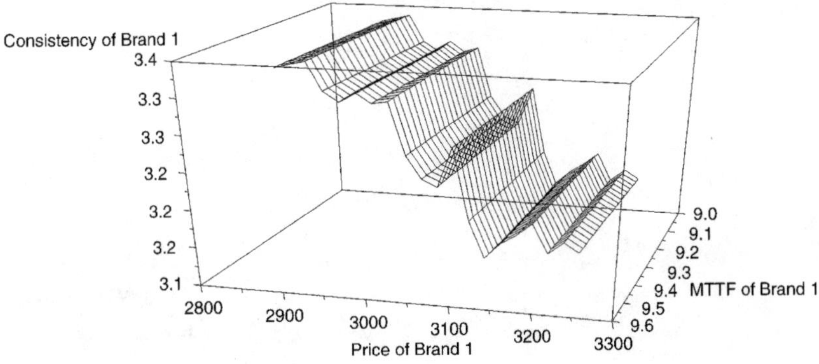

Figure 9.7 Price, *MTTF* and consistency, brand 1, case 4

column. Figure 9.8 reveals the same phenomenon for brand 2 although with dampened amplitudes.

A comparison of firms 1 and 2 using Table 9.10 and Figures 9.7 and 9.8 reveals that both firms move prices, *MTTF* and consistency in similar directions when initiating their own or responding to rival's changes in consonance coefficients. Firm 1 is the greater beneficiary in general of greater cooperation between the firms, although if the Nash equilibrium rules firm 2 does better in an absolute sense; its greater market power forces firm 1 to extend it greater deference than it extends to firm 1. Firm 1's price and quality variable responses are greater than those of firm 2, reflecting the greater sensitivity of firm 2's demand to the quality variable parameters in that function. This becomes most apparent for w_2 whose movements are not detectable to the third decimal place.

Finally, Table 9.11 summarizes the directions of correlation for the relevant variables.

As a last exercise, assume now that sufficient time has passed to permit benchmarks to be affected by firms' values of the quality variables. We adopt the asymmetric Case 4 but permit quality competition to become a *direct* competitive instrument rather than an *indirect* one that affected the quality configurations only via the price impacts of rivalrous consonance. In terms of the first-order conditions listed in (9.9) and (9.10), this means that the derivatives $\delta\mu/\delta\mu_i$, $\delta\sigma/\delta\sigma_i$, and $\delta w/\delta w_i$ are nonzero.

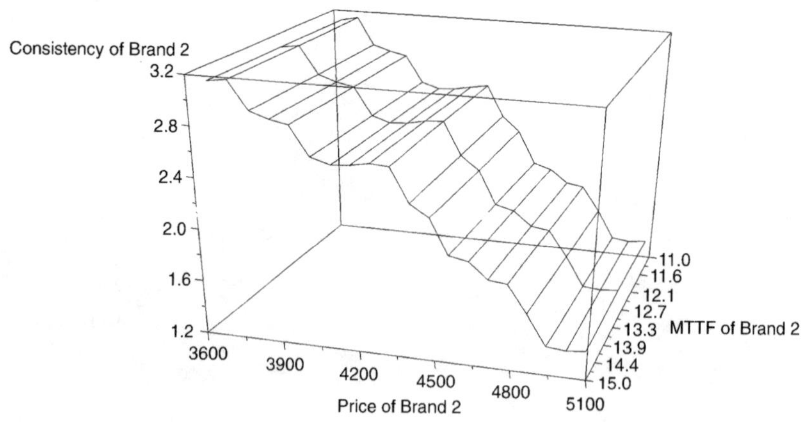

Figure 9.8 Price, *MTTF* and consistency, brand 2, case 4

Table 9.11 Correlation directions for variables in Case 4

	θ_1	μ_1	σ_1	w_1	θ_2	μ_2	σ_2	w_2
μ_1	+	*	−	+	−	−	+	0
θ_1	*	+	−	+	*	−	+	0
σ_1	−	−	*	+	+	+	−	0
w_1	+	+	−	*	+	−	+	0
θ_2	*	−	+	−	*	+	−	0
μ_2	−	−	+	−	+	*	−	0
σ_2	+	+	−	+	−	−	*	0
w_2	0	0	0	0	0	0	0	*

(a) The limitations of the models in long-run analysis

This long-run case carries us into territory in which our simple models are not well suited. First, left without bounds on improvements (upper bounds for μ and w, lower for σ), our quality variables are assumed to have no technologically determined limits which the given technology imposes on their improvement. This is unrealistic, and therefore we have arbitrarily imposed limits $\mu^c = 20$, $\sigma^c = 2$, and $w^c = 10$, which will be found in Table 9.1.

As indicated above, the *reputation parameters* are listed in Table 9.1 as $\mu^* = 8$, $\sigma^* = 4$, and $w^* = 1$. In the long run, however, quality characteristics will be altered by technological innovation and new entrants, which the models cannot handle in their present form. Our results, therefore, must be interpreted within the narrow constraints of a constant technology with fixed product group incumbents operating within quality characteristics' upper and lower bounds.

The outcome of such rivalry with endogenous benchmarks depends upon the relative strength of demand parameters for quality improvements versus quality cost parameters ignoring their interdependence with output changes. As in previous analyses, in the case with which we deal below it is assumed that the quality benchmarks are determined as the sales-weighted average of the firms' quality characteristics. As the model is solved iteratively in the manner discussed in sections 2 and 3 above, the benchmarks are recomputed in this fashion from the values of the immediately preceding iteration.

The usual case is where policy costs are significant. Consumer benchmarking with diminishing marginal sales to favorable quality changes provides an active force leading firms to conform to industry standards, when benchmarks are endogenous and when marginal costs of favorable quality changes rise rapidly. Consumers punish with increasing severity shortfalls from quality standards and reward with decreasing sales positive quality increments above such standards. Firms, therefore, are driven to those standards as competition quickens, and products approach common quality norms. This is somewhat counterintuitive, as it might appear that quality competition would lead to competitive increases in quality. But in the long run, as consumers can adjust their standards to a higher quality product, the firm embarking on such strategies finds sales increasing by relatively small amounts and the marginal costs rising. They rationally regress to the norm in these dimensions.

Consider equations (9.9.2, 9.9.3, 9.9.4), the first-order conditions for the quality variables. Then, say, for firm i, as θ_i approaches 1, *ceteris paribus*, the numerator will shrink (grow) in the cases of μ_i and w_i (σ_i) as the denominator remains unaffected, leading to reductions (increases) in the values of μ_i and w_i (σ_i) These tendencies will be reinforced for firms which have whose quality characteristics values have large impacts in the endogenous quality standards by changes in the numerator and denominator which amplify the effects of rising consonance terms. Therefore, the reputation constraints will bind, forcing μ_i and w_i to their floor values and σ_i to its ceiling value. A similar result will hold for firm j.

Suppose, in period 1, both firms have set prices and quality variables at identical levels, so that their quality variable values are identical to benchmarks and have a neutral impact on demand. Then both firms are motivated to reduce those values and standards to reputation minima (μ_i and w_i) and maximum (σ_i). As they do so demand does not shrink because quality variables affect sales only as differentials from benchmarks, but costs fall because they vary as the values of these variables. Price also will fall since it is positively correlated with improvements or deterioration in qualities, tending to reduce x_i and costs even further. Ultimately quality variable values will approach minimum reputation standards. Moreover, equally interestingly, tacit collusion, reflected in values taken by θ-values will merely delay this approach to these limits: it cannot prevent them. No matter what degree of tacit collusion the firms attempt to establish, each firm is tempted to shade price and quality values in a "Bertrand" process to approach Prisoners' Dilemma variable configurations with minimal profits.

On the other hand, if demand parameters dominate cost parameters, the opposite outcome will occur: firms will be led to shade quality variables above the values of rivals', with accompanying increases in prices, in an attempt to increase sales and profits, but to no avail. Such attempts will be quickly nullified by rivals' reactions. Quality variables will rise to their technological upper bounds, prices will rise, and profits decline toward zero. And, again, tacit collusion can only delay the outcome. This case, however, will be the unusual case, since with costs rising as the absolute values of the quality characteristics change while demand rises at diminishing rates only as the differences of those characteristics from the benchmarks, marginal costs would have to rise by quite small amounts to support this type of rivalry.

Since Hotelling's seminal article on spatial competition[7] economists have been concerned with the conditions under which "minimum differentiation" of products with respect to characteristics occurs. Under both sets of conditions concerning demand and cost parameters, benchmarking with endogenous standards will tend to enforce minimum differentiation. Of course, given the inertia of consumer adjustments to quality standards, these movements to minimal standards will be made over quite long periods – indeed, sufficiently long so that cost and quality innovations and new entry will no doubt interrupt the process. The tendencies toward depreciation of quality and minimum differentiation will underlie competition under conditions of benchmarking nonetheless.

(b) Case 5

To illustrate these tendencies we present below Case 5, which merely takes the asymmetrical model of Case 4 and endogenizes the benchmarks in the manner noted above. Once more we use the incremental $\theta = 0.2$ mesh to make the results more manageable. They are presented in Table 9.12. The first line, in bold face, in each cell contains the benchmark values for the quality variables. Also, it should be pointed out, the Ω-values in general hold only for p_i because the quality characteristics in general are constrained by bounds that prevent full adjustment of the lefthand and righthand side of (9.10.2, 9.9.3, 9.9.4).

Profits as a function of the consonance coefficients follow in general the expected pattern: they rise as other-θs rise and fall as own-θs rise, but with significant exceptions. For given own-θ values, profits for both firms rise monotonically as other-θs rise. However, for given other-θ values, π_1 rises as θ_1 rises for Θ = [0.2,0.2]–[0.2,1], [0.4,0]–[0.4,1], and [0.6,1]. Enhanced tacit cooperation helps firm 1 by significant amounts in these neighborhoods. For firm 2, however, π_2 *falls* as θ_1 rises in Θ = [0.8,0], [0.8,0.2], and [1,0.2]; that is, in the higher ranges of firm 1's deference and lower ranges of its own cooperation. For firm 1 we have seen this same seeming perversity occur in Case 4 (Table 9.9) in about the same region and, for firm 2, in an area not too dissimilar from that in which it occurred in Table 9.12. This leads one to suspect that changes in the quality characteristics have impacts subordinated to those inspired by changes in prices and the consonance coefficients.

This conjecture is indeed borne out by the observation that benchmarking and the taking into account by rivals of the impacts their quality decisions will have upon standards essentially eliminates quality competition. Firms remain at or very close to the values of their reputation parameters, regardless of Θ. In all 36 cells of Table 9.12 firm 1 never budges from those values for any of the three quality characteristics. Except when $\theta_2 = 1$, firm 2

Table 9.12 Case 5 solution for the nonsymmetric duopoly, nonidentical and variable θ-values, for selected θ-values

θ_1 \ θ_2	*0*	*0.2*	*0.4*	*0.6*	*0.8*	*1.0*
0	μ:8;σ:4;w:1.203 μ:8.000;8.000 σ:4.000;4.000 w:1.000;1.370 p:2,814.81;3,427.33 π:4.986510;10.501260 x:45,523;55,381 Ω:2,276.13;2,769.07	μ:8;σ:4;w:1.197 μ:8.000;8.000 σ:4.000;4.000 w:1.000;1.370 p:2,830.73;3,593.40 π:5.118849;10.498841 x:45,784;52,256 Ω:2,289.20;2,969.11	μ:8;σ:4;w:1.189 μ:8.000;8.000 σ:4.000;4.000 w:1.000;1.368 p:2,849.11;3,785.27 π:5.272853;10.352880 x:46,086;48,645 Ω:2,304.32;3,200.34	μ:8;σ:4;w:1.178 μ:8.000;8.000 σ:4.000;4.000 w:1.000;1.365 p:2,870.64;4,009.56 π:5.454239;9.989420 x:46,400;44,424 Ω:2,322.00;3,470.65	μ:8;σ:4;w:1.168 μ:8.000;8.000 σ:4.000;4.000 w:1.000;1.367 p:2,896.13;4,275.42 π:5.670862;9.288198 x:46,859;39,424 Ω:2,342.95;3,970.78	μ:8.687;σ:3.930;w:1.558 μ:8.000;9.658 σ:4.000;3.832 w:1.000;2.347 p:2,917.93;4,650.65 π:5.857645;8.145634 x:47,217;33,436 Ω:2,360.85;4,179.47
0.2	μ:8;σ:4:w:1.203 μ:8.000;8.000 σ:4.000:4.000 w:1.000;1.367 p:2,852.36;3,439.56 π:4.993251;10.626621 x:44,814;55,585 Ω:2,321.38;2,779.23	μ:8,σ:4;w:1.198 μ:8.000;8.000 σ:4.000;4.000 w:1.000;1.369 p:2,868.54;3,606.36 π:5.126074;10.623730 x:45,072;52,449 Ω:2,334.71;2,980.04	μ:8;σ:4;w:1.191 μ:8.000;8.000 σ:4.000;4.000 w:1.000;1.368 p:2,877.26;3,799.07 π:5.280716;10.477839 x:45,371;48,825 Ω:2,350.23;3,209.08	μ:8;σ:4;w:1.182 μ:8.000:8.000 σ:4.000;4.000 w:1.000;1.368 p:2,905.15;4,024.40 π:5.462819;10.112290 x:45,720;44,590 Ω:2,368.32;3,483.56	μ:8;σ:4;w:1.170 μ:8.000;8.000 σ:4.000;4.000 w:1.000;1.368 p:2,935.10;4,291.35 π:5.680486;9.407296 x:46,134;39,573 Ω:2,389.76;3,805.05	μ:8.530;σ:3.961;w:1.447 μ:8.000;9.265 σ:4.000;3.906 w:1.000;2.067 p:2,959.93;4,653.03 π:5.890633;8.232563 x:46,531;33,555 Ω:2,410.29;4,194.39
0.4	μ:8;σ:4;w:1.206 μ:8.000;8.000 σ:4.000;4.000 w:1.000;1.368 p:2,891.41;3,452.41 π:4.993892;10.756090 x:44,077;55,795 Ω:2,891.41;3,452.41	μ:8;σ:4;w:1.200 μ:8.000;8.000 σ:4.000;4.000 w:1.000;1.368 p:2,907.88;3,619.86 π:5.127291;10.754620 x:44,332;52,649 Ω:2,382.15;2,991.40	μ:8;σ:4;w:1.193 μ:8.000;8.000 σ:4.000;4.000 w:1.000;1.368 p:2,926.94;3,813.43 π:5.282504;10.608430 x:44,627;49,012 Ω:2,397.99;3,224.51	μ:8;σ:4;w:1.184 μ:8.000;8.000 σ:4.000;4.000 w:1.000;1.368 p:2,949.22;4,039.74 π:5.465343;10.240980 x:44,972;44,762 Ω:2,416.52;3,497.02	μ:8;σ:4;w:1.171 μ:8.000;8.000 σ:4.000;4.000 w:1.000;1.368 p:2,975.63;4,307.88 π:5.683914;9.531733 x:45,380;39,727 Ω:2,438.49;3,819.90	μ:8.347;σ:3.994;w:1.328 μ:8.000;8.818 σ:4.000;3.986 w:1.000;1.775 p:3,003.77;4,654.76 π:5.918971;8.322206 x:45,816;33,679 Ω:2,461.90;4,209.92

Table 9.12 continued

θ_1	θ_2: *0*	*0.2*	*0.4*	*0.6*	*0.8*	*1.0*
0.6	μ:8;σ:4;w:1.208 μ:8.000;8.000 σ:4.000;4.000 w:1.000;1.368 p:2,932.08;3,465.76 π:4.987838;10.89202 x:43,309;55,014 Ω:2,417.46;2,800.71	μ:8;σ:4;w:1.202 μ:8.000:8.000 σ:4.000;4.000 w:1.000;1.368 p:2,948.86;3,633.95 π:5.121693;10.891350 x:43,560;52,857 Ω:2,431.51;3,003.23	μ:8;σ:4;w:1.195 μ:8.000;8.000 σ:4.000;4.000 w:1.000;1.368 p:2,968.26;3,828.38 π:5.277443;10.744860 x:43,851;49,208 Ω:2,447.74;3,237.34	μ:8;σ:4;1.186 μ:8.000;8.000 σ:4.000;4.000 w:1.000;1.368 p:2,990.95;4,055.71 π:5.460937;10.375520 x:44,192;44,941 Ω:2,466.73;3,511.05	μ:8;σ:4;w:1.173 μ:8.000;8.000 σ:4.000;4.000 w:1.000;1.367 p:3,017.85;4,325.05 π:5.680337;9.661868 x:44,595;39,888 Ω:2,489.25;4,226.25	μ:8.128;σ:4;w:1.218 μ:8.000;8.299 σ:4.000;4.000 w:1.000;1.510 p:3,049.05;4,657.91 π:5.937267;8.418782 x:45,062;33,810 Ω:2,515.37;4,226.25
0.8	μ:8;σ:4;w:1.210 μ:8.000;8.000 σ:4.000;4.000 w:1.000;1,368 p:2,974.67;3,479.67 π:4.974193;11.034260 x:42,509;56,243 Ω:2,468.55;2,812.14	μ:8;σ:4;w:1.204 μ:8.000;8.000 σ:4.000;4.000 w:1.000;1.368 p:2,991.56;3,648.63 π:5.108435;11.034390 x:42,756;53,074 Ω:2,482.95;3,015.56	μ:8;σ:4;w:1.196 μ:8.000;8.000 σ:4.000;4.000 w:1.000;1.367 p:3,011.33;3,843.94 π:5.264690;10.887700 x:43,043;49,411 Ω:2,499.60;3,250.72	μ:8;σ:4;w:1.188 μ:8.000;8.000 σ:4.000;4.000 w:1.000;1.369 p:3,034.44;4,072.39 π:5.448678;10.516180 x:43,378;45,128 Ω:2,519.07;3,525.65	μ:8;σ:4;w:1.176 μ:8.000;8.000 σ:4.000;4.000 w:1.000;1.368 p:3,061.86;4,343.00 π:5.668769;9.797735 x:43,776;40,055 Ω:2.542.16;3,851.46	μ:8;σ:4;w:1.160 μ:8.000;8.000 σ:4.000;4.000 w:1.000;1.369 p:3,094.88;4,668.86 π:5.936547;8.531900 x:44,255;33,949 Ω:2,569.98;4,243.66
1.0	μ:8;σ:4:w:1.212 μ:8.000;8.000 σ:4.000;4.000 w:1.000;1.212 p:3,018.68;3,494.21 π:4.951948;11.183070 x:41,674;56,481 Ω:2,521.85;2,824.05	μ:8;σ:8;w:1.206 μ:8.000;8.000 σ:4.000;4.000 w:1.000;1.368 p:3,036.11;3,663.95 π:5.086539;11.184240 x:41,918;53,300 Ω:2,536.62;3,028.41	μ:8,σ:4,w:1.199 μ:8.000;8.000 σ:4.000;4.000 w:1.000;1.369 p:3,056.26;3,860.29 π:5.243124;11.037265 x:42,200;49,623 Ω:2,553.70;3,264.64	μ:8,σ:4,w:1.189 μ:8.000;8.000 σ:4.000;4.000 w:1.000;1.367 p:3,079.84;4,089.70 π:5.427661;10.663915 x:42,530;45,324 Ω:2,573.69;3,540.93	μ:8,σ:4,w:1.178 μ:8.000;8.000 σ:4.000;4.000 w:1.000;1.369 p:3,107.78;4,361.74 π:5.648242;9.940215 x:42,922;40,230 Ω:2,597.37;3,868.27	μ:8,σ:4,w:1.161 μ:8.000;8.000 σ:4.000;4.000 w:1.000;1.367 p:3,141.46;4,689.16 π:5.916831;8.665078 x:43,393;34,099 Ω:2,625.92;4,262.41

remains at those values for μ_2 and σ_2, and establishes a w_2 value in the neighborhood of 1.368. Only when it is rendering maximum deference to firm 1 is it led to increase the quality of its product for $\theta_1 = 0$ to 0.6, but even then the force of competition induces but grudging movements in the direction of quality.

This is the major conclusion of the simulation: *informed consumers who are knowledgeable about the quality standards of the products they purchase, who remain current with changes in those qualities, and who adjust their purchases in accordance with products' departures from those norms bring about a quality competition among rivals that reduces quality to the minimal reputation parameters of the firms*. Competition then reverts to price competition at those standards, with reduced prices and profits and higher outputs the consequences (see Table 9.9). These conclusions are being seen currently in the movement of increasingly well educated consumers to "house brands" of groceries and analgesics and away from branded products with the indicated consequences for oligopolistic firms. Most dramatically, perhaps, the market for branded aspirin has been drastically reduced as consumers have come to understand that quality standards for the product are set by U.S. Pharmacopeia requirements and render the product of the same quality whoever the manufacturer.

The perverse movements of profits as Θ changes, referred to above, must been seen as manifestations of the same movements discussed in interpreting Case 4 solutions. They hinge upon the "shift and slope" analysis of demand functions as rivals' prices change with changes in θ-values. For firm 1, for example, positive movements of profits as the firm increases its cooperation with firm 2 with no change in reciprocity from firm 2, arise because the change in θ_1 shifts firm 2's demand curve to the right, decreasing its elasticity and leading to a rise in p_2, which in turn shifts firm 1's demand curve to the right, leading it to raise price on an output reduced by the rise in consonance costs. Depending upon the elasticity of the demand function in this region, the proportionate price rise may exceed the fall in quantity and profits will expand.

In Table 9.10 such perverse movements in profits are quite small: indeed, on Figures 9.9 and 9.10, which depict the profits of firms 1 and 2 respectively as functions of θ_1 and θ_2, respectively, these blips are too small to register. The tendency of profits to fall as own-θ rises and rise as other-θ rises – which is especially strong for firm 2 – is well-depicted.

Finally, we can extend the long-run case to include variability of the consonance coefficients as well as the benchmarks, and ask if pure rationality would establish a center of gravity for the industry. After eliminating dominated strategies, we find one Nash equilibrium at $\Theta = [0.4,0]$, with firm 1 deferring to firm 2 in only moderate degree and firm 2 making no effort to cooperate with firm 1. This solution should be compared with the Nash equi-

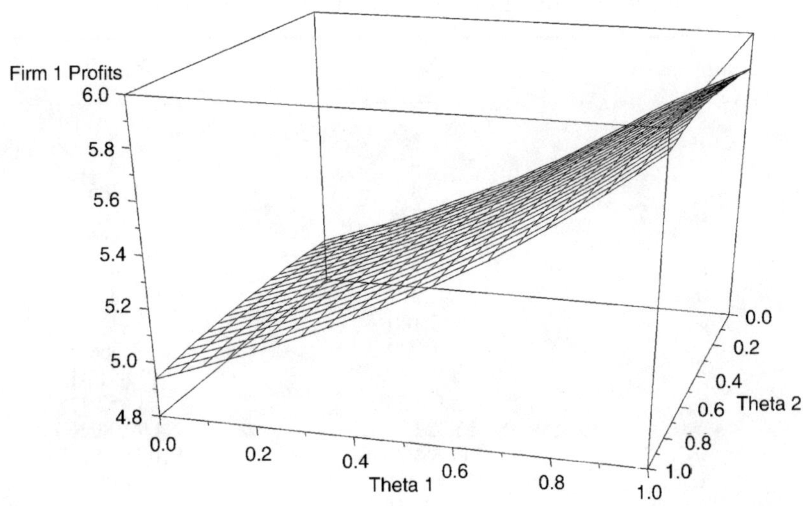

Figure 9.9 Firm 1 profits as a function of θ-coefficients

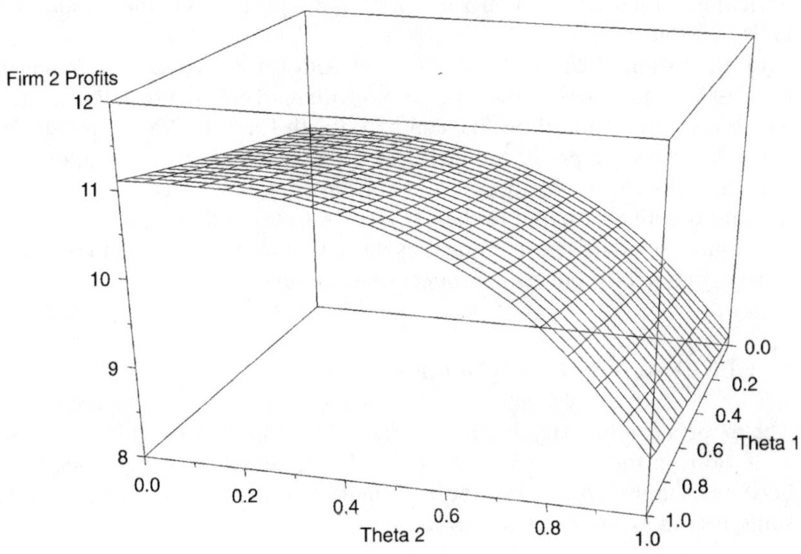

Figure 9.10 Firm 2 profits as a function of θ-coefficients

Table 9.13 Comparison of Nash equilibria for Cases 4 and 5

Parameters	*Case 4*	*Case 5*
μ	8	8
σ	4	4
w	1	1.206
μ_1	9.344	8
μ_2	2.917	8
σ_1	3.232	4
σ_2	2.917	4
w_1	2.160	1
w_2	4.000	1.368
p_1	\$3,034.95	\$2,891.41
p_2	\$3,899.08	\$3,452.41
π_1	\$5.322791E7	\$4.993892E7
π_2	\$11.880770E7	\$10.756090E7
x_1	43,648	44,077
x_2	53,459	55,795
Ω_1	\$2,463.37	\$2,891.41
Ω_2	\$3,037.43	\$3,452.41

librium in Case 4, as shown in Table 9.10, and reproduced in the comparison table of Table 9.13.

In these game-theoretic focal point solutions Case 5 consumers are given more of both products at lower prices but with markedly depreciated quality, and firms have reduced profits, compared with Case 4's Nash equilibrium solution. Firms are producing inefficiently in Case 5 in that reputation and nonnegativity constraints prevent them from equating marginal policy costs per unit of induced output to their Ω factors. Competition under conditions of adaptive standards pushes qualities down to floor values so that minimum differentiation of products in product space occurs.

5 GENERALIZATION TO *n* FIRMS

The models can be extended readily from 2 to n firms with straightforward alterations in the first order conditions. For β_i and x_i the other-price term becomes simply $\Sigma_j b_{ij} p_j$; also, the marginal consonance cost terms become sums, becoming, for example, for μ_i

$$\Sigma_j \theta_{ij} \Omega_j (m_j - n_j(\mu_j - \mu) \frac{\delta\mu}{\delta\mu_i}$$

with similar terms for (9.10.1) and (9.10.3–9.10.4). The term θ_{ij} is the consonance factor of firm i with respect to firm j, where θ_{ij} need not equal θ_{ji}. These terms detail the power structure of the industry as reflected in the degree of deference accorded firms to each other. Neither of these changes results in conceptual complications – a characteristic which is an advantageous feature of the model. Operational solution of the model becomes more cumbersome, of course, with the growth in rival numbers, but it does not experience any qualitative increase in difficulty.

6 CONCLUSIONS

Analysis of the models has been restricted to firms in duopoly, but some interesting insights into the implications of consumer benchmarking and price–nonprice competition among oligopolists in rivalrous consonance have been forthcoming. One result from the closed analysis gave great leverage in analyzing the relations among prices and quality characteristics in comparative statics exercises: the decomposition of first-order conditions into the necessity of price to equal the sum of marginal output, policy and consonance costs when upper and lower bounds on quality variable values are not effective. This permitted the tracing of lines of causation from parameter changes along paths of policy variable interdependence in the abstract, and the application of them in understanding the complex relationships among such variables in the 5 simulation cases chosen to illustrate the principles and to gain further insights.

Our results hinge heavily upon the introduction of consumer benchmarking: the notion that consumers absorb relatively clear notions of the relevant quality standards of brands in product groups and shape their preferences on the basis of differentials from those standards rather than the absolute values of brand qualities. Expectations are that a given brand of a product group should meet certain quality benchmarks and judgments are made on the basis of departures in the positive or negative directions from those standards.

Three periods have been distinguished in the models employed, based in part on whether these benchmarks may be considered exogenous or endogenous. In the short- and medium-run models insufficient time is assumed to have elapsed for consumers to adjust benchmarks to changes in quality characteristics values by firms. In the short run the consonance coefficients are assumed to be fixed as well, whereas in the intermediate run we assume the coefficients are variable and (somewhat hesitantly) search for Nash equilibria or other focal points that firms' profit motives and desires for stability might lead them to use to determine their consonance coefficients. The game theorist might find consonance coefficients a convenient way to deal with different drives to rivalry and cooperation even though he or she might not be ready to adopt the formal framework of rivalrous consonance as an analytical framework. Finally, in the long run, benchmarks are endogenized and we study the implications for firms' price and nonprice decisions of that assumption, when consonance coefficients are fixed and when they are allowed to vary.

In the closed analysis as well as in the simulative theorizing our interest focusses upon the relations among price and the three quality characteristics under consideration: *MTTF* (μ), consistency of *MTTF* (σ), and length of warranty period (w_i). In this we continue and extend our analysis of isolated firms in Chapter 8.

In the short- and medium-run models when tacit collusion increases, quality characteristics tend to improve because price rises, and with it Ω_i, or the marginal revenue of a unit of product taking into account only the marginal cost of enhanced output from marginal changes in the policies. It is to this variable that marginal policy and consonance costs per unit of induced output must be equated in the profit optimum, and when it rises in general the quality characteristics must be improved in order to bring about a new equality. Consumers' surplus is negatively impacted by tacit collusion enhancement because quantities fall, but we do recognize the possibility that improvements in qualities could, conceptually, outweigh reductions in output. In none of our many runs of the 5 cases did this happen, however.

Case 1 features 2 firms, symmetric in demand and cost parameters with low interaction through the demand parameters. The results of the simulation confirmed expectations with respect to correlations among the prices and quality characteristic values as consonance coefficients were varied parametrically, although the changes in such values and in profits were small because the low interdependence in the product space. Social surplus falls as consumers' surplus falls, and the contribution of the quality variables to the consumers' surplus was small as well.

In Case 2 symmetry once again was adopted but the firms' interaction parameter (b_{ij} in the demand functions) was increased substantially and solution values reflected these changed conditions. Prices and quality improvements or depreciations are positively correlated, as expected, and profits are larger and rise faster as tacit collusion increases. One factor that held down changes in the quality variables, however, was the higher output values. Study of the first order conditions of (9.10) reveals that when the outputs are larger the quality variables need make smaller adjustments to bring about equality of the lefthand and righthand side of the relevant equations.

Case 3 maintains the symmetry assumption but increases the firms' identical demand factors for quality characteristics; that is, higher departures from the fixed benchmarks stimulate greater demands and these demands decay more slowly as differentials above or below benchmarks rise. Quality characteristics are much improved as tacit collusion rises, outputs are larger, as are profits. However, the same positive correlations among prices and quality improvements feature the solutions. In the analysis we develop a technique for decomposing consumers' surplus into those portions caused by quantity increases, quality constant, and those caused by quality increases, quantity constant. In no case we analyzed did the rises in quality associated with larger θ values outweigh the downward pull of reduced quantities on consumers' surplus.

In Cases 1, 2, and 3, involving symmetric firms, we assumed that the consonance factors of the firms were kept equal as we varied them parametrically. That is, each firm extended the same deference to the other firm's welfare as the rival did to it. We begin our analysis of unequal deference by permitting the firms in Case 1, the lower interaction case, to adopt unequal θ values. Neither firm is a "dominant" firm by virtue of any demand or cost advantage, but each has the new ability to adopt once-for-all tacit collusion attitudes that are different from the rival's. This step takes our analysis to a higher degree of complexity.

The nice regularity of movements in prices and quality variables and improvements in profits with changes in consonance coefficients disappears when such changes are not reciprocated in full measure or not at all. A rise in other-θ, own-θ constant, does not guarantee a rise in own-profit, and the relations between the price and nonprice variables are no longer as smooth as in Cases 1–3. Indeed, it becomes difficult in some instances to trace the causes of movements in one variable or another. In our transition to the intermediate run, if we interpret the payoff matrix resulting from such assumptions in game-theoretic context our simulation reveals no Nash equilibrium, but the configuration $\Theta = [1,1]$ does emerge as an interesting focal point.

In Case 4 we move into the intermediate run in full fervor by permitting asymmetry in demand and cost factors as well as in θ-values, and studying variable interrelationships with some attention to potential Nash equilibria. The case is created by giving firm 1 its parameters in Case 1 and firm 2 its parameters in Case 2. Firm 2, therefore, must be viewed as the dominant firm by virtue of its large advantage in demand factors and therefore in profit earning. The step-up in complexity noted above continues with respect to price–nonprice variables, but, in general, as θ_i remains fixed and θ_j rises, four tendencies were noted:

1 p_i and p_j both rise
2 firm *i*'s qualities are degraded and firm *j*'s are enhanced or remain unchanged
3 firm *i*'s profits rise and firm *j*'s profits rise, but not without exception
4 firm *i*'s outputs rise and firm *j*'s outputs fall.

The weaker firm gains most from tacit collusion, with the stronger firm's maximum profit cell at a lower own-theta, higher other-theta configuration. A Nash equilibrium does occur in the model, but Pareto superior solutions do exist which would appear to a rivalrous consonance advocate (and to many game theorists) more likely focal points for firms oriented toward cooperation from basic drives.

We now confront in full force results that contradict the experience in the models of Chapter 8 and to this point in this chapter. Price rises may coexist with quality degradation and the relation is to be expected as one firm benefits from another's increasing deference without reciprocity. The deferring firm does follow the previous pattern of a positive correlation among price and quality improvements. Puzzling departures in these patterns may arise without apparent explanation.

In Case 5 we enter a new world of relationships, as we endogenize the benchmarks of Case 4 and assume passage of sufficient time to permit consumer absorption of changes in quality variables as new benchmarks. In our model we assume these new benchmarks are formed from the output-weighted averages of firms' quality variables. For reasons springing from benchmarking and explained in the discussion of section 4a (p. 227), quality competition will lower product quality to conform to lower bounds set by reputation parameters. Price competition and the cost reductions attendant on such low standards will reduce prices and increase outputs: once the reputation parameters are reached quality competition will cease and price competition will be the sole tool of rivalry (with some exceptions in the higher ranges of consonance coefficients).

This certainly is the most dramatic result of our analysis to this point: as consumer cognition of firms' quality standards incorporate them into minimum expectations, firms will be led to reduce product qualities to minima under conditions of benchmarking demand. Minimum differentiation of products in product space will occur, as products become generic in nature and brand distinctions begin to fade in importance.

Although we do not confront it in our simulations, we recognize that quality competition may drive product qualities in the other direction to approach technologically determined upper bounds, in which minimum product differentiation would be achieved at the other end of the spectrum. We indicate that such an occurrence would depend upon slowly rising marginal output and quality costs and should be a rare result. However, the existence of such upper bound parameters does expose the weaknesses of our simple models in long-run contexts where innovation and new entrants may be expected to intrude and alter technology. The long-run tendencies revealed in Case 5, therefore, should be accepted as deeper forces toward product quality degradation that may never eventuate in realistic contexts.

Finally, we examined the payoff matrix of Case 5 for Nash equilibria and found one in roughly the neighborhood in which that for Case 4 was found. This is not unexpected since price competition was the active force in both. Once again, the dominant firm in the Nash equilibrium gave less deference than the weaker firm and it was by no means the only focal point that might emerge in a rivalrous consonance context.

10 Oligopolistic Competition with Scaling of Characteristics

In Chapters 8 and 9 we have assumed that quality characteristics were cardinally measurable and, therefore, capable of immediate incorporation as variables in analytical and simulation analysis. Now we must deal with the difficult task of "scaling" characteristics which are qualities that are not at the present time directly "measurable" in the meaning of Chapter 1 or with attributes which can be measured only in a nominal 0–1 manner. The procedure in this chapter moves from scaling at the product or brand level to study competition without tacit collusion to price–nonprice competition in a collusive context, and from general functional forms in closed analysis to specific forms in simulation runs.

1 SCALING BY QUALITY INDIFFERENCE PREMIA

We begin with the concept of the "brand" as an integral unit of analysis with the aim of characterizing *n* brands with scaling values to locate them in a product space. To do so, we deal with a product which consumers buy only as a single unit if they buy at all: for example, large durable goods such as refrigerators or washing machines. To obtain a scaling of each brand in consumers' preferences we choose brand 1 arbitrarily as an anchor and ask the following three questions of a sample of prospective consumers:

> (1) Suppose you were given a unit of brand 1 at no cost to you, but that you were forbidden to resell it. If you were offered brand *j* instead, how many dollars would you have to receive or give up (independent of your willingness or ability to do so) to make you feel as well off as you feel with brand 1?

These dollar measures I_j are *indifference premia* and will in general be negative and positive with $I_1 = 0$, where negative values are hypothetical payments to the individual and positive values are payments by the individual.

We then again select brand 1 arbitrarily and simply ask each consumer in the sample:

(2) What is the maximum price that you would pay for a unit of brand 1? By adding the indifference premia to the brand 1 valuation of the consumer we may then obtain the preference valuation, v_i, that the consumer gives each remaining brand.[1] As a final question we ask the consumer:
(3) Given your budget resources and the intensity of your desire for the product relative to other goods what is the maximum amount you are prepared to pay for any brand in this product group?

We symbolize this price ceiling p_c.

The valuations v_i represent prices for the brands at which the consumer is indifferent among them. In making his or her choices, however, consumers will (1) eliminate all brands whose prices, p_i, are above p_c, (2) of the remaining subset eliminate those brands whose prices are above valuations, and (3), from the remaining brands choose that brand (not necessarily unique) whose $(v_i - p_i)$ is a maximum. Formally, the consumer acts to

$$\begin{aligned}
&\text{Max}_i (v_i - p_i) \\
&\text{Subject to:} \\
&(p_i - p_c) \leq 0 \\
&(p_i - v_i) \leq 0
\end{aligned} \tag{10.1}$$

Figure 10.1 illustrates the consumer's choice with an example featuring 5 brands.

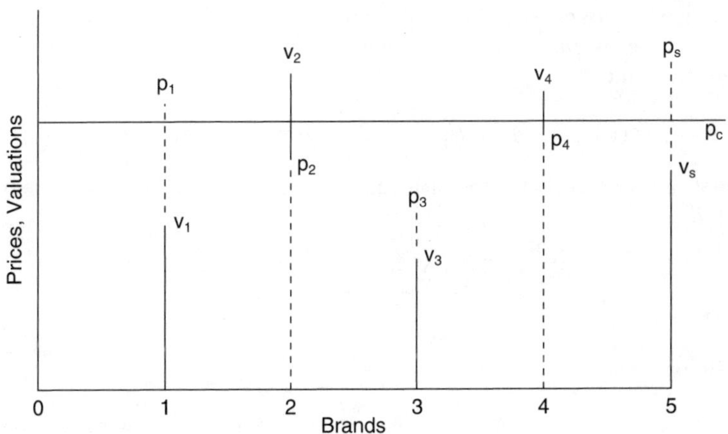

Figure 10.1 The consumer's choice among brands

Their consumer's valuations, v_i, and exogenously given prices, p_i are graphed. Maximum price for any member of the group, p_c, is drawn as a horizontal line. In the solution procedure, any brand whose price is above p_c is eliminated as a possibility, which removes brands 1 and 5 on Figure 10.1. From the remaining brand candidates, those whose valuations are below their prices are eliminated, which reduces the feasible set to brands 2 and 4. The consumer then acts to maximize his or her consumers' surplus, $v_i - p_i$ which leads to the choice of brand 2 by this consumer.[2]

For those brands whose $p_i \leq p_c$, were $v_i = p_i$ for all such brands the consumer would be indifferent among the goods, and indifferent to the purchase of any one of them. In such instances the consumer would be paying exactly what his or her valuation of their utility is, within the limits of his or her budget restraint, and consumers' surplus would be zero with brands' utility exactly equal to their alternative money utility.

Over a large body of consumers with constant tastes and budgets demand functions for the firms are then derivable, which we will assume are continuous:

$$x_i = x_i(p_1, p_2, \ldots, p_n) = x_i(P),\ i = 1, 2, \ldots, n. \tag{10.2}$$

Cost functions are assumed to be

$$C_i = F_i + c_i(x_i)x_i,\ i = 1, 2, \ldots, n, \tag{10.3}$$

where $c_i' > 0$, $c_i'' > 0$. Firms are price setters with profit functions

$$\pi_i = p_i x_i(P) - C_i,\ i = 1, 2, \ldots, n. \tag{10.4}$$

To incorporate possible tacit collusion among the firms, a *rivalrous consonance coefficient matrix*, Θ, is employed, and each firm acts to maximize extended profits:

$$\pi_i^e = p_i x_i(P) - C_i + \Sigma_j \theta_{ij} \pi_j,\ i = 1, 2, \ldots n, j \neq i \tag{10.5}$$

First-order conditions at a Nash equilibrium for optimal prices, P^o, may be written

$$p_i^\circ = \frac{x_i - (c_i' x_i + c_i) x_{ij}' + \Sigma_j \theta_{ij} x_{ji}' (p_i^\circ - c_j' x_j - c_j)}{-x_{i,i}'} \tag{10.6}$$

In (10.6)

$$c_i' = \frac{\delta c_j}{\delta x_i}, x_{i,i}' = \frac{\delta x_i}{\delta p_i}, x_{j,i}' = \frac{\delta x_j}{\delta p_i},\ \text{and } c_j' = \frac{\delta c_j}{\delta x_j}.$$

If we permit noninteger x_i and assume concave extended profit functions these equations can be solved efficiently by closed and iterative analysis.

Note that we may use the indifference premia to place the brands in a product space and compute the distances following some metric in that space. From the individuals' indicated indifference premia we choose some measure of central tendency as an aggregate measure of a good's distance from the origin of the product space at brand 1's location. We may choose the smallest of these values of the indifference premia as the origin of the space at 0 by subtracting its value from all original I-values and then normalizing them by dividing these transformed values by the range. Then we may calculate the relative distances between pairs of brand indifference premia as the differences between the normalized locations of the brands or we may opt for a different metric based on them. In the model developed in section 2 below, however, we shall use the nontransformed, nonnormalized (i.e., the original) indifference premia.

2 MODEL 1: SPATIAL DISTANCES AS METRIC WITH NO TACIT COLLUSION

We begin with the simplest oligopolistic model, using distances in product space as an index of interproduct quality differences. These we shall imagine are derived as means or medians of the indifference premia whose derivation is described above with the origin of 0 shifted to the brand with the minimum I_i. Interproduct distances are computed as simple Euclidean distance, $s_{ij} = \sqrt{(I_i - I_j)^2}$, which has the effect of eliminating the direction of the deviation, which is to say whether good j is more or less preferred to good i. This is to assert implicitly that the degree of quality competitiveness, however determined, is equal for equal distances left or right of the origin good at 0.

Because of the costs of search activity or informational frictions, or to incorporate the variance in the indifference premia eliminated in our choice of a measure of central tendency, we assume that price competition from rival brands diminishes in a greater degree than linear in the s_{ij} by using an exponential decay factor, k. These factors can be customized by brand pairs, k_{ij}, when appropriate. Their most frequent usage is in treating advertising or other marketing expenditures aimed toward increasing the willingness consumers will have to buy brands at higher prices. Instead of reverting to derivation of new interproduct distances, it is possible to change k_{ij} or k to estimate virtual or effective changes in interbrand differences so effected. Their effectiveness is assumed to decline exponentially as brands farther away are impacted by a given firm's campaign. This is a convenient way to treat advertising because it is not a true product quality – it is external to the product – in the sense, for example, that it does not factor directly into consumers' surplus as an increase in durability would do.

Demand functions therefore become:

$$x_i = a_i - b_{ii}p_i - \Sigma_{j \neq i} b_{ij}(p_i - p_j)e^{-k \cdot s_{ij}}, \tag{10.7}$$

where $k \geq 0$ is a parameter, or, after defining

$$\alpha_i = b_{ii} + \Sigma_{j \neq i} b_{ij} e^{-k \cdot sij},$$
$$\beta_i = \Sigma_{j \neq i} b_{ij} p_j e^{-k \cdot s_{ij}},$$

we may rewrite (10.7) as:

$$x_i = a_i - \alpha_i p_i + \beta_i. \tag{10.8}$$

The b_{ii} and b_{ij} are the own- and other-price coefficients per dollar of price that would hold were Euclidean s_{ij} active in determining demand under different price regimes (i.e., if $k = 0$). As noted above, the strength of such price effects, however, are assumed to decay more rapidly than linearly in the s_{ij} as informational frictions grow with distance and price benchmarks are less immediate to the consumer's experience. When $k = \infty$ the brands are isolated from all rival brands and each such brand becomes effectively a different product.

The form of the demand function (10.7) continues our hypothesis that consumers make their choices with the aid of benchmarks – in this case, price differentials among brands. This demand function form is a variant of benchmarking that has been used in Chapters 8 and 9 and has been recommended there as a more realistic approach to consumer decision making in differentiated oligopoly. Given fixed brand locations in quality space, it is assumed that consumers over time, through habit, experience or inertia, adopt one brand as a primary choice but will compare other brands' price differentials with the preferred brands in considering possible switching. In this instance of choice under brand distinctions the benchmark is this preferred brand and the variables of comparison are price differentials. Also, the notion that consumers buy a single "unit" of the product in a time period is not a great limitation on the analysis, because that unit can be defined as multiple physical units of the product where appropriate. For example, it might be 5 quarts of milk or 3 loaves of bread if the time period is one week. The assumption is made, of course, that the consumer buys only the 1 brand during the time period rather than an assortment of brands, but this also seems the only behavior consistent with the logic of the model.

The cost function may be written:

$$C_i = F_i + m_i x_i + n_i x^2. \tag{10.9}$$

Then, we may rewrite (10.6) as:

$$p_i^\circ = \frac{(a_i + \beta_i)(1 + 2\alpha_i n_i) + m_i \alpha_i}{2\alpha_i(1 + \alpha_i n_i)} + \frac{\Sigma_{i \neq j} \theta_{ij} b_{ji} e^{-ks_{ji}} (p_j - m_j - 2n_j x_j)}{2\alpha_i(1 + \alpha_i n_i)},$$

in which form we will solve it iteratively.

When all $\theta_{ij} = 0$, $\pi_i = p_i x_i - C_i$, and setting $\frac{\delta\pi_i}{\delta p_i} = 0$ yields

$$1 \quad p_i^\circ = \frac{(a_i + \beta_i)(1 + 2n_i\alpha_i) + m_i \alpha_i}{2\alpha_i(1 + n_i \alpha_i)} \tag{10.10}$$

$$2 \quad x_i^\circ = a_i - \alpha_i p_i^\circ + \beta_i.$$

Of course, (10.10.1) is simply the condition that marginal revenue $(2p_i - (a_i + \beta_j)/\alpha_i)$ equals marginal cost $(m_i + n_i(a_i + \beta_i) - 2n_i\alpha_i p_i)$.

The model has more severe restrictions in its construction that enforce more limitations on the interpretation of its comparative static propositions than exist in more conventional analyses. The first of these idiosyncrasies concerns the meaning of constancy of consumer preferences, which in the analysis of (10.1) above are reflected in the consumers' ceiling prices and the indifference premia. The demand functions, aggregated from (10.1) and their graphical depiction in Figure 10.1, are based upon such fixed indifference premia and their derivative scalings, interproduct distances. These aggregate functions will shift and change their slope families as product alterations, reflected in new indifference premia, are introduced. Where in conventional analyses movements along or among unchanging indifference surfaces conform to assumptions of constant preferences, the analogs of such surfaces in the model above are the indifference premia, and changes in them are changes in consumer preferences. Hence, for example, we cannot investigate the impacts of changes in the s_{ij} on α_i or β_i without assuming changes in preferences. Strictly speaking, therefore, by assuming small changes in interproduct distances we are violating the model's structure, and we must assume the changes are indeed "infinitesimally" small and be satisfied with qualitative movements wholly.

A second peculiarity in the model is that changes in the values of the *b*-coefficients in the demand functions must be narrowly interpreted as shifts of numbers of consumers among indifference premia that remain constant in value, which in turn implies that changes in such coefficients in one firm's function must be related to offsetting changes in other firms' functions. Under the framing assumptions of the model, with n consumers total sales over all brands must be no more than n in number. We shall again assume that changes in the b-coefficients will be very small indeed, in line with strictly construed comparative statics procedures that are frequently ignored in practice.

Consider, then, a change in s_{ij}, its consequent impacts on α_i and β_i, and movements in p_i and x_i. Movements of brand i are taken to be small enough not to change the cost function, which would be expected for finite movements in product space. When s_{ij} rises, with k given, so that competing brand j becomes less relevant in terms of effective distance for brand i and more or less competitive for remaining brands, then

$$1 \quad \alpha_i' \equiv \frac{\delta\alpha_i}{\delta s_{ij}} = -k \cdot b_{ij} \cdot e^{-ks_{ij}} \tag{10.11}$$

$$2 \quad \beta_i' \equiv \frac{\delta\beta_i}{\delta s_{ij}} = -k \cdot b_{ij} \cdot p_j \cdot e^{-ks_{ij}} = \alpha_i' p_j$$

$$3 \quad \frac{\delta p_i^\circ}{\delta s_{ij}} = \frac{2n_i\alpha_i'(a_i + \beta_i) + (1 + 2n_i\alpha_i)(\beta_i' - 2\alpha_i' p_i^\circ) + m_i\alpha_i'}{2\alpha_i(1 + n_i\alpha_i)}$$

$$4 \quad \frac{\delta x_i^\circ}{\delta s_{ij}} = -\alpha_i \frac{\delta p_i^\circ}{\delta s_{ij}} - \alpha_i' p_i^\circ + \beta_i' = -\alpha_i \frac{\delta p_i^\circ}{\delta s_{ij}} - \alpha_i'(p_i^\circ - p_j).$$

Define:

$$\Psi = p_i^\circ - \frac{MC_i + (1 + 2n_i\alpha_i)p_i}{2(1 + n_i\alpha_i)},$$

where MC_i is the marginal cost of brand i. Then, from (10.10.1, 2) and (10.11.3), after some manipulation we find that:

$$1 \quad \Psi_i > 0 \rightarrow \frac{\delta p_i}{\delta s_{ij}} > 0$$

$$2 \quad \Psi_i = 0 \rightarrow \frac{\delta p_i}{\delta s_{ij}} = 0 \tag{10.12}$$

$$3 \quad \Psi_i < 0 \rightarrow \frac{\delta p_i}{\delta s_{ij}} < 0.$$

In approximation, suppose $n_i\alpha_i \simeq 0$. Then, the sign of Ψ_i is positive if $2p_i > p_j + MC_i$, so that p_i moves in the same direction as s_{ij}. We would expect, therefore, that p_i would move in a direction opposite to s_{ij} only when p_j is substantially greater than p_i.

If we assume that $\frac{\delta p_i}{\delta s_{ij}} > 0$, it follows from (10.11.4) that $\frac{\delta x_i}{\delta s_{ij}} < 0$ if $p_i \geq p_j$.

When $p_i < p_j$ the expression is more difficult to sign. For $\frac{\delta x_i}{\delta s_{ij}} < 0$ it is necessary and sufficient that

$$-\frac{\alpha_i'}{\alpha_i}(p_i^\circ - p_j) < \frac{\delta p_i^\circ}{\delta s_{ij}}. \qquad (10.13)$$

Parameter magnitudes now become important. The absolute value of the ratio on the lefthand side of (10.13) must be expected to be small in that it is the ratio of b_{ij} to the sum of all of the other-price b-coefficients, including itself. It should be expected to shrink toward zero as the number of firms rises. The difference between the prices would have to be very large in general for (10.13) to be violated, and therefore the expectation is that x_i will move in the opposite direction from s_{ij}.

Figure 10.2 depicts those expectations graphically and is based on a different manner of demonstrating their causation. Let $p_{max,1}$ be the price-axis intercept of the original demand function $D_{i,1}$. From (10.2) it is simply $(a_i + \beta_j)/\alpha_i$. When s_{ij} rises, differentiation of the x-axis intercept with respect to s_{ij} reveals that it will always move leftwards. On the other hand, differentiation of $p_{max,1}$ yields $-(\alpha_i'/\alpha_i)(p_{max,\,1} - p_j)$, which will be positive when p_j is less than $p_{max,1}$. Assuming the latter to be true, we find that $p_{max,2}$ will be above $p_{max,1}$, and connecting $p_{max,2}$ with the new, smaller x-axis intercept yields a new demand function $D_{2,i}$ with steeper slope. Then $p_{i,2}$ will be above $p_{i,1}$ when profits are maximized. However, as p_j approaches $p_{max,1}$ so will $p_{max,2}$, placing $D_{i,2}$ below $D_{i,1}$ with a very steep slope, and causing p_j to fall with the rise in s_{ij}. Hence, when brand i is enjoying the sales benefits of a large $(p_j - p_i)$, a rise in s_{ij} reduces that benefit, shifts the demand curve inward, and leads brand i to compete by lowering price.

But, of course, these are only the *ceteris paribus* price and output movements, holding all other prices and interproduct distances constant. However, interproduct distances cannot be kept constant since, if s_{ij} is a distance for an interior brand, some brands will find brand j closer and others farther than previously, and if it is at the highest quality end-point on the brand spectrum all of its rivals will find it farther. Also, the brand which has moved will find all of its own interproduct distances have changed. Prices and outputs will rise and fall as adjustments occur throughout the industry. Because we expect prices to move in the same direction as s_{ij}, it is to be expected that interdependent effects will reinforce the impact movements.

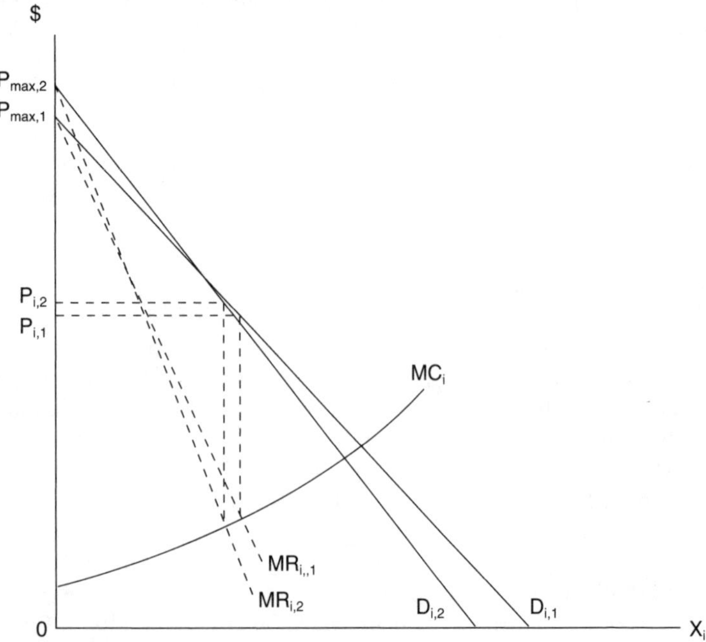

Figure 10.2 Price displacement with a rise in s_{ij}

Such comparative statics become too complex for analytical solution with interesting industry sizes, and therefore we rely upon simulative theorizing to obtain insights through an example.

a A Base Case

We assume a 5-brand industry with the parameters listed in Table 10.1. The profit functions for each of the firms taken separately are strictly concave, and hence first-order conditions for a maximum are both necessary and sufficient for a maximum. (Initial interproduct distances are listed in Table 10.1 without parentheses.) By solving each successively and changing the prices of brands sequentially in a diagonalization algorithm one searches for a convergence which may indeed occur only with negative profits (and elimination) for some firms. With the base case parameters, however, all five firms remain viable with solution values listed in Table 10.2.

A useful index of overall price-quality competitiveness, combining the influence of demand coefficients, prices and interbrand quality distances is the measure

$$E_i = -\frac{\alpha_i p_i}{\beta_i + \alpha_i}.$$

The numerator of E_i rises as sales-damaging forces associated with high p_i (and, through it, high costs), small interbrand distances or large demand coefficients; the denominator rises with favorable demand forces acting through high rivals' prices, large other-price coefficients, large demand function intercepts and expansive interbrand distances. Hence, low values of E_i denote overall competitiveness. They are listed for the brands in the base case in Table 10.2. Clearly, this set of brands falls into two subsets: the highly competitive brands 1, 2, and 3, and the disadvantaged brands 4 and 5. Profits correlate quite well with the E_i, although brand 2 is an exception.

A broader investigation of this correlation is presented in Figure 10.3, and it is not so simply interpreted. A simple linear regression of profits on E_i for 75 observations (21 solutions with 5 brands each, with several outliers omitted) with OLS yields an adjusted r^2 of 0.834. This is, however, somewhat misleading. Figure 10.3 illustrates clearly the persistence of the two clusters of E_i values throughout the 21 solutions (the remaining ones of which will be given below). The steeply negative slope of the estimating equation, graphed in Figure 10.3 is the result of the position of the two clusters identified above. Separate estimating equations have been computed on the diagram for the clusters taken separately, and although a negative relation between profits and E-measures is found in the lower cluster, there is a slightly positive slope in the estimating equation for the upper cluster. Indeed, this equation separates two quite distinct subgroups within the upper cluster, both of which have positive profiles. The lower subset consists of the observations for brand 2 and the upper of those for brands 1 and 3. The use of the E_i measures to index competitiveness, therefore, should, in general be used cautiously. Finally, the relation between the measure and price elasticity of demand will be derived in (10.17) below.

Brands 1 and 3 bound the market interval and are farthest in product space from competitors with average distances of 5.75 and 4.25 respectively, and brand 1 is favored with the lowest variable costs and most favorable "own-price elasticity" coefficient in the industry. Its other-price elasticity coefficients are on the whole the least favorable, however. Its high price, low cost and high profit reflect these advantages, although its quantity is restrained by its other-price demand coefficient drag and its relatively low a_1. Its α_1 and β_1, the lowest in the product group, reflect both its distance advantage and other-price disadvantages.

Brand 3 benefits primarily from a large basic demand for its product (a_3), as reflected in the maximum price it could charge before losing all customers were it completely isolated from other firms' prices. As noted above, it is

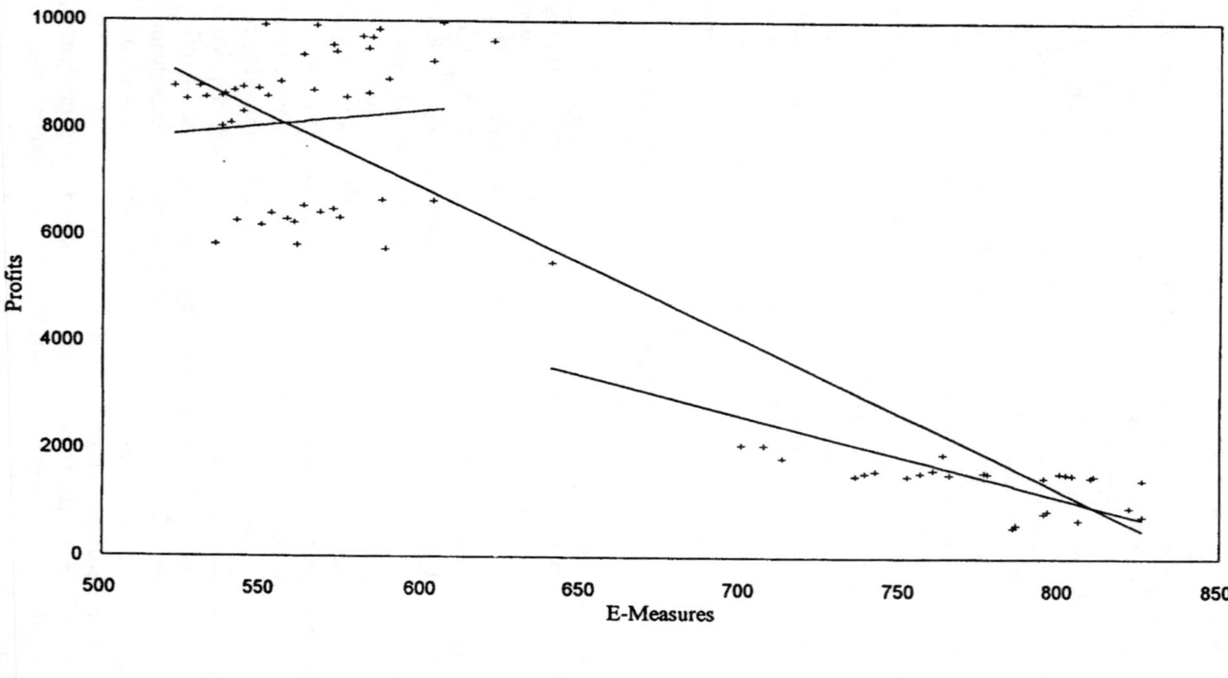

Figure 10.3 Relation of profits to *E*-measures

distant from its competitors, and its cost structure is relatively favorable. Also, other-firm demand coefficients are favorable in the cases of those rivals which are closest to it. One would not have predicted *ex ante facto* that it would enjoy the maximum profit in the product group.

Brand 2 enjoys a good demand and an excellent cost structure, but its competitive position might seem to be penalized by an average distance from competitors of 3 – the smallest of the brands. It does well, being the median profit earner, by virtue of its cost advantages, which permit it to benefit from its favorable price differentials with rivals and its proximity to them. Finally, brands 4 and 5 are the roundly penalized of the group, with average inter-product distances of 3.5 and high cost structures outweighing favorable demand structures.

b Changes in Location in the Quality Space

In the real world we may distinguish 5 types of movements in characteristics space that interest us:

1 Limited or *marginal* moves by incumbents, in which a brand moves a small step closer to an envied rival or farther from a highly competitive brand. In general, this is the form of locational competitive moves we expect to encounter in the short or intermediate run. Firms are limited by patent restraints, technological knowledge limitations, equipment capabilities, marketing reorientation frictions, concerns about consumer reactions to changes in brand images, and so forth, in their consideration of feasible or desirable moves in quality space. Risk-averseness will generally characterize the approach to proposed changes in the characteristics structure of a flagship brand.

2 *Quantum* changes in the location of major brands to meet major competitive challenges from closely competitive rivals or to escape them. Therefore, such moves may involve changes to positions in close proximity to such rivals or to long distances in either direction from them. Such major changes in brand images are rare, for reasons mentioned in 1 above, and in most cases are desperation moves occasioned by threats to survival.

3 *Incumbent multiplicatives* whose producers increase the number of products they sell in order to enhance sales and profits by dispersing new brands in the space. Ready-to-eat breakfast food producers are adept at this, selling new variants under their existing brand names or producing house brands for retailers, but this category also embraces truly innovative products originating within the industry.

4 *Entrant multiplicatives* which are product placements on the quality spectrum by firms previously outside the industry, including competitive

variants of existing brands and innovating products from outside the industry.
5 Brand *eliminations* through competitive failures that widen gaps in the placement profile.

Most characteristics competition in differentiated oligopoly occurs under the first category or as results of this type of competitive process. Quantum leaps pay great costs in abandoning or restructuring in a serious way sunk costs in advertising and marketing infrastructure, brand reputation and consumer recognition – and, perhaps, production efficiency accumulated over many years of learning. Incumbent multiplicatives dilute brand distinctiveness to the extent they are included as variants of the flagship brand(s), are simply ventures in copycat products, or, importantly, are essentially analytically unpredictable innovations. Entrant multiplicatives establish new brands, and may more frequently than incumbent multiplicatives be innovatory, but share the nonpredictability of point of entry into the characteristics spectrum. Finally, brand eliminations occur largely as the competitive outcomes of marginal moves causing negative profits for incumbent firms. Therefore, we confine our analysis to that of such marginal movements as we move into a rivalrous consonance environment.

As a parameter change, and in conformance to the observation above that only small changes are consistent with the logic of the model, we move brand 2 one unit to the right of brand 1 on the product line, so that s_{12} now equals 6 instead of 5. This moves brand 2 with relation to other brands, and where such interproduct distances change they are listed in bold face in parentheses in Table 10.1. Where unchanged, the distances are merely repeated in parentheses in the table.

The model was solved, in *ceteris paribus* fashion brand by brand, holding all base case prices constant but that of the firm under analysis. In Table 10.3, the price and output increments are the direct impacts before computing the indirect effects from changes in all other prices, and are listed in column 2 of the table. Projections of these changes are made from (10.11.3, 10.11.4) and are listed in column 3.

Finally, the *mutatis mutandis* equilibrium was obtained by solving (10.10) sequentially, with changes from the base case values of Table 10.2 found in the last column. These total changes minus the direct impacts yield the price reaction impacts of the *mutatis mutandis* equilibrium in column 4 that temper the direct impacts of the *ceteris paribus* equilibrium.

The direct impacts of brand movements are in line with expectations. Brand 2 moves farther away in product space from brands 1 and 4 and closer to 3 and 5. The prices of the first two rise as their competition lessens and they exploit the shift outward of their demand functions by restricting output. The immediate impact on firms 3 and 5 is to lower their prices to meet the enhanced competition from brand 2 and to raise their outputs. As would be expected brand 2's direct price and output impacts were the largest of all the brands and reflected the necessity to compete with price reductions by brands 3 and 5.

From the b_{2j} row of Table 10.1 it can be seen that brand 2 moved away from brands 1 and 4 with demand function coefficients of 3 and 5 to be closer to brands 3 and 5 with coefficients of 6 and 7, enhancing its ability to increase sales by decreasing its price differentials. Hence, its price declines substantially and output increases even before brands 3 and 5 react to the new situation, by lowering prices, which leads brand 2 to decrease its price further. Brand 2's E-coefficient remains the same and profits increase only slightly (see Table 10. 4 for profit movements).

Note that the projected price and output impacts predicted the directions of *ceteris paribus* changes in every instance and did reasonably well pricewise quantitatively for brands other than brand 2, which was derived by solving (10.11.3 and 10.11.4) for each of the affected brands and summing the projected changes in Brand 2's price and output. Output projections were even more accurate percentagewise but, as in the case of the price estimates, performed relatively well as linear projections of exponentially determined

Table 10.1 Parameters for Model 1 base case

Parameter/Firm	1	2	3	4	5
a_{1j}	800	***	***	***	***
a_{2j}	***	700	***	***	***
a_{3j}	***	***	1100	***	***
a_{4j}	***	***	***	1000	***
a_{5j}	***	***	***	***	950
b_{1j}	15	3	5	8	3
b_{2j}	3	16	6	5	7
b_{3j}	4	7	22	6	9
b_{4j}	8	9	7	25	8
b_{5j}	7	9	11	10	26
s_{1j}	0	5 **(6)**	8	3	7
s_{2j}	5 **(6)**	0	3 **(2)**	2 **(3)**	2 **(1)**
s_{3j}	8 (8)	3 **(2)**	0	5 (5)	1 (1)
s_{4j}	3 (3)	2 **(3)**	5 (5)	0	4 (4)
s_{5j}	7 (7)	2 **(1)**	1 (1)	4 (4)	0
F_j	1000	800	1200	1500	1020
m_j	2	3	5	16	15.5
n_j	0.0005	0.00006	0.00007	0.0001	0.00012
$k_{ij} \equiv k$	0.29	0.29	0.29	0.29	0.29

Table 10.2 Solution values for Model 1 base case

Variables	*Firms*				
	1	*2*	*3*	*4*	*5*
p_i	\$24.24	\$19.56	\$22.84	\$25.02	\$23.22
x_i	435	428	594	336	331
C_i	\$1,963.95	\$2,095.58	\$4,195.66	\$6,890.21	\$6,165.95
π_i	\$8,571.93	\$6,280.272	\$9,374.08	\$1,521.86	\$1,524.28
α_i	19.94	25.94	33.47	37.54	43.32
β_i	118.00	235.53	258.50	275.54	387.26
E_i	0.526	0.542	0.563	0.736	0.752

variables. Also, net total changes in industry output are only 0.84 percent over base case output, approximating unchanged sales as formally required by the assumptions of the individual consumer model that underlies Model 1.

We may summarize the highlights of the indirect effects, as they yield no surprising results that offer enlightening insights. These price-induced modifications to the direct effects were relatively unimportant compared with the direct impacts except for brand 5's output effects. Brand 5's high own-price sensitivity punished its sales severely as differentials between its prices and those of lower cost rivals widened. Further it is strongly sensitive to brands 2 and 3 prices, which fell both initially and after price adjustments, and this was enhanced by brand 2's enhanced proximity. In somewhat the same position as brand 5, brand 3's price fell after total adjustments, although it did benefit somewhat from brand 4's price increase, despite the distance between the two and the low b_{34} demand interaction term. Brand 4 lowered its price slightly on indirect impact account but raised its price substantially on net, benefitting from its most important rival, brand 2, moving away from it as well as its separation from the price cutting of brands 3 and 5. Also, it benefitted somewhat from brand 1's price increase. Brand 1's direct impacts permitted it to raise its price, with price cuts of rivals 2, 3 and 5 having no impact on its new solution. Its nearest and strongest competition, brand 4, was a price raiser, and its favorable cost structure and low own-price demand coefficient were other factors contributing to its rather insulated position. Finally, brand 2 suffered a bit by its movement toward its most important competitors – brands 3 and 5, both severe price cutters – and away from its least important – brands 1 and 4 – who were price raisers.

Consumers' surplus is simply calculated as $CS_j = 0.5x_i[((\alpha_i + \beta_i)/\alpha_i) - p_i]$. Social surplus in the old and new *mutatis mutandis* equilibrium is displayed in Table 10.4. From the equation for consumers' surplus, it is trivial that it will rise with increases in other-firm prices (via β_i), rise with increases in x_i, and, therefore, fall with rises in p_i. Consider, however, a *ceteris paribus* rise in s_{ij}

$$\frac{\delta CS_i}{\delta s_{ij}} = -\left(\frac{CS_i \alpha_i}{x_i} + 0.5x_i\right)\frac{\delta p_i}{\delta s_{ij}} + \frac{\alpha_i'}{\alpha_i}(0.5p_j x_i - CS_i) \tag{10.14}$$

If $\delta p_i/\delta s_{ij} > 0$ then the only positive term on the righthand side of (10.14) is $\frac{\alpha_i'}{\alpha_i} \cdot CS_i$, which, given the expected low value of the ratio as developed above, seems too small to outweigh the sum of the remaining negative terms. Therefore, *ceteris paribus*, we expect consumers' surplus to move in a direction opposite that of distance from the firm initiating movement.

The expectations that for those firms whose locations remain fixed prices will change in the same direction as distances from firm 2, outputs will move in the opposite direction, and that consumers' surplus will move the opposite direction are borne out in Tables 10.3 and 10.4. Note that in Table 10.2 the base case solution values for the prices of firms that were stationary are very close to p_2, the price of the firm whose site is changed. We should expect, therefore, that no counterintuitive movements will occur in prices, outputs or consumers' surplus in the *ceteris paribus* solutions.

Table 10.3 *Ceteris paribus*, projected and *mutatis mutandis* price and output changes

Variable	*Direct impacts*	*Projected impacts*	*Price reaction impacts*	*Total changes*
p_1	+0.12	+0.10	+0.0	+0.12
p_2	–0.33	–0.89	–0.04	–0.37
p_3	–0.3	–0.46	–0.04	–0.34
p_4	+0.25	+0.23	–0.02	+0.22
p_5	–0.21	–0.26	–0.05	–0.26
x_1	–1.53	–1.29	+0.22	–1.31
x_2	+12.10	+8.53	–1.03	+11.07
x_3	+7.17	+8.22	–1.45	+5.72
x_4	–2.03	–1.71	–1.29	–3.32
x_5	+3.44	+3.90	–2.30	+1.14

Table 10.4 Consumers' surplus, profits and social surplus in Model 1 equilibria

	Original equilibrim			*New equilibrium*		
Brands	*Consumers' surplus*	*Profits*	*Social surplus*	*Consumers' surplus*	*Profits*	*Social surplus*
1	$4,664.99	$8,325.20	$12,990.19	$4,678.26	$8,351.88	$13,030.14
2	$3,535.56	$6,270.71	$9,806.27	$3,545.44	$6,290.51	$9,835.95
3	$5,283.07	$9,365.45	$14,648.52	$5,230.92	$9,261.05	$14,491.97
4	$1,504.00	$1,507.65	$3,011.65	$1,526.02	$1,551.78	$3,077.80
5	$1,269.05	$1,515.79	$2,784.84	$1,229.63	$1,438.94	$2,668.57
Totals	$16,256.67	$26,984.80	$43,241.47	$16,210.27	$26,894.16	$43,104.43

Computation of the qualitative movements of CS_i between the original and new equilibria is quite simple. From the definition of CS_i:

$$CS_i = 0.5x_i\left[\frac{a_i + \beta_i}{\alpha_i} - p_i\right] = 0.5x_i y_i, \tag{10.15}$$

where y_i is simply the difference on the price axis of the intercept of the inverse demand function (p_{max}) and the price p_i. Letting the initial and new equilibria be denoted by $k = 1,2$ respectively, we find that

$$\Delta CS_i = CS_{i2} - CS_{i1} \underset{<}{\overset{>}{=}} 0 \Leftrightarrow \frac{x_1}{x_2} \underset{>}{\overset{<}{=}} \frac{y_2}{y_1}. \tag{10.16}$$

As indicated in Table 10.2 and the accompanying discussion, changes in the location of a brand in characteristics space will involve for each brand a shift in the demand function which registers as a new price-axis intercept, p_{max}; a new slope of the demand function arising because of the change in the value of the decay factor involving the distance of the given brand and the moving brand; a change in the price of the stationary brand; and the implied change in the quantity of that brand. We may now broaden our *ceteris paribus* analysis above to include the price–output adjustments of all brands on the basis of the insights from the *mutatis mutandis* example. The first three of these factors determine the changes in the area of the consumers' surplus triangle, and therefore, the sign of δCS_i.

It is interesting in this regard to note two opposing forces that a stationary firm experiences as another brand moves away from it. We have seen that, *ceteris paribus*, the slope of the inverse demand function, $1/\alpha_i$, rises because of the fall in the exponential distance term involving the moving firm, which tends toward a fall in own-price elasticity and a price increase in the face of less intense competition. The rise in the same term in the β_i term will increase the inverse demand curve intercept term enhancing its move to more own-price inelasticity and yielding an even greater likelihood of a price increase. But now we may free all other brand prices. The β_i term will also be affected by the price change of the moving firm, which has a higher likelihood of being positive. But to complicate matters, all other brands will react pricewise to the displacement of the moving firm and these prices will also register in β_i, so that the final resultant reflected in the intercept will be ambiguous. What is interesting, however, is that the initiative of the moving firm sets off advantageous and disadvantageous forces, so that what might appear to be an increase in competition force can actually lead to a fall in competitive position and profits and/or social surplus. From Table 10.4, in the present example, the movement of brand 2 leads to a fall in total consumers' surplus and a fall in profits, so that social surplus also falls. Also, in all of the cases in which brand 2 approached rivals profits fell, and in all cases in which it moved away from rivals profits rose, which we would label the normal expectation. From the welfare standpoints of consumers' and social surplus, however, brand 2's move is not desirable.

This perception of brand competition as one of narrowly bounded movement within a bounded space with fixed total demand in the short- and intermediate-run yields a model with continuous movement and no stable equilibrium, unless one introduces relocation costs and/or minimum profit improvement constraints. Indeed, realistically, such competition among incumbents, without tacit collusion, should be the expectation: continuing marginal adjustments as firms seek profit improvements of worthwhile magnitude. The resort to advertising and other marketing costs as competition alternatives by increasing brand demand with fixed locations is readily understandable in the light of these observations. Further pursuit of Hotelling-model results with costless relocation in these conditions, absent specific industry conditions, is therefore considered realistically unfruitful, and the illustration of means of gaining some insights into the implications of firm movements using brand 2 as an arbitrary mover is deemed sufficient at this stage of the analysis. A wide choice of restrictions on movement necessary to make the analysis realistic is available to the analyst and will change with the industry under study.

c Some Polar Displacements of Distance Discount Factors

The implications of interbrand distances as factors in competition can be seen more clearly by study of two limiting cases, where spatial discount factors k are zero on the one hand and infinite on the other. In the first case interbrand distances derived from indifference premia are undiluted by the spatial impediments of cognition and in the second case brands are completely isolated by their densities so that price differentials play no role in the consumers' choices. Changing these k-coefficients may also be viewed as a way of increasing or decreasing interbrand distances proportionately to s_{ij}.

Table 10.5 displays the solutions to these two extreme cases together with the base case of Table 10.2 for comparison. The profit outcomes are dependent on three factors: (1) the impacts on quantities sold, (2) the implied price at which those quantities are sold, and (3) the average costs of the output. The determinants of the quantities supplied are given by the components of E_i, as explained above. The parameter α_i sums the negative impacts on sales per unit price rise, imposed both directly by b_{ii} and indirectly by the heightening in the price differential $(p_i - p_j)$ as transmitted by $b_{ij}e^{-ks_{ij}}$. The term β_i yields the positive factors acting on sales in the form of a shift in the demand function intercept caused by narrowing of the price differential through rises in the prices of other products discounted by the decay factor. If we add a_i to β_i we obtain the actual horizontal axis intercept fixing the location of the new demand function. Given the changes in p_i and the p_j, the resultant net change in output will be determined by the strength of the changes in shift and slope.

The price reactions of firms are dictated by changes in the own-price elasticities of the demand function as dictated by the changes in shift and slope parameters brought about by the change in k, where the elasticities of the new demand functions in the region of the new equilibrium are determined by the relations of (10.17):

$$\varepsilon_i = \frac{\delta x_i p_i}{\delta p_i x_i} = -\frac{\alpha_i p_i}{\alpha_i + \beta_i - \alpha_i p_i} = -\frac{E_i}{1 - \dfrac{\alpha_i p_i}{a_i + \beta_i}} = -\frac{E_i}{1 - E_i} \tag{10.17}$$

Since the rises in k are effectively increases in the interbrand distances among all brands, on the basis of our previous reasoning we expect all prices to rise and outputs to fall. From Table 10.5 this is indeed the universal rule. All the values of α_i fall monotonically as the $b_{ji}p_i$ terms are attenuated, and the β_i fall towards 0 as the influence of the p_j diminishes. The competitiveness of all 5 brands as indexed by the E_i improve as k rises, or, minimally, remains the same, with brands 4 and 5 – the two high-cost producers – benefitting most from the increasing protection from rivals' price differentials. All of these movements are those we would have predicted *ex ante facto*: there are no surprises.

Moreover, we would have predicted that profits would rise monotonically for all brands as k rose and the pricing power of the firms was enhanced, and for brands 1, 3, 4, and 5 our expectations would have been fulfilled. But for brand 2 we find that although profits did rise as k rose from 0 to 0.29, they fell as k rose further to approach ∞. This is a most interesting instance of a brand actually being injured by gaining greater independence from the pricing decisions of its competitors. Brand 2 is a lower-quality, low-cost product which prospers by offering an attractive price differential to consumers of the other brands. It follows that it must be "in view" by consumers to reap that advantage. A large part of its basic demand is generated by β_2. Hence, when spatial discount factors become too large, Brand 2 is thrown back upon its own weak basic demand (a_2) to the detriment of profits.

A good example of the phenomenon operating in the opposite direction is in the ready-to-eat breakfast food industry where house brands, which are low-cost, unadvertised, and of unbranded but high-quality pedigree, flourish as consumer education decreases the decay factor and the cognitive distance of

Table 10.5 Solution values for polar values of spatial discount factors

Variables	*Firms* 1	2	3	4	5
	Spatial discount factor = 0				
p_i	$18.73	$16.80	$19.36	$21.11	$21.02
x_i	550	508	685	344	342
C_i	$2,251.84	$2,340.72	$4,657.25	$7,055.60	$6,341.21
π_i	$8,055.88	$6,201.26	$8,604.99	$ 593.02	$854.94
α_i	34.00	37.00	48.00	57.00	63.00
β_i	387.17	430.06	514.37	604.77	716.47
E_i	0.54	0.55	0.58	0.79	0.79
	Base case spatial discount factor = 0.29				
p_i	$24.24	$19.56	$22.84	$25.02	$23.22
x_i	435	428	594	336	331
C_i	$1,963.95	$2,095.58	$4,195.66	$6,890.21	$6,165.95
π_i	$8,571.93	$6,280.274	$9,374.08	$1,521.86	$1,524.28
α_i	19.94	25.94	33.47	37.54	43.32
β_i	118.00	235.53	258.50	275.54	387.26
E_i	0.526	0.542	0.563	0.736	0.752
	Spatial discount factor = ∞				
p_i	$27.86	$23.39	$27.53	$28.03	$26.05
x_i	382	326	494	299	273
C_i	$1,837.28	$1,783.43	$3,688.31	$6,296.99	$5,254.99
π_i	$8,808.11	$5,835.88	$9,920.37	$2,091.02	$1,848.06
α_i	15.00	16.00	22.00	25.00	26.00
β_i	0	0	0	0	0
E_i	0.52	0.53	0.55	0.70	0.71

alternatives increases the significance of price differentials. Were marketing strategies by branded products to convince consumers that their quality has been improved and thereby further distanced themselves from house brands, the brand 2 case would be revisited.

3 MODEL 2: SPATIAL DISTANCES AS METRIC WITH THE RIVALROUS CONSONANCE MODE OF TACIT COLLUSION

Suppose now that tacit collusion pervades the relations among the 5 brands of section 2, modeled as rivalrous consonance relations. From (10.6′) and (10.8) the expressions for optimal prices can be solved iteratively for desired values of θ_{ij}. The problem inheres in the choice of the consonance coefficients from their potential infinity of values to obtain useful insights into the nature of competition under varying degrees of tacit collusion while demonstrating the methodology. The base case of Table 10.1 and its solution in Table 10.5 is, of course, Model 1 with $\theta_{ii} = 1$, $\theta_{ij} = 0$. As first cases, therefore, the polar case is presented with perfect collusion when $\theta_{ii} = 1$, $\theta_{ij} = 1$, and subsequently, a midcase with $\theta_{ii} = 1$, $\theta_{ij} = 0.5$, with the base case $k = 0.29$. The solutions are reproduced in Table 10.6 with the base case for comparison.

Prices of all firms rise and outputs fall consistently as rivalrous consonance increases tacit collusion, which is expected. The price rises reflect in large part the inclusion of marginal consonance costs which are found in the last row of each solution set. All of the firms' competitive positions decline (as measured by rises in E_i, which do not include marginal consonance costs) as cooperation rises. In the more competitive cluster of firms, the relative rise in this measure for brand 2 (11.3 percent) is notable and reflects its high marginal consonance cost. Taking into account the small profit rises or losses of brands 4 and 5 reduces its competitive position. Nonetheless profits do increase consistently because of the large rise in price differentials it experiences with these two high-priced brands, and indeed, it enjoys the highest percentage profit increase from zero to perfect consonance of any of the 5 firms.

Interestingly, the two firms that benefit least or suffer most from tacit collusion are brands 4 and 5, which are quite different in quality. From zero to perfect collusion brand 4's profits rise only 1.3 percent and brand 5's actually fall by 6.6 percent. Both firms do benefit modestly from mid-level collusion, but again not to the degree that the three lower quality brands do. One suspects that both of these firms would benefit maximally from tacit collusion at levels somewhat below 0.5.

Brand 5 is a high-quality, high-cost product with weak α_i own-price demand factor and whose β_i other-price demand coefficient rises slowly as competitors' prices rise sluggishly. However, the major culprit causing such profit outcomes in the case of brand 5 is the rise in consonance costs. As consonance coefficients rise the demand functions shift outward with the rise in the β_i coefficients, but (unlike the situation analyzed in Figure 10.2) the slopes of the functions remain the same because the α_i coefficients do not change. Hence, were the marginal cost functions unchanged, outputs, prices, revenues and profits would rise. But marginal cost functions now shift upward by large amounts in the case of brand 5, and outputs and revenues

Table 10.6 Solution values for polar and median values of consonance coefficients θ_{ij}

	Firms				
Variables	*1*	*2*	*3*	*4*	*5*
			Zero consonance case $\theta_{ij} = 0$		
p_i	\$24.24	\$19.56	\$22.84	\$25.02	\$23.22
x_i	435	428	594	336	331
C_i	\$1,963.95	\$2,095.58	\$4,195.66	\$6,890.21	\$6,165.95
π_i	\$8,571.93	\$6,280.27	\$9,374.08	\$1,521.86	\$1,524.28
α_i	19.94	25.94	33.47	37.54	43.33
β_i	118.00	235.53	258.50	275.54	387.26
E_i	0.526	0.542	0.563	0.736	0.752
Mar.con.cost	\$0	\$0	\$0	\$0	\$0
			Median case $\theta_{ij} = 0.5$		
p_i	\$25.11	\$20.99	\$24.05	\$26.63	\$25.11
x_i	425.04	406.63	572.97	292.81	272.43
C_i	\$1,940.42	\$2,029.80	\$4,087.81	\$6,193.57	\$5,251.58
π_i	\$8,731.90	\$6,506.34	\$9,694.66	\$1,603.18	\$1,589.33
α_i	19.94	25.94	33.47	37.54	43.32
β_i	125.73	251.09	278.01	292.41	410.33
E_i	0.541	0.572	0.584	0.773	0.800
Mar.con.cost	\$0.68	\$1.13	\$0.92	\$1.38	\$1.62
			Perfect consonance case with $\theta_{ij} = 1$		
p_i	\$26.02	\$22.49	\$25.33	\$28.29	\$27.07
x_i	414.88	384.04	550.53	248.09	211.74
C_i	\$1,915.81	\$1,960.98	\$3,973.84	\$5,475.62	\$4,307.36
π_i	\$8,879.44	\$6,674.79	\$9,971.06	\$1,542.09	\$1,423.83
α_i	19.94	25.94	33.47	37.54	43.32
β_i	133.74	267.26	298.26	309.99	434.40
E_i	0.556	0.603	0.606	0.811	0.847
Mar.con.cost	\$1.39	\$2.31	\$1.90	\$2.80	\$3.30

fall, with small rises or declines in profits. The marginal consonance costs are high, of course, because the lower quality brands' profits are rising. It is in intense competition with brand 3, whose profits rise steeply when θ_{ij} rise above 0.5.

The marginal consonance cost factor is important in the case of Brand 4, but it is also a high-cost, low-quality brand intensely competitive with firms whose profits are rising. Its high basic demand from a curiously loyal band of customers, saves it from more severe profit deprivation. Its p_{max} shifts upward by a small amount between zero and perfect consonance but its marginal consonance cost shifts the cost curve up from a high base to reduce profits from their mid-level consonance value.

Brand 3 is a highest-quality producer with low marginal production costs and high basic demand, with mid-level α_i own-price impacts and a low β_i other-price factor reflecting its high degree of dependence on other brands' prices. Marginal consonance costs are the second lowest in the industry. Its competitive position weakens only slightly with enhanced tacit collusion, and it is the major winner from enhanced cooperation in the industry.

Finally, brand 1's profit rises steadily as tacit collusion rises, to enjoy a modest 3.3 percent rise from zero to perfect tacit collusion. It is a low-quality, low-cost producer which enjoys a good deal of autonomy from its rivals. The marginal consonance cost, for example, is the smallest in the industry, its α_1 reveals the small impact of rivals' demand coefficients on its sales, and its β_1 value shows that it gains little from rises in rivals' prices.

For $k = 0.29$ the industry's structure reveals a dichotomy. The group of 3 highly competitive firms reveals monotonically rising profits as tacit collusion progresses. Brand 1 enjoys its independence from rivals, brand 2 is highly dependent on its higher-pricing rivals for demand support, and brand 3 is intermediate in its dependence on rival price movements and in its marginal consonance costs. The second group, consisting of brands 4 and 5, is high-cost with large α_i values imposing punishing negative influences on demand, and only moderate offsets in β_i values. Tacit collusion benefits these firms only moderately in mid-ranges and punishes them above those ranges. The steady rise in profits enjoyed by brands 1, 2, and 3 inflict rapidly increasing marginal consonance costs on brands 4 and 5 and reduce profits below the median collusion case and, for brand 5, below the zero collusion case as well. These cost rises force their prices up, increase the differentials between them and group 1 prices, raising the latter group's profits, and thereby shift marginal consonance costs even higher.

As noted above, brand 4 is a lower-quality product produced at high cost in very strong competition with all other firms, most notably, given the distances involved, with group 1 firms. High production costs, large adverse price differentials with these firms, and large profit gains of these firms from tacit collusion result in the poor profit experience related above. Nonetheless, it does hold on to viability rather tenaciously as collusion rises with $k = 0.29$. But firm 5 is something of an anomaly: it is a high-quality product that somehow is in quite high competition with lower-quality products as well as with brand 3, which is higher than it in the quality scale. It is, of course, that highest quality firm that inflicts most damage on it via the large profits it earns, its close distance, and the worsening price differential. But brand 5's large b_{5j}s with such firms as 1, 2, and 4 are difficult to explain in terms of rational consumer preferences. One must wonder if it would remain viable under other rivalrous consonance regimes.

Table 10.7 permits us to probe more deeply into the structure and brand interrelationships in this industry. It records the solutions to combinations of 4 *cluster* categories:

1 The primary organizing cluster is that of *distance discounting* values, with $k = 0, 0.29$, and ∞ successively. These are familiar from Table 10.5, and can be understood as a means of stretching interbrand distances as k rises, from the pure s_{ij} values unaffected by cognitive distortion to an effective complete isolation of each firm from its rivals in product space.
2 For each distance discounting cluster brands are broken down into 3 additional clusters, the first of which are *θ-clusters*. These rivalrous consonance factors are set successively to 0, 0.5, and 1, for all firms, to obtain solutions for zero, median, and perfect tacit collusion levels. They permit study, within each k-cluster, of *generalized* rivalrous consonance – i.e., where the given θ_{ij} value is extended by all firms to all other firms.
3 For each distance discounting cluster and each θ-cluster firms are divided into E_i *clusters*, which groups the firms into the 2 competitive clusters discussed above, with group 1 consisting of brands 1, 2, and 3, and group 2 containing brands 4 and 5. In these solutions each group member extends a θ of 0, 0.5, or 1 to other group members, and of 0 to members of the other group.
4 A last cluster is that constructed by grouping brands by s_{ij} proximity, with firms 1, 2, and 4 in the first group and firms 3 and 5 in the second. For each distance discounting and θ cluster, solution to these s_{ij} *clusters* are obtained with tacit collusion ruling within the clusters only. These cluster conjunctions yield 21 independent solutions for which profit values have been listed.

Brand 1's isolation from its rivals, discussed above, does not prevent it from benefitting from extensive, generalized tacit collusion. As k rises from 0 to ∞ profits rise in the θ-cluster to attain a maximum for perfect consonance when $k = 0.29$, then fall but in general remain higher than in the $k = 0$ configuration. Thus, it generally benefits as virtual distance from all rivals rises and collusion increases. Its low-price places it well to benefit from price differentials and the larger discount factors protect it from suffering large consonance costs. It benefits more from generalized collusion rather than collusion limited to its E-cluster, although profits in it rise as k rises, but clustering by distance in the s-cluster is more profitable than the E-cluster. But the s-cluster profits remain below those obtained in the generalized θ-cluster. In this industry tacit collusion benefits the lowest-quality, cheapest-cost firm by isolating it from negative feedbacks from rivals' policies, and, for median θ-values, permitting it to benefit from large, favorable price differentials.

Although the maximum is attained for $k = 0.29$, profits remain high and almost identical for all 7 solutions when $k = \infty$, accenting the beneficial effects from heightened virtual interbrand distances.

On the other hand, Brand 2 continues to benefit most from proximity to its rivals and, indeed, is the largest relative beneficiary of tacit collusion in the industry: its maximum profit occurs with a zero distance discount factor and perfect generalized tacit collusion. However, for the most part, its profits for the $k = 0.29$ category are higher than corresponding cluster values for $k = 0$ and much higher than those for $k = \infty$. Except for the maximum profit value, therefore, it gains from modest enhancement of virtual distances from its rivals, but as the lowest-priced brand in the industry as k rises brand 2's β_2 depreciates and lessens its price differential advantage. In all three k-clusters the s-cluster profits are higher than the E-cluster values, indicating the greater importance to it of nearness to Brand 4 rather than Brand 3 because the former's price is higher than the latter's as well as its distance being shorter.

Brand 3 is in the happy position of being the highest quality of the five brands, with low costs and a most favorable basic demand. Moreover, the demand coefficients of other firms' price differentials inflict relatively small impacts on α_3 while its price tends to be below that of its closest neighbor, brand 5, so that it draws a large demand benefit from that differential. Its highest profit occurs in the $k = 0$, perfect rivalrous consonance configuration, so that it benefits somewhat from increases in virtual interbrand distancing that increases its end-point advantage. However, as this distancing moves beyond the median k the advantages of tacit collusion pale and it finds it advantageous to revert to zero collusion. When $k = \infty$, the advantage of proximity to brand 5 in the lower k-clusters rather than brands 1 and 2 disappears (that is, the profits in the E-clusters rise to near-parity with those in the s-clusters). In the smaller k-clusters the large price differential with brand 2 relative to that with brand 5 is punishing, while when $k = \infty$ these differences effectively are eliminated and brand 3 is indifferent between the E- and s-clusters. In summary, brand 3, as a low-cost, highest-quality, favorable demand-situated product, benefits to a limited extent from tacit collusion, but even more so in general from greater virtual distance from rivals. Like its polar analog on the quality scale, brand 1, brand 3 is somewhat standoffish

Table 10.7 Summary of firms' profits under various rivalrous consonance regimes

Solution	π_1	π_2	π_3	π_4	π_5
Zero distances discounting: k = 0					
Zero rivalrous consonance: $\theta_{ii} = 1$, $\theta_{ij} = 0$, $k = 0$	$8,055.88	$6,201.26	$8,604.99	$593.02	$854.94
Median riv. cons., $\theta_{ii} = 1$, $\theta_{ij} = 0.5$, $k = 0$	8,332.26	6,446.35	8,936.08	724.39	966.08
Perfect riv. con., $\theta_{ii} = 1$, $\theta_{ij} = 1$, $k = 0$	8,619.52	6,679.37	9,263.10	807.09	984.98
E_i–clusters: $\theta_{ii} = 1$, $\theta_{ij} = 0.5, j,k = 1,2,3; 4,5$, $k = 0$	8,122.38	6,253.37	8,680.70	642.27	905.36
E_i–clusters: $\theta_{ii} = 1$, $\theta_{ij} = 1, j,k = 1,2,3; 4,5$, $k = 0$	8,188.89	6,298.68	8,751.88	692.17	956.21
s_{ij}–clusters: $\theta_{ii} = 1$, $\theta_{ij} = 0.5, j,k = 1,2,4; 3,5$, $k = 0$	8,212.08	6,345.29	8,791.05	655.78	928.01
s_{ij}–clusters: $\theta_{ii} = 1$, $\theta_{ij} = 1, j,k = 1,2,4; 3,5$, $k = 0$	8,369.97	6,491.52	8,979.31	686.33	976.73
Median distance discounting: k = 0.29					
Zero rivalrous consonance: $\theta_{ii} = 1$, $\theta_{ij} = 0$, $k = 0.29$	8,571.93	6,280.27	9,374.08	1,521.86	1,524.33
Median riv. cons., $\theta_{ii} = 1$, $\theta_{ij} = 0.5$, $k = 0.29$	8,731.90	6,506.34	9,694.66	1,603.18	1,589.33
Perfect riv. con., $\theta_{ii} = 1$, $\theta_{ij} = 1$, $k = 0.29$	8,879.44	6,674.79	9,971.06	1,542.09	1,423.83
E_i–clusters: $\theta_{ii} = 1$, $\theta_{ij} = 0.5, j,k = 1,2,3; 4,5$, $k = 0.29$	8,602.74	6,321.23	9,439.08	1,571.82	1,585.54
E_i–clusters: $\theta_{ii} = 1$, $\theta_{ij} = 1, j,k = 1,2,3; 4,5$, $k = 0.29$	8,631.39	6,345.30	9,492.71	1,621.26	1,645.66
s_{ij}–clusters: $\theta_{ii} = 1$, $\theta_{ij} = 0.5, j,k = 1,2,4; 3,5$, $k = 0.29$	8,674.15	6,423.91	9,549.71	1,556.05	1,581.99
s_{ij}–clusters: $\theta_{ii} = 1$, $\theta_{ij} = 1, j,k = 1,2,4; 3,5$, $k = 0.29$	8,767.37	6,563.70	9,719.27	1,507.75	1,578.84

Table 10.7 continued

Solution	π_1	π_2	π_3	π_4	π_5
Total distance discounting: $k = \infty$					
Zero rivalrous consonance: $\theta_{ii} = 1$, $\theta_{ij} = 0$, $k = \infty$	8,808.11	5,835.88	9,920.38	2,091.02	1,848.06
Median riv. cons., $\theta_{ii} = 1$, $\theta_{ij} = 0.5$, $k = \infty$	8,788.06	5,749.23	9,850.30	1,933.73	1,557.14
Perfect riv. con., $\theta_{ii} = 1$, $\theta_{ij} = 1$, k = ∞	8,727.94	5,489.28	9,640.07	1,461.86	684.36
E_i–clusters: $\theta_{ii} = 1$, $\theta_{ij} = 0.5, j,k = 1,2,3; 4,5$, $k = \infty$	8,805.45	5,814.28	9,906.59	2,089.30	1,844.69
E_i–clusters: $\theta_{ii} = 1$, $\theta_{ij} = 1, j,k = 1,2,3; 4,5$, $k = \infty$	8,797.46	5,749.48	9,865.24	2,084.12	1,834.56
s_{ij}–clusters: $\theta_{ii} = 1$, $\theta_{ij} = 0.5, j,k = 1,2,4; 3,5$, $k = \infty$	8,795.85	5,825.55	9,906.23	2,002.92	1,766.13
s_{ij}–clusters: $\theta_{ii} = 1$, $\theta_{ij} = 1, j,k = 1,2,4; 3,5$, $k = \infty$	8,795.07	5,794.58	9,863.79	1,738.63	1,520.32

from its industry confreres, and opts out of increasing tacit collusion at the higher end of the spectrum.

Brand 4's experience is determined by its extremely unfavorable demand and cost conditions. Its own-price demand coefficient is extremely high, it is the highest cost brand in the industry, and it is a low-quality product. In every one of the 21 solutions it suffered from the highest price of the 5 brands, so that it was forced to adjust to negative price differentials in every instance. The crucial variable in meliorating its plight was the distance discount factor and specifically its role in reducing α_i, the own-price demand coefficient. Although rises in k reduce β_i as well – the shift factor in the demand equation – the impact was not comparable with the relief afforded via the reduction in the slope term. For example, for the zero rivalrous consonance cluster, as k rises from 0 to 0.29, α_4 falls from 57 to 38 which, when multiplied by their respective p_4 yield an improvement in the reduction of sales from 1,260 to 951, while β_4 falls only from 387 to 276, or by approximately one-third of the improvement brought about by the fall in α_4. For the same consonance cluster, when k is increased from 0.29 to ∞, all impacts of the price differentials are eliminated, and, with generalized rivalrous consonance equal to zero, brand 4 has zero marginal consonance costs. Its profits reach a maximum for this case.

In general, brand 4 does better in the E-clusters than the s-clusters, indicating that it would prefer to extend collusion to brand 5 rather than to brands 1 and 2. For $k = \infty$, its profits for zero rivalrous consonance are only negligibly different from those earned when it extends tacit collusion to brand 5 only because its consonance costs are so low when only brand 5's profits must be taken into account. Nonetheless, tacit collusion for all three of its θ-values benefits brand 4 when distance discounting is zero and except when perfect with the discount factor at 0.29. In each of the distance discount clusters the α_is are fixed but the β_is rise with the higher prices of rivals that higher values of consonance bring. In discount-cluster 1 the β_4 values rise to shift the demand function with constant slope to the right, making it more inelastic and raising p_4. This effect operates partially in the second cluster, but not at all in the third, where all βs are zero. In that cluster, with infinite discounting of distance all of the firms are harmed as consonance coefficients rise above zero.

Brand 5 is a high-quality product, very close in this respect to brand 3, but with average variable costs roughly triple those of its closest rival and with fixed costs only slightly below. Also, its basic demand intercept is lower and its own-price coefficient higher than brand 3's. It is, in short, highly disadvantaged when compared with its neighbor. Not surprisingly, its performance is comparable with that of brand 4, and its maximum profit about 12 percent below – the worst of the 5 brands. Like brand 4, it benefits from enhanced distancing from rival brands but not greatly if at all from tacit collusion.

4 A SUMMARY AND CONCLUSIONS

Several approaches were adopted in this chapter that permitted consumer preferences over brands to be scaled in an operational manner, which in turn allowed the application of closed and simulative analysis of integrated competition. A formal summary of methodology and major insights derived from it may be useful.

1 The scaling method introduced yields consumer valuations in dollars, making them comparable in dimension to prices, and serving as a means of determining maximum consumers' surpluses over a set of brands. Using measures of central tendency as summary aggregate indices of those preferences permitted the derivation of interbrand differences in a product space, such differences being computed by a simple Euclidean metric in the first instance, but then adjusted by an exponential decay factor. The factor k in this formulation gave us a flexible parameter to adjust advertising effects and other cognitive frictions affecting the consumer, to reflect search costs and to admit into the analysis some of the fuzziness that the failure to take into account the variance of indifference premia for each brand introduces into choice prediction. Setting $k = 0$ restores unadjusted Euclidean distances when desired.
2 Aggregate demand functions for brands are stated in terms of own-price and differentials between own- and rival-prices, instituting usage of benchmark demand theory.
3 First-order conditions are derived for optimal brand prices and outputs when firms do not engage in rivalrous consonance forms of tacit collusion (Model 1) and when they do (Model 2), and diagonalization algorithms are once more used in both cases to obtain numerical solutions to specified models.
4 Parametric displacement analysis of small changes in one firm's location are conducted and necessary and sufficient conditions derived for signing the partial derivatives of output and prices with respect to interbrand distances, s_{ij}. The induced changes are shown to be the result of changes in the intercepts and slopes of the demand functions before (in a *ceteris paribus* analysis) and after (in a *mutatis mutandis* analysis) all brand price changes of firms other than the firm that changed location are taken into account. This is, however, the only experiment in this chapter with firms moving in product space, i.e., with changes in the "quality" of the brand as registered in the valuations of consumers.
5 A base case is designed for simulation analysis, which features 5 brands with differing quality and demand and cost conditions. It is employed both to illustrate the results of the closed analysis and to derive insights

where closed analysis becomes too complicated or incapable of yielding qualitative results absent numerical specifications.

6 A measure of competitiveness, E_i, for each brand i is derived, which varies directly with price elasticity of demand, to index the relative ability to compete for profit under a wide variety of environmental conditions, including the presence and the absence of tacit collusion. It is used to divide the 5 firms into 2 subsets of differential competitiveness. Although the members of these subsets remain the same over the 21 solutions obtained in the chapter, profits do not decline uniformly as the measure rose. Indeed, in the first subset, profits rise slightly with profits, which is counter to expectations. The measure should be used with caution, therefore, as means of gauging profitability, and may be best used as a method of discerning common response subsets of brands in a variety of environments.

7 Distinctions are made among the various types of movements in product or characteristics space, and the analysis is limited to small changes on the basis that they are more realistic in quality competition. With the use of the base case in a simulation exercise, it is seen that the equations for partial derivatives of prices and quantities with respect to changes in interproduct distances give good approximations for finite changes, *ceteris paribus*. When *mutatis mutandis* changes are added, impacts frequently move in the opposite direction from the direct *ceteris paribus* changes, but never enough to enforce a sign change from that predicted by the *ceteris paribus* forecasts. Direct impacts of such movement, in the simulation, always outweigh the indirect impacts imposed by price changes of rivals.

8 Consumers' surplus is shown to move in the *ceteris paribus* analysis in a direction opposite to price for those firms remaining stationary in location.

9 A model with a bounded product space with continuous movement of firms will lead to no stable equilibrium without the introduction of relocation costs or minimum profit improvement constraints. Resort to advertising to affect demand may be explained by realization that brand relocations can be costly to the firm and destabilizing for the industry.

10 Displacements of the base case industry equilibrium through variations in k have two functions: they permit study of disparate brand reactions to changes in the dispersion of consumer brand decisions, or to the costs of search, or other cognitive influences such as advertising, and they permit changes in virtual distances among all brands in the space.

As k rises from 0, through the base case value of 0.29 to ∞, prices of all brands rise and outputs fall monotonically: increasing interbrand distance increasing firms' monopoly power, qualities held constant. Profits also rise over the whole span of k except for brand 2, which suffers a fall in profitability when k rises from 0.29 to ∞. This is an interesting if unsurprising result, revealing that a lower-quality product with important cost advantages but low basic demand, which thrives on favorable price differentials with rivals, suffers as those rival brands increase their distances from it in quality space. Because consumers prefer higher quality to lower at constant price differentials in this example of "vertical differentiation," when such products are thrown back on their own-price demand ($\alpha_i \rightarrow b_{ii}$) and price differential demand wanes ($\beta_i \rightarrow 0$), the extent of sales decline outweighs price rises and revenue losses exceed cost reductions.

11 When tacit collusion is introduced into the industry we encounter the proposition that increases in such cooperation do not necessarily benefit all firms in an industry, even when such firms are mature incumbents with significant market share. Such cooperation imposes marginal consonance costs on firms that reduce competitiveness and that can be quite significant as firms are forced to forgo own-profit possibilities to defer to rivals. The rivalrous consonance approach permits such costs to be isolated.

12 Firms that are likely to be benefitted most by tacit collusion are low-quality, low-cost producers which rely heavily on price differentials – that is, on sheltering under high-price umbrellas. As noted above, brand 2 is such a product, and it is seen to benefit consistently in Table 10.7 from rises in collusion for $k = 0$ and 0.29 both for generalized tacit cooperation and that confined to E- and s-clusters. However, when $k = \infty$, although all other firms benefit when they exploit their effective monopoly positions (brand 2 excluded on grounds explained in 10 above) brand 2 joins all firms in suffering as tacit collusion – generalized and confined to E- and s-clusters – rises. Each firm functions best as an effective monopoly because consonance costs impose penalties that drive up prices and reduce sales.

It is time, now, to examine firms' movements in product space, repositioning their brands to greater advantage, but under realistic constraints upon such movement. To this we turn in Chapter 11.

11 Nodal Changes in Brand Locations in Product Space

In this chapter we turn to an analysis of rational brand relocations in a product space, extending the analysis of Chapter 10 to facility location in conditions of noncooperation as well as rivalrous consonance. To make the analysis feasible – and, more importantly, realistic – important constraints are placed on the movement potentials of brands. For such purposes, a relatively small number of nodes are designated between initial locations as potential relocation sites for brands which bound the intervals in which the nodes lie. For example, if brand 5 is sited at position 7 and brand 3 at position 8, we might designate a node at position 7.5, and ask if brand 3 or brand 5 (but not both) would find it profitable, *ceteris paribus*, to relocate there. The *bounded interval* is the distance between brands 3 and 5, or 1 in the example of Chapter 10. The upper bound of the interval is 8 and the lower bound 7. No firms other than the bounding brands 5 and 3 are allowed to consider movement to the node – that is, brands are not allowed to "leap-frog" other brands. Original sites that are abandoned by relocating firms are also treated as nodes. The number of nodes placed in such subintervals is arbitrary, and current algorithms will permit rather large numbers to be accommodated, so that close approaches to continuous location within the intervals can be approached, but for purposes of obtaining insights and illustrating methodology small numbers will suffice.[1]

These restrictions are consistent with the view taken in Chapter 10 that brand movements in characteristics space tend to be localized, and the mesh of nodes along subintervals can be made arbitrarily fine. Contemplated movement to such nodes entails conjectures by the firm of changes in its functions insofar as such movements affect interbrand locations, demands, and costs. Our assumptions with regards to these coefficient projections will be discussed in detail in section 1. The search is for Nash equilibria, of which there may well be more than one, or none. Which, if any, we find, may be dependent on the order which we assume brands contemplate moving.

1 NODAL RELOCATION ON A PRODUCT SPACE WITHOUT TACIT COLLUSION

It is necessary, then, to model the expectations that (say) brand i, contemplating movement to a node, must form concerning the changes in the a_i and b_{ij} parameters in its own demand function. It is assumed that firms have full knowledge of these parameters for its own and its neighboring rivals' functions at initial locations, and that the parameters are expected to vary with changes in the distance between relevant brands.

The method used depends on the fraction of the bounding interval involved in a contemplated relocation. On Figure 11.1 the product space for the base case example in Chapter 10, with parameters listed in Table 10.1, is graphed with a set of 5 nodes which we designate as possible relocation sites for our simulations. The number of nodes and their placement are arbitrary. The bounded intervals or interbrand distances are shown graphically on Figure 11.1. A network for potential movement is created by arbitrarily selecting five nodal positions, labeled N_1 to N_5, at intermediate positions illustrated on the diagram. The resulting graph is a network, and each firm is selected in arbitrary order for consideration of movement to those intervening nodes between it and its neighbors. If any or all of these hypothetical movements would result in profit rises, the node providing a maximum of profit increase is selected as the new location, and the next firm in the arbitrary sequence is selected for similar analysis. This cycle of examination is repeated until all firms are placed with no incentive to upset the status quo by relocating. A Nash equilibrium has been attained.

As noted above, it is assumed that firms cannot locate at the same position as their neighbors, cannot leap over those neighbors, and can locate only at the designated nodes within this designated interval or at abandoned initial brand sites. To illustrate, let us select nodes in the sequence of their initial positions, proceeding from left to right, or in the order 1, 4, 2, 5, 3. Moreover, it is assumed that a brand contemplating relocation considers its impacts on rivals as confined to changes in their parameters due to interbrand distances from the contemplated node, with the exception of its bounding brand (to be explained below). This assumption is easily dropped if desired to include conjectured changes in other-brand parameters of more distant rivals, but we adopt it as consistent with the view expressed in Chapter 10 that most brand movements are small and rather locally oriented.

Constrained by these limitations on movement, firms form conjectures about the values of their demand and cost function parameters by the following procedure. First, they locate the two original location points that bound the smallest interval containing the new, contemplated location. Second,

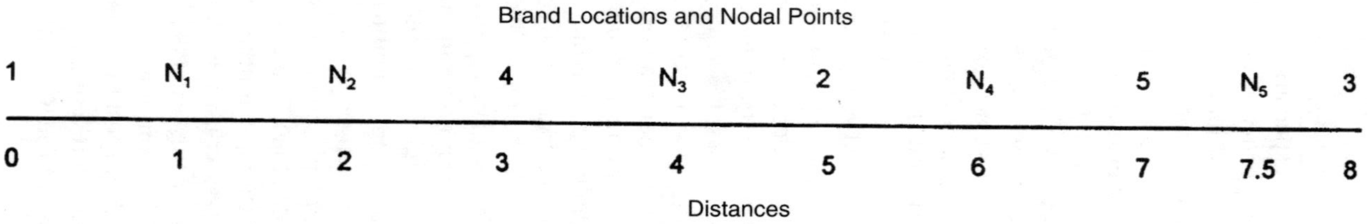

Brand Locations and Nodal Points

1 N_1 N_2 4 N_3 2 N_4 5 N_5 3

0 1 2 3 4 5 6 7 7.5 8

Distances

Figure 11.1 Base case locations with node points for relocation

they assume that the parameter in question changes exponentially between these bounding initial locations. Third, they determine a weight parameter w in the exponential form for a typical parameter, Q, by solving

$$Q_U = Q_L e^{w \cdot s_{LU}}, \tag{11.1}$$

or

$$w = In\left(\frac{Q_U}{Q_L}\right)\frac{1}{s_{LU}}. \tag{11.2}$$

In the expressions, Q_L and Q_U are parameter values for the lower and upper initial location bounds and s_{LU} is the distance between these two initial brand locations (the bounded interval). Lastly, to obtain the value of the parameter at the projected location, Q_N, the firm substitutes s_{LN} for s_{LU} in (11.1):

$$E(Q_N) \equiv Q_N = Q_L e^{w \cdot s_{LN}}. \tag{11.3}$$

As an example of the method of determining conjectured parameter values at a contemplated node, then, assume that brand 1 contemplates moving from position 0 to node N_1 at position 1 on Figure 11.1. Consider brand 1's expectation of a_1 at N_1, which we symbolize $a_{1/1}$. Firm 1's upper bounding node is brand 4's site at 3 and the lower bounding node is its present brand 1 location at 0, and the bounded interval is 3. From Table 10.1, $a_1 = 800$ and $a_4 = 1{,}000$, and from (11.2) $w = 0.074$. With $s_{UN} = 1$, $a_{1/1} = 862$. Note that the initial locations function as the anchoring interval bounds, even when firms no longer occupy them. This procedure is straightforward for the derivation of cost parameters $m_{1/1}$ and $n_{1/1}$. One departure is made for the determination of $F_{1/1}$, the fixed costs parameter. These are treated as sunk costs, and nodal movements are permitted to increase but not to decrease them. When the values derived from the methods discussed above result in a reduced value for the fixed cost term, the initial value of F for the firm is substituted; when they determine a higher value it is adopted for the nodal move.

To obtain $b_{1/1}$ we adopt the view that the defining category is own-price demand coefficients. Hence, in the present case, $Q_L = b_{11}$ and $Q_U = b_{44}$, which are substituted into (11.2 and 0.3) to obtain w and $b_{11/1}$. To estimate $b_{14/1}$ we use $Q_L = b_{14}$ and $Q_U = b_{41}$, derive w from (11.2) and $b_{14/1}$ from (11.3).

One of brand 4's demand parameters will be affected by the contemplated change: b_{41}. Other (nonneighboring) firms' b_{i4} are unaffected and their demand functions will be affected only by the discount factor's new distance $s_{i1/1}$. The new b^*_{41} is determined by letting $Q_L = b_{14}$ and $Q_U = b_{41}$, and using w derived from (11.2) – just as in the calculation in the previous paragraph for $b_{14/1}$, but substituting $-w$ and s_{UN} for the respective terms in (11.3).

The indicated parameters for firms 1 and 4 are changed in accordance with these equations and the algorithm of Chapter 10 is solved to obtain firm 1's expectations of profits. Such expectations are derived for each of firm 1's potential relocation sites (in the present case, N_1 and N_2), and the maximum profit obtained from all of the sites is compared with the firm's profit in the existing base case. If it exceeds the base case profit, the firm is moved to the relevant site and a new base case is named which differs from the old only in the relocation of the firm under analysis. Then the next firm in the sequence is selected and the same procedure is repeated. When analysis of all firms is completed a *cycle* is completed, and the surviving base case is recycled in the same firm sequence until all firms are incapable of improving their profits by relocating. A Nash equilibrium is thereby achieved. It may, of course, not be unique, and other firm sequences can be studied in the same manner to locate other Nash equilibria, if desired. It is possible that one firm may move to a node and preempt movement there by its neighboring rival, so that the order of movement may be significant. It is advisable, therefore, to adopt several sequences to gain some idea of the robustness of solutions with respect to sequencing.

Using the network approach to relocation makes the problem more amenable to solution but does not let us escape the need to use numerical solutions to parametrically specified models to gain insights. Parametric dependence, dimensionality, and the discontinuity of the problem foreclose closed analysis. The discontinuous nature of the movements is particularly troublesome because large jumps in profits can occur with small movements, somewhat in the nature of chaos theory solutions. A firm moving one nodal position into the left portion of the interval can find its profit position much changed from that obtained by such a move into the right portion of the interval. Indeed, even moves within the same portion of the interval can lead to sharp changes in profits. Iterative numerical methods are therefore in order.

a Model 11.1

We begin, therefore, with the initial positions assigned the brands in Chapter 10, as reproduced in Figure 11.1, with the parameters of Table 10.1, and the solution to Model 10.1 of that chapter as listed in Table 10.2. This solution is reproduced in rows 1 through 3 of Table 11.1 and is adopted in all of our sequential experiments with Model 11.1 of this chapter as its base case. We used three sequences for movement: Move 1 moved sequentially in the order of the brands' original placement left to right, or 1, 4, 2, 5, 3; Move 2 reversed this order to yield 3, 5, 2, 4, 1; and Move 3 adopted an "inside out order," 2, 5, 4, 3, 1. All three moves yielded the same Nash equilibrium, reproduced as in Table 11.1 as the relocation solution for Model 11.1. In the

Table 11.1 Base case and relocation solution for Model 11.1 ($k = 0.29$)

Characteristic	*Brand 1*	*Brand 2*	*Brand 3*	*Brand 4*	*Brand 5*
Original model			*Base case for Model 11.1*		
Location	1@1	2@2	3@3	4@4	5@5
Price	$24.24	$19.56	$22.84	$25.02	$23.22
Output	435	428	594	336	331
Profits	$8,512	$6,280	$9,374	$1,522	$1,524
Total output			2,123		
Total profits			$27,272		
Quantity-weighted price			$22.88		
Relocation model			*Relocation solution for Model 11.1*		
Location	1@1	2@2	3@3	4@N_1	5@N_5
Price	$22.67	$19.74	$22.29	$22.33	$21.69
Output	455	403	597	458	502
Profits	$8,308	$5,942	$9,100	$6,844	$5,338
Total output			2,415		
Total profits			$35,532		
Quantity-weighted price			$21.82		
Percentage profit changes	–2.40	–5.38	–2.92	+449.67	+350.26

achieved Nash equilibrium social surplus obviously rises: output expands 14 percent, profits rise 30 percent, and quantity-weighted price decreases 5 percent. The two moves that occur are socially desirable, despite a decline in product differentiation. Brand 4 becomes a neighbor of brand 1 at one end of the spectrum, and brand 5 moves next to brand 3 at the other.

Brand 4's move is driven largely by cost reductions: its linear cost parameter declines from $16 to $4, offset somewhat by a rise in the quadratic cost term from $0.0001 to $0.0003. But total costs (including the sunk costs) fall from $6,890 for an output of 336 to $3,395 for output of 458. This permits a price decline that reverses its price disadvantage with brands 1, 3, and 5, as well as reducing its price disadvantage with brand 2. The α_4 term declines from 38 to 29, which, when multiplied by respective own-prices in the base case and the Model 1 solution, accounts for an incremental rise in sales of 298 units. This results from the decline in p_4 permitted in large part by the decline in marginal costs. However, basic demand a_4 falls by 138 units and the fall in β_4 (from 276 to 238) together reduce sales by 177 units, leaving a gross output increment of 123 units, which closely approximates the net rise on sales (122). The firm's increase in competitiveness is indexed by a fall in the competitiveness index, E_4, from 0.74 in Base Case 10.1 to 0.58 in the Model 11.1 solution.

Brand 5's move is similarly motivated largely by cost advantages obtained by moving closer to brand 3. The linear term in marginal costs (m_5) falls from \$15.50 to \$8.80 and the quadratic term (n_5) from 0.00012 to 0.00009. Despite a rise in sunk costs from \$1,020 to \$1,106, costs fall dramatically, from \$6,166 for output of 331 units in Base Case 1 to \$5,546 for 502 units in Base Case 2. Its own-price reduction (enabled by its costs reductions) and a fall in α_5 accounts for a rise in sales of 156, offset by a fall in β_5 of 57, yielding a gross output gain of 99 units. A rise in a_5 of 72 brings the total gain in sales to 171 units, which equals the actual gain. The fall in costs increases profits greatly. Distances from rivals 1, 2, and 4 increase only by 0.5 spatial units, so the cognitive distance factor does not play a great role in brand 5's dramatic profits gains.

Relocating brands 4 and 5 benefit hugely from their moves, their joint profit gains accounting for more than the total gain of Base Case 11.1 over Base Case 10.1. Brand 1 loses 2.4 percent in profits from brand 4's movement to its vicinity and by price reduction forced by the large fall in p_4. Brand 2 loses 5 percent of its profits as its sales fall and its small price increase does not cover the ensuing revenue loss. Brand 3 is not completely isolated from the relocations, even though brand 5 moves closer by a small amount, but it continues to be the stellar profit earner of the group. The value of α_3 rises as the discounted value of b_{53} rises, leading to a fall in sales of 9, despite the small decline in price between the base cases. However, β_3 rises by 11, leading to a projected rise in sales of 2, compared with an actual rise of 3.

Brands 1 and 3 as the antipodal products were somewhat handicapped in their movement because they can only move in one quality direction, and, in this example, by small amounts. In this cost-driven example, brand 1 marginal costs can only increase sharply as it moves toward brand 4, its neighbor, and brand 3 could only reduce costs substantially if it could leapfrog its neighbor, brand 5. Brand 2 is also bounded by high-cost neighbors – that is, by large marginal cost increases as it moves its quality type in either direction.

The forces that dictate the profitability of moves are indicated more clearly in Table 11.2. In the table the results of movement of the bounding brands of each interval one unit in the direction of its opposite bound are recorded and compared, in each instance, with the base case for Model 11.1 in Table 11.1. Potentially profitable moves occur only for movements from brands 4 in the direction of 2, 5 in the direction of 3, 4 in the direction of 1,

Table 11.2 Model 11.1: parameters dictating movement between bounding locations in the 4 independent intervals

	π	m	a	α	β
From 1 to 4	8,572 to 7,026	2 to 4	800 to 862	20 to 37	118 to 388
From 4 to 2	1,522 to 4,451	16 to 3	1,000 to 700	38 to 33	276 to 281
From 2 to 5	6,280 to 4,979	3 to 15.5	700 to 950	26 to 32	236 to 279
From 5 to 3	1,524 to 8,911	15.5 to 5	950 to 1,100	43 to 40	387 to 363
From 4 to 1	1,522 to 4,975	16 to 8	1,000 to 928	38 to 32	276 to 250
From 2 to 4	6,280 to 5,533	3 to 6.93	700 to 837	26 to 31	236 to 260
From 5 to 2	1,524 to 5,929	15.5 to 6.82	950 to 815	43 to 34	387 to 388
From 3 to 5	9,374 to 4,726	5 to 8.80	1,100 to 1,022	33 to 39	259 to 290

and 5 in the direction of 2. In each case a substantial reduction in the linear marginal cost term occurs. In terms of the parameters of the relocating firm, 3 of the 4 movements result in a reduction in basic demand a, and in only one case is there a substantial rise in β (which can be interpreted directly in terms of changes in sales due to the move). It is true that in all 4 cases there is a fall in α, but when these are multiplied by the change in own-prices to obtain increases in sales, the amounts are relative small. It is marginal costs changes, therefore, that are the greatest determining factor in the relocations. Note that profits for the move of brands 4 toward 1 and 5 toward 3 dominate the profitable moves of brands 4 toward 2 and 5 toward 2.

1 *Some Insights from the First-order Conditions*

One manner of assessing the relative importance of demand and cost forces in determining the relocation solution of Model 11.1 in Table 11.1 is to recall that in both the base case and relocation solutions firms will set their price minus marginal production cost equal to marginal policy costs. Because in locational analyses of our spatially discrete type the only policy is that of price, this condition states that

$$\frac{p_i - m_i - 2n_i x_i}{p_i} = \frac{1}{\varepsilon_i} = \frac{1 - E_i}{E_i}, \tag{11.4}$$

where the lefthand side is the profit margin, ε_i is the price elasticity of demand, and E_i is our measure of competitiveness defined in section 1, Chapter 10. Because α_i is constant in our demand analysis, the elasticity of demand at any given p_i can change only by shifts in the function, which is to say changes in $a_i + \beta_i$, which term is explicit as the denominator of E_i.

In the relocation model the marginal costs of stationary brands (brands 1, 2, and 3) are almost constant: they vary only as x_i changes, and given the small values of n_i, the cost impact will be quite small. The changes in p_i for these stationary firms will be directly motivated by shifts in their demand functions resulting from changes in the prices of relocating firms (brands 4 and 5). These shifts will vary with changes in β_i determined by changes in p_4 and p_5, given the parameters b_{i4} and b_{i5}. If these forces are weak, then ε_i and E_i will not change much from their base case levels.

This holds true in Model 11.1. For base case and relocation solutions respectively, ε_1 is 1.11 and 1.12; ε_2 is 1.19 and 1.18; and ε_3 is 1.29 and 1.30. Between these two solutions β_1 rose by only 42 sales units, β_2 fell by 57 units, and β_3 rose by 11 units. Competitive factors, therefore, are almost constant: E_1 is 0.526 and 0.529, E_2 is 0.542 in both solutions, and E_3 is 0.563 and 0.564. Demand factors instigated by locational changes for brands 4 and 5 do have nonnegligible impacts on the stationary brands, but they are relatively minor, with profit declines in the 4 to 6 percent range.

But, of course, these initiating changes in p_4 and p_5 are motivated largely by marginal cost reductions. Between the base case and relocation solutions ε_4 falls from 2.80 to 1.25 and ε_5 from 3.04 to 1.70, so that high elasticities tumble as marginal cost reductions enable price reductions. Also, for these relocating firms a_4 and a_5 change, and $a_4 + \beta_4$ falls from 1,776 to 1,099 while $a_5 + \beta_5$ falls from 1,407 to 1,350. The moves, therefore, are directly detrimental to both firms' demand functions, shifting them leftward to increase price elasticities at every price and stimulate the large price cuts necessary to reachieve equilibrating sales. But, finally, it is the large marginal cost reductions registering in the profit margin of (11.4) that ultimately explains these price reductions. The model is directly and indirectly cost-driven.

2 *Some Insights from Factor Analysis: A Principal Components Decomposition*

Statistical analysis of the results from Model 11.1 using the econometric tools of multivariate regression analysis must confront the bane of high interrelations among the discounted interbrand distance value variables. If we regress profits of firm i on the s_{ij} observations we face directly the fact that when s_{i1} is changed, s_{i2}, s_{i3}, etc. must also change, so that our regressors are not independent. This makes it difficult to isolate the impacts of any one interbrand distance on profits from that of the others, so that the regression coefficients of the equation are not well defined.[2]

One tool for attempting to isolate meaningful independent relations among the variables in a multivariate analysis is to decompose the variance in a whole set of variables into sets of "supervariables" or factors obtained by maximizing the variance within a sequence of such supervariables while maintaining their complete independence from each other (i.e., each such supervariable is orthogonal to every other). The complete set of such factors decomposes the variance of the original variables additively.

This procedure has two advantages. First, because in general a small number of such supervariables accounts for most of the variance in the whole set of original variables, it is possible to reduce the set of variables in play from the (potentially) large group of initial variables to a much smaller number of significant factors. Second, within such factors, it permits us to study the correlation of its component variables with the factor with knowledge that such relationships are independent of like relationships in other factors, and to determine the percentage of the total variance of each component variable over all factors that is "explained" within the factor under scrutiny. In short, it permits study of the factor structure that may yield deeper insights into variable relationships than multiple regression analysis would allow. The cost, of course, is that predictive regression equations are not derived, but frequently we resort to factor analysis when we reject the usefulness of such equations, so the sacrifice is slight.[3]

Our analysis begins with the three sets of sequences of locational adjustments performed in determining the optimal locations of Model 11.1. For each brand profit was recorded for each of the sequential moves along with the four interbrand distances relevant to each observation. This yielded 5 data sets with 42 observations each. The principal components for each data set were then derived. This procedure requires solution of a characteristic equation to obtain eigenvalues and associated eigenvectors which are then rotated into factor loadings. These factor loadings – 1 set for each eigenvector – are the supervariables mentioned above, whose values are the correlation coefficients of each original variable with the supervariable. By squaring these we obtain the proportion of the variance for each original value captured in the supervariable, which, of course, sum to 1 over all the factors. In the case of our analyses, there are 5 eigenvalues and eigenvectors, rotated into 5 factors with 5 variables in each (one profit variable and four interbrand distances). Each of these factors is orthogonal to all of the others, so that the relationships captured within the factor (the supervariables) are independent of all the relationships in the other factors.

Normally, only those factors whose eigenvalues equal or exceed 1 are analyzed, but because our interests focus on the proportion of the variance of profits explained by the factors we will analyze any set of factors whose proportions add to 0.85 or more. These factors, with relevant information, are reproduced in Table 11.3. The factors for each brand are structured columnwise, with eigenvalues for each selected. Note that multiple factors have been selected for brands 3, 4, and 5. The variables in the factors are brand profits and relevant distances for the brand. The entries for each column are

Table 11.3 Factor structures of Model 11.1

	Brand 1	*Brand 2*	*Brand 3*		*Brand 4*		*Brand 5*		
	Factor 1	*Factor 2*	*Factor 1*	*Factor 4*	*Factor 1*	*Factor 4*	*Factor 1*	*Factor 2*	*Factor 4*
	$\lambda_1 = 2.54$	$\lambda_2 = 1.04$	$\lambda_1 = 1.46$	$\lambda_4 = 0.84$	$\lambda_1 = 3.73$	$\lambda_4 = 0.22$	$\lambda_1 = 2.60$	$\lambda_2 = 0.93$	$\lambda_4 = 0.62$
π	0.88	0.99	0.41	0.47	0.78	0.12	0.31	0.46	0.21
s_{12}	0.20 (+)	0.00 (–)							
s_{13}	0.72 (+)		0.18 (+)	0.05 (–)					
s_{14}	0.14 (+)				0.85 (–)	0.09 (+)			
s_{15}	0.60 (+)						0.82 (+)	0.03 (+)	0.08 (–)
s_{23}		0.00 (–)	0.27 (+)	0.29 (–)					
s_{24}		0.04 (–)			0.53 (+)	0.00 (+)			
s_{25}		0.02 (–)					0.38 (+)	0.21 (–)	0.18 (+)
s_{34}			0.58 (+)	0.00 (–)	0.93 (+)	0.00 (+)			
s_{35}			0.02 (+)	0.03 (–)			0.76 (–)	0.00 (–)	0.15 (+)
s_{45}					0.64 (+)	0.00 (+)	0.35 (+)	0.24 (–)	0.01 (+)

the squares of the correlation coefficients with the factor for each variable in the factor. These have the advantage of indicating the percentage of variance in each variable "explained" by the factor. Thus, for brand 1, its first factor accounts for 88 percent of the variance in brand 1 profits, 20 percent of the variance in s_{12}, and so forth. Were we to add these percentages over each of the 5 factors for brand 1 (of which we have listed only one) the sum would be 1: thus, the two factors listed for brand 3 account for 88 percent of the variance in the principal component decomposition for that brand. In parentheses alongside each of the distance components is placed the direction of the correlation of that distance with the brand's profit. Hence, brand 1's profits in this dominant factor are positively correlated with distances from its rivals: for example, its profits tend to fall as s_{14} moves closer. Note that in the factors where the coefficients of determination did not register at the second decimal point their values were recorded as zero, but the direction of correlation was still recorded.

That said, we turn to the derivation of insights from the factors. Brand 1's profits suffer from nearness to rivals, which makes sense from 3 considerations. First, brand 1 can move only to the right, and when it does it gets closer to all of its competitors: unlike interior brands, distances from rivals do not move in offsetting directions. Second, the b_{1j} are generally smaller than or equal to corresponding b_{j1}, so that on balance when other brands move closer to it its net gains are generally negative. Third, m_1 is the lowest linear marginal cost term of any brand, so that any move to the right toward brand 4 involves a larger marginal cost, somewhat offset by a rise in a_1. The large coefficient for s_{13} is a bit suspect because in the 42 observations this variable differed from its initial value of 8 only 3 times, and in only one of these did we have a *ceteris paribus* observation where it changed and the other distances remained constant. However, in this pair the positive correlation did hold. In all of the analyses brand 3 as a terminal brand only one distance unit away from brand 5 had little ability to move, so that it had little variance. The high correlation with s_{15} has more legitimacy by virtue of the imbalance in the two b demand coefficients. The low coefficient for brand 4 is at first surprising, given its neighboring status and its highly profitable moves to brand 1's proximity, but this is explained by the fact that $b_{14} = b_{41}$: the observations indeed do reveal that π_1 is little affected by brand 4's move to its vicinity.

Brand 2 offers a peculiar profile, in that 99 percent of its variance over 42 observations is accounted for by weak correlations with s_{24} and s_{25}. We have seen that brand 2 suffers from its location between brands 4 and 5 whose marginal and fixed costs are substantially above its own. The strongest relations that can be isolated by the decomposition of the variance comes from the *ceteris paribus* movements in the interbrand distances. But these can occur only when either neighbor – brand 4 or 5 – moves. There are 12 such moves in the data, all of which correlate negatively with π_1, and these lead to the high proportion of variance in profits accounted for by the two distance variables. Yet, the moves represent a small amount of the total variations in the distances, which change when other brands initiate moves. It is this variance that is captured in the unrecorded factors which are of little use in explaining the variance in π_2. It is this ability to distinguish more finely among the variables' contributions to the explanation of the regressand's variation than straightforward regression analysis can which constitutes its superiority in such multicollinear situations as this. The straightforward OLS multiple regression equation gave a higher regression coefficient to s_{12} than to s_{14}, although large standard errors characterize all of the coefficients; moreover, the adjusted R^2 is 0.020, projecting no explanatory power of the interbrand distances in determining profits.

On the other hand, because brand 3 is a terminal brand, the observations are rich in *ceteris paribus* results, and demonstrate the complex nature of the relationships of interbrand distances and π_3. There are two factors of significance in explaining the profits variance, which together explain 88 percent of the variance. One of the factors relates the distances between brand 3 and all of its rivals positively with profits, and the other negatively. Indeed, study of the *ceteris paribus* locational changes reveal this ambivalence. For example, there are 16 *ceteris paribus* changes involving s_{23}, 8 of which are positively correlated with π_3 and an equal number negatively correlated; there are 10 such changes involving s_{34}, 4 of which are positively and 6 of which are negatively correlated with profits; and 3 such changes involve movements of brand 3's neighbor, brand 5, all of which are negatively correlated with π_3. These ambivalences occur because of differences in the *b* coefficients and differential price changes that are imposed as the whole configuration of interbrand distances change. The two dominant factors permit us to see the relative even-handedness of these movements in explaining profit changes, and,permit us, if we wish, to go more deeply into these relationships. The OLS regression, on the other hand, is completely befuddled, asserting that only 3 percent of the variance in π_3 is accounted for by changes in the interbrand distances, even though, in this instance, the Pearson correlation table shows universally small intercorrelations among those distances.

Table 11.3 exihibits brand 4's happy circumstances that permit it to increase its profits by reducing its costs as it moves as close to brand 1 as possible, while at the same time distancing itself from its other rivals to strengthen its profits from these collateral moves as well. More than three-quarters of the variance in its profits is explained by high correlations with factor 1, but we have included factor 4 which boosts this explanatory power somewhat and, more interestingly, introduces a small contrary tendency of reductions in s_{14} to reduce profits. This small contrary influence is buried deep within the relationships of the non-*ceteris paribus* configurations, and, within factor 4, is not supported by the insignificant correlations of the remaining interbrand distance movements. The overall depiction of the profit dependence on distances from its rivals is that suggested in the relocation solution for Model 11.1 in Table 11.1, and given greater precision by the factor relations. The correlation matrix is highly collinear among the interbrand distances and the regression equation is wholly misleading, giving a positive regression coefficient for s_{14} among other anomalies.

For brand 5 it is necessary to include 3 factors to explain 97 percent of the variance in π_5, which reflects several characteristics of the locational process as it affects the brand. The high correlation with s_{15} must be discounted because it reflects primarily just two *ceteris paribus* moves in the data, which are in fact correlated positively with π_5. But there is very little variance in this distance variable because in general brand 4 moved early in the sequences to bind brand 1 in its initial position. The correlation coefficients for s_{25} are much more credible, since we have 15 such moves, 7 of which are positively correlated and 8 negatively correlated with π_5. The pattern revealed by the changes in signs of the correlations is that brand 5 benefitted from nearness to brand 2, but was hurt by it when it was too close, i.e. 0.5 to 1 distance units. However, this is not always true, depending upon the levels at which other distances are held constant, largely because these configurations dictated price adjustments inflicted on brand 5. The ambiguous signs on the s_{25} components in the three factors, therefore, are reflecting existential impact differences. Of course, given that brand 5 moved to N_5 in the locational solution, the strong negative correlation with factor 1 is to be expected. Despite the fact that no *ceteris paribus* moves exist in the data, the general pattern of large profits when brand 5 is 0.5 units from brand 3 rather than 1 or 2, regardless of the positions of other brands, is very strong. Indeed, the existence of a small contrary correlation in the other direction is a surprise dividend of the decomposition. Finally, the bidirectional impacts of s_{45} on π_5 revealed in the factors is reflected in the *ceteris paribus* movements in the data: 4 are positively, 4 negatively correlated with brand 5's profits.

b Model 11.2

With our analyses of Model 11.1's results before us, and their heavy emphasis on costs, we should expect that changes in k that do not affect the m terms in marginal cost will not have much effect in altering these profitable location patterns, but will affect profitabilities of all firms. In Models 11.2 and 11.3 we will allow k to assume values of 0 and ∞ respectively. In view of the results on Model 11.1 we shall test only the first sequence of location adjustments, which is to say, in the order 1, 4, 2, 5, 3.

Our conjecture concerning the relocation pattern for Models 11.2 and 11.3 are correct: they are identical to those of Model 11.1. The implications for profits, prices and outputs are more complicated. Consider first Model 11.2, whose solutions are presented in Table 11.4. As a point of departure, we compute the base case solution for the model before relocation is permitted, in which $k = 0$. This reduces the distance between brands to their initial perceived values, unenhanced by cognitive distortions, when firms are located at those intial positions and before relocations. Compared with the base case solution for Model 11.1 (when $k = 0.29$) prices and profits of all firms fall and outputs increase when the distance enhancements are eliminated. Price competition becomes much more severe, which is to be expected. Profits for brands 4 and 5 are most severely hit as is clear from a comparison of the base case for 11.1 and 11. 2 in Tables 11.1 and 11.4 respectively. Brands 1, 2, and 3 have low marginal costs and adjust to the more intense competition by lowering prices significantly to increase sales and limit losses. But brands 4 and 5, with high marginal costs, see their price differentials with the other firms widen, and are prevented from reducing prices much by these costs.

Table 11.4 Base case and relocation solutions for Model 11.2 ($k = 0$)

Characteristic	*Brand 1*	*Brand 2*	*Brand 3*	*Brand 4*	*Brand 5*
Original model			*Base case for Model 11.2*		
Location	1@1	2@2	3@3	4@4	5@5
Price	\$18.73	\$16.80	\$19.36	\$22.11	\$21.02
Output	550	508	685	344	342
Profits	\$8,056	\$6,201	\$8,605	\$593	\$855
Total output			2,429		
Total profits			\$24,310		
Quantity-weighted price			\$19.31		
Relocation model			*Relocation solution for Model 11.2*		
Location	1@1	2@2	3@3	4@N_1	5@N_6
Price	\$17.83	\$16.04	\$18.51	\$16.47	\$18.15
Output	521	480	657	603	554
Profits	\$7,107	\$5,452	\$7,646	\$5,921	\$4,042
Total output			2,815		
Total profits			\$30,168		
Quantity-weighted price			\$17.46		

Sales hold about steady for these two rivals as the steep rise in their αs, when multiplied by their prices in both solutions, just balance the rise in their βs. Profits plummet, therefore, as their profit margins fall sharply.

In the relocation cases of both models, as noted above, the same new pattern emerges, with brand 4 migrating to within one distance unit of brand 1 and brand 5 moving to within 0.5 distance units of brand 3. The motivation for these moves is the reduction in their m cost parameters, as already noted in our discussion of the relocation model of Model 11.1 above. This permits brands 4 and 5 to reduce prices to values at which they can compete with brands 1, 2, and 3, stealing sales from them and adding new sales as well. The profits of brands 1, 2, and 3 fall from their base case levels while brands 4 and 5 stage a remarkable profits resurgence. Nonetheless, all firms do more poorly in the Model 11.2 solution with respect to profits than they do in Model 11.1, as total industry profits decline by 15 percent. The public, however, is well served as output rises 15 percent and weighted price falls by 19 percent. Measures that serve to lessen the cognitive enhancement of interbrand distances – transport cost decreases, other transaction costs associated with knowledge and information acquisition, lessening persuasive advertising – increases consumer welfare yet still allows comfortable profits for incumbent firms.

c Model 11.3

By setting k to ∞ (i.e., e^{16}), we isolate the firms completely from their rivals, effectively reducing all b_{ij} terms, $i \neq j$, to 0, so that α terms are reduced to b_{ii} and β terms become zero by virtue of the cognitive discount factor. Each firm becomes a monopolist in its own brand domain. The pulls of marginal cost reduction remain strong and dictate the same relocation pattern as we have seen in our previous solutions, so the only information of interest is the impact on profits, prices, and outputs. Table 11.5 yields the solution to the base case for Model 11.3 (before relocation) and the solution to the relocation model.

In the base case for Model 11.3, monopoly distancing benefits all brands except brand 2 when compared with the base cases of Models 11.2 and 11.1. Brand 2 has poor basic demand, but low marginal costs, which permits it to establish large price differentials with its rivals in the latter two base cases. It benefits greatly from moderate distancing from them. This is denied the firm in the present base case, and so its price reduction increases sales from its own demand parameters only and it suffers a large drop in sales that its price rise cannot recover in revenue. Its rivals benefit from larger price increases and larger savings in costs from lower volume.

The solution to Model 11.3 when relocation occurs changes the values of variables only for those firms whose moves have resulted in lower costs:

Table 11.5 Base case and relocation solutions for Model 11.3 ($k = \infty$)

Characteristic	*Brand 1*	*Brand 2*	*Brand 3*	*Brand 4*	*Brand 5*
Original model			*Base case for Model 11.3*		
Location	1@1	2@2	3@3	4@4	5@5
Price	$27.86	$23.39	$27.53	$28.03	$26.05
Output	382	326	494	299	273
Profits	$8,808	$5,836	$9,920	$2,091	$1,848
Total output			1,774		
Total profits			$28,503		
Quantity-weighted price			$26.70		
Relocation model			*Relocation solution for Model 11.3*		
Location	1@1	2@2	3@3	4@N_1	5@N_6
Price	$27.86	$23.39	$27.53	$26.34	$25.81
Output	382	326	494	393	405
Profits	$8,808	$5,836	$9,920	$7,242	$5,766
Total output			2,000		
Total profits			$37,572		
Quantity-weighted price			$26.34		

brands 4 and 5. Their sales and profits rise greatly from reduced prices allowed by such cost decreases, surpassing those of the relocation solutions of Models 11.1 and 2. Monopoly profits surpass those of other relocation models except, of course, for brand 2.

In review of our models when no tacit collusion occurs, we find results are driven by cost factors, directly by the reduction in production expenses permitted and indirectly by virtue of their facilitation of price differential reductions. Model 11.3 permits us to eliminate the effects of price differentials and to study the impacts on own-demand only. Other models also allow this decomposition between own-demand and other-demand effects by study of α and β values. Relocation possibilities permit one degradation of quality and one improvement of quality, both cost inspired, and both robust in terms of the cognitive discount factors determined by k. In the base cases all firms benefit when k rises from 0 to 0.29, although even in this instance of moderate cognitive distancing brand 2's profits rise by only a small amount. As noted, this becomes a fall as k rises to monopoly distancing levels while other brands benefit further, in largest part because brand 2 is denied the advantage of large price differentials because of its low cost. As would be expected, consumers fare best in terms of prices and outputs when k is lower rather than higher. This holds promise for informational advertising which may be expected to reduce cognitive distortions caused by lack of information concerning brands. On the other hand, persuasive advertising, which is aimed toward increasing cognitive distancing, should be inimical to consumer interests. But these impacts will be investigated in Chapter 12: in this chapter, our next investigation will be into the impacts on location of rivalrous consonance.

2 NODAL RELOCATION ON A PRODUCT SPACE WITH TACIT COLLUSION

In Models 11.4 and 11.5 we test the stability of the relocation solution to Models 11.1, 11.2, and 11.3 when rivalrous consonance is introduced at levels $\theta_{ij} = 0.5$ and 1 respectively, for all off-diagonal terms in the Θ matrix, where $\theta_{ii} \equiv 1$. In all of our experiments with rivalrous consonance models in this chapter we assume $k = 0.29$, so that our comparisons with a compatible model without tacit collusion will be with Model 11.1, with solutions given in Table11.1. Both levels of rivalrous consonance adopted feature high degrees of cooperation among the five firms and we address two questions to the models:

1. Will the strong and persistent egoistic drives of firms 4 and 5 to maximize own-profits by relocating be overriden by the cooperative urges of tacit collusion with a retention of their initial product positions? From Table 11.1 we recognize that this would require heroic renunciations by the relocating firms with respect to profit gain without really large gains to any of the stationary brands taken individually.
2. Whatever the answers to question 1, what will be the impacts of tacit collusion on the prices, outputs and profits of the firms, when compared with the levels of Model 11.1 base case and relocation solutions? If the same relocation pattern does emerge, will there be a greater equality in profit and output distributions over the brands, and at what cost to the society? And what will the answers be if we ask the same questions of the models' base cases reflecting the initial product locations?

The answer to the first question can be given immediately: in neither of the models considered did rivalrous consonance deter the relocating firms from moving, or change the pattern of the moves. The locational advantages, which we have seen to be cost-determined, are simply too profitable to be overridden by even these high consonance coefficients. As in Models 11.1–11.3 the cost advantages permitted brands 4 and 5 to be priced substantially below their respective base case levels and to substantially improve their price differentials with rivals or to reverse their disadvantage. The large profit gains of the relocating brands did not come to any great extent if any from reductions in the sales of the stationary brands, but rather through the enforced price reductions set in motion by the cost-enabled falls in p_4 and p_5. This can be seen in the relocation solutions of both models in the tables to follow, along with comparisons with the like solutions in Tables 11.1, 11.4, and 11.5.

a Model 11.4: Rivalrous Consonance at the Universal 0.5 Level

Table 11.6 presents the base case and relocation solutions for the tacit collusion case with all firms' interbrand consonance coefficients at the value of 0.5. A first comparison is of both solutions of the table with their respective analogs in Table 11.1, which features consonance coefficients of 0 (i.e., no rivalrous consonance).

Table 11.6 Base case and relocation solutions for Model 11.4 ($k = 0.29$, $\theta_{ij} = 0.5$)

Characteristic	*Brand 1*	*Brand 2*	*Brand 3*	*Brand 4*	*Brand 5*
Original model			*Base case for Model 11.4*		
Location	1@1	2@2	3@3	4@4	5@5
Price	$25.10	$20.84	$24.05	$26.62	$25.10
Output	425	410	573	292	272
Profits	$8,729	$6,513	$9,685	$1,596	$1,583
Total output			1,972		
Total profits			$28,106		
Quantity-weighted price			$24.13		
Relocation model			*Relocation solution for Model 11.4*		
Location	1@1	2@2	3@3	4@N_1	5@N_6
Price	$24.28	$21.21	$23.94	$23.34	$23.69
Output	428	381	563	447	447
Profits	$8,437	$6,137	$9,439	$7,091	$5,529
Total output			2,266		
Total profits			$36,633		
Quantity-weighted price			$23.38		
Percentage profit changes	–3.35	–5.77	–2.54	+444.30	+345.45

In the base case, before relocation, tacit collusion predictably raises prices and profits of all firms and reduces their outputs. Brands 1, 2, and 3 – the low-cost producers – are the largest winners, each benefitting by $200 or $300, while brands 4 and 5 benefit by only $50–$75. The consumers' surplus falls as output is reduced by about 7 percent, while to the oligopoly rents of Model 11.1's base case is added a "collusion rent" of about 3 percent. It is, then, brands 4 and 5 – the high-cost producers – who pay the highest cost in the form of reduced market share and relative earnings declines.

In the relocation models, once more in Model 11.4 the tables are turned: brands 4 and 5 benefit hugely from cost reductions, and, comparatively with Model 11.1, from the approach to industry profit maximization via consonance. Tacit collusion yields larger profits to all firms in the relocation model than those returns in its absence in Model 11.1, but relatively speaking, the percentage losses and gains that occur between base case and relocation model solutions in Models 11.1 and 11.4 are about the same. That is, in relative terms, the introduction of rivalrous consonance does not punish or benefit the brands: in absolute terms it raises all boats, so to speak, but in relative terms they remain at about the same levels after relocation occurs. Rivalrous consonance, as opposed to relocation, is not a disturber of the power structure in the industry.

b Model 11.5: Rivalrous Consonance with Consonance Coefficients Determined by Relative Profits

Of course, this last result is partly the result of the level values of the θ_{ij} we have assumed. Nonetheless, the result seems quite robust with respect to consonance coefficients within the unit interval. Beyond that, the relocation pattern and that of prices, sales, and profits also remain quite close to those of Models 11.1 and 11.4. Suppose, for example, that each rival set consonance coefficients for its competitors on the basis of their relative profits in the base case of Model 11.1. Then, Θ would be that in Table 11.7, and when solved its base case and relocations solutions are those of Table 11.8.

The smaller overall level of consonance than that which prevails in Model 11.4 results in slightly reduced levels of profit in Model 11.5, for both base case and relocation case solutions, as well as lower prices and higher output levels. But the major characteristics of Model 11.4 are reproduced faithfully. Of notable interest are the percentage changes in profits in the last rows of Tables 11.6 and 11.8: the different consonance levels in the 2 models do not change the relative profit experiences of the rivals, in reinforcement of the argument made at the end of section 2a above. Indeed, even when

Table 11.7 Rivalrous consonance matrix for Model 11.5

Firm i/Firm j	*1*	*2*	*3*	*4*	*5*
1	1	0.23	0.34	0.06	0.06
2	0.31	1	0.34	0.06	0.06
3	0.31	0.23	1	0.06	0.06
4	0.31	0.23	0.34	1	0.06
5	0.31	0.23	0.34	0.06	1

Table 11.8 Base case and relocation solutions for Model 11.5 (k = 0.29, Θ in Table 11.7)

Characteristic	*Brand 1*	*Brand 2*	*Brand 3*	*Brand 4*	*Brand 5*
Original model			*Base case for Model 11.5*		
Location	1@1	2@2	3@3	4@4	5@5
Price	\$24.52	\$20.15	\$23.25	\$25.82	\$24.22
Output	433	420	590	313	297
Profits	\$8,652	\$6,397	\$9,544	\$1,567	\$1,560
Total output			2,053		
Total profits			\$27,720		
Quantity-weighted price			\$23.42		
Relocation model			*Relocation solution for Model 11.5*		
Location	1@1	2@2	3@3	4@N_1	5@N_6
Price	\$22.96	\$20.32	\$22.75	\$22.32	\$22.72
Output	450	394	592	464	468
Profits	\$8,326	\$6,017	\$9,282	\$7,290	\$5,389
Total output			2,368		
Total profits			\$36,304		
Quantity-weighted price			\$22.30		
Percentage profit changes	–3.76	–5.94	–2.75	+465.22	+345.45

consonance is 0 these percentage changes are almost the same, as revealed in the last row of Table 11.1. In these cost-dominated relocation models at least, the levels of consonance thus far encountered have little effect upon the relative profit experiences of the brands, and, to the extent they are an important determinant of the industry's power structure, on that as well.

c Model 11.6: Rivalrous Consonance at the Universal 1.0 Level

As a final exercise in section 2 we increase the rivalrous consonance coefficients to the upper bound of the allowable interval: all $\theta_{ij} = 1$, so that each firm treats rivals' profits as of coordinate value to its own. The base case and relocation case solutions of Model 11.6 are reproduced in Table 11.9.

Table 11.9 Base case and relocation solutions for Model 11.6 ($k = 0.29$, $\theta_{ij} = 1$)

Characteristic	*Brand 1*	*Brand 2*	*Brand 3*	*Brand 4*	*Brand 5*
Original model			*Base case for Model 11.6*		
Location	1@1	2@2	3@3	4@4	5@5
Price	$26.02	$22.49	$25.33	$28.29	$27.07
Output	415	384	551	248	212
Profits	$8,879	$6,675	$9,971	$1,542	$1,424
Total output			1,810		
Total profits			$28,491		
Quantity-weighted price			$25.50		
Relocation model			*Relocation solution for Model 11.6*		
Location	1@1	2@2	3@3	4@N_1	5@N_6
Price	$26.10	$23.10	$25.71	$25.51	$25.83
Output	403	352	528	405	391
Profits	$8,621	$6,269	$9,710	$7,172	$5,543
Total output			2,079		
Total profits			$37,315		
Quantity-weighted price			$25.33		
Percentage profit changes	–2.91	–6.08	–2.62	+465.11	+389.26

As noted above, the relocation solution remains the same as in all previous models, but the high level of tacit collusion now has some notable relative impacts on the firms' individual solutions when compared with previous models. All prices rise in the base case, but, when compared with Model 11.4's base case, profits in this model's base case solution fall absolutely in the cases of firms 4 and 5. The high consonance costs inflicted on these brands prevent them from reducing prices to the extent necessary to preserve sales and profit levels. Marginal consonance costs for brand 4 rise from \$1.37 in Model 11.4's base case solution to \$2.80 in that of Model 11.6; like figures for brand 5 are \$1.62 and \$3.30 respectively. These values reflect the rising profits of their rival firms as consonance levels increase, whereas the latter gain some relief from consonance cost increases because of the falling profits of brands 4 and 5.

The Model 11.6 relocation model solution follows the same pattern as previous solutions in lowering profits for brands 1, 2, and 3 and yielding large increases for brands 4 and 5, when compared with Model 11.6's base case solution. Those relocation profits are higher in each instance than the relocation profits in Model 11.4, although not dramatically: total profits rise less than 2 percent between the two relocation solutions. Once more, however, relative profit changes are not dramatically different from those in previous models. We find that even at these high levels of consonance the relative profit structure remains about the same over all the relocation solutions.

Brands 4 and 5 are once more the grand winners. Despite the large increase in marginal consonance costs, the drop in production costs for both firms permits them to reduce prices and increase their competitive price advantage, as well as their profit margins on higher sales. These results are familiar from previous solutions, however. The most valuable insight from this limiting consonance model is the insensitivity of the results to the large increase in the universal consonance coefficient from 0.5 to 1. This heightens our confidence that costs are driving the models in this section.

3 NODAL RELOCATION WITH COST STRUCTURE EQUALIZATION

To study relocation when demand factors are given greater play we will return to Model 11.1 and equalize the cost parameters F_i, m_i, and n_i for all firms. For those parameters we have selected figures that are close to the sales-weighted average values for the firms in the solution to the Model 11.1 base case. These are, respectively, 1,100, 7.5, and 0.0002. These substitutions penalize brands 1 and 2 greatly, brand 3 somewhat, and benefit brands 4 and 5 greatly.

a Model 11.7: Equalization of Cost Structures in Model 11.1

The base case and relocation solutions for Model 11.7, which incorporate these changed cost configurations, are given in Table 11.10. A comparison of the base cases of Models 11.1 and 11.7 reveals that prices rise for brands 1, 2, and 3 and fall for brands 4 and 5, as is to be expected, and profits follow suit and move negatively for the former three brands and positively for the latter two. Weighted price is a bit better in Model 11.7, consumers are better off with a larger output, and firms in the aggregate benefit as well in a lower-cost industry. In both a consumers' and social surplus sense, therefore, social welfare is improved in Model 11.7.

Relocation, however, brings about a different social judgment. Brands 4 and 5 make their moves toward their terminal node brands as they did in the previous 6 models, so that even in the absence of cost advantages demand improvements dictate such moves. The profit reward for brand 4 is much

Table 11.10 Base case and relocation solutions for Model 11.7 ($k = 0.29$, $\theta_{ij} = 0$)

Characteristic	*Brand 1*	*Brand 2*	*Brand 3*	*Brand 4*	*Brand 5*
Original model			*Base case for Model 11.7*		
Location	1@1	2@2	3@3	4@4	5@5
Price	$26.51	$21.42	$23.77	$20.96	$19.36
Output	376	357	537	498	505
Profits	$6,019	$3,849	$7,589	$5,547	$4,838
Total output			2,273		
Total profits			$27,842		
Quantity-weighted price			$22.26		
Relocation model			*Relocation solution for Model 11.7*		
Location	1@1	2@2	3@3	4@N_1	5@N_6
Price	$24.95	$22.01	$24.20	$22.77	$21.93
Output	406	405	544	466	521
Profits	$5,958	$4,737	$7,934	$5,978	$6,366
Total output			2,342		
Total profits			$30,973		
Quantity-weighted price			$23.16		
Percentage profit changes	–1.01	+23.07	+4.56	+7.77	+31.58

reduced, compared with the result of Model 11.1, although profits rise for firm 5. But the important change is that brand 2 now finds it advantageous to move to a neighboring position to brand 4. This is the result of favorable changes in demand parameters: a_2 rises from 700 to 837, b_{24} rises from 5 to 6.7, b_{42} falls from 9 to 6.7, and β_2 rises from 236 to 248. These favorable changes outweigh the rise in b_{22} from 16 to 20 and the rise in α_2 from 25.94 to 31.23. Sales rise 27 percent and profits 43 percent when compared with the base case. The relocation pattern was identical for all three sequences tested in Model 11.1's solution.

The solutions were also invariant to the degree of tacit collusion at the values of θ_{ij} = 0.5 and 1.0, for which we solved Models 11.7a (θ_{ij} = 0.5) and 11.7b (θ_{ij} = 1.0). Interestingly, but not surprisingly, if we compare the Model 11.1 base case with the Model 11.7 base case we see that the move to cost uniformity reduced the profits of brands 1, 2, and 3, whose costs rose, and benefitted the profits of brands 4 and 5 by virtue of cost reduction. The relocation pattern of Model 11.7 when compared with its own base case yields no surprises either, as brand 1 is further injured, brand 2 benefits from its relocation which in turn, by virtue of its distancing from brand 3 benefits it a bit, while brands 4 and 5 increase their profit advantage. None of this is unexpected.

Movement to tacit collusion also had expected results in enhancing the profits of all brands, in comparisons of base case solutions for the models, relocation model solutions for the models, and for movements from base to relocation model solutions. Table 11.11 presents the base case and relocation solutions for Model 11.7a, showing all firms improving in their base case and relocation profits, with percentage profit increases between the two being of the same order of magnitude as the similar percentages in Model 11.7, except that brand 1 shows a slight improvement in Model 11.7a instead of a small percentage decline in Model 11.7. In both models, relocation increases total output and profits over base case values, although weighted price rises, but outputs are lower, profits and weighted prices higher in Model 11.7a.

This pattern is continued in Table 11.12's presentation of Model 11.7b results, in which θ_{ij} are increased from 0.5 to 1.0. All firms increase their profit levels when compared with Model 11.7a in terms of base case and relocation solutions in both an intrasolution and intersolution sense. Percentage profit increases are once more of the same order of magnitude as those in Models 11.7 and 11.7a. And, once more, both base case and relocation solutions reveal reduced output and increased profits and prices over those of Models 11.7 and 11.7a.

In all of these cases tacit collusion had the classical outcomes of raising prices and profits and lowering output, reducing consumers' surplus, but generating forces too weak even at their strongest to override the relocation drives of brands 2, 4, and 5. As in the case of our models that

Table 11.11 Base case and relocation solutions for Model 11.7a ($k = 0.29$, $\theta_{ij} = 0.5$)

Characteristic	*Brand 1*	*Brand 2*	*Brand 3*	*Brand 4*	*Brand 5*
Original model			*Base case for Model 11.7a*		
Location	1@1	2@2	3@3	4@4	5@5
Price	\$27.54	\$23.06	\$25.17	\$22.47	\$21.17
Output	363	331	510	459	452
Profits	\$6,149	\$4,020	\$7,865	\$5,735	\$5,037
Total output			2,115		
Total profits			\$28,806		
Quantity-weighted price			\$23.81		
Relocation model			*Relocation solution for Model 11.7a*		
Location	1@1	2@2	3@3	4@N_1	5@N_6
Price	\$26.67	\$23.41	\$25.70	\$24.81	\$23.61
Output	382	380	513	424	479
Profits	\$6,190	\$4,924	\$8,193	\$6,204	\$6,579
Total output			2,178		
Total profits			\$32,090		
Quantity-weighted price			\$24.84		
Percentage profit changes	+0.67	+22.49	+4.17	+8.18	+30.61

were cost-driven, these demand-driven models are impotent in forestalling locational impulses. Given the wide range of costs, demand parameters, cognitive distancing factors, and consonance coefficients we have experimented with, our conjecture about realistic collusion and location appears to have substantial theoretical support: *tacit collusion within industries would not generally be expected to alter the location of brands in a quality space.*

4 TACIT COLLUSION AND ENTRY OF NEW FIRMS

As a last exercise in the effects of collusion on location in quality space we experiment with the actions of incumbents to cope with new brand entrants at empty nodal points on the locational network. Beginning with the uniform costs and locational pattern of Models 11.7, 7a, and 7b, would an entrant be

Table 11.12 Base case and relocation solutions for Model 11.7b ($k = 0.29$, $\theta_{ij} = 1$)

Characteristic	*Brand 1*	*Brand 2*	*Brand 3*	*Brand 4*	*Brand 5*
Original model			*Base case for Model 11.7b*		
Location	1@1	2@2	3@3	4@4	5@5
Price	\$28.63	\$24.76	\$26.62	\$24.04	\$23.06
Output	349	303	482	420	397
Profits	\$6,256	\$4,104	8,070	\$5,807	\$5,040
Total output			1,951		
Total profits			\$29,277		
Quantity-weighted price			\$25.41		
Relocation Model			*Relocation Solution for Model 11.7b*		
Location	1@1	2@2	3@3	4@N_1	5@N_6
Price	\$28.46	\$24.84	\$27.26	\$26.93	\$25.36
Output	356	355	481	380	436
Profits	\$6,342	\$5,046	\$8,362	\$6,256	\$6,650
Total output			2,008		
Total profits			\$32,656		
Quantity-weighted price			\$26.57		
Percentage profit changes	+1.37	+22.95	+3.62	+7.73	+31.94

successful in locating at node 2 (vacated by brand 2) if incumbents were not engaging in tacit collusion? We will assume that fixed costs for the entrant are double those of incumbents, and that marginal cost parameters m_i and n_i are 1.5 times those of incumbents. Suppose, then, that incumbents began to engage in tacit collusion with other incumbents in order to drive the entrant out of the product group, if it is successful in entering initially. Is this a feasible goal of the incumbents? In this way we will demonstrate the usefulness of the methods in gaining insights into such questions within a multifirm context.

Table 11.13 summarizes the experience of the product group in dealing with the entrant. The entrant at brand 2's initial position on the quality line is named brand 6 in the table, and we begin with the relocation solution of Model 11.7, in which no tacit collusion among the incumbents is operative, and, of course, no entry has occurred. In Model 11.8 brand 6 enters under

Table 11.13 Profits in rivalrous consonance models confronting entrant brand 6

Models	*Brand 1*	*Brand 2*	*Brand 3*	*Brand 4*	*Brand 5*	*Brand 6*
Model 11.7	$5,958	$4,737	$7,934	$5,978	$6,366	–
Model 11.8	$5,825	$4,792	$7,771	$5,882	$6,333	$1,555
Model 11.8a	$6,026	$4,971	$7,993	$6,088	$6,525	$1,731
Model 11.8b	$5,907	$4,923	$7,874	$5,984	$6,438	$1,631
Model 11.8c	$5,512	$4,484	$7,385	$5,465	$5,935	$1,349

similar conditions of independent decision making, and depresses the profits of all brands but brand 2s, which reduces its price substantially to increase its favorable price differentials with all rivals. Profit declines are not drastic, however, and the entrant's profits are quite modest. Output rises from 2,342 to 2,757, and industry profits rise by about 4 percent, while the output-weighted price falls from $23.26 to $22.49. The new competition is socially welcome, not overly burdensome to incumbents, nor very profitable for the entrant.

We suppose, however, that the incumbents extend to their fellows tacit collusion at the $\theta_{ij} = 0.5$ level, but withhold it from the entrant, which reciprocates the treatment. Model 11.8a raises incumbents' profits above levels attained in Model 11.8 – and, indeed, those in Model 11.7. However, the entrant's profits also rise in step with the collusive levels attained by the incumbents. Total output falls to 2,604, total profits rise above those of Model 11.8 by 3.7 percent, and sales-weighted price rises to $23.81. But positive cooperation among the incumbents combined with the purpose of excluding the entrant is perceived by them as too weak to accomplish the purpose.

In Model 11.8b, therefore, they retain the in-group tacit collusion at the $\theta_{ij} = 0.5$ level, but each sets a value of $\theta_{i6} = -1$, which is a step short of initiating a price war against brand 6, but does limit price increases. The profit results, listed in row 4 of Table 11.13, are not encouraging. At the cost of profit to themselves, the incumbents accept lower prices of their products for a mere 6 percent reduction in the entrant's profit, which leaves it above the Model 11.8 level. Incumbents' profits fall by $477 to achieve a reduction of $100 in the entrant's returns. Sales rise to 2,685 and sales-weighted price drops to $23.10, in benefitting consumers, but once more as means of driving out a troublesome entrant the self-punishing policy, conceived hopefully as a short-run expedient by the incumbents, is ineffective.

As a final, and desperate step, therefore, the incumbents cooperate in a price war, setting the in-group θ_{ij} at a level of –0.5 and at –1.0 for the incumbent. The cost in incumbent profits is evident in the results of Model 11.8c in the table, where they fall to \$28,781 from the \$30,603 level of Model 11.8 – a 6 percent reduction to achieve a 13 percent fall in the entrant's profit, but hardly enough to eliminate the intruder.

Rather clearly, in our example, tacit collusion does not have much potential for preventing entry even when the fixed and variable cost penalties accepted by the entrant are quite high. The incumbents are much wiser to accept the new competition and cooperative tacitly with it than to fight it masochistically. Inducing the entrant to accept and extend cooperation at the $\theta_{ij} = 0.5$ level would raise profits above the Model 11.8a level. Given this result, it would certainly be a mistaken policy of incumbents to attempt to preempt entry by conspiring to set limit prices or minimum outputs. In this instance, with or without the tacit collusion of the potential entrant, the product group would find it costly and ineffective to pursue such policies.

5 SUMMARY AND CONCLUSIONS

This chapter has placed a primary focus on the development of methodology with which to approach the analysis of integrated competition, multioccupant real-world oligopoly, insofar as it relates to placing brands within the quality spectrum. It has done so using the industry created in Chapter 10 to illustrate such applications and, where possible, to gain insights and stimulate conjectures that transcend the narrow confines of the parameter dependence that a realistic methodology demands. Of course, such "simulative theorizing" is disappointing in its failure to obtain "universal" propositions concerning oligopolistic decision making, but one must recognize that such achievement is attained only with simplifications that render the result of doubtful utility. Resort to duopoly or to monopolistic competition are frequent devices to escape parameter dependence or multiple industry incumbents, but the results are frequently disappointing and rather fanciful: one suspects that the problems selected for such closed analysis are more often than not chosen by virtue of their susceptibility of determinateness. To support this contention, the reader is invited to study ingenious but airy-fairy models in the encyclopedic Chapters 7 and 8 of Tirole's *The Theory of Industrial Organization*.

In our studies of relocation of brands in the product space we have adopted a discrete set of nodes whose number is chosen by the analyst in view of the degree of accuracy necessary and the resources available. We experimented with models in which our firms were cost- or demand-driven, and in which they acted independently or in various states of tacit collusion. Two sources of insights into the complex outcomes of such models were illustrated: the marginal conditions derived from first-order profit maximization, which we found so useful in previous chapters, and the all-but-unknown techniques in economic analysis of factor decomposition. We experimented with changes in the degree of cognitive decay (the *k* factor), partially in anticipation of the analysis to come in Chapter 12 where we will study the use of advertising to change such factors. We finished with analysis of several levels of tacit collusion, and concluded that in our cost-driven models the optimal spacing of brands was not susceptible to even quite high degrees of cooperation.

We then equalized the cost structure of our firms to isolate the effects of demand on location, and found that the location solution differed from the cost-driven configuration only by one brand's relocation. The new pattern, like the old, was invariant to high levels of tacit collusion, and we hazarded the conjecture that in realistic oligopolies tacit collusion is not a sufficiently strong force to influence the placement of brands on the quality spectrum.

Finally, we studied the use of tacit collusion to preempt entry or to drive out entrants. In our example, in which we used the demand-driven model, tacit collusion was not strong enough to discourage an entrant from remaining in the product group, even at rather severe cost penalties relative to the incumbents. A corollary was that under the conditions of our models preemptive policies such as limit pricing to forestall entry would be mistaken, and that either accepting the added competition, or, more favorably, enticing the new firm to engage in tacit collusion, would be preferable. On the basis of our analyses and what we interpret to be the rather realistic nature of the parameter values, we again conjectured that tacit collusion, even at high levels, is not in realistic industries an active factor in discouraging entry or punishing entrants, given the short- and intermediate-run costs in incumbents' profit sacrifices such actions entail.

12 Selling Costs and Cognitive Distancing

The last, and very important, component of nonprice competition that we will model is advertising – or, more broadly, selling cost activities – which we will treat as extrinsic characteristics of products. Their costs are distinguished from production and consonance costs as expenditures whose purposes are to affect demand functions for the brands rather than supply conditions.

Selling costs include a wide variety of expenditures, a convenient classification of which for purposes of analysis is the following:

1 *Information Dissemination Costs*: This category of expenditures is for activities encompassing purely "informational" advertising (e.g., department store advertising in newspapers, product specifications for producer goods, capabilities and limitations of medicines for health professionals, and so forth). Importantly for our modeling, it includes advertising of favorable price differentials among brands.
2 *Cognitive Positioning or Distancing Costs*: We distinguish advertising and other costs of purely "persuasive" endeavors which trumpet the alleged advantages of a brand in order to increase the perceived interbrand distances from rivals' offerings (e.g., cigarette advertising), or perhaps to reposition the brand in "virtual product space," a concept to be defined below.
3 *Sales and Sales-supportive Personnel Costs*: Salesmen, sales office support staff, display, catalog, price list, shelf space, telecommunications costs, and so forth, are expenditures for enhancing present and future demand.
4 *Price Inducement Policy Costs*: This heading includes the costs of customer coupons and rebates, wholesaler or retailer rebates, and bona fide "sales."
5 *Experience-inducing and Risk-reduction Program Costs*: Programs such as the offer of free samples, money-back guarantees or free trial periods are means of inducing consumers to experience the product by direct exposure to the brand or by reducing the risk of disappointment.
6 *Post-sales Service Expenditures*: Expenditures on repair or maintenance services, technical support services and product warranties are readily characterized as forms of sales costs designed to enhance future sales.
7 *Reputation Enhancement Costs*: Public relations activities with no direct relation to product sales – charity contributions, institutional advertising,

or sponsorship of community events or institutions are frequent examples – can be treated as broadly targeted sales activities to enhance the image of the firm in consumers' perceptions.

Of course, it is frequently difficult to place a specific activity in any one category, not to mention the problem of separating production costs from sales costs. Informational and persuasive advertising are seldom pure forms. Price reductions necessitated by changes in competitive structure may be viewed as a type of sales inducement policy. Movements of brands in the product space, discussed in Chapter 11, are induced in large part by expectations of affecting the firm's demand function position and/or slope. Warranties partake the characteristics of risk-reduction and post-sales service expenditures. Nonetheless, the categorization will generally give reasonably clear-cut characterizations of expenditures.

1 MODEL 1 – INFORMATIONAL ADVERTISING WITH NO TACIT COLLUSION, REVENUE-DETERMINED ADVERTISING

Previous chapters have dealt with instances of some varieties of selling costs and other issues in those chapters can be readily extended as types of selling cost policies. In Chapters 8–10 we featured the policy costs of price reductions which, as noted above, can be viewed as price-inducement selling activities. Warranties were also dealt with extensively in these chapters, and it would be a straightforward exercise to deal with other post-sales services in similar fashion.

In this section we will confine our analysis to informational advertising, which seeks to enhance sales without changing cognitive distancing among brands. The function fulfilled by the publicity is to accept the position occupied in consumers' cognition and to give voice to the existence of the product and its intrinsic qualities (as well as price). The model is relevant to an oligopoly whose brands are not strongly differentiated in the consumer's mind (i.e., whose indifference premia are relatively small) and in which tacit collusion is not practiced. Examples in the consumer goods sector are major gasoline brands, which have never been successfully differentiated in the consumers mind. Also, producer goods, which are purchased by knowledgeable customers who are swayed in their decisions by product specifications and characteristics to a great degree, are also examples of this genus.

We begin with the demand function of (10.7) which features no advertising:

$$x_i = a_i - b_{ii}p_i - \Sigma_j b_{ij}(p_i - p_j)e^{-ks_{ij}}. \qquad (12.1)$$

Informational advertising is introduced by symbolizing firm *i*'s advertising expenditures by A_i and defining its net impact on brand *i*'s sales as:

$$\Psi_i = A_i \Sigma_j (r_{ij} - t_{ij} A_i) e^{-ks_{ij}} - \Sigma_j A_j (r_{ji} - t_{ji} A_j) e^{-ks_{ji}}. \tag{12.2}$$

where r_{ij} and t_{ij} are parameters in a quadratic expression for the amount of sales transferred from brand *j* to brand *i* by virtue of informational advertising by firm *i* before netting out the impacts of firm *j*'s advertising on firm *i*'s sales. (12.2) yields, therefore, the total net impact on brand *i*'s sales of informational advertising, after discounting by the exponential decay factors that incorporate cognitive distancing in the period of initial determination. Then, by using the form of the demand function in (10.8) and incorporating Ψ we obtain:

$$x_i = a_i - \alpha_i p_i + \beta_i + \psi_i. \tag{12.3}$$

In determining the firm's informational advertising we depart from conventional economic theory. Instead of treating advertising in the manner of firm policies in previous chapters, equating marginal revenue to marginal cost, we take direction from empirical studies. Convincing research indicates that firms tend to determine advertising expenditures largely as a percentage of sales.[1] Advertising is determined as a percentage of revenue modified, plus or minus, by the brand's price differentials with its rivals' prices:

$$A_i = \left(\phi_i + \Sigma_j \lambda_{ij} \left(\frac{p_j}{p_i} - 1 \right) \right) p_i x_i. \tag{12.4}$$

Each firm then, absent rivalrous consonance, maximizes own-profits with respect to price:

$$\max_{p_i} \pi_i = p_i x_i - C_i - A_i. \tag{12.5}$$

Partially differentiating with respect to p_i we obtain the following expression for optimal price that permitted rapid convergence in a diagonalization algorithm:[2]

$$p_i^\circ = \frac{a_i + \beta_i + \psi_i - (m_i + 2n_i x_i)\dfrac{\delta x_i}{\delta p_i} - \dfrac{\delta A_i}{\delta p_i}}{2\alpha_i}. \tag{12.6}$$

Each of the firm's profit functions was strictly concave and robustly so with respect to parameters: the second derivative was negative in all instances of the cases to be solved below.[3]

a A Base Case

To illustrate the model and to gain insights into the interfirm implications of informational advertising we revert to the 5-brand industry base case used in Chapters 10 and 11. The parameters in Table 10.1 are retained in their entirety and the advertising-related parameters in Table 12.1 are added.

Note that all 5 firms are assumed to devote 3 percent of revenues to advertising (ϕ_i) with identical adjustments ($\lambda = 0.005$) times the number of ratio points that the ratios of rivals' prices to own price are above or below 1 applied to total revenue. If the ratio p_j/p_i is greater than 1, advertising rises above the basic expenditure, if below 1 the advertising budget is reduced.

The important distinctions among brands, however, are found in the r_{ij} listings. In Table 12.1 the rows indicate the gross gains in sales (neglecting the t_{ij} terms) for each rival that firms obtain from each dollar of informational advertising before discounting for distance and scale diseconomies, and the columns indicate the sales they lose to each rival's like expenditures. Subtracting column entry r_{ji} from row entry r_{ij} we obtain the undiscounted net impact per dollar of rival- and own-advertising, respectively. These interbrand impacts are listed in the "Total" column of Table 12.2. However, these impacts must be discounted for cognition distance, and this is done in the last column of the table. An index of advertising effectiveness is obtained by totaling the 4 rival discounted net impacts for each firm. These interbrand net impacts are also depicted graphically in Figure 12.1 (totals may not add exactly due to rounding errors), where the arrows point in the direction of the firm in each pair that has a nonnegative benefit balance. Using this index one sees that brand 1 is the largest beneficiary of informational advertising, largely at the expense of brand 2, the largest loser; firm 4 is a net gainer; firm 5 on net is a modest gainer and brand firm 3 a modest loser.

The expectations raised by Table 12.2 are borne out in the base case solution profit comparisons of Table 12.3. In that table performance statistics are compared for the base case solution in Chapter 10, as reported in Table 10.3, in which no advertising occurred (Base Case 0) with the base case solution that occurs with the inclusion of the parameters in Table 12.1 (Base Case 1). In the way of explanation, Advertising-induced Sales (*AIS*) are derived from the solution values of Ψ_i and are the net additions – plus or minus – to a brand's output resulting from own- and other-firm informational advertising. Price-induced-Changes (*PIC*) in advertising are the dollar additions or subtractions to or from the 3-percent-of-revenue basis for advertising obtained by applying the λ_i parameters to the price ratios in (12.4).

Table 12.1 Advertising–relevant base case parameters

$1r_{ij}$					
Brand i/ Brand j	*1*	*2*	*3*	*4*	*5*
1	–	5.00	0.07	0.18	0.06
2	0.12	–	0.18	0.20	0.18
3	0.07	0.19	–	0.10	0.25
4	0.26	0.24	0.18	–	0.30
5	0.09	0.29	0.30	0.13	–
$2t_{ij}$					
Brand i/Brand j	*1*	*2*	*3*	*4*	*5*
1	–	0.01	0.0002	0.00005	0.0003
2	0.001	–	0.0004	0.00003	0.0004
3	0.00015	0.00003	–	0.0002	0.000025
4	0.00003	0.00003	0.00005	–	0.0001
5	0.00017	0.00004	0.00001	0.0002	–
$3\phi_i$					
Parameter/Brand	*1*	*2*	*3*	*4*	*5*
κ_i	0.03	0.03	0.03	0.03	0.03
κ_i					
Brand i/Brand j	*1*	*2*	*3*	*4*	*5*
1	–	0.005	0.005	0.005	0.005
2	0.005	–	0.005	0.005	0.005
3	0.005	0.005	–	0.005	0.005
4	0.005	0.005	0.005	–	0.005
5	0.005	0.005	0.005	0.005	–

In brief summary, from Chapter 10 it will be recalled that brand 1 is the lowest-quality product with low costs and small basic demand at position 0 in the linear product space. Brand 4 is also lower quality, only 3 distance units from brand 1, penalized by high costs and closeness to medium quality brand

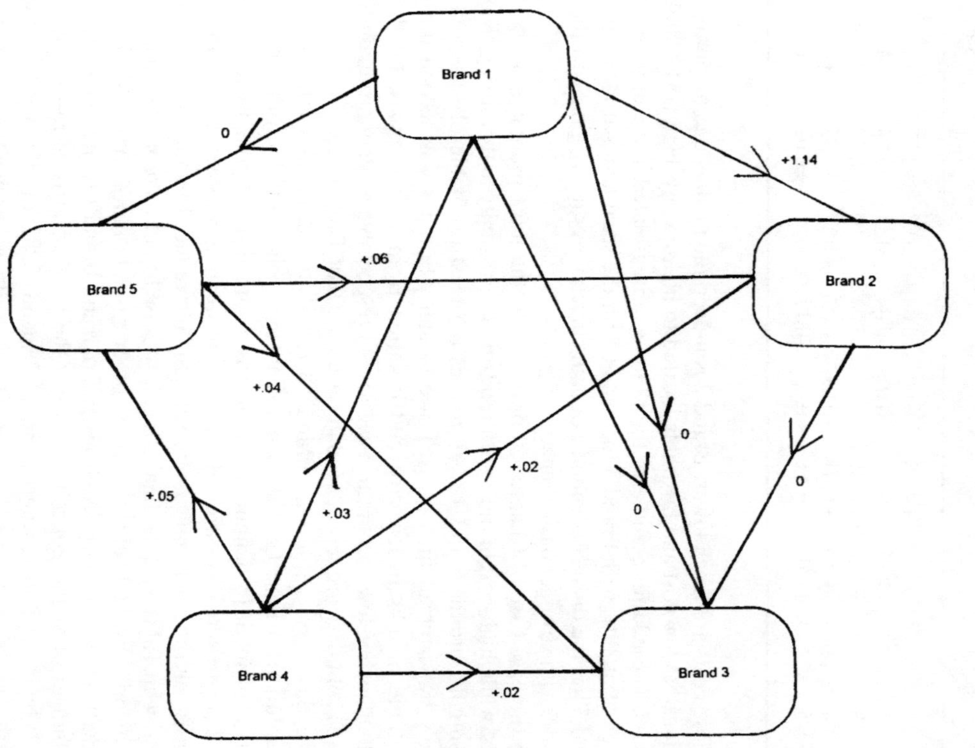

Figure 12.1 Nonnegative discounted interbrand impacts of 1 dollar of own and rival informational advertising expenditures

Table 12.2 Net interbrand impacts of 1 dollar of own and rival informational advertising expenditures

Brand i/Brand j	*1*	*2*	*3*	*4*	*5*	*Total*	*Discounted total*
1	–	+4.88	0.00	–0.08	–0.03	+4.77	+1.11
2	–4.88	–	–0.01	–0.04	–0.11	–5.04	–1.23
3	+0.00	+0.01	–	–0.08	–0.05	–0.12	–0.05
4	+0.08	+0.04	+0.08	–	+0.17	+0.37	+0.13
5	+0.03	+0.11	+0.05	–0.17	–	+0.02	+0.05

2 whose costs are much lower. Brand 2 is indeed the median quality product produced at low cost and favorably located to high-quality, high-cost brands 5 and 3. These latter brands are found to be quite isolated in the uppermost ranges of quality, with brand 3 located at 8 on the scale and 5 at location 7. Brand 3 has the distinct advantage of being much lower in marginal cost than brand 5 with stronger basic demand.

In the base case of Chapter 10 brand 3 was the most profitable of the 5 rivals, while high-cost brand 5 suffered from its proximity to this strong rival. Essentially, brands 5 and 4 were tied as the least profitable of the group, largely by virtue of high costs. Lowest-quality brand 1 was second most profitable, thanks to low cost and isolation from serious rivals. Finally, median quality, low-cost brand 2 was also of respectable median profitability. These profit data are reproduced in Base Case 0 of Table 12.3.

The Base Case 1 solution to Model 1 reveals two dramatic changes from the solution to Base Case 0 – one of obvious origin and the other not so easily explained. In defining the r_{ij} it was assumed that brand 1's informational advertising was extremely effective in stealing net sales from brand 2. Even though the net impacts are substantially reduced by the distance discounting in Table 12.2 the final effect is to raise brand 1's profit 28.2 percent and its price by 22.9 percent. On the other hand, brand 2's profits decline a full 30.9 percent and its price drops 19.5 percent. Brand 1 spends an advertising budget of \$326, reduced \$73 below the base advertising-to-sales ratio (*ASR*) by its price rise, whereas brand 2 spends \$281, or \$80 over the base *ASR* by virtue of its drop in price. These results are projected by the discounted total net impacts of Table 12.2, which give the 2 brands the highest and lowest values of the five.[4]

Of greater interest is the experience of firm 5, which illustrates the unforeseen consequences of modeling general interdependence relationships. The r_{5j} row and r_{j5} column of Table 12.1 indicate that brand 5 is a net advertising gainer from brands 1, 2, and 3, although it suffers a deficit with brand 4, which

Table 12.3 Base case solution comparisons: no advertising versus informational advertising

Parameter	*Base Case 0*	*Base Case 1*	*Percentage Change*
p_1	\$24.24	\$29.78	+22.9%
x_1	435	447	+2.8
C_1	\$1,963.95	\$1994.41	1.6
π_1	\$8,580.45	\$10,997.65	+28.2
A_1	–	\$326.23	–
AIS_1[1]	–	135	–
$PICA_1$[2]	–	–\$73	–
p_2	\$19.56	\$15.74	–19.5%
x_2	428	426	–0.5
C_2	\$2,095.58	\$2,090.05	–0.3
π_2	\$6,276.10	\$4,339.35	–30.9
A_2	–	\$281.10	–
AIS_2	–	–199	–
$PICA_2$	–	+\$80	–
p_3	\$22.84	\$22.92	+0.4%
x_3	594	640	+7.7
C_3	\$4,195.66	\$4,684.48	+11.7
gp_3	\$9,371.30	\$9,532.33	+1.7
A_3	–	\$444.66	–
AIS_3	–	+43	–
$PICA_3$	–	+\$5	–
p_4	\$25.02	\$24.99	–0.1%
x_4	336	372	+10.7
C_4	\$6,890.21	\$7,465.65	+8.4
π_4	\$1,516.51	\$1,567.31	+3.3
A_4	–	\$262.45	–
AIS_4	–	+35	–
$PICA_4$	–	–\$16	–
p_5	\$23.22	\$22.69	–2.3%
x_5	331	341	+3.0
C_5	\$6,165.95	\$6,315.98	+2.4
π_5	\$1,519.87	\$1,178.86	–22.4
A_5	–	\$236.51	–
AIS_5	–	–14	–
$PICA_5$	–	+\$5	–

Notes:
[1]AIS_1 = Advertising-induced Sales.
[2]$PICA_1$ = Price-induced change in advertising.

benefits greatly from its advertising competition with brand 5. After discounting for cognitive distance, however, Table 12.2 suggests that brand 5 is a net gainer in the informational advertising war. But this fails to take into account the *amounts* of advertising undertaken by the firms, as will be shown below.

Brand 4, brand 5's seeming most punishing rival in Table 12.2, lowers price by only $0.03, so that brand 5's $0.53 price reduction is not motivated by brand 4 price action. Brand 3, its closest rival in distance terms, actually raises price. Brand 2, only 2 distance units away from brand 5, does lower price, but Table 12.2 shows brand 5 to be a substantial net gainer from this lower-quality rival. The explanation for brand 5's profit and price plight must lie in the advertising sector, and a deeper analysis of this dimension must be undertaken.

Table 12.4 details the net gains in sales of all firms from rivals across the rows after taking into account the sizes of firms' advertising budgets as well as the r_{ij} and t_{ij} and the decay factor. Note that brand 3 is not a net source of sales for brand 5, as implied by Table 12.2, but the largest cause of its net sales losses on informational advertising account. With brand 4, which does not disappoint Table 12.2 expectations, brand 5 confronts strong pulls downward on its sales which are only partly compensated by its healthy surplus with brand 2. Brand 1 is a competitive nonentity. Brands 3 and 4 emerge as the primary authors of brand 5's profit decline via brand 3's high advertising budget and brand 4's large effectiveness surplus against brand 5's sales. Despite the small positive per dollar surplus in brand 5's favor in Table 12.2, it is a net loser.

Does this indicate that brand 5 should cease advertising, or that it is advertising too much? Brand 5's defensive advertising is a positive factor in its profit experience: absent that effort, sales would have fallen 111 units; advertising reduces this to about 14 units. But suppose firm 5 reduced its advertising by $5. Then the advertising offsetting gains would have fallen to 95.57 units for a net reduction of 1.93 units of output. This reduces revenue by $43.79, but marginal production costs would fall by $77.90, which, with the advertising

Table 12.4 Net flows of benefits from informational advertising among firms, Model 1 base case

Brand:\From brand:	*1*	*2*	*3*	*4*	*5*	*Total*
1	–	+143.82	+0.01	–5.35	–3.18	+135.30
2	–143.82	–	–24.95	–3.96	–26.52	–199.26
3	–0.01	+24.95	–	–9.12	+26.81	+42.64
4	+5.35	+3.96	+9.12	–	+16.39	+34.82
5	+3.18	+26.52	–26.81	–16.39	–	–13.50

budget reduction, reduces total costs by $82.90. *Ceteris paribus*, therefore, the firm is forced to spend more than an optimizing budget would permit.

One interesting aspect of this base case is that advertising expands sales over Base Case 1 by only about 5 percent, so that most of the movement in sales is at the expense of rivals. Marketing specialists are interested in comparing the "voice" of a firm – the percentage that its advertising budget is of the total industry budget – with its market share, or percentage of industry sales. If advertising effectiveness is similar for all firms, then if a firm's voice and its market share are equal, firms should be holding their own in what is in greatest part a zero-sum industry game. In an industry in which the market shares of firms are widely dispersed, one competitive ploy by large firms is to increase its voice, thereby forcing smaller firms to increase their advertising budgets to hold their market share. Smaller firms can be driven to the wall if they are unable to compete in this fashion. In the present case, largely by virtue of the manner in which the advertising budget is determined as a percentage of revenue (and therefore, where prices do not differ greatly, of sales as well) advertising and market shares are quite close. Table 12.5 records the values.

The solution data of Table 12.3 permit us to approximate the effects of price changes versus advertising in the sales of firms. Brand 1's sales rise by 12, but advertising boosts it by 126: hence, the $5.54 price rise induces a sales decline of about 114 units. In the bitter competition between brand 1 and brand 2, the latter loses a net of 2 sales, although advertising reduces them by 197 units. The price decline of $3.82 must account for a sales gain of about 195 units. Brand 3, for all the damage it wreaks on brand 5, is a relatively small profit gainer. Its sales rise by 46 by virtue of advertising, or essentially all of the increase, its price rising only by a few cents. Its large advertising budget penalized the profits one would have expected from this performance, and one suspects that it is too large to be optimal. Firm 4's sales gain of 36 was advertising-driven, the small reduction in price yielding

Table 12.5 A comparison of advertising voice and market share in Base Case 1

Brand	*Market share (%)*	*Voice (%)*
1	20.1	21.0
2	19.1	18.2
3	28.8	28.7
4	16.7	16.9
5	15.3	15.2
Totals	100.0	100.0

a net of 1 unit. Its profits rise by about 3 percent, but its high costs continue to punish the firm. Finally, brand 5 gains 10 sales, losing 14 to advertising, so that its price reduction gains it about 24 units of sales. Profit declines substantially because advertising (which we know is excessive from the profit-maximizing viewpoint) costs add to its high production costs to punish the firm. Brands 4 and 5 continue to be the low profit brands of the product group.

In short, brands 1, 3, and 4 increase their profits through informational advertising and brands 2 and 5 lose. The amount of advertising tends to correlate well with profit for firms who gain, but defensive advertising is engaged in by brands 2 and 3. Informational advertising increases sales for all firms but firm 2, and its sales essentially remain constant. Prices fall for those firms whose profits fall and rise or move negligibly for gainers.

b Some Parametric Ranging with Model 1

In addressing the base case of Model 1 with parameter changes one thinks first of varying the *ASR* values, ϕ_i, to gain insights into which firms are under-advertising or overadvertising relative to profit-maximizing levels. However, in section 2 we will construct Model 2 which includes informational advertising optimization, so it is best to postpone such questions until its base case is available. Therefore, our sensitivity analysis with Model 1 is confined to varying k, the cognitive distance parameter, and the uniform $\lambda_{ij} = \lambda$ parameter that controls the importance of price differentials in determining informational advertising budgets.

Table 12.6 contains the condensed results of increasing and decreasing k to 0.58 and 0.20, and of increasing and decreasing λ to 0.01 and 0.0025. Base Case 1 (the base case of Model 1) is reproduced from Table 12.3 for comparison purposes.

1 Cognitive Distancing through Informational Advertising

Increasing k to 0.58 enhances the decay factor of advertising effectiveness considerably by increasing the perceived distancing of brands by consumers. We should expect, therefore, that firms that suffered from net sales intrusions when $k = 0.29$ – firms 2 and 5 – would be benefitted, as would those who gained modestly from advertising – firms 3 and 4. Brand 1, on the other hand, which gains hugely in the base case, would be expected to be hurt profitswise. All of these expectations are fulfilled when profit comparisons are made with Base Case 1.

Brand 2's profits recover almost to their pre-advertising (Base Case 0) level and its price recovers fully to the level in that state. Sales actually rise above

Table 12.6 Parametric ranging with Model 1

Variable	*Base Case 2*	*k = 0.58*	*k = 0.20*	*λ = 0.01*	*λ = 0.0025*
p_1	$29.78	$27.97	$31.02	$29.08	$29.03
A_1	$326.23	$308.17	$330.34	$270.06	$355.77
x_1	447	409	456	479	446
π_1	$10,997.65	$9,226.19	$11,808.33	$11,597.37	$10,600.26
AIS_1	+135	+32	+185	+145	+109
$PICA_1$	–73	–35	–94	–148	–33
p_2	$15.74	$19.56	$14.04	$15.61	$15.91
A_2	$281.10	$311.88	$248.51	$347.93	$246.38
x_2	426	438	389	418	434
π_2	$4,339.36	$6,136.03	$3,223.84	$4,108.12	$4,540.55
AIS_2	–199	–61	–292	–206	–187
$PICA_2$	+80	+55	+85	+152	+39
p_3	$22.92	$24.60	$22.23	$22.34	$23.20
A_3	$444.66	$429.21	$453.04	$463.28	$437.77
x_3	640	583	666	664	629
π_3	$9,532.33	$9,549.43	$9,517.97	$9,533.92	$9,538.87
AIS_3	+43	–74	+49	+50	+41
$PICA_3$	+5	–1	+9	+18	0
p_4	$24.99	$26.64	$24.31	$24.82	$25.02
A_4	$262.45	$239.46	$284.21	$235.00	$272.21
x_4	372	321	412	362	374
π_4	$1,567.31	$1,660.16	$1,620.23	$1,448.40	$1,590.11
AIS_4	+35	–78	+65	+25	+41
$PICA_4$	–16	–17	–16	–35	–9
p_5	$22.69	$24.00	$22.17	$22.65	$22.69
A_5	35.07	$236.51	$237.98	$232.47	$235.60
x_5	341	320	350	336	343
π_5	$1,178.86	$1,454.58	$1,061.61	$1,134.45	$1,198.17
AIS_5	–14	–92	–26	–20	–18
$PICA_5$	+5	+6	+5	+4	+2

pre-advertising levels and above Base Case 1 values as well, as its net losses on advertising account fall from 199 to 61. Reviving revenues raise advertising expenditures to help achieve the reduction in sales deficit due to such effort. Informational advertising's effectiveness is modified greatly when brands are successful in distancing themselves by product differentiation.

Brand 5's recovery is not so dramatic though substantial, its major antagonist remaining quite close in the new distance configuration. But its price rises above pre-advertising levels, and its profits close within about 4 percent of that state's value. Its sales deficit on advertising account falls slightly due largely to reductions in brand 3 and 4 surpluses in Base Case 1. Advertising remains essentially constant as revenues decline only slightly because rising price offsets the sales decline. Improving price differentials with brands 2, 3, and 4 lead it to increase its advertising budget slightly over Base Case 1.

Brands 3 and 4 are indeed modest profit gainers from the enhanced cognitive distancing. Both brands' profits remain above pre-advertising levels in Base Case 0 as well as those of Base Case 1. Prices of both firms also rise above both base case levels, although outputs fall relative to both base cases not only because of price rises but also because both suffer reductions in their advertising sales surpluses as their advertising is reduced and their surpluses with brands 2 and 5 shrink.

Finally, brand 1 suffers a 16 percent drop in profits, although they remain above pre-advertising levels, and its price is reduced as well. Output falls below both base case values and advertising budget declines 6 percent. Its balance on informational advertising account remains in surplus, but falls by 75 percent because of the large decline in effectiveness with respect to brand 2. Nonetheless, brand 1's benefit from informational advertising holds up quite well, in large part because at its extreme in the linear product space it is well distanced from rivals to start with in both base cases and its costs are so low.

When k is reduced to 0.20, these results are essentially reproduced in opposite directions. Brand 2 suffers a large profit loss compared with Base Case 1, is forced to reduce price substantially and increases its advertising deficit 48 percent. Brand 5 is marginally hurt profitswise relative to Base Case 1 but price declines modestly, output rises a bit, and advertising remains about the same. It is benefitted a great deal because its advertising account sales deficit does not increase greatly as brand 2's deficit rises greatly. Brand 5 continues to demonstrate its rather remarkable isolation in the high quality spectrum from environment changes.

Brand 3's profits are reduced slightly from Base Case 1 levels, its price falls more significantly and its sales rise in consequence; because its advertising budget rises and with it its advertising-induced sales surplus. All changes are small to moderate, however, as the brand, like its polar analog, brand 1, lies at an end-point of the space, achieving high-profit isolation. Brand 4's experience differs somewhat. Compared with Base Case 1 its profit rises moderately and sales increase substantially. These results are largely the result of a rise in its advertising budget and induced sales surplus with every one of its rivals, especially brands 3 and 5. These last two rivals are quite distant from brand 4, and the reduction in k benefits it greatly.

Brand 1 thrives with the reduction in cognitive friction. Profits and price rise above Base Case 2 levels as sales and advertising budget rise. Most notably, of course, its sales surplus on advertising account soars, wholly at the expense of brand 2, with which the surplus grows from about 144 to 218 units.

The results of the variation in *k* do emphasize the importance of cognitive distance, especially when the information friction it creates is approximated by an exponential decay function. Generally, brands at the extremities of a linear product space tend to enjoy relative isolation from rivals' actions, first because rivals attack from only one direction, and second because average distance to interior rivals tend to be large, if those rivals are well dispersed in the space. More centrally located brands (2 and 4 in our example, although brand 2 is exceptional for reasons cited above) tend to be more sensitive to changes in cognitive distance.

2 *Price Sensitivities in Informational Advertising Budgets*

We have used a constant $\lambda = 0.005$ as a parameter applied to price ratios to adjust advertising budgets above or below levels determined by a constant *ASR* applied to revenues. In the first exercise Base Case 1 λ is doubled to 0.01 and in the second is halved to 0.0025, with the results listed in Table 12.6.

When λ is increased it enhances the rise in advertising budgets for firms whose prices are low relative to rivals and reduces such budgets for high-priced firms. Advertising budgets are expected to rise on this account for brands 2, 3, and 5 and to fall for brands 1 and 4. Only brand 5 disappoints these expectations, as its isolation permits it to maintain an essentially constant budget over all four parameter displacements.

Comparing the price-induced change in amounts of advertising (*PICA*) in Base Case 1 to those measures for this solution, we find that brand 1 doubles the reduction in advertising budget despite a substantial reduction in its price. On the other hand, brand 2 almost doubles (\$152 versus \$80) its price-induced budget increase with only a slight price reduction. Brand 3 drops its price substantially and increases its advertising budget by only \$18, of which \$13 was price-induced. Brand 4 reduces advertising by \$27, with a slight fall in price inspiring about \$19 of that. Brand 5, in its splendid isolation, remains all but untroubled in its advertising budget and price particulars.

The increased importance of price differentials does enhance price competition and all prices do fall, with brands 1 and 3 falling more than \$0.50 and the others by minor amounts. Consumers, by increasing price consciousness, do exhibit some ability to inspire price competition.

Brand 2, by increasing its advertising budget and reducing price only slightly, reveals surprising damage control, with its sales deficit on advertising account, its sales, and its profit declining only moderately. Nevertheless, despite the fact that it had the lowest price in the industry in the base case, while brand 1 had the highest, it is brand 2 whose profits suffer from an enhanced importance of price differentials in determining advertising budgets and brand 1 which prospers! Our methods permit us to track the causes of the outcome rather exactly, but once more we experience the tangled web of interdependence in situations of relevant dimensionality, and the necessity of resorting to modeling rather than parameter-free closed analysis.

Brands 3, 4, and 5 emerge from the experience essentially unscathed. Brand 3 does reduce its price significantly and its advertising budget somewhat, but sales and profits remain about the same. Brands 4 and 5 lose some profit but are not grievously damaged, nor are they forced to make important advertising budget or price adjustments.

When price differentials are reduced to half their Base Case 2 importance in advertising budget determination, our expectations are the reverse of those in the case of increased importance: high-priced brands should benefit by raising prices, low-priced brands should suffer and lower prices to maintain advantage. But, of course, the outcomes are not so simple, depending largely on whether firms are overspending or underspending on advertising budget in Base Case 1. For example, brand 1 lowers price and increases advertising, while suffering profit losses, while brand 2 increases price, advertising budget, and profits. Brand 2's price rise and steady sales raise revenue and its reduction in advertising by virtue of reducing price spreads with rivals permits a profit rise. Both firms show evidence of overadvertising in the base case.

Firms 3, 4, and 5 reveal expected behavior: prices rise or remain constant; sales, advertising budgets, and balances on advertising account remain at base case levels; and profits rise significantly. In both parameter λ shocks price changes are relatively minor given the degrees of parameter change inflicted. The model is robust with respect to parameter λ. It must be remembered that it impacts price only indirectly via changes in advertising budgets. The assumed values of λ are set by producers, not consumers, reflecting producers' views of the productivity of advertising when their prices depart from those of rivals. Moderately-priced brands – brands 3, 4, and 5 in our example – are fairly immune from price and profit shocks inflicted. Reactions of significance occur largely in brands whose prices lie in the extremities. But given the rather complex interactions set off in the advertising budget and price dimensions in these cases, outcomes can be counterintuitive though ultimately explainable by tracing flows of advertising-induced sales changes among the rivals. This is done by disaggregating each firm's ϕ_i to trace changes in flows of advertising-induced sales with rivals.

2 MODEL 2 – INFORMATIONAL ADVERTISING WITH NO TACIT COLLUSION, PROFIT-OPTIMAL ADVERTISING

We now revert to determining both price and informational advertising levels by profit maximization, treating each as a sales policy whose marginal costs must be equated in the optimal solution. The expressions derived in this fashion that were used to solve for the variables by diagonalization methods are the following:

$$1 \quad p_i = \frac{a_i + \beta_i + \alpha_i(m_i + 2n_i x_i) + \psi_i}{2\alpha_i} \qquad (12.7)$$

$$2 \quad A_i = \frac{(p_i - m_i - 2n_i x_i)(\Sigma_j r_{ij} e^{-ks_{ij}}) - 1}{2(p_i - m_i - 2n_i x_i)(\Sigma_j t_{ij} e^{-ks_{ij}})}.$$

Through the use of our techniques of previous chapters, we can rewrite these equations as:

$$1 \quad (p_i - m_i - 2n_i x_i) = \frac{x_i}{\alpha_i} \qquad (12.8)$$

$$2 \quad (p_i - m_i - 2n_i x_i) = \frac{1}{\Sigma_j (r_{ij} - 2t_{ij} A_i) e^{-ks_{ij}}}.$$

which state that the marginal policy cost of price and advertising policies must equal the marginal gross profit after marginal production cost only. (The numerator of the righthand side of (12.8.2) is the price of advertising ($1) and the denominator is marginal sales effecitiveness, $\delta x_i/\delta A_i$, so the fraction is the marginal policy cost of advertising.) The lefthand sides of these equations are price minus marginal cost in the usual sense of production cost, or $(p_i - MC_i)$. Now divide both sides of both equations by p_i to obtain:

$$1 \quad \frac{p_i - MC_i}{p_i} = \frac{1}{\varepsilon_p} \qquad (12.9)$$

$$2 \quad \frac{p_i - MC_i}{p_i} = \frac{1}{\dfrac{\delta x_i}{\delta A_i p_i}} = \frac{\dfrac{A_i}{x_i}}{\varepsilon_A p_i} = \frac{ASR}{\varepsilon_A},$$

where ε_p is the price elasticity of demand, ε_A is the elasticity of output with respect to advertising expenditure and ASR is the advertising sales ratio. These are the Dorfman–Steiner conditions (1954), as treated by Cable

(1972) and Schmalensee (1972). Condition (12.9.2) is especially convenient for our purposes in that it permits us to derive the optimal *ASR* in the profit-maximization solution to compare it for each firm with the 3 percent value we assumed in Model 1.

a A Base Case

The solution to the model for our five firms is given as Base Case 2 in Table 12.7, and, for comparative purposes, Base Case 1 (Model 1's base case) is reproduced.

A glance at Table 12.7 indicates that when informational advertising is moved to an optimization regime momentous changes in firms' behaviors and welfares occur. To disentangle the causal flows, consider the net flows in sales resulting from advertising budgets in Model 2's Base Case. These are recorded in Table 12.8, along with the like values for Model 1's Base Case reproduced in parentheses from Table 12.4.

Row 4 of the table reveals that the major energizing force behind the changes is the freeing of brand 4 to exploit the advertising effectiveness that was severely constrained by the rules of Model 1 and dimly foreseen in the parenthesized data in the row taken from Model 1. Those data show that it is the only firm in the earlier base case to run a positive advertising account sales surplus with every rival: yet by similar criteria, brand 3 might have been expected to prosper as well, which we shall see is not borne out. Brand 4 inflicts massive account deficits on each of its rivals, and views its overall surplus rise over 16 times as its advertising expenditure rises over 700 percent. The shift rightward of its demand function permits it to raise prices and expand output, and, most importantly, to enjoy a profit rise of 260 percent. It emerges as the "dominant firm" in the product group, severely punishing its neighboring brands, brands 1 and 2, impacting high-quality, low-cost brand 3 only slightly less severely, and inflicting a sales deficit even on brand 5, somewhat lessening its image in Model 1 as enjoying isolation from the advertising expenditures of its rivals.

Brand 4 sells 28.5 percent of the group's output, rising from 16.7 percent in Base Case 2, and it captures 20.7 percent of industry profits, up from 5.7 percent in Base Case 2. It is the only brand to enjoy a rise in profits in Base Case 2. In part because of its high costs its price becomes the highest in the group despite its relatively low quality. It is an advertising phenomenon, in a sense overcoming its initial inferiority in consumers' eyes by informing those consumers of its existence and its quality rather than altering its cognitive distance from its rivals.

Hardest hit by the new advertising regime is brand 2, which sees its advertising sales deficit with brand 4 rise from 4 to 202 and that with brand 5 from 27 to 176. Mercifully, its deficit with firm 1, which was featured in the Base

Table 12.7 Base case solution comparisons: Model 1 versus Model 2

Parameter	*Base Case 1*	*Base Case 2*	*Percentage Change*
p_1	$29.78	$25.31	–15.01%
x_1	447	456	2.01
C_1	$1,994.41	$2,015.20	1.04
π_1	$10,997.65	$9,265.81	–15.75
A_1	$326.23	$251.47	–22.92
ε_{A1}	0.0327	0.0241	–26.30
ASR_1	0.03	0.0218	–27.32
p_2	$15.74	$8.39	–46.70
x_2	426	139	–67.37
C_2	$2,090.05	$1,218.97	–41.68
π_2	$4,339.35	–$152.19	–103.51
A_2	$281.10	$101.17	–64.01
ε_{A2}	0.0372	0.1353	363.68
ASR_2	0.03	0.0866	288.75
p_3	$22.92	$21.17	–7.64
x_3	640	517	–19.22
C_3	$4,684.48	$3,971.33	–15.22
π_3	$9,532.33	$5,719.75	–40.00
A_3	$444.66	$1,249.60	281.02
ε_{A3}	0.1279	0.1565	22.36
ASR_3	0.03	0.1142	280.72
p_4	$24.99	$31.85	27.45
x_4	372	591	58.87
C_4	$7,465.65	$10,986.21	47.16
π_4	$1,567.31	$5,648.59	260.40
A_4	$262.45	$2,181.17	731.08
ε_{A4}	0.0841	0.2347	179.03
ASR_4	0.03	0.1159	286.40
p_5	$22.69	$24.09	6.17
x_5	341	368	7.92
C_5	$6,315.98	$6,742.72	6.76
π_5	$1,178.86	$724.71	–38.42
A_5	$236.51	$1,400.07	491.97
ε_{A5}	0.0958	0.4475	367.14
ASR_5	0.03	0.1579	426.29

Table 12.8 Net flows of benefits from informational advertising among firms, Model 2 base case

Brand:\ From brand:	*1*	*2*	*3*	*4*	*5*	*Total*
1	–	+146.33 (+143.82)	+14.91 (+0.01)	–160.2 (–5.35)	+26.71 (–3.18)	+27.79 (+135.30)
2	–146.33 (–143.82)	–	–73.93 (–24.95)	–202.03 (–3.96)	–175.53 (–26.52)	–597.82 (–199.26)
3	–14.91 (–0.01)	+73.93 (+24.95)	– –	–80.24 (–9.12)	–95.07 (+26.81)	–116.29 (+42.64)
4	+160.16 (+5.35)	+202.03 (+3.96)	+80.24 (+9.12)	–	+121.83 (+16.39)	+564.26 (+34.82)
5	–26.71 (+3.18)	+175.53 (+26.52)	+95.07 (–26.81)	–121.83 (–16.39)	–	+122.06 (–13.50)

Case 1 analysis, remains about steady, but its overall deficit rises from 200 to 600 sales units. The firm's profits become negative, although revenues cover variable costs, price is almost halved, and sales fall 67 percent. The firm's advertising becomes wholly defensive and is reduced by 64 percent from the Base Case 2 level, even though its *ASR* rises to about 9 percent. From a comfortable median profit and quality position the firm becomes a potential long-run casualty from effective informational advertising from all firms on both sides of the product space.

Brand 1 – another of brand 4's major victims – fares much better than brand 2 because its surplus with brand 2 remains about the same and it *benefits* from the huge increase in the advertising budgets of brands 3 and 5. Their advertising impact on brand 1 reaches the saturation point and turns negative, actually harming their sales to brand 1. As a result brand 1's surplus falls to only 21 percent of its Base Case 1 level, but its profits hold up to about 85 percent of that case's amount and its sales actually rise a bit because of its price reduction. Advertising budget falls by 23 percent, but a portion of this is permitted by the reduction in the necessity of combating the former impacts of brands 3 and 5. Brand 1 is a victim of brand 4's effectiveness, but escapes major damage by virtue of its retention of a sales surplus with brand 2 on advertising account as well as the negative effectiveness of the heavy advertising of its other rivals.

Brands 3 and 5 – the highest-quality products in the group – are both losers with the new advertising regime, suffering profit losses of about 40 percent. Both are forced to increase their informational advertising – most particularly, brand 5. Their price–output solutions do differ, however, with brand 3 lowering both variables and brand 5 raising them. A look at Table 12.8 explains the difference: brand 5 suffers a rise in its deficit with the aggressive brand 4, but its large advertising increase converts brand 3's Base Case 1 surplus into a substantial deficit. Overall, brand 3's advertising account sales surplus in Base Case 1 becomes a substantial deficit in Base Case 2, forcing the firm to increase advertising budget (which does increase its surplus with brand 2) and reduce its price to stem profit losses.

Firm 5 suffers even more grievously from brand 4's competition on advertising account, but recoups the loss by positive gains from brands 2 and 3, so that its previous deficit on advertising sales account is converted to a surplus. However, despite the rise in price and output and therefore revenue, the 500 percent increase in advertising and its high cost structure reduce profit levels. Hence, brand 4's advertising foray directly and indirectly via brands 2 and 3 enhance brand 5's advertising sales account, but only at the cost of defensive advertising expenditures that reduce the isolation from rivals' policies enjoyed in Base Case 1.

Institutional restrictions on informational advertising budgets, in the form of common *ASR*s, serve in our example to constrain brand 4' s emergence as a dominant firm, and therefore is a form of tacit collusion or tacit cooperation among its rivals to enforce a policy which benefits them all. But what of the public policy implications of both advertising regimes, in the way of consumers', producer and social surpluses? Table 12.9 displays these magnitudes from Base Cases 0, 1 and 2, with consumers' surpluses computed from (10.15).

Informational advertising does increase consumers' and producers' surplus when a relatively low *ASR* is set uniformly on all firms; in our example, this prevented firm 4 from exercising a large enhancement in market power by virtue of its effectiveness in the art. Thus, when profit motivation is permitted to determine advertising budgets, consumers' and producers' surplus both decline: it is not in the interest of the industry as a whole to permit informational advertising restrained only by profits. All firms but firm 4 would

Table 12.9 Consumers', producers', and social surplus for base Cases 0, 1, and 2

Variable	*Base Case 0*	*Base Case 1*	*Base Case 2*
Consumers' surplus	\$16,318.88	\$17,064.14	\$15,783.50
Producers' surplus	27,272.42	29,264.23	21,206.67
Social surplus	43,591.30	46,328.37	36,990.16

welcome governmental restrictions on such endeavor. Consumers' surplus, of course, varies with industry output, and informational advertising in Base Case 1 increases total sales by about 100 units over Base Case 0 levels; but the market power derived in Base Case 2 reduces total sales by about 50 units below Base Case 0 levels, with attendant decline in consumers' surplus.

Table 12.10 gives a rather graphic view of the changes in market power among the brands by comparing market shares and voice, as we did in Table 12.5 for Base Case 1. In the latter case market shares and voices were kept close to parity by virtue of the rule determining advertising expenditure. In Base Case 2, however, the discrepancies between market shares and voice become marked. Firm 4, of course, spends 42 percent of the industry advertising budget to obtain 29 percent of its sales, rising from values of about 17 percent for both variables in Base Case 2. Brand 3 dips slightly in both values from Base Case 2 but maintains proportionality in both industry shares. Brand 5 is forced to spend 27 percent of the industry's advertising expenditures to increase its sales just slightly. Even though brand 1's voice dips from 21 percent to 5 percent, its market share declines only by about 2 percentage points. But firm 2 is savaged, reduced from shares in both categories of about 19 percent to only 7 percent of market share and 2 percent of advertising budget. With its negative profits it lies at the mercy of firm 4, which, by increasing voice beyond its short-run profit maximization point, could eliminate brand 2 from the product group.

Introducing a profit-maximization regime in our industry example in lieu of a constrained competition fixed *ASR* results in a destabilizing realignment of the group in which 4 of the 5 firms suffer. Nonprice competition in this instance is not a competitive outlet that channels rivalry into more peaceful precincts. It will be interesting to see if rivalrous consonance – to be introduced in Model 4 – restrains these disruptive competitive forms significantly.

Table 12.10 A comparison of advertising voice and market share in Base Case 2

Brand	*Market Share*	*Voice*
1	22.0%	4.9%
2	6.7	2.0
3	25.0	24.1
4	28.5	42.0
5	17.8	27.0
Totals	100.0%	100.0%

b Some Parametric Ranging with Model 2

Conditions (12.8) permit us to form expectations of *ceteris paribus* reactions by a firm to changes in parameters before taking into account the complex interdependence among the firms. For example, suppose a parameter change results in a reduction in the sales on firm i's informational advertising account, α_i assumed for the moment to be constant because k is constant. The impact effect is to reduce the righthand side of (12.8.1), since α_i is a positive constant. Also, the reduction in x_i reduces marginal production cost on the lefthand side of the expression. Price p_i must fall to reequate both sides of the equation, which means that marginal gross profit (the lefthand side) falls, which stimulates a bit of rise in x_i. This lower marginal gross profit now must impact the righthand side of (12.8.2) by forcing it to fall. The denominator of the righthand side is the marginal sales impact of informational advertising, so that it must rise: that is, the marginal policy cost of advertising must equal the lower marginal policy cost of price reduction. With diminishing marginal returns to advertising expenditure this must reduce A_i (k assumed constant) which should reduce x_i even more, reacting back upon (12.8.1). Interaction of price reductions and advertising reductions must continue until both conditions are met once more with lower price, lower output and lower advertising budget. But then, of course, the flows of causation on firm i from the similar adjustments of its rivals impose further adjustments whose complexity force us into simulative modeling for insights. We are led to expect, however, that parameter changes affecting advertising accounts negatively (positively) will lead to declines (advances) in p_i and x_i: the price and advertising policies should be positively correlated unless external interdependence shocks are powerful and disruptive.

In this section we will gauge, among other factors, the viability of these expectations with two sets of parameter changes: changes in k, the decay parameter, to 0.58 and 0.20 from the base case value of 0.29, and changes in all r_{ij} and t_{ij} parameters to 0.5 and 1.1 times their base case values. The solutions to these four parameter shocks to the base case solution, along with Base Case 2 values, are displayed in Table 12.11.

With a rise in k the impacts of advertising budgets on rivals will be diminished compared with those experienced with $k = 0.29$, so that firms that suffer from rivals' advertising budgets, especially those that are more rather than less distant, will obtain a lessening of the deficits on advertising accounts with those rivals. From our analysis above, we should expect brands that are especially benefitted from such a change to reveal higher prices, outputs, and advertising expenditures. On the other hand, firms that are hurt by increases in the decay factor should reveal lower values for these variables. In the first camp we find brands 2 and 5, and in the second brand 4. Brand 1 raises price but lowers output and advertising, while brand 3 raises price and advertising budget but suffers lower output.

Table 12.11 Parametric ranging with Model 2

Variable	*Base Case 2*	*k = 0.58*	*k = 0.20*	$0.5r_{ij}$, *.5tij*	$1.1r_{ij}, 1.1t_{ij}$
p_1	$25.31	$26.45	$24.88	$24.97	$25.43
x_1	456	401	498	449	458
A_1	$251.47	$235.83	$251.73	$242.18	$252.33
π_1	$9,265.81	$8,487.82	$10,011.82	$8,969.00	$9,371.72
p_2	$8.39	$14.19	$5.99	$15.35	$6.89
x_2	139	234	85	319	101
A_2	$101.17	$130.27	$35.26	$119.69	$63.87
π_2	–$152.19	$1,687.97	–$582.77	$3,019.02	–$472.47
p_3	$21.17	$22.64	$20.39	$22.98	$20.84
x_3	517	486	531	575	506
A_3	$1,249.60	$1,900.32	$1,035.61	$971.33	$1,274.69
π_3	$5,719.75	$5,302.64	$5,734.98	$7,928.43	$5,365.42
p_4	$31.85	$30.74	$31.83	$27.36	$32.77
x_4	591	445	653	423	625
A_4	$2,181.17	$1,688.50	$2,206.53	$1,395.17	$2.242.84
π_4	$5,648.59	$3,359.05	$6,581.34	$1,892.48	$6,696.68
p_5	$24.09	$26.13	$23.29	$23.26	$24.24
x_5	368	380	364	333	375
A_5	$1,400.07	$2,189.82	$1,171.76	$778.25	$1,454.95
π_5	$724.71	$818.77	$631.39	$767.24	$785.41

Table 12.12 sheds light on these results by tracing the sales flows on advertising account among firms in this first displacement solution and by comparing them with the parenthesized flows in Base Case 2. Brand 2 is clearly the major beneficiary reducing its deficits with all brands substantially and its overall sales-from-advertising deficit by 50 percent. Price, sales and advertising rise, as expected, and it emerges from a loss to a respectable profit. Brand 5's solution also can be explained straightforwardly. It enjoys a 32 percent increase in its overall sales surplus. Price, output, and profits rise modestly, but its advertising budget jumps by 56 percent and its *ASR* to 42 percent from 16 percent.

On the basis of the analysis above based on (12.8) one might not expect that the small rise in x_5 would set in motion adjustments in (12.8.2) leading to such a large increase in advertising budget. But the marginal effectiveness of

Table 12.12 Net flows of benefits from informational advertising among firms, Model 2 parameter displacements: k = 0.58 and 0.20

	1k = 0.58					
Brand:\ From brand:	*1*	*2*	*3*	*4*	*5*	*Total*
1	–	+34.39 (+146.33)	+4.00 (+14.91)	–55.08 (–160.2)	+10.62 (+26.71)	–6.07 (+27.79)
2	–34.39 (–146.33)	–	–41.43 (–73.93)	–92.22 (–202.03)	–133.73 (–175.53)	–301.77 (–597.82)
3	–4.00 (–14.91)	+41.43 (+73.93)	–	–38.16 (–80.24)	–125.53 (–95.07)	–126.26 (–116.29)
4	+55.08 (+160.16)	+92.22 (+202.03)	+38.16 (+80.24)	–	+88.04 (+121.83)	+273.50 (+564.26)
5	–10.62 (–26.71)	+133.73 (+175.53)	+125.53 (+95.07)	–88.04 (–121.83)	–	+160.60 (+122.06)

	2k = 0.20					
Brand:\ From brand:	*1*	*2*	*3*	*4*	*5*	*Total*
1	–	+229.09 (+146.33)	+18.84 (+14.91)	–211.56 (–160.2)	+30.59 (+26.71)	+66.96 (+27.79)
2	–229.09 (–146.33)	–	–87.12 (–73.93)	–252.37 (–202.03)	–187.05 (–175.53)	–755.63 (–597.82)
3	–18.84 (–14.91)	+87.12 (+73.93)	–	–97.37 (–80.24)	–86.55 (–95.07)	–115.64 (–116.29)
4	+211.56 (+160.16)	+252.37 (+202.03)	+97.37 (+80.24)	–	+133.61 (+121.83)	+694.91 (+564.26)
5	–30.59 (–26.71)	+187.05 (+175.53)	+86.55 (+95.07)	–133.61 (–121.83)	–	+109.40 (+122.06)

informational advertising (the denominator of (12.8.2)) and therefore the marginal policy cost of advertising is greatly affected by the steep rise in k. This is displayed graphically in Figure 12.2, which displays the configurations of marginal advertising policy costs for brand 5 as functions of advertising

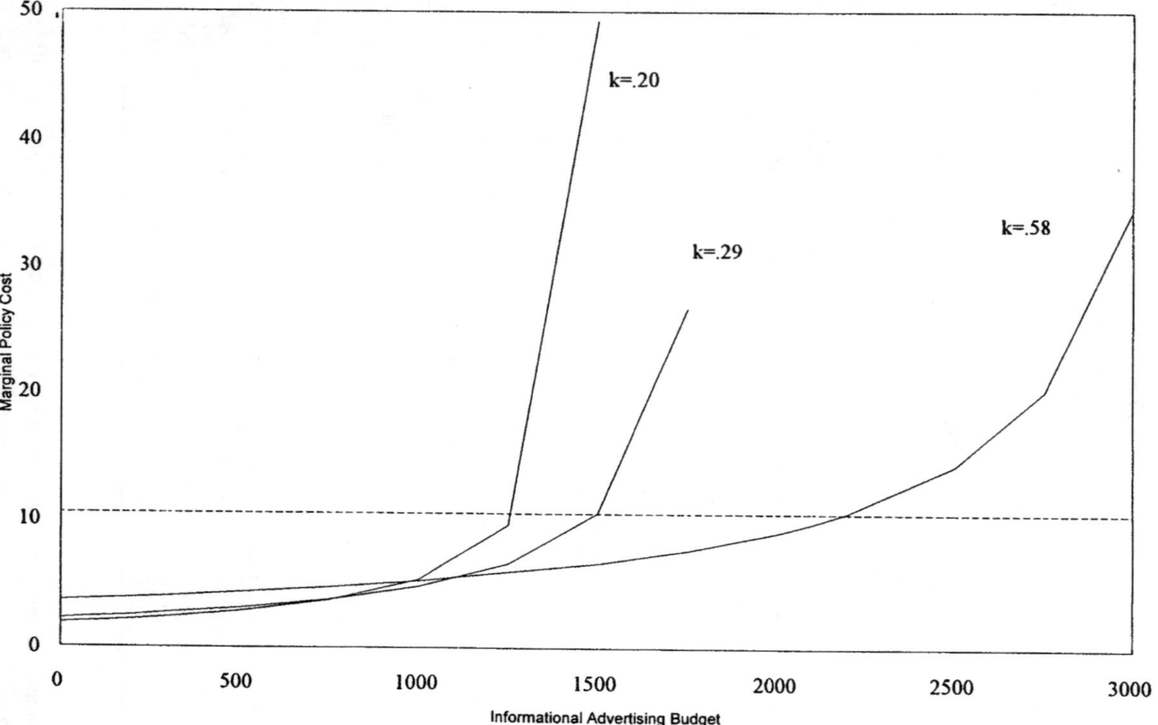

Figure 12.2a Marginal advertising policy costs: marginal policy cost – brand 2

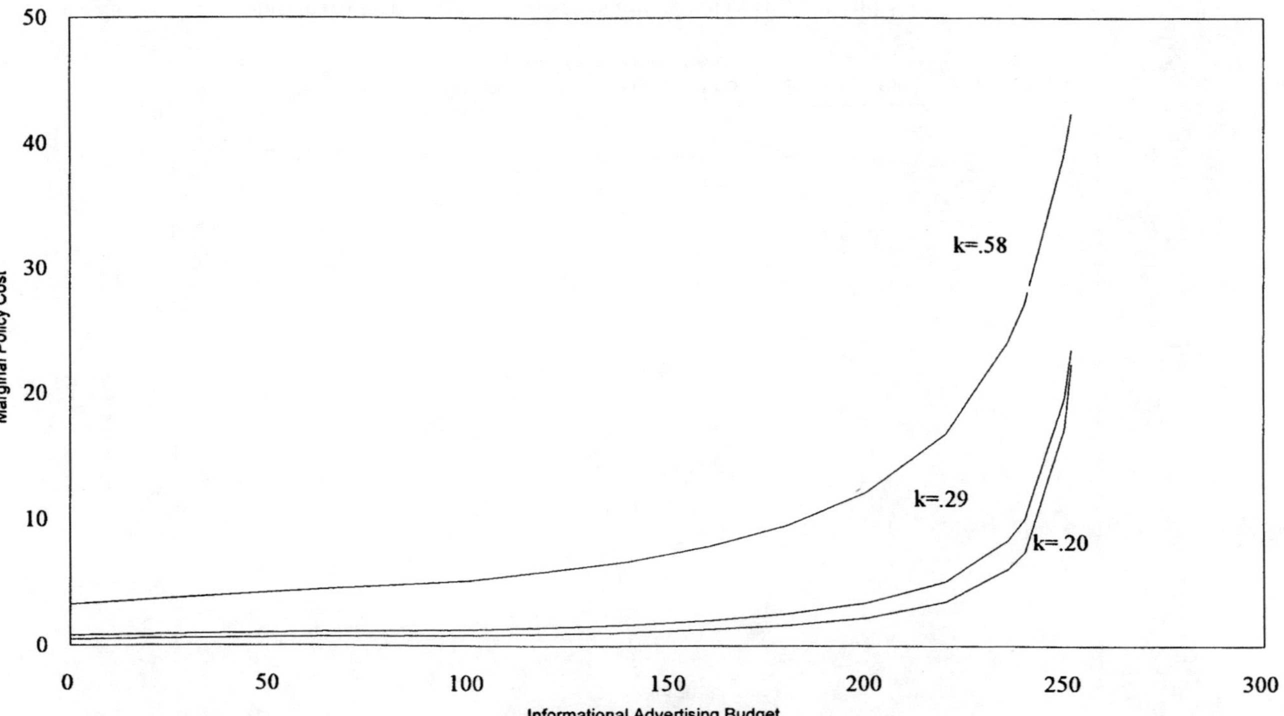

Figure 12.2b Marginal advertising policy costs: marginal policy cost – brand 1

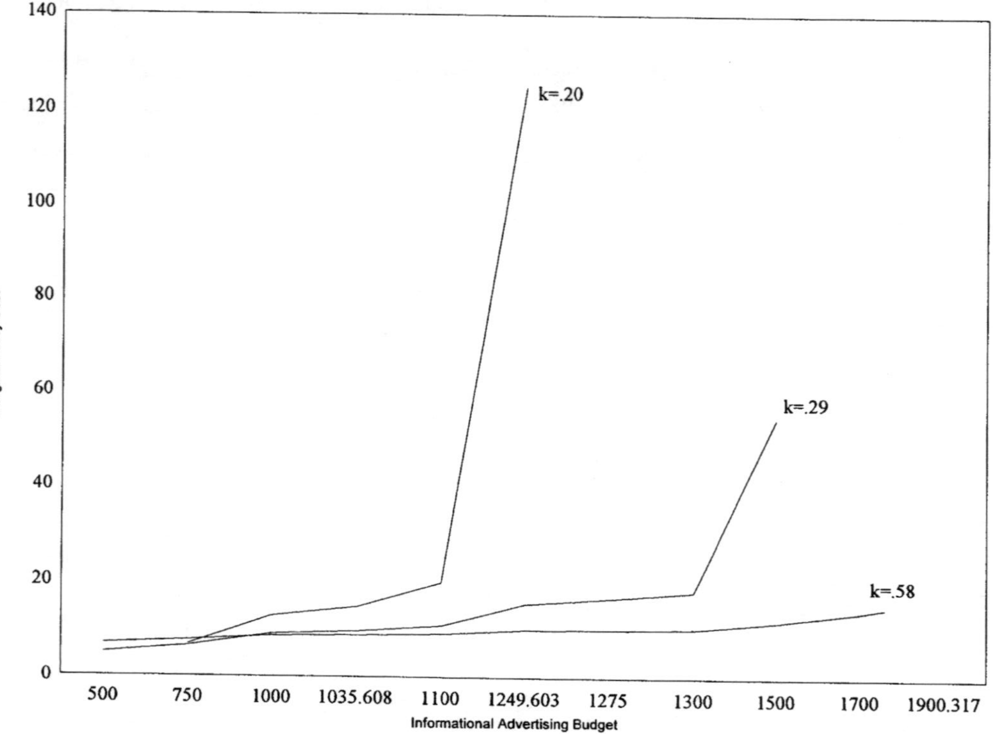

Figure 12.2c Marginal advertising policy costs: marginal policy cost – brand 3

budgets and the three relevant k values in our displacement analysis. The horizontal line is the solution value of marginal gross profit for brand 5 when $k = 0.58$ that must be equated to marginal price and advertising policy costs. Note how higher values of k yield much lower marginal advertising costs in the moderate and upper domains of advertising budgets. Were the value of marginal gross profit to be equated to marginal advertising policy cost with $k = 0.20$ or 0.29, advertising budgets would be much lower than with $k = 0.58$: for the latter value the budget must rise to \$2,190 to achieved the necessary equality in (12.8.2).

Brand 4 suffers greatly from its lessened advertising effectiveness and its solution values can be explained as the inverses of the experiences of brand 5. A 52 percent drop in surplus on advertising account is counteracted sales-wise by the drop in p_4. The price reduction contrasts with price rises for all of its rivals, and with this improvement in its price differentials cushions the sales drop. The large reduction in advertising budget can be explained by the substantial fall in sales and the slow fall in marginal advertising policy costs illustrated for brand 5 in Figure 12.2a and applicable to brand 4 as well.

Brands 1 and 3 are the mavericks in the solution results. Brand 1 sees its small surplus in the base case all but disappear and its sales fall considerably, and reacts as expected by lowering its advertising budget, yet raises its price. It suffers only a moderate loss in profit. In the introductiory discussion of the adjustment process illuminated by (12.8) we assumed that α_i was constant. But when k is changed this will not be true, because the b_{ij} coefficients in its definition will be modified by different decay factors. With a rise in k the firms' α_is will fall. When the proportionate fall in α_i is greater than that of x_i the marginal policy cost of price policy will rise, requiring a rise in p_i and a consequent fall in the firm's marginal advertising effectiveness The important factor in this solution is that the optimal marginal policy costs are the highest of all the rivals because although x_1 falls by 12 percent α_1 falls by 16 percent as the price impacts of b_{41} and b_{51} are lessened by the rise in k. The optimal gross marginal profit from \$22.85 in the base case to \$24.05 in the present case reflects the rise in price that is necessary to reequate both sides of (10.8.1).

This rise in gross marginal profit requires also that marginal advertising policy cost must rise through a decrease in the marginal effectiveness of advertising. But this may be brought about by either a rise or a fall in A_i depending on the strength of the change in the decay factors. If the rise in k enhances the marginal effectiveness of advertising greatly the righthand side of (12.8.2) may actually have to be adjusted downward by a reduction in A_i rather than an increase that would be necessary were k held constant. When k rises from the base case level of 0.29 to 0.58, the optimal marginal policy cost increases from \$22.85 to \$24.05. This would ordinarily be brought about by an increase in advertising budget with consequent rise in its marginal policy cost. What accounts for this perverse behavior?

Figure 12.2b yields the clues that provide the answer. Note that the marginal advertising cost curves are in descending sequence of their k values when compared with those of Figure 12.2a: such costs rise as the decay factor diminishes. The reason for this is that we have permitted marginal advertising effectiveness to become negative rather than give it a lower bound of zero. Since the firm has no ability to alter its advertising budget rival-by-rival, and because we assume that a firm's informational advertising may be oversaturating some rivals' consumers and causing them to reduce purchases of its product, requilibration to the higher marginal policy cost may occur by decreasing advertising budget, lowering marginal effectiveness and raising marginal advertising cost. This is what is happening in the case of brand 1: because of the large expenditures on advertising necessary to exploit brand 1's huge advantage with respect to brand 2, the marginal effectiveness of brands 3, 4, and 5 become importantly negative as advertising expenditures approach \$200, reducing overall effectiveness and raising marginal advertising advertising cost.

Brand 3 is a somewhat simpler case. Its output falls 6 percent but α_3 falls 14 percent, so marginal price rises, marginal policy cost rises, and advertising budget rises to increase marginal advertising policy cost. Figure 12.2c reveals that this cost rises so modestly in the higher ranges of advertising due to saturation with respect to brands 1 and 4 and the decline in marginal effectiveness relative to brands 2 and 5, that the budget must increase substantially to reequilibrate (12.8).

The comparative statics results of a reduction in k to 0.20 can be interpreted rather straightforwardly by inverting the analysis of its rise, and we shall save space by omitting further discussion of these displacements.

Parametric changes in the r_{ij} and t_{ij} values affect advertising effectiveness directly, so the analysis of their effects is best begun by considering their impacts on marginal advertising policy cost in (12.8.2). Initially we will analyze adjustments in *ceteris paribus* fashion, ignoring reactions to external factors. These external factors influence firms' decisions via their β variables, which transmit price change impacts of rivals, and Y variables, which carry the changes in demand springing from rivals' advertising budget changes.

Halving all advertising effectiveness parameters raises marginal advertising costs as a function of advertising budget above the base case function and raising them by 10 percent shifts the function below its base case counterpart. (See Figure 12.2 for examples of such marginal policy cost functions used in the analysis of changes in k.) We shall start with the marginal policy cost value in the base case that is common to marginal price and advertising policies in its Nash equilibrium.

Suppose, now, all advertising effectiveness parameters are halved, reducing firm *i*'s marginal advertising effectiveness and raising its marginal advertising costs for all values of the advertising budget. Suppose, also, that the firm's advertising budget in the new regime is adjusted to equal its common base case policy cost derived from the conditions in (12.8). This requires a reduction in A_i, the advertising budget, which in turn must lower sales, x_i. Because the α_i terms are unaffected by the parameter changes, marginal price policy must fall, which in turn reduces the advertising budget, and so a sequence of moves occurs until a new equilibrium is established. At that new equilibrium, prices, outputs and advertising purchases will be lower than in the base case optimum, everything else being equal. Symmetrically, when the *r*- and *t*-parameters are raised by 10 percent, A_i, x_i, and p_i will rise to a higher common marginal policy cost for the firm. The results of these parameter changes are listed in Table 12.13.

These expectations are fully met by brands 1, 4, and 5: reactions to external changes are not strong enough to override the internal adjustments. In the case of brand 2 the movements of A_2, x_2, and p_2 are exactly the reverse of *ceteris paribus* expectations, rising with a halving of parameters and falling with an increase in them. Brand 2 is the major victim of informational advertising. Despite its rather large price changes, brand 2's influences from changes in β_2 are quite small (–4.7 percent reduction in sales and a 0.7 percent increase for the parameter-reduction and parameter-increase respectively). It is rather changes in Ψ_2 which explain the divergences. A halving of advertising effectiveness across the board reduces that of brand 2's formidable rivals so that its deficit sales balance falls from a base case value of –599 to –226. This external effect, therefore, boosts x_2 significantly and with it A_2 and p_2, accounting for the "perverse" movements. The reverse effect is registered when the parameters are increased, the deficit rising from –599 to –678, reducing the three variables.

Brand 3's experience is not so straightforwardly explained. β_3 changes in the two parameter displacements from a base case value of 242 units of sales to 250 and 240 for the parameter decrease and increase respectively. Price differentials play a small role in the result. Once again the Ψ-value does most of the explanation of the perverse movements in p_3 and x_3, with its fall from a base case value of –116 to –6 for the parameter reductions and rise to –136 for the parameter increases. However, advertising budgets do move in the *ceteris paribus* directions, falling with the parameter decreases and rising with their increase. These results are explained by the steep rates of rise in the marginal advertising policy cost functions. Despite a rise in common marginal policy cost to $17.17 from a base case value of $15.44 when parameters are decreased, this was not sufficient to attain or surpass the base case budget level. A similar result holds in the opposite sense when parameters are increased.

Table 12.13 Net flows of benefits from informational advertising among firms, Model 2 parameter displacements: all r_{ij} and t_{ij} coefficients halved and increased by 10 percent

Brand:\ From brand:	*1 Coefficients halved*					
	1	*2*	*3*	*4*	*5*	*Total*
1	–	+73.31 (+146.33)	+3.87 (+14.91)	–55.24 (–160.2)	+1.96 (+26.71)	+23.90 (+27.79)
2	–73.31 (–146.33)	–	–29.42 (–73.93)	–70.81 (–202.03)	–51.97 (–175.53)	–225.51 (–597.82)
3	–3.87 (–14.91)	+29.42 (+73.93)	–	–28.78 (–80.24)	–3.06 (–95.07)	–6.29 (–116.29)
4	+55.24 (+160.16)	+70.81 (+202.03)	+28.78 (+80.24)	–	+38.22 (+121.83)	+193.05 (+564.26)
5	–1.96 (–26.71)	+51.97 (+175.53)	+3.06 (+95.07)	–38.22 (–121.83)	–	+14.85 (+122.06)

Brand:\ From brand:	*2 Coefficients Increased by 10 Percent*					
	1	*2*	*3*	*4*	*5*	*Total*
1	–	+160.52 (+146.33)	+17.23 (+14.91)	–179.73 (–160.2)	+32.50 (+26.71)	+30.53 (+27.79)
2	–160.52 (–146.33)	–	–84.60 (–73.93)	–230.79 (–202.03)	–201.64 (–175.53)	–677.55 (–597.82)
3	–17.23 (–14.91)	+84.60 (+73.93)	–	–90.23 (–80.24)	–112.98 (–95.07)	–135.84 (–116.29)
4	+179.73 (+160.16)	+230.79 (+202.03)	+90.23 (+80.24)	–	+139.33 (+121.83)	+640.07 (+564.26)
5	–32.50 (–26.71)	+201.64 (+175.53)	+112.98 (+95.07)	–139.33 (–121.83)	–	+142.79 (+122.06)

3 MODEL 3 – INFORMATIONAL AND COGNITIVE POSITIONING ADVERTISING WITH NO TACIT COLLUSION

A second form of advertising is that whose purpose is to persuade consumers by means beyond the mere provision of information of the comparative desirability of the firm's brand relative to rivals'. This is done by enhancing the distinctiveness of the brand; exaggerating the product's quality by trying to move the product farther upscale in the product space than consumers initially placed it; downplaying the quality of a competing brand with which its product is in intense competition; decreasing the decay factor in its advertising effectiveness by more attractive or memorable media presentations; and so forth. We shall introduce all of these advertising functions into the demand functions of the brands by viewing them as attempts to relocate the brands in "virtual" product space. That is, we view the consumers' initial perceptions of the brands' desirabilities as formulated in the absence of informational and persuasive advertising and therefore as reflecting objective qualities more faithfully in the placements in the product space. In Chapter 11 we dealt with firms' contemplated movements in the product space by actual changes in the characteristics of the brands – flavor, durability, and so forth. Now we hold those characteristics constant at their initial levels and study firms' attempts through the use of advertising only to move those brands away from the initial perceptions.

The distinction between informational and persuasive advertising is not sharply defined except for their prototypes, but it is nonetheless a useful one. Informational advertising accepts the brand's current position in product space and attains effectiveness by publicizing its existence and qualities. In so doing it must cope with the interproduct brand distances and the cognitive decay factor, k. The targets of a firm's persuasive advertising may well be chosen on the basis of the success or failure reflected in its informational sales balances. The advertising achieves its effectiveness by tailoring a k to enhance its distance from brands making inroads in its sales by their informational advertising or decreasing its cognitive distance from those with whom that advertising is achieving success. To this end we specify:

$$k^* = k + u_i D_i - v_i D_i^2, \tag{12.10}$$

where k^* is the revised cognitive distance factor; u_i is the linear effectiveness factor of brand i's targeted advertising dollar in altering cognitive distance; v_i is the quadratic term in the distance expression; and D_i is the size of the persuasive advertising budget. When $u_i > 0$, k^* is increased above k for $D_i > 0$ and decreased for $u_i < 0$.

Our manner of incorporating persuasive advertising in Model 3 is indeed to identify its effectiveness in moving the firm in virtual product space relative to its rivals. Firm i shapes its persuasive advertising to get closer to those brands to which it is a successful competitor and to distance itself in virtual product space from those brands which make inroads into its net sales. Because D_i is the total budget applied to execute all of these diverse programs, the allocation of D_i among them is a compromise determined by overall profit maximization.

We may then respecify the demand functions of the firms as

$$x_i = a_i - \alpha_i^* p_i + \beta_i^* + Y_i^*, \quad (12.11)$$

where:

$$1 \quad \alpha_i^* = b_{ii} + \Sigma_{j\neq 1} b_{ij} e^{-k_i^* s_{ij}} \quad (12.12)$$

$$2 \quad \beta_i^* = \Sigma_{j\neq 1} b_{ij} p_j e^{-k_i^* s_{ij}}$$

$$3 \quad Y_i^* = A_i \Sigma_{j\neq 1}(r_{ij} - t_{ij}A_i)e^{-k_i^* s_{ij}} - \Sigma_j A_j(r_{ji} - t_{ji}A_j)e^{-k_i^* s_{ji}}.$$

Maximizing firm i's profits

$$1 \quad \pi_i = p_i x_i - C_i - A_i - D_i, \quad (12.13)$$

with respect to p_i, A_i and D_i yields the following first-order conditions:

$$1 \quad p_i = \frac{a_i + \beta_i^* + Y_i^* + \alpha_i^*(m_i + 2n_i x_i)}{2\alpha_i^*} \quad (12.14)$$

$$2 \quad A_i = \frac{(p_i - m_i - 2n_i x_i)\Sigma_j r_{ij} e^{-k_i^* s_{ij}}) - 1}{2(p_i - m_i - 2n_i x_i(\Sigma_j t_{ij} e^{-k_i^* s_{ij}})}$$

$$3 \quad p_i - m_i - 2n_i x_i = \frac{1}{\Sigma_j(b_{ij}[(p_i - p_j) - A_i(r_{ij} - t_{ij}A_i)](u_i - 2v_i D_i)s_{ij} e^{-k_i^* s_{ij}}},$$

where (12.14.3) is in the implicit form which permitted its solution by numerical search and iteration. These conditions may be cast in the same form as (12.8), which (as in (12.14.3)) reveal them to equate the marginal policy cost of each variable to the marginal production cost of the good:

$$1 \quad (p_i - m_i - 2n_i x_i) = \frac{x_i}{\alpha_i^*} \quad (12.15)$$

$$2 \quad (p_i - m_i - 2n_i x_i) = \frac{1}{\Sigma_j(r_{ij} - 2t_{ij}A_i)e^{-k_i^* s_{ij}}}$$

$$3 \quad (p_i - m_i - 2n_i x_i) = \frac{1}{\Sigma_j (b_{ij}[(p_i - p_j) - A_i(r_{ij} - t_{ij}A_i)](u_i - 2v_i D_i)s_{ij}e^{-k_i^* s_{ij}}}.$$

As shown throughout this book, these are useful forms with which to reveal the *ceteris paribus* reactions of the righthand sides of the equations to changes in the common lefthand side, and we will employ it below to gain insights into the movements of newly introduced variables k_i^* and D_i. However, because of the variability of the k^*-factors with respect to persuasive advertising, the interdependence among the three conditions is more complicated and makes such interpretations more difficult. Because of this it becomes extremely difficult to trace through *mutatis mutandis* changes in the system. Suppose, for example, the lefthand sides of the equations in (12.15) were lowered from a Nash equilibrium value. Changes in the righthand sides of (12.15.2 and 12.15.3) will depend in the first instance on whether u_i is positive or negative. Assume it is positive. Then the marginal policy cost (*MPC*) of A_i must fall, implying that its marginal sales effectiveness (*ME*) must rise, which in turn requires that A_i must fall. That may be expected to lower x_i and have no effect on α_i^*, moving the *MPC* of price policy toward equilibration with the righthand side. The *MPC* of D_i must also fall, which requires the *ME* of D_i to rise. A fall in D_i will lower the exponential term in the denominator of the lefthand side of (12.15.3) and lower the term that precedes it, leaving us with ambiguous effects on the *ME* and *MPC*. The effects on x_i and α_i^* are similarly indeterminate. Bringing in the interrelationships with other equations leaves us with a perfect tangle of parameter-specific results which can only be approached through simulative theorizing.

a A Base Case

Base Case 3 is constructed by using the parameters of Tables 10.1 and 12.1, with the addition of the D_i effectiveness parameters of Table 12.14. The negative u_i were given to those brands whose balances on informational

Table 12.14 Advertising-relevant Base Case parameters, Model 3

Brand i	u_i	v_I
1	–0.0000001	0.00000001
2	0.000001	0.0000004
3	0.0000001	0.00000008
4	–0.000001	0.0000007
5	0.00002	0.0000003

advertising account as recorded in Table 12.8 were positive, and positive values to those with negative balances in the Total column. The basis for so doing was that those firms with positive balances would seek to move closer in virtual space to their rivals and those negative balances would seek to distance themselves from competing firms.

The solution to Model 3 – Base Case 4 – is reported in Table 12.15 with Base Cases 2 and 3 for comparative purposes. One notable result is that persuasive advertising lowers the profits of all firms below Base Case 2 levels where informational advertising was employed, and, indeed, except for firm 4, below Base Case 1 levels where no advertising was used. The industry as a whole is ill served by such advertising, each firm employing it defensively against its rivals' efforts, which moves the industry into a Prisoners' Dilemma trap. Compared with Base Case 2 results, industry sales do rise, from 2,071 to 2,203 units, and consumers' surplus rises to $16,172.60, but with the fall in industry profits to $17,512.07, social surplus falls to $33,684.67. Persuasive advertising, somewhat paradoxically, does benefit consumers at the expense of firms' profits.

Some insights into the causation of the individual firms' experiences in Base Case 4 can be obtained by computing a measure of their *relative* movement in virtual space. This was done by weighting each $e^{-k_j^* s_{ij}}$ by the ratio of sales gained from brand j by informational and persuasive advertising to the total of such gains over all rivals, treating this scaling as a weighted average distance factor, and solving for that average distance. The interbrand flows on advertising account are recorded in Table 12.16.

Formally, the calculation of the weighted average distances was the following:

$$s_i = \ln\left(\frac{(\Sigma_j (r_{ij} - t_{ij}A_i)A_i e^{-k_i^* s_{ij}})}{\Sigma_j (r_{ij} - t_{ij}A_i)A_i}\right)\frac{1}{-k_i^*}, \qquad (12.16)$$

where s_i is the "average virtual distance from rivals" in the product space ascribable to informational and persuasive advertising. These scalings index the pulls toward competitors with whom the firm has favorable balances on advertising account and the pushes from firms with whom it runs deficits, as they register in the firm's experience with A_i and with k_i^* with adjustments in D_i. These scalings were altered to provide a 0 origin by subtracting the smallest value of the s_i from the other 4, but it should be remembered that the resulting translations represent relative interbrand distances in virtual space only.

The resulting relative changes in virtual space are depicted in Figure 12.3. The numerals at the end of the tick lines are the brands with subscripts referencing Model 2 or Model 3, and the decimal numbers are the positions in the space.

Table 12.15 Base case solution comparisons: Model 1, Model 2, and Model 3

Parameter	*Base Case 1*	*Base Case 2*	*Base Case 3*
p_1	\$29.78	\$25.31	\$25.94
x_1	447	456	495
C_1	\$1,994.41	\$2,015.20	\$4,627.38
π_1	\$10,997.65	\$9,265.81	\$8,217.59
A_1	\$326.23	\$251.47	\$252.01
D_1	–	–	\$2,262.26
k_1	0.29	0.29	0.239
AIS_1	+135	+27.79	+87
p_2	\$15.74	\$8.39	\$7.37
x_2	426	139	124
C_2	\$2,090.05	\$1,218.97	\$1,746.54
π_2	\$4,339.35	–\$152.19	–\$834.12
A_2	\$281.10	\$101.17	\$96.05
D_2	–	–	\$477.96
k_2	0.29	0.29	0.199
AIS_2	–199	–598	–673
p_3	\$22.92	\$21.17	\$20.12
x_3	640	517	587
C_3	\$4,684.48	\$3,971.33	\$4,375.48
π_3	\$9,532.33	\$5,719.75	\$5,031.20
A_3	\$444.66	\$1,249.60	\$808.81
D_3	–	–	\$1,591.87
k_3	0.29	0.29	0.087
AIS_3	+43	–116	–77
p_4	\$24.99	\$31.85	\$31.17
x_4	372	591	566
C_4	\$7,465.65	\$10,986.21	\$12,809.70
π_4	\$1,567.31	\$5,648.59	\$4,847.60
A_4	\$262.45	\$2,181.17	\$2,162.52
D_4	–	–	\$51.97
k_4	0.29	0.29	0.288
AIS_4	+35	+564	+524
p_5	\$22.69	\$24.09	\$22.64
x_5	341	368	431
C_5	\$6,315.98	\$6,742.72	\$9,515.30
π_5	\$1,178.86	\$724.71	\$249.80
A_5	\$236.51	\$1,400.07	\$964.58
D_5	–	–	\$822.10
k_5	0.29	0.29	0.104
AIS_5	–14	+122	+139

Table 12.16 Net flows of benefits from persuasive advertising among firms in Base Case 3, with Base Case 2 flows in parentheses

Brand:\ From brand:	*1*	*2*	*3*	*4*	*5*	*Total*
1	–	+188.94 (+146.33)	+21.36 (+14.91)	–157.19 –(–160.2)	+33.79 (+26.71)	+86.90 (+27.79)
2	–188.94 (–146.33)	–	–95.64 (–73.93)	–200.15 (–202.03)	–187.96 –(–175.53)	–672.69 (–597.82)
3	–21.36 (–14.91)	+95.64 (+73.93)	–	–69.08 (–80.24)	–82.20 –(–95.07)	–77.00 (–116.29)
4	+157.19 (+160.16)	+200.15 (+202.03)	+69.08 (+80.24)	–	+97.30 (+121.83)	+523.72 (+564.26)
5	–33.79 (–26.71)	+187.96 (+175.53)	+82.20 (+95.07)	–97.30 –(–121.83)	–	+139.06 (+122.06)

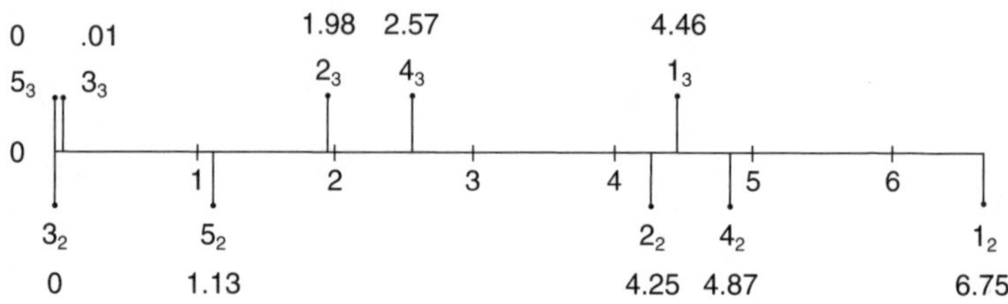

Figure 12.3 Relative locations in virtual product space, Base Cases 2 and 3

Note that in Model 3's base case solution the dispersion in virtual space is lessened when compared with Model 2's base case: persuasive advertising in general has served to lessen the cognitive distance separating the firms. Brand 1's k^* decreases from 0.29 to 0.24 and moves inward on the virtual space interval, but maintains the same distance from brands 4 and 2. Its deficit with brand 4 remains about the same, but it does increase its surplus with brand 2 as the latter decreases its informational advertising and engages in a modest persuasive advertising program. It does reduce its distance to brands 3 and 5, however, by substantial distances, increasing its surpluses with both slightly. But overall, on a net basis, its advertising sales surplus rises by only about 60 units which, even with a higher price, does not recoup the huge persuasive advertising expenditures the move entails. Brand 1's profit suffers seriously. We must conclude that the move is reactive to the attempts of brands 2, 3, and 5 to escape proximity to it.

Brand 2 has deficits with all of its rivals, but is hindered in its attempts to distance itself by the moves of brands 1 and 4 – with which it runs major deficits – to keep very close to it. Movement to the right would lessen the distance to firm 1 as well as to its other major rival, brand 4. These moves also decrease distances from 3 and 5 increasing their surpluses with hapless brand 2. Through no choice of its own its k_2^* declines to 0.20 with increases in three of its deficits and a negligible decline in its deficit with brand 4. The introduction of persuasive advertising is a disaster for this firm, its losses rising almost sevenfold.

Brand 3's primary concerns in its persuasive advertising are to increase its distance from brand 4 at the same time as maintaining proximity to brand 2. In so doing it cannot escape some increase in its deficit with brand 1 – given the latter's large jump toward it, but the firm is successful in its maneuvers with these 3 rivals in reducing its deficit by more than 26 units, although in so doing it moves closer to brand 5, with which it runs a deficit. However, it reduces this deficit despite the greater proximity and this result is one of two movements on Figure 12.3 that we cannot explain on the basis of our movements in virtual product space. Surpluses and deficits are also affected by the amounts of informational advertising engaged in, but firms 3 and 5 reduce their expenditures by about the same amounts (as seen in Table 12.15). Also, firm 5 lowers price by more than firm 3, adding to the puzzle of why firm 3's deficit falls (firm 5's surplus falls) with reduced proximity of the 2 rivals. Our tentative explanation is the difference in the cross-elasticities of the products in the neighborhood of the Model 3 solution. For brand 3, $\varepsilon_{3,5}^*$ = 0.19 and for brand 4 $\varepsilon_{5,3}$ = 0.46. Hence, x_3's response to the fall in p_5 is somewhat smaller than x_5's response to the fall in p_3. Its large expenditure on persuasive advertising reduced k_3^* from 0.29 to 0.09, with a substantial reduction in its advertising sales deficit; but profits fall, although they remain comfortably positive.

Brand 4's slight movement in virtual space is reflected in its k_4^* value of 0.29, unchanged from its fixed Model 2 value. Its persuasive advertising budget is negligible. Relative distances to brands 1 and 2 remain almost unchanged, as did the surpluses it enjoys with both firms. Its closer proximity to firms 3 and 5, however, would have led us to expect increases in its advertising sales surpluses with those firms. Yet, surpluses with both decline somewhat. However, this can be explained by these brands' expenditures on persuasive advertising against brand 4's almost nonexistent expenditures.

Brand 5's concerns are to reduce its distance to brand 2 and increase its distance from brand 4, with whom it runs its largest surplus and deficit respectively on advertising sales account. It succeeds in the first endeavor, with a rise in its surplus, but fails in its second – yet enjoys a substantial decline in its deficit nonetheless. Both these counterintuitive results are discussed above. The net result is that its overall surplus with all firms rises, but, like all other firms in the product group, its profits decline in large part because of the increases in cost incurred by its advertising efforts.

4 MODEL 4 – INFORMATIONAL AND COGNITIVE POSITIONING ADVERTISING UNDER RIVALROUS CONSONANCE

We now introduce rivalrous consonance as a means of analyzing tacit collusion. Introduction of the marginal consonance cost term in each of the three first-order necessary conditions results in the equations of (12.15):

$$1 \quad p_i = \frac{a_i + \beta_i^* + Y_i^* + \alpha_i^*(m_i + 2n_i x_i)}{2\alpha_i^*} + \frac{\Sigma_j \theta_{ij}(p_j - m_j - 2n_j x_j) b_{ji} e^{-k_i^* s_{ji}}}{2\alpha_i^*} \tag{12.17}$$

$$2 \quad A_i = \frac{(p_i - m_i - 2n_i x_i)\Sigma_j r_{ij} e^{-k_i^* s_{ij}} - \Sigma_j(\theta_{ij}(p_j - m_j - 2n_j x_j) r_{ij} e^{-k_i^* s_{ij}}) - 1}{2[(p_i - m_i - 2n_i x_i)\Sigma_j t_{ij} e^{-k_i^* s_{ij}} - \Sigma_j(\theta_{ij}(p_j - m_j - 2n_j x_j)(t_{ij} e^{-k_i^* s_{ij}}))]}$$

$$3 \quad (p_i - m_i - 2n_i x_i) = \frac{1 - \Sigma_j \theta_{ij}[(p_j - m_j - 2n_j x_j)(A_i(r_{ij} - t_{ij}A_i)(u_i - 2v_i D_i) s_{ij} e^{-k_i^* s_{ij}}]}{(u_i - 2v_i D_i)[\Sigma_j((p_i - p_j) b_{ij} - A_i(r_{ij} - t_{ij}A_i)) s_{ij} e^{-k_i^* s_{ij}}]}.$$

Each of the 3 policy variables has its own marginal consonance cost appended to its own proper marginal policy cost. Price changes, therefore, are included in the oligopolistic decision making: advertising competition is not used as an alternative to price competition even when tacit collusion exists.

a A Base Case

The potentials for tacit collusion in the illustrative product group when advertising of both types is active is quite small. When all θ_{ij} were set at 0.3 or more, the system would not converge. The maximum value for a universal θ_{ij} that led to convergence (when 1 decimal point values are used) is 0.2, and this value was used for the base case, termed Base Case 4 (Table 12.17).

Profitswise the beneficiaries of such tacit collusion are brands 1, 4, and 5, and the losers are brands 2 and 3. Brand 4, and to a lesser extent brand 1, are the major winners, with brand 5 scoring only a slight gain. These profit changes are fairly well correlated with the changes in the advertising-induced surpluses and deficits. All of the firms are led to increase prices in the face of rivals' like actions, and to vary A_i and D_i in the competitive struggle. This

Table 12.17 Base Case 4 solution values for strategic variables, with Base Case 3 solution values in parentheses for comparisons

Brand	p_i	A_i	D_i	π_i	AIS_i
1	\$27.16 (\$25.94)	\$251.02 (252.01)	\$2,273.94 (\$2,262.26)	\$8,930.67 (\$8,217.59)	111 (87)
2	\$7.73 (\$7.37)	\$0 (\$96.05)	\$482.01 (\$477.96)	–\$927.91 (–\$834.12)	–723 (–673)
3	\$20.41 (\$20.12)	\$936.57 (\$808.81)	\$1,520.47 (\$1591.87)	\$4,744.85 (\$5,031.20)	–106 (–77)
4	\$32.64 (\$31.17)	\$2,095.84 (\$2,162.52)	\$67.79 (\$51.97)	\$5,852.23 (\$4,847.60)	579 (524)
5	\$23.45 (\$22.64)	\$1,178.04 (\$964.58)	\$723.31 (\$822.10)	\$291.47 (\$249.80)	140 (139)

conforms to the expectation that firms will hold prices constant or increase them and engage in nonprice competition when profits pressure is felt; but it is interesting that most of such variation in advertising budgets affects informational advertising. This implies the desire to maintain the position in virtual product space purchased in Base Case 3.

Firm 1, revealed to be an end-point brand in virtual product space in Base Case 3 of Figure 12.3, is especially desirous of retaining the greater proximity to rivals 3 and 5, without sacrificing that to brand 2 or increasing the nearness to brand 3. By holding both types of advertising essentially constant and increasing price substantially to meet rivals' price rises – especially brand 2's – it increases its surplus sales on advertising account and its profits.

Brand 2 also retains its Base Case 3 D_2 value but reduces its small investment in informational advertising to 0, despite the fact that its effectiveness parameters were relatively good except against brand 1. It does increase its price but actually increases the price differential with brands 1, 4, and 5, although the differential with brand 3 narrows by only a few cents. Nonetheless the resulting rise in the deficit on advertising account from its reduction in A_2 overwhelms this differential-induced sales increase, and profits decline further into negative territory.

Brand 3 also loses profits in Base Case 4, although it remains in healthy surplus. Its strategy is to increase price slightly to lessen the price differential with its neighboring rival in virtual space, brand 2, while benefitting from increased price differentials with other rivals. It increases its informational advertising budget, although it is not especially effective in this activity, and decreases D_3; the result is to increase its advertising sales deficit, reducing sales, whose cost reduction is offset by a rise in advertising budget, with a consequent profit loss.

Brand 4, on the other hand, prospers magnificently from this small movement toward tacit collusion. Sandwiched among rivals 1, 2, and 5 – its major beneficiaries on advertising sales account – it has no incentive to vary D_4 much and it holds A_4 about constant, yet increases its sales surplus. Net sales rise slightly, as do revenues at a nicely higher price, and despite its high costs it enjoys the highest profit increase of any firm.

Brand 5 does little better than hold its own in the industry, in terms of profits and advertising sales surplus. Major sources of that surplus – brands 2 and 3 – increase or decrease persuasive advertising only slightly, and brand 5 has little incentive to move closer to them. Its major deficit on this account occurs with brand 4, which also retains its position in virtual space. Hence, brand 5 finds it profitable to reduce D_5. This reduction is more than offset by a rise in A_5, to take advantage of its great effectiveness against rivals 2 and 3. Sales fall slightly, however, as its price increase chokes off sales, but profits do manage a rise of about \$40.

In summary, the introduction of rivalrous consonance into this regime of price and advertising competition does not benefit all firms. Firms 4 and 1 gain a great deal, firm 5 essentially is affected in a neutral fashion, and firms 3 and 2 lose profits, the latter deepening its losses. Prices are raised by all firms, while most firms hold their persuasive advertising steady (firm 5 is an exception), with the result that their k^* coefficients change very little from Base Case 3 levels. They do raise and lower informational advertising – generally by small amounts – in accordance with its specific effectiveness with major rivals.

b Stage 1: Firm 2 Opts Out

As a first reaction to this initial step toward tacit collusion, let us now assume that firm 2 refuses to participate and sets θ_{2j} to 0, although other firms make no adjustment to their base case $\theta_{ij} = 0.2$, including firm 2 as a beneficiary. The solution to the new system is reproduced in Table 12.18, with Base Case 4 in parentheses for comparisons:

Support of brand 2 without reciprocation is a costly enterprise for rivals: jointly they sacrifice \$630.16 in profits to save brand 2 \$41.56 in losses. Brand 2's price reduction leads to similar price falls of \$0.15 to \$0.20 for all of its rivals, allthough its price differentials widen. Brand 2 essentially restores its Base Case 3 informational advertising level, but this constitutes the only significant change in advertising expenditures by any firm, so that k^* values remain little changed from those of Base Case 4 (and Base Case 3). The change by brand 2 does reduce its advertising sales deficit by 28 units,

Table 12.18 Stage 1 solution values for strategic variables, with Base Case 4 solution values in parentheses for comparisons

Brand	p_i	A_i	D_i	π_i	AIS_i
1	\$27.11 (\$27.16)	\$251.02 (251.02)	\$2,278.95 (\$2,273.94)	\$8,886.55 (\$8,930.67)	111 (111)
2	\$7.13 (\$7.73)	\$89.09 (\$0)	\$481.89 (\$482.01)	–\$886.35 (–\$927.91)	–695 (–723)
3	\$20.22 (\$20.41)	\$933.02 (\$936.57)	\$1,520.27 (\$1,520.47)	\$4,563.50 (\$4,744.85)	–114 (–106)
4	\$32.42 (\$32.64)	\$2,091.06 (\$2,095.84)	\$68.74 (\$67.79)	\$5,607.26 (\$5,852.23)	567 (579)
5	\$23.28 (\$23.45)	\$1,177.74 (\$1,178.04)	\$726.49 (\$723.31)	\$164.39 (\$291.47)	132 (140)

adversely affecting the balances of firms 3, 4 and 5 by small amounts. Given the essential constancy of advertising, the defection of brand 2 impacts the profits of its rivals by imposing the need to adjust to the defector's price reduction. Here we have an occurrence of constancy in nonprice rivalry and the use of price competition to reachieve equilibrium, somewhat contrary to conventional expectations of the opposite. Finally, although brand 2's profit position is somewhat improved, it is worse off than it was in Base Case 3 before tacit collusion and its future viability in an advertising regime is still in question.

c Stage 2: Firm 2's Rivals Withdraw Support from It

As a next move we hypothesize that firm 2's rivals reduce their θ_{i2} to 0, so that it does not get collusive protection in face of continued collusion at $\theta_{ij} = 0.2$ among the rivals. The solution is given in Table 12.19.

Firm 2 now suffers from losses that are worse than those in Base Case 3 in which rivalrous consonance was absent, despite its desperate price reduction and maintenance of both types of advertising expenditure at Stage 1 levels. It is now clear that in the medium or long run it is not a viable rival in the advertising or collusive environment.

Most interesting in this case is to see which rivals received indirect benefit from the product group's unreciprocated support of firm 2. Brands 3 and 5 are those which are hurt by withdrawal of support to brand 2. Brand 3's profits fall a good deal below those earned in Stage 1 and in Base Cases 3 and

Table 12.19 Stage 2 solution values for strategic variables, with Stage 1 solution values in parentheses for comparisons

Brand	p_i	A_i	D_i	π_i	AIS_i
1	$27.19 ($27.11)	$250.98 (251.02)	$2,221.46 ($2,278.95)	$9,024.02 ($8,886.55)	113 (111)
2	$7.03 ($7.13)	$86.20 ($89.09)	$488.78 ($481.89)	–$913.75 (–$886.35)	–703 (–695)
3	$20.03 ($20.22)	$966.97 ($933.02)	$1,493.23 ($1,520.27)	$4,312.51 ($4,563.50)	–132 (–114)
4	$32.64 ($32.42)	$2,123.51 ($2,091.06)	$66.16 ($68.74)	$5,896.30 ($5,607.26)	587 (567)
5	$23.33 ($23.28)	$1,274.45 ($1,177.74)	$691.09 ($726.49)	$113.90 ($164.39)	13 (132)

4. These results imply that brand 3 does not benefit from rivalrous consonance, with or without the participation of brand 2, but that its fortune is much affected by that brand's active presence. Brand 3's only advertising sales surplus is with brand 2, so that its sales are dependent on that firm's deficit. Equally important, its sales are strongly affected by its price differential with brand 2, and that rival's further price reduction in Stage 2 is a further blow, leading it to a deep price reduction below its Stage 1 price. The combination of a price and a sales reduction leads to a fall in profits, although it remains comfortable in these regards: its viability is not threatened.

Brand 5, on the other hand, approaches closer to zero profit, despite a small rise in price, an essential constancy in its advertising sales surplus, and constancy in sales. Its problem is that the departure of brand 2's protection leads it to increase its informational advertising to protect against brand 4's increase in such advertising, and this is enough to reduce the small positive profits it earns in Stage 1.

Brands 1 and 4 improve profit positions with the elimination of support to brand 2. The changes are not dramatic. In brand 1's case advertising levels are modestly reduced, advertising sales surplus is about constant, and sales are essentially unchanged. The improvement is the rise in price permitted by price rises in brands 4 and 5 together with the saving on its D_1 budget. Brand 4's profit rise is ascribable to the same developments. A large jump in price with constant sales yields a rise in revenue almost all of which accrues as profit after a small reduction on advertising account. Both brands 1 and 4, therefore, are the beneficiaries of the elimination of the price umbrella the industry held over brand 2. Nonetheless, brand 2's low price in Stage 2 remains a restraining force on industry prices and profits that one expects to feature typical rivalrous consonance solutions. The stage is an example of the profit impact of a weak firm's fight for survival with desperate price discounting, as exemplified for example in the United States by the recent state of the airline industry when bankrupt carriers were kept in existence by courts resolved to protect workers' jobs.

d Stage 3: Firm 2 Fails and Withdraws from the Product Group

It is a assumed now that Firm 2 fails and leaves the industry, while remaining rivals regroup and retain their consonance coefficients of $\theta_{ij} = 0.2$. The solution is found in Table 12.20. The removal of brand 2 effects a major structural change on the functioning of the product group and the interbrand relationships. Table 12.21 traces the net flows on advertising account that occur in the new rivalrous consonance Nash equilibrium. It will also be useful to plot the new locations in virtual product space using the methods discussed above in the presentation of Base Case 4. The rather drastic changes are graphed on Figure 12.4, with Base Case 4 locations also included for comparison.

The void in the virtual distance spectrum left by the departure of firm 2 is filled by moves of brands 1 and 3 into the interior of virtual space rather than staying near the end-points. Brand 1's loss of its large advertising sales surplus with brand 2 devastates its profits and motivates it to gain distance

Table 12.20 Stage 3 solution values for strategic variables, with Stage 2 solution values in parentheses for comparisons

Brand	p_i	A_i	D_i	π_i	AIS_i
1	\$19.69 (\$27.19)	\$212.55 (250.98)	\$5,446.06 (\$2,221.46)	\$2,312.92 (\$9,024.02)	–92 (113)
2	– (\$7.03)	– (\$86.20)	– (\$488.78)	– (–\$913.75)	– (–703)
3	\$22.43 (\$20.03)	\$512.55 (\$966.97)	\$1,871.63 (\$1,493.27)	\$7,218.59 (\$4,312.51)	4 (–132)
4	\$29.52 (\$32.64)	\$1,353.32 (\$2,123.51)	\$117.79 (\$66.16)	\$2,175.15 (\$5,896.30)	186 (587)
5	\$21.93 (\$23.33)	\$239.25 (\$1,274.45)	\$953.79 (\$691.09)	–\$32.90 (\$113.90)	–97 (134)

Table 12.21 Net flows of benefits from informational and persuasive advertising among firms in Stage 3, with Stage 2 flows in parentheses

Brand:\ From brand:	*1*	*2*	*3*	*4*	*5*	*Total*
1	–	–	+9.44	–91.36	–10.00	–91.90
	–	(+186.97)	(+30.40)	(–155.85)	(+51.75)	(+113.27)
2	–	–	–	–	–	–
	(–186.97)	–	(–104.34)	(–199.40)	(–212.47)	(–703.17)
3	–9.44	–	–	–38.68	+51.70	+3.57
	(–30.40)	(+104.34)	–	(–89.00)	(–116.52)	(–131.59)
4	+91.36	–	+38.68	–	+55.65	+185.67
	(+155.85)	(+199.40)	(+89.00)	–	(+142.83)	(+587.08)
5	+10.00	–	–51.70	–55.65	–	–97.35
	(–51.75)	(+212.47)	(+116.52)	(–142.83)	–	(+134.41)

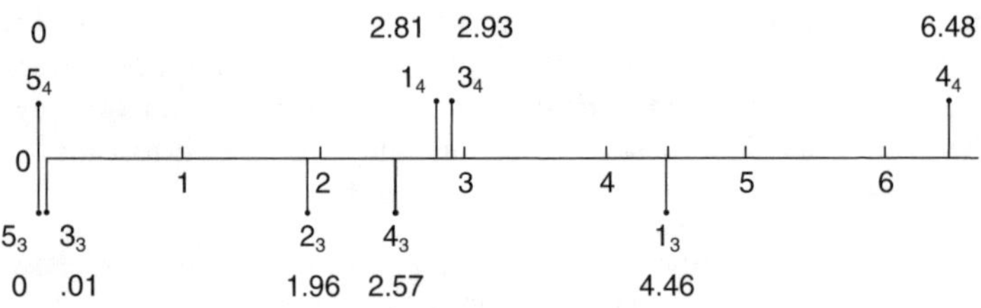

Figure 12.4 Relative locations in virtual product space, stage 3 Base Case 3

from brand 4, at the same time as maintaining proximity to brands 3 and 5. It finds it profitable to reduce A_1 slightly while more than doubling D_1. Despite its efforts, its advertising sales surplus of Stage 2 is turned into a deficit of almost equal magnitude, and its profit falls to about one-quarter of its Stage 2 level.

Brand 3, on the other hand, is, somewhat paradoxically, a large profit gainer. It loses its large surplus on advertising sales account with brand 2, but by distancing itself from brand 5 it turns its deficit with that brand into a surplus and by moving farther from brand 4 it reduces its deficit with it. It eliminates the overall deficit it ran in Stage 2, thereby increasing sales, which, with reduced informational advertising expenditures and heightened price, increases its profit – the only firm in the group to do so.

Firm 4 is grievously hurt by loss of its surplus with firm 2, yet it retains reduced surpluses with the three remaining rivals. One would suspect that the firm would find it profitable to move inward from the end-point and attain closer proximity to all of these rivals, especially as Table 12.14 shows that its persuasive advertising is among the most effective of the group. Yet it increases D_4 to a low absolute figure, although it does almost double its expenditure from that in Stage 2. Thus, k_4^* is reduced from the k value of 0.29 to 0.28. This must be admitted to being a puzzling reaction by the firm, and is one more instance of the frequent surprises of interdependence modeling. With the reduction in price and sales, profit falls to less than half its Stage 2 level, although it remains well above negative levels.

Brand 5 suffers a fall in profits from positive to negative levels in Stage 3, largely because of the loss of its large surplus with brand 2 and firm 3's movement from its neighborhood. These blows are somewhat softened by brand 4's movement to the opposite end-point, thereby reducing brand 5's deficit with it, and, to a lesser extent, brand 1's similar distancing. But in the end, surplus on advertising sales account has turned to deficit, price and sales are reduced, and profits fall despite the large cutback in informational advertising.

Sales in the product group fall by 262 units, or somewhat more than the loss of firm 2's output of 115 in Stage 2. Most of these excess sales losses can be accounted for by the decline in informational advertising from $4,702 in Stage 2 to $2,318 in Stage 3.

e Stage 4: Remaining Brands Reduce Consonance Coefficients to 0.1

Under the motivation of its losses, brand 5 resolves to reduce its level of collusion by setting $\theta_{5j} = 0.1$, and its rivals decide to follow its lead and set their consonance coefficients to the same level. The solution values are reproduced in Table 12.22, with Stage 3 values parenthesized for comparison.

Firms 1 and 3 suffer profit reductions in the new equilibrium, the former only about 4 percent but the latter a more severe 12 percent. But firm 4 gains about 1.5 percent and firm 5 moves into positive profits on a modest scale. Prices of firms 1, 3, and 4 fall, as we would expect with a reduction in tacit collusion, but firm 5 raises price in the face of increased demand. In this respect, the most active cause is the large increase in A_5 which impacts brand 3 exclusively and converts the surplus that it runs in Stage 3 to a deficit. The whole tableau of advertising-induced flows is presented in Table 12.23.

Indeed, as can be seen from the table, this interchange contains the only significant change in the advertising sales accounts of the firms. In terms of the direct impacts, firm 3's profit reduction is chargeable to firm 5, although the secondary adjustment of price to match rivals' changes must also be given its fair due. The reason for this strong increase in firm 5's advertising sales balance *vis à vis* firm 3 is revealed in Tables 12.1 and 12.22: firm 5's

Table 12.22 Stage 4 solution values for strategic variables, with Stage 3 solution values in parentheses for comparisons

Brand	p_i	A_i	D_i	π_i	AIS_i
1	\$19.34 (\$19.69)	\$219.43 (\$212.55)	\$5,450.15 (\$5,446.06)	\$2,217.32 (\$2,312.92)	–92 (–92)
3	\$21.69 (\$22.43)	\$522.14 (\$512.55)	\$1,797.70 (\$1,871.63)	\$6,342.43 (\$7,218.59)	–52 (+4)
4	\$29.17 (\$29.52)	\$1,436.42 (\$1,353.32)	\$97.99 (\$117.79)	\$2,207.44 (\$2,175.15)	+193 (+186)
5	\$22.23 (\$21.93)	\$440.61 (\$239.25)	\$914.28 (\$953.79)	\$27.01 (–\$32.90)	–49 (–97)

Table 12.23 Net flows of benefits from informational and persuasive advertising among firms in Stage 4, with Stage 3 flows in parentheses

Brand:\\ From brand:	*1*	*3*	*4*	*5*	*Total*
1	– –	+9.46 (+9.44)	–95.28 (–91.36)	–5.80 (–10.00)	–91.62 (–91.90)
3	–9.46 (–9.44)	– –	–39.69 (–38.68)	–3.10 (+51.70)	–52.25 (+3.57)
4	+95.28 (+91.36)	+39.69 (+38.68)	– –	+57.69 (+55.65)	+192.67 (+185.67)
5	+5.80 (+10.00)	+3.10 (–51.70)	–57.69 (–55.65)	– –	–48.80 (–97.35)

informational advertising effectiveness against firm 3 is especially strong, and given increased play as firm 5 increases A_5 greatly while firm 3 raises A_3 by very little.

Stage 4 may indeed provide a focal resting point for the product group. Brand 5 has been restored to profitability and only brand 2 has suffered substantial losses, although it remains the greatest profit earner of the four rivals. However, when comparison is made with Base Case 4 – which no longer is really relevant because brand 2 is no longer in the mix – brands 1, 4, and 5 are doing worse than in this starting point, and only brand 3 is benefitting from the rivalrous consonance. We suppose, then, that the firms resolve to return to the environment of non-cooperation, with brand 2 absent.

f Stage 5: Surviving Brands Revert to Zero Rivalrous Consonance

We next suppose that firm 5, dissatisfied with its losses in Stage 4, signals its intent to set its θ_{5j} at 0 for all j, and other firms decide to follow suit, therewith eliminating rivalrous consonance. The product group, therefore, reverts back to a Base Case 3 environment, but with firm 2 no longer existent. The solution is given in Table 12.24, with Stage 4's solution parenthesized for comparison.

The move is not a happy one for the group. Profits of all firms fall except those of brand 4, which rise by only 0.9 percent. Prices fall as is to be expected, intensifying rivalry, and informational advertising budgets increase universally in further support of such competition. Persuasive advertising falls, or in the case of brand 1, rises negligibly, indicating that firms do not try to alter their virtual positions in the product space. And brand 3's advertising sales deficit widens to the benefit of brand 5, for reasons discussed in section e. above.

g The Search for a Focal Resolution

If we remain, for demonstration purposes, at the 1-digit consonance coefficient level, none of the Base Case 4 or five stages examined yields a Nash equilibrium. Moreover, $\theta_{i,j} \geq 0.3$ for all i,j yield results that do not

Table 12.24 Stage 5 solution values for strategic variables, with Stage 4 solution values in parentheses for comparisons

Brand	p_i	A_i	D_i	π_i	AIS_i
1	\$19.03 (\$19.34)	\$224.98 (\$219.43)	\$5,459.15 (\$5,450.15)	\$2,107.71 (\$2,217.32)	–92 (–92)
3	\$21.18 (\$21.69)	\$521.01 (\$522.14)	\$1,765.95 (\$1,797.70)	\$5,938.04 (\$6,342.43)	–75 (–52)
4	\$28.83 (\$29.17)	\$1,509.48 (\$1,436.42)	\$84.45 (\$97.99)	\$2,227.06 (\$2,207.44)	+200 (+193)
5	\$22.11 (\$22.23)	\$523.12 (\$440.61)	\$907.45 (\$914.28)	–\$13.54 (\$27.01)	–33 (–49)

converge. In Chapter 9 we have ruled out of consideration mixed strategies as realistically irrelevant and side-payments as illegal. Our search for a product group consensus that brings industrial stability by reasonable compromises with realistic competitive clout leads us to a search for a "focal resolution": some nonequilibrium solution that can be expected to have an attractiveness on rational and conventional equity grounds.

On these bases, Stage 5 can be eliminated from consideration. 3 of the 4 firms are worse off than in Stage 4 and the other is negligibly better off. Moreover, brand 5 is incurring a loss and can correct this by moving back to Stage 4. But can it be accepted as a viable resolution? By moving from it to Stage 3 brand 3 experiences a sharp profit increase and brand 1 a moderate rise, while brand 4 suffers only a minor loss. The major drawback is that brand 5 moves into a loss situation that it will be reluctant to endure. Moreover, the other firms, given their relative prosperity, may be sympathetic to its plight. Movements to Stages 1, 2, and Base Case 4 involve the resurrection of brand 2, which is not desirable or practical.

Suppose, then, firms tacitly agree to permit brand 5 to seek a positive profit outcome by reducing its θ_{5j} to 0.1, while the other 3 rivals hold theirs at 0.2. Stage 6 results are reported in Table 12.25, as are Stage 5 solutions in parentheses and Stage 4 values – based on all θ_{ij} = 0.1 – in curly brackets.

Stage 6 accomplishes the desirable mission of lifting brand 5 to positive profits. A variety of measures are adopted to accomplish this. Firm 5 decreases D_5 to further distance itself from brands 3 and 4 in virtual product space, reducing its deficit on advertising sales account with those firms, while increasing its informational advertising substantially. The result is to shift its demand curve to the right, decreasing its elasticity and permitting price to rise yet still permitting some increase in sales, even in the face of declining β_5^*. The small movement into positive profit (after inclusion of fixed costs) is the net result.

Firm 1 benefits profitwise in small degree, but is otherwise little affected: its price and advertising expenditures remain about constant, but it does benefit somewhat from the rise of p_4 and p_5 in its sales. Firm 4 is similarly little affected, but its profits rise a bit. Firm 3, however, sees its profits reduced by virtue of its proximity to brand 5 and the size of b_{35}. As noted above, firm 5's improvement is largely at the expense of this rival. Its sales fall despite a sizeable price reduction and the rise in k_5^* due to a reduction in its targeted advertising reduces β_5^* and helps to put it in advertising sales deficit. Still, its profits remain the greatest of the 4 rivals by a large amount, about 2.65 times that of the second most profitable firm.

The suggestion arises, then, that firm 3 might "agree" to this small fall in its profitability to bring firm 5 back into profitability and to benefit the remaining members of the product group. Reverting to Stage 4 in which all rivals adopt consonance coefficients of 0.1 is not a likely reaction, as shown

Table 12.25 Stage 6 solution values for strategic variables, with Stage 5 solution values in parentheses and Stage 4 solution values in curly brackets for comparisons

Brand	p_i	x_i	A_i	D_i	π_i	α_i^*	β_i^*	AIS_i
1	$19.69	522	$212.24	$5,469.80	$2,410.18	32	434	–85
	($19.69)	(515)	($212.55)	($5,446.06)	($2,312.67)	(32)	(429)	(–92)
	{$19.34}	{520}	{$219.43}	{$5,450.15}	{$2,217.63}	{32}	{424}	{–92}
3	$21.96	600	$533.92	$1,802.82	$6,389.92	39	410	–52
	($22.43)	(636)	($512.51)	($1,871.73)	($7,218.32)	(40)	(437)	(+4)
	{$21.69}	{606}	{$522.13}	{$1,797.72}	{$6,342.41}	{39}	{403}	{–52}
4	$29.59	385	$1,358.80	$117.28	$2,247.61	33	164	+191
	($29.51)	(383)	($1,353.32)	($117.82)	($2,175.00)	(33)	(164)	(+186)
	{$29.17}	{399}	{$1,436.44}	{$98.01}	{$2,207.61}	{33}	{160}	{+193}
5	$22.34	354	$450.94	$881.95	$55.62	48	526	–54
	($21.93)	(341)	($239.26)	($953.98)	($–32.84)	(51)	(601)	(–97)
	{$22.23}	{359}	{440.01}	{$914.01}	{$27.03}	{49}	{547}	{–49}

in Table 12.25, where profits of all firms drop below their Stage 6 levels. We conclude then by signaling Stage 6's solution as a potentially acceptable basis on which to establish product group stability even though it is not a Nash equilibrium. Our purpose is wholly to illustrate the complexity of the problem, not to "solve" it in some determinate manner. There may indeed be one or more Nash equilibria in the domain of acceptable consonance coefficients which are 2 or more digits, and had we a deeper interest in the solution as such we might spend more time seeking them out. But our purposes to demonstrate methodology and give an idea of the essential unpredictable outcomes by virtue of parameter dependence have been served.

5 SUMMARY AND CONCLUSIONS

Our approach to advertising is to distinguish between "informational" and "persuasive" varieties, granting them a definitional separability that is admittedly somewhat distorting. It is analytically useful, however, in disentangling the two most important functions of selling costs: disseminating the existence of the product, its price, and its characteristics on the one hand, and seeking to alter the consumer's cognitive positioning of the product without changing the qualities that locate it originally or relocate it in the competitive process discussed in Chapter 11.

In Models 1 and 2 informational advertising is modeled under two decision regimes: that which sets its budget as a fixed percentage of revenues modified by the extent and direction of a firm's price differentials with rivals, and that which treats the budget as a profit-driven endogenous variable. Model 3 brings persuasive advertising into the profit-maximizing of the firm along with informational advertising, but with no tacit collusion among the firms. Model 4 introduces the decision making of Model 3 with rivalrous consonance active.

As revealed in previous chapters, the casting of first-order maximization conditions in the form of equating the marginal policy cost of each policy (including its associated marginal consonance costs in Model 4) to marginal production cost yields good light into the *ceteris paribus* adjustments of such variables in the wake of parameter changes. But, again, as seen in the solutions of previous chapters, the great degree of interfirm interdependence that is the very essence of oligopolistic decision making, limits our ability to project *mutatis mutandis* results when the number of firms is greater than two. Dimensionality enhances the importance of parameter dependence exponentially, restricting the generality of analytic results derived by resort to simulative theorizing. But nonetheless some insights into this black box of causal forces are gained by our modeling.

The same 5-firm product group is used in the modeling of this chapter that is employed in Chapters 10 and 11. Brand 1 is perceived by consumers to be the lowest-quality product and brand 3 the highest. Brand 2 is of median quality, with brand 4 somewhat less highly regarded and brand 5 very close to brand 3's highest rating. Brands 1, 2, and 3 are low marginal-cost providers – so that firm 3 is doubly blessed with highest quality position and low variable costs – while brands 4 and 5 are high marginal-cost firms, complicating brand 4's low-quality positioning.

In the nonadvertising environments of Chapter 10, low-cost firms 1, 2, and 3 prospered in the absence of tacit collusion while brands 4 and 5 received more modest profits. Highest quality and low cost gave brand 3 the greatest profit and low quality with high cost gave brand 4 the smallest in the base case (Table 10.2). Reduction of the spatial discount factor from 0.29 to 0 lowered the profits of all the firms but retained the profit rankings of the base case. Raising the discount factor to ∞ benefitted all brands except brand 2 which suffered from its weak basic demand, but again the profit rankings were unchanged.

The results for these pre-advertising environments are largely cost-driven, although brand 3's highest quality rating contributes to its best performance results. Rivalrous consonance is beneficial for all firms in the middle range but in comparison with the base case lowers brand 4's performance when extended to a perfect consonance value of 1. However, the results for consonance and nonconsonance environments are more complex when advertising is introduced.

In the base case solution with advertising determined as 3 percent of sales revenue with price-differential adjustments (Base Case 1, Table 12.3) firms' discretion in varying their informational advertising budgets is quite limited. Varying as these do with revenue, advertising budgets in this case cause some firms to exceed and some to fall short of profit-maximizing levels. For brands 1 and 3 prices and sales rise and advertising budgets are high, and both raise profits above those obtained in the pre-advertising model with no tacit collusion in Chapter 10 (Base Case 0, Table 12.3). Brand l's profits rise above those of brand 3 by virtue of the large effectiveness its advertising has in stealing sales from brand 2. That firm suffers a deficit on advertising sales account as well as a substantial fall in profit. Brand 4 gains a small amount in profit, but brand 5 loses when compared with the solution to Base Case 0.

One suspects, however, from the small values of advertising sales balances, that firms 2 and 5 are protected from much greater profit deprivation by the revenue-constrained advertising expenditures of their competitors. This proves to be correct: in Base Case 3 (Table 12.7) brands 3 and 4 increase their advertising by large amounts and with them their surpluses on advertising sales accounts with brand 2 (Table 12.8). That brand's deficit rises by 2.5 times and its profits fall to negative levels.

But several surprises do occur in the solution. Firm 1 actually reduces its advertising budget, holding its surplus with firm 2 constant, and also seeing its own surplus melt down by virtue of brand 4's depredations. With those sales reductions on advertising account a fall in its profits occurs.

Firm 3 – the favored firm in all previous solutions – takes a large profit hit, despite its increase in advertising, because of a competitive price reduction and a sales reduction caused by increases in its advertising sales account deficit with brands 1 and 4 and the conversion of its surplus with firm 5 to a sizeable deficit. Table 12.12.1 reveals its vulnerability to firm 5. The advantages it receives from its position of highest quality and lowest cost is countered by its sensitivity to firm 5's advertising and its proximity to this major rival.

But brand 5, despite its sales gains at the expense of brand 3 and its large increase in advertising budget, also suffers a large profit reduction, despite price and sales increases. High production costs and large advertising expenditures which are mainly defensive to hold down brand 4 depredations, cut into profits.

In Model 3 we introduce persuasive advertising as a second advertising strategy. Our methodology views the function of such advertising to be that of altering the position of a brand in "virtual " space by changing the cognitive parameter k to an endogenous variable k_i^* which is a function of persuasive advertising expenditures, D_i. The firm seeks to position itself with respect to consumers' perceptions of its qualities at a point that maximizes profits, *ceteris paribus*, by varying D_i. Such positioning is distinguished from that in Chapter 11 in that product qualities are not actually changed.

The interdependence of such efforts in our product group's Base Case 3 (Table 12.5) is to lower profits below Base Case 2 levels for all firms and, excepting firm 4, below Base Cases 0 and 1 levels as well. Such "brand" advertising serves to neutralize rivals' similar efforts, enforce price reductions in general, and add substantially to costs. It leads the product group into a Prisoners' Dilemma trap. Brand 2 is seriously jeopardized as its losses deepen substantially and brand 5 sees a worrisome decline in its profits as well. Brand 1 maintains its rank as maximum profit earner in the industry which it gained in Base Case 1, and widens its lead in that respect over Brand 3. Interestingly, the general tendency is for D_i to substitute for A_i, but the amounts of the reductions in A_i vary greatly.

Our last study is to determine whether tacit collusion might increase firms' profit positions. We remain with symmetric rivalrous consonance coefficients for the most part (all firms adopt the same θ_i coefficients and apply it uniformly to all rivals) at the single decimal point level. When $\theta_i \geq 0.3$ the solutions did not converge and so we remained with $\theta_i \leq 0.2$ for our illustrative examples. Base Case 4 (Table 12.17) adopts a universal $\theta_i = 0.2$ and improved the profits of firms 1, 4, and 5, but lowered those of firms 2 and

3 when compared with those in Base Case 3. Through a succession of stages involving changing values of θ_i in search of a potentially stable focal resolution in the absence of a Nash equilibrium we arrive at a solution with firm 2 eliminated as a brand and brands 1, 3, and 4 with $\theta_i = 0.2$ and $\theta_5 = 0.1$.

Except for firm 3, rivalrous consonance worsens profits for all firms – eliminating brand 2 and raising brand 5 just barely into a positive profits position – when compared with Base Case 3 where $\theta_i = 0$. Tacit collusion worsens the condition of 4 of the 5 brands in the industry, in general reducing prices, reducing A_i, and increasing D_i from Base Case 3 levels. After this overview, let us probe more deeply into the results, firm by firm, to distill some insights into the plights of our sample of firms, constructed to present a broad variety of demand, cost, and advertising circumstances.

In the discussions to follow we shall note that firms' experiences depend heavily upon their usage of D_i, the levels of their persuasive advertising budgets. The motivations behind the use of this variable to alter k_i^* from the base value of $k = 0.29$ are quite complicated. When k_i^* approaches 0 (which requires an increase in D_i when $u_i < 0$ and a decrease when $u_i > 0$) the discount factor $e^{-k_i^* s_{ij}}$ approaches 1, which means that the informational advertising effectiveness coefficients r_{ij} and t_{ij} as well as the b_{ij} demand factors are not reduced from their stated values in Tables 12.14 and 10.1, respectively. Persuasive advertising has overcome the cognitive decay factor k. On the other hand, as k_i^* approaches ∞ the discount factor approaches 0, and persuasive advertising reduces the two types of factors to impotence. The firm is isolated from its rivals' pricing actions and reduces its own informational advertising impacts on its advertising sales balance to zero. In general, then, as k_i^* increases by virtue of the firm's changes in D_i two forces pull in opposite directions, reducing the impact of rivals' prices and reducing the effectiveness of that firm's informational advertising on other firms' demand.

From scenario to scenario a firm's expenditures on D_i will depend on the like expenditures of its rivals. In general, a firm will adopt a value, given the like actions of competitors, that will lower k_i^* to increase its advertising effectiveness and raising β_i, the contribution of rivals' prices to its sales, taking into account (1) the movements in k_j^* of its rivals and (2) the impact of rising D_i on its costs.

The simultaneous workings of these intrabrand and interbrand adjustments are difficult to trace when studying changes between two solutions. They are additionally complicated because advertising sales balances between firms are also determined by the levels of informational advertising adopted, AD_i. Such balances can be increased by rises in AD_i or reductions in k_i^* and hence the relative effectiveness of \$1 of expenditure on the balance, AIS_i enters into the determination of AD_i and D_i magnitudes.

a Brand 1

Table 12.26 presents a detailed reproduction of brand 1's solution values for the models with profit-maximizing determination of informational and persuasive advertising with zero tacit collusion (Base Case 3) and tacit collusion (Base Case 4 and Stages 1–6). C_1 is costs including advertising costs.

Brand 1's profits benefit when all firms move to tacit collusion with $\theta_{ij} = 0.2$, rising to a peak when it no longer must shelter brand 2 although it remains in the product group. In the Base Case 4 through Stage 2 scenarios prices, sales, advertising sales surpluses, β_1s and k_1^*s remain about the same, although in Stage 2 profits reach a maximum because of a small rise in p_1 and a fall in D_1.

But brand 1's profits in this regime are highly dependent on its ability to prey on brand 2's sales through its informational advertising effectiveness. With quite small AD_1 values it maintains large advertising sales surpluses for the most part derived from hapless brand 2, and despite a large deficit with brand 4. When brand 2 exists in the group, brand 1's profits fall to 26 percent of their Stage 2 level, and drastic changes are necessary to salvage the situation. Most importantly, this requires reducing the deficit with brand 4.

Fortunately for brand 1, brand 4 maintains its k_4^* level through all 8 scenarios at about the base level of $k = 0.29$. Brand 1, therefore, holds its informational advertising budget about steady, but increases its per dollar effectiveness r_{14} from a discounted value of 0.088 to an undiscounted value (when $k_1^* = 0$) of 0.18. This reduces its deficit with brand 4 on advertising account by 65 units, which introduces some damage control. Large price

Table 12.26 Brand 1 experience with advertising

Variable	*Base Case 3*	*Base Case 4*	*Stage 1*	*Stage 2*	*Stage 3*	*Stage 4*	*Stage 5*	*Stage 6*
p_1	25.94	27.16	27.11	27.19	19.69	19.34	19.03	19.69
x_1	495	500	499	501	515	520	524	522
AD_1	252	251	251	251	213	219	225	212
D_1	2262	2274	2279	2221	5446	5450	5459	5470
C_1	4627	4650	4654	4600	7820	7845	7870	7862
π_1	8217	8931	8887	9024	2313	2217	2108	2411
α_1	21	21	21	21	32	32	32	32
β_1	156	163	162	161	429	424	420	434
AIS_1	87	111	111	113	–92	–92	92	–85
k_1^*	0.238	0.238	0.238	0.240	0	0	0	0

reductions are also necessary to maintain sales but reduce revenues which, with the increases in D_1, account for the severe profit declines.

The principle of significance is that the disappearance of a weak competitor who provides an easy target for persuasive advertising hurts a brand severely by forcing it to compete more actively with other rivals with whom it enjoys less advertising effectiveness and also may lead to a price reduction as another means of maintaining sales. The disappearance of a competitor may be a severe disadvantage to a firm heavily dependent on it as a target for its advertising campaigns.

b Brand 2

Brand 2 in the full advertising regime cannot survive under zero or positive rivalrous consonance (Table 12.27). Extending consonance at the 0.2 level to rivals leads it to raise price and eliminate informational advertising, with a resultant large fall in sales. Its advertising sales deficit widens, and even when rivals protect it in Stage 2 while permitting it to extend no consideration to them, losses fall only moderately. When that protection by rivals is withdrawn losses deepen again, and the firm goes bankrupt. Advertising is defensive and, surrounded on both sides by all of its rivals, with all of whom it runs advertising sales deficits, persuasive advertising offers no escape.

The evidence here is that a highly disadvantaged firm in the advertising wars is unlikely to be benefitted by tacit collusion within rational bounds. Its existence is likely to be a convenience to some healthier rivals but unless they are benefitting unanimously all are not willing to give it the level of collusion necessary for survival.

Table 12.27 Brand 2 experience with advertising

Variable	*Base Case 3*	*Base Case 4*	*Stage 1*	*Stage 2*	*Stage 3*	*Stage 4*	*Stage 5*	*Stage 6*
p_2	7.37	7.73	7.13	7.03	*	*	*	*
x_2	124	75	117	115	*	*	*	*
AD_2	96	0	89	86	*	*	*	*
D_2	478	482	482	489	*	*	*	*
C_2	1747	1507	1724	1720	*	*	*	*
π_2	–834	–929	–886	–914	*	*	*	*
α_2	28	29	29	29	*	*	*	*
β_2	306	319	316	319	*	*	*	*
AIS_2	–673	–723	–695	–703	*	*	*	*
k_2^*	0.199	0.198	0.198	0.195	*	*	*	*

c Brand 3

As shown in Table 12.28, this brand is a median profit earner in the profit-maximizing advertising scenario but loses profit in all rivalrous consonance regimes where brand 2 is present, even though it runs a large advertising sales surplus with that brand. Deficits are suffered with the other 3 rivals with large deficits overall. Defensive needs lead it to large informational advertising budgets. Moreover, its persuasive advertising expenditures are large because it wishes to reduce k_3^* from its $k = 0.29$ base value, and because with $u_3 > 0$ it can do that only by applying a large D_3^2 to its v_3 parameter in its k_3^* equation. It is forced to keep its price low in this scenario set Base Case 4 through Stage 2 to maintain sales and widen its price differentials with rivals, taking advantage of its price-elastic demand function (1.41 and 1.50 in the neighborhoods of solutions to Base Cases 3 and 4 respectively).

But when brand 2 departs the industry, brand 3's profits bound ahead by a substantial sum. For the first time it benefits from tacit collusion. It raises price, but its lost sales in doing so are more than compensated by a rise in D_3 that raises β_3 greatly despite the reduction in surviving rivals' prices. This occurs because the discount factor in virtual space is reduced to almost zero, making the brand's position in virtual space effectively that in original product space. This increases the r_{3j} effectiveness factors as brands 4 and 5 do not reduce their discount factors so drastically despite the loss of surpluses with brand 2. As rivalrous consonance is reduced in Stages 4–6, brand 3 loses some of its Stage 3 profit, but remains a substantial winner from brand 2's demise. The associated result is to eliminate its deficit on advertising sales account: the rise in β_3 and deficit elimination raises sales a total of 194 units, so that although the price rise reduced sales by 102 units a net rise of 92 units results.

Table 12.28 Brand 3 experience with advertising

Variable	*Base Case 3*	*Base Case 4*	*Stage 1*	*Stage 2*	*Stage 3*	*Stage 4*	*Stage 5*	*Stage 6*
p_3	20.12	20.41	20.22	20.03	22.43	21.69	21.18	21.96
x_3	587	559	555	544	636	606	598	600
AD_3	809	937	933	967	513	522	521	534
D_3	1592	1521	1530	1493	1872	1798	1766	1803
C_3	6776	6673	6652	6589	7048	6810	6727	6789
π_3	5031	4745	4563	4313	7219	6342	5938	6390
α_3	41	41	41	40	40.31	39	38	39
β_3	399	392	390	379	437	403	387	410
AIS_3	–77	–106	–114	–132	4	–52	–75	–52
k_3^*	0.087	0.105	0.103	0.112	0.001	0.003	0.041	0.030

Brand 3 is a low-cost, high-quality producer which is punished by a poor persuasive advertising strategy devised to increase its distances to rivals in virtual product space when it should be aimed at reducing those distances. Its persuasive advertising budget is large but therefore inefficient. Its proximity to brand 2 and sensitivity to its price in its β_3 require it restrain its price increases and to compete with that brand through this inefficient advertising. Unlike brands 1, 4, and 5 it finds the presence of this weak competitor a burden and recovers only when firm 2 leaves the industry.

d Brand 4

Brand 4's experience is in some ways inverse to that of brand 3. Profits rise above the Base Case 3, zero consonance, value and remain there until brand 2 leaves the group. Then they fall to less than half their State 2 value in Stages 3–6. Informational advertising is high in the first subset of stages but is reduced in the second, and D_4 expenditures are extremely small in all consonance scenarios. The result is that $k_4^* \sim k = 0.29$ in all solutions: the firm does not seek to reduce its discount factors in virtual product space to enhance the effectiveness of its advertising and demand parameters. This is because its b_{4j} factors are about equal in value and it location makes it about evenly spaced from its rivals. Large D_4 expenditures would add more to costs than revenues, since its persuasive advertising effectiveness is not among the strongest, although u_4 is negative and D_4 outgo lowers k_3^* directly (in contrast to brand 3's predicament). Another factor in the firm's poor performance after brand 2's demise is that surviving rivals lower prices which reduces β_4 and sales substantially.

Table 12.29 Brand 4 experience with advertising

Variable	*Base Case 3*	*Base Case 4*	*Stage 1*	*Stage 2*	*Stage 3*	*Stage 4*	*Stage 5*	*Stage 6*
p_4	31.17	32.94	32.42	32.64	29.51	29.17	28.83	29.59
x_4	566	574	566	578	382	399	416	385
AD_4	2163	2096	2091	2124	1353	1436	1509	1359
D_4	52	68	68	66	118	98	84	117
C_4	12810	12877	12753	12971	9094	9440	9769	9157
π_4	4848	5852	5607	5896	2175	2207	2227	2248
α_4	38	38	38	38	33	33	33	33
$_*gb_4$	215	225	221	220	164	160	157	164
AIS_4	524	579	567	587	186	193	200	191
k_4^*	0.288	0.287	0.287	0.287	0.280	0.283	0.285	0.280

With brand 2 out of the industry firm 4 sees its surplus on advertising account fall by about two-thirds and its overall sales by about one-third, even with reductions in p_4. Each of its rivals trims its deficit on advertising sales account with brand 4 by sizeable amounts through substantial increases in D_j, while firm 4 follows the stand pat posture noted above. It is a rather puzzling immobility despite the relative ineffectiveness of its persuasive advertising.

e Brand 5

Firm 5, never a robust profit earner in the advertising wars before rivalrous consonance, becomes a basket case when brand 2 leaves the product group. A high-cost, high-quality firm with small basic demand, its informational advertising effectiveness is strong only against brands 2 and 3, although its persuasive advertising effectiveness is the strongest of any of the firms in the group. It does engage in heavy informational advertising levels when firm 2 is competing, as well as adequate persuasive advertising given its demand and cost restrictions. D_5 is effective in reducing k_5^* to about half its base k value, and its advertising sales account is in overall surplus. Still, its sales remain moderate while production and advertising costs keep profits low (Table 12.30).

The firm's modest good fortune, however, depends heavily on the advertising sales surplus with brand 2, and its disappearance is too great a blow from which to recover. Its predicament is complicated by the conversion of a large surplus with firm 3 to a deficit as that firm increases its persuasive advertising to reduce its k_3^* to near-zero. Although brand 5 does increase D_5 to lower k_5^*, it lowers its informational advertising because of the elimination of brand 2, with consequent loss of leverage against brand 3. Its profits fluctuate in these

Table 12.30 Brand 5 experience with advertising

Variable	*Base Case 3*	*Base Case 4*	*Stage 1*	*Stage 2*	*Stage 3*	*Stage 4*	*Stage 5*	*Stage 6*
p_5	22.64	23.45	23.28	23.33	21.93	22.23	22.11	22.34
x_5	431	407	400	398	341	359	371	354
AD_5	965	1178	1178	1274	239	441	523	451
D_5	822	723	726	691	954	914	907	882
C_5	9515	9244	9137	9174	7514	7955	8220	7860
π_5	250	291	164	111	–33	27	–14	56
α_5	53	50	50	49	51	49	49	48
β_5	547	494	489	467	600	547	532	526
AIS_5	139	140	132	134	–97	–49	–33	–54
k_5	0.104	0.148	0.146	0.161	0.036	0.058	0.061	0.074

Stage 3 to Stage 6 solutions between small positive and negative profits. Profit margins are low because of the need to restrain prices, and the firm becomes a casualty of the basic demand and cost conditions noted above, low informational advertising effectiveness against surviving firms, and firm 3's aggressive advertising. The advent of advertising is an adverse development for this firm, especially after it switched to a profit-maximizing basis and its rivals' advertising budgets are no longer constrained by revenue. It becomes increasingly burdensome when rivalrous consonance is introduced and brand 2 succumbs.

f A Final Overview

This last modeling effort in our work, introducing advertising at several levels of complexity, presents at once the most complicated of the integrated oligopolistic competition studies we have conducted and makes the case for our concerns about current and alternative approaches to such analysis most cogently. Theoretical attempts to derive general propositions concerning the outcomes of such decision making in parameter unspecified models by restricting dimensionality to duopoly do not yield satisfying insights even if solutions are forthcoming. Resort to simulative theorizing via modeling, as defined in Chapter 1, is the only chance to derive insights into the tangled causal paths determining outcomes. Those insights may indeed be of limited generalizability, but the very nature of oligopoly is that of the *sui generis*. Worthwhile analysis with realistic numbers of firms must begin with a rather narrow definition of the types of actors, the historical context within which they interact, the state of their information, the existing power structure, and so forth. This is true when the goals of modeling are to understand a specific industry's functioning, but it holds true also when that modeling has simulative theorizing ambitions.

A persistent result of the experiments in the advertising regimes of this chapter is the recurrence of unpredictable, and frequently inexplicable, movements in the variables. In previous chapters where product characteristics were intrinsic we found policy variables moving in the same patterns: price rises and improvements in quality tended to move in the same direction, and when exceptions occurred, explanations were generally derivable. In the present models this no longer generally true. Prices, quantities, profits, and the two different types of advertising expenditures no longer reveal stable covariation patterns, are frequently of surprising magnitude, and often counterintuitive. *Ceteris paribus* analysis is of little help in aiding understanding. Increases in rivalrous consonance coefficients generally worsen the profit positions of most brands. Had our interests centered on some one particular specification, certainly more intensive sensitivity analysis in the neighborhood of solutions would yield deeper understanding of the forces at work. But our goals of illustration forestall that, and we are entitled to doubt that we would thereby penetrate some of the more densely obscured processes.

Perhaps the case can be made that the primary usefulness of the methods, therefore, is as a set of operational models applicable to the analysis of oligopoly cases in the real world. Deriving most of the parameters from a detailed study of the industry should be feasible, perhaps as interval estimates bracketed by upper and lower bounds. Plausible guesses in bracketed intervals and scaling methodology are accepted alternatives when necessary. Econometric analysis, in all its sophistication, may be of some usefulness, but its methodology is still too crude to cope with the body of interdependence we have modeled. But – we have said all this in Chapter 1. In coming to the end of our analyses of integrated rivalry we have circled back to the beginning.

Part IV
Epilog and Prospectus

13 A Final Word

1 IN THE WAY OF A RECAPITULATION

This work was written with a framing vision of process that may now be stated in a more coherent manner than was possible in the piecemeal presentations of the individual chapters. The economics of oligopoly are ill suited to exclusive or even dominant analysis by the rigid formalism of modern microeconomics. At best, that methodology may provide partial insights into questionably simplified abstractions of oligopolistic environments – much in the manner that metaphor or analogy may provide enlightening guidance in the literary artist's struggle to understand the complex motivations of the human personality. The economic theorist is more frequently motivated to derive determinate theorems from his efforts, and shapes the model's assumptions with that overriding goal in mind, than he is to assure the realistic relevance of those theorems.

What may originate with a desire to analyze oligopoly ends with the comforting determinism of monopoly or monopolistic competition, or results in structures so hag-ridden with instrumental postulates designed to obtained closed model solutions that realistic applicability is a casualty. But that is of no consequence to the theorist: the purpose of the exercise is to demonstrate his methodological virtuosity above all else. The field becomes cluttered with "famous victories" in the form of theorems relating to airy-fairy realms of fantasy.

In this book we have placed emphasis on well known characteristics of realistic oligopolistic rivalry that make the search for universally applicable theorems so fruitless. These include the integrated nature of the competitive process, featuring price, product qualities, advertising, innovation, and reputation among the more important. The problem of measurability arises in many of these dimensions, along with the need to accept "nonscientific" scaling methodologies to obtain "fuzzy" metrics. Dominating all else, of course, is the defining characteristic of the market structure – the mutually recognized interdependence of decision making by three-dimensional, flesh-and-blood managements. In such environments the importance of individualized, idiosyncratic factors loom, such as the personalities of management with their differing multiple objectives, the history of the industry and its "ethos", or the mores and folkways that shape the directions of and constrain firms' rivalries, as well as the nature of government regulation or monitoring with its differential impacts on the firms in an industry or product group. Implied by the structure is a pervasive uncertainty that transcends that found in other market environments and features concerns about destabilizing actions of incumbents or potential entrants.

What such conditions require is, first, the abandonment of a search for some universal theory of oligopoly, modern counterparts of Cournot, Bertrand, or von Stackelberg frameworks. Methodologies must be capable of tailoring to specific industry artifacts with ambitions limited largely to deriving insights into the functioning of that industry. This requires that the analytical frameworks be capable of including informal information as well as characteristics capable of formal statement as mathematical functions. Those methods, second, and importantly, must permit the distillation of the *power structure* that encapsulates the binary relations among a rather large number of firms that go far in determining the decision making in the industry. Those relations will emphasize the rivalrous, of course, but must also include the specific cooperative impulses that inform the actions of the incumbent firms.

My own suggested means of incorporating both competition and cooperation in variable degrees between specific pairs of firms is via a power structure captured in a nonsymmetric matrix, Θ, whose elements express degrees of dominance or deference by incorporating those rivals' profits with own-profits at varying discount rates. I have featured *mature oligopoly*, in which incumbents are well established, respectful of rivals' survivability, and averse to destabilizing initiatives. The discount factors that brand i applies to firm j's profits, θ_{ij}, therefore, vary between 0 and 1. I believe this method has the virtues of simplicity, flexibility, and parameter derivability using both formal and informal observations. The advantages that in my view it has over game-theoretic approaches I have discussed at some length in the book, especially in Chapter 3.

A third requirement of the methodology design is to incorporate parameters capable of derivation from the data in numerical form, either in "measurable" form or by scaling methods. The complexity and dimensionality of the frameworks militates against qualitative assessment of solutions and parametric displacements, so that such solutions that emerge will be parameter-dependent. Insights into the industry's functioning will be obtained largely by standard displacement techniques, in which alteration of parameter values permits "what if" questions to be posed to explore potential developments in the industry and also to examine the sensitivity of solutions to specific parameter values.

Such efforts I have termed "modeling" as distinguished from "theorizing". In this definition a *model* is parameter-specified and incapable of yielding determinate results in the absence of such numerical specification. *Theory*, on the other hand, seeks determinate answers in closed analysis which is parameter-dependent only in the sense that it requires qualitative information about them. Its aim is insights in the form of theorems with a greater generality than modeling permits. I have used the term *simulative theorizing* to describe the process of employing models with differing sets of specified parameters with the goal of extending the narrow insights concerning the industry's performance obtained through parametric displacement to obtain hypotheses and conjectures concerning other industries or industry groups.

A useful analogy may be borrowed from aerodynamics. Theory, of course, is the body of deductive analysis that aims to obtain the qualitative properties of air flow around an aircraft in flight from qualitative specifications of relevant parameters in its environment. Modeling is concerned with the mockup of a specific aircraft design in the wind tunnel, in which the parameters are quantitatively under the control of the modeler and the characteristics of the air flow specific to the aircraft model under analysis can be mapped accurately. Simulative theorizing involves the use of the model in a more generic sense to gain insights into the air flow properties of different types of craft, perhaps a close air support craft from the mockup of a fighter-attack plane.

In the past microeconomic theorists – as opposed to empiricists or experimental economists – have disdained modeling as a means of obtaining insights, struggling instead to employ mathematical techniques that would lessen dependence on the qualitative properties of parameters or to gain greater predictive leverage from a given body of qualitative information. To obtain determinate results they have frequently reduced the dimensionality of realistic environments, employed functional forms that restrict generality in uncertain ways, or operated in market structures which permit determinate results at the expense of realism. The argument in this book is that there is simply no alternative to modeling when dealing with oligopolistic decision making.

An example of the validity of that assertion is the experience of game theory. It began with strong theoretic ambitions to construct a universal theory of strategic interaction directly applicable to oligopolistic decision making. Over time, however, especially as game theorists became more interested in cooperative behavior, in supergames extending over time, and in asymmetric or imperfect information it has evolved into what is largely a modeling technique in the meaning defined above. Insights are obtained by solving examples with numerically specified parameters, and pretensions to universal theorems and concepts of what constitutes an "equilibrium" solution have yielded to a recognition of the importance of the idiosyncratic characteristics of specific "games." Indeed, one of the major contributions of game theorists is their demonstration of the large number of potential solutions in many games and the inability to choose one or narrow the set in the absence of specific knowledge of the personalities of the players, the folkways and mores that have developed to constrain players' actions, as well as the power structure or pecking order recognized by them.

Although I have criticized game theory for its excessive rationalism and its failure to incorporate broader socio-economic characteristics in its assumption set when dealing with oligopoly, and have argued the preferability of rivalrous consonance frameworks in oligopolistic contexts, one must emphasize the importance of the contributions it has made to such analysis. It has provided a framework for reasoning about the market structure, criteria for restricting expected outcomes to logical subsets, and a body of hypotheses concerning strategy choices by firms which are invaluable to the modeler. The methodologies put forward in this work have benefited hugely from them, as has been acknowledged in their discussion. I do believe, however, that the ultrarationalism of the approach leads to an excessive emphasis on rivalry in oligopoly and a failure to accord to cooperative impulses their rightful role, especially in mature oligopolistic decision making. In this respect, and in respects the operationalism of the technique, in the sense of the ease of obtaining empirical estimates of the crucial parameters of the modeling, I believe that rivalrous consonance is a preferable usage in studying realistic oligopoly.

The role of theory in the modeling process is to guide the construction of the model through the insights its manipulations yields. In no sense is modeling a replacement for theory, but rather it is its complement. Because the modeler is freer in his or her constructions than the theorist, he or she can frequently construct more realistically complicated or functionally more flexible frameworks with numerically specified parameters – at the cost, of course, of generalizability.

In the spirit of these beliefs (and biases?) the major contributions of this book are in the form of modeling methodologies with demonstrations of their usage in the analysis of integrated competition among oligopolies. Chapters 10–12 deal with a 5-firm industry which was constructed with some care to include high-, medium- and low-cost producers, making brands of higher and lower qualities with varying basic demand functions and with the occasional realistic anomaly. By maintaining a common set of firms it was possible to study the continuities in firm behavior with and without rivalrous consonance collusion in the determination of prices, outputs and qualities under conditions of informational and persuasive advertising and constrained relocations in the product space.

One last unusual treatment is to be found in the models: consumer benchmarking. Our treatment of consumers' choices among differentiated goods in a product group is to assume that buyers judge brands' characteristics by comparing them with their conceptions of a "standard" characteristic level. A brand's differential quality, therefore, receives merits or demerits only on the basis of its departure from such standards, and with lessening incremental benefit as a firm raises the quality content above that standard and increasing punishment as it falls below the standard. This view is introduced in the belief that it reflects a realistic attitude in consumers' choice. Its practical impact on firms is to create a centripetal force that acts to pull brands' qualities toward the standards.

2 RESULTS AND CONJECTURES

In the preparatory material of Part I we placed great emphasis on scaling, or the development of quasi-measurement techniques to bypass the obstacles to analysis created by the non-measurability of many characteristics. Cross-factor analysis was introduced and illustrated as a means of bringing individuals' intuitive judgments and preferences into numerical scales for mathematical operations. Notably, its applicability to the difficult task of determining the elements of the rivalrous consonance matrix Θ was mentioned and the author's usage of the techniques to obtain this power structure for the OPEC cartel was referenced. Also, an extensive experiment by the author in testing the consistency of subjects' scalings of characteristics of rather hazy description for varied groups of persons was presented and shown to be initially promising in establishing the methodology's ability to yield meaningful, i.e., nonrandom, values. Scaling was also introduced in Chapter 2 to derive consumers' preferences over characteristics and brands using the dollar as a unit. Some such body of techniques, whether applied to characteristics or to brands, seems indispensable if progress is to be made in analyzing nonprice competition.

On the basis of analysis in Chapter 3 we demonstrated the practical necessity of moving welfare analysis away from its ideals defined in purely competitive environments into a world of oligopolistic interdependence. In such an imperfect world the ideal welfare point – either for social or consumers' surplus – is what we termed the Cournot point, where firms ignore their interdependence with other firms but exercise the pricing power inherent in their nonhorizontal demand functions. That, too, is only an ideal in the sense that it is irrational to assume that oligopolistic firms will ignore this interdependence in their decision making. The question then becomes how large a departure from the Cournot point into the rivalrous consonance polygon is a society willing to tolerate? This is to say, how much tacit collusion, as measured by the θ_{ij} consonance coefficients, will society view as inescapable or impractical of combat? But in the face of these realities the continuing usage of a welfare economics by economists based upon universalized price equal to marginal cost is fatuous.

An important principle which guided our analyses throughout the book was derived from maximization theory: maximization of own- or extended-profit for price and nonprice policies requires that the marginal gross revenue of a policy *less* its marginal production cost equal the marginal policy cost *plus* the marginal consonance cost when rivalrous consonance is active. This in turn requires that the marginal policy cost *plus* marginal consonance cost be equal for all price and nonprice policies. By tracing through the implications of these conditions in the solutions of our models it was frequently possible to isolate the forces at work in moving the relevant price and nonprice variables. These conditions also made possible the algorithms by which the models were solved in iterative fashion.

One continuous result observed in those model solutions was that prices and product quality generally moved together: firms did not meet price competition by changing product qualities, even in cases where price was not driven by quality costs. This was somewhat surprising, in that it occurred in conditions of non-collusion as well as those of tacit collusion of varying degrees.

Among the more frequent characteristics of importance in products are durability, consistency in durability and length of warranty period. We examined the covariation of these characteristics, along with price, under conditions of nonaging and aging with time. One surprising result of this modeling at initial perusal was the relatively small warranty periods that were optimal in the case of nonaging products compared with those of aging products. This can be explained by the "front-loaded" failures of nonaging products, since the probability of failure in any interval remains constant over time, and consequently yields relatively more failures in early periods of use than aging products.

Rivalrous consonance was introduced into duopoly in Chapter 8 with cases that featured symmetric consonance coefficients for the two firms, symmetric coefficients with increased other-price demand coefficients, and symmetric coefficients with enhanced demand factors for qualities. All of these moved in expected directions pricewise, profitwise and outputwise, and the positive relations among price and the quality characteristics (implying opposite movements in durability consistency) persist. In Cases 4, 5, and 6 we introduced asymmetry in consonance, demand and cost coefficients with much more complicated consequences. For example, holding both θ_i constant but allowing θ_j to rise led to 4 strong results. Both prices rise, but the quality factors degrade for firm *i* and are enhanced or remain the same for firm *j*. Tacit collusion introduces negative relations among price and quality for the firm that does not change its degree of collusion. Both firms' profits rise in general, but with exceptions for certain Θ, and firm *i*'s outputs rise while firm *j*'s fall. Firm *j* is the deferential firm and follows the expected patterns in terms of price, profit, output, and qualities, but firm i finds it most profitable to raise price and output, but to reduce the quality of its product.

Endogenization of benchmarks drives the quality standards of both firms to their minimum "reputation" levels to approach minimum differentiation when marginal policy costs of the qualities are substantial. We conjecture that were such costs nonexistent or slowly rising, the opposite result would occur with competition among the rivals driving quality to technologically determined upper bounds. On the assumption that costs of creating quality would generally be significant, we conjecture on the basis of our results that consumer benchmarking drives quality down to benchmark standards. Over time, however, as consumers become accustomed to higher quality products and adjust benchmarks upward, product quality would be expected to rise even as greater homogenization of quality in the industry characterized the shorter- and medium-term outcomes. Finally we did search for and found several Nash equilibria in the cases but speculated that in rivalrous consonance realistic solutions might occur for Θ conjunctures that were not Nash resting points.

In Chapter 10 we introduced a 5-firm industry designed as noted above to meet a variety of differential demand and cost conditions. Also introduced in this chapter was the scaling of consumers' preferences to obtain demand functions and positioning of brands in the product space. Benchmarking was extended to prices in this chapter, with consumers making selections among brands on the basis of price differentials. Quality of product was associated with position in the product space as determined by consumers' cognition of the brands, with the impact of brands on one another declining exponentially with distance in the space. The degree of such decay was regulated by a cognition parameter, k, which was varied between 0 and ∞ to study the differing experiences of the firms at various positions in the (linear) space with such changes in the "virtual" product space caused by changes in k. Firms were assumed to be operating under regimes of noncollusion in Model 1 and rivalrous consonance in Model 2.

In the noncollusion case, as k rose, increasing interbrand distances in the virtual space, prices rose and quantities fell monotonically for all brands, and as actual quality, designated by its actual (as opposed to its cognitive) site in the space, was held constant. Profits also rose over the k span for all firms except one which had a low basic demand but depended for its sales on price differentials made possible by its low costs. When k rose above moderate levels that firm's profits declined.

But when tacit collusion is introduced, it is this brand and its compeers – lower-quality, low-cost producers which shelter under the higher prices induced by collusion – which benefit most as consonance levels rise from 0 to 1. However, when $k = \infty$, when all firms function as effective monopolies, all firms suffer profit declines from higher levels of tacit collusion. An important point is that different firms benefit or lose to different extents as marginal consonance costs are introduced into their cost functions and competitiveness is reduced, and the rivalrous consonance approach allows such costs to be isolated.

In Chapter 11 we studied *actual* (as opposed to cognitive, or virtual) changes in firms' quality positions in product space, but in accordance to reality, limit their moves in product space to the intervening space between their immediate neighbors. It employs the 5-firm industry introduced in Chapter 10. Our primary results were that such moves were infrequent and cost-driven, with only 2 of the 5 firms making moves, one in the direction of decreasing quality and one in movement toward higher quality, but both motivated largely by reduced costs. Experiments with rivalrous consonance did not change the patterns of movement, leading us to conjecture – given what we consider to be realistic cost parameters – that tacit collusion is not powerful enough in realistic industries to influence the location of products in quality space. Further, tacit collusion was not an effective way of preempting entry into the space, even at high levels among the incumbents. The costs of such action outweighed the deterrent effect on the entrant, and incumbents were much better off permitting entry and then enticing the entrant to engage in tacit collusion.

Finally, a long Chapter 12 deals with the introduction of informative and persuasive advertising by the 5 firms. The results of the extensive modeling runs were the most complicated we conducted, and generalizations from the results ranged from the difficult to obtain to the impossible. Departures from the *ex ante* expected were frequent, and, unlike such occurrences in our previous models, proved extremely difficult to explain by tracing out the movement of causation among the first-order conditions between iterations of the algorithms. In this chapter we concluded that our methodology will be useful almost wholly for the analysis of a specific industry rather than the gathering of information for broader conjectures, and even in such instances the industry's solutions will partake from time to time the characteristics of black-box emissions.

3 DEFICIENCIES IN MODELS AND MODELING METHODOLOGY

What we have accomplished, hopefully, in this work is to establish in the reader's purview of differentiated oligopoly the necessity of modeling, including techniques for scaling the nonmeasurable, devising operational manners of combining cooperation and rivalry into measures of industry power structure, and dealing with quality-dictated locations of brands within an industry's product space as well as means of analyzing actual and cognitive changes in such space. Finally, the necessity is for such models to incorporate the integrated competition among price and quantity characteristics simultaneously.

Our models are relatively simple in structure – to some extent that probably will characterize improved models – and would benefit from broadened views of the nature of consumers' choices among differentiated brands. We may have overemphasized or underemphasized benchmarking as a component of such processes. The treatments of informative and persuasive advertising can probably be improved with more intensive research attention to their complications. Perhaps the concept of nodal or network treatments of firms' movements in the product space can be improved upon, and the important issues of multibrand deployment by incumbents and new entrant placements in the space be introduced more satisfactorily. Innovation, patent races, research and development have been entirely ignored in our presentations, but could be incorporated into the types of models developed here. And, importantly, a more extensive consideration of the social welfare implications of differentiated oligopoly and the need to develop more realistic ideals to guide policy are certainly clear from our deficiencies.

All of which is to say that this work offers introductory frameworks which are believed to be valuable for the applied economist interested in gaining insights into the structure and functioning of a specific oligopolistic industry as well as the more theoretically oriented researcher searching for broader insights into wider spectra of industries. Progress in the construction of such models would be greatly enhanced by the development of an "econometrics" of simulative theorizing. We need a well thought-out and integrated body of guidelines for proceeding efficiently to the construction of models and for their manipulation to gain comparative statics insights. At its best, simulation is an exercise in applied statistics. How can the modeling researcher derive from the data that estimates the model's parameters the measures that permit statistical inference to be performed on its solutions? How do we bracket in statistically efficient manners the values of parameters to be used in displacements? Can such sampling inference techniques help us to isolate in timely fashion those parameters that are strategic as solution drivers? What factors can be determined to be crucial in establishing the limits of ambition of a model: what determines the maximum effective number of rivals that can be included, the numbers of characteristics that can be considered, or the fineness of the mesh adopted to determine the potential nodes for location in a product space? Can the multivariate techniques of the psychometrician and biometrician aid in simplifying the model structure and complement econometric techniques? How can the research of the experimental economists be adapted for usage in the construction of models?

Perhaps the most difficult problem will be to convince the young economist of the rich vein of analysis to be mined in oligopoly theory using modeling techniques. Far more tempting is the prospect of deriving theorems empty of utility from structures of low dimensionality whose primary virtue is determinateness. One can only hope for the future of economics that the day will soon be when the curtain falls on this theater of the absurd.

Notes

1 On Definitions and the Problems of Measurement

1. In my view Chamberlin's work differs significantly in these concerns about product qualities from those of Sraffa and Robinson. The latter pair treat product differentiation rather narrowly in terms of preferences of buyers among sellers, partly on the basis of location, rather than on differences that inhere in (are *intrinsic* to) the product itself. See Kuenne (1967, Ch. 10, and 1992, Ch. 11).
2. I shall term properties that are capable of continuous measurement or scaling "qualities" or "variables" and 0–1 properties "attributes," with "characteristics" referring to both types.
3. Of course, there are instances when price may affect preferences, as in the Veblenian "snob effect," in which it becomes a characteristic. See Leibenstein (1950).
4. Becker (1965).
5. Hotelling (1929).
6. Lancaster (1966, 1971, 1972, 1975, 1979, 1991; Kuenne, 1967). See also Salant (1980) and Salop (1979).
7. The following section draws heavily upon, but expands on Kuenne (1974), reprinted in (1992, pp. 296–318). The heavy reliance on real analysis can be skipped without great sacrifice in the continuity of the presentation.
8. I neglect the Kelvin scale with its value of absolute zero.
9. See, for example, the discussion in Torgeson (1958, p. 62).

2 Core Characteristics Analysis

1. Hotelling (1929).
2. Kuenne (1967, 1986).
3. See Kuenne (1967, reprinted as Chapter 11 in Kuenne, 1992). This paper was written in 1965 and 1966 without knowledge of or reference to Lancaster's initial probings.
4. Triffin (1949), especially pp. 3, 5–7, 9–10, 12, 49, 67, 77, 141, 189.
5. "Lastly, it [attribution measures] must be used where the indexes available to establish numerical measures along a continuum by ordinal or cardinal methods are dependent on consumer or firm preferences, as for example the 'atmosphere' or 'tone' of a restaurant or store" Kuenne (1974, p. 234).
6. This is exactly true only for three sets of values $[\alpha, \beta]$: $[2+\sqrt{2}, 2-\sqrt{2}]$, $[2-\sqrt{2}, 2+\sqrt{2}]$, and $[3,3]$. However, it is a reasonably good approximation for the range of Z values of relevance to characteristics analysis.
7. Luce and Galanter (1963, p. 251).
8. That is, the characteristics matrix is post-multiplied by the vector of raw weighting factors to obtain the vector of weighted sums.

3 Rivalrous Consonance: An Approach to Mature Oligopolistic Competition

1. See Kuenne (1986, 1992), and the bibliography cited in those works.
2. Empirically, competition within the industry is a much more threatening force than potential entrants from without. In my view, too much attention has been paid in the analysis of oligopoly to "barriers to entry" or "contestable" industry structures. Entrants have succeeded largely in converting monopolies to oligopolies in deregulated industries, but were notable failures, for example, in the airline industry. Cf. Shepherd (1984).
3. In (Kuenne, 1986) I constructed some relatively simple examples of oligopolistic interdependence and attempted to isolate the patterns of association using econometric methods. Similarly, in (1992, Ch. 7) I employed a broad-scale econometric modeling of the OPEC organization.
4. Over the years, one solution technique that has proved quite trustworthy even for finding local maxima when the firms' models are not convex is the Sequential Unconstrained Minimization Technique (SUMT), a penalty function algorithm designed and programmed by A. Fiacco and G. McCormick (1968). It is discussed in (Kuenne, 1968). A convergence proof is presented for problems that are convex, and in my experience the success rate for locating local maxima in nonconvex problems is quite high. An additional advantage is that it accommodates equality as well as inequality constraints.
5. The solution obtained is not actually the joint profit maximization solution, for this would require that aggregate industry profits be maximized with respect to all firms' prices or outputs. In the rivalrous consonance framework the firms maximize the function with respect to their own prices or outputs only. The latter solution will depart further from the joint profit maximization point as the other-output terms in the inverse demand functions rise.
6. For positive values of own-outputs, both firms' second derivatives are strictly negative and hence extended profit functions are strictly concave in own outputs. When outputs are zero, so are the second-order derivatives. Hence each firm's solution for given consonance coefficients is a global extended profit equilibrium.

   The general solution for prices is the following. Let:

$$
\begin{aligned}
&1\quad t_1 = 2(b_{11} + b_{11}^2 c_{12} + b_{21}^2 c_{22}) \\
&2\quad t_2 = a_1(1 + 2b_{11}c_{12}) + c_{11}b_{11} - \theta_1 b_{21}(c_{21} + 2c_{22}a_2) \\
&3\quad t_3 = b_{12}(1 + 2b_{11}c_{12}) + b_{21}(\theta_1 + 2b_{22}c_{22}) \\
&4\quad t_4 = 2(b_{22} + b_{22}^2 c_{22} + b_{12}^2 c_{12}) \\
&5\quad t_5 = a_2(1 + 2b_{22}c_{22}) + c_{21}b_{22} - \theta_2 b_{12}(c_{11} + 2c_{12}a_1) \\
&6\quad t_6 = b_{21}(1 + 2b_{22}c_{22}) + b_{12}(\theta_2 + 2b_{11}c_{12}) \\
&7\quad t_7 = 1 - \frac{t_3 t_6}{t_1 t_4}.
\end{aligned}
\qquad (1)
$$

Then, prices may be written:

$$1 \quad p_1^{\circ} = \left(\frac{1}{t_1 t_7}\right)\left(t_2 + \left(\frac{t_3 t_5}{t_4}\right)\right) \tag{2}$$

$$2 \quad p_2^{\circ} = \left(\frac{1}{t_4 t_7}\right)\left(t_5 + \left(\frac{t_2 t_6}{t_1}\right)\right)$$

7. The reaction functions in general form are the following:

$$1 \quad p_1 = \frac{a_1 + b_{11}c_{11} + 2a_1 b_{11} c_{12}}{2b_{11}(1 + b_{11}c_{12})} + \frac{b_{12} + 2b_{11}b_{12}c_{12} + \theta_1 b_{21}}{2b_{11}(1 + b_{11}c_{12})} p_2 \tag{1}$$

$$2 \quad p_2 = \frac{a_2 + b_{22}c_{21} + 2a_2 b_{22} c_{22}}{2b_{22}(1 + b_{22}c_{22})} + \frac{b_{21} + 2b_{21}b_{22}c_{22} + \theta_2 b_{12}}{2b_{22}(1 + b_{22}c_{22})} p_1.$$

8. Let

$$b_{11}^{*} = \frac{b_{11}}{(b_{11}b_{22} - b_{12}b_{21})} \tag{1}$$

$$b_{12}^{*} = \frac{b_{12}}{(b_{11}b_{22} - b_{12}b_{21})}, \text{etc.}$$

Then, the *solution* values for prices may be written:

$$p_1 = a_1 b_{22}^{*} + a_2 b_{12}^{*} - b_{22}^{*} x_1 - b_{12}^{*} x_2 \tag{2}$$

$$p_2 = a_2 b_{11}^{*} + a_1 b_{21}^{*} - b_{11}^{*} x_2 - b_{21}^{*} x_1.$$

For firm 1,

$$\pi_1^e = x_1 p_1 - c_{10} - c_{11}x_1 - c_{12}x_1^2 + \theta_1 (x_2 p_2 - c_{20} - c_{21}x_2 - c_{22}x_2^2), \tag{3}$$

and,

$$\frac{\delta \pi_1^e}{\delta x_1} = p_1 - b_{22}^{*} x_1 - c_{11} - 2c_{12}x_1 - \theta_1 b_{21}^{*} x_2 = 0, \tag{4}$$

which may be rewritten as

$$p_1 - b_{22}^{*} x_1 = (c_{11} + 2c_{12}x_1) + (\theta_1 b_{21}^{*} x_2). \tag{5}$$

The lefthand side is marginal revenue, which is equated to the sum of marginal production cost, or the first term on the righthand side, and marginal consonance cost, the second term.

9. For example, when $\theta_2 = 1$, in our example, firm 2's profits fall uniformly as θ_1 rises. But these are the only instances in the example for either firm in which this counterintuitive movement occurs.
10. The other-good offset is obtained by taking the difference between the integrals of the inverse shifted demand function and the inverse of the initial demand function between 0 and x_2:

$$dCS = \int_0^{x_2}\left(\frac{a_2}{b_{22}} - \frac{x_2}{b_{22}} + \frac{b_{21}}{b_{22}}\left(p_1 + dp_1\right)\right)dt - \int_0^{x_2}\left(\frac{a_2}{b_{22}} - \frac{x_2}{b_{22}} + \frac{b_{21}}{b_{22}}p_1\right)dt.$$

11. This argument reflects the position of Posner (1975) that profits are the result of expenditures to obtain oligopoly rents which are largely cancelled out by such costs.
12. See Chapter 7, n. 3 for a fuller explanation of this determination.

4 Hotelling Models and Other Spatial Analogs

1. See, for example, Spence (1976), Dixit and Stiglitz (1977), and Salop (1979) to be analyzed below.
2. Sraffa (1926). Sraffa's paper is as precise a published beginning as can be discerned for the analysis of competition with differentiated products and the mixture of competition and monopoly it implied. It should be noted that Chamberlin was at work at this time upon his thesis and derived book (1948).
3. Hotelling does refer explicitly to a multidimensional characteristics space but does not develop the concept formally.
4. Salop's quality space is the circle, i.e., the boundary of a disk; it does not include the interior of the disk. This type of space has been used since Chamberlin (1948) to eliminate the end-points of a linear space and thus make the space continuous rather that discrete. As Eaton and Lipsey (1975) have shown, the existence of end-points has important implications for optimal firm location, and the circular market area changes solutions drastically; this will be reviewed in section 3. However, circular product quality spaces have little interest for analysts of quality "location". For two quality characteristics it is unlikely that they will be forced to vary in a circular manner. Generally, each will vary independently, perhaps bounded from above by technological limits and from below by technological and maintenance-of-reputation limits. It is the planar or hyperplanar quality space, therefore, that is relevant for quality characteristics analysis.
5. Most of the asserted advantage seems to hinge upon its relieving the Sweezy rationalization for the kinked demand curve from conjectures about rivals' reactions by providing an alternative explanation. This seems to be that if a firm raises its price above the kink-price, marginal consumers will buy the composite good, and if the firm lowers price it will gain consumers at the expense of neighboring firms, but demand will expand more slowly than it does above the kink. See Salop (1979, pp. 145, 155).
6. Salop adopts the circular market area to eliminate analytically bothersome end-points of the finite linear market and the pairing of peripheral firms. The

reader may assume instead a linear market of infinite extent and interpret distances from most-preferred brands in terms of straight-line distance.

7. Salop specifies sufficient conditions to escape the Roberts–Sonnenschein demand curve discontinuity. See Roberts and Sonnenschein (1977).

8. Necessity is easily established:
   1 If Condition 1 does not hold a firm can improve its profit by pairing with another
   2 If Condition 2 does not obtain, a peripheral firm can increase its market by moving towards its neighbor.

   Sufficiency requires more complicated proofs which are referenced in Eaton and Lipsey (1975).

9. Eaton and Lipsey give extremely concise derivations for these bounds which, in the interest of clearer comprehension, are expanded below. Five characteristics should be kept in mind:
   1 There are $2n$ half-markets that must be accounted for
   2 No half-market can be greater than Y, the peripheral firms' whole market size (Condition 1)
   3 No interior firm's half-market can be smaller than $0.5Y$ (Condition 1)
   4 Each peripheral firm must have one half-market equal to zero (Condition 2)
   5 Neighboring half-markets must be equal in size.

1 PERIPHERAL FIRMS' LOWER BOUND

Set the 4 peripheral firms which establish (1) 4 half-markets of Y, (2) 4 half-markets of 0, and 2 neighboring firms' half-markets of Y. Then, Y is minimized by setting the $2n - 10$ remaining markets equal to Y,

$$6Y + (2n-10)Y = 1$$
$$Y = \frac{1}{(2n-4)}. \tag{1}$$

2 PERIPHERAL FIRMS' UPPER BOUND

When n is odd, pair all but 1 firm, yielding $n - 1$ half-markets of Y, $n - 1$ half-markets of 0, and the interior firm with 2 half-markets of Y. Hence,

$$(n-1)Y + 2Y = 1$$
$$Y = \frac{1}{n+1}. \tag{2}$$

When n is even, pair all firms, to obtain n half-markets of Y and n of 0, so

$$Y = \frac{1}{n}. \tag{3}$$

Since $n < n + 1$, the upper bound is $1/n$.

3 INTERIOR FIRMS' LOWER BOUND

Peripheral firms have 4 half-markets of 0 and, taking into account neighboring firms, imply 6 half-markets of Y. Let 1 firm have the minimum half-market of $0.5Y$, implying 2 more neighboring half-markets of $0.5Y$. Hence, we have accounted for 14 half-markets, with 6 of them at Y, 4 at $0.5Y$ and 4 at 0. Let the remaining $2n - 14$ half-markets be Y. Then

$$6Y + 4(0.5Y) + (2n-14)Y = 1 \qquad Y = \frac{1}{(2n-6)}. \tag{4}$$

4 INTERIOR FIRMS' UPPER BOUND

If n is odd, pair all firms but 1, to get $n + 1$ half-markets of Y. That interior firm will have the largest whole market, consisting of 2 half-markets of $1/(n + 1)$ length, so

$$Y = \frac{1}{(n+1)}, \quad M_1 = \frac{2}{(n+1)}. \tag{5}$$

If n is even pair all but 2 firms, to get $n + 2$ half-markets of Y and $n - 2$ of 0, for a half-market size of $1/(n + 2)$. The maximum whole market is then

$$Y = \frac{1}{(n+1)}, \quad M_l = \frac{2}{(n+1)}. \tag{6}$$

which is less than the upper bound when n is odd.

10. To motivate these bounds, consider that Condition 1 alone is now necessary and sufficient since Condition 2 is not applicable. Hence, no firm's half-market can exceed any other firm's whole market, and neighboring half-markets must be equal. If x is the maximum whole market for n firms, no firm can have a whole market less than $0.5x$. Then:

1 LOWER BOUND

Assume $n - 1$ firms have a market area of x each, and the firm with the minimum market has $0.5x$. Then

$$(n-1)x + 0.5x = 1 \qquad x = \frac{1}{(n-0.5)}, \tag{1}$$

so the minimum market area is half of this, or

$$M_l = \frac{1}{(2n-1)}. \tag{2}$$

2 UPPER BOUND

Let $n - 1$ firms get the minimum market area of $0.5X$, and the nth firm a maximum area of x:

$$0.5(n-1)x + x = 1$$
$$x = M_l = \frac{2}{(n+1)}. \tag{3}$$

11. To establish necessity only:
 1 Conditions 1 and 2 are identical to those in Models EL1–EL4
 2 The definition of firm i's profit is

$$1 \quad \pi_i = M_i(p-m)$$
$$2 \quad \pi_i = \left(\int_{B_L}^{x_i} c(x)dx + \int_{x_i}^{B_R} c(x)dx\right)(p-m) \tag{1}$$
$$3 \quad \pi_i = (C(B_R) - C(B_L))(p-m),$$

where M_i is firm i's market in customers and m is marginal cost.

But because half-market boundaries lie halfway between firm i's location and that of its neighboring firms,

$$B_L = \frac{(x_{i-1} - x_i)}{2}, \; B_R \frac{(x_i - x_{i+1})}{2}, \tag{2}$$

Substituting (4) into (3) and maximizing with respect to X_i yields

$$\frac{\delta \pi_j}{\delta X_\iota} = 0.5(c(B_L) - c(B_R))(p-m) = 0, \tag{3}$$

which implies the first-order condition that the marginal profit at the boundaries of firm i's market be equal, or, more simply,

$$c(B_L) = c(B_R). \tag{4}$$

Condition 4 is just a variant of Condition 3 for peripheral pairs. Because by definition such a firm cannot move within its short half-market, the equilibrium condition concerns its profit experience were it to move marginally into its long half-market. For an equilibrium, should it do so it must suffer a loss or zero gain, and if Condition 4 holds that will hold true. Hence, it will settle for the locational status quo.

12. The proof requires consideration of interior firms and peripheral firms. For an interior firm, Condition 3 implies that each firm's market interval must contain in its interior at least one point of inflection of the density function that is a maximum. Second-order profit conditions would be violated if the turning point were a minimum.

For any pair of firms not at a mode, $c(x)$ must rise for at least one of them in the direction of its long-side half-market boundary. Hence, the interior of that half-market must contain at least one mode if Condition 4 holds. If the firms are paired at a mode, that node is a short-side half-market boundary.

If all firms are interior firms $n \leq s$, the number of modes. If all firms are paired, $n \leq 2s$. Combinations of the two types of firm configurations set bounds between these limits. Hence, the upper bound on n is $2s$.

Note that this is not a sufficient condition for an equilibrium. It is quite possible for n to be within the bound and yet for Condition 3 or 4 to fail to hold.

13. Eaton and Lipsey (1975, pp. 35–6).
14. Motivation of these conditions begins with the observations that under maximum loss conjectural variation the firm seeks to minimize its larger half-market, preferably by equalizing both, and that when a firm moves from x_i to $x_i + dx$ *its lefthand and righthand boundaries shift also by* dx. Suppose it shifts in the direction of its left-side half-market. The customer content of the new half-market will diminish by $c(x_i)dx$ but increase at the boundary by only $0.5c(B_L)dx$, because "half" of the incremental market it will have already controlled. Similarly, the righthand market will gain $c(x_i)dx$ but lose $0.5(B_L)dx$.

    If Condition 1 holds but the relevant part of Condition 2 does not, so that (say) $0.5c(B_R) > c(x_i)$ *and* $0.5c(B_L) \leq c(x_i)$: then both sides of the market can be enlarged by a shift in the righthand direction, and the firm cannot be in an optimal location.

    If Condition 1 does not hold but Condition 2 does hold, the firm can increase its small side by moving in the direction of its large side, so it cannot be in market loss conjectural equilibrium.
15. See Lösch (1954).

5 Characteristics as Objects of Consumer Preference

1. The use of the characteristics approach to the derivation of characteristic shadow prices (hedonic prices) predates Lancaster's extensive formalization, with most of its usage in deriving such prices for different types of labor skills. See Court (1941); Tinbergen (1956); and Mandelbrot (1962).
2. For example, Lancaster asserts that "beauty" is not a characteristic but a psychological reaction to a host of complex characteristics which are probably not capable of identification. Hence, when aesthetic reactions are dominant in consumer choice, his characteristics framework may not be operationally useful. See (1971, p. 114).
3. "Characteristics bear a double relation to any situation. On the one hand characteristics are technically related to goods through the characteristics–goods relationship or consumption technology. On the other hand, they have a human relationship to the consumers' involved in the situation through the characteristics–people relationship, embodied in preferences. Although the two relationships cannot be entirely separated, we shall find it extremely useful to divide the criteria for irrelevance into those which are concerned mainly with the structure of technology and those which are concerned mainly with the structure of preferences. A characteristic may be ruled out as irrelevant for primarily technical reasons or for primarily human reasons." Lancaster (1971, p. 141).
4. The x_j may be defined as consumption activities if they consist of complementary collections of goods *that are not in the same product group*: coffee, sugar and cream, for example. An activity is defined as fixed amounts of each component good per unit of consumption, **B** has a larger number of characteristics (sweetness, for example, in beverage consumption), and the *composite good*

must be priced for use in (5.2) below. The concept of production activities is discussed in Lancaster (1966, pp. 14–15; 1971, pp. 47–49; and 1972, p. 53). However, Lancaster for purposes of simplifying the analysis, moves quickly to the assumption that the consumption activity contains only one good so that a 1 to 1 correspondence between activities and goods exists.

It is important to note that the concept of a composite good is not identical to or subsumed in the definition of *combinable* goods to be discussed below – a distinction that Lancaster does not make clear. The important distinguishing property is that composite goods are formed from products that are not members of the same product group while combinable goods are contained in a single group.

5. The approach is discussed in (1979).
6. I cannot find any direct extension by Lancaster of the notion of noncombinable goods to include multiple purchases of the same brand. If a consumer purchases two automobiles some characteristics may be increased in quantity and some may not. For example, "time availability" will rise because one automobile will be available during those periods when the other is being repaired or serviced. But "roominess" will not be changed. Hence, in a two-dimensional characteristics space, with "roominess" along the horizontal axis and "time availability" on the vertical axis, the image vectors of all brands defined in physical units will have images in characteristics space that are rays from the origin to the end-point defined by the combination yielded by a single unit, and then become horizontal as further units are added. This property seems to be implicit in the notion of noncombinable goods.
7. Recall that product units are scaled to amounts obtainable by applying the "resource" (i.e., income) depicted by PDC wholly to acquisition of any brand. Hence, any brand's unit of measure is the distance of a ray from the origin to its intersection with PDC. Since increases in resource shifts all PDCs in parallel fashion, all such rays will rise in proportion as they intersect higher PDCs such as PDC′, and therefore depict the same number of brand units. Hence, if PDC′ depicts an increase of 10 percent in resource, 0C might rise 8 percent (although in the case of the consumer facing fixed prices it should rise 10 percent), to represent 1.08 units of Z'. Homotheticity, however, makes this comparable to the unit length of $0\mathbf{Z}^0$, and hence the compensating ratio given above is meaningful.
8. Lancaster terms assumptions 2 and 3 to follow as preconditions for the *uniformity property* of the compensating functions, to be discussed below. I have included assumption 1 in such preconditions because it seems to me to require such inclusion.
9. Note, however, that this does not imply a uniform density of consumers along the transformed PDC.
10. Reproduced from (1979, p. 48).
11. Since goods in the own-group are assumed to have no characteristic in common with goods in the other-group, given fixed money income the optimal available good chosen in the own-group is independent of relative prices between the two groups. However, the amount of the best available good to buy (and consequently the amount of income to spend on it) is dependent on the relative prices of own- and other-group goods. See Lancaster (1979, pp. 142–43).
12. In his treatment of optimality in Chs. 3 and 4, (1979), and in his analysis of perfect monopolistic competition (p. 180), Lancaster assumes all brands in the target group are sold at the same price.
13. Cf. Lancaster (1979, pp. 61, 212–13).

14. See Lancaster (1979, pp. 282–313, 1991, pp. 206–29).
15. Even these restrictive assumptions are not sufficient to obtain desired results in one operational area in which the characteristics approach has achieved its greatest usage: the calculation of hedonic prices to correct price indices for quality changes. In order for prices of goods to equal the sum of their characteristics quantities times the shadow prices of such characteristics, necessary and sufficient conditions when consumer utility functions over characteristics are strictly concave and twice differentiable and goods are divisible are that the functions also be identical for all consumers and homothetic.

    These conditions are required to permit the marginal rates of substitution among characteristics to be equal for all consumers – and hence characteristics prices to be proportional – in conditions where characteristics are not traded directly but only indirectly in goods bundles. In general it is not possible to bring about marginal rate of substitution equalities unless the stated conditions hold. Consumers purchasing different goods, even when utility functions have only total levels of characteristics as arguments, will in general fail to meet the usual marginal conditions for Pareto optimality. Hence, prices predicted from the linear model based on characteristics contents will overestimate actual prices. See Jones (1988).

    For a discussion of the econometric problems involved in estimating simultaneous equation equilibrium models in which hedonic prices are derivative, see Epple (1987).

6 Game-theoretic and Monopolistic Competition Analyses

1. There is debate among game theorists as to the best manner of handling "tacit collusion." Tirole (1993, pp. 206–207), for example, suggests that such motivations are fundamentally self-serving and, hence, rational in the usual sense. As such, they may be best included as alternative actions or strategies and incorporated into the noncooperative game as such. Myerson (1991, pp. 370–3), on the other hand, argues that such collusion is best approached by altering the concepts of equilibrium because of the large number of actions that would have to be incorporated. It does seem a bit strained to treat tacit collusion as just another form of noncooperative game. Rivalrous consonance accommodates a spectrum of competitive–cooperative environments within the same framework by merely changing parameter values.
2. Cf. Meyerson (1991, p. 420): "The key assumption that distinguishes cooperative game theory from noncooperative game theory is this assumption that players can negotiate effectively." But negotiation among oligopolistic rivals can only be imperfect, primarily implicit through signaling. This must limit the effectiveness of cooperative game theory in oligopoly analysis, especially in coalition games.
3. See, for example, R. Myerson's usage in (1991, p. 107):

    > In general, a *solution concept* is any rule for specifying predictions as to how players might be expected to behave in any given game. However, when we represent a real conflict situation by a mathematical model ... we must suppress or omit many "non-game theoretic" details of the actual situation, which we may call *environmental variables*. For example, in the strategic form [of the game] there is no indication of any player's height, weight, socio-economic status or nationality. We cannot a priori rule out the possibility that the outcome of the game might depend in some way on such environmental

variables. So we should allow that a solution concept may specify more than one prediction for any given game, where the selection among those predictions in a specific real situation may depend on the environment.

4. Kreps (1990, pp. 408–409), is also cautious in embracing the notion of a mixed Nash equilibrium. The implication of the Nash equilibrium is that one's rivals must find that none of their alternative strategies can improve their payoffs over their Nash strategies given that one is playing one's Nash strategy. Therefore, a mixed strategy Nash equilibrium requires that one choose the probability mix over one's strategies in such manner that one's *rivals* are indifferent over their strategy set or any probability mixture of them. That is, one does not choose those probabilities to make oneself indifferent over the play of one's own strategies.

   Therefore, Kreps writes:

   > One randomizes to keep one's rivals guessing and not because of any direct benefit to oneself. Put another way, in a mixed strategy Nash equilibrium each player has no *positive* incentive to randomize according to the called-for mixing probabilities; as long as the other player is fulfilling his part of the equilibrium, there are many best responses for the first.
   >
   > For this reason, many people find the idea of a mixed strategy Nash equilibrium incredible. Are we to believe that individuals faced with real economic decisions decide what to do by flipping a coin? And if we believe that individuals will bother to perform just the right randomization, when doing so is not particularly to their advantage? Nothing said so far should be taken to imply that the answer is yes. Remember that being a Nash equilibrium is necessary for "the obvious way to play the game", if an obvious way to play exists. It is in the eye of the players (or the analyst) whether mixed strategies ever can constitute the obvious way to play the game.

5. Although rivalrous consonance has been criticized for the difficulty in isolating the power matrix Θ, one seldom encounters discussions of the difficulties of isolating such constructions as the "type" density or "belief" density functions of Bayesian game forms.
6. "Although we regard these results about the *structure* of the equilibrium strategies to be the main achievement of the theory, most of the results in the literature focus instead on the set of *payoffs* that can be sustained by equilibria, giving conditions under which this set consists of nearly all reasonable payoff profiles. These "folk theorems" have two sides. On the one hand they demonstrate that socially desirable outcomes that cannot be sustained if players are short-sighted can be sustained if the players have long-run objectives. On the other hand they show that the set of equilibrium outcomes of a repeated game is huge, so the notion of equilibrium lacks predictive power. "Folk theorems" are the focus of much of the formal development of this chapter. Nevertheless, we stress that in our opinion the main contribution of the theory is the discovery of interesting stable social norms (strategies) that support mutually desirable payoff profiles, and not simply the demonstration that equilibria *exist* that generate such profiles." (p. 135)
7. In coalitional cooperative games once the power structure is defined in a characteristic function, analysts assume usually that after the bargaining involving threats and side payments, the players form the grand coalition of all n players and allocate the gains according to the power structure in some focal equilibrium. But this is clearly not the case of oligopolistic behavior absent cartel formation. The power structure is more complex than the ability to hurt or harm

the coalitions. For the narrower interpretation of the power structure cf. Myerson (1991, p. 427):

> Once a representation in coalitional form has been specified, we can try to predict the outcome of bargaining among the players. Such an analysis is usually based on the assumption that the players will form the grand coalition and divide the worth $v(n)$ among themselves after some bargaining process, but that the allocation resulting from a focal equilibrium of this bargaining process will depend on the power structure rather than on the details of how bargaining proceeds. A player's *power* is his ability to help or hurt any set of players by agreeing to cooperate with them or refusing to do so. Thus, a characteristic function is a summary description of the power structure of the game.

8. This is an interpretation adopted by Luce and Raiffa (1957, pp. 250–252). Their caveat that Shapley never interpreted his measure in this way should be repeated here.
9. This is the axiom that is hardest to motivate. Luce and Raiffa (1957, pp. 251–2) criticize it on the basis that it assumes that one can combine two games into one, and obtain the allocations of the new game by adding the allocations of its two components, firm by firm. They illustrate by example a case in which such a procedure would yield an implausible allocation, and argue that a new solution must be derived on its own merits. However, they admit they have no axiom to substitute for it. Osborne and Rubinstein (1994) seem to support these concerns. Myerson (1991, pp. 437–40) converts the axiom to an expected value linear combination.
10. See Kuenne (1992, Ch. 6, pp. 148–168).
11. See Harsanyi (1963), Aumann and Drèze (1974), Aumann and Myerson (1988), and Owen (1977) for modifications and extensions of the Shapley value.
12. Myerson (1991, p. 456) adopts a similar view of the inadvisability of taking equilibria of the core or Shapley values too literally as realistic solutions:

> Like the Nash bargaining solution, the Shapley value and other equitable solutions can be interpreted as arbitration guidelines, or as determinants of focal equilibria in bargaining. We only need to assume that the unspecified bargaining process has a sufficiently large set of equilibria and that the focal equilibrium will be determined by the properties of equity and efficiency. Here we use 'equity' to mean that each player's gains from cooperating with others should be commensurate (in some sense) with what his cooperation contributes to other players. So equitable solutions should depend on the power structure that is summarized by the representation of the game in coalitional form.

As noted in the discussion of game theory, Luce and Raiffa (1957) stressed the interpretation of coalition solutions as guidelines for objective arbitrators. And it is interesting that Myerson is a member of that large group of economists who automatically equate "theory of equity" with only a single member of that group: contributory theory. A bias in the profession is to project the notion that the principles of economic equity must be grounded in rational self-interest.

13. Hart's major contribution to the study of this market structure (1979) is the extension of the concept of the "large" economy to market structures with differentiated commodities. His argument is that as the size of a firm's market relative to the number of consumers falls, the firm's demand curve approaches

the horizontal and, absent other interferences with social welfare, Pareto optimality. It is, therefore, not the absolute size of the firm that determines price behavior but size relative to the number of consumers. Monopolistic competition approaches the purely competitive solution under these circumstances as long as the firm's output potential is bounded. Declining average costs restrict the number of firms as long as the economy's resources are limited. Thus, the standard treatment of the large group case is that of a "small" economy where firms are large relative to the consumer base. Hart does not investigate the relation between the optimal number of goods produced and the actual number produced in the monopolistically competitive structure. His contribution in this regard in a later work (1980) is to examine the complementarity problem raised by Spence(1975) and Dixit–Stiglitz (1977). For a discussion of this work see n. 16.

14. See Green (1978, pp. 150–56).
15. More realistically, consider the case of hydrogen-powered motor vehicles and service stations selling hydrogen for refueling. Firms do not wish to produce such vehicles until facilities for refueling are available to the public, and such facilities will not be built until the automobiles are on the road.
16. This insight was examined more fully by Hart (1980), who shows that such possibilities are ruled out if consumer preferences are differentiable and convex. The complementarity problem is to be distinguished from the usual definition of complementarity involving negative cross-derivatives between products, which can occur when preferences are nonconvex and nondifferentiable. Joint production of the goods (e.g., nuts and bolts, hotels and ski-runs) may not be feasible for firms because of the expense of acquiring information concerning feasibility or reduced efficiency of a merger of the two goods because of different skills required in their production. Hart shows that this market failure can occur even in pure competition.

7 Pure Competition and Monopoly: A Beginning

1. Leffler (1982) has stressed this aspect of quality characteristics. He distinguishes between characteristics of products which are measured and priced and those which are measured but not explicitly priced. Thus, milk is sold by the quart, a liquid measure characteristic, with that price varying with butterfat content, the latter a characteristic that is measured but not identifiably priced. Quarts of milk with different butterfat contents are treated as the same brand of milk in Leffler's treatment, from which the price of butterfat can be derived as a shadow price. Of course, the distinction between units of characteristics which serve as pricing units and those that do not is implicit in Lancaster's work.
2. Of course it is somewhat fanciful to assume that the units of warranty sold are independent of the number of automobiles sold. It is assumed throughout the analysis of section 1 that $x > 0$, but even with that qualification to independence the element of unreality lingers. One advantage of that neglect of interdependence is that the reader may apply the framework and results to the welfare aspects of two totally unrelated industries or firms. In section 2 the interdependence will be fully integrated into the analysis.
3. Let the general equation of the second degree be

$$Az^2 + Bzx + Cx^2 + Dz + Ex + F = 0 \qquad (1)$$

Then, in general, if $B^2 - 4AC < 0$ the equation is elliptic (or has no locus); if positive it is hyperbolic; and if zero is parabolic. Since in the present instance $B = 0$ and A and C are positive, the W-equation is elliptic. When $B = 0$ (no interaction between z and x) and $Az^2 + Cx^2 + Dz + Ex + F = 0, AC > 0$, then the axes are parallel to the coordinate axes. Because we have solved for z as a function of given x values, our expression is $Az^2 + Dz + (Cx^2 + Dz + Ex + F = 0$, and parallelism with the coordinate axes is established. When $B \neq 0$, $Az^2 + Bzx + Cx^2 + Dz + Ex + F = 0, B^2 - 4AC < 0$, the axes of the ellipse are oblique to the coordinate axes.

4. This concept may be illuminated by considering the price elasticity of demand for a commodity:

$$\varepsilon_p = \frac{p \cdot dx}{X \cdot dp}.$$

The numerator is the gross incremental benefit of (say) a price reduction and the denominator is the marginal policy cost of the price reduction. Price elasticity of demand may be interpreted as the marginal gross revenue gain per dollar of marginal policy cost.

5. See n. 3 above.
6. It may seem peculiar that consumers' surplus at T, with firm 1 in pure competition and firm 2 a monopoly, yields a higher consumers' surplus than at W_{max} where both firms are in pure competition. This occurs because, in the example,

$$CS = .1x_1^2 + .3x_2^2, \tag{1}$$

so the CS rises as the square of outputs. When firm 1 is a pure competitor and firm 2 a monopolist, the rise in p_2 leads to a large rise in x_1 above the level of twin pure competition, and a disproportionate rise in x_1's contribution to CS. A 16 percent rise in x_1, from 174 to 202, leads to a 35 percent rise in CS, while the 47 percent fall in x_2 results in only a 23 percent fall in x_2's contribution.

8 The Isolated Firm and Consumer Benchmarking of Measurable Characteristics

1. An initial version of this chapter was delivered at the International Economic Modeling Symposium, University of Göteborg, Göteborg, Sweden (August 18–20, 1992). It has been substantially extended and altered in its present form.
2. As will be shown, the negative exponential density function is a special form of the Weibull.
3. See Chapter 3 for a brief introduction and Kuenne (1986), for a more extended presentation.
4. Here, and throughout the chapter, the firm's (and product's) subscript i is suppressed in the interests of unburdening notation, except where necessary to avoid ambiguities.
5. Note that the firm is assumed to have four rivals who do not react to firm 1's decisions. Their prices are parameters in the analysis.
6. The requirements for a negative definite or semi-definite Hessian are a rather uninformative combination of marginal production costs, marginal policy revenues, and costs (see the discussion to follow) and the slopes of the marginal policy revenue and marginal policy cost of μ_i. For the base case, the determinant

of the Hessian was consistently positive for all displacements, equaling 426,525 for the solution values of p and μ_i.

7. See Dorfman and Steiner (1954).
8. The values of the derivatives are:

$$1 \quad \frac{\partial p}{\partial a} = \frac{1+2hb_{11}\omega}{2b_{11}(1+b_{11}h\omega)} \tag{1}$$

$$2 \quad \frac{\partial \mu_i}{\partial a} = \frac{-[(j-u)(1+2hx)+2h\delta\omega+\mu_i hx((k-v)+1)+\mu_i]}{[D+(j-u)(1+2h\delta x)+2\delta^2\omega h+\eta\delta(1+2hx)+\mu_i\delta+\mu_i hx\delta(1+(k-v))]},$$

where D is the denominator of (8.7.2).

The sign of $\partial u_i/\partial a$ is unambiguously negative.

Hence, when μ_i is constant, an increase in a will raise p, and when p is constant, a rise in a will reduce μ_i. The flows of causation as one variable changes in response to the level of the other set are ignored.

9. The algorithms used to solve for the optima in sections 2 and 4, however, yield the global, as they begin at $w_i = 0$ and move through a wide domain of w_i to obtain the maximum profit configuration.
10. (8.23) is truncated. The expression actually used in calculations contained terms through the 26th power of z. It is reproduced in U.S. Department of Commerce, National Bureau of Standards, *Handbook of Mathematical Functions* (Washington, D.C., U.S. Government Printing Office, 1972, p. 256), reproduced from H. T. Davis, *Tables of Higher Mathematical Functions* (Bloomington, Indiana, Principia Press, 1935), with corrections due to H. E. Salzer.
11. From (8.21),

$$\frac{d\sigma^2}{dc} = -\frac{2b^2}{c^2}\{\Gamma'(z_2)-\Gamma(z_1)\Gamma'(z_1)\} \tag{1}$$

The sign of (1) will be negative, because the expression in curly brackets is positive. From the approximation to $\Gamma(z)$ in (20) and its expansion discussed in n. 6, for $z > 1$, $\Gamma(z) > 0$ and $\Gamma(z_2) > \Gamma(z_1)$ for $z_2 > z_1$, since $\Gamma'(z) > 0$. Also, from (17), $\Gamma(z_1) = \mu_i/b_i$. Hence, we may rewrite (1) as

$$\frac{d\sigma^2}{dc} = -\frac{2b}{c^2}\{\Gamma'(z_2)-\frac{\mu_i}{b_i}(\Gamma'(z_1)\}. \tag{2}$$

But $\mu_i \,\varepsilon\, [0.866b_i, b_i]$. Therefore, the expression in curly brackets is positive and $d\sigma^2/dc < 0$.

9 Oligopolistic Competition and Consumer Benchmarking in a Rivalrous Consonance Market Structure: Measurable Characteristics

1. An early version of this chapter was delivered as a paper at the International Economic Modelling Symposium, University of Piraeus, Piraeus, Greece (June 2–4, 1993), and published as a portion of R. Kuenne (1994).
2. The reader may interpret this stable pattern of rivalry and tacit cooperation as the outcome of a supergame played over an infinite time horizon or indefinite

time period. Game theory is not extremely successful in isolating unique or small subsets of such patterns as Nash equilibria with some claim to credibility as outcomes. In Kuenne (1986, 1992) I have been critical of the game theorist's approach to determining strategies in oligopoly as placing too much emphasis on the competitive aspects of market behavior and failing to incorporate adequately the strong motivation to cooperate at the possible expense of short-run profits. In recent years, with the greater attention game theorists have accorded to cooperative game theory, the basis of this criticism has attenuated to a large degree. However, the ultrarationalist approach to the formation of strategies under complex interdependence does not adequately reflect the simpler patterns that real-world decision makers employ, nor does the technique feature the sociological aspects that are unique to each industry. Finally, in the analysis of the functioning of the industry I am not interested in the path of approach to a Nash equilibrium that so fascinates the game theorist: my concern lies in isolating the existing power relationships that characterize the industry and that motivate its decisions.

3. The expressions for the elements of the Hessian are available upon request from the author.
4. Consumers' surplus is simply

$$CS = 0.5\frac{x_i^2}{b_{i,i}},$$

for each firm's sales. For the society as a whole consumers' surplus is double this value.

5. This quasi-decomposition was performed by computing $\beta_i - x_i$ to obtain the terms in the demand function (9.1) involving all of the quality variables and subtracting this term from x_i in the expression for consumers' surplus for both firms:

$$CSCCOR = \frac{\beta^2}{b_{ii}}.$$

This is only an approximation to the contribution of quality characteristics to consumers' surplus because it is assumed that price would remain at its solution value if the sales impacts of those characteristics were neutralized.

6. Most economists accept the notion that Nash equilibria are at best necessary, not sufficient, conditions for credible solutions, and indeed are not credible in many instances of cooperative games where pregame communication or signaling during plays of repeated games are recognized, as for example the game of chicken. For a healthily skeptical approach to the interpretation of game theoretic solutions see Kreps (1990).
7. Hotelling (1929).

10 Oligopolistic Competition with Scaling of Characteristics

1. Question 2 does bring into play the consumers' valuation of money and, indirectly, his income. The indifference premia also will be affected by such

circumstances, much as the compensating variation of conventional demand theory. Our operational manner of deriving consumer preferences over brands, therefore, does not have the same degree of independence between preferences and the budget line that conventional demand theory does.

2. This scaling approach is similar to that discussed in Tirole (1993, pp. 96–97), in which he employs a "quality index", s, and a "taste parameter", θ, and defines the utility function

$$U = \begin{cases} \theta s - p, \text{ if the consumer buys a good with quality } s \text{ at price } p, \\ 0 \text{ if he does not buy.} \end{cases}$$

He refers to θ as a positive real number, but θs must have a dollar dimension for meaningful comparison with p. The valuation measure, v_i, in (10.1) may be looked upon as serving the function of Tirole's θs, derived empirically, with more readily interpretable meaning than θs. Tirole, in his treatment of preferences over multiple brands, assumes a cumulative density function for consumers over θ to determine demands for brands whereas the use of the valuation approach yields these directly, albeit with the use of a measure of central tendency that ignores variance among individuals' valuations. We attempt to include this variance via the use of k parameters to alter effective interbrand distances.

11 Nodal Changes in Brand Locations in Product Space

1. The topic is well-covered in Miller, Friesz and Tobin (1996), in which facility location in networks is related to Hotelling models with elastic demands and in which a 2-stage algorithm based on variational methods of solution of nonlinear programming problems is presented in great detail.
2. This problem is a general one in econometrics that is not sufficiently recognized, and goes beyond the problem of high multicollinearity. Let $\mathbf{R}_{xx}$ be the correlation matrix for the regressors of the equation, $\mathbf{R}_{yx}$ the vector of correlation coefficients of the regressand and the regressors, and $\mathbf{B}$ the vector of regression coefficients. Then,

$$\mathbf{B} = \mathbf{R}_{xx}^{-1}\mathbf{R}_{yx},$$

so that the regression coefficients, which purport to be the measures of the net impact of a regressor on a regressand, are affected in their definition by every off-diagonal covariance term in $\mathbf{R}_{xx}$. It is difficult to accept them as representing the net impacts on the regressand when $\mathbf{R}_{xx}$ is not a diagonal matrix.

3. For a more extensive discussion of principal components methodology as well as similar multivariate analytical techniques, the reader is referred to a variety of texts in the field, frequently oriented to psychometrics or educational psychology. One recommended text is Cooley and Lohnes (1971).

12 Selling Costs and Congnitive Distancing

1. Strickland and Weiss (1976, pp. 1109–21), in a study of 417 4-digit Standard Industrial Classification (SIC) manufacturing industries in 1963, estimate that a rise of 1 percentage point in the advertising–sales ratio (*ASR*) would raise the price–cost margin 1.396 percent points for producer good industries. The same study gave average *ASR*s, as computed by Martin (1979, pp. 639–47), of a little less than 4 percent for consumer goods industries, with a wide range of 0 to 29 percent, and 1 percent for producer goods industries with a range from 0 to 4 percent.

   In a study at the firm level of 231 large companies in the period 1960–1969, Shepherd (1972) found an average *ASR* of 2.5 percent, with a large variance. His regression results indicate that a 1 percentage point rise in *ASR* increased after-tax rate of return on equity by 0.6 percentage points.

   In (12.4) I have assumed that the *ASR* is determined by a fixed percentage of revenue (3 percent in the base case) plus adjustments determined by the sum of interbrand price differentials.
2. Note that when $A_i = 0$, $\alpha_i = 0$, and $\beta_i = 0$ then (12.6) becomes identical to (10.10.1).
3. The second-order partial derivative of profit with respect to price is:

$$\frac{\delta^2 \pi_i}{\delta p_i^2} = 2\frac{\delta Y_i}{\delta p_i} - 2\alpha_i + p_i\frac{\delta^2 Y_i}{\delta p_i^2} - (m_i + 2n_i x_i)\frac{\delta^2 x_i}{\delta p_i^2} - 2n_i\left(\frac{\delta x_i}{\delta p_i}\right)^2 - \frac{\delta^2 A_i}{\delta p_i^2}$$

4. Note that firm 1 is spending much less on advertising than it would were it to equate price policy and advertising policy marginal profits to zero. From Table 12.2, 1 dollar of advertising yields approximately 1.11 additional sales, or about \$33.06 in revenue. Marginal production plus advertising cost is about \$3.46, leaving a marginal profit of \$29.60 per dollar of advertising. Obviously, r_{12} is not a realistic parameter but an outlier defined to obtain a result with clear lines of causation.

   Although the net impacts of the advertising environment are to reduce profits of brand 2, it does not follow that the firm would be better off not advertising. From the r_{2j} row and r_{j2} column it can be seen that its advertising substantially dampens its rivals' incursions. If $A_4 = 0$ the discounted total net impact on brand 2 sales would be –1.55 rather than –1.23, or an additional loss of \$5.04 in revenue per average dollar dollar of rivals' expenditures. A marginal dollar of advertising generates 0.32 units of sales, or \$5.04 in marginal revenue at a marginal production and advertising cost of \$2.08. Clearly informational advertising reduces firm 2's losses.

Bibliography

Aumann, R. and J. Drèze (1974) "Cooperative Games With Coalition Structures," *International Journal of Game Theory*, 3 (1974), pp. 217–38.

Aumann, R. and R. Myerson (1988) "Endogenous Formation of Links Between Players and Coalitions: An Application of the Shapley Value," in A. Roth, ed. (1988), pp. 175–91.

Becker, G. (1965) "A Theory of the Allocation of Time," *Economic Journal*, 75 (1965), pp. 493–517.

Beckmann, M. and T. Puu (1985) *Spatial Economics: Density, Potential, and Flow*. Amsterdam: North-Holland.

Cable, J. (1972) "Market Structure, Advertising Policy and Intermarket Differences in Advertising Intensity," in K. Cowling (1972), pp. 105–24.

Chamberlin, E. H. (1948) *The Theory of Monopolistic Competition*, Sixth Edition. Cambridge, Mass.: Harvard University Press.

Cooley, W. and P. Lohnes (1971) *Multivariate Data Analysis*. New York: Wiley.

Court, L. M. (1941) "Entrepreneurial and Consumer Demand Theories for Commodity Spectra," *Econometrica*, 9 (1941), pp. 135–62, 241–97.

Cowling, K., ed. (1972) *Market Structure and Corporate Behavior: Theory and Empiricial Analysis of the Firm*. London: Gray-Mills.

d'Aspremont, C., J. Gabszewicz and J. F. Thisse (1979) "On Hotelling's Stability in Competition," *Econometrica*, 47 (1979), pp. 1145–150.

Dixit, A. and J. Stiglitz (1977) "Monopolistic Competition and Optimum Product Diversity," *American Economic Review*, 67 (1977), pp. 297–308.

Dorfman, R. and P. Steiner (1954) "Optimal Advertising and Optimal Quality," *American Economic Review,* 44 (1954), pp. 825–36.

Eaton, B. and R. Lipsey (1975) "The Principle of Minimum Differentiation Reconsidered: Some New Developments in the Theory of Spatial Competition," *Review of Economic Studies*, 45 (1975), pp. 27–49.

Epple, D. (1987) "Hedonic Prices and Implicit Markets: Estimating Demand and Supply Functions for Differentiated Products," *Journal of Political Economy*, 95 (1987), pp. 59–80.

Fiacco, A. and G. McCormick (1968) *Sequential Unconstrained Minimization Technique*. New York: Wiley.

Friedman, J. (1983) *Oligopoly Theory*. Cambridge: Cambridge University Press.

Green, H. A. J. (1978) *Consumer Theory*. New York: Academic Press.

Harsanyi, J. (1963) "A Simplified Bargaining Model for the *n*-Person Cooperative Game," *International Economic Review*, 4 (1963), pp. 194–220.

Hart, O. (1974) "Monopolistic Competition in a Large Economy With Differentiated Commodities," *Review of Economic Studies*, 46 (1979), pp. 1–30.

Hart, O. (1980) "Perfect Competition and Optimal Product Differentiation," *Journal of Economic Theory*, 22 (1980), pp. 279–312.

Hein, R. and O. Moeschlin, eds (1977) *Essays in Mathematical Economics and Game Theory*. Berlin: Springer-Verlag.

Hotelling, H. (1929) "Stability in Competition," *Economic Journal*, 39 (1929), pp. 41–57.

Isard, W. (1956) *Location and Space Economy*. New York: Wiley.

Jones, L. (1988) "The Characteristics Model, Hedonic Prices, and the Clientele Effect," *Journal of Political Economy*, 96 (1988), pp. 551–67.

Kleiman, E. and T. Ophir (1966) "The Durability of Durable Goods," *Review of Economic Studies*, 33 (1966), pp. 165–78.

Kreps, D. (1990) *A Course in Economic Theory*. Princeton: Princeton University Press.

Kuenne, R. (1967) "Quality Space, Interproduct Competition, and General-Equilibrium Theory," Ch. 10 in R. Kuenne (1967).

Kuenne, R., ed. (1967) *Monopolistic Competition Theory: Studies in Impact*. New York: Wiley.

Kuenne, R. (1974) "Interproduct Distances in a Quality-Space: Inexact Measurement in Differentiated Oligopoly Analysis," *Applied Economics*, 6 (1974), pp. 255–73.

Kuenne, R. (1986) *Rivalrous Consonance: A Theory of General Oligopolistic Equilibrium*. Amsterdam: North-Holland.

Kuenne, R. (1992) *The Economics of Oligopolistic Competition: Price and Nonprice Rivalry*. Oxford: Blackwell.

Kuhn, H. and A. Tucker, eds (1953) *Contributions to the Theory of Games, II*, Annals of Mathematical Studies, 24, Princeton: Princeton University Press.

Lancaster, K. (1966) "A New Approach to Consumer Theory," *Journal of Political Economy*, 74 (1966), pp. 132–57.

Lancaster, K. (1971) *Consumer Demand: A New Approach*. New York: Columbia University Press.

Lancaster, K. (1972) "Operationally Relevant Characteristics in the Theory of Consumer Behavior," in M. Peston and B. Corry, eds (1972).

Lancaster, K. (1975) "Socially Optimal Product Differentiation," *American Economic Review*, 65 (1975), pp. 567–85.

Lancaster, K. (1979) *Variety, Equity and Efficiency*. New York: Columbia University Press.

Lancaster, K. (1991) *Modern Demand Theory*. Aldershot: Elgar.

Leffler, K. (1982) "Ambiguous Changes in Product Quality," *American Economic Review*, 72 (1982), pp. 956–67.

Leibenstein, H. (1950) "Bandwagon, Snob and Veblen Effects in the Theory of Consumer's Demand," *Quarterly Journal of Economics*, 64 (1950), pp. 183–207.

Lerner, A. and H. Singer (1937) "Some Notes on Duopoly and Spatial Competition," *Journal of Political Economy*, 45 (1937), pp. 145–86.

Leyland, H. (1977) "Quality Choice and Competition," *American Economic Review*, 87 (1977), pp. 127–37.

Lösch, A. (1954) *The Economics of Location*. New Haven: Yale University Press.

Luce, R. and H. Raiffa (1957) *Games and Decisions*. New York: Wiley.

Luce, R., R. Bush, and E. Galanter, eds (1963) *Handbook of Mathematical Psychology*. New York: Wiley.

Luce, R. and E. Galanter (1963) "Psychophysical Scaling," in R. Luce, R. Bush, and E. Galanter, eds (1963).

Mandelbrot, B. (1962) "Paretian Distributions and Income Maximization," *Quarterly Journal of Economics*, 76 (1962), pp. 57–85.

Martin, S. (1979) "Advertising, Concentration and Profitability: The Simultaneity Problem," *Bell Journal of Economics*, 10 (1979), pp. 639–47.

Mas-Colell, A., M. Whinston, and J. Green (1995) *Microeconomic Theory*. New York: Oxford University Press.

Miller, T. C., T. L. Friesz, and R. L. Tobin (1996) *Equilibrium Facility Location on Networks*. Berlin: Springer-Verlag.

Myerson, R. (1991) *Game Theory*. Cambridge, Mass.: Harvard University Press.
Negishi, T. (1961) "Monopolistic Competition and General Equilibrium," *Review of Economic Studies*, 38 (1961), pp. 196–201.
Osborne, M. and A. Rubinstein (1994) *A Course in Game Theory*. Cambridge, Mass.: MIT Press.
Owen, G. (1977) "Values of Games With A Priori Unions," in R. Hein and O. Moeschlin, eds (1977), pp. 76–88.
Palander, Tord (1935) *Beiträge zur Standortstheorie*. Uppsala: Almqvist & Wiksell.
Peston, M. and B. Corry, eds (1972) *Essays in Honour of Lord Robbins*. London: Weidenfeld & Nicolson.
Predöhl, A. (1928) "The Theory of Location in Its Relation to General Economics," *Journal of Political Economy*, 36 (1928), pp. 371–90.
Posner, R. (1975) "The Social Costs of Monopoly and Regulation," *Journal of Political Economy*, 83 (1975), pp. 807–27.
Roberts, J. and H. Sonnenschein (1977) "On the Foundations of the Theory of Monopolistic Competition," *Econometrica*, 45 (1977), pp. 101–13.
Robinson, Joan (1948) *The Economics of Imperfect Competition*. London: Macmillan.
Roth, A., ed. (1988) *The Shapley Value: Essays in Honour of Lloyd S. Shapley*. Cambridge: Cambridge University Press.
Salant, S. (1980) *Quality, Location Choice and Imperfect Competition*, doctoral dissertation, University of Rochester.
Salop, S. (1979) "Monopolistic Competition with Outside Goods," *Bell Journal of Economics*, 10 (1979), pp. 141–56.
Shapley, L. (1953) "A Value for *n*-Person Games," pp. 307–17, in H. Kuhn and A. Tucker, eds (1953), pp. 307–17.
Schelling, T. (1960) *The Strategy of Conflict*. Cambridge, Mass.: Harvard University Press.
Schmalensee, R. (1972) *The Economics of Advertising*. Amsterdam: North-Holland.
Shaked, A. (1975) "Non-existence of Equilibrium for the Two-Dimensional Three-Firm Location Problem," *Review of Economic Studies*, 45 (1975), pp. 51–5.
Shepherd, W. (1972) "The Elements of Market Structure," *Review of Economics and Statistics*, 54 (1972), pp. 25–37.
Shepherd, W. (1984) "Contestability" vs. Competition," *American Economic Review*, 74 (1984), pp. 572–86.
Spence, A. M. (1975) "Monopoly, Quality and Regulation," *Bell Journal of Economics*, 6 (1975), pp. 417–29.
Spence, M. (1976) "Product Selection, Fixed Costs and Monopolistic Competition," *Review of Economic Studies*, 43 (1976), pp. 217–35.
Spence, M. (1984) "Cost Reduction, Competition, and Industry Performance," *Econometrica*, 52 (1984), pp. 101–21.
Sraffa, P. (1926) "The Laws of Return Under Competitive Conditions," *Economic Journal*, 36 (1926), pp. 535–50.
Strickland, A. and L. Weiss (1976) "Advertising, Concentration and Price-Cost Margins," *Journal of Political Economy*, 84 (1976), pp. 1109–21.
Thünen, J. von (1929) *Der isolierte Staat*. Jena: Waentig.
Tinbergen, J. (1956) "On the Theory of Income Distribution," *Weltwirtschaftliches Archiv*, 77 (1956), pp. 155–73.
Tirole, J. (1993) *The Theory of Industrial Organization*. Cambridge, Mass.: MIT Press.
Torgeson, W. S. (1958) *Theory and Methods of Scaling*. New York: Wiley.

Triffin, R. (1949) *Monopolistic Competition and General Equilibrium Theory*. Cambridge, Mass.: Harvard University Press.

Weber, A. (1909, 1929) *Theory of Location of Industries*, trans. C. J. Friedrich. Chicago: University of Chicago Press.

Index